Dictionary of Literary Biography • Volume Twelve

American Realists and Naturalists

Dictionary of Literary Biography

1: *The American Renaissance in New England*,
   edited by Joel Myerson (1978)

2: *American Novelists Since World War II*,
   edited by Jeffrey Helterman and Richard Layman (1978)

3: *Antebellum Writers in New York and the South*,
   edited by Joel Myerson (1979)

4: *American Writers in Paris, 1920-1939*,
   edited by Karen Lane Rood (1980)

5: *American Poets Since World War II*, 2 volumes,
   edited by Donald J. Greiner (1980)

6: *American Novelists Since World War II*, Second Series,
   edited by James E. Kibler, Jr. (1980)

7: *Twentieth-Century American Dramatists*, 2 volumes,
   edited by John MacNicholas (1981)

8: *Twentieth-Century American Science-Fiction Writers*, 2 volumes,
   edited by David Cowart and Thomas L. Wymer (1981)

9: *American Novelists, 1910-1945*, 3 volumes,
   edited by James J. Martine (1981)

10: *Modern British Dramatists, 1900-1945*, 2 volumes,
    edited by Stanley Weintraub (1982)

11: *American Humorists, 1800-1950*, 2 volumes,
    edited by Stanley Trachtenberg (1982)

12: *American Realists and Naturalists*,
    edited by Donald Pizer and Earl N. Harbert (1982)

Yearbook: 1980,
edited by Karen L. Rood, Jean W. Ross, and Richard Ziegfeld (1981)

Yearbook: 1981,
edited by Karen L. Rood, Jean W. Ross, and Richard Ziegfeld (1982)

Documentary Series, volume 1,
edited by Margaret A. Van Antwerp (1982)

Documentary Series, volume 2,
edited by Margaret A. Van Antwerp (1982)

Dictionary of Literary Biography • Volume Twelve

American Realists and Naturalists

Edited by Donald Pizer
Newcomb College, Tulane University
and
Earl N. Harbert
Northeastern University

A Bruccoli Clark Book
Gale Research Company • Book Tower • Detroit, Michigan 48226
1982

Manufactured by Braun-Brumfield, Inc.
Ann Arbor, Michigan
Printed in the United States of America

Library of Congress Cataloging in Publication Data

Main entry under title:

American realists and naturalists.

(Dictionary of literary biography; v. 12)
"A Bruccoli Clark Book."
Includes index.
1. American literature—19th century—Bio-bibliography.
2. American literature—20th century—Bio-bibliography.
3. Authors, American—Biography—Dictionaries. 4. American
literature—History and criticism. 5. Realism in literature. 6.
Naturalism in literature. I. Pizer, Donald. II. Harbert, Earl N.,
1934- . III. Series.

PS201.A46   1982   810'.9'004   82-9258
ISBN 0-8103-1149-6   AACR2

In memory of
Richard P. Adams
and
C. Hugh Holman

Contents

Contents

Foreword

The closely related American literary movements known as realism and naturalism are conventionally placed between the close of the Civil War and the beginning of World War I. The historiography of late nineteenth- and early twentieth-century American literature differs in this respect from that of both England and France. The terms realism and naturalism are seldom used in accounts of English literature of this period. Instead, Victorianism and Edwardianism (and occasionally such more specialized terms as decadence and aestheticism) serve as historical markers. And though French literary historians do rely on realism and naturalism to designate specific phases of French literary expression, they place these phases much earlier in the nineteenth century, with naturalism reaching its climax in the late 1870s with Zola's most significant work.

These differences in terminology and chronology have suggestive implications for the origin and nature of realism and naturalism in America. The placing of the movements between the two wars reveals the importance of these traumatic moments in the history of American life and thought. The Civil War, with its central metaphor of brother killing brother (as in one of Ambrose Bierce's most memorable stories), brought to an end not only transcendental idealism but also the very notion of a patrician society with deep roots in family, land, and education. Somewhat as in early eighteenth-century England, there arose as a dominant force in postbellum America a largely commercial and urban middle class with interests in literature which could best be met by the normative, commonplace, pragmatic world of the realistic novel—by the novels, in short, of William Dean Howells during the 1870s and 1880s. American realism in Howells's conception and practice of fiction moved during these decades toward Rene Wellek's definition of realism as "the objective representation of contemporary social reality." The movement achieved its annus mirabilis in 1885, when Mark Twain's *Adventures of Huckleberry Finn*, Howells's *The Rise of Silas Lapham*, and Henry James's *The Bostonians* appeared in American magazines. These works sought to render Ameri-

can life in "the light of common day," to use Edwin Cady's phrase for the writer's effort to express a vision of life which most men share. And they did so with a combination of autobiographical and comic threads and an objective, scenic method (a detached author revealing theme through action) which also characterizes the movement at its best.

To stress the Civil War as a turning point in the American consciousness, however, is to obscure, as Robert Falk has pointed out, that American realism is also a form of Victorianism. The Civil War did not destroy the American writer's penchant for moral idealism, melodrama, and sentiment; it only drove these characteristics of high Victorianism into more mixed forms and more indirect expression. Victorianism flourished within realism most openly in the highly popular local-color movement which dominated the American short story for over thirty years. From Bret Harte in the 1860s to Hamlin Garland in the 1890s, this form of fiction often combined a preoccupation with verisimilitude of local detail (the writer's homage to what Alfred Kazin has called the American absorption in "the material surface of things") and powerful currents of ethical idealism, sentimentality, and melodramatic plotting. In the work of the major realists, moral idealism is expressed more obliquely but is still a characteristic of their fiction. A Huck Finn or a Silas Lapham or an Isabel Archer possesses a "good heart" which is capable of defeating or at least withstanding the evil forces of life.

World War I and its aftermath were, of course, to cast considerable doubt on this faith in man's innate ethical nature as well to mark the beginning of American modernism, a literary movement in which an elitist high art often joins with a deeply jaundiced view of the human condition. As Hemingway noted in a famous passage in *A Farewell to Arms*, after the inhuman carnage of modern battle the traditional language of moral idealism rings obscene. But to view World War I as the abrupt conclusion of a literary period is as misleading as to view the Civil War as its abrupt beginning. Just as Victorianism did not die at Appomattox, so American modernism has its roots in a group of young turn-of-the-century writers (most of whom were born in the early 1870s) who helped create the modern temper in America. Labeled even in their own time as naturalists, these writers have often been overidentified with Emile Zola's more extreme pronouncements on the function and nature of the naturalistic or "experimental" novel, a novel in which character is depicted as conditioned and determined by heredity and environment. In fact, aside from the early fiction of Frank Norris and Jack London, the work of this generation of American writers is seldom so simplistically doctrinaire. Other than a frequently shared desire to depict the sensationalistic underside of urban life, these writers had widely ranging interests. From Henry Adams's and Theodore Dreiser's accounts of the failure of the American Dream to Edith Wharton's and Kate Chopin's brave attempts to deal honestly with the fate of being a woman in America to Stephen Crane's ironic deflation of most human pretensions to wisdom and strength, they sought to respond to American life with a richness and fullness appropriate to the disparate yet increasingly confining and destructive American world they saw around them. Though they seldom revealed their characters as triumphing in any expression of heroism, love, or even common integrity, these writers nevertheless still rendered experience with a sense of its tragic pathos which is an oblique reflection of traditional humanistic faith.

There were thus no "pure" realists or naturalists in late nineteenth- and early twentieth-century American writing. American literary expression of the period was too diffuse in its origins and in general too instinctively unideological in its fundamental impulses to adhere to specific theories of literature. But there were two distinctive generations of writers, with the writers of each generation sharing a broadly similar set of assumptions about literature. The biographies and critical commentaries of this volume represent a collective effort to describe these assumptions as they appear in the life and art of the principal figures of a major phase of American literature.

It might be helpful to provide some comments on the principles of selection which have guided Professor Harbert and myself in our choices of which writers to include in this volume. We have sought to include every significant writer of fiction who flourished between the wars and whose work exhibits characteristics which can be designated realistic or naturalistic. On the one hand, this principle has resulted in the omission of figures who wrote exclusively in poetry or nonfictional prose, such as Walt Whitman or William James, despite their frequent presence in historical surveys of the period. On the other, it has resulted in the inclusion of such writers of fiction as Ambrose Bierce, Edward Bellamy, and Richard Harding Davis whose work is only marginally realistic or naturalistic. In short, because our emphasis has been on fiction, we have sought to be as inclusive as possible in this area. We have also omitted several novelists who, though published between 1865 and 1914, are usually viewed principally as antebellum or post-World War I writers. Thus, Oliver Wendell Holmes and Willa Cather are not in this volume, though their biographies and those of similar figures can be found in other volumes in this series.

—Donald Pizer

Permissions

The following people and institutions generously permitted the reproduction of photographs and other illustrative materials: The Granger Collection, New York, pp. 3, 14, 37, 43, 174, 203, 221, 242, 251, 270, 295, 398, 418, 426; Culver Pictures, New York, pp. 5, 24, 49, 79, 90, 125, 127, 137, 143, 145, 156, 163, 172, 210, 227, 237, 239, 245, 252, 264, 286, 291, 292, 298, 326, 338, 374, 392, 409, 422, 425, 430, 456; The Bettmann Archive, Inc., New York, pp. 7, 253, 303, 333, 334, 395, 417, 433, 438; Massachusetts Historical Society, Boston, pp. 8, 12; Courtesy of Lilly Library, Indiana University, pp. 9, 31, 229; University of Virginia Library, pp. 20, 21, 47, 98, 101, 107, 109, 135, 216, 217, 236, 266, 267, 312, 313, 331, 428, 429, 442, 459; Bancroft Library, University of California at Berkeley, p. 27; Courtesy of Mrs. A. L. Suman, p. 28; Courtesy of the California Historical Society, San Francisco, p. 29; Courtesy of the New York Historical Society, p. 46; Courtesy of Tulane University Library, p. 51; Cleveland Public Library, pp. 52, 54, 57; The New York Public Library, Astor, Lenox and Tilden Foundations, p. 148; University of Pennsylvania Library, pp. 154, 155, 160; Wide World Photos, New York, p. 161; The Newberry Library, Chicago, pp. 191, 195, 196, 199, 200, 201; University of Chicago Library, pp. 256, 257, 258, 259; The Huntington Library, San Marino, and the estate of Jack London, pp. 362, 363; estate of Harriet Beecher Stowe, pp. 428, 429.

Acknowledgments

This book was produced by BC Research.

Karen L. Rood, senior editor for the *Dictionary of Literary Biography* series, was the in-house editor.

The production staff included Mary Betts, Joseph Caldwell, Patricia Coate, Angela Dixon, Lynn Felder, Joyce Fowler, Patricia S. Hicks, Nancy L. Houghton, Sharon K. Kirkland, Cynthia D. Lybrand, Shirley A. Ross, Walter W. Ross, Joycelyn R. Smith, Robin A. Sumner, Cheryl A. Swartzentruber, Carol J. Wilson, and Lynne C. Zeigler.

Anne Dixon did the library research with the assistance of the staff at the Thomas Cooper Library of the University of South Carolina, particularly Michael Freeman, Michael Havener, David Lincove, Roger Mortimer, Donna Nance, Harriet Oglesbee, Loretta Shepherd, Paula Swope, Jane Thesing, Ellen Tillett, and Beth Woodard. Special thanks are due to Alexander Gilchrist and Jean Rhyne of Thomas Cooper Library. Photographic copy work for this volume was done by Pat Crawford of Imagery, Columbia, South Carolina, and Charles Gay of Columbia, South Carolina.

We have frequently called on the services of special collections librarians and we are indebted to Joan Crane at the University of Virginia Library; Neda Westlake at the University of Pennsylvania Library; the staff at the Lilly Library, Indiana University; and Diana Haskell at The Newberry Library, Chicago.

The following collectors and researchers served us well: Sal Noto, Mary V. McLeod, and Jurek Polanski.

Dictionary of Literary Biography • Volume Twelve

American Realists and Naturalists

Dictionary of Literary Biography

Henry Adams

Earl N. Harbert
Northeastern University

BIRTH: Boston, Massachusetts, 16 February 1838, to Charles Francis and Abigail Brooks Adams.

EDUCATION: A.B., Harvard University, 1858.

MARRIAGE: 29 June 1872 to Marian Hooper.

AWARDS AND HONORS: Loubat Prize for *History of the United States of America During the Administrations of Thomas Jefferson and James Madison*, 1894; elected president of the American Historical Association, 1894; Pulitzer Prize for *The Education of Henry Adams*, 1919.

DEATH: Washington, D.C., 27 March 1918.

SELECTED BOOKS: *Chapters of Erie, and Other Essays*, by Adams and Charles F. Adams, Jr. (Boston: Osgood, 1871);
The Life of Albert Gallatin (Philadelphia & London: Lippincott, 1879);
Democracy: An American Novel, anonymous (New York: Holt, 1880; London: Macmillan, 1882);
John Randolph (Boston & New York: Houghton, Mifflin, 1882; revised, 1883);
Esther: A Novel, as Frances Snow Compton (New York: Holt, 1884; London: Bentley, 1885);
History of the United States of America During the Administrations of Thomas Jefferson and James Madison:
History of the United States of America During the First Administration of Thomas Jefferson (Cambridge, Mass.: Privately printed, 1884; revised edi-

tion, 2 volumes, New York: Scribners, 1889);
History of the United States of America During the Second Administration of Thomas Jefferson (Cambridge, Mass.: Privately printed, 1885; revised edition, 2 volumes, New York: Scribners, 1890);

Henry Adams

3

History of the United States of America During the First Administration of James Madison (Cambridge, Mass.: Privately printed, 1888; revised edition, 2 volumes, New York: Scribners, 1890);

History of the United States of America During the Second Administration of James Madison, 3 volumes (New York: Scribners, 1891);

Historical Essays (New York: Scribners, 1891; London: Unwin, 1891);

Mont-Saint-Michel and Chartres, anonymous (Washington, D.C.: Privately printed, 1904; revised and enlarged, 1912; Boston & New York: Houghton Mifflin, 1913; London: Constable, 1914);

The Education of Henry Adams (Washington, D. C.: Privately printed, 1907; Boston & New York: Houghton Mifflin, 1918; London: Constable, 1919);

A Letter to American Teachers of History (Washington, D. C.: Privately printed, 1910);

The Life of George Cabot Lodge (Boston & New York: Houghton, Mifflin, 1911);

The Degradation of the Democratic Dogma (New York & London: Macmillan, 1919).

Henry Adams owes his popular reputation to a single work, *The Education of Henry Adams*. That book, which was privately printed in 1907 but not commercially published until just after the author's death in 1918, quickly made Adams famous, as he was posthumously awarded the Pulitzer Prize for it in 1919. At the same time, the sudden notoriety of this one book put into critical eclipse the substantial literary work that Adams had accomplished earlier: essays, biographies, novels, letters, and especially a magisterial nine-volume historical study of the presidencies of Thomas Jefferson and James Madison—a classic of American historiography. In the years since 1919, some of that shadow has disappeared, and a larger, fairer-minded sense of Henry Adams's proper place in the cultural history of the late nineteenth and early twentieth centuries has gradually emerged. With the passage of time, we have come to see that Adams stands apart even while he belongs to his age; as an artist and a man, he must be understood on his own terms, as a thoroughly independent participant and observer, yet in and of his time, and even perhaps as a unique American who contributed in a special way to the richness of American intellectual life. Finally, no label like that of *realist* can possibly do full justice to Henry Adams.

In a seemingly simple anecdote, *The Education of Henry Adams* proposes to teach its readers the primary lesson of its author's birth and life: "The Irish gardener once said to the child: 'You'll be thinkin' you'll be President too!' The casualty of the remark made so strong an impression on his mind that he never forgot it. He could not remember ever to have thought on the subject; to him, that there should be a doubt of his being President was a new idea. What had been would continue to be. He doubted neither about Presidents nor about Churches, and no one suggested at that time a doubt whether a system of society which had lasted since Adam would outlast one Adams more."

The truth is that Henry Adams never quite outgrew "thinkin' you'll be President too!" Almost all of his life and nearly everything he wrote showed signs of a powerful family influence, the results of his fourth-generation membership in the Adams clan, that most remarkable of American political families, which had provided two presidents, John Adams and John Quincy Adams, and a minister to the court of St. James, Charles Francis Adams, before Henry Adams's own generation reached maturity.

At his birth in 1838, Henry Brooks Adams entered the special world of the Massachusetts Adamses, as the third son of Abigail Brooks Adams and Charles Francis Adams, the grandson of John Quincy Adams, and the great-grandson of John Adams. It was hardly an inauspicious beginning. All three illustrious forebears exemplified the principle of duty before pleasure, especially political duty to their state and nation. But, as their heir soon learned, the Adamses were also habitually committed to the equally demanding role of lifelong authorship—to being writers as much as politicians and statesmen. From their collective efforts has emerged the remarkable four-generation collection of diaries, documents, and letters that is known as the Adams Papers. Along with a political name, Henry inherited a duty to celebrate, explain, defend, and often to justify in simple words the complex experiences that were his life.

The earliest surviving evidence of Henry's attempt to satisfy this family demand for authorship dates from his years as an undergraduate student at Harvard College, 1854-1858. His essays on such subjects as the reading habits of his fellow students were printed in the *Harvard Magazine*, and they helped to establish for Adams a college popularity that led to his election as class orator for 1858. After graduation and the usual grand tour of Europe, he took up residence in Berlin, to begin the study of civil law and of the German language. In 1859 and 1860, Adams moved around Europe, touring in

Henry Adams, circa 1875

throughout the American Civil War and until 1868. Again, the effects of place and time were lasting, as Adams never quite got over feeling that he had missed participating in the single most significant historic event of his lifetime. Yet, during these years, the young private secretary made good literary use of his time. He served perhaps the most important part of his apprenticeship, learning to shape his own thoughts on politics, history, and science into the essay form. Adams's most ambitious pieces appeared in the prestigious *North American Review*: "Captaine John Smith" (1867) and an extended essay-review (1868) of Sir Charles Lyell's tenth edition of *Principles of Geology*, a key text in evolutionary theory. Returning to Washington after the Civil War, Adams continued his career as an essayist, writing now in a more popular style a series of political studies aimed at practical reform. These essays began appearing in periodicals during 1869-1870 and were later collected in *Chapters of Erie*, along with similar efforts written by Henry's brother, Charles Francis Adams, Jr. Both of the fourth-generation sons were at this moment dedicated to the task of shaping a practical force of public opinion, one sufficiently powerful to effect reform in American political life.

Soon disillusioned by a failure to achieve any real results and with strong encouragement from his family, Henry Adams moved back to Boston and Harvard in 1870, to become both an instructor of history at Harvard College and editor of the *North American Review*. His marriage on 29 June 1872 to Marian ("Clover") Hooper, a young lady he had met first in London and a member of proper Boston society, led next to a lengthy wedding journey to England, continental Europe, and Egypt. The newlyweds carried with them written introductions to political and intellectual leaders in the countries they would visit, and some of the resulting friendships lasted throughout their lives. Back at Harvard, Adams took up his work with new seriousness, as he taught courses in medieval and American history, introduced within the university the first graduate seminars organized on the German model, in which a professor led a small group of students in an investigation of primary sources, and published the historical writings of his best graduate students along with some of his own in *Essays in Anglo-Saxon Law* (1876). Adams's chief contribution, the essay "The Anglo-Saxon Courts of Law," stands as an impressive demonstration that the academic had mastered traditional techniques for scholarly research and publication. In December 1876, Adams gave further evidence of his

northern Italy with his sister, Louisa Adams Kuhn, and later taking advantage of an unusual opportunity to interview Garibaldi, the most popular revolutionary figure of the moment. Based on these experiences, Adams wrote colorful travel letters that were published in the *Boston Daily Courier*, thus marking his initiation into the adult world of newspaper journalism.

Returning to Massachusetts in 1860, Adams was soon recalled to family duty. He packed up and moved to Washington, where he served a double function: private secretary to his father, now Congressman Charles Francis Adams, and Washington correspondent for the *Boston Daily Advertiser*. Once settled in the capital Henry Adams found that the combination of activities seemed to satisfy both the political and literary demands of his complex nature, and certainly he took to Washington with enthusiasm. In fact, Adams never recovered from Potomac fever, as the city played an important role in most of the remainder of his long life. In 1861, however, when President Lincoln appointed Charles Francis Adams to be minister to the Court of St. James, Henry Adams transferred his residence to London, where he continued to serve as his father's secretary. There he remained, a remote although especially well-informed spectator,

versatility, as he presented a carefully prepared paper on "The Primitive Rights of Women" to a popular audience at the Lowell Institute. This talk argued for a greater appreciation of the legal and political importance of women in earlier times, and marked a path of investigation that would lead Adams to some of the most significant conclusions in his later writing.

Impressive fruits of his serious work in American history began to appear under the title *Documents Relating to New England Federalism, 1800-1815* (1877), a volume which he edited. Adams made this volume a spirited defense of his grandfather John Quincy Adams against the old attacks from Federalist party loyalists.

Adams resigned his appointment at Harvard during 1877 and once again moved to Washington, where he began to sort through the private papers of Albert Gallatin, secretary of the treasury in the Cabinet of President Thomas Jefferson. Adams's hard work soon made itself known to the public. In 1879 both *The Writings of Albert Gallatin*, edited by Adams, and *The Life of Albert Gallatin*, a biography by Adams, were published. During the first of these years in Washington, Adams joined a small circle of Washingtonians with whom he was to have permanent friendships: then assistant Secretary of State John Hay and his wife, Clara; Sen. James Donald (Don) Cameron and his wife, Elizabeth; Secretary of the Interior Carl Schurz; and Clarence King of the U. S. Geological Survey. More important for the moment, however, was the fact that his work on Gallatin announced a sense of high purpose in Adams's literary career.

In substance *The Writings of Albert Gallatin*—an edition commissioned by Gallatin family heirs, along with the biography of their kinsman—was a collection of private materials made available to scholars and to the general public for the first time. As editor of these papers, Adams learned something new about using source materials in an attractive and historically meaningful way. This ability he would convincingly demonstrate with even greater skill in the years ahead. At the time he took on the burden of editing Gallatin, however, his technique and editorial style still owed much to the hours he had spent laboring alongside his father, helping Charles Francis Adams put into print his massive editions of the writings of both John and John Quincy Adams. *The Life of Albert Gallatin* also shows something of an antique flavor, as if it were the work of a much older man. This quality, reviewers of the biography, including his brother Charles Adams, noted immediately. The profuse quotations from

Gallatin's writings did not mix easily with the narrative portions. Yet, even if it was from first appearance regarded as something less than an artistic success, *The Life of Albert Gallatin* remains a sound scholarly job, a biography that offers the portrait of Gallatin as an ideal statesman for his time, a man who might have been a worthy successor to Jefferson as president except for the uncontrollable historical accident of foreign birth. Over time, Adams's biography required little correction; the book held its place as the standard treatment of Albert Gallatin until the middle of the twentieth century.

After finishing the biography of Gallatin, Adams felt confident enough to extend his range and to begin a more ambitious historical study, which would gradually take shape and finally be made available to the general public during the years 1889-1891, as the *History of the United States of America During the Administrations of Thomas Jefferson and James Madison*. This nine-volume work mixes social, diplomatic, and intellectual history of the period 1800-1817 in an impressive way. It was unparalleled in Adams's day and still represents one of the most significant achievements in his entire literary career. The *History of the United States* is, in fact, one of the true classics in American historical writing. Adams's research for the book was extensive, especially in the archives of England, France, Spain, and America. In many cases Adams brought into public view for the first time archival materials that he had been able to see and use only because he was an Adams and the great-grandson and grandson of American presidents. Once he had gained access to these papers, the historian worked with copyists, translators, and personal secretaries to compile a massive documentary foundation, one that could support a deep yet broad reconsideration of a crucial period in the development of his nation. A scientific inquiry, the *History of the United States* came to represent in Adams's mind an act of patriotic duty.

While he was at work on the *History of the United States* Adams also found time to use writing as a pleasurable diversion for Marian Adams and himself when he turned his attention to critical biography and fiction. His vitriolic attack on Southern politician John Randolph of Roanoke, Virginia (1773-1833), in the short biography, *John Randolph* (1882), remains interesting, colorful reading. It was highly seasoned by the author's clear dislike for his subject—an opposite feeling from the one he had entertained for Gallatin—and the result was an enduring picture of an unattractive, enigmatic man, one that demanded response from Randolph's

Adams in his study, circa 1883, at work on the History of the United States During the Administrations of Thomas Jefferson and James Madison. *Photograph by Marian Adams.*

more sympathetic biographers. In this book, Adams was trying out a biographical style quite different from the one he had used in *The Life of Albert Gallatin*. He drew upon new materials to fashion a savage critique in *John Randolph*, one that would later be incorporated in a larger and more significant historical work, the *History of the United States*, as would much of the material in his biography of Gallatin. In *John Randolph* Adams proved that he was learning more about the difficult art of biography. Meanwhile, striking off in another direction, Adams also added to his artistic skills by writing, more for fun than financial gain, his two novels: *Democracy: An American Novel* (1880) and *Esther: A Novel* (1884). Neither of these fictional works displayed its author's real name; instead Adams published the first anonymously and the second pseudonymously, seeking to protect his reputation as a serious historian and man of letters, at least until the appearance of the *History of the United States*, on which his real literary hopes were staked.

Of the two novels—all that Henry Adams ever wrote—*Democracy* has enjoyed the greater reputation. Set in post-Civil War Washington, the book stands as an extension into fiction of its author's persistent interest in political reform, the same interest that had generated the essays in *Chapters of Erie* but equally, a moralistic impulse that could find no easy outlet in the more objective *History of the United States*. As the first of many novels set in the nation's capital, *Democracy* treats the chief questions of political power with a skeptical realism that broke with the prevailing myths of sentimental patriotism. The chief characters, like their real-life counterparts, people whom Adams knew in Washington, play out the moral and ethical dramas of personal and national right and wrong, set against a backdrop of political turmoil and reconciliation in the period of Reconstruction just after the Civil War. As the lessons of politics and life are taught to the heroine, Madeleine Lee, they are also made available to the reader. Senator Ratcliffe, the political villain from the American West, and Carrington, the noble but impecunious Southerner who was

*Henry Adams in Beverly Farms, Massachusetts, summer 1884.
Photograph by Marian Adams.*

once a Confederate soldier but never a secessionist, engage in a romantic contest not only for the hand of the widowed Mrs. Lee, an attractive and intelligent woman who has come to Washington to learn political and human truths at first hand, but by implication, for control of her nation's future. Adams uses the male suitors to illustrate the dangers yet inherent in geographical sectionalism (so recently tested in the Civil War) and human imperfectability. All promises of a rosy, virtuous future—national and personal—demand some further test. In the end, Mrs. Lee (along with author Adams) recoils at what she does find—pragmatism instead of patriotic idealism and personal corruption in the men (and perhaps the women) who seem to determine our national destiny. Confronted by a virtuous woman, Ratcliffe remains unreformed, although not untouched by the feminine principles she represents. For although she finds herself not immune to temptations of power and sexual attraction, Madeleine concedes no part of her moral code in action. Despite the promptings of ambition, she will not accept expediency as an adequate motive for an alliance with Ratcliffe. Yet he will never renounce American politics as usual, with its increments of graft and corruption and its overwhelmingly seductive invitation to POWER (as Adams insisted it be printed). In Adams's view, no idealistic

solution to the problems inherent in democracy was as yet possible. Many critics seemed to deny that he had done more than dress American government in romantic attire to make a clever novel, but a large reading public in England and America believed that the author had taken them behind the scenes to show what really went on in the corridors of power.

Perhaps to forestall the journalistic speculations concerning the authorship of the anonymously published *Democracy*, Adams chose to sign *Esther* with the pseudonym Frances Snow Compton. He never again used a pseudonym, although he continued to hide his authorship of various works throughout the remaining years of his life. *Esther* is another "problem" novel, but one that focuses on religion rather than politics. The chief male characters surround Esther Dudley (who owes her name and Puritan origins to Hawthorne's character in the short story "Old Esther Dudley"), trying their best to help the heroine find a usable personal philosophy that will get her through life. She searches for a set of modern—scientifically, aesthetically, and religiously—up-to-date ideas that will provide answers to her shrewdly posed, but often old-fashioned, questions about human experience. She studies, or more often talks about, geology, art, and theology, expecting that each in turn might supply just that degree of truth and certainty that seems required for her own life. Esther's need is sympathetically defined: she desperately wishes to function as a forceful, effective person in a post-Darwinian world. To her, in her dilemma as a woman, Adams brings what aid he can see around him, most obviously from a conventional tradition of romantic love, but more substantially from the worlds of art (represented by Wharton), science (George Strong), and religion (Stephen Hazard). None of these proves adequate for Esther's adjustment to life. Adams would later describe this plight as an "impasse" and recognize its lack of popular appeal as an ending for a novel. The practical effect for *Esther* was extremely poor sales, and the novel also failed to attract the attention of important critics.

Esther's own solution (final in the book) is to flee from the complications of her dilemma—a possibility that would later prove congenial to the real-life creator of this fiction, who put much of his thinking about his own experience into the novel. For even though he claimed with some justice in later years that the heroines of *Esther* and, to a lesser extent, *Democracy* owed their best qualities to his high-spirited wife, Marian Adams, it is equally clear that both characters are somewhat autobiographi-

Front cover for Adams's anonymous first novel, an examination of Washington politics during the Hayes administration

puritanical, duty-bound Boston, Adams also had transferred his mind to the more worldly, less serious points beyond. For him, there would be no turning back.

Aside from writing during the 1880s Adams spent much time with his wife and their closest friends, the Hays, planning for the elegant new house the two families would occupy, just across Lafayette Park from the White House. Their lives seemed the best that financial security and select Washington society could offer. But before the *History of the United States* was finished or the new house constructed, Henry Adams's life was shattered by the suicide of his wife in 1885. From this blow, he never could recover fully. Yet, at that time, Adams seemed to continue in the normal patterns of his married life, moving into the new house on H Street, spending hours with the Hays and Camerons, finishing the writing of his history, and traveling when he found opportunity and good companionship available to him. As a memorial to Mar-

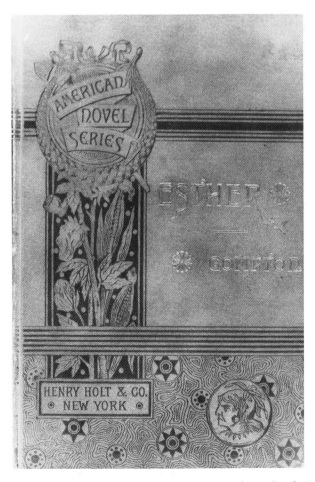

Front cover for Adams's pseudonymous second novel. The heroine closely resembles the author's wife, Marian.

cal. Yet, as he developed the most feminine traits of his heroines, Henry Adams knew that he was using his fiction to compliment his wife and to repay the interest she had displayed in his writing. Because of its great reliance on abstract discussion, *Esther* lacks the appeal that *Democracy* has as an insider's guide to real politics. Yet, in both novels Adams was testing the first rough outlines of his theory of feminine force, the hypothesis that would later be developed more fully in *Mont-Saint-Michel and Chartres* and *The Education of Henry Adams*, where he would derive from his study of women in ancient and modern times the theory that women have served both as a standard for moral behavior and, historically, as a source of power. In another way, the novels signaled a new freedom in Adams's thought and work. He showed that he could write without the discipline of historical scholarship and avoid the traditional family demands for serious nonfiction and moral purpose. Just as he had moved his home from

ian Adams, Adams commissioned the American sculptor Augustus Saint-Gaudens to create the bronze figure of a weeping woman, a symbol of his enduring grief, that marks her gravesite in Washington's Rock Creek Cemetery.

History of the United States of America During the Administrations of Thomas Jefferson and James Madison stands as the first important example of "scientific" history written in the United States. Borrowing from both German and English models, and even more from what Adams knew of the scientific method used in geology, biolog , and physics, the historian attempted to study the presidential years of Jefferson and Madison as an experiment crucial to the fate of American democracy. Between the framing chapters at the beginning and end of his nine volumes—a frame that painted in contrasting colors two grand pictures, the United States in 1800 and again in 1817, in a novel and ambitious form of social and intellectual history—Adams sought to recount the seventeen-year story of the American nation with near-scientific precision, by arranging "facts in their sequence." Just such facts, Adams believed, were the proper business of the historian,

Augustus Saint-Gaudens monument for Marian Adams's grave, Rock Creek Cemetery, Washington, D.C.

who should write history as a way of inviting others to observe and compare their conclusions with his own. His ideal reader must be a student who viewed this scientific demonstration with the purpose of increasing his personal understanding by participating in the exercise. This reader did not exist merely to be entertained.

Yet, even as Adams was setting down his "facts" about the lives and thoughts of Jefferson, Gallatin, John Quincy Adams, John Randolph, and others, his historical "sequence" took on the coloration of his own prejudices and limitations in understanding, so that the objectivity he prized and aimed to achieve inevitably escaped from his artistic grasp. For later readers, who have been inclined to deny any real possibility of "scientific" history of the kind that Adams sought in this work and in later essays, the limitations of the *History of the United States* are less remarkable than its achievements. By skillful handling of original source materials in several languages, effective portrayal of character and personality, breadth of historical vision, and more, Adams made of the most ambitious literary project that he ever undertook a milepost on the road to modern historical writing. Yet the *History of the United States* was not a popular success. If his most appreciative readers have been scholars, rather than members of a more general public, that fact should not be allowed to diminish his overall achievement. For he succeeded beyond question in changing an old-fashioned narrative form of history into something quite different, a kind of history that would challenge every serious reader to improve upon its findings. In a personal way, moreover, Adams could point to the *History of the United States During the Administrations of Jefferson and Madison* as the first literary work of his life that demonstrated a full use of his abilities and talents.

Except for an extension of his travels to Japan, Cuba, Hawaii, and elsewhere, and a deeper cultivation of his platonic friendship with Elizabeth Cameron and her daughter, Martha, after 1885 Adams seemed to withdraw increasingly into a private existence. Publication of the final volumes of the history in 1891 (along with a companion volume, *Historical Essays*, to complete the ten-volume set) brought significant professional recognition but no public acclaim. Overall, the reviews were favorable, and the accuracy of Adams's "facts" drew special praise. The author was selected president of the American Historical Association, but he did not receive an important diplomatic appointment, such as those given his father and to some of his own friends. Accepting his largely symbolic role in the

Adams's home at 1603 H Street, Washington, D.C., one of two attached townhouses built for Adams and John Hay by the architect H. H. Richardson. Adams lived here, across Lafayette Park from the White House, for the last thirty-two years of his life.

historical association, Adams chose not to appear in person to read his presidential address but had it printed in the *Annual Report of the American Historical Association for the Year 1894* (1895). In that paper, "The Tendency of History," the author drew upon his personal experiences with his *History of the United States* by inviting his colleagues to find new and better ways to teach and write their own versions of history, ancient and modern. Meanwhile, from his vantage point in Washington, across the park from the White House, Adams watched his friend John Hay become first, Minister to the Court of St. James (the position Henry Adams's father had held in England during the Civil War) and later, Secretary of State (following, after many years, John Quincy Adams). Whatever ironies Henry Adams might have noted in the flight of real political power from his family during the course of American history, he managed to keep to himself. Yet, in the years of grief that followed Marian Adams's death, his mind

and pen remained active, as he turned away from political subjects to use his considerable skills in writing, among other things, two important works of private rather than public history. These two works marked the final decade of Henry Adams's full mental and physical capabilities, a decade that ended with the partial paralysis caused by a cerebral thrombosis that afflicted him in 1912.

In that final decade of full performance, Henry Adams wrote the two best-known of all his works, *Mont-Saint-Michel and Chartres* (privately printed, 1904; commercially published, 1913) and *The Education of Henry Adams* (privately printed, 1907; commercially published in October 1918, after the author's death the previous March). He also brought forth several essays and two memorial volumes for friends who died before him, editing *Letters of John Hay and Extracts from Diary* (1908) and writing *The Life of George Cabot Lodge* (1911). These two works have remained largely unread. On the other hand, along with the earlier *History of the United States*, *Mont-Saint-Michel and Chartres* and *The Education of Henry Adams* must be taken to represent the chief pillars on which Henry Adams's modern reputation as a man of letters rests.

Even so, the attractions of *Mont-Saint-Michel and Chartres* are difficult to define in any satisfactory way. The book is less an attempt to write either serious or popular history than a compelling invitation to travel and enjoy (as the author so obviously does) the aesthetic and emotional benefits of immersion in medieval life and culture. Where the pedant might have written a textbook for classroom use, Adams casts himself in a different role. As tour guide, he insists goodnaturedly on leading a procession of favorite "nieces in wishes" along a path to appreciation based on knowledge. Despite objections from serious-minded historians who want their history "straight," testimonials to the artistic success of *Mont-Saint-Michel and Chartres* abound. It has captured readers who are sympathetic to a kindly uncle and who know that the study of history as a cultural exercise can offer something more than mere instruction, just as studying religion is more than learning catechism and studying art is something more than gallery hopping. Overall, *Mont-Saint-Michel and Chartres* offers those who pick it up in the right frame of mind a reading experience that is greater than any possible listing of its parts.

Most complex and problematical of all, *The Education of Henry Adams* stands alone among Adams's writings. As a culmination of Adams's thinking on the subject of feminine force, it draws on the novels and on *Mont-Saint-Michel and Chartres*

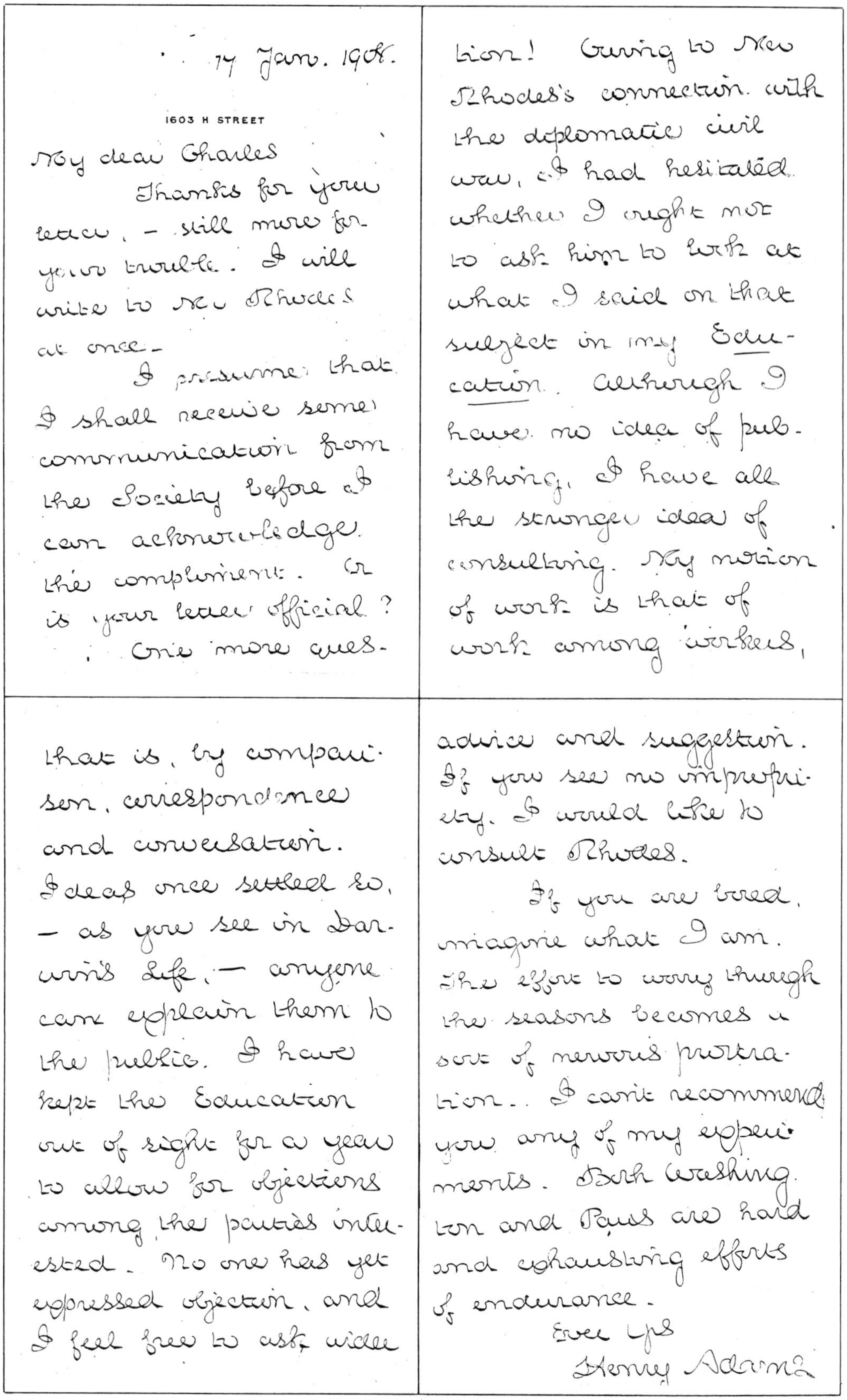

14 Jan. 1908.

1603 H STREET

My dear Charles

Thanks for your letter, — still more for your trouble. I will write to Mr Rhodes at once —

I presume that I shall receive some communication from the Society before I can acknowledge the compliment. Or is your letter official?

One more question! Owing to Mr Rhodes's connection with the diplomatic civil war, I had hesitated whether I ought not to ask him to look at what I said on that subject in my Education. Although I have no idea of publishing, I have all the stronger idea of consulting. My notion of work is that of work among workers,

that is, by comparison, correspondence and conversation. Ideas once settled so, — as you see in Darwin's Life, — anyone can explain them to the public. I have kept the Education out of sight for a year to allow for objections among the parties interested. No one has yet expressed objection, and I feel free to ask wider

advice and suggestion. If you see no impropriety, I would like to consult Rhodes.

If you are bored, imagine what I am. The effort to worry through the seasons becomes a sort of nervous prostration. I can't recommend you any of my experiments. Both Washington and Paris are hard and exhausting efforts of endurance.

Ever Yrs
Henry Adams

In this letter Adams explains to his brother Charles some reservations concerning the commercial publication of
The Education of Henry Adams.

to make a compelling argument for the superiority of woman over man and for the primacy of feminine understanding. Appealing as this case may be, *The Education of Henry Adams* is too often the only work by Adams that commentators use as a basis for generalizations about its author, and even about the world of his time. Yet, the accomplishments of the book deserve our admiration. *The Education of Henry Adams* is at once an accounting for a single private life, written in a tradition of great autobiography that includes St. Augustine, Rousseau, Franklin, Thoreau—and Henry James among Adams's contemporaries—and a panoramic representation of one man's version of American history in his time. That highly personalized history begins with the optimistic phrases of Thomas Jefferson and John Adams and ends for Henry Adams in the moral decadence of Grantian politics and the virtual disappearance of public concern and interest. For the Henry Adams of this book, as much as for the nation he represented as a kind of modern Everyman, decline and fall seemed the only possible conclusion. Yet the richness of Adams's art, and his reluctance to accept an unalterable pessimism as the only possible working philosophy, leads him to explore each alternate possibility and to reject oversimplification of experience at every point in his account. Wherever we hear his private voice, the author tells us insistently that all experience is dense and complex, and that living—for an Adams and for Everyman—may not be simple or easy. If decline in human greatness (for whatever reasons) had proved an unappealing truth for a fourth-generation heir to presidents, statesmen, and constitution writers, what was left to Henry Adams was yet an unmistakable legacy of intelligence and talent. While *Democracy* and *Esther* proved to Adams that his own skills in fiction did not match his ambitious intellectual designs, *The Education of Henry Adams*, along with *Mont-Saint-Michel and Chartres* and *The History of the United States of America During the Administrations of Jefferson and Madison*, provides ample evidence that, whatever loss had occurred in political distinction, the family reputation for perceptive thought and skillful writing remained secure in Henry Adams's hands.

Other:

Essays in Anglo-Saxon Law, edited, with an essay, by Adams (Boston: Little, Brown / London: Macmillan, 1876);

Documents Relating to New-England Federalism. 1800-1815, edited, with a preface, by Adams (Boston: Little, Brown, 1877);

The Writings of Albert Gallatin, edited, with a preface, by Adams, 3 volumes (Philadelphia & London: Lippincott, 1879);

"King," in *Clarence King Memoirs* (New York & London: Putnam's, 1904), pp. 157-185;

Letters of John Hay and Extracts from Diary, edited by Adams, 3 volumes (Washington: Privately printed, 1908).

Letters:

Letters to a Niece And Prayer to the Virgin of Chartres, edited by Mabel La Farge (Boston & New York: Houghton Mifflin, 1920);

A Cycle of Adams Letters, 1861-1865, edited by Worthington Chauncey Ford, 2 volumes (Boston & New York: Houghton Mifflin, 1920);

Letters of Henry Adams (1858-1891), edited by Ford (Boston & New York: Houghton Mifflin, 1930);

Letters of Henry Adams (1892-1918), edited by Ford (Boston & New York: Houghton Mifflin, 1938);

Henry Adams and His Friends, edited, with a biographical introduction, by Harold Dean Cater (Boston: Houghton Mifflin, 1947).

Biographies:

James Truslow Adams, *Henry Adams* (New York: A. & C. Boni, 1933);

Ernest Samuels, *The Young Henry Adams* (Cambridge: Harvard University Press, 1948);

Elizabeth Stevenson, *Henry Adams: A Biography* (New York: Macmillan, 1955);

Samuels, *Henry Adams: The Middle Years* (Cambridge: Harvard University Press, 1958);

Samuels, *Henry Adams: The Major Phase* (Cambridge: Harvard University Press, 1964).

References:

Max I. Baym, *The French Education of Henry Adams* (New York: Columbia University Press, 1951);

R. P. Blackmur, *Henry Adams* (New York & London: Harcourt Brace Jovanovich, 1980);

John J. Conder, *A Formula of His Own: Henry Adams's Literary Experiment* (Chicago & London: University of Chicago Press, 1970);

William Dusinberre, *Henry Adams: The Myth of Failure* (Charlottesville: University Press of Virginia, 1980);

Earl N. Harbert, ed., *Critical Essays on Henry Adams* (Boston: G. K. Hall, 1981);

Harbert, *The Force So Much Closer Home: Henry Adams and the Adams Family* (New York: New

York Univ. Press, 1977);

Harbert, *Henry Adams: A Reference Guide* (Boston: G. K. Hall, 1978);

George Hochfield, *Henry Adams: An Introduction And Interpretation* (New York: Barnes & Noble, 1962);

Robert A. Hume, *Runaway Star: An Appreciation of Henry Adams* (Ithaca: Cornell University Press, 1951);

William H. Jordy, *Henry Adams: Scientific Historian* (New Haven & London: Yale University Press, 1952);

J. C. Levenson, *The Mind and Art of Henry Adams* (Boston: Houghton Mifflin, 1957);

Melvin Lyon, *Symbol and Idea in Henry Adams* (Lincoln: University of Nebraska Press, 1970);

Robert Mane, *Henry Adams on the Road to Chartres* (Cambridge: Harvard University Press, 1971);

Ernst Scheyer, *The Circle of Henry Adams: Art and Artists* (Detroit: Wayne State University Press, 1970);

Vern Wagner, *The Suspension of Henry Adams: A Study of Manner And Matter* (Detroit: Wayne State University Press, 1969);

Henry Wasser, *The Scientific Thought of Henry Adams* (Thessalonica, Greece: Privately printed, 1956).

Papers:

Most of Henry Adams's papers and his personal library are housed at the Massachusetts Historical Society, Boston, Massachusetts.

Edward Bellamy
(26 March 1850-22 May 1898)

Tom H. Towers
University of Rhode Island

SELECTED BOOKS: *Six to One: A Nantucket Idyl*, anonymous (New York: Putnam's, 1878; London: Low, 1878);

Dr. Heidenhoff's Process (New York: Appleton, 1880; Edinburgh & London: Douglas/Hamilton, Adams, 1884);

Miss Ludington's Sister: A Romance of Immortality (Boston: Osgood, 1884; London: Douglas & Hamilton, 1884);

Looking Backward: 2000-1887 (Boston: Ticknor, 1888; London: Reeves, 1889);

Equality (New York: Appleton, 1897; London: Heinemann, 1897);

The Blindman's World and Other Stories (Boston & New York: Houghton, Mifflin, 1898);

The Duke of Stockbridge: A Romance of Shays' Rebellion (New York, Boston & Chicago: Silver, Burdett, 1900);

The Religion of Solidarity (Yellow Springs, Ohio: Antioch Bookplate Company, 1940).

Edward Bellamy owes his entire literary reputation to a single work, *Looking Backward* (1888), one of the relatively few American books to have an indisputable effect on society and politics. Along with *Uncle Tom's Cabin* (1852) and *Ben-Hur* (1880), *Looking Backward* was one of the best-selling books of the nineteenth century. Probably more directly than any other American novel, except perhaps *Uncle Tom's Cabin*, *Looking Backward* rendered in comprehensible terms its readers' deepest social anxieties. Bellamy's analysis of the dislocations of an increasingly industrialized America and his mix of cultural and technological solutions to the most disturbing social problems, at once confirmed and resolved doubts his generation had begun to express about the moral and material future of the nation. Bellamy clubs and publications advocating Bellamy's reformism sprang up throughout the United States, and his ideas were translated into legislative acts and party platforms. *Looking Backward* inspired a host of utopian and dystopian novels, and within a few years of its publication was the most widely familiar "socialist" work of its time. It influenced a generation of American and European reformers, and its place as the most important American depiction of utopia remains secure and unchallenged.

Although it might be possible to discover hints of some of Bellamy's mature thought in published and unpublished writings of his earlier years, there is little in either Bellamy's life or work prior to 1888 to suggest his sudden emergence as an important social thinker. Bellamy was born in Chicopee Falls, Massachusetts, the son of a Baptist minister, Rufus King Bellamy, and Maria Putnam Bellamy. He was a descendant, on both sides of his family, from generations of solid, earnest, but otherwise unexceptional New England clergymen, educators, and merchants. Family tradition held that Bellamy's paternal great-grandmother had been related to Roger Sherman, a signer of the Declaration of Independence. The author's great-grandfather, Joseph Bellamy, was a student and friend of Jonathan Edwards, and became a locally renowned preacher in Connecticut. Joseph Bellamy was perhaps most notable as an unbending defender of Calvinist orthodoxy; his unwavering commitment to principle was passed on to his children and grandchildren, and probably constituted the most important family influence on Edward Bellamy. Bellamy's father was revered in Chicopee Falls, where he held the same pastorate for nearly thirty-five years. However, unlike his ancestor, Rufus Bellamy departed significantly from his Puritan heritage, most notably in his implicit disbelief in hell, predestination, and eternal damnation. Edward inherited the family tradition of rectitude and responsibility, and more specifically, his father's optimistic and benevolent view of mankind. However, there is nothing in his family background to

Bellamy's birthplace, Chicopee Falls, Massachusetts

suggest his eventual social and economic ideas.

In 1867, after failing the physical examination for West Point, Bellamy entered Union College. However, his career there was cut short when his parents urged him to join his brother Packer in Europe. Bellamy spent about a year (1868-1869) in Germany and was rather casually moved by his observation of industrial conditions there. When he returned to America, he undertook the study of law with a Springfield, Massachusetts, attorney, and in 1871 was admitted to the bar. After accepting a single case as a lawyer, Bellamy abandoned the law in favor of journalism. He worked briefly (1871-1872) on the *New York Evening Post*, and in 1872 returned home to take a position as editorialist and book reviewer with the *Springfield Union*. Ill health caused him to give up that position in 1877 and to take a recuperative cruise to Hawaii in the company of his brother Frederick. He returned home in 1878 and two years later, in partnership with his brother Charles, began what became the *Springfield Daily News*. However, after less than a year as a publisher, Bellamy left newspaper journalism for good and devoted himself to the writing that would culminate in *Looking Backward*. On 30 May 1882 Bellamy married Emma Sanderson. Their children, Paul and Marion, were born in 1884 and 1886.

During his newspaper days Bellamy wrote a number of short stories (many of them later collected in *The Blindman's World*, 1898) and four novels. For the most part these early fictions are significant only as they anticipate ideas developed more importantly in *Looking Backward*. *Six to One* (1878) is a static novel of summer romance in which Bellamy explores romantic concepts of the relation of the individual to the cosmos—ideas first expressed in his essay *The Religion of Solidarity*, written in 1873 but not published until 1940. In both the essay and the novel Bellamy posits the familiar romantic notion of a wholly immanent God or "All-soul" present in all individuals. While that universally shared presence makes all men spiritual brothers, individuating desires and experiences tend to hold them apart. In *Six to One* the hero is an ailing newspaper editor convalescing at a shore resort where he becomes involved with six young women representing various aspects of materialism or spirituality. The hero and eventual heroine find that they are similarly attracted by the power of the universal life force symbolized by the sea, and in the end discover that their growing love for one another is the best means of breaking free from

individual isolation and of realizing the "All-soul" within them.

Bellamy's most realistic early fiction, *The Duke of Stockbridge*, was published serially the year after the appearance of *Six to One*. (It was not published in book form until Bellamy's cousin Francis Bellamy edited it and had it published in 1900.) *The Duke of Stockbridge* is a historical novel of Shays's Rebellion in 1786-1787, and is the fullest early expression of Bellamy's political ideas. Bellamy's sympathies lie emphatically with the villagers and small farmers whose hopes for a truly democratic order had been frustrated by the great merchants and landowners of post-Revolutionary America. In Bellamy's view the Revolution's implications had been as much social and economic as merely political, and American independence should have led to a society of general equality. Instead he saw it as ending with the substitution of plutocracy for royal authority. The resulting class structure, acting ironically in the name of freedom, oppressed the commonalty of citizens and denied them any but the most literal and hollow political liberty. Bellamy made a serious effort to study the popular uprising that was his subject, and his account differed significantly from the view of most nineteenth-century histories, but *The Duke of Stockbridge* evokes the concerns of Bel-

Frontispiece for Bellamy's first book, Six to One

lamy's own time more powerfully than it does the spirit of western Massachusetts in the 1780s. What is most striking in the novel, at least in terms of Bellamy's later works, is the conviction that politics is inescapably rooted in economics, and that no degree of merely political change can genuinely effect the transformation of society.

Bellamy's remaining early novels return to the post-Emersonian romanticism of *Six to One*. Both *Dr. Heidenhoff's Process* (1880) and *Miss Ludington's Sister* (1884) are moral-psychological romances concerned with the influence of the past upon individual lives. The "process" of the first of these novels is a vaguely mesmeric means of literally blotting out the memory of the past. Dr. Heidenhoff believes that most men are slaves to memory because the memory perpetuates the sense of sin by holding constantly before one the specter of his past misdeeds. So oppressed, the individual can be conquered by his sense of personal depravity and destroy himself in endless guilt, or he can try to desensitize himself, making himself perhaps less vulnerable to the torment of memory, but also increasing his propensity for repeated sin. As it obliterates the past, Heidenhoff's process leaves men free to do good according to their true nature—here as in *Six to One* and *Looking Backward* implicitly defined by their common participation in the benevolent "All-soul."

In *Miss Ludington's Sister*, Bellamy attacks the problem of the past from a somewhat different perspective. Ida Ludington was once a beautiful, active young woman; now she is an embittered spinster held captive by the memory of her youth, whose potential she believes she has betrayed. In a series of dialogues between Ida and her nephew Paul, Bellamy develops the idea of a discontinuous self, one that is not the cumulative totality of experience, but a series of separate selves, each with a distinct chronological duration. Thus Ida's age and desolation are not betrayals of her youthful self. That self, along with other later selves, has lived and died into its own special immortality, and the present Ida is neither the product nor the destroyer of those earlier selves. Freed from her guilt, Ida is enabled to accept the present and look without fear to the future. Ideas similar to those in the early novels are developed in most of Bellamy's short stories of these years.

Almost none of Bellamy's fiction before *Looking Backward* has much intrinsic appeal or value. He seldom created compelling or even convincing actions. His characters lack dimension or, except for the ideas put into their mouths, interest. His style is

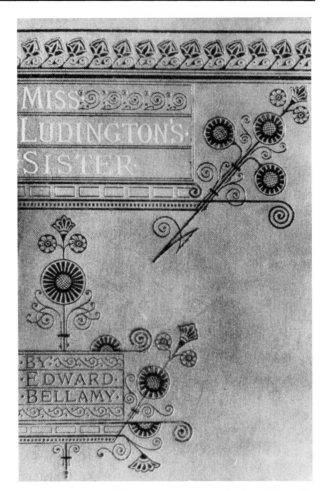

Front cover for Bellamy's 1884 novel, which continues his examination of the past's enslaving power

at best serviceable, and in the more specifically romantic novels which William Dean Howells admired somewhat, it is not always appropriate to Bellamy's "spiritual" subjects. In all of the earlier novels, as in *Looking Backward*, idealogical dialogue or debates predominate over plot and character development. However, his early writing shows Bellamy examining some of the important notions of *Looking Backward*. The idea of human brotherhood informed by universal participation in transcendent spirituality, the recognition of the need for self-realization founded in that same transcendence, the perception of the primacy of economics to politics, and the theory of a discontinuous history admitting an infinitude of "fresh starts" are all important to the utopian vision of Bellamy's major work.

Looking Backward appeared at the end of two decades of rapid, unsettling change in American life. Industrialization, urbanization, immigration, the opening of the trans-Missouri West, the apparently uncontrollable power of trusts and political machines had radically altered society. Business panic followed expansionist boom in an ever-quickening cycle. The old ideal of the self-sufficient farmer in benevolent nature was undermined by exploitive banks and railroads and by the distinctly unpastoral rigors of the new lands—and by the militance of the emergent Grangers and Populists. Trade unions challenged both the trusts and middle-class complacency in an epidemic of violent strikes. Surrounded by what appeared to be social chaos, many Americans of Bellamy's age and class sensed, sometimes vaguely, that while they had won a great Civil War to preserve their nation, they had somehow in the process been cheated and dispossessed of the America that was properly their heritage. Both the serious and popular literature of the period is suffused with nostalgic idealization of the pre-Civil War village, where, in Howells's phrase, "everybody had enough and nobody had too much." At the same time the middle-class Americans who felt deprived of their birthright were often participants in and beneficiaries of the very progress responsible for the cultural upheaval. In the flood of reformist writing of the period, *Looking Backward* is distinguished by its promise to restore the idealized culture of village America while retaining all the more attractive fruits of industrialization, technology, and economic centralization. It is probably that double, not to say contradictory, character of the book which accounted for both its vast popularity and its considerable influence upon the reform movement.

The double focus of *Looking Backward* makes it in a sense two books. More familiarly it appears to be a blueprint for a more or less socialist utopia; but that blueprint is framed in a narrative of nineteenth-century cultural unrest. Bellamy often spoke of the latter aspect of the book—the personal story of his hero, Julian West—as a "sugar-coating" for his utopian message. Julian's story conveys the cultural reassurance that is ultimately the justification for Bellamy's social and economic reforms.

West is both narrator and hero, a wealthy, educated Bostonian, who, under hypnosis, falls asleep in the chaotic America of 1887, and is revived in the new, perfected society of the year 2000. Most of the book consists of a series of dialogues between West and his twenty-first-century host and mentor, Dr. Leete, who explains the workings of the new order, corrects West's nineteenth-century prejudices and false assumptions, and allays his fears and misgivings. In his nineteenth-century life Julian re-

garded himself as a typical New England aristocrat, living on the income from inherited wealth and "occupied only with the pursuit of the pleasures and refinements of life." But in West's lifetime the graceful calm of generations had been shattered. Society generally had been paralyzed by a seemingly endless series of strikes, and even the West family mansion had been surrounded on all sides by factories and industrial slums. Recalling those times from the perspective of the twenty-first century, Julian perceives that what he had thought to be "the hum of peaceful industry" had in fact been "the clangor of swords" and that "mills and shops were so many forts, each under its own flag, its guns trained on the mills and shops about it, and its sappers busy below, undermining them." Such social malaise predictably affected personal life as well. In the nineteenth century Julian had suffered from chronic insomnia induced by the general turmoil and relieved only by hypnosis. He had lived in constant anticipation of class warfare, and had converted his own underground sleeping quarters to a combination bunker and bank vault. Worst of all, his marriage, potentially the means of personal peace, had been repeatedly postponed because of the strikes that prevented completion of the new home in which he and his bride might escape the pervasive strife of the modern world.

In the twenty-first century, when Julian awakes from the hypnotic spell, he finds that all the social and economic conflicts he has known in his previous life have been resolved—and without the dreaded bloodiness of revolution. Dr. Leete explains that toward the end of the nineteenth century the trusts had grown and merged to the point where a few great corporations had effectively controlled society. Yet those same trusts had become so vast that traditional private control became increasingly unworkable. In a single evolutionary step, the nineteenth-century industrial organization had been nationalized, the trust in effect became the state, and public ownership was declared. With the end of private control of the economy, the way had been easy to a new egalitarianism. The energy wasted in all forms of competition, cultural as well as economic, had been directed to the genuine service of the populace. Thus unshackled from their earlier wasteful functions, technology and industrialism had created a utopia.

The end of economic competition meant also the end of political parties and of all varieties of social and political conflict. In the same fashion, war with all its human and material waste had been eliminated. The new Americans are organized as a universal industrial army, led by technocrats who have themselves advanced through the ranks, and who at the close of their active service have been elevated by their peers to preside over a system of benevolent authoritarianism. The prescription of a military style of government has troubled many of Bellamy's twentieth-century readers. Bellamy, growing up during the Civil War, had cultivated an adolescent infatuation with the military and for a

LOOKING BACKWARD

2000—1887

BY

EDWARD BELLAMY

Author of " Miss Ludington's Sister"; " Dr. Heidenhoff's Process"; " A Nantucket Idyl," &c., &c.

BOSTON
TICKNOR AND COMPANY
211 Tremont Street.
1888

Title page for Bellamy's crusading novel, which sold 200,000 copies in the first two years after its publication

time had hoped to enter West Point. No doubt his idea of an industrial army derived in part from that enthusiasm. But authoritarianism is also a useful means of reconciling the inherent dynamism of an industrial order and the static, essentially preindustrial culture depicted in the book. In the end, the social and cultural effects of economic evolution are much more important in *Looking Backward* than are the political and economic consequences.

The perfection of technology and its redirection for the general good have obviated much tra-

ditional labor, and economic equality has eliminated the old idea of a working class. All citizens, as members of the army, have their appointed tasks, but these are now determined by aptitude and desire, not by class identity or financial necessity. The efficient use of the industrial plant for the general good has meant that economic equality, instead of leading to the downward leveling so feared by the nineteenth century, has produced an upward leveling, so that in the twenty-first century all enjoy what had earlier been beyond the reach of even aristocrats like West. As Dr. Leete explains in *Equality* (1897), the sequel to *Looking Backward*, "the revolution has made us all capitalists." The consequence has been the extension of traditional middle-class values and culture to the entire society. Education and leisure have become universal. The congestion of slums and factories that offended West's nineteenth-century sensibilities has disappeared. Despite what must have been a century of intense industrial development, twenty-first-century Boston is marked by the pastoral calm of the pre-Civil War village. Moreover, the new order has produced cultural effects quite beyond the imagining of the nineteenth century. For example, twenty-first-century women, because they are equal sharers in the economy, are free from financial dependence on men; love, not necessity, governs relations between men and women, and once-common sexual frustrations have disappeared. Similarly, because there is no longer a hierarchy of social status, all the psychic and other energies once spent in gaining and keeping one's position can be redirected, without sacrifice, to the spiritual fulfillment of the self. And there is no more of the socially induced anxiety and resentment that had earlier brought West and his contemporaries to a desperation bordering on madness.

The cultural—and by extension psychological—fruits of reform are most clearly perceived in the changes wrought upon Julian himself. His guide in the twenty-first century is aptly a physician, Dr. Leete, whose lectures on political economy have the ultimate purpose of restoring West to a health that his first life had stolen from him. As his frustration in love and his insomnia were the principal indices of his nineteenth-century malaise, so his engagement to Edith Leete (a descendant of Julian's nineteenth-century sweetheart, Edith Bartlett) and his slow progress to untroubled sleep suggest a recovery of psychological soundness. In the end, the institutional reforms of the new order liberate Julian from the destructive spiritual divisions of his earlier life. The self is reintegrated,

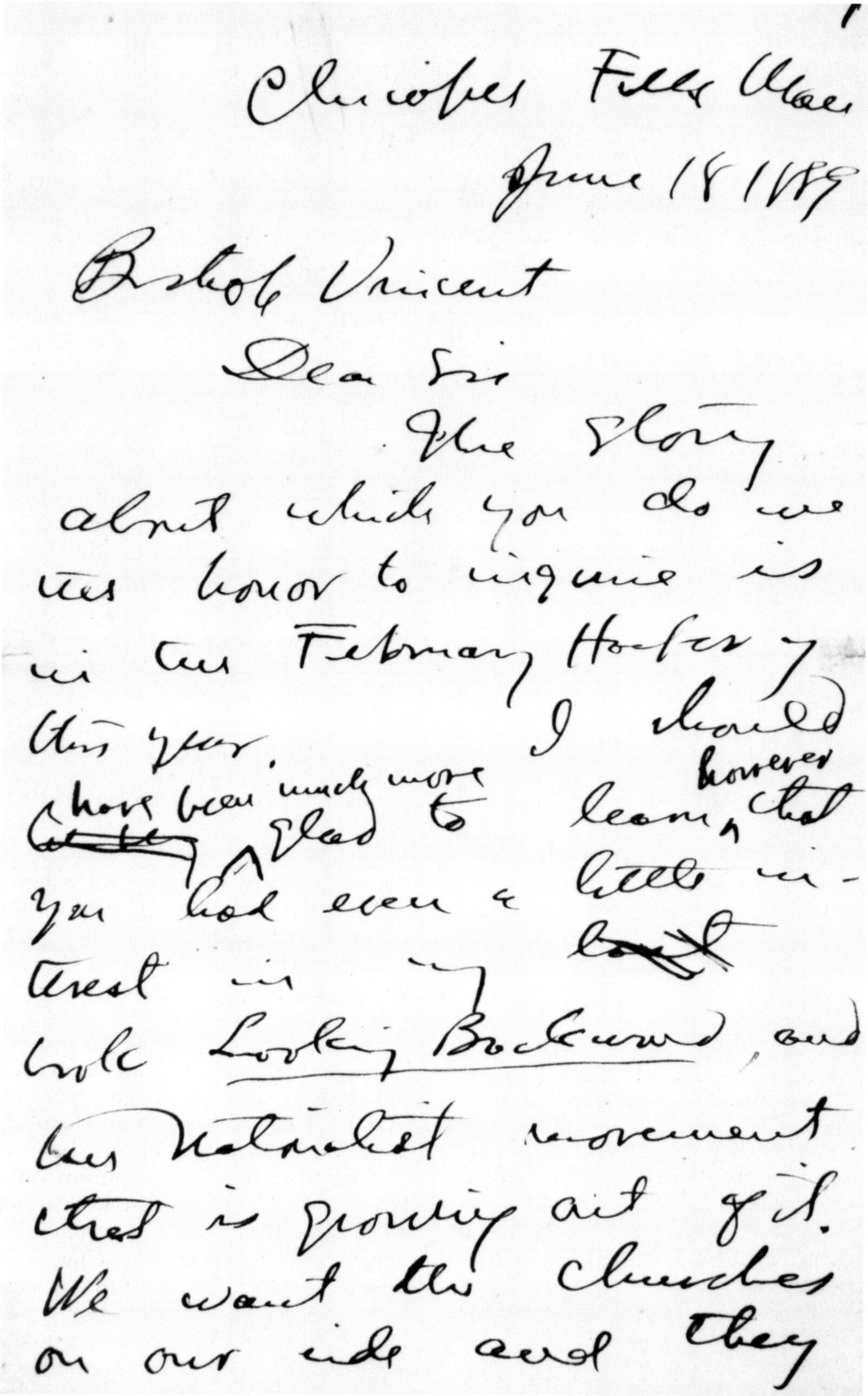

Chicopee Falls Mass

June 18 1889

Bishop Vincent

Dear Sir

The story
about which you do me
the honor to inquire is
in the February Harper's of
this year. I should
however
have been much more ~~lately~~ glad to learn that
you had even a little in-
trest in my ~~book~~
book Looking Backward, and
the Nationalist movement
that is growing out of it.
We want the churches
on our side and they

A letter about Bellamy's Nationalist movement, written a year and a half after the publication of Looking Backward, *the book that introduced Nationalist principles*

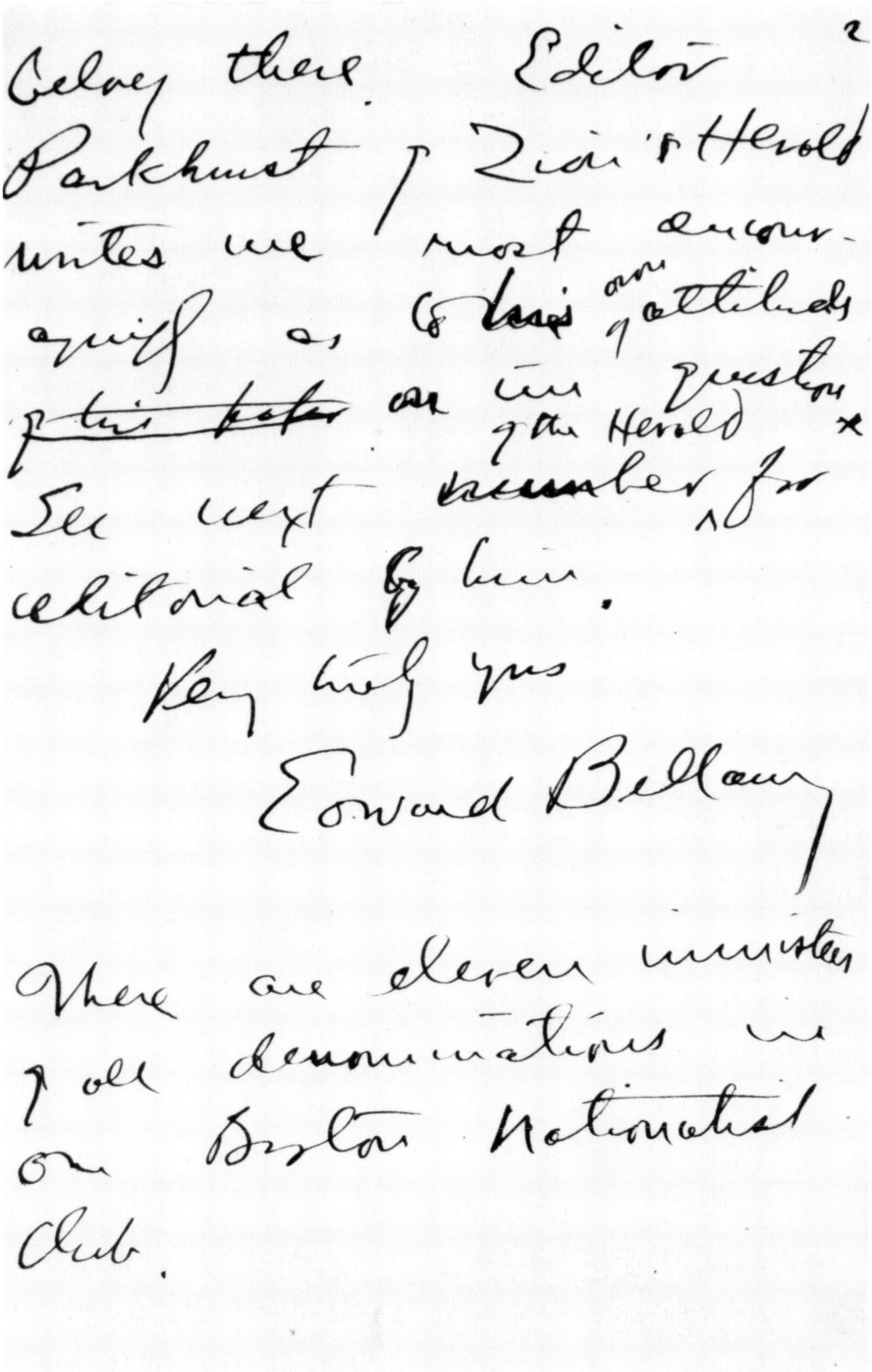

Below there. Editor [2]
Parkhurst of Zion's Herald
writes me most encour-
agingly as to his own attitude
& this paper on the question
of the Herald. ×
See next number for
editorial by him.

Very truly yours

Edward Bellamy

There are eleven ministers
of all denominations in
our Boston Nationalist
Club.

and Julian stands on the threshold of the self-realization that is the great desideratum of nineteenth-century romanticism.

Looking Backward, like many descriptions of utopias (including Sir Thomas More's), ironically seeks through its futurism the recovery of a lost golden age—in Bellamy's case one characterized by the myth of pastoral America and the dream of romantic selfhood. Although that nostalgic vision probably accounts for the otherwise surprising popular acceptance of the book, the prescription for economic and political reform understandably provoked a more fully articulated response. However, while his outline of an egalitarian society had excited great public interest, Bellamy had in fact only sketchily developed his reformist ideas in *Looking Backward*. As those ideas became part of the currency of contemporary political debate, Bellamy felt the need to fill in the programmatic chinks of *Looking Backward* and to answer his critics. In the preface to *Equality* he explains, "*Looking Backward* was a small book, and I was not able to get into it all I wished to say on the subject. Since it was published what was left out of it has loomed up as so much more important than what it contained that I have been constrained to write another book." As such a statement suggests, the resultant book, *Equality*, is wholly didactic and makes little pretense to being a novel. Even more than *Looking Backward*, it is devoted to lectures by Julian's twenty-first-century mentors, chiefly again Dr. Leete. But in abandoning the novelistic core of *Looking Backward*, the story of Julian West by which the book's cultural and psychological themes were developed, Bellamy shifts his emphasis almost entirely to theories of political economy, and the result is not merely a supplement to *Looking Backward*, but to some extent, a significant revision of the earlier work. One of the most striking differences between *Looking Backward* and its sequel is the virtual absence from *Equality* of any emphasis on the industrial army. And in *Equality* Leete confesses that the new America has been born out of revolution—complete with limited violence and general upheaval—rather than the scarcely discernible "evolution" suggested in the first book. Finally, there is little concern in *Equality* for the socially determined self-realization that is at the center of *Looking Backward*. Chapter titles such as "Private Capital Stolen from the Social Fund," "Economic Suicide of the Profit System," "Foreign Commerce under Profits," "Hostility of Vested Interests to Progress," "Inequality of Wealth Destroys Liberty," and "Life the Basis of the Right of Property" suggest the more or less orthodox socialism espoused in *Equality*. Whereas *Looking Backward* had promised that through painless evolution technological progress would end in the recovery of idyllically pastoral culture, *Equality*, by contrast, seems only a relatively charming but essentially predictable recipe for a socialist economy. The sales of *Equality* were insignificant in comparison to those of *Looking Backward*, and while the book does clarify many of Bellamy's ideas, it had little discoverable public impact.

The excitement generated by *Looking Backward* translated itself into the formation of clubs dedicated to the discussion and advancement of the book's ideas. The first such Nationalist Club was founded in Boston in December 1888, and within a year there were enough clubs nationwide to justify speaking of a Nationalist movement. The primary goal of Nationalism was the transfer of corporate property—in the beginning utilities and other quasi monopolies—to public ownership. For Bellamy and his followers Nationalism meant what would now be called nationalization; it had no overtones of devotion to a single state, and as it was concerned with world politics was distinctly internationalist. Nationalist ideas strongly influenced the Populist platform of 1892, and Bellamy himself became increasingly involved in political activism and in 1891 started his own magazine, the *New Nation*. As Nationalism became more and more identified with and influenced by other reform movements—for example, Populism, Theosophy, and Christian Socialism—it seemed to Bellamy to drift further and further from what he considered the spiritual and religious foundations of his ideas. Inevitably the movement became fragmented, and Bellamy's became increasingly a solitary voice. Nationalism as a political force had all but disappeared by 1895; in 1896 Bellamy abandoned the *New Nation* and devoted his dwindling energies to writing *Equality*. Bellamy had never been particularly robust. Since the 1870s he had suffered from recurrent pulmonary and digestive disorders, and by the early 1890s he had contracted tuberculosis. He died in Chicopee Falls on 22 May 1898.

References:

George Becker, "Edward Bellamy: Utopia, American Plan," *Antioch Review*, 14 (June 1954): 181-194;

David Bleich, "Eros and Bellamy," *American Quar-*

terly, 16 (Fall 1964): 445-459;

Sylvia E. Bowman, *The Year 2000: A Critical Biography of Edward Bellamy* (New York: Bookman Associates, 1958);

Howard Bruce Franklin, *Future Perfect: American Science Fiction of the Nineteenth Century* (New York: Oxford University Press, 1966), pp. 276-282;

William Dean Howells, "The Romantic Imagination," in *Criticism and Fiction and Other Essays*, edited by Clara Kirk and Rudolph Kirk (New York: New York University Press, 1959), pp. 250-255;

Arthur Morgan, *Edward Bellamy* (New York: Columbia University Press, 1944);

Vernon Lewis Parrington, Jr., *American Dreams: A Study of American Utopias* (New York: Russell & Russell, 1964), pp. 69-97;

Kenneth Roemer, *The Obsolete Necessity: America in Utopian Writings* (Kent, Ohio: Kent State University Press, 1976);

Charles Sanford, "Classics of American Reform Literature," *American Quarterly*, 10 (Fall 1958): 295-311;

Joseph Schiffman, "Edward Bellamy's Altruistic Man," *American Quarterly*, 6 (Fall 1954): 195-209;

Schiffman, "Edward Bellamy's Religious Thought," *PMLA*, 68 (September 1953): 716-732;

Tom H. Towers, "The Insomnia of Julian West," *American Literature*, 47 (March 1975): 52-63.

Papers:
Bellamy's manuscripts, notebooks, and other unpublished materials are deposited in the Harvard College Library, and typed copies of many items are held by the Library of Congress, the Huntington Library, and the Antioch College Library.

Ambrose Bierce
(24 June 1842-January 1914)

M. E. Grenander
State University of New York at Albany

See also the Bierce entry in *DLB 11, American Humorists, 1800-1950*.

SELECTED BOOKS: *The Fiend's Delight*, as Dod Grile (London: John Camden Hotten, 1873; New York: A. L. Luyster, 1873);

Nuggets and Dust Panned Out in California, as Dod Grile (London: Chatto & Windus, 1873);

Cobwebs from an Empty Skull, as Dod Grile (London & New York: Routledge, 1874);

The Dance of Death, by Bierce and Thomas A. Harcourt, as William Herman (San Francisco: Privately printed, 1877; corrected and enlarged edition, San Francisco: Henry Keller, 1877);

Tales of Soldiers and Civilians (San Francisco: E. L. G. Steele, [1892]); published simultaneously as *In the Midst of Life* (London: Chatto & Windus, 1892; revised and enlarged edition, New York & London: Putnam's, 1898);

Black Beetles in Amber (San Francisco & New York: Western Authors Publishing, 1892);

Can Such Things Be? (New York: Cassell, 1893; London: Cape, 1926);

Fantastic Fables (New York & London: Putnam's, 1899);

Shapes of Clay (San Francisco: W. E. Wood, 1903);

The Cynic's Word Book (New York: Doubleday, Page, 1906); enlarged as *The Devil's Dictionary*, volume 7 of *The Collected Works of Ambrose Bierce* (New York & Washington: Neale, 1911);

A Son of the Gods and A Horseman in the Sky (San Francisco: Elder, 1907);

The Shadow on the Dial and Other Essays, edited by S. O. Howes (San Francisco: A. M. Robertson, 1909); revised and republished as *Antepenultimata*, volume 11 of *The Collected Works of Ambrose Bierce* (New York & Washington: Neale, 1912);

Write It Right (New York & Washington: Neale, 1909);

The Collected Works of Ambrose Bierce, twelve volumes (New York & Washington: Neale, 1909-1912)—1) *Ashes of the Beacon, The Land Beyond the Blow, For the Ahkoond, John Smith, Liberator, Bits of Autobiography;* 2) *In the Midst of Life;* 3) *Can Such Things Be?, The Ways of Ghosts,*

Ambrose Bierce

Soldier-Folk, Some Haunted Houses; 4) *Shapes of Clay, Some Antemortem Epitaphs, The Scrap Heap*; 5) *Black Beetles in Amber, The Mummery, On Stone*; 6) *The Monk and the Hangman's Daughter, Fantastic Fables, Aesopus Emendatus, Old Saws with New Teeth, Fables in Rhyme*; 7) *The Devil's Dictionary*; 8) *Negligible Tales, The Parenticide Club, The Fourth Estate, The Ocean Wave, "On with the Dance!," Epigrams*; 9) *Tangential Views*; 10) *The Opinionator, The Reviewer, The Controversialist, The Timorous Reporter, The March Hare*; 11) *Antepenultimata*; 12) *In Motley, Kings of Beasts, Two Administrations, Miscellaneous*;
Battlefields and Ghosts, edited by Hartley E. Jackson and James D. Hart (Palo Alto: Harvest Press, 1931);
Selections from Prattle by Ambrose Bierce, edited by Carroll D. Hall (San Francisco: Book Club of California, 1936);
Enlarged Devil's Dictionary, edited by Ernest J. Hopkins (Garden City: Doubleday, 1967);
The Ambrose Bierce Satanic Reader, edited by Hopkins (Garden City: Doubleday, 1968).

The late Carey McWilliams, an astute observer of the national scene, has pointed out that every American should have some familiarity with Ambrose Bierce, that aloof and independent iconoclast who was in the thick of some of the most important developments of our history. Like other gallant young men of his generation, he sacrificed his youth to the military holocaust that blazed through and almost destroyed the United States in 1861-1865. As he grew older, his magnetic personality attracted respect and esteem in England, California, and Washington, D.C. Many of his admirers recorded their impressions of him; and his incisive journalism, witty epigrams, and brilliant stories are now part of the American heritage. Nevertheless, for more than 100 years his life and his writings have resisted easy generalizations.

The reason lies in the fact that Bierce was the completely self-reliant man, whose nonconformity permeated almost every aspect of his thinking. He set his face not only against literary fashion, but against dominant social and political theories as well. Basic to his position was his dark view of the human soul. Given the nature of man, he felt, programs based on rigid principles of any stripe were doomed to failure. What might be abstractly preferable was irrelevant to the solution of problems whose answers must be devised and implemented by human beings. The starry-eyed idealist who oversimplified issues did more harm than good in the long run, said Bierce; his visionary promises deluded the very people he sought to help, leading them to cynicism and despair. Not only about theological and scientific matters, but about literary, moral, ethical, social, and political ones as well, men and women should reserve judgment on problems which cannot be solved by reason. They should not leap blindly into an uncritical acceptance of dogma by faith. Anyone holding such views is unlikely to maintain doctrinaire tenets, and here lies the crux of Bierce's nonconformity. He could hardly be expected to follow the majority, but what is perhaps more interesting is that he refused to enlist in any minority *-ism*, either. Such a man is clearly provocative rather than popular, since there is no group for whom he will have mass appeal. Rather, his charm lies in his affinity for the small number of people in any age who are as strongly individualistic as he.

Ambrose Gwinnett Bierce was born on a farm in southeastern Ohio on 24 June 1842, the tenth of thirteen children (all of whose first names began with *A*) born to Marcus Aurelius and Laura Sherwood Bierce and the youngest to survive to adulthood. Although the Ohio of his early childhood furnished the background for two of his short stories, "The Suitable Surroundings" and "The Boarded Window," his family moved to northern Indiana near the village of Warsaw four years after his birth, and he grew up a Hoosier except for a brief period in 1859-1860 when he studied draftsmanship, surveying, and engineering at the Kentucky Military Institute in Franklin Springs, Kentucky. His nonconformity was nurtured when, as a teenager, he worked on an antislavery paper in Warsaw, the *Northern Indianan*. And in April 1861, when the Civil War broke out, he enlisted at the age of eighteen as a private in the Ninth Indiana Infantry.

This decision, at the beginning of four of the most impressionable years of his life, was to have lasting consequences in molding his character. He fought bravely and skillfully throughout the war, rising eventually to the rank of first lieutenant and the staff position of topographical engineer. As a brigade headquarters officer, he was in a position not only to engage in firsthand combat, but also to understand the larger strategic picture of some of the Civil War's most famous battles: Shiloh, Stones River, Chickamauga, Missionary Ridge, and Kennesaw Mountain, where he was shot in the head in June 1864. After hospitalization and a brief convalescent furlough he returned to service in September, in time to participate in the battles of Franklin and Nashville. During Reconstruction after the war, he worked as a U.S. Treasury agent in Alabama for several months in 1865. The next year, however, he joined his wartime commander, Brig. Gen. William Hazen, as engineering attache on an army mapping expedition from Omaha to the West Coast. But when he arrived in San Francisco, he resigned his army post, angered at not receiving the captain's commission he had been promised. (He was brevetted to major in 1867 for his distinguished military service.)

In 1867, while holding minor, undemanding jobs at the U.S. Sub-Treasury in San Francisco, he began having his work published in the *Californian*, the *Golden Era*, and the *Alta California*, as well as in the *San Francisco News Letter and California Advertiser*, of which he became editor in December 1868. In 1871 his "Grizzly Papers" began to appear in the *Overland Monthly*, then under Bret Harte's editorship. These essays contain some of Bierce's best and most distinctive early work. For example, in a public statement of the principles that governed his own life, he attacked conformity to fickle public opinion and defended self-reliance, on the ground that "If a man have a broad foot, a stanch leg, a strong spine,

and a talent for equilibrium, there is no good reason why he should not stand alone. . . . A mind that is right side up does not need to lean upon others: it is sufficient unto itself. The curse of our civilization is that the 'association' is become the unit, and the individual is merged in the mass." According to Bierce, civilization owed its advances to the courageous minority, not to the powerful but mediocre majority. His first published story, "The Haunted Valley," a tale of murder and mystery which was republished in *Can Such Things Be?* (1893) also appeared in the *Overland Monthly*.

On Christmas Day 1871, Bierce married Mary Ellen (Mollie) Day, the daughter of a well-to-do miner; and in March 1872, financed by his father-in-law, he and Mollie Bierce left for England. They lived there from 1872 to 1875, a period he later characterized as "the happiest and most prosperous period of his life." Tall, well-dressed, and handsome, with gray eyes and blond hair and mustache, the witty Bierce appealed to the British, and he quickly became active in London journalism and publishing. He wrote for Tom Hood's *Fun*, a humorous weekly; for *Figaro*; and for the San Francisco *Alta California*, to which he sent accounts of English current events. He also wrote in their entirety the two issues of the *Lantern*, a gorgeously polychromatic publication which appeared on 18 May and 15 July 1874. A footnote to the French revolution of 1870-1871, which had toppled Napoleon III from his throne and established the short-lived Paris Commune, the *Lantern* was subsidized by the Empress Eugénie, Napoleon's widow and a wealthy exile in England.

Using the pen name Dod Grile, Bierce also had his first three books published in England: *The Fiend's Delight* and *Nuggets and Dust Panned Out in California* in 1873, and *Cobwebs from an Empty Skull* in 1874. Four thousand copies of *Cobwebs from an Empty Skull* were printed, with a second printing of 4,000 several years later. All three of these early books were composed of sketches, paragraphs, short narratives, epigrams, and fables collected from Bierce's journalistic writings. *The Fiend's Delight* shows him at his epigrammatic best in selections such as "Those who are horrified at Mr. Darwin's theory, may comfort themselves with the assurance that, if we are descended from the ape, we have not descended so far as to preclude all hope of return." *Nuggets and Dust* included appreciative little essays on aspects of England that had appealed to Bierce: "St. Paul's," "The Size of London," and "Stratford-on-Avon," his homage to Shakespeare. Typical of the short fables in *Cobwebs from an Empty*

Skull is one in which an oak agrees to let an ivy vine climb him: "So she started up, and finding she could grow faster than he, she wound round and round him until she had passed up all the line she had. The oak, however, continued to grow, and as she could not disengage her coils, she was just lifted out by the root. So that ends the oak-and-ivy business, and removes a powerful temptation from the path of the young writer." Such fables, with their compression, wit, stylistic elegance, and reversal of conventional opinion, were admired by Mark Twain, and he included seven of them in his *Library of Humor* (1888), their first publication in America. Bierce, however, always expressed contempt for his early London books and refused to have them republished during his lifetime. Nevertheless, they were moderately successful in England, where Prime Minister William Ewart Gladstone, twenty years after their original appearance, started a Bierce boom by praising their wit. And in spite of his announced distaste for them, Bierce culled from all three books for Volumes 6, 8, 9, and 12 of his *Collected Works* (1909-1912).

Bierce's chronic asthma had prevented the Bierces from settling permanently in London. They lived in a number of attractive places: Bristol, where their first son, Day, was born in 1872; Bath; and Leamington, birthplace of their second son, Leigh, in 1874. However, Mollie Bierce, burdened with two small children and pregnant with a third, was not as enchanted with England as her husband, and in April 1875 she returned to San Francisco. Bierce joined her in September, and on 30 October their third child—a daughter, Helen—was born there. Bierce had had to leave a promising writing career in England, and it took him more than a decade to establish himself professionally in the United States. Initially he got a job in the assay office of the San Francisco branch of the U.S. Mint and wrote a column, "The Prattler," for a newly founded magazine called the *Argonaut*, beginning the satiric definitions which later became famous in *The Devil's Dictionary* (1911—after an intermediate appearance in *The Cynic's Word Book*, 1906). With T. A. Harcourt he concocted an elaborate hoax called *The Dance of Death* (1877), supposedly written by a William Herman. The book purported to be a vicious attack on the waltz, but was so suggestively written as to be a popular success whose appeal Bierce augmented by stern strictures against it in his column.

However, his most serious efforts at establishing himself in a career were devoted to an ill-starred gold-mining venture in the Dakota Territory. Financed by Wall Street capitalists, the Black

Hills Placer Mining Company was run by incompetents and headed by a president who later barely escaped being sent to Sing Sing on charges of graft and corruption. In the spring of 1880 Bierce was appointed general agent of the struggling mining company and left for Deadwood, his wife and children remaining in California. For four months he worked ably and conscientiously for the company, but its affairs were so snarled by foolish and dishonest managers that, despite his skill and hard work and the mine's potential for success, the enterprise collapsed. He wound up with little money for his exhausting labors and the burden of a complicated lawsuit which dragged on for nine years, ending up in the U.S. Supreme Court. As nominal plaintiff Bierce won the suit, but he got nothing out of it and even had to pay the court costs. Although this single episode was not the only basis for his continuing satire against the law and lawyers, it could hardly have failed to add to his disillusionment with them.

In 1881 he returned to San Francisco and his family, and once again had to find a new career. This time, however, he was able to secure the editorship of the weekly *San Francisco Wasp*, with which he was associated from 1881 to 1886. He continued his column in this journal, renaming it "Prattle" and including in it many more of the definitions collected in *The Cynic's Word Book*, and published "What I Saw of Shiloh," an eyewitness account of one of the Civil War's most memorable battles. The *Wasp* also offered Bierce a journalistic outlet for attacking the "Big Four," whose depredations were later to be documented by Gustavus Myers in his *History of the Great American Fortunes* (1910). Primarily through the Central Pacific and Southern Pacific Railroads, they had seized control of California, dominating not only the press but the state's corrupt politicians in Washington as well as in Sacramento. Bierce denounced these malefactors of great wealth—Mark Hopkins, £eland $tanford (as Bierce called him), Collis P. Huntington, and Charles Crocker—while they were at the very height of their power. An honest and courageous man, he was throughout his life filled with disgust at the chicanery and greed that scarred American life after the Civil War. He had seen these traits of the national character while still a young man, in the days of his Alabama service during the Reconstruction; and one of the reasons he had been so taken with England in the three and a half years he lived there was that he felt Englishmen were morally superior to Americans. His months in the Black Hills, when he watched what could have been a valuable gold mine destroyed by incompetent and

Portrait of Bierce by English artist J. H. E. Partington exhibited at 1893 World's Fair in San Francisco

changes, he sold his periodical in 1886, and Bierce was once more out of a job.

But the next twelve years were to be the most significant of his personal and professional life. In 1887 the young William Randolph Hearst hired him, at a generous weekly salary, to write for his newly acquired *San Francisco Examiner*, and Bierce henceforth had a powerful weapon at hand for attacking the objects of his scorn, which included not only political and economic malfeasance but also bad writing. The scourge of poetasters, he became the literary dictator of the West Coast. His living arrangements, however, were controlled by the asthma which prevented his settling in any of the Bay Area cities where he earned his living—San Francisco, Berkeley, and Oakland. Instead, he retreated to lonely hotels in out-of-the-way mountain resorts, his solitude mitigated by an occasional visitor and by a number of pets, not only cats, birds, and squirrels but also those rejected by most people: horned toads, lizards, and snakes. Troubled by insomnia as well as bronchial ailments, he spent much time in the open air, hiking and bicycling along woodland trails.

Two crises blighted this period. One was his separation from Mollie Bierce, which occurred after he discovered some indiscreet letters an ardent admirer had written her. Although nothing seriously improper had occurred, Bierce refused to compete for the affection of his own wife; the rupture was complete and final. Even more shattering was the death of the Bierces' older son, Day, at the age of sixteen, when he and a young rival killed each other in a gun duel over a girl.

fraudulent management, had reinforced his contempt for deceit and graft. Much of his reputation on the West Coast stemmed from his audacity and skill in attacking the Big Four, whom he called feudal overlords. Bierce accused these men of holding the economic and political life of California in their viselike grip and demonstrating on a grand scale the worst qualities of America's Age of Plutocracy. Unfortunately, however, the *Wasp's* owner was too vacillating and dependent to succeed in journalism. After an embarrassing series of policy

Bierce's 1867 cartoon of the Aerial Steam Navigation Company's heavier-than-air balloon

Bierce in Washington, D.C.

Bierce confronted these tragedies stoically, and he wrote in rapid succession, between 1888 and 1891, the series of short stories on which his reputation today largely rests: "One of the Missing," "A Son of the Gods," "A Tough Tussle," "Chickamauga," "One Officer, One Man," "A Horseman in the Sky," "The Suitable Surroundings," "The Affair at Coulter's Notch," "A Watcher by the Dead," "The Man and the Snake," "An Occurrence at Owl Creek Bridge," "Parker Adderson, Philosopher," and "The Death of Halpin Frayser." These tales, published initially in ephemeral periodicals, deal with the psychological traumas of a protagonist suddenly forced into agonizing and deadly straits. For most of the settings, Bierce returned to the Civil War battles of his youth. Now,

however, he distilled those experiences, catalyzed by a polished craft, through the alembic of a mature wisdom. The results, among the English-speaking world's greatest creations in the demanding art of the short story, were eventually collected in two volumes. The first was published simultaneously in 1892 in San Francisco by E. L. G. Steele as *Tales of Soldiers and Civilians* and in London by Chatto and Windus as *In The Midst of Life*. The London title, derived from the burial service in the Anglican Book of Common Prayer ("In the midst of life we are in death"), was a brilliant contribution of Andrew Chatto's. Bierce was slow to appreciate this title, although in 1898 he took it over himself for the new American edition. The book was favorably received on both sides of the Atlantic, with Bierce

TALES

OF

Soldiers and Civilians

BY

AMBROSE BIERCE

SAN FRANCISCO
E. L. G. STEELE
208 CALIFORNIA STREET
1891.

IN THE MIDST OF LIFE

Tales of Soldiers and Civilians

BY

AMBROSE BIERCE

London
CHATTO & WINDUS, PICCADILLY
1892

Title pages for the simultaneously published American and British editions of Bierce's 1892 collection of Civil War stories, the first of his books to be published under his name

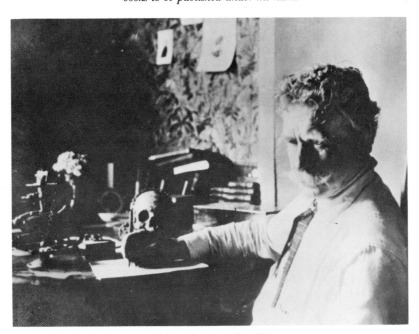

Bierce in his study, 1899

being ranked alongside Poe and Hawthorne. It suffered, not from lack of critical appreciation, but from a failure of business acumen. Steele was not a publisher, but a moderately well-to-do friend of Bierce's. Two subsequent publishers of the book went bankrupt as did the publisher of a second collection of Bierce's stories which appeared as *Can Such Things Be?*, a title derived from Shakespeare's *Macbeth*.

Meanwhile Bierce was becoming involved in one of the most tangled episodes of his career. A young German-Jewish dentist, Gustav Adolph Danziger, had brought him a rough translation of a short novel by Richard Voss, *Der Mönch von Berchtesgaden*, which had appeared in a German monthly. Bierce rewrote the story from Danziger's translation, and the two signed a complicated contract dividing the rewards they expected to get. Their work appeared serially under the title *The Monk and the Hangman's Daughter* in the *Examiner*; then it was published by F. J. Schulte of Chicago, who went bankrupt. For years Danziger squabbled with Bierce over *The Monk and the Hangman's Daughter*.

Bierce's next book, a volume of satirical verse, *Black Beetles in Amber* (1892), was published by the Western Authors Publishing Company, a shaky vanity enterprise formed by Danziger and William M. Langton. This company also failed. Although Bierce's satire was superb, its targets were so insignificant that a new firm in Cambridge, Stone and Kimball, decided not to go through with their plans for publishing a selection from his book. Bierce defended his concentration on minor insects, however, by referring to the examples of Byron and Pope and revealing his theory of satire: "I cannot see how the quality or interest of a piece is affected by application to a real, though unknown, person instead of presenting it as a general satire, with perhaps a fictitious name. If the verse is good it *makes* the victims known; if not good it is not worth publishing anyhow." But his work was soon taken in hand by a competent firm. In 1898 G. P. Putnam's Sons published a revised and enlarged edition of *In the Midst of Life*, which earned favorable reviews and royalties on the sale of over 3,000 copies; Chatto and Windus brought out a second printing; and in 1899 Putnam's published *Fantastic Fables*, whose sales approached 1,000.

In journalism, too, this period saw Bierce's greatest triumphs. Hearst had decided to direct his minions to attack a railroad refunding bill introduced in Congress in 1896. The bill would have written off the tremendous sums the federal government had loaned the railroads, gouging the American taxpayers for $130 million. Collis Huntington, only surviving member of California's Big Four, was leading the Washington lobby favoring the bill; Bierce was sent to the nation's capital to head the opposition deployed by Hearst, who had recently acquired the *New York Journal*. Bierce wrote for both the *Journal* and the *San Francisco Examiner*, traveling frequently from Washington to New York, and pointing out in powerful prose in these two widely circulated papers the web of deceit on which the funding bill rested and its cost to the nation. Telegrams and letters streamed from the *Examiner's* San Francisco staff, furnishing him a constant source of ammunition that he supplemented with what he picked up himself on the East Coast. The bill was eventually defeated, and the railroads paid off their debt in twenty semi-annual installments from 1899 to 1909.

Bierce had planned to join his second son, Leigh, in New York, but poor health and changes in the political scene caused his return to California in 1896. Although he had numerous conflicts with the editorial staffs of both the *Examiner* and the *Journal* because they mangled his copy and failed to print some of what he considered his best work, Hearst himself insisted on paying his weekly salary, leaving him free to decide when and what he wanted to write. Bierce then began a journalistic crusade with a column, "War Topics," that, contrary to Hearst's own stand, opposed the Spanish-American War. Bierce considered it unnecessary and imperialistic, describing it as the first step in America's march to world power, global wars, and eventual destruction of the planet by airborne superbombs.

Meanwhile his ties to California were loosening. Most of his early literary friends were his "pupils"—young writers such as George Sterling, Gertrude Atherton, and Danziger—who lived in California and who had come to him with their manuscripts for advice and encouragement. But as his fame spread, his friends were admirers of his work who were not necessarily Californians. Moreover, he wanted to be nearer Leigh Bierce, a reporter for the *New York Journal*. Consequently Bierce left San Francisco in December 1899 to return to Washington, where he lived for most of the remainder of his life.

His last thirteen years were shaken by two further tragedies: the death of his second son, the twenty-six-year-old Leigh Bierce, from pneumonia in 1901; and the death of his wife, Mollie Bierce, four years later, shortly after their divorce. Yet his daughter Helen, despite a serious illness and repeated marital difficulties, remained a solace to him. And, most important, Carrie Christiansen, a middle-aged schoolteacher whom the Bierces had befriended when she was a young girl, moved to Washington and lived near him as friend and secretary. Consequently this period was in many ways the most serene and contented of Bierce's life. He joined the Army and Navy Club, where military friends revived his post-Civil War brevet rank of major; his writing enjoyed a growing reputation; and he was earning a steady salary from William Randolph Hearst, contributing to the *San Francisco Examiner*, the *New York Journal*, the *New York American*, and *Cosmopolitan* magazine. Although such former "pupils" as Sterling, Herman Scheffauer, and Danziger (who changed his name to De Castro) created friction in his life, other young men and women made much of his work: Gertrude Atherton, Percival Pollard, H. L. Mencken, and, most important, an aggressive publisher, Walter Neale.

Shapes of Clay, a second volume of satirical verse, came out in 1903. Although in this book Bierce calls the pun the bequest of a "dying idiot," the following stanza from "For Merit" is typical:

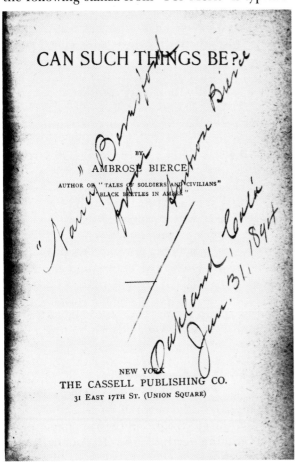

Inscribed title page for Bierce's 1893 collection of short stories dealing with the Civil War and the California frontier

Let meaner men the poet's bays
Or warrior's medal wear;
Who cooks potatoes fifty ways
Shall bear the palm—de terre.

In 1906 Bierce's satirical definitions, which are still current, appeared in book form as *The Cynic's Word Book*, a weak title insisted upon by a timorous publisher afraid of his author's forthright choice, *The Devil's Dictionary*. In 1907 two of his short stories were published in book form as *A Son of the Gods and A Horseman in the Sky*; and Neale brought out *The Monk and the Hangman's Daughter*, Danziger having turned over his rights in it to Bierce in 1902. In 1909 Neale also published a small handbook of grammatical usage, *Write It Right*, which is not included in Bierce's *Collected Works*. *Write It Right* was reprinted many times and remained a newspaperman's bible for decades; much of the advice in it is still valuable. Typical of its strictures is the following: "*Badly* for *Bad*. 'I feel badly.' 'He looks badly.' The former sentence implies defective nerves of sensation, the latter, imperfect vision. Use the adjective." Still another book appeared under the aegis of Silas Orrin Howes, a young Texas newspaperman, who edited a collection of Bierce's essays bearing the title *The Shadow on the Dial and Other Essays* (1909); it reappeared as *Antepenultimata* in the *Collected Works*, volume 11.

By far the most important publishing project of Bierce's entire life was his *Collected Works*, a twelve-volume set he prepared himself, which Neale published from 1909 to 1912 and marketed through subscription. Bierce was not always discriminating in what he chose to include, and since he was a prolific journalist throughout his life, much is left out. Nevertheless, this collection, which contains much material that had not previously been published in book form, is essential for any serious study of its author. Bierce expended years of devoted labor on its twelve volumes—gathering, revising, editing, and proofreading.

After this monumental task was completed in 1912, Bierce's thoughts began turning to death. He had stated repeatedly that he did not want to die in bed, and after more than a decade of relative quiet, he craved action. Consequently he began writing farewell letters to his friends and relatives, telling them that he intended to visit Mexico to observe the revolutionary forces of Pancho Villa, who was leading a popular insurrection against the reactionary government. Early in October 1913 Bierce left Washington and made a leisurely tour of his old Civil War battlefields. Reaching New Orleans, he

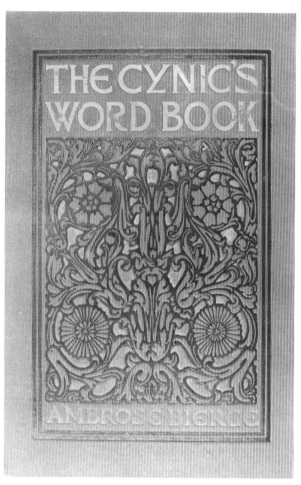

Front cover for first book publication of Bierce's cynical dictionary. An enlarged edition was later published under Bierce's original title, The Devil's Dictionary, *which was unacceptable to Doubleday, Page.*

granted interviews to newspaper reporters, then traveled to Texas. From El Paso he went to Juarez, which Villa had captured on 15 November. Thence he proceeded to Chihuahua, occupied by Villa on 8 December. Bierce's last letter was dated 26 December 1913. In it he stated that he intended to go from Chihuahua to Ojinaga the next day. Circumstantial evidence indicates that almost certainly he was killed in the battle of Ojinaga, which took place on 11 January 1914. Although many fanciful theories, outlining his continued activities in Mexico or South America after this date, were advanced, none of them was convincing, and none stood up to investigation. His disappearance, the most dramatic exit from life in American literary history, still causes a flurry of excitement when his name is mentioned. His mysterious end had an effect that he himself would have deplored: for years interest

focused not on his work, but on his colorful life and commanding personality. Even today the student of Bierce is often forced to preface any discussion of his writing by answering the question: "What happened to him after he went to Mexico?"

However, serious critical examination of his work is now well under way. Bierce wrote entirely in short forms, and while in some cases, to be sure, he strikes a false note that spoils their tone, many are masterly. At his best, Bierce makes us think: about ourselves, about our relations with others, and about our society.

His short stories fall into four broad categories: didactic tales, mimetic tales of passion, mimetic tales of moral choice, and mimetic tales of action. Didactic tales like "Haita the Shepherd," "Parker Adderson, Philosopher," and "The Famous Gilson Bequest" are arguments persuading the reader to accept particular theses about such questions as the nature of happiness, the meaning and acceptance of death, and the destructive effects of avarice. All the mimetic tales, however, are imitations of human experience so represented as to arouse in the reader a sequence of expectations and emotions. In mimetic tales of passion like "An Occurrence at Owl Creek Bridge," "A Resumed Identity," and "The Death of Halpin Frayser," the protagonists undergo changes in thought and feeling as reactions to the situations in which they find themselves. Mimetic tales of moral choice—like "The Affair at Coulter's Notch," "A Son of the Gods," and "A Horseman in the Sky"—place their protagonists in situations where they must make crucial decisions involving a conflict between two value systems, both of which they adhere to. And finally, the mimetic tales of action present protagonists who act in relation to their situation. Examples of these stories are "Jupiter Doke, Brigadier-General," "A Watcher by the Dead," and "The Suitable Surroundings."

Bierce's plots are represented in such a way as to create different kinds of emotional effects on the reader: ironic terror, pathos, tragic pity and fear, the moral satisfaction of retributive tragedy, uncanny dread, or moral indignation. The effect may even be one of absurdity, in tales like "Jupiter Doke, Brigadier-General," "The Widower Turmore," "My Favorite Murder," and "An Important Conflagration." Such stories force the reader to reexamine accepted values in human ties and social relationships, an aim accomplished by a reversal of genuine standards, hyperbolic exaggeration, and understatement.

But Bierce's fame also rests on forms which are even briefer than the short story: fables, epigrams, verse satires, and sardonic definitions. Although enormous variety exists in these works, four features Bierce explicitly aimed at can be found in them: clear thinking, wit, precision, and taste. In *Write It Right*, he had stated that good writing, "essentially, is clear thinking made visible." Wit, he believed, was different from humor, conveying a sudden, sharp insight that reverses conventional attitudes and overturns stereotyped values; it "stabs, begs pardon—and turns the weapon in the wound." Precision was achieved through writing so that the "reader not only may, but must, understand." Bierce was a linguistic liberal, not a purist; he believed that dictionaries were poor guides to the precise use of language because they tended to rigidify usage. For taste, since "there are neither standards nor arbiters," what the reader gets, of course, is Bierce's own.

Certain subjects run through his short forms: international relations, politics, religion, medicine, business, the pleasures of good food and drink, science, law, and the war between the sexes. Illustrating the last is his definition of *Marriage* in *The Devil's Dictionary*: "The state or condition of a community consisting of a master, a mistress and two slaves, making in all, two." An epigram also illustrates this theme: "For study of the good and the bad in woman two women are a needless expense." Thus, Bierce claimed that "A virtuous widow is the most loyal of mortals; she is faithful to that which is neither pleased nor profited by her fidelity." And he also wrote this forthright definition of *Widow*: "A pathetic figure that the Christian world has agreed to take humorously, although Christ's tenderness towards widows was one of the most marked features of his character."

Although it is a scholarly convention to call the period in which Bierce wrote the Age of Realism and Naturalism, he does not fit neatly into either of these categories. Nevertheless, the dominant trends in a period can sometimes be defined by their opponents as well as by their adherents. From this point of view, Bierce helps to explain realism and naturalism by exposing the limitations of the movement. In his critical writings he repeatedly attacked realism and realists, his favorite target being William Dean Howells. One reason he preferred the short story to the realistic novel, with its slow, painstaking accretion of detail, was that his artistic aims were radically different from those of the realists. A third movement—international in scope—dominant during the late nineteenth and early twentieth centuries was literary impressionism. Bierce fits far better under the heading of

impressionism than he does under the rubrics of either realism or naturalism.

According to the impressionists, a verifiable description of reality is impossible; rather, the writer must concentrate on the perceptual awareness which links the subjective response of the perceiver to the objective reality he perceives. It is this interaction between perceiver and perceived that constitutes "reality" for the literary impressionist. Moreover, neither space nor time is regarded as a fixed and rigid category. Both are fluid, depending on how the observer apprehends them. Consequently time can be either speeded up tremendously or slowed down to an extraordinary degree. Space, likewise, can be expanded exponentially or contracted to the merest pinpoint. Finally, the protagonist in impressionistic writing experiences a moment of epiphany, a flash of illumination during which he has an immediate and blinding revelation of what constitutes for him the ultimate nature of reality.

These defining characteristics of literary impressionism—which have already been explored in connection with Henry James—fit the work of Ambrose Bierce much better than do those of realism and naturalism. Indeed, the focal point of many of his stories is precisely the relativistic perception of the external world. In "An Occurrence at Owl Creek Bridge" and "Chickamauga," Peyton Farquhar and the deaf-mute boy misperceive lethal military situations as ones in which the appropriate responses are happiness and glee. And the sensations of time and space are both radically affected by the protagonists' emotional states. Moreover, Bierce's impressionistic attitude toward time was not limited to his stories. In "The Chair of Little Ease," an essay on the newly introduced electric chair as a device for capital punishment, he questioned the easy assumption that execution by such means would be mercifully quick and painless. He pointed out that it is impossible for any observer to tell whether the dying criminal, his body jolted by electric shocks and his face contorted, perceives his death as quick or not. Indeed, an "unnatural exaltation of the senses" might commute a moment "into unthinkable cycles of time."

The epiphany, too, is of extraordinary importance in Bierce's work. In his short stories he is, above all, interested in the brief but devastating crises most individuals face only once or twice in the course of their lives, when they must confront not only other people or dangerous situations but, at the most fundamental level, themselves. The unwary reader is often lured into believing a tale to be one of the supernatural. The real terror, however, derives from the irrational powers of the human psyche, whose depths Bierce was probing long before Freud. His investigations reveal his great understanding of and deep compassion for the soul tortured by circumstances it can face only with the agonized courage of supreme suffering. Given this philosophy, it is not surprising that many of Bierce's stories deal with the Civil War. But in the midst of civilian life, too, his protagonists may find themselves in death.

While Bierce's work is impressionistic rather than realistic, it does express a sense of the determinism that is characteristic of naturalism. Bierce was keenly interested in tracing effects to their ineluctable causes, and his brand of determinism was precisely the secular one held by the naturalists: he believed that all human events were necessarily controlled by ancestry and environment. His interest in the transmission of character traits from one generation to another is discussed theoretically in his essay "The Ancestral Bond." He uses the theory in various ways in such stories as "Beyond the Wall," "John Bartine's Watch," "The Death of Halpin Frayser," and especially "One of Twins." Even the actions of the deaf-mute boy in "Chickamauga" are explained in large part by tracing his genealogy, and "A Watcher by the Dead" concerns the influence of racial memory in antipathy to cadavers. In other stories, Bierce traces the interlocking relationships of past events moving onward into the present to determine a given incident which may be the subject of his story. In "One of the Missing," for example, Jerome Searing, a Federal scout, has been sent out on a reconnaissance mission during the Civil War engagement at Kennesaw Mountain, Georgia. Seeing a column of retreating Confederate troops in the distance, he raises his rifle and plans to shoot into their midst: "But it was decreed from the beginning of time that Private Searing was not to murder anybody that bright summer morning, nor was the Confederate retreat to be announced by him. For countless ages events had been so matching themselves together in that wondrous mosaic to some parts of which, dimly discernible, we give the name of history, that the acts which he had in will would have marred the harmony of the pattern. Some twenty-five years previously the Power charged with the execution of the work according to the design had provided against that mischance by causing the birth of a certain male child in a little village at the foot of the Carpathian Mountains, had carefully reared it, supervised its education, directed its desires into a military channel, and in due

time made it an officer of artillery. By the concurrence of an infinite number of favoring influences and their preponderance over an infinite number of opposing ones, this officer of artillery had been made to commit a breach of discipline and flee from his native country to avoid punishment." Arriving in New Orleans, he has enlisted in the Confederate army and eventually ended up commanding a Confederate battery that at the moment was standing

Portrait of Bierce by Roulé Campbell

about two miles away from Searing. "Nothing had been neglected—at every step in the progress of both these men's lives, and in the lives of their contemporaries and ancestors, and in the lives of the contemporaries of their ancestors, the right thing had been done to bring about the desired result. Had anything in all this vast concatenation been overlooked Private Searing might have fired on the retreating Confederates that morning, and would perhaps have missed. As it fell out, a Confederate captain of artillery, having nothing better to do while awaiting his turn to pull out and be off, amused himself by sighting a field-piece obliquely to his right at what he mistook for some Federal officers on the crest of a hill, and discharged it."

The aspect of naturalism in which Bierce was primarily interested was the moral determinism examined in depth by Jonathan Edwards in *Freedom of the Will*. For him, as for Edwards, it is morally impossible for a man with a certain character to respond to a given situation other than as he does respond. His character determines the way in which he thinks and feels, makes crucial choices, and acts at decisive points in his life. Bierce's interest in determinism and its relation to freedom of the will is apparent in a civilian tale, "The Death of Halpin Frayser." Bierce not only traces Halpin Frayser's ancestry back through several generations; he also peels away layer after layer of Frayser's personality to expose his underlying character structure, determined in large part by what today would be called the Oedipus complex, in order to explain why he must necessarily act as he does act.

Because Bierce does not fit easily into the literary *-isms* of his time, literary historians have had difficulty in placing his work, and a good part of his reputation has always rested on his appeal to readers as independent and iconoclastic as he was. Only in the last three decades have scholars and critics begun to recognize that their theoretical concepts must be expanded if they are to include a writer as nonconformist as Ambrose Bierce.

As more biographers investigate Bierce's life and more critics examine his work, misinterpretations of his personality and his writing are fading. Scholars have begun to dispel the fog of innuendos and falsehoods (which originated with people who had known him and created a smokescreen after his death to conceal the nature of their relations with him) that have marred many biographical studies. It is no longer said that "Bitter" Bierce's output is mediocre and that he is interesting only as a misanthropic cynic incapable of human emotions. But if he is not to remain elusive as a man, future investigations will have to be undertaken on the careful, detailed model of Paul Fatout's *Ambrose Bierce and the Black Hills*, an authoritative and absorbing account of Bierce's abortive mining venture in the Dakota Territory.

Critics, too, are now evaluating his work on its merits. Even as a young man he had a reputation in several English-speaking countries. After his death his work was translated into French, German, Spanish, Italian, and Japanese. His writing has been popular with Russians since Czarist times. Much of the best work on Bierce is found in doctoral dissertations which began to appear after World War II, both in the United States and abroad. It is therefore safe to say that his place in American literature is secure. And those who give Bierce's work their careful attention will be able to render him a juster homage than the interest accorded a fascinating newspaperman who disappeared mysteriously in Mexico.

Other:
Mark Twain's Library of Humor, contains contributions by Bierce (New York: Webster, 1888);
Richard Voss, *The Monk and the Hangman's Daughter*, Gustav Adolph Danziger's translation, revised by Bierce (Chicago: Schulte, 1892).

Letters:
The Letters of Ambrose Bierce, edited by Bertha Clark Pope (San Francisco: Book Club of California, 1922).

Bibliographies:
Vincent Starrett, *Ambrose Bierce, A Bibliography* (Philadelphia: Centaur Book Shop, 1929);
Joseph Gaer, ed., *Ambrose Gwinett* [sic] *Bierce, Bibliography and Biographical Data* (1935; republished, New York: Burt Franklin, 1968);
Paul Fatout, "Ambrose Bierce (1842-1914)," *American Literary Realism, 1870-1910*, 1 (Fall 1967): 13-19.

Biographies:
Carey McWilliams, *Ambrose Bierce, A Biography* (New York: A. & C. Boni, 1929);
Paul Fatout, *Ambrose Bierce, the Devil's Lexicographer* (Norman: University of Oklahoma Press, 1951);
Fatout, *Ambrose Bierce and the Black Hills* (Norman: University of Oklahoma Press, 1956);
Richard O'Connor, *Ambrose Bierce, A Biography* (Boston: Little, Brown, 1967).

References:
Howard W. Bahr, "Ambrose Bierce and Realism," *Southern Quarterly*, 1 (July 1963): 309-331;
Lawrence I. Berkove, "Arms and the Man: Ambrose Bierce's Response to War," *Michigan Academician*, 1 (Winter 1969): 21-30;
Cathy N. Davidson, ed., *Critical Essays on Ambrose Bierce* (Boston: G. K. Hall, 1982);
Davidson, "Literary Semantics and the Fiction of Ambrose Bierce," *ETC.: A Review of General Semantics*, 31 (September 1974): 263-271;
Paul Fatout, "Ambrose Bierce, Civil War Topographer," *American Literature*, 26 (November 1954): 391-400;
Fatout, "Ambrose Bierce Writes about War," *Book*

Club of California Quarterly News Letter, 16 (Fall 1951): 75-79;

Wilson Follett, "Ambrose Bierce—An Analysis of the Perverse Wit that Shaped His Work," *Bookman*, 68 (November 1928): 284-289;

M. E. Grenander, *Ambrose Bierce* (New York: Twayne, 1971);

Grenander, "Ambrose Bierce and Charles Warren Stoddard: Some Unpublished Correspondence," *Huntington Library Quarterly*, 23 (May 1960): 261-292;

Grenander, "Ambrose Bierce and *Cobwebs from an Empty Skull*: A Note on BAL 1100 and 1107," *Papers of the Bibliographical Society of America*, 79 (Third Quarter, 1975): 403-406;

Grenander, "Ambrose Bierce and *In the Midst of Life*," *Book Collector*, 20 (Autumn 1971): 321-331;

Grenander, "Ambrose Bierce Describes Swinburne," *Courier*, 14 (Fall 1977): 22-26;

Grenander, "Ambrose Bierce, John Camden Hotten, *The Fiend's Delight*, and *Nuggets and Dust*," *Huntington Library Quarterly*, 28 (August 1965): 353-371;

Grenander, "Au Coeur de la vie: a French Translation of Ambrose Bierce," *Boston University Studies in English*, 1 (Winter 1955-1956): 237-241;

Grenander, "Bierce's Turn of the Screw: Tales of Ironical Terror," *Western Humanities Review*, 11 (Summer 1957): 257-263;

Grenander, "California's Albion: Mark Twain, Ambrose Bierce, Tom Hood, John Camden Hotten, and Andrew Chatto," *Papers of the Bibliographical Society of America*, 72 (Fourth Quarter, 1978): 455-475;

Grenander, "H. L. Mencken to Ambrose Bierce," *Book Club of California Quarterly Newsletter*, 22 (Winter 1956): 5-10;

Grenander, "A London Letter of Joaquin Miller to Ambrose Bierce," *Yale University Library Gazette*, 46 (October 1971): 109-116;

Grenander, "Seven Ambrose Bierce Letters," *Yale University Library Gazette*, 32 (July 1957): 12-18;

Carroll D. Hall, *Bierce and the Po? Hoax* (San Francisco: Book Club of California, 1934);

F. J. Logan, "The Wry Seriousness of 'Owl Creek Bridge,' " *American Literary Realism*, 10 (Spring 1977): 101-113;

Fred H. Marcus, "Film and Fiction: 'An Occurrence at Owl Creek Bridge,' " *California English Journal*, 7 (1971): 14-23;

Jay Martin, "Ambrose Bierce," in *The Comic Imagination in American Literature*, edited by Louis D. Rubin, Jr. (New Brunswick: Rutgers University Press, 1973), pp. 195-205;

Robert C. McLean, "The Deaths in Ambrose Bierce's 'Halpin Frayser,' " *Papers on Language and Literature*, 10 (Fall 1974): 394-402;

Carey McWilliams, Introduction to *The Devil's Dictionary* (New York: Sagamore Press, 1957): pp. v-xii;

H. L. Mencken, *A Book of Prefaces* (New York: Knopf, 1917);

Mencken, "Ambrose Bierce," in his *Prejudices, Sixth Series* (New York: Knopf, 1927), pp. 259-265;

Frank Monaghan, "Ambrose Bierce and the Authorship of *The Monk and the Hangman's Daughter*," *American Literature*, 2 (January 1931): 337-349;

Matthew C. O'Brien, " Ambrose Bierce and the Civil War: 1865," *American Literature*, 48 (November 1976): 377-381;

James W. Palmer, "From Owl Creek to *La Rivière du hibou*: The Film Adaptation of Bierce's 'An Occurrence at Owl Creek Bridge,' " *Southern Humanities Review*, 11 (Fall 1977): 363-371;

Lois Rather, *Bittersweet: Ambrose Bierce & Women* (Oakland, Cal.: Rather Press, 1975);

J. V. Ridgely, "Ambrose Bierce to H. L. Mencken," *Book Club of California Quarterly News Letter*, 26 (Fall 1961): 27-33;

Eric Solomon, "The Bitterness of Battle: Ambrose Bierce's War Fiction," *Midwest Quarterly*, 5 (January 1964): 147-165;

William Bysshe Stein, "Bierce's 'The Death of Halpin Frayser': The Poetics of Gothic Consciousness," *ESQ: Emerson Society Quarterly*, 18 (Second Quarter, 1972): 115-122;

Franklin Walker, *San Francisco's Literary Frontier* (New York: Knopf, 1939);

David R. Weimer, "Ambrose Bierce and the Art of War," in *Essays in Literary History*, edited by Rudolf Kirk and C. F. Main (New York: Russell & Russell, 1965);

Napier Wilt, "Ambrose Bierce and the Civil War," *American Literature*, 1 (November 1929): 260-285.

Papers:

The most important holdings of Bierce's papers are in the Bancroft Library of the University of California at Berkeley; the Clifton Waller Barrett Collection at the University of Virginia; the University of Cincinnati; the Huntington Library in San Marino, California; the Berg Collection of the New York Public Library; the Division of Special Collections at Stanford University; the George Arents Research Library at Syracuse University; and the Beinecke Library of Yale University.

Hjalmar Hjorth Boyesen

(21 September 1848-2 October 1895)

Robert S. Fredrickson
Gettysburg College

SELECTED BOOKS: *Gunnar: A Tale of Norse Life* (Boston: Osgood, 1874);

A Norseman's Pilgrimage (New York: Sheldon, 1875);

Tales from Two Hemispheres (Boston: Osgood, 1877);

Goethe and Schiller: Their Lives and Works (New York: Scribners, 1879);

Falconberg (New York: Scribners, 1879);

Ilka on the Hill-Top and Other Stories (New York: Scribners, 1881);

Queen Titania (New York: Scribners, 1881);

Idyls of Norway and Other Poems (New York: Scribners, 1882);

A Daughter of the Philistines (Boston: Roberts, 1883; London: Douglas, 1883);

The Story of Norway (New York & London: Putnam's, 1886; London: Low, 1886);

The Modern Vikings: Stories of Life and Sport in the Norseland (New York: Scribners, 1887; London: Low, 1887);

Vagabond Tales (Boston: Lothrop, 1889);

The Light of Her Countenance (New York: Appleton, 1889);

Against Heavy Odds: A Tale of Norse Heroism (New York: Scribners, 1890; London: Low, 1890);

The Mammon of Unrighteousness (New York: Lovell, 1891);

Essays on German Literature (New York: Scribners, 1892; London: Unwin, 1892);

Boyhood in Norway: Stories of Boy-Life in the Land of the Midnight Sun (New York: Scribners, 1892); republished as *The Battle of the Rafts: Boyhood in Norway* (London: Nelson, 1893);

The Golden Calf: A Novel (Meadville, Pa.: Flood & Vincent, 1892);

Social Strugglers: A Novel (New York: Scribners, 1893);

A Commentary on the Writings of Henrik Ibsen (New York & London: Macmillan, 1894; London: Heinemann, 1894);

Literary and Social Silhouettes (New York: Harper, 1894);

Norseland Tales (New York: Scribners, 1894; London: Nelson, 1895);

Essays on Scandinavian Literature (New York: Scribners, 1895; London: Nutt, 1895).

Crayon portrait of Boyesen at age twenty-nine, by Wyatt Eaton

Remembered mainly as a staunch apologist for literary realism, Hjalmar Hjorth Boyesen produced a sizable body of his own variety of realistic fiction. William Dean Howells praised Boyesen for his enthusiastic support: "Boyesen indeed out-realisted me, in the polemics of our aesthetic," although Howells goes on to imply that Boyesen had overdone it. Howells also criticized Boyesen for being too prolific, saying he wrote "more and more when he should have written less and less." Boyesen's zeal as a theorist grew from his belief that realism was a new philosophy—not just a literary method—and that realism's job was to demonstrate how scientific law could explain the mystery of life. His zeal led to his writing eight novels, eight short-story collections, and eight other book-length works including children's books. Nearly a hundred stories, essays, poems, and reviews were published in periodicals—an astonishing number for a man who died at forty-seven. Boyesen was involved with the great literary figures of his time in both Europe and America and invented his own peculiar theoretical synthesis, linking Howells's belief in truthful treatment of material with his own faith that such material, if selected properly, would reveal the truth about man's evolutionary spiral toward perfection. Yet, Boyesen's work is now largely forgotten. His mixture of bourgeois sentimentalism and grandiose theory resulted in work that often lacks the particularity which is exciting in the work of classic realists. He had facile, optimistic ideas, and he lacked an eye and ear for the color of American life and the vitality of American culture.

Perhaps Boyesen's problem as an American realist is best explained by his Norwegian birth. The grandson of a Norwegian judge, Boyesen, born in Fredrikvaern, was a prosperous immigrant who came to America in 1869 because it was the land of literary opportunity, not because he sought wealth or freedom which was unavailable in Norway. From his father he had acquired a romantic notion of America as a land of destiny. A well-educated immigrant, Boyesen had attended Latin school in Drammen, gymnasium in Christiania, and the Royal Fredriks University, where he had received an advanced degree in 1868. As a European and a gentleman, his analysis of the American situation was more the study of cultural forces (the historical contest of feudalism and democracy) and more theoretical and more detached (he could not share in populist anger) than that of American realists and naturalists. Vernon Parrington places Boyesen's work somewhere between the polite realism of Thackeray's drawing-room novels and the city realism which culminates in Edith Wharton's fiction. Boyesen's position seems to be in the middle in other ways as well. He is between Europe and America, between popular art and serious work, and between a realism based on particulars and a naturalism based on theories. Boyesen's early novels develop a contrast between old and new worlds, often placing the protagonist with a foot on each continent. His later novels develop a contrast between bitter struggles in society and possibilities for moral evolution. He straddles the gap between pragmatism and idealism.

Boyesen did not begin his American career with a realistic work, although it was a realist acquaintance who arranged for its publication. Upon arriving in America in 1869, Boyesen had gone to

teach at Urbana University, a small Swedenborgian college in Urbana, Ohio. Discontented with Swedenborgianism, he went to Chicago to edit *Fremad*, a Norwegian weekly. Then, unhappy working in Norwegian rather than English, he returned to Ohio. Feeling isolated there Boyesen escaped to Boston in the summer of 1871 to work on improving his English. There he met Howells and showed the realist his manuscript for *Gunnar*, a romance set in Norway, which he had written out of homesickness while in Ohio. Howells, the editor of the *Atlantic Monthly*, accepted *Gunnar* for serialization during 1873 and also began publishing Boyesen's reviews and poems in the magazine. Before long, Boyesen's work began to appear in other magazines, such as *Lippincott's, Galaxy,* and the *North American Review*.

Howells also helped Boyesen establish an academic career in America. Through Howells's Boston connections, Boyesen secured a position at Cornell University, but before going to Ithaca as a German professor, he returned to Europe in 1873,

Title page for Boyesen's first book. William Dean Howells helped to launch Boyesen's career by accepting the novel for serialization in the Atlantic Monthly *before it was published by Osgood.*

and studied for a half year at the University of Leipzig. While at Cornell he produced his first scholarly book, *Goethe and Schiller: Their Lives and Works* (1879) which at that time was considered the best English-language treatment of Goethe, and he married Lillie Keen. Aspiring to support himself by writing alone, he moved to New York in 1880 to do free-lance writing. Unable to earn enough, however, he took an appointment the next year at Columbia University, where he worked until his death, continuing to produce scholarly books and earning a reputation as a dynamic teacher. Yet throughout his career, which was cut short by pneumonia in 1895, he remained committed to his vocation as a writer.

Gunnar, published in book form by Osgood in 1874, is a parable about the development of the artist that takes place among the romantic fjords and alpine pastures of a Norway where legendary creatures, spirits, trolls, and fairy princesses still cavort. The hero is a youth who wishes to escape the confines of his peasant-class background by becoming an artist, an aristocrat's vocation. Gunnar proves his worth by succeeding at a series of tests of physical derring-do, and finally by winning a prize as an artist. Along with this success, he is rewarded with the hand of a beautiful maiden from a higher class. To be an artist, Boyesen seems to be saying, one must have both imagination and the savvy to deal with the real world, a message he reiterates throughout his career. Significantly Boyesen proves how successful Gunnar is in dealing with reality by sending him to America at the end of the novel.

Boyesen's second and third novels, *A Norseman's Pilgrimage* (1875) and *Falconberg* (1879), while purporting to be realistic, also contain elements of the romance. Dealing with the difficult struggle of immigrants for a new identity, they also tell of the inevitable success which awaits the young man brave enough to dream. The goal of both protagonists is to overcome the false romanticism of the old world and to acquire a new, supposedly realistic, American view. *A Norseman's Pilgrimage* is a story of Americanization. Olaf Varberg, a Norwegian-born American, travels to Europe, where he meets a totally American phenomenon, a brash girl much like Henry James's Daisy Miller. At first cultural differences keep the two apart (he is a sentimental European, and she is a hardheaded American), but eventually the two marry, marriage offering the romantic solution for their realistic conflict. In *Falconberg*, Einar Falconberg, who has left Norway in disgrace, proves his virtues as a journalist in a small

Norwegian settlement in Minnesota. The plot, like those of many stories Boyesen wrote during this period, involves a wayward son's vindicating himself to a conservative father. Like *Gunnar* and *A Norseman's Pilgrimage*, in which differences are resolved through marriage, these stories of fathers and sons also end in reconciliation, with Boyesen's synthesizing European tradition and the new world. Boyesen, who had left Norway against his grandfather's wishes and who was struggling for literary success in this country, was writing solutions to his own problems.

Yet these novels also attempted to depict life realistically and dispassionately while working toward their sentimental ends. In *A Norseman's Pilgrimage*, Boyesen manages to satirize both the hyperromantic European and his bold American ladyfriend. In *Falconberg* Boyesen depicts in detail characteristic problems of an immigrant community. Realistic episodes include a contest between prospective church organists, the inside workings of a small-town newspaper, a tarring and feathering, a Norwegian Independence Day celebration, and an election.

The increasingly realistic Boyesen, writing in the 1880s, turned his attention to a classic problem of the nineteenth-century novel: whom should a young person marry? In *A Daughter of the Philistines* (1883), Alma Hampton, the child of a social-climbing mother and a businessman father, chooses a geologist, a mistaken choice according to her mother, who believes the only men eligible for her daughter are rich. Alma's husband, however, teaches her moral values which set her free from her Philistine past. She learns the evils of the financial world and the shallowness of high society. She learns to be subservient to her husband, a lesson all Boyesen women learned since Boyesen believes the evil world of society is a matriarchy. Perhaps in reaction to her husband's literary misogyny, Lillie Keen Boyesen, a society woman, disdained association with writers. (She would not allow the Authors' Club to meet in their home.)

In *The Light of Her Countenance* (1889) Boyesen tells of a somewhat decadent American, who, having little else of significance with which to occupy himself, goes to Europe and meets Constance Douglas, a heroine Boyesen treats with ambivalence. Boyesen wished in part to satirize this expatriate Southern belle who lives in Rome because her gracious homeland was spoiled by the late unpleasantness, that is, the Civil War. Yet, Boyesen wished to idealize her as well. In a similar vein, another of Boyesen's characters is a coarser version of James's

Henrietta Stackpole, the wholly un-Europeanized American in *The Portrait of a Lady*. Delia Saunders, like James's character, is partly admired and partly ridiculed.

Boyesen's best fiction was written during the last five years of his life when it appears his talent and theory had coalesced. In numerous periodical articles published during the 1880s, he had developed an evolutionary overview of American culture. He became able to identify the larger forces which contended in the struggle for survival in modern society, and now he possessed enough novelistic flair to give characters in the struggle individual identities. *The Mammon of Unrighteousness* (1891), possibly his best novel, contrasts examples of moral evolution with examples of ruthless Darwinian survival of the fittest. Two brothers, Horace and Aleck Larkin, sons of an upstate New York university president, represent this opposition. Aleck intends to do good; Horace aims for success. Horace is coldly calculating, both in setting up a legal and political career and in his choice of the wealthy and

THE MAMMON

OF

UNRIGHTEOUSNESS

BY

HJALMAR HJORTH BOYESON

AUTHOR OF

"GUNNAR," "IDYLS OF NORWAY," "THE LIGHT OF HER COUNTE-
NANCE," ETC., ETC.

NEW YORK.

JOHN W. LOVELL COMPANY

150 WORTH ST., COR. MISSION PLACE

Title page for Boyesen's 1891 novel, expressing his evolutionary view of American life

unprincipled Kate Van Schaak for his wife. Aleck, however, resigns his position with his brother for moral reasons (Horace is using his office for political advancement), goes to the city to set up his own ethical legal practice, and later marries purely for love. Their adopted sister, Gertrude, is impractical in her romantic idealism and needs to become more realistic. She gets engaged to a romantic phony, and then, after breaking it off, she foolishly rebels against her just but authoritarian father and goes to New York on a futile mission to rescue her drug-addicted real mother. Helpless and unable to return home, Gertrude is rescued by Aleck, the sensible romantic, and the battle between foolish impulses and good instincts is resolved. Pitted against rational calculation, however, even impulsive behavior seems morally superior and more humane. Evidently Boyesen believed that a benign naturalistic force counteracts the prosaic realistic world of business and society. In natural man, removed from society, there is an instinct to do good. Moral evolution is a transcendent force.

The Golden Calf (1892) is an American success story which is simultaneously a story of spiritual failure. Oliver Tappan fails "by a series of successes" after he leaves his New England small-town home to win fame, wealth, and power in the city. He gets what he seeks, but loses his soul in the process. Tutored as a child by a German idealist, Dr. Habicht, the adult Tappan moves farther from his earlier principles with each step he takes toward success. Like Horace Larkin in *The Mammon of Unrighteousness*, he chooses an unprincipled woman for a wife. This woman encourages Tappan to succumb to the temptations of power in Washington, D.C. There Tappan sees how "human depravity is less restrained under our form of government" and loses the softening influences of ideals and poetry.

Tappan may have been ruined by power, but Boyesen makes it clear that man need not be caught in a deterministic struggle for survival of the fittest. Instead man is capable of altering the course of evolution, a truth Tappan discovers too late. Tappan, characteristically American and modern, learned standards of right and wrong in his childhood which do not seem to apply in the city, where only success is admired. So Tappan seeks material wealth, as American young men were supposed to do, and he dies spiritually. Although cosmic law does not destroy him as it might the protagonist of a naturalistic novel, it is clear that humanistic values are in trouble. In modern cities, men thwart the noble possibilities of moral evolution.

Boyesen's last major work, *Social Strugglers*

Hjalmar Horth Boyesen

(1893), also represents the absence of values in an American city. Here a midwestern family flounders when the social-climbing mother takes them into the moral chaos of New York. Here again, matriarchy is identified as a source of evil. The Peleg Lemmuel Bulkley family has become rich because of the father's hard work in a midwestern tailoring concern. After Mr. Bulkley has made the fortune, Mrs. Bulkley moves the family east to spend it. There she tries vainly to gain an entrance into society so that her daughters can find the right kind of husbands. One of the girls, Maud Bulkley, is offered an opportunity to marry an apparently rich but caddish man. After his caddishness comes to light, Maud accepts instead an offer from the poor but aristocratic Warburton, who works as a sort of Christian social worker. Warburton as a paragon, in fact, differs from earlier Boyesen representations of goodness in that he seems effective. He has a strength that Aleck Larkin and Dr. Habicht lack. Warburton also has a habit, annoying for readers, of preaching his reformist philosophy at inopportune moments.

He interrupts his proposal of marriage, for example, to offer his social program.

The novel's title has several meanings. The book is about social climbers, about those who must struggle just to survive, and about those who struggle to change society. Warburton shows men how to fight back against the world of chance and matriarchy, how to alter the direction of evolution. Maud demonstrates, as Alma Hampton did in *A Daughter of the Philistines*, that daughters at least can be better than their mothers. If we must be social strugglers, Boyesen tells us, let us help make others aware of what the real struggle, the moral struggle, is about. Boyesen ended his career by creating a protagonist who is both effective and good.

Ultimately Boyesen had little direct influence on other writers, but through the European writers, including Turgenev and Ibsen, whom he introduced to American readers and through his steady support for an optimistic social Darwinism in his essays, he helped create the climate for naturalism. Boyesen's essays, particularly those which celebrated evolution toward the ideal, may in the long run be more important than his novels. As a theorist he was fashionable, since he represented the place where the popular ideology of social Darwinism and avant-garde realism meet. While for many science was undermining religious faith, Boyesen was among those who saw in nineteenth-century progress a reason for new faith. As an ambitious immigrant making his way in an exciting new world of wealth, expanding cities, and stimulating change, Boyesen felt a sense of possibility in the material world he described.

Periodical Publications:
"Reminiscences of Turgeniev," *Harper's*, 27 (29 September 1883): 615;
"The Danger of Immigration," *Independent*, 36 (2 October 1884): 1113-1114;
"The Hope of the Nations," *Independent*, 40 (19 January 1888): 66-67;
"Victims of Progress," *Independent*, 40 (17 May 1888): 610;
"Mars and Apollo," *Chautauquan*, 8 (July 1888): 584-586;
"Philistinism," *Independent*, 40 (27 September 1888): 1225-1226;
"On Howells' Work," *Cosmopolitan*, 12 (February 1892): 502-503;
"Juxtaposition of Races," *Cosmopolitan*, 15 (August 1893): 504-505;
"A New World Fable: The World's Fair," *Cos-*

mopolitan, 16 (December 1893): 173-186;

"The Evolution of the Heroine," *Lippincott's*, 54 (September 1894): 425-428.

References:

Robert Fredrickson, *Hjalmar Hjorth Boyesen* (Boston: Twayne, 1980);

Fredrickson, "Hjalmar Hjorth Boyesen: Howells " 'Out-Realisted,' " *Markham Review*, 3 (February 1973): 93-97;

Clarence Glasrud, "Boyesen and the Norwegian Immigration," *Norwegian-American Studies and Records*, 19 (1956): 15-45;

Glasrud, *Hjalmar Hjorth Boyesen* (Northfield, Minn.: Norwegian-American Historical Association, 1963);

Laurence M. Larson, "Hjalmar Hjorth Boyesen," in his *The Changing West and Other Essays* (North-

field, Minn.: Norwegian-American Historical Association, 1937);

Marc Ratner, "Georg Brandes and Hjalmar Hjorth Boyesen," *Scandinavian Studies*, 33 (November 1961): 218-230;

Ratner, "Howells and Boyesen: Two Views of Realism," *New England Quarterly*, 35 (September 1962): 376-390;

Ratner, "The Iron Madonna: H. H. Boyesen's American Girl," *Jahrbuk fur Amerikastudien*, 9 (1964): 166-172;

George Leroy White, Jr. "H. H. Boyesen: A Note on Immigration," *American Literature*, 13 (January 1942): 363-371.

Papers:

Boyesen's papers are in the Butler Library at Columbia University.

George Washington Cable

(12 October 1844-31 January 1925)

Michael Kreyling
Tulane University

SELECTED BOOKS: *Old Creole Days* (New York: Scribners, 1879);

The Grandissimes (New York: Scribners, 1880; revised 1883);

Madame Delphine: A Novelette and Other Tales (London: Warne, 1881);

Madame Delphine (New York: Scribners, 1881);

The Creoles of Louisiana (New York: Scribners, 1884);

Dr. Sevier (Boston: Osgood, 1884; Edinburgh: Douglas, 1884);

The Silent South (New York: Scribners, 1885; expanded, 1889);

Bonaventure: A Prose Pastoral of Acadian Louisiana (New York: Scribners, 1888);

Strange True Stories of Louisiana (New York: Scribners, 1889);

The Negro Question (New York: Scribners, 1890);

John March, Southerner (New York: Scribners, 1895; London: Low, 1895);

Strong Hearts (New York: Scribners, 1899; London: Hodder & Stoughton, 1899);

The Cavalier (New York: Scribners, 1901; London: Murray, 1901);

Bylow Hill (New York: Scribners, 1902; London:

Hodder & Stoughton, 1902);

Kincaid's Battery (New York: Scribners, 1908; London: Hodder & Stoughton, 1909);

"Posson Jone' " and Père Raphaël (New York: Scribners, 1909);

Gideon's Band (New York: Scribners, 1914);

The Amateur Garden (New York: Scribners, 1914);

The Flower of the Chapdelaines (New York: Scribners, 1918; London: Collins, 1919);

Lovers of Louisiana (To-day) (New York: Scribners, 1918).

George Washington Cable was the most significant Southern writer in the crucial years from the Civil War and Reconstruction to the first decades of the twentieth century. When he was born in New Orleans in 1844, *Walden* (1854) and *Moby-Dick* (1851) were not yet written. When he died in Florida in 1925, Fitzgerald's *This Side of Paradise* (1920) and Eliot's *The Waste Land* (1922) had been published, and Hemingway was working on *The Sun Also Rises* (1926). Cable was lauded as the successor to Hawthorne, and lived to negotiate the motion-picture rights for some of his stories. Cable was a

major participant with Mark Twain and William Dean Howells in widening the scope of realism in fiction, and he is a focal point for critics and literary historians who continue to debate the nature of the Southern literary imagination. He wrote about a host of social issues (the convict lease system, corruption in state government, race) that put established New Orleans society on the defensive. In New Orleans today there are parents who will not mention to their children the alleged slanders of Creole society in Cable's fiction of a century earlier. Finally, Cable the man and artist provides a fascinating subject for the literary biographer (chief among whom is Arlin Turner), for he mustered his talent against a host of foes—editorial pressure, economic need, his felt obligation to take a stand on current social issues, his own fame—and yet, like so many American writers, he did not sustain his early achievement.

George Washington Cable was the fifth of six children born to George W. Cable, Sr. and Rebecca

Boardman Cable. Two siblings died soon after young G. W. Cable's birth. Cable's father's family had moved from Virginia to Pennsylvania, and George Washington Cable, Sr., had moved on to Indiana and then New Orleans. The Cable family had freed its slaves after their move to Pennsylvania. The author's mother, Rebecca Boardman, was an Indianian with New England antecedents. The author's father found his livelihood on the Mississippi River. He had supported his growing family, before their move to New Orleans, as a cooper and a tavern keeper. But the financial opportunities of the river trade lured him south. In New Orleans he began as a wholesale grocer, supplying goods to river merchants who provisioned river craft and upriver communities. As Cable's father prospered, his fortunes became ever more connected with the river. At the peak of his success he owned interests in several steamboats. But as quickly as he had risen, he fell into bad luck. A cargo or two was lost, and to pay debts the steamboats had to be auctioned. George W. Cable, Sr., took work on the boats, but neither his fortune nor his health reached former peaks. He died in 1859, on his forty-eighth birthday, and young Cable was forced to go to work to support his mother and sisters. At the age of nineteen he enlisted in the Confederate cavalry and was wounded in battle.

After the war, although Cable was meticulous and considered invaluable to the company, his work in his old job as a bookkeeper for a cotton commission merchant did not fully occupy his mind. In his free time he walked about the city picking up odd scraps of information, vignettes, and bits of Creole legend and song. He also knew the members of the flourishing literary circle that included Grace King, Charles Gayarré, and on occasion Lafcadio Hearn as its most illustrious local personalities. Cable began as a writer by contributing columns written under the pseudonym "Drop Shot" to the *New Orleans Picayune* in 1870. The discipline of writing a column and the influence of literary companions and conversation led Cable to attempt to incorporate the settings, characters, and bits of narrative he had collected into a few sketches and tales. He wrote mostly in the cooler hours of the night and early morning—after his growing family (Cable and his first wife, Louisa Stewart Bartlett, whom he had married in 1869, had six children) had retired and before he was due at work.

Cable, a talented and disciplined writer, produced stories employing the dialects, scenes, and flavor of an exotic Southern city at a time when the victorious North was deeply curious about its former enemy. It was a case of writer and moment meeting. The catalyst was Edward King, a literary scout sent to the South in the early 1870s by *Scribner's Monthly* magazine (which became the *Century* in 1881) with the commission to write a series of descriptive pieces about conditions in the conquered Confederacy and to discover new literary talent. Cable was his biggest find.

In 1873 King sent Cable's story, "Bibi," a condensed version of the Bras Coupé story that appears in *The Grandissimes* (1880), to Richard Watson Gilder, the editor of *Scribner's Monthly*. Gilder declined the story, as did George Parsons Lathrop at the *Atlantic Monthly*. Both men found the story "distressing." But Gilder accepted a second Cable story, " 'Sieur George," and Cable's career and his relationship with this influential editor were underway.

During the 1870s Cable was a popular regional writer. At times Gilder even praised him as a major national writer, one deserving comparison with the great writers of American literature (the name most frequently invoked was Hawthorne's). Twain called Cable the "South's finest literary genius," a potential antidote to the romantic influence of Scott.

Cable's early reputation was based almost exclusively on his short stories. Stories such as " 'Sieur George," "Jean-ah Poquelin," and "Belles Demoiselles Plantation" brought to the readers of the *Century* and other magazines more than the exotic colors and radiance of New Orleans, its strange denizens and their enchanting speech. Although few of Cable's contemporary readers were aware of the qualities that placed him ahead of other local-color writers, later critics such as Louis Rubin and Edmund Wilson have concurred that Cable was the preeminent local colorist. He is one of the few writers of his time who was consistently able to mesh the superficial aspects of his setting—those traits usually considered indigenous to Southern local color—and the interior structures, values, drives, moods, and temperaments that his characters have assumed from the world that has shaped them. For his ability to suggest this state of consciousness by attention to the surfaces of character (habits, gestures, visage, costume) Cable merits comparison with Henry James. 'Sieur George, for example, is of a piece with the romantic and shabby, forever decaying world that makes him. The revelations of sexual depravity with which the story ends have been preceded by suggestions that run throughout the story. A similar stylistic feature occurs in "Belles Demoiselles Plantation" as the dying

Colonel De Charleu utters "Charl-," the root of his name which he shares with his half-breed relative Injin Charlie—thus revealing that this story has actually concerned the sin of divided heritage that has plagued the South. Cable saw deeply into the complex heart of his place and time, and presented the unresolved and unresolvable as he found them. By contrast, other writers of Southern local color, such as Mary Noailles Murfree and Grace King, used the surface characteristics of the time and place but imposed contrived or derivative plots. Cable's ability to impart inner truths through surface descriptions has infused his early stories with a power and vitality that have survived the years. The stories of his contemporaries have become dated.

When he could control the tension between his material and the need for form, Cable wrote powerful stories. Most of these stories can be found in his first published volume, *Old Creole Days* (1879). To cap the successful 1870s Cable completed a novel, *The Grandissimes* (serialized in *Scribner's* in 1879 and published as a book in 1880) that shows much of the same suggestive power. It has been regularly in print since its publication.

In *The Grandissimes*, a novel set at the time of the Louisiana Purchase, Cable balances the romantic love plot involving Honoré Grandissime and Aurore Nancanou, inheritors of a long-standing family feud, against the tempestuous triangle of Honoré's half brother of mixed blood (also named Honoré), the beautiful quadroon practicer of voodoo Palmyre Philosophe (who loves the white Honoré but is loved by the other Honoré) and the majestic slave Bras Coupé. The story of Bras Coupé, originally told some years earlier in the rejected story "Bibi," occupies the central position in *The Grandissimes*. Thematically, morally, and structurally it is the mark against which the rest of the novel—taken by most of its contemporary readers as a delightful portrait of Creole society at its myriad social rituals—is continually measured. The result is a powerful and unresolved question about Creole and, by extrapolation, Southern, society: have the foundations of slavery been so morally rotten from the start that no society can call itself legitimate, much less claim excellence, if it is founded on an institution that maims its fellow man?

This question haunts Honoré, pure white son of Numa Grandissime and the object of his clan's total loyalty. He tries to reconcile the moral absolutism of Joseph Frowenfeld, a newcomer from Philadelphia who espouses idealistic reforms that would destroy the Creole society in order to reform it, with the need to preserve some of the threads of social coherence from which to weave change. Between Frowenfeld's vision of immediate redress for the racial crimes of centuries and Agricole Fusilier's commandment to stand by the family right or wrong, Honoré must steer a complex course between ideal and pragmatic that affords no room for traditional heroism. Even though Honoré wears the mask of the romantic hero and lover in his courtship of Aurore Nancanou—thereby entertaining a reading audience that was enthralled by the tantalizing route that eventually leads them to each other—he must also make his way in an ironic realm of no-win alternatives. He sighs at Frowenfeld's naive claim that he, Honoré, possesses the "noble part" in the drama of correcting the wrongs of the past: "Ah, my-de'-seh! The noble part! There is the bitterness of the draught! The opportunity to act is pushed upon me, but the opportunity to act nobly has passed by."

Each time the story of Bras Coupé's defiance of his white master, flight, capture, hamstringing,

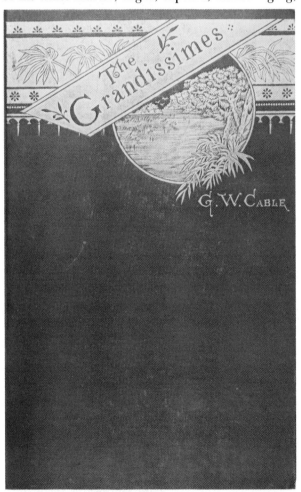

Front cover for Cable's first novel, expressing his ambiguous attitude toward Creole society

and death is told, the proud and xenophobic civilization headed by the patriarch Agricole, Honoré's uncle, is called into question. And each retelling further clarifies Honoré's dilemma: he is trapped between causes deeply rooted in the past and solutions determined by realities of the present. Honoré knows too much of both to believe that nobility is possible. The resolution in the denouement of the novel is not complete, for Honoré's act of moral courage in publicly establishing a business partnership with his quadroon half brother has only limited impact on the rest of the clan. Frowenfeld's Yankee moral perfectionism is shown to be too extreme and too deficient in social rootedness to be effective in the long range. The problem of race, as Cable saw it, demanded a long-standing commitment to gradual change and a wariness of the instant solution. In expressing this point of view, he offended both Northern and Southern readers who, well aware of the novel's relevance to the social and political situation in 1880, wanted a reassuring report that all was well with the black man.

A few readers in the South detected Cable's doubt about Southern society and raised their voices against him, and his Yankee ancestry was brought up. His editors in New York had suspected that certain aspects of *The Grandissimes*—namely Cable's treatment of racial relations and his portraits of black and white mentalities as basically the same human mentality—would not be universally palatable. But Cable, showing a stubborn streak of moral commitment that at other times appeared as a kind of fastidious piety, insisted upon his vision. *The Grandissimes* shows the tension between his admiration for the Creole way of life, apparent in the love plot of which Honoré is the handsome hero, and his awareness of the maze of racial sin and guilt that lies behind its gracious facade.

It is often argued that after the short stories in *Old Creole Days* and the novel *The Grandissimes* Cable never again achieved such high quality in his work, never again balanced the inner vision with the demands of an audience that wanted entertainment. Wilson, for instance, blamed the Genteel Tradition for "strangling" Cable. Rubin has written that Cable's talent simply ran down after years of working against the opposition that greeted his demands for racial justice. Any single explanation, however, seems insufficient.

After the deaths from yellow fever in 1878 of his only son and several other relatives, whose survivors he undertook to support, Cable needed a large income to sustain his household of both in-laws and blood kin. He had resigned his accountant's position with the Cotton Exchange in December 1881 and had embarked on the risky career of the professional writer. But income from his pen was unsteady and smaller than he had hoped. To make ends meet he had accepted invitations to read his Creole stories to audiences hungry for the exotic dialects and scenes of New Orleans.

In 1884 he agreed to Samuel Clemens's proposal that the two of them go on a lecture tour.

Samuel Clemens and George Washington Cable in 1884, the year of their lecture tour

Clemens would repeat his popular Mark Twain platform performance, and Cable would read his Creole stories and sing a few Creole dialect songs. The money was good, $450 a week, but the grueling schedule often tired Cable. Some mild trouble arose over Cable's insistence on keeping the Sabbath, and the tour ended in confusion. Clemens and Cable were never boon companions, but their friendship and mutual respect survived the tour and Cable spoke at the Carnegie Hall memorial service for Clemens in 1910.

The lecture tour also opened up the rest of the country to Cable. As he came to see the South in contrast with other regions, he came to like it less and to believe that the Northeast, which he called the intellectual treasury of the nation, was the only place where he could live as a writer. He made several visits to New York, discovered that he could write successfully there, and began to ask his editorial friends about the possibilities of living by his pen in the North. In 1885 he took his household to Northampton, Massachusetts, where he bought a house, which he named Tarryawhile.

In the 1880s Cable's writing had taken a pronounced turn toward controversy that made his continued residence in the South uncomfortable. "The Freedman's Case in Equity," which appeared in the *Century* early in 1885, is a vigorous yet subtle exposition of the self-deceptions inherent in the belief that the problem of slavery had been solved by such events as Emancipation and Appomattox. Cable saw the establishment of genuine equality as a much more time-consuming and rigorous process of peeling away myths about black mentality and character. He wrote that mutual education of the races was essential, and that the New South's claim that the freedman's fate was best left in the hands of his former masters was a ruse.

This position antagonized both the old-line Confederates and the New South boosters. Henry Grady, champion of the latter, attacked Cable's argument in the pages of the *Century* a few months later. Such criticism continued. In 1891 Thomas Nelson Page, who almost single-handedly created the Old South as literary myth, diagnosed Cable's literary genius as terminally infected by his social and political heresies. And Edwin Mims, writing of Cable in the prestigious *History of Southern Fiction* (1909), pronounced Cable's literary talent dead at the hands of his political causes. Cable's polemical essays were published in *The Silent South* (1885; expanded 1889) and in *The Negro Question* (1890). These two works enhanced Cable's reputation as critic of New South progressivism and of the condition of interracial relations in the South. The tension between art and polemic was not always constructive.

The didacticism of *Dr. Sevier* (1884), the novel with which he had followed *The Grandissimes*, dismayed Gilder so strongly that Scribners refused to publish it, and Cable had to take it to James R. Osgood in Boston for publication. *Dr. Sevier* is set in New Orleans between 1856 and 1865, but Cable does not focus on the exotic and picturesque New Orleans of his earlier stories. Instead he examines the workings of the municipality during a yellow-

25

IV

A Riddle.

"Madame Zenobia," said Mrs. Richling one day, "don't you think I might sit up, eh? Just to scare Mr Richling when he comes in, eh? Don't you?"

The quadroon smiled irresponsibly:—

"If you thing?"— spreading her eyes and elbows suddenly in the manner of a crab, with palms turned upward and thumbs outstretched,—"well?"— and so dropped them, but presently threw up one hand again with the forefinger lifted alertly forward:—"I'll mek a lill fi' biff."

She made a fire. Then she helped the young wife to put on a few loose drapings. She gave the aid with pleasure. A man's clothing is his defense; but with woman all dress is adornment, and adornment—for reasons that you may see lying on the bottom through the clear depths of philosophy,—adornment is their most natural delight. And above all, the adorning of a bride There centres the gay consent of all mankind and womankind to an inno-cent, sweet treason against the ranks of both. The value of

A page from the manuscript for Dr. Sevier, *Cable's second novel*

fever epidemic and under occupation by Union forces. Cable's aim is not to enchant but to inform the reader about the unglamorous drainage system of the city, the health establishment's inability to cope with the fever, and the improvements wrought by some of the Yankee occupiers. Gilder liked only the typical and vintage Cable "darky" character Narcisse; he spoke for the majority of readers.

This controversial polemical streak culminated in Cable's next novel, *John March, Southerner* (1895), another novel that Gilder begged Cable not to write. But Reconstruction and what Cable believed to be widespread and dangerous misconceptions about its success were topics that he could not and would not ignore. Once convinced of his moral duty, Cable would do anything to fulfill it. With *The Grandissimes* this perseverance preserved a fine novel in the face of much editorial hand wringing. The same cannot be said in the case of *John March, Southerner.*

The novel is set in the fictitious state of Dixie after the Confederacy's surrender. John March, son of a judge whose mind and vocabulary are saturated with the Chesterfieldian eighteenth century, was too young to fight in the Civil War, but the upheavals of Reconstruction sweep him up. He must reconcile the traditional values of his father's generation—the acceptance of slavery included—with the highly suspect tactics of carpetbagger and scalawag developers who have flocked to Dixie and the March plantation with schemes to transform it into an industrial village. The mountains are surveyed for mineral deposits; the streams are gauged for water power. John March's naive attempts to retain the good in the old order while adapting to the new make him a hero in the mold of Honoré Grandissime. But Cable does not execute this portrait clearly and it is difficult to decide whether March is an admirable hero or a saintly fool.

March's role as go-between is difficult for Cable to represent dramatically. He often puts forward characters who preach, and an ornate, often cloying love plot further lengthens the novel and obscures the ending, making the reader uncertain that the central issues of money versus tradition, New South versus Old, have been resolved. *John March, Southerner* was neither a critical nor a financial success for Cable. There are many veins of potential interest: the dilemmas facing veterans who return to a social condition in which the old hierarchy has fallen, the Reconstruction's corruption of politics for both black and white, the personal struggle with one's father's past, and the complex ways in which one section's myths about

another inhibit full understanding. *John March, Southerner* remains an interesting failure, and Cable's final polemical excursion. After this experience he was determined to turn his hand to the production of entertainment. He had already begun *The Cavalier* (1901).

In the new century Cable heeded the calls of his publishers and of the market for a historical romance of the Civil War. In *The Cavalier* he gives himself wholeheartedly to the romance of the dashing hero, to the clash of the sword and the dust of battle, and to the sighs of parted lovers. It is the story of the medieval paladins wrought out of his own experience in the Confederate cavalry, and his readers responded by buying 100,000 copies. *The Cavalier* was so popular that Cable began to write a dramatic adaptation for Julia Marlowe, a popular actress of the day. The play, which opened in New York on 8 December 1902 and ran for seventy performances, did not bring Cable the comfortable income that he had anticipated.

The success of the novel did, however, relax the financial pressure temporarily. During the early 1900s Cable devoted his time to many of the programs for civic improvement that he had always conducted. The Home Culture clubs, which he had started as early as 1886, had become a large operation that consumed more and more of his time. The clubs grew out of Cable's humanitarian concern for "elevating the masses." Sensing the dangers in an increasingly industrial and urban society, Cable established clubs for the reading and discussion of works of literature and other cultural topics. The clubs were small—the ideal number of members was around ten—and were to meet regularly in the homes of the members. This arrangement was intended to couple the twin ideals of the larger culture, represented by literature and art, and the traditional seat of all value, the home.

Entertaining literary visitors such as James Barrie at Tarryawhile also took time away from his writing. His publishers still urged him to write stories about New Orleans Creoles, but he felt that part of his life had closed. As the twentieth century and its historical and literary movements sped by, Cable fell farther behind. He tried a novel set outside the South, *Bylow Hill* (1902). Somewhat in the vein of Edith Wharton's *Ethan Frome* (1911), it was not a success. *Kincaid's Battery* (1908), in which Cable tried to shift the success of his cavalry novel to one about the artillery, was a tepid work that did not repay his publisher's advances. *Gideon's Band* (1914), a romance in which Cable mined his memories of his father's exploits in the Mississippi

George Washington Cable, 1902

River trade, was a disappointment as well. Although Cable approaches the themes of race and wealth in *Gideon's Band*, he devotes too much time to the hackneyed story of the steamboat owner's daughter who falls in love with the son of her father's bitter rival. Critics and readers alike found it colorless.

In debt to his publishers, Cable continued to write as his powers waned. He kept hoping for income from stage adaptations or from motion-picture rights, but very little cash materialized. His friend Andrew Carnegie provided a pension, and Cable was able to combine several of his longer stories into *The Flower of the Chapdelaines* (1918). His daughters contributed to his support from time to time. There were few bright spots in Cable's later years. In 1920 his doctor told him that he could no longer work, but Cable continued on a reduced schedule. He could still afford to winter in Florida or Bermuda, but the deaths of so many friends kept the outlook bleak. His first wife, Louise Bartlett, had died in 1904, his second, Eva Stevenson, in 1923. Clemens had died in 1910 and Howells in 1920. Still Cable remained cheerful and married a

Northampton widow, Hanna Cowing. He took a manuscript with him to Florida in the winter of 1924, and was at work on it when he died in St. Petersburg on 31 January 1925.

Cable's work is the uneven achievement of a writer whose genius was not monumental, whose craft was dependable but not great. The stories in *Old Creole Days* are still anthologized, and *The Grandissimes* was, until 1982, still in print. In his polemical works Cable was a courageous critic of his society, one who could see the manifold ways in which it deceived itself about its successful solution to the problem of race. But he was too much the idealistic believer in the eventual triumph of good to lapse into a cynical silence or an antagonistic naysaying. He was a devout reader of Emerson, Thoreau, and Whitman—a subscriber to American optimism.

In his later fiction there are no unrecognized masterpieces. *Dr. Sevier* is flawed by preaching and a lack of dramatic action. *John March, Southerner* remains an intriguing failure which generates much discussion among scholars but does not engage a popular audience. *The Cavalier* and the novels that followed it trace Cable's disappearance into the mists of romantic entertainment; the reader can glimpse only here and there a remnant of his former power. The reviewer for the *Atlantic Monthly* said of *The Cavalier* that it was "good reading for a dull, materialistic day."

Cable's career, however, is by no means the record of a failure. For a brief period of his long life he was ahead of or at least abreast of his times, but then the times outstripped him. At his peak he anticipated Faulkner's probing of the tangled psychology of racial identities. In the complex brotherhood brought about by miscegenation, Cable found a metaphor for the relationship between the races that likewise anticipated Faulkner and, in his own times, challenged the paternalistic point of view that served to maintain the status quo.

In his polemical writings Cable sought to influence social conditions. He saw that the problem of race was not a problem of inadequate or compromised institutions, but was a complex matter of individual and social psychology. A way of thinking had to be altered before the social manifestations of that thinking, the institutions and laws, could be successfully changed. In this position, Cable was far ahead of his audience. That loneliness eventually took its toll, and Cable abandoned his causes for the comfortable surroundings of a genteel literary and social environment.

Compared with Twain, Howells, and James, the preeminent realists of American literature in

Cable in his study at Tarryawhile, his house in Northampton, Massachusetts

the nineteenth century, Cable is a secondary figure. He pioneered the use of dialect in fiction, opened up to a wide national audience the picturesque scenes of New Orleans, and bore unflinching witness to the fate of the black American under slavery and emancipation. Cable's attempt to combine his polemical topics—prison reform, the care of the indigent, the political and financial misdeeds of Reconstruction—and the forms of fiction were decreasingly successful. The achievement of the early stories and *The Grandissimes*, however, has never been challenged. For these works alone Cable is entitled to a permanent place among the writers of the latter half of the nineteenth century in America.

Biographies:
Lucy Leffingwell Cable Biklé, *George W. Cable: His Life and Letters* (New York: Scribners, 1928);
Arlin Turner, *George W. Cable: A Biography* (Durham: Duke University Press, 1956);
Philip Butcher, *George W. Cable: The Northampton*

Years (New York: Columbia University Press, 1959);
Louis Rubin, Jr., *George W. Cable: The Life and Times of a Southern Heretic* (New York: Pegasus, 1969).

References:
Philip Butcher, *George W. Cable* (New York: Twayne, 1962);
Guy A. Cardwell, *Twins of Genius* (East Lansing: Michigan State College Press, 1953);
Richard Chase, *The American Novel and Its Traditions* (Garden City: Doubleday, 1957), pp. 167-176;
Jay B. Hubbell, *The South in American Literature, 1607-1900* (Durham: Duke University Press, 1962);
Edwin Mims, *History of Southern Fiction* (Richmond: Southern Historical Publication Society, 1909);
Edmund Wilson, *Patriotic Gore* (New York: Oxford University Press, 1962).

Charles Waddell Chesnutt

(20 June 1858-15 November 1932)

Charles W. Scruggs
University of Arizona

SELECTED BOOKS: *The Conjure Woman* (Boston &
New York: Houghton, Mifflin, 1899; London:
Gay & Bird, 1899);

Frederick Douglass (Boston: Small, Maynard, 1899;
London: Kegan Paul, Trench & Trubner,
1899);

The Wife of His Youth and Other Stories of the Color Line
(Boston & New York: Houghton, Mifflin,
1899);

The House Behind the Cedars (Boston & New York:
Houghton, Mifflin, 1900);

The Marrow of Tradition (Boston & New York:
Houghton, Mifflin, 1901);

The Colonel's Dream (New York: Doubleday, Page,
1905; London: Constable, 1905);

The Short Fiction of Charles W. Chesnutt, edited by
Sylvia Lyons Render (Washington, D.C.:
Howard University Press, 1974).

Charles W. Chesnutt

Charles Waddell Chesnutt was America's first
important black writer of fiction; no black American before him had created a sustained body of
significant work. Since his life spanned nearly two
halves of two different centuries, his writing reflects
both the new and the old. Despite the often clumsy
and artificial plot devices in his novels, his portrayal
of black character is both varied and realistic. No
one until Chesnutt had invested the Negro common
man (such as Josh Green in *The Marrow of Tradition*,
1901, and Uncle Julias in *The Conjure Woman*, 1899)
with a dignity which does not strain the bounds of
credulity. Yet although Chesnutt knew the seamy
side of black life, he remained very much a child of
the century of his birth. Genteel in his social habits
and aspirations and fastidious in his taste for moral
literature, he disapproved of many of the Harlem
Renaissance writers who arrived a generation later.

Chesnutt's fiction chronicles the small Southern town of the late nineteenth century. He was
born in Cleveland to Andrew J. and Maria Sampson
Chesnutt, free Negroes who had moved from
Fayetteville, North Carolina, to the North before
the Civil War, but in 1866, the family returned to
Fayetteville, and Chesnutt's father started a grocery
store there. Young Charles heard folktales and
other country lore in his father's market, but he
preferred Latin authors and the English and
American classics. At first his reading made him a
snob. He said of the country people around him
that they were "the most bigoted, superstitious,
hardest-headed people in the world," believing in
"ghosts, luck, horseshoes, cloud signs, witches and
all other kinds of nonsense." Later, however, his
reading, especially of Latin authors such as Ovid,
would give him another perspective on these "uneducated" black people. Their myths would appear
to him to be universal; their sufferings and humor,
part of their humanity.

When he was fourteen, he was given a position
of pupil-teacher at the normal school for Negroes in
Fayetteville, but his father's poverty soon made him
seek elsewhere for other work. Between the ages of

The Howard School, where Chesnutt was first a pupil-teacher and then principal, was on the second floor of this building in Fayetteville, North Carolina.

fifteen and eighteen, he taught briefly in Spartanburg, South Carolina, and for two and a half years in Charlotte, only to return to Fayetteville in 1877 to become assistant principal of the normal school under Robert Harris. The pattern of those years has been well described by a recent biographer, Frances Richardson Keller: "He rose at six, read till breakfast, ate, studied until school time, taught until three in the afternoon, then left for home and read again until dusk." At night he would reflect upon what he had read.

In 1878, Chesnutt married Susan Perry, and two years later, when Harris died, he became principal of the normal school in Fayetteville. Yet instead of settling down, Chesnutt became restless. He began to study languages—Latin, German, French, Greek—and even shorthand. It was this last skill which was to provide him with a passport to the business world.

Chesnutt had made a trip to Washington, D.C., in 1878, but had hurried back to Fayetteville

filled with loneliness. Now he decided to try urban life again. In 1883, he resigned his position as principal, went to New York City, and worked for six months as a reporter of Wall Street news for the *New York Mail & Express*. Later he was to use this experience in New York in some of his short stories and in his last novel, *The Colonel's Dream* (1905), which begins and ends in New York. Yet Chesnutt's New York is never more than a backdrop for his characters.

In 1883 Chesnutt settled in Cleveland and sent for his wife and children, two little girls and a baby boy. He immediately got a job as a clerk with a railway company, and eventually became a stenographer for the company's lawyer, Judge Williamson. He soon turned this job into an opportunity to learn law, studying under Williamson's guidance just as John Walden studies under Judge Straight's in *The House Behind the Cedars* (1900). In 1887, he passed the Ohio bar exams with the highest marks in his class, and in the meantime he had formed his own stenographic service, which developed into a lucrative business.

As early as 1880, however, Chesnutt had seen an opportunity to gain both fame and fortune in literature. Having read *A Fool's Errand* (1879) by Northern white novelist Albion Tourgée, Chesnutt wondered if a "colored man," someone "who has lived among colored people all his life; who is familiar with their habits, their ruling passions, their prejudices, their condition, their public and private ambitions, their religious tendencies and habits . . . and who besides had possessed such opportunities for observation and conversation with the better class of white men in the South as to understand their modes of thinking," would not be able to "write a far better book about the South than Judge Tourgée or Mrs. Stowe has written." He speculated further that the audience for his work would not be black but white; he would be concerned with "not so much the elevation of the colored people as the elevation of the whites." The "high, holy purpose" of his writing would be to elevate the souls of his audience. Thus, Chesnutt's aim was twofold: to write well and to educate his audience. He could not see at the time that the two impulses might someday conflict.

Although he had previously had several short stories published, his work was not noticed until the publication of "The Goophered Grapevine" in the August 1887 issue of the *Atlantic Monthly*. This publication brought him to the attention of writers Albion Tourgée and George Washington Cable. Walter Hines Page, a fellow North Carolinian and the editor of the prestigious *Altantic Monthly*, took a personal interest in Chesnutt's career and encouraged him to put together a collection of his stories. Chesnutt thought that a book could be made from a mixture of "conjure" stories and "mulatto" stories, but Page insisted that a group of "conjure" stories would work better as a separate entity. Chesnutt took Page's advice and a collection of his "Uncle Julius" tales was published as *The Conjure Woman*.

Although *The Conjure Woman* does not have the unity of a novel, it has an overall framing device. The Northern narrator has purchased a post-Civil War plantation in the Cape Fear area of North Carolina, and in the opening story, "The Goophered Grapevine," he meets an old retainer who has been quietly living on the plantation. The narrator feels an obligation to keep Uncle Julius on as a general handyman and coachman, but it so happens that the old man has even greater talents: he is a marvelous raconteur and (as the narrator comes to

suspect) an adept con man. The tales Uncle Julius tells have their source in the folklore of the region, and for this reason they can be considered part of the realistic tradition in American literature. Not only are they accurate pictures of the folk imagination but Uncle Julius himself escapes the traditional stereotype of the shuffling, happy-go-lucky "darky."

Chesnutt always insisted that his conjure stories were not mere "transcriptions" like Joel Chandler Harris's Uncle Remus stories but "the fruit of my own imagination." And Chesnutt's imagination was as much a product of his reading as his listening. Almost all of the stories which make up *The Conjure Woman* deal with metamorphosis, and several of them have classical antecedents. For example, in the story, "The Conjurer's Revenge," Primus steals a conjure man's pig and is changed into a mule as punishment. Chesnutt probably got this idea both from a local folk story which he heard and from his reading of Apuleius's *The Golden Ass*. Similarly, Ovid's *Metamorphoses* and Vergil's *Aeneid* are sources for "Po' Sandy," a tale about a man whose wife turns him into a tree. Other characters in *The Conjure Woman* are metamorphosed into a bird (Little Mose in "Sis' Becky's Pickaninny") and a wolf (Dan in "The Gray Wolf's Ha'nt"), and Henry in "The Goophered Grapevine" is even transformed into a kind of vineyard deity reminiscent of Chloris's transformation into the goddess of Spring in Ovid's *Fasti*.

A year before the publication of *The Conjure Woman*, Chesnutt's short story "The Wife of His Youth" appeared in the July 1898 issue of the *Atlantic Monthly*. A delicately comic tale about the separation and reunion of a mulatto husband and his "Negro" wife, this story was soon to head the collection of "mulatto" stories, *The Wife of His Youth and Other Stories of the Color Line* (1899). As Chesnutt told Houghton, Mifflin in 1899, "the backbone of this volume is not a character, like Uncle Julius in *The Conjure Woman*, but a subject, as indicated in the title—*The Color Line*." Yet *The Wife of His Youth and Other Stories of the Color Line* deals with more than the theme of color; it also deals with the theme of law. The title story, with which the collection opens, is a good indication of the breadth of Chesnutt's concerns. It alludes to the first two verses in chapter 15 of Ecclesiasticus in the Apocrypha: "he who holds to the law will obtain wisdom. She will come to meet him like a mother, and like the wife of his youth she will welcome him." The law in this story is the higher law of moral obligation. Ryder, who has made a

Mars Jeems's Nightmare   97   98   *The Conjure Woman*

how er nuther I doan lak yo' looks since I come back dis time, en I'd much ruther you would n' stay roun' heah. Fac', I's feared ef I'd meet you alone in de woods sometime, I mought wanter ha'm you. But layin' dat aside, I be'n lookin' ober dese yer books er yo'n w'at you kep' w'iles I wuz 'way, en fer a yeah er so back, en dere's some figgers w'at ain' des cl'ar ter me. I ain' got no time fer ter talk 'bout 'em now, but I 'spec' befo' I settles wid you fer dis las' mont', you better come up heah ter-morrer, atter I 's look' de books en 'counts ober some mo', en den we straighten ou' business all up.'

"Mars Jeems 'lowed atterwa'ds dat he wuz des shootin' in de da'k w'en he said dat 'bout de books, but howsomeber, Mars Nick Johnson lef' dat naberhood 'twix' de nex' two suns, en nobody 'roun' dere nebber seed hide ner hair un 'im sence. En all de darkies t'ank

de Lawd, en 'lowed it wuz a good riddance er bad rubbage.

"But all dem things I done tol' you ain' nuffin 'side'n de change w'at come ober Mars Jeems fum dat time on. Aun' Peggy's goopher had made a noo man un 'im enti'ely. De nex' day atter he come back he tol' de han's dey neenter wuk on'y fum sun ter sun, én he cut dey tasks down so dey did n' nobody hab ter stan' ober 'em wid a rawhide er a hick'ry. En he 'lowed ef de niggers want ter hab a dance in de big ba'n any Sad'day night, dey mought hab it. En bimeby, w'en Solomon seed how good Mars Jeems wuz, he ax' 'im ef he would n' please sen' down ter de yuther plantation fer his junesey. Mars Jeems say sut'n'ly, en gun Solomon a pass en a note ter de oberseah on de yuther plantation, en sont Solomon down ter Robeson County wid a hoss 'n' buggy fer ter fetch his junesey back. W'en de nig-

100   *The Conjure Woman*   *Mars Jeems's Nightmare*   101

Peggy's goopher had turn't Mars Jeems ter a nigger, en dat dat noo han' wuz Mars Jeems hisse'f. But co'se Solomon did n' das' ter let on 'bout w'at he 'spected, en ole Aun' Peggy would 'a' 'nied ef she had be'n ax', fer she 'd a got in trouble sho' ef it 'uz knowed she 'd be'n cunj'in' de w'ite folks.

"Dis yer tale goes ter show," concluded Julius sententiously, as the man came up and announced that the spring was ready for us to get water, "dat w'ite folks w'at is so ha'd en stric' en doan make no 'lowance fer po' ign'ant niggers w'at ain' had no chanst ter l'arn, is li'ble ter hab bad dreams, ter say de leas', en dat dem w'at is kin' en good ter po' people is sho' ter prosper en git 'long in de worl'."

"That is a very strange story, Uncle Julius," observed my wife, smiling, "and Solomon's explanation is quite improbable."

"Yes, Julius," said I, "that was powerful goopher. I am glad too, that you told us the moral of the story; it might have escaped us otherwise. By the way, did you make that up all by yourself?"

The old man's face assumed an injured look, expressive more of sorrow than of anger, and shaking his head he replied : —

"No, suh, I heared dat tale befo' you er Miss Annie dere wuz bawn, suh. My mammy tol' me dat tale w'en I wa'n't mo'd'n knee-high ter a hoppergrass."

I drove to town next morning, on some business, and did not return until noon ; and after dinner I had to visit a neighbor, and did not get back until supper-time. I was smoking a cigar on the back piazza in the early evening, when I saw a familiar figure carrying a bucket of water to the barn. I called my wife.

Page proofs for The Conjure Woman *with Chesnutt's corrections*

Front cover for Chesnutt's first book

nutt told the editors at Houghton, Mifflin as early as 1891, he wanted to give people of mixed blood "their day in court," because they had been subjected to so many biased attitudes. For instance, he complained to George Washington Cable that many intelligent people saw the mulatto as "unnatural." One gentleman, he went on, had called the person of mixed blood "an insult to nature" and "a kind of monster." Chesnutt wanted to correct this view in his art by treating the mulatto as a real human being, and not as a moral aberration.

Eighteen ninety-nine seemed to be an eventful year for Chesnutt; in addition to the two collections of short stories, he produced a small biography of Frederick Douglass, a man who had appealed to him because of his strong will and uncompromising principles. Like Douglass, Chesnutt was determined to make a name for himself through his writing, and in 1899, his future as a writer did indeed look bright. Thus on 30 September 1899, he gave up his business as a legal stenographer to become a full-time writer. He was especially encouraged by a favorable review of both books of his short stories by the Dean of American letters, William Dean Howells, in the May 1900 issue of the *Atlantic Monthly*. Howells emphasized Chesnutt's artistry rather than his racial origins, and said, in effect, that Chesnutt was not only a realist but a new American writer of great promise. Chesnutt was pleased with the review because he had been treated as an artist and not as a special case. In the advertisements for *The Conjure Woman*, Houghton, Mifflin had not mentioned Chesnutt's race because they wanted the book to be received on its merits alone, but by the time of Howells's review, everyone knew that Chesnutt was a Negro.

Just as Howells was writing this praise, Chesnutt had finished *The House Behind the Cedars*, a novel which he hoped would live up to Howells's expectations. His friend Page had moved to Doubleday, and Chesnutt thought of changing publishers. Houghton, Mifflin was already considering another novel by Chesnutt ("The Rainbow Chasers"—a nonracial love story still unpublished) but chose to publish *The House Behind the Cedars* before Doubleday could get a chance at it.

Chesnutt had been working on the story of Rena Walden for years. In 1890, he had sent a draft of a short story about her to *Century Magazine*, only to have it rejected. Chesnutt told Cable at the time that the magazines seemed to want stories that reworked stale material about the loyal darky servant. "I can't write about those people," he said, "or rather I won't write about them." He hoped that he

name for himself among the light-skinned "colored" set of Groveland (Cleveland), has no legal tie to his former wife, for he married her when they were slaves and hence their marriage is not legally binding. Older than he (and considerably darker in color), she sought him out in the North after the Civil War. Although she fails to recognize her husband when she meets him, she explains her mission to him. At the annual ball that evening, Ryder tells his wife's story to the members of the society; and in the reader's mind, he is transformed into a person of real consequence (as opposed to the earlier view of him as a commonplace social climber). He renounces his personal and social aspirations (marriage to a handsome, rich widow) for his responsibility to his past, thus giving the lie to his previous cynical statement that "Self-preservation is the first law of nature."

Other stories in the volume explore the relationships between natural law and societal law, higher law and lower law (social custom). As Ches-

would not "have to drop the attempt at realism" to give his readers the kind of characters they expected.

In *The House Behind the Cedars*, Chesnutt did make some concessions to his audience, but not many. For instance, the unpublished "Rena Walden" had presented a realistic portrait of a young girl's calculated attempts to pass for white; in the published novel, however, Rena is more saintly than human. Also, the plot of *The House Behind the Cedars* suffers from the creakiness of Victorian melodrama, and what could have been a fine realistic novel descends, at crucial moments, to the world of the penny dreadful. Yet despite these flaws, the story has great power, and it deserves to be Chesnutt's most popular novel.

Chesnutt did make some happy additions to the original story, most of them having to do with his desire to create realistic portraiture. In one early version, Rena's white lover, George Tryon, is a completely unsympathetic character; but in the published novel, he is more complicated than con-

Front cover for Chesnutt's first novel

temptible, his love for "colored" Rena making him a truly tragic figure. Like Rena, he is star-crossed, but in this instance, it is his own character which brings about his tragedy—not improbability.

Another happy addition to the original story was the introduction of John Walden, Rena's brother. A courageous young man, he studies law and leaves Patesville (in North Carolina) for South Carolina, where the laws governing his mulatto status are flexible enough to make him white. (The legislature had decided that octoroons like John and Rena are officially white, even though custom may still be against them.) When he arrives in South Carolina, he takes the name of Warwick and becomes a successful lawyer. After the death of his wife, he convinces his sister to live with him in South Carolina and thereby to enter Southern high society as a white woman. Almost immediately, a white man, George Tryon, falls in love with her and thus begins a chain of events which will cause her doom and his unhappiness.

A tangle of philosophical beliefs entrap the three major characters. John Walden, like Thoreau, believes that a man can recreate himself out of the ashes of his past. Having read Paine's *The Age of Reason*, he subscribes to the concept of natural rights, which he believes to be his on the basis of natural law, but he has not counted on the irrational force of social custom which is built into the framework of Southern life. Although he and his sister are both legally white in South Carolina, they are standing on very shaky ground. Once the truth is known about Rena's ancestry, Tryon's dream of Rena as the perfection of white womanhood and Rena's dream of Tryon as the gallant Southern gentleman are destroyed. At this point Chesnutt focuses on the conflict between Tryon's natural affection for Rena and the subtle social pressure which alienates that affection. A good man whose soul is warped by social convention, Tryon wavers until it is too late, his final decision taking the shape of a revolt against society: "Never in the few brief delirious weeks of his courtship had he felt so strongly drawn to the beautiful sister of the popular lawyer, as he was now driven by an aching heart toward the same woman stripped of every adventitious advantage and placed, by custom, beyond the pale of marriage with men of his own race. Custom was tyranny. Love was the only law." Yet "being stripped of every adventitious advantage" has placed Rena in Hobbes's state of nature where "Love" is not the only law. Threatened by the villainy of one man (Jeff Wain, a mulatto who lusts after her) and by the ambiguous motives of another

(Tryon), Rena has nowhere to turn. One day she is literally forced into a swamp to escape both men, and she dies in a storm from pneumonia. The ending is fraught with irony. Although Tryon has decreed that natural law (love) is superior to the laws of man, the fates have judged differently; their laws are the final arbiters.

Chesnutt's next novel was to be his epic, a challenge to Harriet Beecher Stowe's *Uncle Tom's Cabin*, for he intended to treat the whole gamut of racial relationships and tensions in the South. His title, *The Marrow of Tradition*, is an indication of its scope, but he decided that he would use a small Southern town as a microcosm of the larger macrocosm. Chesnutt had been upset by the racial violence in Wilmington, North Carolina, in 1898 and he had even visited the town in order to determine the causes of the riot. He discovered that it began as an attempt by white people to wrest all political power from the Negro. Hence, Chesnutt saw the riot as an American Revolution in reverse, an action which signified the destruction of man's natural rights rather than their restoration.

The novel itself suffers from having too many plot lines and is much too didactic, but it is an insightful picture of the social structure of the post-Reconstruction South. Chesnutt documents the failure of a well-intentioned newspaper editor, Major Carteret, to provide intelligent political leadership in Wellington (Wilmington) because of his belief in "the divine right of white men." Thus he is victimized by an unscrupulous thug, Captain McBane, and a political opportunist, General Belmont, and his campaign to purify the town results in his own moral corruption and the end of all civil order.

Coupled with the spiritual sickness of the New South is the retribution for the sins of the Old South. Chesnutt was fascinated by the burden of Southern history, especially the history of miscegenation. For instance, Carteret's wife has a black half sister whom she refuses to recognize and to whom she has done a grave injustice. Her sister's husband, Dr. William Miller, is a European-trained physician of considerable ability. However, because he is also part black, his positive influence on the town's social health is stifled. At the end of the novel, the Millers' child has been killed in the riot, and Carteret's wife must beg her sister to have Doctor Miller save her son. The final scene is as melodramatic as any in

Chesnutt in his library at 9719 Lamont Avenue, Cleveland

Uncle Tom's Cabin. The novel's strength lies in its indictment of a society which has allowed its baser instincts to prey upon itself.

The reception of *The Marrow of Tradition* was not what Chesnutt had hoped. The critics were generally indifferent to the novel, and the public ignored it. Chesnutt was especially disturbed by Howells's criticism. Howells recognized the justice of Chesnutt's argument but found the novel "bitter." The novel *is* bitter, because Chesnutt felt strongly about what was happening in an area which he once called home.

Chesnutt was to try his hand once again at dissecting the small Southern town. Published by Doubleday in 1905, *The Colonel's Dream* was Chesnutt's attempt to write a popular novel. Concerned with regaining his audience, he even asked Page to advise him on narrative elements which would please readers. Unfortunately, his "purpose novel" (as he was later to describe it to Carl Van Vechten) was the least popular of his three novels. Thomas Dixon, Jr.'s historical romances of the post-Civil War South (*The Leopard's Spots*, 1902, and *The Clansman*, 1905) had captured the public's imagination, and Chesnutt's point of view, so directly opposed to Dixon's theme of white supremacy, was not fashionable in its day.

Chesnutt's antagonist is not a remnant of the old aristocracy but rather a Captain McBane with brains. Fetters is a man of lowly origins who has made good by exploiting the weaknesses of others. Because he is seen from a distance throughout much of the novel, his evil seems insidious and pervasive. Once he actually appears, however, he simply becomes a stock character out of a dime novel.

The hero of *The Colonel's Dream* is Henry French. Having grown up in Clarendon, North Carolina, he has made a fortune in business in New York. Now he has returned to his hometown hoping to revive it, for civilization seems to have passed it by after the Civil War. However, his plans are frustrated by Fetters's greed, Fetters's desire for personal revenge against him, and by the town's strange perversity. The citizens of Clarendon prefer their deteriorating town to a healthy, thriving community based on the equal rights of blacks and whites. Chesnutt's perceptive study of the mentality of a small town foreshadows later American novels such as Sherwood Anderson's *Winesburg, Ohio* (1919) and Sinclair Lewis's *Main Street* (1920).

Colonel French's return to New York is also Chesnutt's farewell to Fayetteville. Never again would he write about the small Southern town, although he did continue writing. The success of his short story "Baxter's Procrustes," which appeared in the *Atlantic Monthly* in 1904, was encouraging after the commercial failure of *The Marrow of Tradition*. One of the best things he ever wrote, "Baxter's Procrustes" is a delightful tale about a huckster who pulls an elaborate hoax on a society of book lovers. There is not a black person in the entire story, whose themes nevertheless touch upon the power of convention to mold men's minds so that they do not see the truth in front of their faces. Unfortunately, Chesnutt was never again to write with such subtlety. He tried to have a play about white middle-class life, "Mrs. Darcy's Daughter," published in 1906, but it was rejected. In 1919, he put together a collection of "conjure" stories which he entitled "Aunt Hagar's Children," but no one wanted it.

In 1902, Chesnutt realized that he could not support himself and his family as a writer, and he returned to his business of legal stenography. As the years went by, he continued to be a polemicist and a platform speaker for Negro rights. He corresponded with both Booker T. Washington and W. E. B. Du Bois, and tried to steer clear of their basic disagreements. Washington wanted to take a conciliatory approach to the harsh racial problems of the new century, whereas Du Bois had urged Negroes to take a militant stand against racism. Chesnutt believed with Du Bois that without the ballot, the Negro's future was doomed; and yet he was reluctant to attack Washington in public, for he thought that Washington's presence in the South *had* made a difference.

Although Chesnutt remained active in public affairs throughout the 1920s, his reputation as a writer diminished after World War I. In fact, he was even forgotten by some of the black writers of the early 1920s. In 1923, Walter White claimed to H. L. Mencken that his soon-to-be-published novel was a first for black literature, despite the fact that White's *The Fire in the Flint* (1924) dealt with a situation already treated by Chesnutt: the tragedy of a black doctor who returns to his provincial hometown in the South.

As the 1920s progressed, however, Chesnutt was rediscovered. Carl Van Vechten praised Chesnutt in his novel *Nigger Heaven* (1926) and in an article in the *New York Herald Tribune Books* (20 December 1925). In 1928, Chesnutt was awarded the NAACP's Spingarn medal even though little of his work had been published for over twenty years.

Because publishing houses such as Knopf and Boni & Liveright had opened their doors to black writers in the 1920s, Chesnutt thought he would try once more to write a novel on black life. He submitted a manuscript called "The Quarry" to Knopf in 1930, but it was rejected. Chesnutt's black hero was just too perfect; by this time, Chesnutt had forgotten his original reason for writing, his desire to create realistic portraits of black people. In 1932, he died of arteriosclerosis in his home in Cleveland.

Periodical Publications:
"What Is a White Man?," *Independent*, 51 (30 May 1889): 5-6;
"Superstitions and Folk-Lore of the South," *Modern Culture*, 13 (May 1901): 231-235;
"The Disenfranchisement of the Negro," in *The Negro Problem: A Series of Articles by Representative American Negroes of To-day*, by Booker T. Washington and others (New York: James Pott, 1903), pp. 79-124;
"Race Prejudice: Its Cause and Its Cure," *Alexander's Magazine*, 1 (July 1905): 21-26;
"The Negro in Art," *Crisis*, 33 (November 1926): 28-29;
"Post-Bellum—Pre-Harlem," *Colophon*, 2, no. 5 (1931).

References:
William L. Andrews, "Charles Waddell Chesnutt: An Essay in Bibliography," *Resources for American Literary Study*, 6 (Spring 1976): 3-22;
Andrews, *The Literary Career of Charles W. Chesnutt* (Baton Rouge: Lousiana State University Press, 1980);
Andrews, "A Reconsideration of *Charles Waddell Chesnutt: Pioneer of the Color Line*," *CLA Journal*, 19 (December 1975): 136-151;
Helen M. Chesnutt, *Charles Waddell Chesnutt: Pioneer of the Color Line* (Chapel Hill: University of North Carolina Press, 1952);
Curtis W. Ellison and E. W. Metcalf, Jr., *Charles W. Chesnutt: A Reference Guide* (Boston: G. K. Hall, 1977);
J. Noel Heermance, *Charles W. Chesnutt: America's First Great Black Novelist* (Hamden, Conn.: Shoe String Press, 1974);
Frances Richardson Keller, *An American Crusade: The Life of Charles Waddell Chesnutt* (Provo: Brigham Young University Press, 1978);
Sylvia Lyons Render, *Charles W. Chesnutt* (Boston: Twayne, 1980);
Robert P. Sedlack, "The Evolution of Charles Chesnutt's *The House Behind The Cedars*," *CLA Journal*, 19 (December 1975): 125-135.

Papers:
The Charles Waddell Chesnutt Collection of the Erastus Milo Cravath Memorial Library, Fisk University, contains Chesnutt's unpublished journals, letters, and novels.

Kate Chopin

Sara deSaussure Davis
University of Alabama

BIRTH: St. Louis, Missouri, 8 February 1851, to Thomas and Eliza Faris O'Flaherty.

MARRIAGE: 9 June 1870 to Oscar Chopin; children: Jean, Oscar, George, Frederick, Felix, and Lelia.

DEATH: St. Louis, Missouri, 22 August 1904.

BOOKS: *At Fault* (St. Louis: Privately printed, 1890);
Bayou Folk (Boston & New York: Houghton, Mifflin, 1894);

A Night in Acadie (Chicago: Way & Williams, 1897);
The Awakening (Chicago & New York: Herbert S. Stone, 1899);
The Complete Works of Kate Chopin, edited by Per Seyersted, 2 volumes (Baton Rouge: Louisiana State University Press, 1969).

Kate Chopin introduced to the reading public a new fictional setting: the charming, somewhat isolated region along the Cane River in north central Louisiana, an area populated by Creoles, Acadians, and blacks. Beginning in the 1960s, her fiction was also recognized for its new psychological terrain, especially in her depiction of women who experience the power of passion that often brings them into conflict with society. Instead of comparing Chopin to the Louisiana local colorists—George Washington Cable, Ruth McEnery Stuart, or Grace King; or even to Mary E. Wilkins Freeman and Sarah Orne Jewett, the local colorists of New England—critics now compare her exploration of new themes to the innovations of other daring writers of the 1890s: Stephen Crane, Hamlin Garland, and Frank Norris. It is true that her first published novel, *At Fault* (1890) and her two published collections of short fiction, *Bayou Folk* (1894) and *A Night in Acadie* (1897), are set in or refer to the Cane River area and convincingly portray the distinctive customs, language, and atmosphere of the region. The popularity in her own time of such local-colorist qualities, combined with the condemnation of her frank depiction of female sexuality in *The Awakening* (1899) have somewhat obscured Chopin's other achievements. Literary historians of the first half of this century perpetuated some important misjudgments or misinformation about her fiction and her career, typically praising her as the author of "Désirée's Baby" (a short story about, among other things, the tragic effects of miscegenation) while seldom mentioning *The Awakening*, now considered her masterpiece. On occasion the plot of the short story has been attributed to the novel. A corrective

to the stale second- or thirdhand assessments of her work came in 1946, when the French critic Cyrille Arnavon called attention to Chopin's place in the realistic tradition of France and America. Although she treats in *The Awakening* what are basically naturalistic ideas of heredity and environment, the essence of her work remains best described as realistic. Since Arnavon's work, a Chopin revival has taken place, in part stimulated by the work of another European scholar, Per Seyersted, who wrote the definitive biography and edited *The Complete Works of Kate Chopin* (1969).

Most of the important experiences that shaped Kate Chopin's temperament and subject matter occurred in the first thirty-three years of her life, before she began to write professionally. Born in St. Louis to secure and socially prominent parents, Eliza Faris O'Flaherty, of French-Creole descent, and Thomas O'Flaherty, an Irish immigrant and successful commission merchant, Katherine O'Flaherty attended the St. Louis Academy of the Sacred Heart; she graduated in 1868 and participated in the social life of a belle for two years before she married a Creole, Oscar Chopin of Louisiana, in June 1870.

Kate O'Flaherty's great-grandmother, Mme. Victoria Verdon Charleville, lived in the O'Flaherty household and directed young Kate's mental and artistic growth until her death when Kate was

Kate and Oscar Chopin, 1870

eleven. She cultivated in the young girl a taste for storytelling, a relish for the intimate details about such historical figures as the earliest settlers of the Louisiana Territory, and an unabashed, unhesitant, even unjudgmental intellectual curiosity about life. Additionally, she superintended the girl's piano lessons and her French, the language especially important in their bilingual home. Chopin's interest in music was lifelong, as was her willingness to explore unconventional ideas. The young Kate was known in St. Louis as the town's "Littlest Rebel" for having taken down and hidden a Union flag from her home where "the Yanks tied it up." A Unionist neighbor managed to keep her from being arrested, but the severity of her offense may be judged by the fact that in New Orleans a man was shot for the same violation.

During her childhood, Kate Chopin endured the death of her father, as well as several other family deaths. Although she always recovered, the depth of her grief may be sensed by her reaction as an eleven-year-old to the deaths (that occurred within a month) of both Mme. Charleville and her half brother George, who fought on the Confederate side during the Civil War. For about two years Chopin withdrew from school, from friends, even somewhat from her family, and spent much of the time reading in the attic. Yet in her fiction— "Ma'ame Pélagie," for example—as in her life, she stressed the moral and psychological value of living in the present.

In 1869, before she had met her future husband, she met a German woman in New Orleans who combined fame as a singer and actress with a respectable place in society and a wealthy, loving husband. This meeting exhilarated the recently graduated Kate Chopin. She also began smoking during this trip, a pleasure she indulged with relish and humor all her life.

Kate and Oscar Chopin lived for almost a decade in New Orleans, until his cotton factoring business failed in 1879, whereupon they moved to Cloutierville, Natchitoches Parish, in north central Louisiana. In both New Orleans and in Cloutierville she absorbed impressions that she would later employ in her fiction. The combination of her gift as a mimic with her talent as a musician—she played by note and by ear and had a remarkable memory for music—allowed her to capture the distinctive cadences, nuances, gestures, and diction of the residents of Louisiana who would, years later, people her fiction. She was at home in New Orleans and Cloutierville society, partly because of her personal magnetism but also because of her faultless French

and her Southern sympathies.

In the fertile cotton land around the Cane River, the Chopins lived on inherited property, with income from the management of several small plantations and the ownership of a plantation store. Although they were not living on a plantation themselves, they were intimately involved in the festive plantation society. By 1879, Kate Chopin had borne her sixth child and only daughter, and by 1883 she was a widow, her husband dead of swamp fever. For a year she successfully managed his business duties, but in 1884 returned with her family to St. Louis, to live with her mother. Her mother's death followed shortly afterward in 1885, leaving Chopin without family—except for her six children—and with a small, diminishing income.

Her only close friend during this time was Dr. Frederick Kolbenheyer, her mother's neighbor and her own obstetrician for three of her children, a learned man whose encouragement is believed to have led her to study contemporary science, to give up her religious beliefs, and to start writing professionally. Following a visit to Natchitoches in 1887, she wrote a poem, "If it might be," published 10 January 1888 in *America*, a progressive Chicago magazine; this publication marked her first appearance in print. She also began working on two pieces of fiction, one titled "Euphrasie," which was much later revised and published as "A No Account Creole" in *Century* (1894), and one she referred to in a notebook as "An Unfinished Story—Grand Isle—30,000 words," which she later destroyed. In an unpublished draft of an essay written in 1896, she describes herself as she struggled initially to shape her personal self into a fictive one and credits Guy de Maupassant with helping her find a vision as well as technique and theme: "It was at this period of my emerging from the vast solitude in which I had been making my own acquaintance, that I stumbled upon Maupassant. . . . Here was a man who had escaped from tradition and authority, who had entered into himself and looked out upon life through his own being and with his own eyes." She particularly responded to his spontaneity and his ability to create genuine impressions "without the plots, the old fashioned mechanism and stage trapping that in a vague, unthinking way I had fancied were essential to the art of story making."

Her first two stories to reach print, "Wiser than a God" and "A Point at Issue!," were written and published in 1889; both concern the unconventional attitude of the heroine toward marriage as a reflection of her unconventional attitude toward herself. This subject would become a persistent but not single-minded theme in Chopin's work, culminating in *The Awakening* as well as in the unpublished short story "Charlie," written in 1900. She came to the theme naturally, not ideologically, partly at least through the strong influence of her great-grandmother, Mme. Charleville. In "Wiser than a God" Paula Von Stolz chooses a musical career rather than a loving, wealthy husband; she explains to him that music "courses with the blood through my veins. . . . it's something dearer than life, than riches, even than love." Paula's devotion to art is humanized somewhat by her association of musical success with love for her dead parents. The pianist's independence, her renown, her German origin as well as her triumph in Leipzig reveal Chopin's debt to her first visit to New Orleans.

In the other 1899 story, "A Point at Issue!," Eleanor Gail and Charles Faraday begin with a modern, emancipated marriage; they share a "free masonry of intellect." The test of their freedom occurs as a result of her year in Paris (why not *Hades*, say their friends) to study French, while he remains in the United States. During this separation each becomes jealous because of false appearances. She attenuates her rational conception of marriage to accommodate jealous passion; he comforts himself with, "my Nellie is only a woman, after all." And Chopin's satiric comment closes the story, "With man's usual inconsistency, he had quite forgotten the episode of [his own jealousy]." Chopin also includes a reference to the woman's suffrage movement's busying itself with the question of clothes "which while stamping their wearer with the distinction of a quasi-emancipation, defeated the ultimate purpose of their construction by inflicting a personal discomfort that extended beyond the powers of long endurance." In contrast to such superficial attempts at creating equality is the integrity of Eleanor and Charles's struggle to maintain individual freedom while dealing with essentials like passion.

Chopin's first novel, *At Fault*, was written after "Euphrasie," the first draft of "A No Account Creole." These works are the first to employ the region, families, concerns, and ambiance of Natchitoches Parish. Written between July 1889 and April 1890, *At Fault* presents the intertwined questions of divorce and moral idealism and announces a number of Chopin's future themes: the relation of the individual to change and to society, the problems of romantic love and unrestrained passion, and the dilemma of the modern woman. Like many first novels, *At Fault* does not satisfactorily balance its various themes; furthermore, the resolution as

well as two major premises of the work seem contrived. The main character, Thérèse Lafirme, who initially seems somewhat like Kate Chopin after the death of her husband, is a young Creole widow who takes over the management of her husband's plantation as a way to cope with her grief. Her healthy accommodation to that painful change in her life is characteristic of her ability to accept such other changes as the new railroad that causes her to move her house, and the sawmill that, because of the allure of money, she permits to alter the landscape she loves; yet she is unable to change or even to question her religious and moral views. Her belief in moral absolutes leads to her attempt to shape the lives of those who work for her. When she discovers that the man she loves, David Hosmer, the sawmill owner, is divorced, she sacrifices their happiness to her rigid morality. If it is nearly incredible that Thérèse asks Hosmer to remarry his alcoholic wife, it is even harder for the reader to believe that he does and returns with her to live on the Lafirme plantation. When Thérèse's interference in the lives of Fanny and David Hosmer, as in the lives of others, begins to produce questionable results, she finally asks herself, "What reason had she to know that a policy of non-interference in the affairs of others might not after all be the judicious one?" Despite her startled discovery that Fanny might not be worth the sacrifice that she and David have made and despite a dream that suggests she is killing David while rescuing Fanny, the solution to her dilemma comes arbitrarily when Fanny is drowned in a surging river, which she is crossing in search of whiskey. Her death renders moot the question of her worth and allows David to marry Thérèse. Thérèse's final realization suggests her growing awareness of moral complexity and personal change: "I have seen myself at fault in following what seemed the only right. I feel as if there were no way to turn for the truth. Old supports appear to be giving way beneath me." David responds, "the truth in its entirety isn't given to man to know—such knowledge, no doubt, would be beyond human endurance." Divorce is neither condemned nor openly endorsed, yet it serves as an appropriate metaphor for those social realities that refuse to be contained within absolute beliefs.

The question of woman's role in society is related to the problem of divorce, though the connection is only tangentially made in the novel. Nevertheless, Chopin creates several psychologically astute vignettes that suggest the varied uses and misuses of a woman's freedom. Fanny's St. Louis friends Belle and Lou are "finished and pro-

Kate Chopin with four of her sons: Frederick, George, Jean, and Oscar, circa 1877

fessional time-killers," who squander their time on matinees, gossip, and in Lou's case, on an extra-marital affair. After their marriage, Thérèse will continue to run the plantation and David will operate the sawmill, a division of labor that suits their interests and abilities. This happy ending, which implies the fulfillment of personal, sexual, and social ideals, seems at odds with many of the antiromantic qualities of the novel.

Contemporary reviews of *At Fault* praised its author's characterizations, style, and humor, while complaining about its breaches of respectability in diction and action. By and large, *At Fault* was seen as a promising first novel. Now, the novel's refusal to condemn divorce is recognized as a first in fiction, and Chopin's willingness to describe a female alcoholic is also a departure from conventional expectations.

In 1890 Chopin worked primarily on her second novel, "Young Dr. Gosse," which was finished in January 1891 and sent to several publishers but was never accepted. She then returned to shorter fiction, completing about forty pieces in the next three years. Twenty-three of these stories, four previously unpublished, were collected in *Bayou Folk*,

published by Houghton, Mifflin in March 1894. By then, Chopin had broken out of the local St. Louis periodicals and children's magazines that first published her work and into the eastern literary market, though the subject matter of several of the stories caused delays as she searched for more tolerant forums. In 1894 her stories appeared in *Century*, *Atlantic*, and *Vogue*. *Vogue*, in fact, published nineteen of her stories from 1893 to 1900, among them her most provocative and outspoken on the themes of a woman's sexual nature and her situation in marriage, including "Désirée's Baby," "La Belle Zoraïde," "A Respectable Woman," "The Story of an Hour," "The Kiss," "Her Letters," "An Egyptian Cigarette," and "The White Eagle."

Bayou Folk depicts more fully the Louisiana milieu of *At Fault*. The tales are unified by setting, recurring characters, a prevailing theme, and the author's tone—cool and distant but with humor and insight. The setting is occasionally New Orleans but predominately Natchitoches Parish, whether the village of Natchitoches, the plantations along Cane River, the small farms and squalid cabins, or the houses on the bayous. Chopin reveals herself here as a practitioner of Howellsian realism—portraying ordinary people in their everyday concerns. Except for two stories set during the Civil War, the tales take place after the war, the effects of which are apparent in the narratives. The war indirectly provides the main plot in four of the twenty-three stories, but in each the family at home supplies the angle of vision.

The major theme of the *Bayou Folk* collection is love, whether loyal devotion, romantic love, love of honor, sexual passion, or some combination of these. Love is a positive force for the individuals involved and for their community. Devotion to another takes many forms. Yet even devotion has complexity when examined from Chopin's ironic perspective. For example, in "A Lady of Bayou St. John" a childlike wife whose husband is fighting with Beauregard falls in love with a neighboring Frenchman and plans to flee to Paris with him. But before she does, word comes that her husband is dead. Instead of marrying the Frenchman she devotes herself to the memory of her husband. Is devotion to an ideal more satisfying than love itself, and is a dead husband more capable of inspiring fidelity than a living one, or has the passion she experienced with the Frenchman enabled her, ironically, to sacrifice as well as to love? Chopin leaves the enigma unresolved.

Chopin convincingly portrays the simplicity of romantic love in Natchitoches Parish, partly through her use of setting. In such stories as "Love on the Bon-Dieu," the act of falling in love at first sight is given plausibility by the characters' rootedness in a small, homogenous community, where everyone's knowing one another lays the groundwork for what only seems an impetuous act.

Sexual passion as the basic force in love is wrought with complexity and sometimes with tragedy. The tragic effects of miscegenation loom in the background of two stories of passion, "Désirée's Baby" and "La Belle Zoraïde." The justly famous "Désirée's Baby" dramatizes the rage of a planter, Armand, whose name is one of the oldest and proudest in Louisiana, when he discovers that his infant son has Negroid features. Blaming his wife, whom he has loved passionately, and sending her away, he "thought that God had dealt cruelly and unjustly with him; and felt somehow that he was paying him back in kind when he stabbed thus into his wife's soul." She walks into the bayou, carrying her baby, while Armand, in burning all her possessions, discovers a letter from his mother telling of her own Negro blood. In "La Belle Zoraïde" preventing the marriage of a young mulatto girl and the black man for whom she has developed a spon-

taneous erotic attraction ends in the girl's insanity.

Reviewers of *Bayou Folk* were enthusiastically favorable, praising its freshness, charm, realistic subject matter, and unpretentious style. Chopin was perceived as more than a local colorist, with the *Atlantic Monthly* reviewer commenting, "Now and then she strikes a passionate note, and the naturalness and ease with which she does it impress one as characteristic of power awaiting opportunity." Modern reaction is in accord with these early appraisals. *Bayou Folk* was reprinted by Houghton Mifflin in 1895, 1906, 1911, and 1968.

The success of *Bayou Folk* no doubt contributed to Chopin's continuing to write short stories. She was not receiving much encouragement for her still unpublished second novel, *Young Dr. Gosse*; in 1895 it was rejected again, and in 1896 she destroyed it. Her working methods and living conditions probably also influenced her to write shorter fiction. Valuing spontaneity in art as in life, she often composed a story in one sitting and most of her stories were printed as they were first written. She said of her own writing, "I am completely at the mercy of unconscious selection. To such an extent is this true, that what is called the polishing up process has always proved disastrous to my work, and I avoid it, preferring the integrity of crudities to artificialities." Chopin worked in the living room, subject to the demands of her family. Her children remember her sitting in their midst with a lapboard and writing materials, refusing to exclude them, even though she wished to at times. The youngest of her six children was eighteen when Chopin began her next novel, *The Awakening*. Throughout her career, she wrote only one or two days a week, leaving the rest of the time for such activities as musicales, concerts, and the theater. She also presided over the equivalent of a French salon, which attracted St. Louisians of various intellectual interests.

Chopin's second collection of tales, *A Night in Acadie*, which came out in 1897, contains twenty-one stories, all but one of which had first been published in a periodical. Way and Williams, the book's Chicago publisher, was not well known, and this work received less notice than *Bayou Folk*. The milieu and some of the characters are the same as in *Bayou Folk*, but the themes of this second volume are more diverse. The number of stories about devotion falls to two. In place of charmingly depicted romantic love is a more complicated sexual passion. The demands of passion, the reconciliation of public with private self, and the resurrection from a static life are interrelated themes in this collection and point toward Chopin's next book and finest achievement, *The Awakening*. Fifteen tales are equally divided among these three topics; three of the remaining four are miscellaneous sketches, brief insights into character.

In *A Night in Acadie* love is an overwhelming force, irrational in its demands; impervious to caste, class, honor; and dangerous to physical well-being. In "Azélie" the plantation-store manager, 'Polyte, first gives Azélie whatever she wants for her shiftless father so that she will not steal the items; then he falls desperately in love with her, gives up his job as well as his notion of honor and follows her helplessly to Little River, a place which, he says, "always make me sad—like I think about a graveyard. To me it's like a person mus' die, one way or otha, w'en they go on Li'le river. Oh, I hate it!" When in "At Cheniere Caminada" a clumsy island fisherman falls desperately in love with a wealthy New Orleans girl, his whole life is radically altered, and his despair is so intense that he finds himself glad that she is dead rather than married to someone else. His passion is depicted as inevitable, natural: "He obeyed [this powerful impulse] without a struggle, as naturally as he would have obeyed the dictates of hunger and thirst." A tantalizingly ambiguous story, "A Respectable Woman," shows the dilemma of a married woman who becomes physically attracted to her husband's friend, Gouvernail. As she would later do in *The Awakening*, Chopin details the physical aspects of the wife's attraction, "Her mind only vaguely grasped what he was saying. Her physical being was for the moment predominant. She was not thinking of his words, only drinking in the tones of his voice. She wanted to reach out her hand in the darkness and touch him with the sensitive tips of her fingers upon the face or the lips. She wanted to draw close to him and whisper against his cheek—she did not care what—as she might have done if she had not been a respectable woman." To avoid seeing him again, she leaves to visit the city before his stay has ended. Later she dissuades her husband from inviting him again; but by the end of the year she proposes that he visit, and when her husband is pleased that she has overcome her dislike for him, she replies, "Oh, . . . I have overcome everything! you will see. This time I shall be very nice to him." This ending was ambiguous enough for her audience not to take offense, as they would with Chopin's treatment of passion and adultery in *The Awakening*.

One of Chopin's best stories, "Athénaïse," suggests the degree to which love and passion sometimes go against the demands of the self for both husband and wife. The childlike, passionate, willful bride of two months, Athénaïse, runs away from her husband twice, not because he is in any way objectionable but because marriage does not suit her: "It's jus' being married that I detes' an' despise. I hate being Mrs. Cazeau, an' would want to be Athénaïse Miché again. I can't stan' to live with a man; to have him always there; his coats an' pantaloons hanging in my room. . . ." In spite of his deep love for her, Cazeau does not go after his wife the second time because doing so reminds him of his father's bringing home a runaway slave: "the loss of self-respect seemed to him too dear a price to pay for a wife." He would have her return voluntarily or not at all. Yet passion also reconciles the couple. After a month of hiding out in a New Orleans pension, missing her home and family and nearly beginning an affair, Athénaïse discovers she is pregnant; then, thinking of Cazeau she experiences "the first purely sensuous tremor of her life." Chopin's astute characterization makes Athénaïse's joyous return home credible.

"The dual life," as Chopin called it in *The Awakening*, "that outward existence which con-

Kate Chopin, 1894

forms, the inward life which questions," touches five stories in *A Night in Acadie* but is most powerfully realized in "Ozéme's Holiday" and "Nég Créol." Unlike Edna Pontellier in *The Awakening*, who in totally shedding her social self leaves herself nowhere to go but death, the main characters in these stories strike a balance between the two worlds, accommodating self to society in a way that does not extinguish the self; Chopin ironically suggests that some portion of society's demands in fact nourish some aspect of the self. In five other stories, an adult frozen in a kind of emotional or social isolation (or both) is rejuvenated by an encounter with a child, or in the case of "Regret," several children. Chopin uses the symbolism of spring and, sometimes, of Easter to reinforce the awakenings, but the religious motifs in "After the Winter" and "The Lilies" here, as in "Odalie Misses Mass," serve only to heighten the significant experiences that take place in the natural rituals of life, not in those of the church.

The few reviews *A Night in Acadie* attracted praised Chopin as a local colorist but reacted against the book's sensual themes. The collection is now praised both for its success in the local-color genre and for its indication of Chopin's maturing artistry.

From 1897 to 1900 or 1901, Chopin tried unsuccessfully to market a third collection of stories, called "A Vocation and A Voice." It contained in its final version twenty-one stories, one written before 1894, sixteen written between 1894 and 1897, and four written after 1897. About half of the stories had been published in *Vogue*, a number had been difficult to place because of their subject matter, and five were not to see print until many years after Chopin's death. *Vogue* was clearly aware that Chopin's themes were often daring, and its editors gave her her most consistently tolerant forum.

The variation of themes begun in *A Night in Acadie* increases in this collection, and Chopin moves away from her usual Louisiana setting. Moreover, the characters and themes establish themselves authentically without the Louisiana dialect or setting (present in only three tales), and for the first time Chopin experiments effectively in several pieces with first-person narration. Among these stories are three brief sketches that concern nature as a means of knowledge, specifically a knowledge of God. The remaining tales are almost equally divided: about half deal frankly with the imperatives of passion; the rest can be grouped together not so much by theme as by their most salient quality—an ironic tone, closest in spirit perhaps to Stephen Crane's irony.

Many of the stories treat extramarital sex as a subject of interest for what it reveals of human psychology, not as a subject of lament or moralizing, anticipating Chopin's handling of the theme in *The Awakening*. Furthermore, in the title story, "A Vocation and a Voice," as well as in "Lilacs," "Two Portraits," and "Juanita," she suggests in a Whitmanesque fashion that to obey erotic impulses is to participate in the natural rhythms of life itself. Eschewing all moralizing, Chopin leaves herself free to explore as well the varied consequences within society of such sexuality; they might be painful, tragic, humorous, dangerous, joyous, or pleasurable; they are not, however, wrong. As she implies in "A Vocation and A Voice" and in "Two Portraits," frequently the ardor that makes a good member of a religious order is the same that makes a good lover, and vice versa.

One of the ironic stories, "The Story of an Hour," now frequently anthologized because of its commentary on marriage and its relationship to *The Awakening*, turns on a series of artfully modulated ironies that culminate in a somewhat contrived ending. After an outburst of grief over the news that her loving husband has been killed in a train accident, Mrs. Mallard, who has a heart condition, goes to her room alone, where she fearfully tries to ward off the realization that she is glad to be free and then becomes intoxicated with the vision of freedom: "she would live for herself. There would be no powerful will bending hers in that blind persistence with which men and women believe they have a right to impose a private will upon a fellow-creature. A kind intention or a cruel intention made the act seem no less a crime as she looked upon it in that brief moment of illumination." When her husband returns unharmed (he did not even know of the accident), Mrs. Mallard has a fatal heart attack, her shock emphasizing the completeness of her new commitment to freedom. The final irony comes from the physician, who declares that she died "of joy that kills."

It is unfortunate that "A Vocation and A Voice" has never been published as a collection, because it would confirm what has been generally recognized by critics, that Chopin was interested in 'universal human nature; Natchitoches Parish or New Orleans merely provided a specific setting for many of her works. This setting was no doubt fresh and piquant to her as to her contemporary audience, but it is not the major basis for her achievement as an artist. "A Vocation and A Voice" offers

Manuscript for "The Storm," written in July 1898. The story was not published during Chopin's lifetime.

convincing evidence that her insights into character, her narrative voice, her prose style are her finest achievements.

In addition to some forty poems and several translations (including seven of Maupassant's tales), Chopin also wrote and had published a small number of essays, among them literary reviews. With the exception of one piece that appeared in the *Atlantic Monthly*, most of the essays were published in St. Louis journals from 1894 to 1897. Not surprisingly, she proves as a critic to be consistent with her own practice of art. For example, in two 1894 essays she chastises Hamlin Garland for dismissing "from the artist's consideration such primitive passions as love, hate, etc.," and she criticizes Zola's method in "Lourdes" because the story is "more than two-thirds of the time swamped beneath a mass of prosaic data, offensive and nauseous description and rampant sentimentality." While her criticism was often acute, Chopin's major achievement remains her fiction, particularly *The Awakening*.

Now often republished and acclaimed as a masterpiece, *The Awakening* was during Chopin's lifetime the subject of scandal and censure. Certain contemporary reviews of the novel depicted the moral and literary biases of her critics, who termed the book "moral poison," "sordid," "unhealthy," "repellent," and "vulgar" with "disagreeable glimpses of sensuality." Accusing Chopin of "out Zola-ing Zola," reviewers were offended because the author did not condemn her adulterous heroine, Edna Pontellier, or, worse, that she seemed at times to sympathize with Edna. In spite of the moral outrage it engendered, the novel also drew some reluctant praise for its artistry and insight. Typical was the comment of her friend, writer C. L. Deyo: "It is sad, and mad and bad; but it is all consummate art." Libraries in St. Louis banned the book, and acquaintances and even some friends cut Chopin socially. In fact, reactions to the novel were later credited with paralyzing Chopin's creativity.

The vehemence of the hostile reviews of *The Awakening*, which assuredly contributed to its half century of neglect, is attributable to the novel's special power. That power derives not so much from Chopin's violation of several nineteenth-century principles of womanly and literary decorum, although that violation raised indignant protests, as from the novel's intense poetic unity: the prose style, the characterization of the heroine, and the symbolism all lead inevitably to the novel's tragic resolution. Indeed, Chopin's contemporary re-

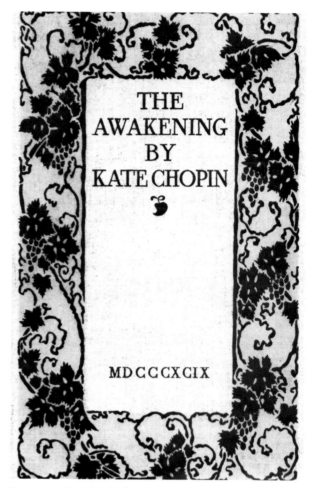

Front cover for Chopin's last novel, which was considered shocking in its portrayal of adultery

viewers often seem to protest loudest against their own sympathy with Edna.

The poetic beauty of *The Awakening* derives from its organic unity of symbolism and plot, traceable in part to Chopin's methods of composition and in part to Chopin's mature mastery of form and theme. Just as she tended to write a short story in a burst of concentrated writing, Chopin worked on *The Awakening* from about mid-1897 until 21 January 1898, during which time she probably wrote only one other work, the short story "A Family Affair"; thus she gave the novel her full creative effort. The manuscript was submitted to Way and Williams but when they went out of business, they transferred it in November 1898 to Herbert S. Stone and Company, and the novel was published 22 April 1899. According to the author's notebooks, *The Awakening* earned $145 between 1899 and 1901.

The Awakening was in many ways—despite all

the 1890s' celebration of the New Woman—a novel ahead of its time. At a Louisiana summer resort, Edna Pontellier, a native of Kentucky, gradually and unexpectedly discovers the possibilities for a life outside her safe but dull marriage of convenience. At Grand Isle, not far from New Orleans, she is exposed to the sophistication, the sensuality, and the customs of the Europeanized Catholic Creoles, whose values are much different from those of her own Protestant heritage of Kentucky. The lush, languid, and tropical ambiance of the island provides the right setting for Edna's awakening to her sensual and psychic needs, as she falls in love with a young Creole, Robert Lebrun. Robert, concerned for their honor and frightened that his dalliance is taken seriously, leaves abruptly for Mexico. Returning to New Orleans, Edna begins to change her life in accordance with her summer discoveries, moving toward a free and independent existence. To her husband's great astonishment, she gives up her day for receiving guests, neglects housekeeping activities and her children (though they continue to flourish), refuses to share her husband's bed, resumes her painting, and, finally, moves out of her husband's house into a small cottage around the block.

Léonce Pontellier has been advised by the family physician that Edna's "peculiarities" will "pass happily over. . .if you let her alone." Léonce is no villain; he is considerate and loving in his way, as Edna recognizes; but he regards his wife, Chopin indicates, much as he would a valuable piece of furniture in his house. The irrevocable split between the Pontelliers is suggested by their inverse actions: as she turns resolutely away from society toward inner realities, he scrambles feverishly to keep up social appearances. He represents the conformity of society, believing his wife is crazy: "He could see plainly that she was not herself. That is, he could not see that she was becoming herself and daily casting aside that fictitious self which we assume like a garment with which to appear before the world." Because he believes the changes in Edna are a passing mood he is unconcerned about leaving her alone while he goes to New York on business.

Edna's circle of friends changes too. She spends time with an eccentric musician, Mlle. Reisz, imbibing her passionate music along with her perorations on individuality and nonconformity; but she also visits her friend Adèle Ratignolle, one of the "mother-women" who typify Creole culture. Very much as Kate Chopin delighted in doing, Edna wanders the streets unescorted, finding out-of-the-way retreats, exploring the city, observing its people. Most significantly, she succumbs to the seductions of a roue, Alcée Arobin, without shame or remorse, only with regret that he is not Robert.

In spite of her quest, Edna finds no complete or lasting realization of her desires. She is not a first-rate artist; she despairs of the value of the Ratignolles' intimate but boring domesticity; nor does she love Alcée, though he meets her sexual needs. Nowhere does she find "the taste of life's delirium," though she seems to have the chance when Robert returns from Mexico. After expressing her feelings openly, in an "unwomanly" fashion, and initiating the caresses between them, she announces, "I am no longer one of Mr. Pontellier's possessions to dispose of or not. I give myself where I choose." In the middle of her declaration of love to him, she is summoned to help with the birth of Adèle Ratignolle's child. She leaves, proclaiming, "Now you are here we shall love each other, my Robert. We shall be everything to each other. Nothing else in the world is of any consequence." He begs her to stay with him, but upon her return, he has gone, leaving a farewell note: "Good-by— because I love you." Shattered both by the "scene of torture" at Adèle's and by Robert's second desertion, Edna goes to Grand Isle, strips off her clothing, and swims out to sea to drown.

Two crucial scenes—the delivery of Adèle's child and Edna's suicide—dramatize the novel's major themes. Through the description of the delivery and the subsequent conversation between the physician and Edna, Chopin expresses the idea that children (and by implication, marriage) control the lives of women because of the imperatives of biology as well as of society. Dr. Mandelet observes, "The trouble is . . . that youth is given up to illusions. It seems to be a provision of Nature; a decoy to secure mothers for the race. And Nature takes no account of moral consequences, or arbitrary conditions which we create, and which we feel obliged to maintain at any cost." Edna, though stunned by what she has seen, replies, "perhaps it is better to wake up after all, even to suffer, rather than to remain a dupe to illusions all one's life." Earlier Edna has commented to Adèle that for her children she would "give up the unessential . . . my life . . .; but I wouldn't give myself." What she realizes after her conversation with the doctor is at least partly responsible for the fact that she does give her life.

Edna's idealized love for Robert sustains her in the face of her disillusionment, but after she finds him gone, she seems to believe it inevitable that she will never find such compensation again. After a long night's meditation, she journeys to Grand Isle, where the only embrace and comfort she finds are those promised by Death as both lover and self-realization. An evocative, musical refrain that recurs throughout the book has foreshadowed this paradoxical symbolism of the waters at Grand Isle:

> The voice of the sea is seductive; never ceasing, whispering, clamoring, murmuring, inviting the soul to wander for a spell in abysses of solitude; to lose itself in mazes of inward contemplation.
> The voice of the sea speaks to the soul. The touch of the sea is sensuous, enfolding the body in its soft, close embrace.

The original title of the novel, "The Solitary Soul," points to the essential, radical aloneness of Edna, whose transcendent self is only realized in death, a "defeat," as Donald Ringe says, "that involves no surrender." Chopin's sympathies were no doubt engaged by Edna's tragic dilemma, yet she refrains from all moralizing about Edna's suicide, content to examine with courage and honesty without reaching for easy moral judgments.

The treatment of eros in *The Awakening* has rightly been compared to Greek tragedy, to Whitman's poetry, and to D. H. Lawrence's novels, while in its analysis of a woman's role in marriage and society, the novel bears a strong though not derivative resemblance to both *Madame Bovary* and *The Portrait of a Lady*. The public outcry stirred by *The Awakening* makes it comparable to *Sister Carrie*, published in 1901; Chopin, like Dreiser, was unwilling to compromise her artistic vision.

The effect of the unfavorable reviews for *The Awakening* was compounded in 1900 by another rejection of Chopin's third collection of stories, as well as by the return of her piece "Ti Démon" from the *Atlantic*, which termed the story "too sombre." Nevertheless, she did not completely cease writing as a result of these disappointments, as has been popularly maintained. She wrote some nine stories after April 1899, three of which were published before her death.

Of the works unpublished in her lifetime, two deserve special mention: "The Storm" was written in July 1898, before the reviews of *The Awakening* appeared; "Charlie" was written afterward, in April 1900. In "The Storm" Chopin portrays the momentary sexual ecstasy of two lovers—although they are married to others, to call them adulterers violates the spirit of the story—who, caught together accidentally in a violent storm, move in their passion as naturally as the rhythms of the storm. Two qualities of the tale are noteworthy: its explicitness for its day in describing the beauty and power of sexuality and the amoral, happy way the event is described, concluding with, "So the storm passed and every one [both the lovers, their respective spouses, and their children] was happy." Chopin's view of the possibilities for such fulfillment are indicated unobstrusively in the comparison of the lovers' passion with the storm itself, a cyclone, relatively rare even in Louisiana; and in the fact that this exquisite pleasure, a first for both lovers, occurs outside of marriage.

"Charlie," a tale of a tomboy-poet's development into a woman, is also one of Chopin's best (and longest) stories. The main character has much in common with the author herself, and more significantly the sustained power of the writing—complex, ironic, ambiguous—bespeaks an artist in control of her talent.

Although she had not been in good health since 1903, and had not written anything since then, Kate Chopin became an enthusiastic daily visitor to the 1904 St. Louis World's Fair. Following one day at the fair she suffered a cerebral hemorrhage and died two days later, on 22 August 1904.

Lacking a good editor who might have provided encouragement or simply good editing for her sometimes artless diction, Kate Chopin did not accomplish what she might have during a career shortened by her death. Nevertheless, she is distinguished for the frankness with which she approached sexuality, the amorality with which she described such problems as divorce and adultery, and for the serious consideration she gave to the restrictions of marriage and childbearing and the uses of freedom. Freed from conventional American male viewpoints by an inheritance that came naturally to Chopin—her French culture and her female perspective—possessed of a graceful wit and an intelligent honesty, Kate Chopin spoke of woman's condition in American society in a way that her contemporaries could not or would not. But she also, in both male and female characters, explored that persistent American concern, the relationship between self and society.

Biographies:

Daniel S. Rankin, *Kate Chopin and Her Creole Stories* (Philadelphia: University of Pennsylvania Press, 1932);

Per Seyersted, *Kate Chopin: A Critical Biography*

(Baton Rouge: Louisiana State University Press, 1969);

References:

George Arms, "Kate Chopin's *The Awakening* in the Perspective of Her Literary Career," in *Essays on American Literature in Honor of Jay B. Hubbell*, edited by Clarence Gohdes (Durham: Duke University Press, 1967), pp. 215-228;

Cyrille Arnavon, "Les Débuts du Roman Réaliste Américain et l'Influence Française," in *Romanciers Américains Contemporains*, edited by Henri Kerst, *Cahiers des Langues Modernes*, no. 1 (Paris: Didier, 1946), pp. 9-35;

Robert Arner, "Kate Chopin," *Louisiana Studies*, 14 (Spring 1975): 11-139;

Kenneth Eble, "A Forgotten Novel: Kate Chopin's *The Awakening*," *Western Humanities Review*, 10 (Summer 1956): 261-269;

Lewis Leary, "Kate Chopin's Other Novel," *Southern Literary Journal*, 1 (Autumn 1968): 60-74;

Donald Ringe, "Cane River World: Kate Chopin's *At Fault* and Related Stories," *Studies in American Fiction*, 3 (Autumn 1975): 157-166;

William Schuyler, "Kate Chopin," *Writer*, 7 (August 1894): 115-117;

Cynthia G. Wolff, "Thanatos and Eros: Kate Chopin's *The Awakening*," *American Quarterly*, 25 (October 1973): 449-471.

Papers:

The major collection of Chopin's papers is held by the Missouri Historical Society, St. Louis. Among other items, it includes manuscripts, a commonplace book, a diary, and two notebooks. A few letters are available in the Century Collection of the New York Public Library and in the Houghton Library, Harvard University.

Samuel Langhorne Clemens
(Mark Twain)

Hamlin Hill
University of New Mexico

See also the Clemens entry in *DLB 11, American Humorists, 1800-1950*.

BIRTH: Florida, Missouri, 30 November 1835, to John Marshall and Jane Lampton Clemens.

MARRIAGE: 2 February 1870 to Olivia Langdon; children: Langdon, Olivia Susan (Susy), Clara, Jane Lampton (Jean).

DEATH: Redding, Connecticut, 21 April 1910.

SELECTED BOOKS: *The Celebrated Jumping Frog of Calaveras County, and Other Sketches* (New York: C. H. Webb, 1867; London: Routledge, 1867);

The Innocents Abroad, or The New Pilgrims' Progress (Hartford, Conn.: American Publishing Company, 1869); republished in 2 volumes as *The Innocents Abroad* and *The New Pilgrims' Progress* (London: Hotten, 1870);

Mark Twain's (Burlesque) Autobiography and first Ro- *mance* (New York: Sheldon, 1871; London: Hotten 1871);

"Roughing It" (London: Routledge, 1872);

The Innocents at Home (London: Routledge, 1872);

Roughing It, enlarged edition (Hartford, Conn.: American Publishing Company, 1872)—combines *"Roughing It"* and *The Innocents at Home*;

A Curious Dream; and Other Sketches (London: Routledge, 1872);

The Gilded Age: A Tale of Today, by Twain and Charles Dudley Warner (Hartford, Conn.: American Publishing Company, 1873; 3 volumes, London: Routledge, 1874);

Mark Twain's Sketches, New and Old (Hartford, Conn.: American Publishing Company, 1875);

The Adventures of Tom Sawyer (London: Chatto & Windus, 1876; Hartford, Conn.: American Publishing Company, 1876);

Old Times on the Mississippi (Toronto: Belford, 1876); republished as *The Mississippi Pilot* (London: Ward, Lock & Tyler, 1877); expanded as *Life on the Mississippi* (London: Chatto & Windus,

1883; Boston: Osgood, 1883);

An Idle Excursion (Toronto: Rose-Belford, 1878); expanded as *Punch, Brothers, Punch! and Other Sketches* (New York: Slote, Woodman, 1878);

A Tramp Abroad (London: Chatto & Windus/Hartford, Conn.: American Publishing Company, 1880);

[Date 1601] *Conversation, As It Was by the Social Fireside, in the Time of the Tudors* (Cleveland, 1880);

The Prince and the Pauper (London: Chatto & Windus, 1881; Boston: Osgood, 1882);

The Stolen White Elephant (London: Chatto & Windus, 1882); republished as *The Stolen White Elephant, Etc.* (Boston: Osgood, 1882);

The Adventures of Huckleberry Finn (London: Chatto & Windus, 1884); republished as *Adventures of Huckleberry Finn* (New York: Webster, 1885);

A Connecticut Yankee in King Arthur's Court (New York: Webster, 1889); republished as *A Yankee at the Court of King Arthur* (London: Chatto & Windus, 1889);

The American Claimant (New York: Webster, 1892; London: Chatto & Windus, 1892);

Merry Tales (New York: Webster, 1892);

The £1,000,000 Bank-Note and Other New Stories (New York: Webster, 1893; London: Chatto & Windus, 1893);

Tom Sawyer Abroad by Huck Finn (New York: Webster, 1894; London: Chatto & Windus, 1894);

Pudd'nhead Wilson, A Tale (London: Chatto & Windus, 1894); expanded as *The Tragedy of Pudd'nhead Wilson and the Comedy of Those Extraordinary Twins* (Hartford, Conn.: American Publishing Company, 1894);

Personal Recollections of Joan of Arc by the Sieur Louis de Conte (New York: Harper, 1896; London: Chatto & Windus, 1896);

Tom Sawyer Abroad, Tom Sawyer, Detective, and Other Stories (New York: Harper, 1896);

Tom Sawyer, Detective, as told by Huck Finn, and Other Stories (London: Chatto & Windus, 1896);

How to Tell a Story and Other Essays (New York: Harper, 1897);

Following the Equator (Hartford, Conn.: American Publishing Company, 1897); republished as *More Tramps Abroad* (London: Chatto & Windus, 1897);

The Man That Corrupted Hadleyburg and Other Stories and Essays (New York & London: Harper, 1900); enlarged as *The Man That Corrupted Hadleyburg and Other Stories and Sketches* (London: Chatto & Windus, 1900);

A Double Barrelled Detective Story (New York & London: Harper, 1902);

A Dog's Tale (New York & London: Harper, 1904);

King Leopold's Soliloquy: A Defense of His Congo Rule (Boston: P. R. Warren, 1905);

Eve's Diary Translated from the Original Ms (London & New York: Harper, 1906);

What Is Man? (New York: De Vinne Press, 1906); expanded as *What Is Man? and Other Essays* (New York & London: Harper, 1917);

The $30,000 Bequest and Other Stories (New York & London: Harper, 1906);

Christian Science with Notes Containing Corrections to Date (New York & London: Harper, 1907);

A Horse's Tale (New York & London: Harper, 1907);

Is Shakespeare Dead? (New York & London: Harper, 1909);

Extract from Captain Stormfield's Visit to Heaven (New York & London: Harper, 1909);

Mark Twain's Speeches, edited by F. A. Nast (New York & London: Harper, 1910);

The Mysterious Stranger, a Romance, edited by Albert Bigelow Paine and Frederick A. Duneka (New York & London: Harper, 1916); expanded as *The Mysterious Stranger and Other Stories*, edited by Paine (New York & London: Harper, 1922);

The Curious Republic of Gondour and Other Whimsical Sketches (New York: Boni & Liveright, 1919);

Mark Twain's Speeches, edited by Paine (New York & London: Harper, 1923);

Europe and Elsewhere, edited by Paine (New York & London: Harper, 1923);

Mark Twain's Autobiography, edited by Paine, 2 volumes (New York & London: Harper, 1924);

Sketches of the Sixties, by Twain and Bret Harte (San Francisco: Howell, 1926);

The Adventures of Thomas Jefferson Snodgrass, edited by Charles Honce (Chicago: Pascal Covici, 1928);

Mark Twain's Notebook, edited by Paine (New York & London: Harper, 1935);

Letters from the Sandwich Islands Written for the Sacramento Union, edited by G. Ezra Dane (San Francisco: Grabhorn, 1937);

The Washoe Giant in San Francisco, edited by Franklin Walker (San Francisco: Fields, 1938);

Mark Twain's Travels With Mr. Brown, edited by Walker and Dane (New York: Knopf, 1940);

Mark Twain in Eruption, edited by Bernard DeVoto (New York & London: Harper, 1940);

Mark Twain at Work, edited by DeVoto (Cambridge: Harvard University Press, 1942);

Mark Twain, Business Man, edited by Samuel Charles Webster (Boston: Little, Brown, 1946);

Mark Twain of the ENTERPRISE, edited by Henry Nash Smith (Berkeley: University of California Press, 1957);

Traveling with the Innocents Abroad: Mark Twain's Original Reports from Europe and the Holy Land, edited by Daniel Morley McKeithan (Norman: University of Oklahoma Press, 1958);

Mark Twain's Autobiography, edited by Charles Neider (New York: Harper, 1959);

Letters from the Earth, edited by DeVoto (New York: Harper & Row, 1962);

Mark Twain's "Which was the Dream" and Other Symbolic Writings of the Later Years, edited by John S. Tuckey (Berkeley: University of California Press, 1966);

Mark Twain's Satires and Burlesques, edited by Franklin R. Rogers (Berkeley: University of California Press, 1967);

Clemens of the "Call": Mark Twain in San Francisco, edited by Edgar M. Branch (Berkeley: University of California Press, 1969);

Mark Twain's Hannibal, Huck, and Tom, edited by Walter Blair (Berkeley: University of California Press, 1969);

Mark Twain's "Mysterious Stranger" Manuscripts, edited by William M. Gibson (Berkeley: University of California Press, 1969);

Mark Twain's Fables of Man, edited by Tuckey (Berkeley: University of California Press, 1972);

"What Is Man?" and Other Philosophical Writings, edited by Paul Baender (Berkeley: University of California Press, 1973);

Mark Twain's Notebooks and Journals, volume 1, 1855-1873, edited by Frederick Anderson, Michael B. Frank, and Kenneth M. Sanderson; volume 2, 1877-1883, edited by Anderson, Lin Salamo, and Bernard L. Stein; volume 3, 1883-1891, edited by Robert Pack Browning, Frank, and Salamo (Berkeley: University of California Press, 1975, 1979);

Mark Twain Speaking, edited by Paul Fatout (Iowa City: University of Iowa Press, 1976);

Mark Twain Speaks for Himself, edited by Fatout (West Lafayette: Purdue University Press, 1978);

Early Tales & Sketches, volume 1 (1851-1864), edited by Branch and Robert H. Hirst (Berkeley: University of California Press, 1979);

The Devil's Race-Track: Mark Twain's "Great Dark" Writings, edited by Tuckey (Berkeley: University of California Press, 1979).

COLLECTIONS: *The Writings of Mark Twain,* Autograph Edition, 25 volumes (Hartford, Conn.: American Publishing Company, 1899-1907);

The Writings of Mark Twain, Hillcrest Edition, 25 volumes, edited by Paine (New York & London: Harper, 1906);

The Writings of Mark Twain, Definitive Edition, 37 volumes, edited by Paine (New York: Wells, 1922-1925).

In the early spring of 1835, John Marshall Clemens and his wife, Jane, loaded up their possessions, their five children, and their single slave, in Three Forks, Tennessee, to move to Missouri. It was another in a long series of migrations which the family undertook, seeking the success and affluence which always eluded them. As Dixon Wecter has noted, the Clemenses "appeared to lack the golden touch, even in an age when the riches of inland America hung ripe for the plucking." Their destination, Florida, Missouri, was an unpromising village with two muddy streets, a hundred inhabitants, and the Salt River, which farfetched optimists predicted would be navigable in the near future; but their family's journey this time would produce a legacy more impressive than all their schemes for wealth and status combined. Along the way, John Marshall and Jane Lampton Clemens conceived their sixth child. At his birth, on 30 November 1835, they named him Samuel, after his grandfather, and Langhorne, purportedly to honor an old-time Virginia friend.

The Clemenses lived—Sam, born prematurely, in precarious health—in Florida for four years. Then the cycle of movement-enthusiasm-disillusionment-movement uprooted them and sent them to the edge of the Mississippi, to Hannibal, thirty miles away. There young Sam spent his youth, living and absorbing the childhood memories that have become a part of American legend and folklore.

His rudimentary formal education lasted only until 1847, when his father died, leaving the family nearly destitute. John Marshall Clemens's steady procession of business failures and the family's frequent moves from house to house in Hannibal undoubtedly impressed upon Sam the goading obsession for success and conspicuous consumption that marked his own mature years.

In addition to the schooling, Sam's education

continued in the woods outside Hannibal, on the Mississippi River which served as a dangerous playground for the boys of the town, and at his uncle's farm back in Florida, Missouri, where Sam spent most of his summers. Hannibal was a mixture of slaveholding outpost, frontier jumping-off point, and orthodox Calvinist bastion, and infused with the idyllic, pastoral, carefree world he recollected in *The Adventures of Tom Sawyer* was a layer of violence, horror, and inhumanity that surfaced in his writings only in his middle and old age.

From 1847 until 1853, Sam Clemens served as apprentice and typesetter for various Hannibal newspapers, finally ending up as assistant to his brother, Orion, whose failures were as persistent as John Marshall's. As Orion bankrupted journalism along the Mississippi—with his ownership of the *Hannibal Western Union* and *Journal*, the *Muscatine Journal*, and the *Keokuk Daily Post*—Sam absorbed that brand of frontier humor called the humor of the Old Southwest, a staple as filler for small newspapers along the river. Sam's own first, inept, comic story, "The Dandy Frightening the Squatter," an amateurish version of such humor, appeared in the *Carpet-Bag* in May 1852.

In 1853, Sam Clemens broke loose from the family ties that Jane Clemens struggled to preserve. That year he went to St. Louis, New York, and Philadelphia; in 1854, he visited Washington, D.C.; in 1855 and 1856, he lived in St. Louis; and in 1857, he lived briefly in Cincinnati. He recorded his compulsive wanderings in travel letters, which Orion published in whatever newspaper he owned at the time.

In April 1857, Sam boarded the *Paul Jones* in Cincinnati, bound for New Orleans as the first stop on a trip up the Amazon to make a fortune growing cocoa, as he later exaggerated. The pilot, Horace Bixby, agreed to take Clemens on as a cub pilot, the profession he later called the "one permanent ambition among my comrades in our village." His apprenticeship to Bixby marked the end of his youthful vagabondage and completed the phase of his life that was later to be transformed into *The Adventures of Tom Sawyer* (1876), *Adventures of Huckleberry Finn* (1884), and some of the most poignant recollections in *Mark Twain's Autobiography* (1924).

For almost two years, Clemens served as Bixby's "cub," receiving his own license in April 1859 and becoming a pilot, the "only unfettered and entirely independent human being that lived in the earth." Until the outbreak of the Civil War and the closing of the Mississippi River traffic, Clemens wallowed in his prestige, conspicuousness, and

Clemens at the time he received his steamboat-pilot's certificate, 1859

grandeur. The only tragedy that interrupted his idyll was the death of his younger brother, Henry (fictionalized as Sid in *Tom Sawyer*), in the explosion of the *Pennsylvania*—a death for which Sam was to hold himself responsible for the rest of his life because he had secured his younger brother's passage on the ship.

His profession as effectively closed to him by the war as the river was, Clemens briefly joined an irregular band of Confederate sympathizers who skylarked around the rural surroundings of Hannibal, trying unconvincingly to look like soldiers. Years later, Mark Twain was to boast, "I was a *soldier* two weeks once in the beginning of the war, and was hunted like a rat the whole time. . . . My splendid Kipling himself hasn't a more burnt-in, hard-baked and unforgettable familiarity with that death-on-the-pale-horse-with-hell-following-after which is a raw soldier's first fortnight in the field." But that was embroidery for an escapade that was closer to one of Tom Sawyer's "adventures."

Orion Clemens meanwhile had received an appointment as secretary to the governor of the Territory of Nevada but was, embarrassingly but predictably, unable to pay his passage on the overland stage to claim his position. With money from Sam Clemens, the two left St. Joseph, Missouri, on 26 July 1861, headed for Carson City, Nevada. Twenty days later, Orion claimed his sinecure and Sam went off, as he later described the opportunities in *Roughing It*, to "maybe go out of an afternoon . . . and pick up two or three pailfuls of shining slugs, and nuggets of gold and silver on the hillside." For a year, he tried to cash in on the speculation fever in silver, sending some humorous correspondence to the *Virginia City Territorial Enterprise* for comic relief. In August 1862, he joined the staff of that paper and for two years contributed both "straight" reporting and Far-West humor, wildly improbable hoaxes and burlesque assaults on

competing reporters, to its pages. On 2 February 1863, he employed the pseudonym Mark Twain for the first time on one of his contributions.

Virginia City was a boom town, raw and raucous; its first twenty-six graves, Mark Twain was later to claim, were those of murdered men. Its life-style, like its humor, tended to violence, insult, and aggression. Though he was making a name in the Far West as a humorist, Mark Twain overstepped even the liberal tolerance of Virginia City when he accused the wife of the editor of a rival newspaper of collecting money for a society to promote miscegenation. In a town strongly Union in its sympathies during the Civil War, it is no surprise that the husband of the outraged wife challenged Mark Twain to a duel.

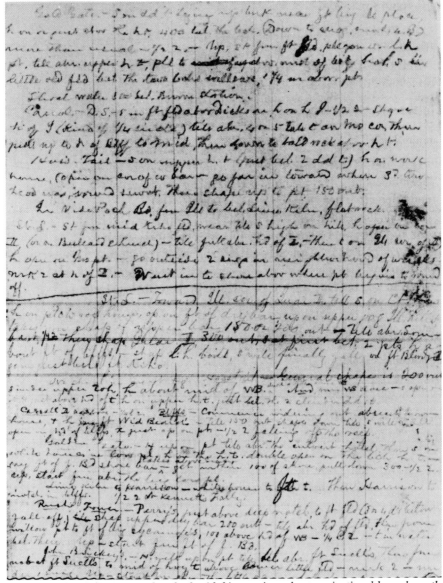

Page from Clemens's April-July 1857 memorandum book with his notations about navigational hazards on the Mississippi River

Clemens took the stage for San Francisco to avoid the duel, and became affiliated with a number of newspapers and magazines on the Pacific Coast. He contributed sketches to the *Golden Era,* the *Californian,* the *San Francisco Call,* the *Sacramento Union,* and the *Alta California,* for two and a half years, from mid-1864 to the end of 1866. Mixed with humor was sufficient moral indignation and editorial outrage that Mark Twain became known as the "Moralist of the Pacific Slope." In late 1864, his attacks on the San Francisco police department produced a libel suit and another hurried departure—this time a three-month vacation at Jackass Hill and Angel's Camp in the California Sierras, which Walter Blair has called "a turning point in the author's career." Between early December and late February 1865, he spent his time pocket mining (seeking small hordes of pure gold, as he describes it in chapter 40 of *Roughing It*) and listening to two raconteurs who wove yarns about a frog filled with shot, a bluejay who tried to fill a cabin with acorns, a cat blown up in an explosion.

Returning to San Francisco after the police had found other diversions, Clemens found a letter from Charles Farrar Browne, the United States' most popular humorist, who wrote under the pen name Artemus Ward and who had spent a riotously liquid three weeks with Mark Twain in Virginia City, back in December 1863. The letter requested a contribution for a book of humor; Mark Twain wrote up the story of the frog stuffed with bird shot, "Jim Smiley and His Jumping Frog," later retitled "The Celebrated Jumping Frog of Calaveras County." It arrived on the East Coast too late for inclusion in Ward's book, but it appeared in the *New York Saturday Press* on 18 November 1865.

The story was an immediate success, and it stretched the Western humorist's name and reputation across the continent. Complexly narrated to a humorless listener by a humorless tale teller, the story typified Mark Twain's later dictum that "the humorous story may be spun out to great length, and may wander around as much as it pleases, and arrive nowhere in particular. . . . The humorous story is told gravely; the teller does his best to conceal the fact that he even dimly suspects that there is anything funny about it."

The following spring, the *Sacramento Union* commissioned Mark Twain to sail for the Sandwich Islands (as the Hawaiian Islands were then called) and to write a series of travel letters from there for the paper. The humorist left San Francisco on 7 March 1866, and remained in the Sandwich Islands for four months. His letters back to the West Coast combined factual and informative writing with the raucous humor his audience expected of him. They also exploited, for the first extended period, the comic contrast between two fictional characters, Mark Twain and Mr. Brown. The Mark Twain character was a sentimentalist and an idealist, who went into raptures over the picturesque beauties of the islands; Mr. Brown was a practical, semiliterate vulgarian, who undercut Mark Twain's highfalutin rhapsodies by uncouth, but realistic, evaluations of the identical object. The formula worked so effectively that Mark Twain was to employ it for two more series of travel letters and to continue to use it, with significant modulations, for the rest of his career.

In December 1866, commissioned by the *Alta California* to continue a travel-letter correspondence, Clemens left San Francisco for New York, sailing down the West Coast to Nicaragua, crossing the isthmus, sailing up the Atlantic Coast to New York, and sending twenty-six letters, later collected as *Mark Twain's Travels With Mr. Brown* (1940), back to the *Alta.* Although he was to send another set of letters to the *Alta,* Clemens's departure from San Francisco marked the end of his apprenticeship and symbolized his turning from the wild and extravagant humor of the West to a mode that would capture a national audience.

His background, training, and instinct through the first fifteen years of his writing career made the frontier tradition of humor natural. Vigorous, "masculine" stories, burlesques of wild invention and, quite often, off-color hue, verbal gymnastics which exploited quick laughs by punning and word play were his main stock-in-trade. In later years, he would call "The Celebrated Jumping Frog of Calaveras County" a villainous backwoods sketch and refer to his letters to the *Alta* as "those wretched, slangy sketches." But when he decided, as he told Orion Clemens on 19 October 1865, that he "had a 'call' to literature, of a low order—*i.e.* humorous," he was already well on his way in exploiting a mode of humor that was realistic in its overtones; as a newspaperman, he was required to report as objectively as possible the mundane world around him; as a travel writer, his function in part was to render the unusual in terms which would reproduce an accurate image in his audience's imagination; and as a Westerner, he saw a world in which violence determined fate and the frustration of ambitions and goals was more frequent than their realization.

In New York, Clemens heard of the impending "pleasure excursion" of the *Quaker City* to Europe and the Holy Land, and persuaded the editors of the *Alta* to advance his $1,250 passage in return for a continued series of travel letters. The trip, which Mark Twain was later to call "a funeral excursion without a corpse," was his extended introduction to eastern gentility, sobriety, and decorum; Henry Ward Beecher, the pastor of one of the largest Protestant congregations in the United States, had to back out of the trip, but his spirit was on board. When this excursion was over, Mark Twain wrote for the *New York Tribune,* "The venerable excursionists were not gay and frisky. They played no blindman's buff; they dealt not in whist; they shirked not the irksome journal, for alas! most of them were even writing books. They never romped, they talked but little, they never sang, save in the nightly prayer-meeting. . . . A free, hearty laugh was a sound that was not heard oftener than once in seven days about those decks or in those cabins, and when it was heard it met with precious little sympathy." Nevertheless, Mark Twain joined the mourners and sailed on 8 June 1867, for a five-month sentence in their midst.

Almost immediately he gravitated toward the lunatic fringe on board, a group whose irreverence and devilry matched his own. Delighted to shock the "Pilgrims," as he was later to call the more sedate passengers, the iconoclasts were a slightly older version of Tom Sawyer's gang. They played practical jokes on guides throughout Europe, scoffed at the artifacts of the Old World and its culture, and refused proper reverence at the sacred locations in the Holy Land. Throughout this trip, Mark Twain sent his vivid and mocking letters back to the *Alta* and the *New York Tribune,* restrained only by the occasional admonitions of Mary Mason Fairbanks, wife of the owner of the *Cleveland Herald,* and at least briefly Mark Twain's monitor of gentility and propriety.

As he made his way through France, Italy, and the Holy Land, he befriended Charles Langdon, the young and pampered son and heir of Jervis Langdon, a wealthy Elmira, New York, coal magnate. In Charlie's cabin, probably while the *Quaker City* was anchored in the Bay of Smyrna, Clemens spotted a cameo portrait of the young man's older sister, Olivia; and, as legend would have it, he fell immediately in love with the likeness. He was to meet Olivia during that Christmas season of 1867, court her through the end of the decade, and to marry her on 2 February 1870.

Meanwhile, his career as a newspaper humorist flourished after the return of the *Quaker City;* he contributed humorous articles to newspapers and magazines; he mounted two lecture campaigns

Olivia Langdon, whom Clemens married on 2 February 1870

during the 1868-1869 and 1869-1870 seasons; and he accepted an offer from Elisha Bliss, of the American Publishing Company in Hartford, Connecticut, to edit his *Quaker City* letters for publication as a subscription book.

The revising, with one eye on a national rather than a western audience and the other on the standards of propriety and decorum that both "Mother" Fairbanks and the Langdon family felt Clemens lacked, attempted to clean up what the humorist himself called "wretched, slangy letters." He added new material that accounted for almost half the published book, eliminated allusions to western personalities and places, removed Mr. Brown as his straight man, and deleted the coarsest elements of the humor.

The result was a curious but typically anomalous product of Mark Twain's pen. The narrator shifts from Mr. Brown, irreverent and caustic about American adulation of European culture, to Mark Twain, reverent and purple-prosed before the Sphinx; from low comedy of the broadest burlesque to scathing ridicule of the other passengers' "Christian" piety; from imaginative genius to tedious statistics and lengthy passages "borrowed" from other travel writers. If it was—as it has been called—America's literary declaration of independence, it was also a case study of a group to become known in the twentieth century as "ugly Americans."

Fortunately, but coincidentally, the audience which was to make *The Innocents Abroad* a best-seller when it appeared in July 1869 was unconcerned with literary unity or consistency. The American Publishing Company was one, probably the best, of a new kind of publisher which flourished in the three decades after the Civil War. Using veterans as door-to-door salesmen, subscription-book publishers reached a readership for whom a bookstore was unavailable. Late in his life, Clemens was to call this audience his "submerged clientele." Bibles and bible commentary, medical and self-help volumes, and Civil War memoirs were their stock in trade; but Bliss was convinced that the humor of a Mark Twain would also appeal and sell to the rural and small-town, middle-class audience who were his customers. He was correct; *The Innocents Abroad* sold almost 70,000 copies in its first year, a record which Mark Twain boasted only *Uncle Tom's Cabin* had beaten.

Still, he considered himself a newspaper humorist rather than an author of books. And after his marriage, he and Olivia Clemens moved to Buffalo, New York, where he had purchased a part ownership of the *Express* with money borrowed from his father-in-law. The first few years of the marriage were turbulent ones: his father-in-law

died on 6 August 1870; Olivia gave birth prematurely to their son, Langdon, on 7 November; and Mark Twain's writing schedule was a hectic and frenzied one. He wrote columns for the *Buffalo Express*, edited one called "Memoranda" for the monthly magazine, the *Galaxy*, and began piecing together the recollections and earlier writings which would become his second book, *Roughing It*, in 1872. In addition, he confronted for the first time in his life, an eastern gentility and decorum which were foreign to his own personality and background.

The Langdons were impressively wealthy, and their standards of propriety were ones which fitted Samuel Clemens uncomfortably. Olivia served as arbiter of taste for his writings throughout most of her life, with Clemens voluntarily seeking her advice and accepting practically all of her suggestions. Her own standards of refinement were enforced in October 1871 when the family moved to Hartford, Connecticut, a stronghold of literary conservatism. Harriet Beecher Stowe and Charles Dudley Warner became neighbors when the Clemenses built their spectacular home on Farmington Avenue in 1874, and William Dean Howells, the genteel editor of the genteel *Atlantic Monthly*, became Clemens's closest friend and literary adviser.

Roughing It appeared from the American Publishing Company's presses in early 1872; and, although it was not the commercial success which *The Innocents Abroad* had been, it marked a signifi-

Frontispiece for The Innocents Abroad

Clemens at the time Roughing It *was published*

manuscript to the required length. He embedded anecdotes that rank with his best fiction—"The Mexican Plug," "Bemis and the Bull," "Buck Fanshaw's Funeral," and "Grandfather's Old Ram," for instance—in his book. And he showed, at least briefly, the seamier side of frontier egalitarianism in rigged juries, violence, and rampant speculation.

The Hartford years lasted into the early 1890s, and at first they were idyllic. Langdon's death in 1872 marred an otherwise pleasant domestic scene. Susy was born in 1872, Clara in 1874, and Jean Clemens in 1880. The family summered at Quarry Farm in Elmira, New York, when they were not on trips to Europe. They entertained sumptuously and lived ostentatiously. And Clemens lectured frequently as Mark Twain, and even tried his hand (usually with disastrous results) at writing drama.

His books, always published by the subscription method, poured forth throughout the 1870s: after *Roughing It*, *The Gilded Age* in 1873, written in collaboration with his neighbor, Warner; *Mark Twain's Sketches, New and Old* in 1875; *The Adventures of Tom Sawyer* in 1876; and *A Tramp Abroad* in 1880. He broke into the prestigious *Atlantic Monthly* with "A True Story" in November 1874 following it in 1875 with the series "Old Times on the Mississippi" in seven installments (which became chapters 4 through 15 of *Life on the Mississippi*).

He wrote for a variety of different audiences, and occasionally he made mistakes about them. *The Gilded Age* was one of the earliest uses of the novel in America for political satire. Mark Twain's share of the loosely joined plots brought Colonel Beriah Sellers, the ineffectual but constantly optimistic speculator, to life. It included thinly disguised portraits of corrupt senators and representatives, lobbyists, and cabinet members, all of whom Mark Twain expected his audience to recognize. It exposed corruption and greed tainting the nucleus of American government with the firsthand knowledge its author had gained from his own experience in Washington. But it contained chapter mottoes, written by the Hartford savant James Hammond Trumbull, which were pedantic in their display of esoteric and erudite language—inappropriate to his "submerged," middle-class audience.

Both *The Adventures of Tom Sawyer* and "Old Times on the Mississippi" represented an attempt to cultivate the genteel, Eastern seaboard audience currently enthralled by local-color fiction. The "acceptable" literary magazines of the 1870s (and later) wallowed in sentimentality, nostalgia, and pathos brought on—as they believed—by the disappear-

cant advance in Mark Twain's literary artistry. He succeeded in adapting the Mark Twain and Mr. Brown dichotomy by having the narrator of *Roughing It* begin as a naive, childish sentimentalist who undergoes an initiation into western and pragmatic ways so that he becomes a wise insider in Nevada culture as the book progresses. As he loses his illusions about silver mining, the Indians, and instant wealth, he becomes a realist about the world in which he lives. That education process was to serve him in most of his later fiction: the cub pilot of "Old Times on the Mississippi," Tom Sawyer, Huckleberry Finn, David "Pudd'nhead" Wilson, and a host of characters in shorter works all begin as "outsiders" and attempt with varying degrees of success to come to terms with a society in which they were originally misfits.

But the book was significantly flawed. Still unable to compose a long narrative with consistency, Mark Twain used old articles from the *Territorial Enterprise* and the *Sacramento Union* to pad out the

True Williams illustration for the whitewashing scene in
The Adventures of Tom Sawyer

ance of regional distinctions and quirks as a result of the Civil War. By reverting to his own childhood in antebellum Missouri, Mark Twain joined the tidal wave of lachrymose reminiscers who chose the good old days for their subject. The cub pilot of "Old Times on the Mississippi" was made deliberately younger, more childlike, less perceptive than Clemens had been when he began his course of instruction, in order that, as narrator, he might ignore some of the vulgar realities of steamboat life. But he captured the flavor of the river, however muted and selected he filtered it, with relentless accuracy. The challenge of memorizing the river, both ways, in dark and daylight, in high water and low, with the realization that channels changed, "points" shifted, sandbars built up, landmarks disappeared between trips, was the basic theme of the articles; and Mark Twain achieved his goal so impressively that Howells said, "It almost made the water in our ice-pitcher muddy."

Tom Sawyer was also aimed at the local-color

audience, even though it was sold by subscription. Uncertain whether it should be aimed at a youthful or an adult audience, Mark Twain once more submerged in shadow the realistic aspects of puberty, removing portions of the book which might offend younger readers. Like the cub in "Old Times on the Mississippi" Tom undergoes an initiation, learning to act maturely and to gain the adulation of the grown-ups in St. Petersburg. As he takes Becky's punishment, testifies at Injun Joe's trial, saves Becky in the cave, he moves into society rather than out of it. His wealth makes him prominent; his antics, like returning to town in the middle of his own funeral, relieve the boredom of village life; and his rebellions from conformity have none of the subversive quality Huck's were to show just a few years later. Tom is a conformist pretending to be a rebel, with one eye closely on the limits which his society would permit for token assaults on its institutions.

While writing his book, Mark Twain debated about taking Tom into adulthood (to his midforties, according to one note), but he decided, as he told Howells, that the protagonist of such a novel should not be "Tom Sawyer—he would not be a good character for it." Perhaps Mark Twain realized that Tom was too socially oriented, too other-directed to accomplish the goals which the author's increasingly pessimistic philosophy required. Clemens had discovered W. E. H. Lecky's *History of European Morals from Augustus to Charlemagne* (1869) in the early 1870s, and it became a favorite whipping boy for his own thought. Lecky had proposed that morality was determined by either altruistic selflessness or by self-serving utilitarianism. Clemens denied the existence of the former and insisted—in a running battle he carried on in the margins of his copy of Lecky—that only the latter existed. He embodied in a paper he read to a gathering of friends in the late 1870s some of his ideas in *What Is Man?*; and in other lesser works, he began questioning democracy ("The Late Revolution on Pitcairn," 1879), universal suffrage ("The Curious Republic of Gondour," 1875), and human control over conscience ("The Recent Carnival of Crime in Connecticut," 1876). Under the circumstances, Tom Sawyer's rigid adherence to "authorities" might have made the author conscious that Tom was unsuited for the book he had in mind.

Almost immediately, he began work on what he told Howells was "Huck Finn's autobiography. I like it only tolerably well, as far as I have got, & may possibly pigeonhole or burn the MS when it is done" (9 August 1876). Fortunately, he chose pigeonhol-

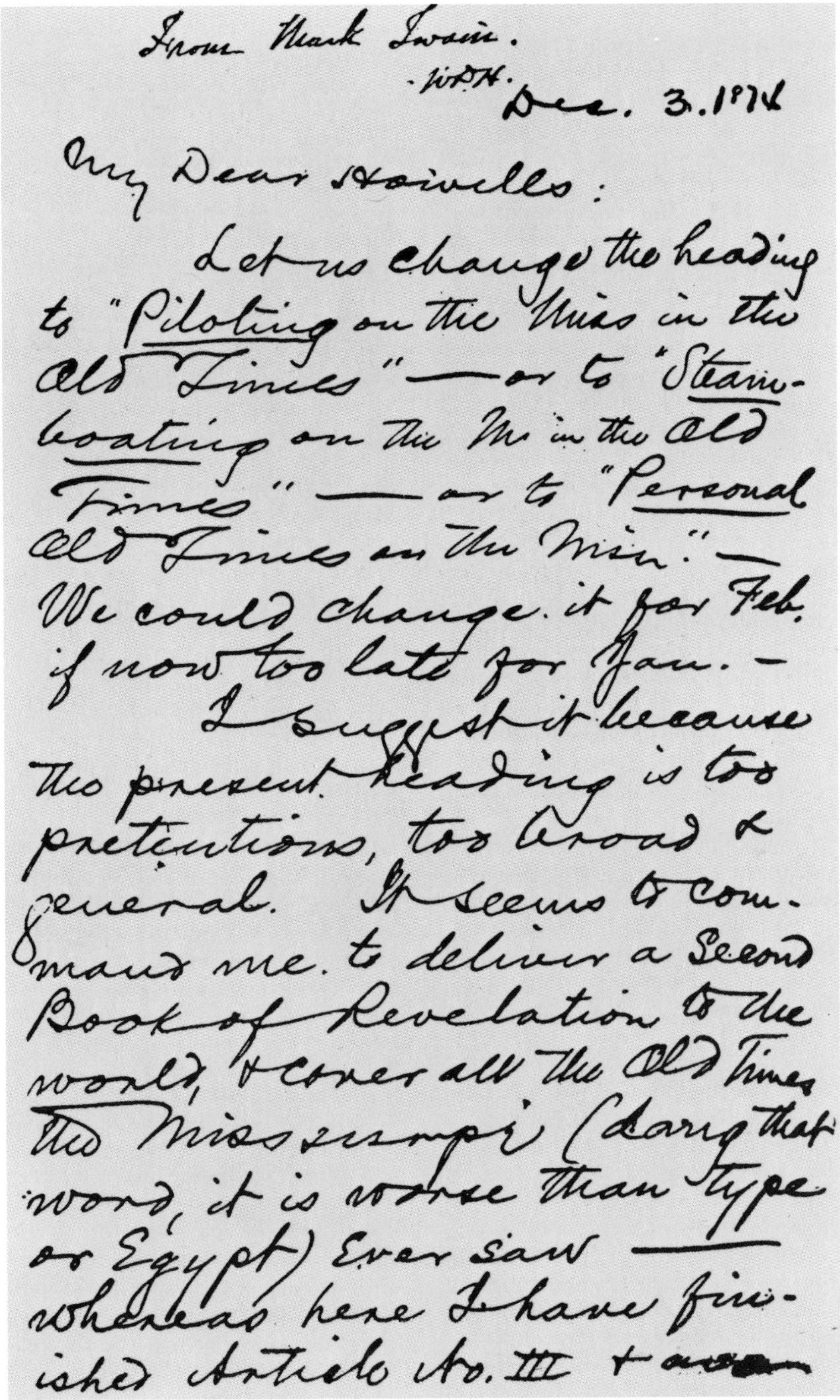

From Mark Twain.

·WDH·

Dec. 3. 1874

My Dear Howells:

Let us change the heading to "<u>Piloting</u> on the Miss in the Old Times" — or to "<u>Steam-boating</u> on the M in the Old Times" — or to "<u>Personal</u> Old Times on the Miss." — We could change it for Feb. if now too late for Jan. —

I suggest it because the present heading is too pretentious, too broad & general. It seems to command me to deliver a Second Book of Revelation to the world, & cover all the Old Times the <u>Mississippi</u> (dang that word, it is worse than type or Egypt) Ever saw — whereas here I have finished Article No. III + ~~aa~~

Clemens's letter to Howells suggesting title change for "Old Times on the Mississippi," which was appearing serially in the Atlantic, *the magazine Howells edited. This series eventually became part of* Life on the Mississippi.

ing and worked sporadically on his masterpiece for the following seven years.

Meanwhile, on 17 December 1877, he committed what he was later convinced was the greatest disgrace of his career by miscalculating his audience one more time. Invited to address the celebration of John Greenleaf Whittier's seventieth birthday dinner, Mark Twain delivered a raucous hoax. Offering Western humor to a New England audience by ridiculing Ralph Waldo Emerson, Henry Wadsworth Longfellow, and Oliver Wendell Holmes, quoting (and more often misquoting) their poetry, and representing them as three cutthroat, gambling vagrants in the Far West, he was greeted, he later remembered, with stunned silence. Condemnation of his flippant attitude filled several New England newspapers, and Clemens wrote letters of apology to his three comic foils, all of whom had been in the audience during the speech.

In fact, the Whittier birthday speech might well be used to mark the end of the domination of American literature by its New England monopoly, the freeing of American literature from the restraints that first Calvinism and then secular Brahminism had imposed on it. As its author was later to admit, it is a hilariously funny parody, but Clemens felt humiliated; he believed that further appearances of his work in the *Atlantic Monthly* would damage the reputation of that magazine, and within three months he fled with his family for a seventeen-month trip to Europe.

From April 1878 to September 1879 Clemens wandered through the major cities of Europe—in Germany, Switzerland, and Italy. Of course, a third travel book was the expectation, and *A Tramp Abroad* (1880) was the result. Although less lively and energetic than *Innocents Abroad* or *Roughing It* and less profitable to its author, *A Tramp Abroad* was punctuated with such cameo masterpieces as "Baker's Blue-Jay Yarn," "The Awful German Language," and a recounting of a long and placid raft trip down the Neckar River, which has some obvious parallels to Huck's trip down the Mississippi.

Settled back in Hartford, Mark Twain worked on the manuscript which was to become *The Prince and the Pauper*. More important, he also decided to become his own publisher, and to secure the bulk of the profits from his books. Leaving the American Publishing Company, he set up a subscription-book department for the firm of James R. Osgood, publishing *The Prince and the Pauper* with its imprint in 1882 and *Life on the Mississippi* in 1883. He secured the New York agency for *The Prince and the Pauper* for his nephew-in-law, Charles L. Webster, and

after Osgood went bankrupt, established the subscription-book firm of Charles L. Webster and Company in the early 1880s.

Publishing his own books became only one of a number of extraliterary occupations. He invested in the Kaolatype, an engraving process, began copyrighting and manufacturing children's games, and in late 1881, he became almost obsessively concerned with speculation in the Paige typesetter, an invention in which he was ultimately to invest almost $300,000. Other, smaller investments diverted his time and energy from literature and finally contributed to his bankruptcy in the Panic of 1893. Clemens's mania for speculation and get-rich-quick schemes was an integral part of his personality; so was its predictable corollary, threats of litigation and actual law suits against his partners, his competitors, and anyone whom he suspected of cheating him. (It is probably no coincidence that so many of his books use courtroom scenes and trials for their climaxes.)

His life throughout the 1880s was frenzied. *The Prince and the Pauper* appealed to his genteel audience as an elegant costume piece; but its archaic language, its syrupy and contrived plot, and its lack of the anticipated humor defeated it with the subscription audience. Only its satire directed at legal abuses and its basic plot of mixed identities command critical attention. Its failure was financial as well as literary.

Life on the Mississippi (1883) fared little better. Clemens took his old *Atlantic Monthly* sketches, "Old Times on the Mississippi," and padded them out with firsthand reports of the river from a trip there in 1882. The modern river was as colorless as Mark Twain's prose, and only the "Old Times on the Mississippi" opening has literary merit. Deliberately omitted from the book was a scathing attack on Southern romanticism, the "Walter Scott disease," he called it, which ridiculed duels, feuds, and lynchings, because, it was decided, the attack would damage potential sales south of the Mason-Dixon line. (The subject would appear in fictional form in *Huckleberry Finn*, however.)

As Clemens told Osgood, "The Prince and the Pauper and the Mississippi are the only books of mine which have ever failed." For an author who was financing his wildcat speculations and inventions with anticipated royalties, it was a disaster. So Clemens drafted Webster to head a new publishing company, in addition to an overwhelming list of other chores and duties, and to publish the American edition of *Adventures of Huckleberry Finn*.

The book had moved slowly to its completion.

The first 400 pages had been the overflow of enthusiasm and energy from *Tom Sawyer*, in 1876. Twain added more chapters in 1879 or 1880, and in 1883, after the river trip, he wrote the latter half of the novel. The story of Huck and Jim's raft trip down the Mississippi toward "freedom" has become so imbedded in the American imagination that it is disconcerting to the modern reader to realize that

E. W. Kemble drawing of Huckleberry Finn

its composition was haphazard, its immediate reception uniformly hostile, and its recognition as a masterpiece delayed until the twentieth century. Ernest Hemingway's famous judgment that all American literature begins with *Huckleberry Finn* is a relatively recent one (*The Green Hills of Africa,* 1935).

The opening and concluding chapters of the novel are burlesque in their main action; Tom plays the superior, informed romantic who, in both sections, manipulates Huck into following his suggestions. It is only when Huck, isolated from Tom, goes to Jackson's Island, meets Jim, and heads south on the Mississippi, that the book takes on its serious meaning. Huck and Jim's search for freedom becomes increasingly somber and increasingly omi-

nous as they head helplessly in the exact opposite direction from their goal, controlled by the flow of the Mississippi until they can head north only after reaching the Ohio River at Cairo, Illinois. Moving deeper and deeper into slave territory, they encounter increasing violence and treachery. Their isolation is violated by the King and Duke, as the raft is commandeered; and Huck's vision of human cruelty increases as he visits the towns on shore. Mark Twain used the linear structure of his novel, as Huck and Jim follow the course of the Mississippi in a straight descending line, to unleash the satire against the South which he had felt constrained from including in *Life on the Mississippi*.

The characters of the King and Duke, Colonel Sherburn, the Grangerford family, the townspeople in the Wilks's town, and the rural folk at Uncle Silas's are not only a panoramic cross section of the South; their meanness, greed, and violence are universal human traits. In his speech on mob behavior and human behavior, Colonel Sherburn condemns "the average all around," not merely the Southerner; and Huck universalizes that "human beings can be awful cruel."

Beneath the surface conflicts of freedom versus slavery, *Huckleberry Finn* explores whether any human being can transcend his society, violate his training, achieve independence from external pressure and judgment. In his later years, Mark Twain was to decide insistently that he could not. But in *Huckleberry Finn*, the issue is more complex. Huck has wrestled with his conscience three times in the novel, trying to decide whether to help Jim escape: on Jackson's Island, he concludes that he can help Jim because no one in St. Petersburg will know about his action; when he encounters the slave hunters, in chapter 16, he makes an argument on the basis of expediency—"What's the use you learning to do right, when it's troublesome to do right and ain't no trouble to do wrong, and the wages was just the same." In his final debate with his conscience, in chapter 31, he must confront the theological implications of his decision . . . damnation. He decides to "go to hell," rather than turn Jim in. As readers, we cheer Huck's ability to loose the shackles of convention and conformity.

But the final chapters seem anticlimactic to many readers. Huck allows Tom to orchestrate Jim's escape, letting Tom delay it too long with his ornate and ridiculously embellished plans, without protesting Tom's silliness. Huck appears to descend from the height he had reached in chapter 31, allowing Tom to usurp his own role as Jim's liberator. Discovering that Tom knew Jim was "free" all along

Clemens's copy of The Adventures of Huckleberry Finn, *marked for oral delivery*

reduces him and his thrill seeking even further in readers' estimations.

Much of the continuing critical debate about the final chapters and the ultimate meaning of the novel is a result of Mark Twain's strategy in allowing Huck to narrate his own novel. Huck is not an abstract reasoner; he lacks critical judgment. He admires, for instance, the Grangerfords' house and Emmeline's sentimental poetry, and he fails to perceive the irony in Pap's speech about the "gov'ment." As a result, readers pierce through Huck's literal descriptions and discern a number of value judgments that Huck himself does not make. We hear Mark Twain's voice beneath Huck's and perhaps, with the benefit of that double vision, yearn for more heroism than Huck can possibly achieve.

Contemporary reaction was microscopically small and almost entirely negative. Louisa May Alcott is reported to have decided that "if Mr. Clemens cannot think of something better to tell our pure-minded lads and lasses, he had best stop writing for them." *Life* magazine also condemned it as unsuitable reading for children. The Concord, Massachusetts, public library set the precedent which continues sporadically to the present of banning it from its shelves. Brander Matthews praised it in the London *Saturday Review,* and T. S. Perry was ultimately favorable in the *Century,* but theirs were minority reports.

Fortunately, another book diverted Clemens from concern about his own novel. Former President Ulysses Grant, dying of throat cancer, finally agreed to allow Charles L. Webster and Company to publish his *Personal Memoirs* by subscription. The country, knowing of his condition, subscribed for over 300,000 volumes of his autobiography; and the Webster marketing apparatus was strained almost to the point of rupture to produce and sell the book. After Grant's death, Clemens delivered to his widow a royalty check for $200,000, which he boasted was the largest one ever paid an author.

But the publishing company had established a network of agents which it was never able to use again. Webster and Clemens began a prodigal publishing campaign, publishing the autobiographies of other Civil War generals, a biography of Pope Leo XIII, and similar volumes which never managed to attract a fraction of the market Grant's volumes had. In the late 1880s, the company was financially overextended and heading precipitously for serious danger.

There was one fringe benefit of the Grant volume for Mark Twain. Matthew Arnold, the English critic, had reviewed Grant's *Personal Memoirs* in a supercilious tone which infuriated its publisher. First Twain planned to launch a direct assault on Arnold; but when the Englishman died, the humorist decided to reaim—this time at all English culture. The result was *A Connecticut Yankee in King Arthur's Court* (1889).

The idea for the novel had occurred to Mark Twain in December 1884 and he recorded in his notebook, "Dream of being a knight errant in armor in the middle ages." As he worked on the novel over the next four years, the tone and the theme of the work was to change from lighthearted burlesque to venomous satire, partly at least as a result of Arnold's criticism of Grant.

Hank Morgan, a foreman in the Colt Firearms Factory in Hartford, has been hit in the head during a fight and awakens in sixth-century England at King Arthur's court. With his common sense, inventiveness, and practical knowledge, he sets out to enlighten the kingdom, with its superstitiousness and ignorance, most fully embodied in Merlin. Hank strings telephone lines, establishes a newspaper, uses gunpowder and lightning rods to create explosive "miracles." But these trappings of civilization from the nineteenth century eventually become destructive rather than beneficial. Hank's own actions become more and more despotic rather than humanitarian, and his attitude toward the common men of King Arthur's realm, increasingly inhumane. Finally, as a result of manipulations on the stock market which Hank has created, the nation rises against him. At the end of the book, he and 52 boys destroy 25,000 knights with dynamite, electrified barbed wire, and Gatling guns. Merlin puts Hank in a trance, and he awakens back in the nineteenth century, with "an abyss of thirteen centuries yawning between me and . . . all that is dear to me, all that could make life worth the living!"

On the surface, Hank is Mark Twain's

"I SAW HE MEANT BUSINESS."

Frontispiece by Dan Beard for A Connecticut Yankee in King Arthur's Court

spokesman for democracy in preference to monarchy, freedom in preference to servitude and the caste system, a free economy in preference to a controlled one. Indeed, he wanted a twenty-five cent version of the novel to circulate among the working men in the new labor unions forming in the United States. But beneath that chauvinism, there is another message that questions technology and the machine civilization of the late nineteenth century, that confronts the dangers of absolute power, and that ponders whether human beings can ever be enlightened or altered by education.

A Connecticut Yankee in King Arthur's Court infuriated the British; his English publisher even asked for permission to censor some of the more inflammatory passages in the London edition. And even though he refused permission, Mark Twain wrote a curious letter to distinguished English critic Andrew Lang in defense of his novel. He insisted that his audience was not the cultivated reading public but what he called "the Belly and Members" section of society. "I have never tried," he went on, "in even one single little instance to help cultivate the cultivated classes. I was not equipped for it, either by native gifts or training. And I never had any ambition in that direction, but always hunted for bigger game—the masses. I have seldom deliberately tried to instruct them but have done my best to entertain them. . . . My audience is dumb, it has no voice in print, and so I cannot know whether I have won its approbation or only got its censure." No matter how simplistic and ingenuous that description sounds, it does mark off the major audience for Mark Twain's books.

Neither *A Connecticut Yankee* nor the sumptuous, multivolume Library of American Literature which Webster was publishing on the installment plan produced the revenue necessary to keep the firm afloat. In February 1888 after a series of bitter accusations and recriminations, Charles L. Webster was replaced as head of the company which bore his name by Fred J. Hall, who managed to keep the foundering organization afloat for five more years, but only by borrowing larger and larger amounts of money from the banks. The Paige typesetter drained funds like an enormous brass leech.

Both of the Clemenses were suffering from rheumatism and Olivia Clemens had a heart condition, which convinced them that it would be both beneficial and economical to close the Hartford house and spend some time in European health spas. On 6 June 1891, the family left the United States, embarking on a nightmare that was to end only with their deaths, and closing the doors of the Hartford residence for what would be the last time as residents.

Throughout the early 1890s, while the girls and their mother lived on the eastern side of the Atlantic, Clemens made frenzied and frequent trips across the ocean to bolster his failing financial condition. His frantic hopscotching was futile: in the depths of the Panic of 1893-1894, Charles L. Webster and Company declared bankruptcy (on 18 April 1894). Eight months later, the typesetter failed its trial run and no capital was available for further manufacture. Just turned sixty, Clemens was virtually penniless.

He had just one possible source of substantial revenue—a manuscript for a subscription book on which he had been working for the several years he was in Europe—*The Tragedy of Pudd'nhead Wilson*. Since Webster was bankrupt, he returned to the American Publishing Company with his new volume and in November 1894, that publisher published the novel together with its burlesque counterpart, *The Comedy of Those Extraordinary Twins*.

After contemplating black slavery in *Huckleberry Finn* and universal slavery to convention and training in *A Connecticut Yankee*, Clemens chose to return to the antebellum South in *Pudd'nhead Wilson*. There, a young lawyer, relegated to the status of "pudd'nhead" because of a chance remark he makes when he disembarks at Dawson's Landing, Arkansas, spends most of the next two decades collecting fingerprints of all the residents of the town. Meanwhile, Roxy, a "black" slave whose skin is white and whose eyes are blue, has exchanged her baby with her owner's shortly after their births. As the plot unravels, Tom Driscoll (the black who has usurped the master's position) grows up as the petted heir of a Virginia lineage while Valet de Chambre (the white child relegated to slave status) matures in the slave quarters. Tom gambles, steals to pay his debts, and sells his own mother "down the river" in order to raise cash. Finally, he murders his "uncle" in order to protect his inheritance. At the predictable trial scene, Pudd'nhead Wilson uses his collection of fingerprints to reveal that Tom is in fact the slave and Valet the master. And therefore Tom, who was to be executed for murder, is now another man's property and is himself sold down river to settle his "uncle's" estate.

Beneath the contrivances and melodrama of the novel runs the darkest vein of Mark Twain's thought. Neither half of Dawson's Landing is in fact free. Both master and slave are conditioned by generations of slavery to accept white superiority and black inferiority. Even Roxy attributes Tom's in-

A TALE BY MARK TWAIN

THERE is no character, howsoever good and fine, but it can be destroyed by ridicule, howsoever poor and witless. Observe the ass, for instance: his character is about perfect, he is the choicest spirit among all the humbler animals, yet see what ridicule has brought him to. Instead of feeling complimented when we are called an ass, we are left in doubt. — *Pudd'nhead Wilson's Calendar.*

A WHISPER TO THE READER.

 PERSON who is ignorant of legal matters is always liable to make mistakes when he tries to photograph a court scene with his pen ; and so I was not willing to let the law chapters in this book go to press without first subjecting them to rigid and exhausting revision and correction by a trained barrister — if that is what they are called. These chapters are right, now, in every detail, for they were rewritten under the immediate eye of William Hicks, who studied law part of a while in southwest Missouri thirty-five years ago and then came over here to Florence for his health and is still helping for exercise and board in Macaroni Vermicelli's horse-feed shed which is up the back alley as you turn around the corner out of the Piazza del Duomo just beyond the house where that stone that Dante used to sit on six hundred years ago is let into the wall when he let on to be watching them build Giotto's campanile and yet always got tired looking as soon as Beatrice passed along on her way to get a chunk of chestnut cake to defend herself with in case of a Ghibelline outbreak before she got to school, at the same old stand where they sell the same old cake to this day and it is just as light and good as it was then, too, and this is not flattery, far from it. He was a little rusty on his law, but he rubbed up for this book; and those two or three legal chapters are right and straight, now. He told me so himself.

Given under my hand this second day of January, 1893, at the Villa Viviani, village of Settignano, three miles back of Florence, on the hills — the same certainly affording the most charming view to be found on this planet, and with it the most dream-like and enchanting sunsets to be found in any planet or even in any solar system — and given, too, in the swell room of the house, with the busts of Cerretani senators and other grandees of this line looking approvingly down upon me as they used to look down upon Dante, and mutely asking me to adopt them into my family, which I do with pleasure, for my remotest ancestors are but spring chickens compared with these robed and stately antiques, and it will be a great and satisfying lift for me, that six hundred years will.

Mark Twain.

CHAPTER I.

TELL the truth or trump — but get the trick. — *Pudd'nhead Wilson's Calendar.*

THE scene of this chronicle is the town of Dawson's Landing, on the Missouri side of the Mississippi, half a day's journey, per steamboat, below St. Louis.

In 1830 it was a snug little collection of modest one- and two-story frame dwellings whose whitewashed exteriors were almost con-

stood wooden boxes containing moss-rose plants and terra-cotta pots in which grew a breed of geranium whose spread of intensely red blossoms accented the prevailing pink tint of the rose-clad house-front like an explosion of flame. When there was room on the ledge outside of the pots and boxes for a cat, the cat was there — in sunny weather — stretched at full length, asleep and blissful, with her furry belly to the sun and a paw curved over her nose. Then that house was complete, and its content-

The first installment of Pudd'nhead Wilson, *in* Century *magazine, December 1893*

ability to live up to his aristocratic expectations to his black blood: "Thirty-one parts o' you is white, an on'y one part nigger, an dat po' little one part is yo' *soul*." The entire town sees "blood" as determining human behavior and fate; but, beneath the town's self-deception, is Mark Twain's increasingly insistent belief that "training is everything." Not only does Tom revert to property, but Valet, now a wealthy white aristocrat, "could neither read nor write, and his speech was the basest dialect of the negro quarter." Moreover, "His gait, his attitudes, his gestures, his bearing, his laugh—all were vulgar and uncouth; his manners were the manners of a slave. Money and fine clothes could not mend these defects or cover them up; they only made them the more glaring and the more pathetic. The poor fellow could not endure the terrors of the white man's parlor, and felt at home and at peace nowhere but in the kitchen. The family pew was a misery to him, yet he could nevermore enter into the solacing refuge of the 'nigger gallery'—that was closed to him for good and all." Most ironic, however, is Pudd'nhead Wilson's fate. It is he who revealed the truth about identity to the town, who should liberate it from its false standards. But he accepts its standards and is elected mayor of Dawson's Landing; "he was a made man for good." Like a series of transcendent strangers in Mark Twain's later works, he should strip the absurdities and vanities from human self-deception and reveal the truth about human character and motivation. Only in "Pudd'nhead Wilson's Calendar," epigrams that open each chapter of the novel, does David Wilson reveal those thoughts:

> Whoever has lived long enough to find out what life is, knows how deep a debt of gratitude we owe to Adam, the first great benefactor of our race. He brought death to the world.

> . . . .

> Why is it that we rejoice at a birth and grieve at a funeral? It is because we are not the person involved.

> . . . .

> All say, "How hard it is that we have to die"—a strange complaint to come from the mouths of people who have had to live.

> . . . .

> If you pick up a starving dog and make him prosperous, he will not bite you. This is the principal difference between a dog and a man.

Perhaps it is no accident that the novel is called David Wilson's tragedy.

Clemens's own impending tragedies were soon to overshadow Pudd'nhead Wilson's, however. Since September 1893, he had placed almost all of his financial affairs in the capable hands of Henry Huttleston Rogers, a vice-president of Standard Oil and ultimately one of Clemens's closest friends during the last fifteen years of his life. Rogers negotiated the dissolution of the Paige typesetter agreement, arranged for the contracts for editions of Mark Twain's collected works, oversaw the repayment of the Webster bankruptcy claimants. But Clemens's financial situation was still so complicated that debts, barely alleviated by the sales of *Pudd'nhead Wilson*, plagued both Clemenses. The family returned to the United States in May 1895 to deliver the manuscript of *Personal Recollections of Joan of Arc* (1896), to deposit Jean and Susy at Quarry Farm, and to embark with Clara for an around-the-world lecture tour intended to get the family debt free.

Clemens, Olivia, and Clara sailed from Vancouver on 23 August 1895; he lectured in Australia, New Zealand, India, and South Africa to throngs of listeners. And when the family arrived in England on 31 July 1896, Mark Twain had materials for his final travel volume, *Following the Equator* (1897).

But the family received first a letter and then a cable advising that Susy was ill; Olivia and Clara boarded a ship for the United States, and while they were in mid-ocean, on 15 August 1896, Susy died of meningitis. Clemens, alone in London, unable to reach the United States before the funeral, poured forth his grief and self-blame at having left Susy in the United States, at having separated Olivia from her, and at the loss of the family's "prodigy." The family, reunited in London after Susy's funeral, moved into deep mourning, not celebrating Thanksgiving or Christmas; only furious work on the travel book served, as he told Twichell, as "the 'surcease of sorrow' that is found there. I work all the days, and trouble vanishes away when I use that magic." But additional tragedies were looming: in 1896, Jean's erratic behavior was diagnosed as epilepsy, and she was to undergo almost constant treatments until her death in 1909; Olivia's health, weakened by Susy's death and (Clemens insisted) the lecture tour, seemed fragile.

It is important to notice the elements of pessimism, determinism, and contempt for humanity that formed a part of Mark Twain's belief long before the domestic catastrophes occurred; it is equally important to be aware that the Clemens family was less the Victorian ideal than its head felt it necessary to describe for the public. Nevertheless, after the blows of the late 1890s, his attitude became persistently misanthropic and mechanistic, with fewer interludes of light comedy or optimism. Though he read none of the major naturalists, his own instincts and beliefs began to parallel theirs. That man was a machine, without free will, whose behavior was determined by biology or environment or chance, incapable of altering his life's course, became Mark Twain's credo at the same time Crane, Dreiser, and Norris were proclaiming it.

Following the Equator was published by the American Publishing Company in November 1897 with a $10,000 advance against sales (by the following March, all the creditors' claims would be settled). Although, like his earlier travel volumes, this one was basically autobiographical, even it showed Mark Twain's increasing disillusionment with the human race. He attacked imperialism, colonialism, the torture and exploitation of slave labor by rulers. Shocked at the poverty and squalor he found in India—and by the brutality of the ruling class—he turned *Following the Equator*, probably the most unjustifiably neglected of his works, into a preview of his condemnation of imperialism among the early twentieth-century colonial nations in "To the Person Sitting in Darkness," *King Leopold's Soliloquy*, and "The Czar's Soliloquy." Admittedly, the book is overly long, but it seethes with a sense of injustice and man's inhumanity to man that merits more attention than it has received.

Creditors paid off—Olivia read their letters of appreciation to Mark Twain for making good on his debts and, as Clemens reported to Rogers, experienced "the only really happy day she has had since Susy died"—the family moved to Vienna, and Mark Twain plunged into work on a number of significant manuscripts. Most of them were never finished, and only a few saw publication during his lifetime; but they marked a dramatic turn in the twilight decade of his literary career.

He had tried unsuccessfully to revive Tom Sawyer and Huck Finn, in *Tom Sawyer Abroad* (1894) and *Tom Sawyer, Detective* (1896). In 1897 he attempted "Tom Sawyer's Conspiracy" and "Hellfire Hotchkiss" (not published until *Mark Twain's Hannibal, Huck, and Tom*, 1969, and *Mark Twain's Satires and Burlesques*, 1967) using his Hannibal childhood as the skeleton for the stories. In 1898 he attempted to write a Hannibal version of *The Mysterious*

Stranger called "Schoolhouse Hill," with Tom and Huck as characters. But the charm, the magic, and the captivation of childhood in Hannibal were gone. Mark Twain wrote in his notebook as the epitaph for the creative inspiration he found in his boyhood,

> Huck comes back sixty years old, from nobody knows where—crazy. Thinks he is a boy again and scans always every face for Tom, Becky, etc.
>
> Tom comes at last from sixty years' wandering in the world and attends Huck and together they talk of old times; both are desolate, life has been a failure, all that was lovable, all that was beautiful is under the mold. They die together.

This plot outline was never converted into fiction.

In the summer of 1899, the family stayed in Sanna, Sweden, where Jean underwent treatments for her epilepsy; that winter they spent back in London. And on 15 October 1900, the family returned to the United States—to a house in New York City rather than to Hartford. Mark Twain became a social butterfly and a political gadfly, attending banquets, giving after-dinner speeches, delighting in reporters' interviews, and speaking out frequently and forcefully against a wide range of injustices.

He assaulted Christian missionaries in China, the British role in the Boer War, American lynchings, the United States' exploitation of the Philippines, King Leopold's butchery in the Belgian Congo, Czar Nicholas's depravity in Russia, New York City politicians, and Mary Baker Eddy's manipulation of Christian Science with particular venom and endurance (perhaps because he believed Susy might have been cured had she not been practicing Mental Science and refused the help of a physician). Between 1900 and 1907, he launched into polemics with equal energy and exhaustion. He even wrote against bullfighting (in *A Horse's Tale*, 1907) and vivisection (in *A Dog's Tale*, 1904).

The intellectual premises of his polemical writing contradicted the themes in his later, usually unfinished, fiction. In "The Chronicle of Young Satan" (written in 1897, but not published until 1969 in *Mark Twain's "Mysterious Stranger" Manuscripts*), *What is Man?* (1906), *Letters from the Earth* (written in 1909, published in 1962), and "The Turning Point of My Life" (collected in *What Is Man?* in 1917) he repeated his refrain that human fate was outside the individual's control, that man

Drawing by Clemens in Metropolitan *magazine (1903): "the features are Mr. Howells's, while the expression is Mr. Laffan's."*

sumptuous Villa di Quarto, she continued to fail and died on the evening of 5 June 1904, from syncope. The remnants of the family returned to New York, Clara to a sanatorium, Clemens and Jean to a house on Fifth Avenue. There he brought to fruition a lifelong project, his autobiography.

Mark Twain had contemplated, and even written portions of, his autobiography earlier in his life; but in 1905 and 1906 (with less frequent additions from 1907 to 1909), he amassed a staggering amount of autobiographical materials. He proposed that, since he intended to withhold the book from publication until after his death, he could speak the absolute truth "as from the grave." Each day a stenographer would record his thoughts, which had no chronological sequence, type them, and have him proofread them. He wandered wherever his fancy led him: "Start it at no particular time in your life; talk only about the thing which interests you for the moment; drop it the moment its interest threatens to pale, and turn your talk upon the new and more interesting thing that has intruded itself into your mind." This was his plan.

As a result, the autobiographical dictations are impressively modern; almost like a patient on a couch talking to a stenographer rather than a

was merely a machine, following the "law of his make." Neither blame nor praise, neither vices nor virtues were possible when the universe operated purely on biological law. Thus, in one of his voices and moods he criticized mankind, while in another he absolved it of any alternative and preferable behavior.

Another large body of manuscripts that remained unfinished and unpublished during Mark Twain's lifetime concerned the confusion of dream and reality. "Which Was the Dream?," "The Great Dark," and "No. 44, The Mysterious Stranger," all explored dream and waking selves to question whether external reality existed at all. In small part, the theme might have been a device for negating the factual tragedies for which he felt guilty.

Those tragedies were not yet ended. On 12 August 1902, Olivia Clemens suffered a major illness; Clemens was not permitted to see her for long stretches of time—for three months, in late 1902. As soon as she improved sufficiently, in the summer of 1903, the family traveled to Florence, Italy, where the climate might improve her health. There, in a

Samuel Clemens, circa 1905

psychiatrist, Mark Twain moved by free association, ignoring both chronology and cohesiveness, in order to record the biography of a personality, of a mind at work unrestricted by form. While certainly not the absolute truth he promised, the first several years of the autobiographical dictations capture more convincingly than any other document the spirit, the vanity, the viciousness, and the tenderness which were essential aspects of Mark Twain's personality.

In October 1906, Jean entered the first of a series of sanatoriums which were to separate her from her father for almost three years. Clara pursued a singing career with more perseverance than success. The daughters were replaced by a coterie of admirers—Albert Bigelow Paine, the official biographer; Isabel Lyon, personal secretary; and Ralph Ashcroft, business manager—who insulated Clemens as much as possible from the outside world, and who fought out internecine skirmishes

Twain's note about his autobiographical material, explaining why he insisted on posthumous publication

for his attention. In 1907, Clemens was awarded the Litt. D. degree from Oxford University, which he traveled across the Atlantic to accept.

In June 1908, he moved from New York City to an ornate villa outside Redding, Connecticut, which he christened Stormfield after his story "Captain Stormfield's Visit to Heaven," an extract from which, published as a small book in 1909, had helped pay for the building. Jean joined him there in April 1909, and Clara married Ossip Gabrilowitsch there on 6 October 1909 and departed for Germany. On Christmas Eve 1909, Jean suffered an epileptic seizure in her bathtub and drowned. Too infirm to accompany the body to Elmira, Mark Twain wandered the huge, empty house, composing "The Death of Jean" which he considered the last chapter of his autobiography. A few days later, he made one of the frequent trips of his last years to Hamilton, Bermuda, where he hoped the mild climate might alleviate his worsening angina. In April, Paine received reports of his weakening condition, went to Bermuda, and accompanied Clemens back to Stormfield. There, just a few days after Clara and

The last known photograph of Clemens, taken on his return to New York from Bermuda, 14 April 1910

Gabrilowitsch arrived from Germany, Mark Twain died, on 21 April 1910.

Mark Twain's unpublished literary legacy probably almost equalled the works published during his lifetime. Paine, as literary editor, carefully selected manuscripts—a scissors-and-paste version of *The Mysterious Stranger* in 1916, two volumes of *Mark Twain's Letters* in 1917, *Mark Twain's Speeches* in 1923, two volumes of *Mark Twain's Autobiography* in 1924, and a heavily abridged and edited *Mark Twain's Notebook* in 1935. After his tenure as literary executor ended in 1937, the unpublished collections were opened for scholarly scrutiny, and in 1967, the University of California Press began publishing The Mark Twain Papers, which will ultimately print all the previously unpublished material by the humorist. There is little chance, however, that the new documents and manuscripts will cause any significant change in Mark Twain's reputation and significance.

Even if he was a fictional character himself, Mark Twain was a unique American writer. His experiences ranged by good fortune through the exact events that captivated the American imagination—the river during its golden age, the Far West of its bonanza days, the first waves of middle-class American tourists to Europe, the mania for material wealth—conspicuous consumption, as Thorstein Veblen was to label it—of the last quarter of the nineteenth century. His chauvinistic pride in democracy and technology began to turn to shame as the United States became a fledgling superpower at the beginning of the twentieth century, as did the pride of many of his countrymen. Because he was a reasonably accurate barometer of their own sentiments and beliefs, he gained acceptance as the spokesman of the common man. And his major voice and prose style—vernacular, commonsensical, pragmatic—struck resonant echoes among his subscription audience. With a mixture of pride and wistfulness, he wrote in his notebook in 1886, "My books are water; those of the great geniuses are wine. Everybody drinks water."

He captured, with amazing fidelity, essential aspects of the American experience and the American stance. The adulation of a highly romanticized childhood, the compulsion of the westward migration, the persistence of the Horatio Alger myth of fame, wealth, and success as somehow synonymous; these he embodied in both his major literature and his spectacularly public life.

From his western background, he learned the use of colloquial speech, an egalitarianism only occasionally tarnished by his doubts about human perfidy until his later years, and a love of the lusty, earthy facts of life which New England literature had struggled for a century to ignore. His journalism and his travel writings had compelled him to photographic detail and descriptive accuracy. His honesty—William Dean Howells said after Clemens's death, "At the last day he will not have to confess anything, for all his life was the free knowledge of any one who would ask him of it"—however filtered through Victorian convention, was resolute in every significant way—language, behavior, morality.

If he was a realist in his language and a naturalist in his final philosophy, he was also an archromantic. Neither Howells's smiling aspects of life nor Frank Norris's drama of a broken teacup is a part of Mark Twain's fiction. Wild coincidences (like Tom's unexpected arrival at the Phelps's farm at the end of *Huckleberry Finn*), improbable changelings (Edward and Tom Canty in *The Prince and the Pauper*; Tom Driscoll and Valet de Chambre in *Pudd'nhead Wilson*), melodramatic courtroom climaxes, deus ex machina denouements (fingerprints in *Pudd'nhead Wilson*, Tom Sawyer's reappearance in *Huckleberry Finn*), supernatural visitors (in many of the later works), dream visions (in *A Connecticut Yankee* and many of the unfinished fragments) are the stuff of pure romanticism.

His own personality was predominantly romantic, as well. He abided by most of the domestic conventions of his time; he paraded down Fifth Avenue in his old age in his white suit, simply for its shock value. He needed to be center-stage front in the drama he made of his own life. Perhaps his most endearing quality as a public performer who imposed himself indelibly as an American folk hero was the all-too-human frailty which he refused to camouflage.

His literature explored questions of freedom, independence, identity. In a steady evolution, he moved from the confidence and self-reliance of the brash Westerner to the questioning and contradictory stance of the agnostic, until he could write in his notebook in the last years of the century, "The human race consists of the damned and the ought-to-be-damned." It could be argued that, almost singlehandedly, he liberated American fiction from the rigid conventions of the mid-nineteenth century—its stilted dialogue, its stereotyped characters, its didactic impulse, its optimistic impetus. At the same time, he lowered American literature to the plane of the mass audience and elevated it to a distinct, indigenous height which no one else has reached.

Letters:

Mark Twain's Letters, 2 volumes, edited by Albert Bigelow Paine (New York: Harper, 1917);

Mark Twain the Letter Writer, edited by Cyril Clemens (Boston: Meador, 1932);

Mark Twain's Letters to Will Bowen, edited by Theodore Hornberger (Austin: University of Texas Press, 1941);

The Love Letters of Mark Twain, edited by Dixon Wecter (New York: Harper, 1949);

Mark Twain to Mrs. Fairbanks, edited by Wecter (San Marino: Huntington Library, 1949);

Mark Twain's Letters to Mary, edited by Lewis Leary (New York: Columbia University Press, 1961);

Mark Twain–Howells Letters, 2 volumes, edited by Henry Nash Smith and William M. Gibson (Cambridge: Harvard University Press, 1966);

Mark Twain's Letters to His Publishers, edited by Hamlin Hill (Berkeley: University of California Press, 1967);

Mark Twain's Correspondence with Henry Huttleston Rogers, edited by Leary (Berkeley: University of California Press, 1969).

Bibliographies:

Merle Johnson, *A Bibliography of the Works of Mark Twain*, revised and enlarged edition (New York & London: Harper, 1935);

Thomas Asa Tenney, *Mark Twain: A Reference Guide* (Boston: G. K. Hall, 1977);

Alan Gribben, "Removing Mark Twain's Mask: A Decade of Criticism and Scholarship," *ESQ: Journal of the American Renaissance*, 26 (1980): 100-108, 149-171.

Biographies:

William Dean Howells, *My Mark Twain* (New York & London: Harper, 1910);

Albert Bigelow Paine, *Mark Twain, A Biography*, 3 volumes (New York & London: Harper, 1912);

Bernard DeVoto, *Mark Twain's America* (Boston: Little, Brown, 1932);

Minnie M. Brashear, *Mark Twain, Son of Missouri* (Chapel Hill: University of North Carolina Press, 1934);

Ivan Benson, *Mark Twain's Western Years* (Stanford: Stanford University Press, 1938);

DeLancey Ferguson, *Mark Twain: Man and Legend* (Indianapolis & New York: Bobbs-Merrill, 1943);

Kenneth Andrews, *Nook Farm: Mark Twain's Hartford Circle* (Cambridge: Harvard University Press, 1950);

Dixon Wecter, *Sam Clemens of Hannibal* (Boston:

Houghton Mifflin, 1952);

Paul Fatout, *Mark Twain in Virginia City* (Bloomington: Indiana University Press, 1964);

Edith Colgate Salsbury, *Susy and Mark Twain* (New York: Harper & Row, 1965);

Justin Kaplan, *Mr. Clemens and Mark Twain* (New York: Simon & Schuster, 1966);

Hamlin Hill, *Mark Twain: God's Fool* (New York: Harper & Row, 1973).

References:

Howard Baetzhold, *Mark Twain and John Bull* (Bloomington: Indiana University Press, 1970);

Gladys Bellamy, *Mark Twain as a Literary Artist* (Norman: University of Oklahoma Press, 1950);

Walter Blair, *Mark Twain & Huck Finn* (Berkeley: University of California Press, 1960);

Edgar M. Branch, *The Literary Apprenticeship of Mark Twain* (Urbana: University of Illinois Press, 1950);

Van Wyck Brooks, *The Ordeal of Mark Twain* (New York: Dutton, 1923; revised, 1933);

Louis J. Budd, *Interviews with Samuel L. Clemens, 1874-1910* (Arlington: University of Texas at Arlington, 1977);

Budd, *Mark Twain, Social Philosopher*, (Bloomington: Indiana University Press, 1962);

George C. Carrington, *The Dramatic Unity of Huckleberry Finn* (Columbus: Ohio State University Press, 1976);

James M. Cox, *Mark Twain, The Fate of Humor*, (Princeton: Princeton University Press, 1966);

Paul Fatout, *Mark Twain on the Lecture Circuit* (Bloomington: Indiana University Press, 1960);

Robert L. Gale, *Plots and Characters in the Works of Mark Twain,* 2 volumes (Hamden, Conn.: Archon Books, 1973);

Alan Gribben, *Mark Twain's Library, A Reconstruction*, 2 volumes (Boston: G. K. Hall, 1980);

Fred W. Lorch, *The Trouble Begins at Eight* (Ames: Iowa State University Press, 1968);

Kenneth S. Lynn, *Mark Twain and Southwestern Humor* (Boston: Little, Brown, 1959);

Arthur G. Pettit, *Mark Twain and the South* (Lexington: University Press of Kentucky, 1974);

Robert L. Ramsay and Frances G. Emberson, *A Mark Twain Lexicon* (Columbia: University of Missouri Press, 1938; New York: Russell & Russell, 1963);

Arthur L. Scott, *On the Poetry of Mark Twain with Selections from His Verse* (Urbana: University of Illinois Press, 1966);

David E. E. Sloane, *Mark Twain as a Literary Comedian* (Baton Rouge: Louisiana State University Press, 1979);

Henry Nash Smith, *Mark Twain, The Development of a Writer* (Cambridge: Harvard University Press, 1962);

Albert E. Stone, *The Innocent Eye, Childhood in Mark Twain's Fiction* (New Haven: Yale University Press, 1961).

Papers:

The major collection of Mark Twain materials is The Mark Twain Papers at The Bancroft Library, University of California, Berkeley. Other major collections are at Yale University Library, the Henry W. and Albert A. Berg Collection of the New York Public Library, Vassar College, and the Alderman Library of the University of Virginia.

Rose Terry Cooke

(17 February 1827-18 July 1892)

Perry D. Westbrook
State University of New York at Albany

BOOKS: *Poems* (Boston: Ticknor & Fields, 1861);
Happy Dodd (Boston: Hoyt, 1878);
Somebody's Neighbors (Boston: Osgood, 1881);
Root-Bound and Other Sketches (Boston: Congregational Sunday-School & Publishing Society, 1885);
The Sphinx's Children and Other People's (Boston: Ticknor, 1886);
No (New York: Phillips & Hunt, 1886);
Poems (New York: Gottsberger, 1888);
Steadfast: The Story of a Saint and a Sinner (Boston: Ticknor, 1889);
Huckleberries Gathered from New England Hills (Boston & New York: Houghton, Mifflin, 1891).

Rose Terry Cooke has been called by Jean Downey the first New England "short story writer to make the transition from sentimentalism to the beginnings of realism"—a transition which first became apparent in the mid-1850s in her tales dealing with rural scenes and characters in her native Connecticut. Not only was she one of the earliest New England regionalists in fiction, but she was having her local-color stories published ten years before the 1868 appearance of Bret Harte's "The Luck of Roaring Camp," which many literary historians credit with initiating the local-color movement. Not all of Cooke's approximately 200 published stories are realistic, but a number of them rank with the best realistic fiction of such New England authors of Cooke's generation as Sarah Orne Jewett and Mary E. Wilkins Freeman.

Born on a farm six miles outside of Hartford on 17 February 1827, to Henry Wadsworth and Anne Hurlbut Terry, Rose Terry was descended from two old and respected Connecticut families. Her grandfather on her mother's side, John Hurlbut, was a shipbuilder and first mate on the first American ship to sail around the world. On her father's side her grandfather had a varied career as a congressman, a legislator, a bank president, an insurance company president, and mayor of Hartford. Her father, Henry Wadsworth Terry, was a landscape gardener—a calling which brought him neither fame nor financial success. It is re-

ported that Rose could read when she was three. When Rose was six years old, the family moved from their farm to the imposing mansion of her grandmother Terry in Hartford. During a girlhood marred by periods of ill health which continued to plague her throughout life, she was quite often outdoors with her father, learning from him much about nature and gardening. When she was sixteen, she graduated from the Hartford Female Seminary, and the same year she underwent the religious conversion, or spiritual awakening, which was necessary for one to join the Congregational church as a full member. Soon after graduation and a brief period of teaching in Connecticut, she went to Burlington, New Jersey, to teach a school of five pupils in the home of the Reverend William Van Rensselaer, a Presbyterian clergyman, and to serve as governess in his family. Four years later she was back in Hartford and its vicinity teaching and writing. In 1848 a small inheritance enabled her to cease teaching.

Her early publications were poems, the first of which appeared in the *New York Tribune* in 1851. It was followed by poems in *Putnam's Magazine*, *Harper's New Monthly Magazine*, and later in the decade in the *Atlantic Monthly*. In 1861 Ticknor and Fields of Boston brought out a volume of her verse. By preference she wrote poetry, but few, if any, of her approximately 300 poems have survived the test of time. In conventional meters and stanzaic forms, she wrote on many subjects—nature, New England scenes, religion, the Civil War. Surprisingly she came closest to originality in composing several frontier ballads, which won praise from James Russell Lowell. According to Harriet Prescott Spofford (Cooke's friend and biographer), this religious, blue-blooded New England young woman was the first to write in this genre.

Cooke's only notable contributions to American literature were short stories, some of which still appear in anthologies. Her first short story of any consequence, "The Mormon's Wife," which appeared in *Putnam's Magazine* in 1855, is a sentimental tale of a Connecticut girl whose husband becomes a Mormon and takes two other wives, with the result that the heroine dies of a broken heart. Since *Putnam's* opposed Mormonism and statehood for Utah, Cooke's story borders on propaganda, whether or not she intended it as such. During the next three years she contributed some half dozen other stories to *Putnam's*, all dealing with rural New England people, whose dialect she faithfully reproduced and whose peculiar traits she carefully represented, drawing from observations made earlier while she was teaching in country schools in northern Connecticut. These stories combined humor and some sentimentality with social comment. She did not hesitate to reveal the poverty, the narrowness, and other grim aspects of life in the villages or on the farms of backcountry New England, and she was particularly insistent in describing the monotonous and toil-filled lives of the country women, whom she found to be little appreciated, if not abused and exploited, by their menfolk; but she was not blind to the humor, some of the lighter aspects, in the way of life she was recording.

Among these early stories "Uncle Josh" (*Putnam's*, September 1857) is typical and perhaps the best written. Humorously it recounts the effort of a villager, Uncle Josh, who, after years as a sailor, returns home addicted to swearing, a habit he has picked up while at sea, which is deeply offensive to the villagers. After being converted to religion, he struggles to overcome his swearing and finally succeeds by marrying the most ill-tempered woman in town, who cures him with her scathing, vinegarish tongue. The story is much more than farce, for it displays a small gallery of lifelike rural characters engaged in the day-to-day activities of village life. Cooke's listing of widely used rural nostrums, for example, might shake the faith of present-day devotees of folk medicine. A dying farm woman diagnosed by the local doctor as having "successively 'a spine in the back,' a 'rising of the lungs,' and 'a gittaral complaint of the lights'. . . [was] blistered, plastered, and fomented, dosed with Brandreth's pills, mullein-root in cider, tansy, burdock, bittersweet, catnip, and boneset teas; sow-bugs tickled into a ball and swallowed alive; dried rattlesnake's flesh; and the powder of a red squirrel, shut into a red-hot oven living, baked till powderable, and then put through that process in a mortar, and administered while fasting." The recipient, or victim, of this medication is a farm wife typical of scores of other such women who appear in Cooke's writing—women worn down by a ceaseless, lifelong grind of bearing and rearing children, cooking for large, hungry families and the hired help, sweeping, washing, mending, and spinning. Cooke describes those women as "martyrs by the pang without the palm, of whom a noble army shall yet rise out of New England's desolate valleys and melancholy hills to take their honor from the Master's hand." Yet, though the bleak, often loveless and hopeless, lives of the women in her stories aroused Cooke's compassion and, at times, indignation, she was never an active feminist and even complains of having herself been "hustled and bustled by the Rights Women" while "weakly and meekly protesting against their ways and works."

During the 1850s Cooke, in addition to the local-color fiction she contributed to *Putnam's*, placed in *Harper's Monthly Magazine* four sentimental tales of unrequited love and the deaths of jilted heroines, but at the end of the decade there appeared in *Harper's* "Alcedema Sparks; or Old and New," which ranks with "Uncle Josh" as one of her most realistic studies of life in the New England countryside. In this tale Cooke, always concerned with religious matters, contrasts the Old-School

Calvinists, who in Puritan fashion "believed in the Law and only tolerated the Gospels," with the New-School Calvinists, who were guided primarily by the Gospels, especially by the Sermon on the Mount, and regarded religion as best expressed in "a life of duty" rather than in a rigid adherence to "doctrines." Cooke is clearly of the New School. Old-School Deacon Sparks, for whom the story is named, emerges as typical of dozens of deacons in Cooke's work. "Six days Deacon Sparks ground the faces of the poor, snarled and snapped at his wife, looked like a Yankee Gorgon at every child that he passed, overworked his horses and underfed his hired men. The seventh day he held his tongue and read the Old Testament, or went to church and sung psalms with much fervor and no tune." Deacon Sparks, indeed, embodies his town's dominant spirit of intolerance and meanness. In such towns, as Cooke presents them, the storekeepers, frequently deacons, sell sanded sugar and watered rum; and at town meetings the voters literally auction off the paupers to the townsperson who bids the lowest price for caring for them.

"Alcedema Sparks" is one of many of Cooke's stories depicting spiritual atrophy in rural New England. Most notable of these are "Grit" (*Harper's*, January 1877), "Freedom Wheeler's Controversy with Providence" (*Atlantic*, July 1877), and "Mrs. Flint's Married Experience" (*Harper's*, December 1880), the last a bleak account of a deacon's victimizing his wife. The fictional and representative town of Bassett, which is the setting of many of Cooke's grimmer stories, is not a pastoral Eden and belies most of the idealized notions that urban romantics of her time and later have had concerning rural living. Yet even in her most somber accounts Cooke does not abandon a religious conviction that the granitic heart of even a deacon can be softened; and frequently, but not always, her tales end with a change for the better in her offending characters. In her best stories, however, the change of heart is plausible. In "Freedom Wheeler's Controversy with Providence" Cooke assures her readers that there will be no sudden conversions in her stories. "Facts," she states, "are stubborn things; and if circumstances and the grace of God modify character, they don't change it."

Cooke capped her literary successes in the 1850s by placing four stories in volume 1 (1857) of the *Atlantic Monthly*; altogether in her lifetime she contributed twenty-one stories to the *Atlantic*. John Greenleaf Whittier admired one of these, "Eben Jackson" (March 1858), for its accurate rendition of rural New England speech. Another, "Miss Lu-

cinda" (August 1861), is notable not only as a fine tale but also for containing its author's statement of her ideas about realism: "But if I apologize for a story that is nowise tragic, nor fitted to 'the fashion of these times,' possibly somebody will say at its end that I should also have apologized for its subject, since it is as easy for an author to treat his readers to high themes as vulgar ones, and velvet can be thrown into a portrait as cheaply as calico; but of this apology I wash my hands. I believe nothing in place or circumstance makes romance. I have the same quick sympathy for Biddy's sorrows with Patrick that I have for the Empress of France and her august, but rather grim lord and master. . . . and I have a reverence for poor old maids as great as for the nine Muses. Commonplace people are only commonplace from character, and no position affects that. So forgive me once more, patient reader, if I offer you no tragedy in high life, no sentimental history of fashion and wealth, but only a little story about a woman who could not be a heroine."

During the 1860s caring for her dead sister's children, the war, and her own illnesses combined to reduce Cooke's literary output, but by 1870 her productivity had greatly increased. While her contributions to the *Atlantic* and *Harper's* were less frequent, and her fiction no longer was appearing in *Putnam's*, the bulk of her material, in prose at least, was being placed in the *Independent* and the *Christian Union*. Though her writing for these periodicals was religiously slanted and often unabashedly didactic, her characters and settings were drawn from the same rural New England background as those in her less tendentious fiction. Many of these stories and sketches were later reprinted in *Root-Bound*, published by the Congregational Sunday-School and Publishing Society in 1885.

In 1873, at the age of forty-six, Rose Terry married Rollin H. Cooke, a thirty-year-old widower with two young daughters. Though at that time in New England women often married men many years their junior, the Terry family considered that she had made a misalliance, and there were reasons other than disparity in age for this view. Rollin Cooke had tried, and continued to try, many jobs—bank clerk, real-estate agent, factory representative, genealogist—and had prospered in none. According to one rather unlikely account the two had met in a boardinghouse in Boston, where she was studying art; according to another Rollin Cooke had read and admired her stories and had looked her up in Winsted, Connecticut, where she lived at that time. After the marriage, it soon became apparent that Rose Cooke's writing would be

150

2517 words
C.P.

Old Cool.

regiment

He wasn't old at all, not a day
over twenty when he joined the regiment,
a great tall bulking fellow, with a
big honest face like a boy's, weighed
a hundred and seventy-five pound if
he did an ounce, and answered to the
name of Joseph Cooley; we called him
Joe to begin with, and this yarn is
to tell how he got his other name.
We shipped aboard a river steamer at
New York for Ship Island; fifteen
hundred of us; maybe you boys don't
know what that means; aboard of a river
steamer? It means that every berth had
two men in it, lyin' heads and p'ints,
and glad to get one at that; the unlucky
ones lyin' side by side on the floor like
herring in a box, thick as they could
lie. Lots of 'em were dreadful sick
to begin with, some for one day, some

the chief support of the family. As she reveals in a sketch, "About Our House" (*Independent*, 12 February 1885), they were constantly on the move, living in such unlikely places as a country hotel and the upper floor of an opera house, until Rose Cooke finally located and bought a dilapidated house, which she and her husband made livable by their own labor. Her marriage had cost her money and peace of mind and had more or less alienated her from her family.

In 1881 the first of Rose Terry Cooke's short-story collections, *Somebody's Neighbors,* was published. This volume was followed by three other collections: *Root-Bound* (1885), *The Sphinx's Children and Other People's* (1886), and *Huckleberries Gathered from New England Hills* (1891). Yet these publications, plus her steady output of stories, sketches, and poems, did not bring financial security. Moreover, she was finding it more and more difficult to place her work with the prestigious journals like the *Atlantic* and *Harper's*. A major portion of her income now came from her sales to juvenile magazines, especially *The Youth's Companion*. A Sunday-school novel for boys, *No* (1886), brought only meager recompense. She reported that, though she wrote from nine to fifteen thousand words a week during this period, she in no year made as much as $1,000.

In 1887, when Cooke was sixty, she and her husband moved to Pittsfield, Massachusetts, where he had found work in a bank and as a real-estate broker. Already in 1885, on Whittier's urging, she had been working on an adult novel (the only one she ever attempted), *Steadfast,* which has its setting in colonial Connecticut. Based in part on actual events in Wallingford, Connecticut, the novel is an expose of the bigotry of the rigid Puritanism of the eighteenth century. Published in 1889, *Steadfast* cannot be called a success, and indeed it attracted little critical attention. Though its depictions of village characters and setting are firmly and convincingly drawn, the novel's theme had been treated frequently by the time she was writing about it. Also in 1889, her husband, predictably, failed in his business ventures, and in their consequent desperate financial straits, Rose Cooke wrote to Ticknor in Boston, begging for any kind of literary work. Nothing came of this effort, and in 1892, weakened by a bout of pneumonia, she contracted influenza and died. She was buried in Collinsville, Connecticut.

In American literature Rose Terry Cooke is not a major figure; yet her work deserves attention. Her significance has been best assessed by William Dean Howells, who pointed out that Cooke began to write realistic New England stories "when truth in art was considered a minor virtue if not a sordid detail." However, Howells found her stories to be "looser in structure" than Mary E. Wilkins Freeman's and "not so fine" as Sarah Orne Jewett's. To Fred Pattee her chief merit lay in "picturing the odd and the whimsical, in tenderness and sympathy, and in the perfect artlessness that is the last triumph of art." Hers is not a naturalistic realism, Pattee points out, but a poetic realism like that of the early Howells, "a realism that sees life through a window with an afternoon light on it."

Bibliography:
Jean Downey, "Rose Terry Cooke: A Bibliography," *Bulletin of Bibliography,* 21 (May-August and September-December 1955): 159-163 and 191-192.

References:
Van Wyck Brooks, *New England Indian Summer* (New York: Dutton, 1940), pp. 85-88;
Harriet Prescott Spofford, *A Little Book of Friends* (Boston: Little, Brown, 1917), pp. 143-156;
Spofford, "Rose Terry Cooke," in *Our Famous Women* (Hartford: A. D. Worthington, 1884), pp. 174-206;
Susan A. Toth, "Rose Terry Cooke," *American Literary Realism,* 42 (Spring 1971): 170-176;
Perry D. Westbrook, *Acres of Flint: Sarah Orne Jewett and Her Contemporaries* (Metuchen, N.J.: Scarecrow Press, 1981), pp. 78-85.

Stephen Crane

James B. Colvert
University of Georgia

BIRTH: Newark, New Jersey, 1 November 1871, to the Reverend Dr. Jonathan Townley and Mary Helen Peck Crane.

EDUCATION: Lafayette College, 1890; Syracuse University, 1891.

DEATH: Badenweiler, Germany, 5 June 1900.

SELECTED BOOKS: *Maggie: A Girl of the Streets*, as Johnston Smith (New York: Privately printed, 1893); revised edition, as Stephen Crane (New York: Appleton, 1896; London: Heinemann, 1896);

The Black Riders (Boston: Copeland & Day, 1895; London: Heinemann, 1896);

The Red Badge of Courage (New York: Appleton, 1895; London: Heinemann, 1896);

George's Mother (New York & London: Edward Arnold, 1896);

The Little Regiment (New York: Appleton, 1896; London: Heinemann, 1897);

The Third Violet (New York: Appleton, 1897; London: Heinemann, 1897);

The Open Boat (New York: Doubleday & McClure, 1898; London: Heinemann, 1898);

War is Kind (New York: Stokes, 1899);

Active Service (New York: Stokes, 1899; London: Heinemann, 1899);

The Monster (New York & London: Harper, 1899; enlarged edition, London & New York: Harper, 1901);

Whilomville Stories (New York & London: Harper, 1900);

Wounds in the Rain (New York: Stokes, 1900; London: Methuen, 1900);

Great Battles of the World (Philadelphia: Lippincott, 1901; London: Chapman & Hall, 1901);

Last Words (London: Digby, Long, 1902);

The O'Ruddy, by Crane and Robert Barr (New York: Stokes, 1903; London: Methuen, 1904);

The Sullivan County Sketches of Stephen Crane, edited by Melvin Schoberlin (Syracuse: Syracuse University Press, 1949);

Stephen Crane: Uncollected Writings, edited by O.W. Fryckstedt (Uppsala: Studia Anglistica Upsaliensia, 1963);

The War Dispatches of Stephen Crane, edited by R. W. Stallman and E. R. Hagemann (New York: New York University Press, 1966);

The New York City Sketches of Stephen Crane, edited by Stallman and Hagemann (New York: New York University Press, 1966);

Sullivan County Tales and Sketches, edited by Stallman (Ames: Iowa State University Press, 1968);

The Notebook of Stephen Crane, edited by Donald and Ellen Greiner (Charlottesville, Va.: A John Cook Wyllie Memorial Publication, 1969);

Stephen Crane in the West and Mexico, edited by Joseph Katz (Kent, Ohio: Kent State University Press, 1970);

The Red Badge of Courage: A Facsimile Edition of the Manuscript, 2 volumes, edited by Fredson Bowers (Washington, D. C.: Bruccoli Clark/ NCR Microcard Editions, 1973).

COLLECTIONS: *The Work of Stephen Crane*, 12 volumes, edited by Wilson Follett (New York: Knopf, 1925-1926);

The Collected Poems of Stephen Crane, edited by Follett (New York & London: Knopf, 1930);

The Poems of Stephen Crane, edited by Katz (New York: Cooper Square, 1966);

The Works of Stephen Crane, 10 volumes, edited by Bowers (Charlottesville: University Press of Virginia, 1969-1976).

A precursor of the imagists in poetry and of the novelists writing the new fiction of the 1920s, Stephen Crane was one of the most gifted and influential writers of the late nineteenth century, noted for his brilliant and innovative style, his vivid, ironic sense of life, and his penetrating psychological realism. Unusually precocious, he wrote his first novel, *Maggie: A Girl of the Streets* (1893), when he was only twenty-one and had his masterpiece, *The Red Badge of Courage* (1895), published before he was twenty-four. When he died in 1900 at the age of twenty-eight, from tuberculosis and the effects of his exhausting life as adventurer and war correspondent, he had written, in addition to his voluminous war reportage and numerous incidental pieces, six novels, well over a hundred stories and sketches, and two books of poems—enough all to-

Crane, age seventeen, as a student at Hudson River Institute in Claverack, New York

gether to fill ten large volumes in the University Press of Virginia edition of his collected works. Neglected for two decades after his death, he was rediscovered in the 1920s by poets and novelists (such as Amy Lowell, Willa Cather, Sherwood Anderson, and Joseph Hergesheimer) who recognized in his experiments with new subjects, themes, and forms something of the spirit of their own literary aims.

Although these aims were derived originally from such nineteenth-century realists as Hamlin Garland, William Dean Howells, Rudyard Kipling, Tolstoy, and others of perhaps more indeterminant influence, he radically altered their principles and methods to serve his own unique vision and purposes. He eschewed the conventional plot, shifting the focus from the drama of external event or situation to the drama of thought and feeling in the mental life of his subjects. He substituted for the conventional expository, descriptive style a highly metaphorical, imagistic representation of psychological effects. And he denied, in his most telling work, assumptions about norms of reality,

often depicting unfolding experience as gradual revelation of its ultimate mystery. A relativist, ironist, and impressionist, he anticipated the modernism of Hemingway, Fitzgerald, Anderson, and Faulkner by thirty years. Like Hemingway, he was preoccupied with violence, finding in the reaction of his hero under the stress of ultimate crisis the mystery and poignancy of the hero's character and fate. Like Anderson, Fitzgerald, and Faulkner, he dramatized the powers of illusion to shape events and destinies. He does, indeed, seem closer to these writers in manner and spirit than to the writers of his own day.

The experience which contributed most importantly to the shaping of Crane's modernist ideas and attitude was probably his early life as a minister's son. He was born 1 November 1871, in Newark, New Jersey, the last of fourteen children of the Reverend Dr. Jonathan Townley Crane, a well-known Methodist clergyman, and Mary Helen Peck Crane. Mrs. Crane, a descendant of a long line of Methodist preachers "of the old ambling-nag, saddle-bag, exhorting kind" (as Crane once described them), was active in church and reform work, serving at one time as an officer in the New Jersey Women's Christian Temperance Union. Her uncle, the Reverend Jesse Peck, a Methodist bishop and one of the founders of Syracuse University, was the author of a minatory religious treatise "redolent with the fumes of sulphur and brimstone," *What Must I Do to Be Saved?* (1858), a copy of which Stephen Crane inherited from his father in 1881. The bishop's view of God as a God of wrath was apparently shared, to some extent at least, by Crane's mother; but his father, who resigned from the Presbyterian church as a young man in protest against the harshness of its doctrine of infant damnation, was apparently of a gentler persuasion, stressing in his milder books on Christian conduct a view of God as a God of mercy and compassion. The religious poems in Stephen Crane's first book of poems, *The Black Riders* (1895), written about the same time he was writing *The Red Badge of Courage*, reflect the anguish of a spiritual crisis in which he attempted to exorcise the Pecks' God of wrath and, beyond that, to test his faith in general against the moral realities he observed as a young newspaper reporter in Asbury Park, New Jersey, and New York City in the early 1890s. The religious issue haunted Crane's imagination to the end. As Amy Lowell observed, "He disbelieved it and hated it, but he could not free himself from it." The effect of his preoccupation with questions of faith is not only evident in his poetry but appears, more obliquely, in his fiction as well, notably in its striking evocation of man's poignant alienation in a God-abandoned world of menace and violence.

Two years after his father died in 1880, Mrs. Crane moved to Asbury Park, New Jersey, a popular resort town on the coast where one of his older brothers, Townley, operated a news agency for the *New York Tribune.* Left much to his own devices, since Mrs. Crane was often busy with church and reform projects, Stephen roamed the beaches, indulged his passion for baseball (one of the pastimes his father cautioned against in his book *Popular Amusements,* 1869), and under the influence of his mentor Townley and another older brother, Will, who advised him once to ignore the hell-fire warnings of his visiting preacher-uncles, began to develop a decidedly secular point of view. In the summers he helped Townley Crane gather news and gossip for his *Tribune* column, "On the Jersey Coast." By 1888, when he enrolled at Claverack College and Hudson River Institute, a quasi-military prep school at Claverack, New York, he was already in full revolt against his Methodist heritage. As one of his classmates reported, he was bohemian in dress and manner, aloof and taciturn except on the baseball field, where he was companionable and "giftedly profane." He violated no rules, but he was known to the faculty for his indifference to the school's official ideals and apparently "enjoyed a certain reputation for villainy." He was even then approaching that break with the current social, intellectual, and literary norms and conventions which H. G. Wells described a dozen years later, after Crane's death, as his "enormous repudiations."

His single year of higher education, at two different colleges, was notably unsuccessful. At Lafayette College, where he enrolled in the fall of 1890, he played baseball and delivered self-assured literary opinions—Tolstoy, whose novel of the Crimean War, *Sebastopol* (1855), he had read, was the world's greatest writer; Flaubert's *Salammbô* (1862) was too long; Henry James's *The Reverberator* (1888) was a bore—but he did no work, and at the end of the term was advised to withdraw. At Syracuse University for the spring semester of 1891, he haunted the baseball diamond and, as a part-time reporter for the *Tribune,* scouted the Syracuse tenderloin and police court, studying "humanity," as he explained, rather than the "cut and dried" lessons of the classroom. He was known to his classmates and professors for his unconventionality and undisciplined brilliance. When the famous reformer Emma Willard visited, he refused to meet her on the ground

that she was a fool, and he shocked a professor by declaring in class that he disagreed with St. Paul. Sometime that spring he decided definitely to be a writer and began spending his afternoons in the cupola of the Delta Upsilon fraternity house reading and writing. Classmates recalled that he started a story about a prostitute, perhaps the first draft of *Maggie,* based on his observations in the Syracuse slums. He was also writing stories and sketches in imitation of Twain's tall tales and Poe's satirical hoaxes: a spoof on international politics, a yarn about a swarm of gigantic "electric-light" bugs stalling a locomotive, and a tale about a New York tenor's misadventure on a concert tour in Africa. But he neglected classwork, and by the end of the semester, when only one grade was reported for him, an *A* in English literature, he had already decided not to return.

At Asbury Park he apparently took charge of Townley Crane's *Tribune* column in the summers of 1891 and 1892, gathering news and gossip at the resort hotels, recording events at the Methodist religious conferences at nearby Ocean Grove, and reporting on the annual seminars in the arts and sciences at another neighboring community, Avon-by-the-Sea. During this time he was also working out a theory of art, evidently basing it partly on theories of realism advanced by Hamlin Garland and William Dean Howells, partly on ideas expressed by the realist painter-hero of Kipling's novel *The Light That Failed* (1891), and partly on the practical demonstration of the uses of irony and the handling of psychological realism in Tolstoy's *Sebastopol.* Strolling the beach with a friend who asked his advice about writing, Crane tossed a handful of sand in the air and said, "Treat your notions like that. Forget what you think about it and tell how you feel about it." "I cannot see," he wrote about this same time, "why people hate ugliness in art. Ugliness is just a matter of treatment. The scene of Hamlet and his mother and old Polonious behind the curtain is ugly, if you heard it in a police court. Hamlet treats his mother like a drunken carter and his words when he has killed Polonious are disgusting. But who cares?" This point of view, daring for the times, could have come from the radical-minded Garland, who declared with special emphasis in an 1890 article about Ibsen in the *Arena* magazine that "realism has only one law, to be true, not to the objective reality, but to the objective reality *as the author sees it.*" Crane met Garland in August 1891 when the critic was at Avon delivering lectures on Howells, "The City in Fiction" and "Sharpening Social Contrasts." The accuracy of the young reporter's *Tribune* summary of the lecture on Howells called Crane to Garland's attention. Crane's meetings with this pioneer realist in the two weeks of the critic's stay, when they talked literature and pitched baseball, may mark the real beginning of Crane's literary career. Garland's theory of realism ("Veritism"), based on Howells's and modified by his study of Eugene Veron's aesthetics and the theory of impressionism in painting, may have given shape to Crane's ideas; and Garland's stress on the importance of social problems of the city as a subject for the new fiction may have directed him to the slums of New York that fall in search of materials.

Meanwhile, he was practicing his literary skills in the satirical sketches of life on the Jersey coast he was sending the *Tribune* for Townley Crane's column, probably without his brother's supervision since Townley Crane was apparently more interested in the gambling games at the hotels than in the details of Stephen Crane's newspaper copy. Aware that his bailiwick was a kind of microcosm concentrating tendencies in American religious, cultural, and popular social life, Crane skillfully exploited the potential of its contrasts, picturing its scenes with irreverent irony and enthusiastic hyperbole. Describing preachers congregating at Ocean Grove for a religious conference, he notes that "sombre-hued gentlemen . . . are arriving in solemn procession, with black valises in their hands and rebukes to frivolity in their eyes," that "they greet each other with quiet enthusiasm and immediately set about holding meetings." At the resort hotels, in contrast, "pleasure-seekers arrive by the avalanche" and descend on the amusement park where a new "razzle-dazzle" (which is, "of course, a moral machine") is being installed and where an upright wheel revolves "carrying little cars, to be filled evidently with desperate persons, around and around, up and down." Later he reports that the "sombre-hued gentlemen" complained "that the steam organ disturbed their pious meditations on the evils of the world" and that "thereupon the minions of the law violently suppressed the wheel and its attendants." At Avon faculty and students at the School of Biology "are constantly engaged in inspecting great glass jars filled with strange floating growths," and "they vary this exciting pursuit by taking a boat and going to dig ecstatically for singular things in the mud flats. . . ."

Studying the middle-class vacationers at the hotels, he began to create a character type which would appear more fully developed in his fiction: the poignantly muddled, morally powerless egotist victimized by his sentimental heroic fantasies and delusions. "The average summer guest," he reported, "stands in his two shoes with American self-reliance, playing casually with his watch-chain, and looks at the world with a clear eye." He presumes a vast worldly knowledge even as he foolishly submits to the "arrogant prices" and deceits of the hotel proprietors. "However, deliberately and baldly attempt to beat him out of fifteen cents and he will put his hands in his pockets, spread his legs apart and wrangle in a loud voice until sundown." Crane describes the vain "golden youth," a "rose-tint and gilt-edge" swaggerer who appears on the beach with his narcissistic "summer girl, a bit of interesting tinsel flashing near the sombre-hued waves." And he presents the millionaire owner of the beach, James A. Bradley, as a pompous gentleman who displays signs advertising his principles of piety and gentility and cautioning guests against unseemly conduct on his beaches and who considers it a matter of import that the "ocean of the Lord's" lies "adjacent to the beach of James A. Bradley."

Vain illusion in context of a vast, remote, somber nature is the main theme of his first fiction, written about this time and published in the *Tribune* in the summer of 1892. Based on his hunting and fishing outings in the wilds of Sullivan County, New York, where he often went with friends in the summers, these stories, first collected and published as *The Sullivan County Sketches of Stephen Crane* in 1949, develop elaborately a metaphor of man at war against nature. The hero is the unnamed "little man," an outdoorsman who wanders over the landscape challenging what seems to him its inimical spirit, ludicrously assaulting caves, bears, mountains, and forests. He declares his courage in heroic orations which, as his three mocking companions understand because they share his anxieties, mask an almost hysterical dread of what he perceives as powers of an alien and hostile world. It is the apparent ambiguity, or the indeterminate reality, of the landscape that he finds particularly sinister: it sometimes seems terrifyingly hostile; sometimes serenely Edenic, in harmony with his own visions of the ideal; and sometimes both at once. This uncertainty challenges and enrages him, and when the landscape threatens he assaults it violently in desperate efforts to subdue it to his will. He is moved to explore a cave "because its black mouth gaped at him," he assaults a mountain which he thinks glowered at him, he hurls imprecations at the dreaded dark and kills a bear from ambush "with mad emotions, powerful to rock worlds." But in Crane's perspective, the cave's black mouth is merely "a little tilted hole" on a hillside, the phantom that haunts the night is merely a starving dog, the sinister mountain, once mastered, is after all merely "motionless under his feet," and the dead bear is only a dead bear.

The lurid light the little man's fancy casts on this problematic nature is represented in Crane's remarkable imagery, the impressionistic style he had been developing in some of his "news" reports since 1891. The style transmutes the real Sullivan County landscape into a dreamlike evocation of the little man's distraught fancy, a world curiously animistic, alternately menacing and tender or maddeningly enigmatic. Night masquerades "weird features . . . awfully in robes of shadow" and the sun gleams "merrily" upon waters that hold in their depth "millions of fern branches that quavered and hid mysteries." Religious imagery occurs frequently and often seems faintly facetious, as when tender, sentient pines in a field of snow "huddled together and sang in quavers as the wind whirled among the gullies and ridges," while a "dismal choir of hemlocks crooned over one that had fallen." Crane's irony is directed at the absurdity of his hero's swagger, his pompous oratory, and his outrageous self-esteem—vanities that conjure demons in the landscape.

Perhaps at Garland's suggestion Crane began his firsthand study of city life in the summer of 1891, going into the Bowery from his brother Ed's house in Lake View, New Jersey, within easy commuting distance of New York, to study the color of the city and the effect of the slums on the morals and manners of the poor. A year or so later, in August, 1892, his propensity for satire got the Crane brothers in trouble: the owner-editor of the *Tribune*, a Republican candidate that year for the vice-presidency of the United States, fired both Stephen and Townley Crane when the young satirist's graphic and ironic description of a labor-union parade in Asbury Park aroused the ire of the politically influential unionists. His ties with Asbury Park broken with the sudden demise of Townley Crane's agency, Stephen Crane now moved to the city, taking up precarious residence in the semibohemian quarters of aspiring actors, medical students, and commercial illustrators and beginning his study of tenement life in earnest. He disappeared for days into the Bowery disguised as a derelict, gathering material for sketches and newspaper stories, which he occasionally sold to the *Herald*, and perhaps for his novel *Maggie*, begun either at Syracuse in the spring of 1891 or, more likely, in the late fall after his first excursions into the city. He revised the novel in March 1892 and

showed it to Richard Watson Gilder, the editor of the *Century* magazine, who thought it "cruel" and "too honest" in its description of the sordid life of the slums. Crane revised it again that winter, but after it was rejected by editor after editor, Crane gave up. Borrowing money from his brother Will and raising some on the coal-mine stock he inherited from his father, he had the novel privately printed. It appeared in February or March 1893 under the pseudonym Johnston Smith, an ugly, yellow, little book no bookstore would take, except Brentano's, which stocked twelve copies and returned ten.

The novel studies the career of Maggie Johnson, a tenement girl driven by the cruelty, neglect, and selfishness of her family and acquaintances into the streets and ultimately to suicide. Hatred and violence dominate her childhood. She and her brother Jimmie are victims of a brutal, alcoholic mother who alternately beats them and smothers them with sentimental protestations of affection. Their sullen father objects to the beatings only because they disturb his rest. As a young man, Jimmie cultivates the friendship of Pete, a swaggering bartender who at sixteen wears the "chronic sneer of an ideal manhood," and who seems to the blossoming Maggie a man of infinite prowess and sophistication. The abusive mother finally drives Maggie to Pete's protection, and after he has seduced her, the Johnson family, outraged at this affront to their respectability, drive her from the tenement. When Pete abandons her, Maggie drifts into prostitution and finally, in a fit of despair, drowns herself. The book ends with the self-righteous mother shouting to her neighbors, "Oh, yes, I'll fergive her! I'll fergive her!"

The novel's sordid subject, its air of relentless objectivity (despite the implicit editorializing in its irony), and its sense of fatalism have led some historians to claim it as the first American naturalistic novel, a claim supported somewhat by Crane's statement that he intended it "to show that environment is a tremendous thing in the world and frequently shapes lives regardless." But later he noted other forces besides environment at work in the lives of the people he depicted. "I do not think much can be done with the Bowery," he wrote in 1896, "as long as the people there are in their present state of conceit. A person who thinks himself superior to the rest of us because he has no pride and no clean clothes is as badly conceited as Lillian Russell." In his sketch "An Experiment in Misery," a description of slum life published a few months after *Maggie,* he said he "tried to make it plain that the root of Bowery life is a sort of cowardice. Perhaps I mean a lack of ambition or to willingly be knocked flat and accept the licking." His stinging verbal irony constantly chastises the Johnsons and other characters for their moral blindness, which clearly is caused by their absurd and self-indulgent illusions about their world and themselves. This moralistic overtone casts doubt on the theory that *Maggie* is a naturalistic novel. It in fact seems closer to the Sullivan County sketches than it does to Emile Zola's *L'Assommoir* (1877) or other naturalistic novels which have been cited as possible models.

Maggie shares with the Sullivan County sketches the premise that self-aggrandizing conceit is a fundamental human motive and principal source of moral confusion. Like the little man, the swaggering Pete and Jimmie apprehend a world of menace which challenges their assumptions about their special virtues and their dreams of heroic destinies. Pete's manner stamps him as a man who has a "correct sense of his personal superiority," and Jimmie, sitting high on the driver's seat of his delivery truck, turns his sneer on the world below and

Price, 50 Cents

MAGGIE

A Girl of the Streets

(A STORY OF NEW YORK)

By

JOHNSTON SMITH

Copyrighted

Front wrapper for Crane's pseudonymous first novel

wonders at the crowd's "insane disregard for their legs and his convenience." The brutish Mrs. Johnson imagines herself "a good mudder," and the father, who complains to bartenders that his "home is a livin' hell," beats Jimmie with a beer pail for amusement. Everywhere in this world is evidence of the power of aggressive conceit to distort reality and twist moral vision.

Like the irony of the sketches, *Maggie*'s irony marks the contrast between reality and fantasy which is the basis of the novel's structure. In the opening sentence—"A very little boy stood upon a heap of gravel for the honor of Rum Alley"—a mean tenement alley is set against an embattled gang's false sense of the heroic. At the theater with Pete, Maggie is transported "by plays in which the dazzling heroine was rescued from the palatial home of her treacherous guardian by the hero with beautiful sentiments." To her these melodramas, with their "pale-green snow-storms," "nickel-plated revolvers," and daring rescues, are "transcendental realism." These sentimental distortions of reality are of course projections from the myths of popular culture, but they are also indications of a more pervasive perceptual distortion. The tenement world is pictured in metaphors which give it an almost surrealistic aura, a displacement of time and space, as, for example, when a looming tenement house is described as having "a hundred windows" and "a dozen gruesome doorways" that "gave up loads of babies to the street and gutter" while "withered persons . . . sat smoking pipes in obscure corners." Descriptions abound in unexpected perspectives and analogies. The inanimate world, like that of the little man, is fantastically alive ("The open mouth of a saloon called seductively. . . ."), and attributes of things observed seem often to be projections of the psychological world of the observer, as when Maggie, plying her trade as a prostitute, encounters "a stout gentleman, with pompous and philanthropic whiskers, who went stolidly by, the broad of his back sneering at the girl." These are the characteristics of style Frank Norris described memorably when he reviewed the novel in 1896, shortly after Appleton gave it, slightly revised, its first commercial publication. "The picture he makes," Norris wrote, "is not a single carefully composed painting, serious, finished, scrupulously studied, but rather scores and scores of tiny flashlight photographs, instantaneous, caught, as it were, on the run."

Impressive as it is, *Maggie* is by no means without flaws. Its unrelieved irony sometimes seems shrill and contrived, and the closing chapters are faulty in pacing and scale, though the saloon scene in which the "woman of brilliance and audacity" fleeces the sorry drunken Pete is as effective as any in the novel. The remarkable vitality of the language, the brilliance of its method, and the originality of its conception point toward the skillful, innovative art of *The Red Badge of Courage* and "The Open Boat."

But hardly anyone noticed it in 1893 except Howells and Garland, both of whom tried to interest editors in the young novelist's work, though without success. Howells invited him to tea and read some of Emily Dickinson's poems; shortly after which Crane himself began writing poems—or, as he preferred to call them, "lines." He continued his study of the tenements, writing a series of three stories about the adventures of a slum child named Tommie and more sketches of the Bowery. He began another novel of the slums, a companion piece to *Maggie,* but he laid it aside to finish a novel about the Civil War he began in the early spring of

1893, taking up the new tenement story in May 1894 when he wrote Garland that his new novel was "a bird." In November he wrote that it was finished and described it enthusiastically as "a New York book that leaves 'Maggie' at the post." Though not published until 1896, after his war novel, *The Red Badge of Courage,* had brought him international fame, the New York book, *George's Mother* (originally titled "A Woman Without Weapons") should be read in the context of *Maggie,* since both deal with similar subjects and themes.

George's Mother is a study of the relationship between a doting widow, Mrs. Kelcey, and her weak, self-indulgent son, George. Although the Kelceys share part of their gloomy tenement building with the Johnsons of *Maggie,* the pious Mrs. Kelcey, who is devoted to religion and her son's welfare, miraculously maintains in this moral chaos a decent, respectable home; and young George, though somewhat spoiled and selfish, is at first a steady and

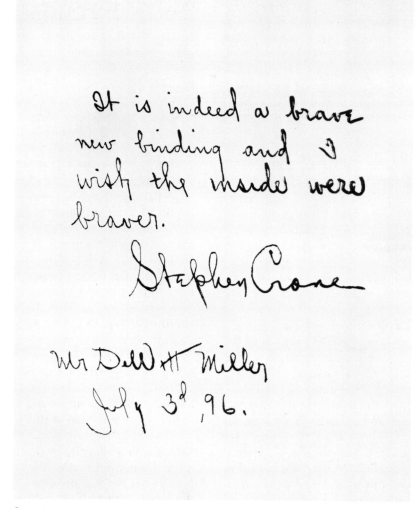

Crane's inscription in the revised 1896 edition of Maggie, *which was bound in cloth*

dependable provider. But when he joins an amiable crowd of saloon loafers whose flattery seems to confirm his high opinion of himself, he begins to change for the worse. Resentful of his mother's sentimental moralizing and her criticism of his conduct, convinced that only his saloon friends fully appreciate his moral and intellectual superiority, he rejects her authority, openly expressing his contempt for her religion and abusing her when she upbraids him for neglecting prayer meetings or queries him about his frequent absences. When he loses his job and tries to borrow money from his friends, they become suddenly indifferent. He drifts into a gang of neighborhood toughs and joins them in bullying people in the streets and cadging drinks at the corner saloon. Mrs. Kelcey is convinced almost to the last that these aberrations are temporary and that George is actually a brilliant and devoted son who under her loving care and firm moral guidance will one day make his mark in the world as a great man. When events finally dispel these illusions, she seems to lose her will to live, and as she lies dying from a sudden stroke, George is in a nearby vacant lot preparing to fight a member of his gang, Blue Billy, to settle a quarrel over a bucket of beer and their relative prowess with their fists.

Although it has been suggested that Crane drew on Zola's *L'Assommoir* for *George's Mother* as well as for *Maggie*, it seems clear enough that its sources are Crane's personal experience and the popular culture of his time. The germ for the mother-son relationship is in his own life, his mother being clearly the model for Mrs. Kelcey and Crane himself for George. One of Crane's nieces gave testimony of the attitude which enabled him to project his mother as the critically contemplated Mrs. Kelcey: "His mother's memory was dear to him, and although he never questioned her ways when he was outside the family portals, he did marvel always that such an intellectual woman, a university graduate . . . could have wrapped herself so completely in the vacuous, futile, psalm-singing that passed for worship in those days." George is a partial, guilt-inspired, self-portrait: "I used to like church and prayer meetings when I was a kid," Crane wrote in later years, "but that cooled off. . . ." Once, he remembered, an Italian on the beach at Asbury Park gave him "a long drink out of a nice red bottle," and arriving home feeling "ecstatic," he amiably agreed, to Mrs. Crane's surprise, to accompany her to prayer meeting. "Mother was tickled to death. I have frequently wondered how much mothers ever know about their sons."

The literature of the antisaloon movement, in

Corwin Knapp Linson portrait of Crane

which his mother actively participated and to which his father contributed a book, *Arts of Intoxication* (1870), is also a source for *George's Mother*, as are the views sentimentally dramatized in the popular temperance literature of the time, examples of which are Timothy Shay Arthur's famous *Ten Nights in a Barroom* (1854) and its sequel *Three Years in a Man Trap* (1872). The common elements of these melodramatic fictions are the ruined victim of drink, the blighted career, the impoverishment of the victim's family, and the death of a loved one—child, wife, or mother—from shame or drink-induced poverty. This stereotypical plot Crane merged with elements of his personal history, basing the character of George partly on himself and partly on the swaggering hero he created in the Asbury Park reports and the Sullivan County sketches, the pompous little man. This amalgamation of disparate elements, transmuted by the distancing effect of Crane's critical irony, suggests the undoubted complexity and ambivalence of his feelings about his Methodist heritage and the sentimental heroics celebrated in the popular literature of the 1890s.

Although *George's Mother* is somewhat less dramatic than *Maggie*, more explicitly satirical and more discursive in style, there are passages which are as effective as some of the best parts of its predecessor. The vulgarity of the amiable saloon brotherhood George so much admires—the banality of their talk and interests, their cheap sentiment, and above all their comical swagger and self-congratulatory complacency—are admirably portrayed. In the back room of the saloon, which is their retreat "from a grinding world filled with men who were harsh," these sympathetic comrades "understood that they were true and tender spirits," that they possessed "various virtues which were unappreciated by those with whom they were commonly obliged to mingle." The theme of fraternal order is prominently developed, as it is in much of Crane's work. In *The Red Badge of Courage* and "The Open Boat" it is treated sympathetically, but in *George's Mother*, as in the Sullivan County sketches, comradeship is problematical and uncertain, vitiated by swelling emotions of the self. The description of old Bleecker's party, which satirizes the stereotyped tastes, crippled thought, and vulgar emotions of the guests, of whom George is typical, is especially memorable. Mr. Zeusentell's nervous recitation of "Patrick Clancy's Pig," the comical social helplessness of the timid, the pompous self-confidence of Bleecker, and the ultimate dissolution of the party in an absurd blur of alcoholic violence are brilliantly rendered in Crane's best impressionistic style.

During the years 1893 and 1894, when he was reworking *Maggie* and writing *The Red Badge of Courage*, the poems in *The Black Riders*, and *George's Mother*, Crane continued, apparently by choice, to live in wretched poverty, convinced that suffering was beneficial to his art. This conviction he probably owed to Kipling's *The Light That Failed*, which he most likely read as early as 1891 and which apparently exerted considerable influence on his literary ideas. The hero of the novel, a realist painter who theorizes a good deal about realistic art, advocates poverty as a spur to creativity. "There are few things more edifying unto Art," he says, "than the belly-pinch of hunger," an idea Crane echoed later when he stated that the fact that *The Red Badge of Courage* was "an effort born of pain, despair, almost" made it "a better piece of literature than it otherwise would have been." Seeking firsthand experience of the bitter life of the poor, he lived in a gloomy, run-down, ill-heated old building, often as cold and hungry as the derelicts he studied in the Bowery. He slept in a tenement-district flophouse and stood in a breadline in a blizzard for the experiences he described vividly in the fine sketches "An Experiment in Misery" and "The Men in the Storm." During this period he wrote three stories about the street adventures of the toddler Tommie Johnson, whose death is mentioned in *Maggie*, and miscellaneous sketches about life in artists' studios, the police court, the saloon, and the amusement park.

But he also wrote during this time, beginning in March or April of 1893, *The Red Badge of Courage*, the novel of the Civil War which made him famous when it was published in 1895 and which has long been regarded as one of the classics of American literature. Unlike *Maggie* and *George's Mother*, which seem to honor a basic tenet of his theory of realism—namely, that truth in art is grounded in actual observation and experience—*The Red Badge of Courage* was apparently a pure invention, written years before its author ever actually saw a battle. But in an important sense real-life experience probably contributed little more to *Maggie* than to the war novel, for although he doubtless observed in the slums most of the particulars of *Maggie*, Crane appropriated the major elements of the novel from the myth of the slum girl, a myth readily accessible in the popular literature of the time—in Edgar Fawcett's *The Evil That Men Do* (1889) and in articles about slum life in the *Arena* magazine, for example. In these writings he found the character types (the pure, betrayed slum girl, the drunken parents, the vicious brother), the attitudes (the scorn of hypocritical respectability, the veneration of purity in women), actions (the fights, the seduction, the suicide of the heroine), and ideas (the powers of vanity and social forces)—all elements which he incorporated in the plot of *Maggie*. *The Red Badge of Courage* apparently originated in much the same way, deriving similarly from a popular myth of war. As Stanley Wertheim has shown, the numerous memoirs of war veterans which appeared in the 1860s, 1870s, and 1880s had established by 1890 "a distinctive literary convention for Civil War narratives, embodied in literally dozens of exemplars," many of which Crane, with his lifelong obsession with war, must have known. He obviously drew upon the common pattern of these chronicles for the major elements of plot in *The Red Badge of Courage*: the sentimental expectation of the young recruit moved to enlist by patriotic rhetoric and heroic fantasies of war, the resistance of his parents to his enlistment, his anxiety over the apparent confusion and purposelessness of troop movements, his doubts about his personal courage, the dissipation of his heroic illusions in his first battle, his grumbling about the incompetency of generals, and other such motifs, incidents, and situations. H. T. Webster has demonstrated that "everything [except style and execution] that makes up *The Red Badge of Courage* exists at least in germ" in Wilbur Hinman's *Corporal Si Klegg and His Pard* (1887), a story about a

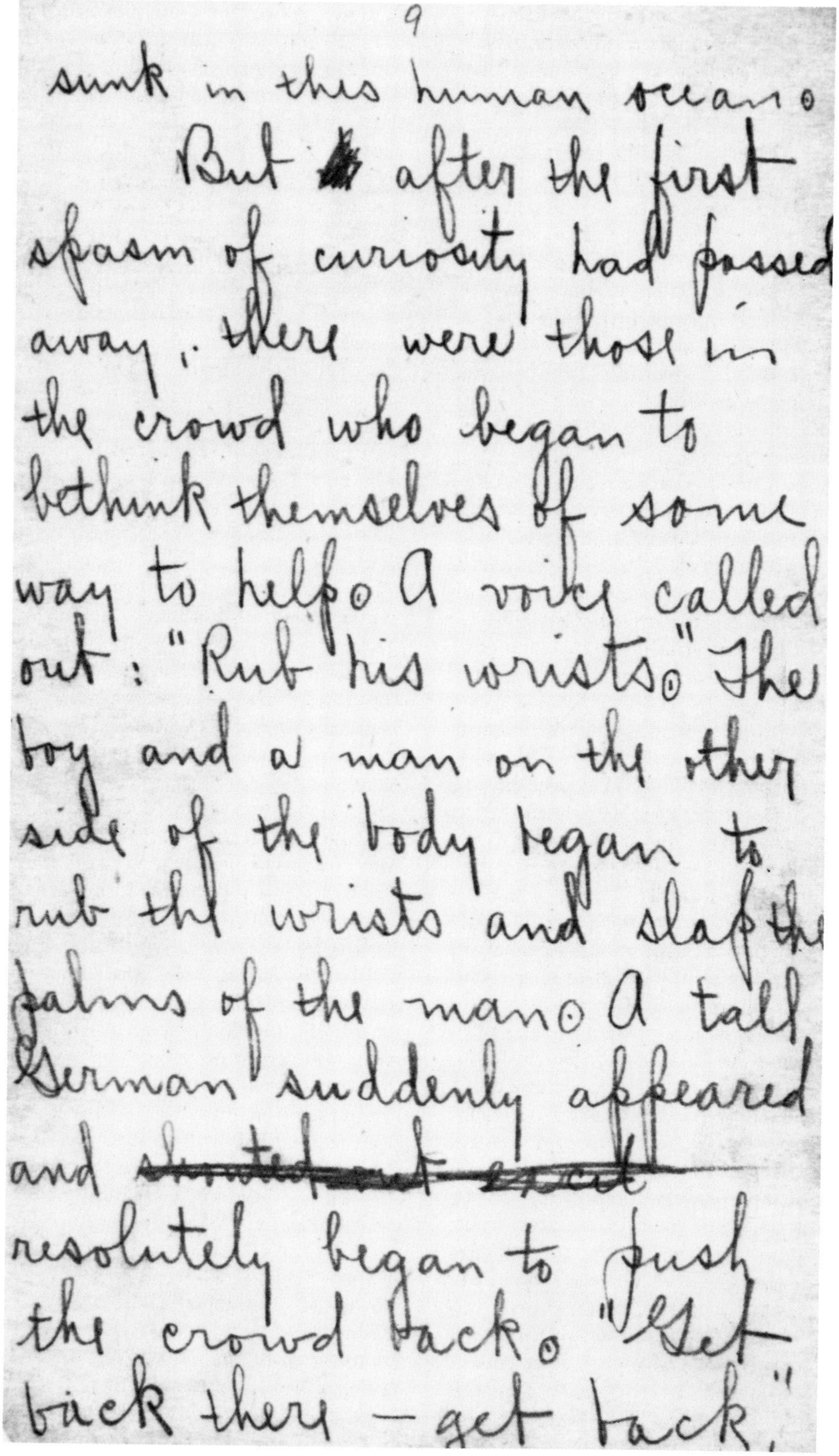

9

sunk in this human ocean.

But ~~the~~ after the first
spasm of curiosity had passed
away, there were those in
the crowd who began to
bethink themselves of some
way to help. A voice called
out: "Rub his wrists." The
boy and a man on the other
side of the body began to
rub the wrists and slap the
palms of the man. A tall,
German suddenly appeared
and ~~shouted out excu~~
resolutely began to push
the crowd back. "Get
back there — get back."

Draft of "When Man Falls a Crowd Gathers" in Crane's notebook

raw recruit who, like Crane's Henry Fleming, is given to romantic self-dramatization and anxious worry about his personal courage but who eventually proves himself in battle and is praised for heroism by his colonel.

It is style and execution directed by a powerful imagination which transmutes these commonplace narrative conventions into literature; in a sense, the literary method and the ideas Crane developed in his *Tribune* pieces and New York writings are more relevant to the question of origins than any of these historical accounts. He probably developed his method chiefly on the model of Tolstoy's ironic, impressionistic *Sebastopol*, which demonstrates the powerful dramatic effect of representing reality in the imagery of the hero's psychological life. He may have found in Kipling's *The Light That Failed* an adaptable illustration of the dramatic use of color, as his repetitive use of Kipling's wrathful red-sun image in *The Red Badge of Courage* and other works suggests. The style he shaped from these models was validated theoretically by Howells's concept of realism as the truthful treatment of materials and by Garland's idea that truth is the artist's subjective view of it. Thus when Crane turned to his imaginary war in the spring of 1893, he was in command of formidable literary resources: the plot elements provided by the conventionalized Civil War story, an attitude toward it sanctioned by contemporary theories of realism, a literary character developed in his studies of the little man in his Asbury Park and Sullivan County pieces, and a vivid impressionistic style inspired by Tolstoy and Kipling.

Another force at work in the shaping of the novel was the effect on Crane's imagination of his intense preoccupation at this time with religious questions, the explicit evidence for which is in his book of poems, *The Black Riders*. More than half of the sixty-eight poems of the volume are on religious themes—the inscrutability of God, man's futile quest for God, God's wrath, the terrors of a Godless universe, and man's pride and impotence—which express Crane's anguished uncertainty about God's character and man's relation to him. Is God dead and man abandoned to an indifferent universe, the questioning runs, or is he, on the contrary, terribly present in the world, a God of wrath breathing hatred and malice on helpless, sinful man? Occasionally he appears in visions of poignant yearning as kindly and compassionate, and again as removed to impossible distances, far beyond the range of human knowledge. Worrying about these puzzling contradictions, the speaker is torn between piety and blasphemy. "I hate Thee, unrighteous picture,"

he rages against the God of wrath. "So, strike with Thy vengeance / The heads of those little men / Who come blindly. / It will be a brave thing." To a man who says the roaring thunder is the voice of God, the speaker says, "not so. / The voice of God whispers in the heart / So softly / That the soul pauses." And once he agonizes over the thought that in "the mighty sky" is nothing "But a vast blue, / Echoless, ignorant, —." The God of wrath and the God of indifference often appear in images of hostile or stolidly impassive mountains. In one poem, angry mountains appear as an army of vengeance against a defiant little man: "On the horizon the peaks assembled; / As I looked, / The march of the mountains began"; and in still another: "Once I saw mountains angry, / And ranged in battle-front. / Against them stood a little man; / Aye, he was no bigger than my finger." And yet another man, "clambering to the house-tops" to appeal to the heavens, finds God, at last, in "the sky . . . filled with armies."

The recurrent motif of the little man against the hostile mountain first appears in expanded form as one of the 1892 Sullivan County stories, "The Mesmeric Mountain," a fablelike narrative of the little man's war against nature which not only outlines the plot of *The Red Badge of Courage* but also explains the symbolic meaning of the motif in the novel, where it occurs a number of times at crucial points in the narrative. The hero of the fable is the little man, who, contemplating the "ecstatic mystery" of a road leading into a pine forest, decides to follow it, certain that "it leads to something great or something." Making his way through the forest, battling "hordes of ignorant bushes" and "obstructing branches," he pauses at sundown to rest near the foot of a mountain. Gazing idly at the mountain in the fading light of "the red silence" of the sinking sun and the "formidable" shadows of the pines, he suddenly perceives that the mountain has eyes and is watching him. It appears about to attack, and the little man springs to his feet and flees in terror. Later, he pauses and, returning cautiously, is horrified to see that the mountain "has followed him" and is now about to crush his head with its heel. In a blind rage, he attacks, flinging pebbles against its face and scrambling wildly up toward its summit, which he perceives as "a blaze of red wrath." When he reaches the top at last, he thrusts his hands "scornfully in his pockets" and swaggers victoriously about, confidently identifying distant landmarks. He does not notice that "the mountain under his feet was motionless."

Nearly all of the elements of the war novel are

First page of the final manuscript for The Red Badge of Courage

in the fable. Like Henry Fleming in *The Red Badge of Courage*, the little man is motivated to his adventure by heroic expectations of "great things," and like Henry's mother, the little man's camping companion disapproves of the undertaking. Both heroes project their anxieties on the landscape, animating it in their morbid fancies with menacing life. Both are obliged to force their ways against an unfriendly nature, "ignorant bushes" and "obstructing branches." Both are terrorized by perceptions of hostile supernatural forces which seem to threaten their destruction, and both are driven in desperation to attack them. Finally, both entertain illusions of victory and celebrate their delusive triumphs in secret ceremonies of self-congratulation.

The prominence of the imagery of menace and threat in the landscape in *The Red Badge of Courage*, particularly in the images of mountains and hills, clearly shows that the novel, the fable, and the poems all have a common origin in Crane's imagination. Although the novel enlarges the metaphor of the angry mountain to include nature in general, the mountain is nevertheless a central symbol. A passage in chapter 17 describes Henry's reaction when his lieutenant praises him for his violent assault against the attacking enemy: "He had been a tremendous figure, no doubt," Henry thinks complacently. "By this struggle he had overcome obstacles which he had admitted to be mountains. They had fallen like paper peaks, and he was now what he called a hero." Obviously, Henry is symbolically identical with the vainglorious hero of the fable who struts like a victor on the peak of the motionless mountain.

The passage suggests that Henry from the beginning has been as much concerned about how he measures up to nature—and, by extension, to God—as he has about how he measures up to war. For in his imagination, the terror of war—"the blood-swollen god"—and the terror of nature become one. Mountains, fields, streams, the night, the sun, appear in his disordered fancy in guises of living creatures, monstrous and terrible. He sees the "red eye-like gleam of hostile campfires set in the low brows of distant hills" and "the black columns [of enemy troops] disappearing on the brow of a hill like two serpents crawling from the cavern of night." Crossing a little stream, he fancies that the black water looks back at him with "white bubble eyes," and that "fierce-eyed hosts" lurk in the shadows of the woods. When he deserts in his first battle he flees, not the attack of enemy troops alone, but the "onslaught of redoubtable dragons," the approach of the "red and green monsters." Al-

though as these examples show, nature appears in a variety of metaphorical forms—monsters, dragons, ogres, demigods—the figure of the sinister mountain recurs often and crucially, bearing, it would seem, the symbolic meaning given it in the poems in *The Black Riders*.

But the meaning of the landscape shifts with Henry's moods and fortunes: his fear is its hostility, his complacency is its sympathy. Humiliated by his panicky flight from his first battle, he turns to nature for solace and comfort. Wending his way in a peaceful forest, he is gratified to observe that nature is "a woman with a deep aversion to tragedy." He reaches a secluded place where "high arching boughs made a chapel," and he supposes that tender nature has furnished it for his need and convenience. He pushes the "green doors" aside and is suddenly transfixed with horror. Sitting on the "gentle brown carpet" in the "religious half-light" is a rotting corpse, an abomination in the very nave of peaceful nature. When he tries to flee, it seems to him that nature turns on him in a fury, that the snagging branches and brambles at the threshold of the delusive chapel now try to throw him on the unspeakable corpse. But at a distance, the aspect of the horrible chapel seems to change, like the enraged mountain in the fable: "The trees about the portal of the chapel moved soughingly in a soft wind. A sad silence was upon the little, guarding edifice." Earlier, after his company has beaten off an enemy attack, he has glanced upward and felt "a flash of astonishment at the blue sky and the sun gleaming on the trees and fields"; it has seemed to him "surprising that nature had gone tranquilly on with her golden processes in the midst of so much devilment." Such shifts in Henry's perception are signs of his spiritual disorder. A victim of his vain expectations, he can never be certain whether nature is hostile or sympathetic, or merely indifferent.

When Henry is returned to his regiment by the humble and competent "cheery soldier," he finds that his braggart friend Wilson, "the loud soldier," veteran now of a battle, has undergone a remarkable change: he no longer regards anxiously "the proportions of his personal prowess" but shows now a "fine reliance" and "quiet belief in his purposes and abilities." "He was no more a loud young soldier." Henry wonders "where had been born these new eyes" and notes that Wilson "apparently had now climbed a peak of wisdom from which he could perceive himself as a very wee thing." The meaning of the mountain image has clearly shifted: it is no longer the angry mountain driving an exasperated little man to desperate but futile assault, but

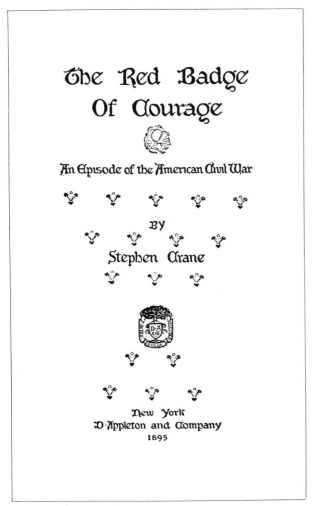

Title page for the novel that established Crane's reputation

"a peak of wisdom" from which he is able to perceive correctly his humble place in the scheme of things. Having exorcised his corrupting vanity, Wilson sees himself and the world clearly and truly, as Henry later does also after he yields himself to the larger purposes of the regiment and heroically leads a charge against the enemy.

But the problem with Henry is different. Wilson's conversion is merely given; Henry's must, according to the narrative logic, be demonstrated. Figuratively, he is the little man at war against God as well as against the Confederate enemy, and the war against God he cannot win. When Crane describes Henry's moral transformation in the final chapter, he simply drops the issue of his hero's adversary relation to the landscape. Revising the text before submitting it to Appleton for publication, he deleted in the last chapter all crucial reference to Henry's experience with nature. He struck the sentence "Echoes of his terrible combat with the

arrayed forces of the universe came to his ears," and he struck also Henry's thought that the God of wrath could have justly commanded his obeisance—"that he had been wrong not to kiss the knife and bow to the cudgel." He deleted references to the indifference of nature and to Henry's momentary impulse to see himself "once again fraternizing with nature," remembering presumably the harmony he felt with it in the forest before finding the corpse in the little chapel-like bower. Crane deleted also Henry's reflection that he could "no more stand upon places high and false, and denounce the distant planets." As these cancellations suggest, Crane's attitude toward God was markedly ambivalent, as it is in *The Black Riders,* and his purpose in the revision was apparently to avoid the problem of resolving the whole uncertain issue of Henry's war against God. This evasion is undoubtedly the reason for the diminished vitality of the chapters describing Henry's heroic battlefield exploits: the slackness of the irony, as in the notoriously sentimental description of Henry's feeling about the rescued flag, and the weakening of the symbolic resonance of the imagery.

The irreconcilable tension between Crane's religious and heroic imaginations is clearly revealed in this weakness in construction. If the second half of the novel is much like the conventional heroic war story (expressive certainly of one side of Crane's nature), the first half is powerfully and originally imaginative. The pathos of Henry's alienation in an incomprehensible world, of his helplessness under the spell of his vanity, and of his poignant yearnings for a sign is brilliantly rendered. Generations of readers have found memorable the fantastic descriptions of the landscape, the gay humor of the country maiden's heroic battle to rescue her cow from the fat thieving soldier, the horror of the discovery in the little forest chapel, the awesome death of Jim Conklin, the patient and selfless suffering of "the tattered man," the manliness of the anonymous "cheery soldier," and other scenes, incidents, and characters.

The first publication of *The Red Badge of Courage,* like that of *Maggie,* was irregular and discouraging. *McClure's Monthly* accepted it, presumably intending to publish it as a serial. But after six months of waiting, Crane, doubtful that any such plan would ever be carried out, withdrew it and sold it for ninety dollars to Irving Bacheller, who carved away two-thirds of the text and distributed this abridged version to his newspaper syndicate. It appeared in the *Philadelphia Press,* the *New York Press,* and many other newspapers across the nation (in serial form in many) in early December 1894. Pleased by the favorable response of editors and readers and impressed by Crane's demonstrated powers of description, Bacheller engaged him as a special correspondent and ordered him on a journalistic expedition to Mexico via Nebraska, Louisiana, Arkansas, and Texas. Hastily completing arrangements for the publication of *The Black Riders,* which an editor friend had recommended to a Boston publisher of experimental poetry, and of *The Red Badge of Courage,* the newspaper version of which had attracted the attention of the publisher D. Appleton, Crane departed on his four months' journey west in late January 1895.

The first leg of his trip took him to Lincoln, Nebraska, where he arrived, via St. Louis and Kansas City, in early February 1895. He was already known to the young Nebraskan Willa Cather, a part-time reporter for the *Nebraska State Journal,* who hoped to become a novelist also, and she queried him about writing as he lounged about the newspaper offices, shabby and dispirited, waiting for money from Bacheller. He journeyed into surrounding counties in search of information for an article about Nebraska farmers and their battles against the fury of their weather. In imagery like that he had used in depicting the landscapes of Sullivan County and Chancellorsville, where Henry first encountered "the blood-swollen god" of war, Crane described the agony of a land scorched by a "terrible and inscrutable wrath of nature," a screaming wind, "hot as an oven's fury," that raged over the rich, brown crops "like a pestilence" while the farmers stood by in helpless despair. "It was as if upon the massive altar of the earth, their homes and their families were being offered in sacrifice to the wrath of some blind and pitiless deity." This powerful description he wrote, paradoxically, during a blizzard which brought upon the people another "strange and unspeakable punishment of nature," winds from the north that swept over the devastated country like "wolves of ice." The graphic imagery of tempest-driven snowflakes "fleeing into the south, traversing as level as a line of bullets, speeding like the wind" he adapted nearly three years later in his masterful little tragedy of the Nebraskan plains, "The Blue Hotel": "great whirls and clouds of flakes, swept up from the ground by the frantic winds, were streaming southward with the speed of bullets."

In an article from Galveston, Texas, which he reached in early March after brief visits to New Orleans and Hot Springs, Arkansas, he noted ironically the disparity between the tourist's romantic expectations, conditioned by heroic legends of the West, and the actuality of the city's paved streets, webs of telegraph wires, clamorous trolleys and other such indications of industrial progress. He noted the contrast again in an article from San Antonio in which he protested "an eloquent description of the city which makes it consist of three old ruins and a row of Mexicans sitting in the sun" when it is actually "a totally modern" city with "rows of handsome business blocks" and "the terrible almighty trolly car." This diminishment of the mythical Old West by the encroaching reality of civilization is the theme of three of his western stories, "The Blue Hotel," "The Bride Comes to Yellow Sky," and its sequel, "Moonlight on the Snow."

His attraction to the legendary, however, was by no means diminished by his discovery that an "eloquent description" of the Old West is more valuable as a "masterly literary effect" than as a guide to reality. His romantic imagination was profoundly stirred by the heroic legend of the Alamo, "the greatest memorial to courage which civilization has allowed to stand." In recounting the story of a man named Rose, the only member of the Alamo band to refuse Colonel Travis's call for volunteers to defend the mission to the death, Crane's imagination created a poignant moment. Rose stepped forward "with a strange inverted courage" and announced his decision. "He bade them adieu and climbed the wall. Upon its top he turned to look down at the upturned faces of his silent comrades." The suspended moment seems to concentrate the entire question of courage, a question Crane explored more elaborately in "The Five White Mice," a story he wrote in 1896 about a Mexican adventure of a character called the New York Kid. The Kid, facing in a despair of terror a deadly knife-wielding caballero on a gloomy night street in Mexico City, discovers when he at last finds the courage to draw his revolver that his formidable adversary has also been in a kind of despair of terror. His adversary leaps back with a startled cry and melts into the darkness. From a distance he calls, "Well, señor, it is finished?" The story ends: "Nothing had happened."

By mid-March 1895 Crane was in Mexico, "hungry for color, form, action," as he noted in one of his articles, and as his dispatches show, the color and movement of Mexican life registered powerfully on his imagination. He found in the mysterious landscape and impassive mien of the people intimations of some alien and impalpable reality and drew once again on the tropes he used to describe Henry's feverish sense of the battlefields in

The Red Badge of Courage. He was struck by "the inscrutable visage" of a sheepherder, by "the masses of crimson rays" from household fires in a village at dusk "where dark and sinister shadows moved," by the empty, blazing skies of Mexican noons, and by mountains which "stand like gods on the world" and silence the speech of men who "fear that they might hear." Such intimations of menace, he discovered, were not always merely literary or metaphysical. On an excursion in the Mexican backcountry, he and his guide, Miguel Itorbe, were asleep in a primitive village inn when they were awakened by the arrival of a gang of horsemen led by the bandit Ramon Colorado. Crane overheard their discussion of a plan to rob and perhaps murder him, but Colorado was distracted at the crucial moment by the arrival of a band of women. At dawn Crane and his guide fled into the desert on horseback, but the bandits, discovering their flight, gave chase and were gaining steadily on them when a company of mounted police appeared suddenly and drove Colorado and his men away. The hero of the story, which Crane wrote in September 1895 under the title "Horses—One Dash," is the swift little horse which responds to the crisis with supreme courage and determination. It is a masterful evocation of a sense of crisis, furious motion, and rapport between horse and rider.

The best of the stories based on the western adventure, however, are "The Bride Comes to Yellow Sky" (written in 1897) and "The Blue Hotel" (written in 1898). "The Bride Comes to Yellow Sky" introduced some of the themes and situations that later became standard conventions in the plots of commercial Westerns in pulp magazines and cowboy movies: the conflict between gunman and lawman, the climactic "face off" or "walkdown," the yielding of the lawless West to the irresistible influences of civilization. The six-gun wizard Scratchy Wilson, "about the last one of the old gang that used to hang out along the river," periodically goes on drunken rampages and shoots up the little plains town of Yellow Sky, Texas. For years Marshall Jack Potter has restored order on these occasions by facing Scratchy down, but one day when Jack is in San Antonio secretly getting married, the gunman launches an attack. Clad in boots that had "red tops with gilded imprints of the kind beloved in winter by little sledding boys on the hillsides of New England" and a "maroon-colored flannel shirt . . . made, principally, by some Jewish women on the east side of New York," he strides up and down the street with revolvers in both hands, firing at everything that moves. The marshall and his bride arrive on the 3:42 from San Antonio, and as they round a corner of the depot, encounter Scratchy face to face. Dropping the revolver he has paused to load, the old outlaw whips the other from its holster like lightning and flings a ferocious challenge at his old adversary. When the marshall advises him that he is unarmed and, moreover, married, Scratchy is paralyzed with astonishment. "Married?" he stammers finally, noticing at last "the drooping drowning woman at the other man's side." Gradually the full meaning of the situation dawns on him. "Well," he says, "I 'low it's all off, Jack." "He was not a student of chivalry," Crane writes; "it was merely that in the presence of this foreign condition he was a simple child of the earlier plains. He picked up his starboard revolver, and placing both weapons in their holsters, he went away."

Scratchy clearly plays—not too seriously—a role created partly by the legend-mongering Eastern imagination, as his costume was created largely by the New York garment industry. In "The Blue Hotel" Eastern influences have dire consequences. The hero, a half-crazed Swede newly arrived in Rompers, Nebraska, his head full of fantasies of violence, is convinced that the blue hotel, where he is the guest of a genial Irishman, old Scully, harbors desperadoes intent on his murder. The terrified Swede's odd behavior leads him finally into a fight with Scully's son, whom the Swede soundly thrashes as Scully and two other guests look on. Flushed with victory, the Swede leaves the hotel, pushing arrogantly through a raging blizzard as if he has defeated it as well as young Scully. In the local saloon he orders whiskey, and blustering and boasting, invites a gambler and his table companions to drink with him. When the gambler refuses, the Swede wrathfully seizes him by the throat. Suddenly a blade "shot forward, and a human body, this citadel of virtue, wisdom, power, was pierced as easily as if it had been a melon. The Swede fell with a supreme cry of astonishment."

"The Blue Hotel" is an ingenious adaptation of the theme of *The Red Badge of Courage* and some of the Sullivan County stories. Like Henry Fleming and the little man, the Swede is at war against nature, and, like them, he can imagine personal victories over it. At one time the vainglorious Henry entertains visions of his triumph over fallen "paper peaks," and once congratulates himself as the deserving recipient of nature's warm sympathy and friendly solicitude. The Swede, having battled his way to the saloon through the blizzard, finds himself likewise equal to this adversary: "I like this weather," he tells the bartender. "I like it. It suits me." Describing this hero's brave progress through the fury of the storm, Crane reflects, more darkly than anywhere in *The Red Badge of Courage,* on man's awesome presumptuousness: "One viewed the existence of man then as a marvel, and conceded a glamour of wonder to these lice which were caused to cling to a whirling, fire-smote, ice-locked, disease-stricken, space-lost bulb. The conceit of man was explained by this storm to be the very engine of life." Like *The Red Badge of Courage,* "The Blue Hotel" is rooted in the deepest sources of Crane's imagination: his radical sense of man's alienation in a problematical universe.

His western adventure contributed significantly to Crane's literary resources, providing not only new subjects and settings but confirmation of the themes and ideas of the earlier fiction. The vast plains of Nebraska and Texas, the awesome mountains of Mexico, the violent western weather, seemed to confirm his convictions about the ways of nature. The primitive, half-lawless settlements like his fictional War Post, Yellow Sky, Rompers, and Tin Can stimulated his sense of the legendary Old West and its theatrical myth of acute crisis and exquisite personal challenge. And tales of courage and commitment in face of supreme dangers sharpened his ambivalent sense of the heroic ideal which, as in the war novel, he paradoxically both celebrated and ironically mocked.

When he returned to New York City in mid-May 1895, he paused to distribute signed copies of *The Black Riders,* which had appeared a few days before his arrival, and then went west to his brother Edmund's house in Hartwood, in Sullivan County, where he lived, with frequent sojourns in the city and other places, for more than a year. Here he received the first reviews of *The Black Riders,* most of which complained of his eccentric disregard for conventional poetic forms, though a few also praised his power and originality. One well-known reviewer, Harry T. Peck of the *Bookman,* praised the poet as "a bold—sometimes too bold—original, and powerful writer of eccentric verse," characteristics which Peck and others thought linked him to Whitman and Dickinson. By early summer his literary reputation among editors and writers such as Richard Harding Davis, Irving Bacheller, S. S. McClure, R. W. Gilder, and Willis Hawkins was well established, and on the strength of it he was invited to join The Lantern Club, a literary society headed by Bacheller. Crane was apparently searching at this time for a salaried position on some newspaper, for he was in Philadelphia in early September to discuss his possible appointment as drama critic for the *Philadelphia Press;* but he was not hired, despite the editor's personal admiration of the short version of *The Red Badge of Courage* the *Press* had printed in 1894. Crane stayed on in Philadelphia for a while, writing "Horses—One Dash" and basking in his local fame as a war writer. He was in New York when *The Red Badge of Courage* was published in October (1895), then in Hartwood, eagerly following the reviews and pondering his literary situation.

As his letters of late 1895 and early 1896 suggest, his literary situation was somewhat problematic, paradoxically because of the immense success of *The Red Badge of Courage.* It created something of a sensation in late 1895, and before the end of that year Crane was a famous man, an international celebrity known on both sides of the Atlantic for his brilliant and uncompromisingly realistic portrayal of war. But the novel seemed to prove that he was more a realist in theory than in practice, and he was painfully aware that his literary mentors, Howells and Garland, would take it as clear evidence of his abandonment of serious literary purpose, a view Howells more than hinted when he wrote Crane early in 1896: "For me, I remain true to my first love, 'Maggie.' That is better than all the Black Riders and Red Badges." Crane had anticipated the point, however, for in November 1895, about the time he was expressing surprise at his sudden fame and reporting that his incoming mail at Hartwood had "reached mighty proportions," he felt obliged to reaffirm his program as a literary realist: "I decided [in 1892]," he wrote an editor, "that the nearer a writer gets to life, the greater he becomes as an artist, and most of my prose writings have been toward the goal partially described by that misunderstood and abused word, realism." He complained about the war novel, as if he blamed it for the predicament it had put him in by making him an authority on war, which he had never seen, and by establishing him as a master of realism, whose first principle he had conspicuously violated. He began in those early months of his fame to derogate the novel: "I suppose I ought to be thankful to 'The Red Badge' but I am much fonder of my little book of poems, 'The Black Riders.' My aim was to comprehend in it the thoughts I have had about life in general, while 'The Red Badge' is a mere episode in life, an amplification" (a comment which may suggest, incidentally, that he was conscious of a significant relationship in the themes of the two books). And he referred to it variously as the "damned 'Red Badge,' " "that damned book," "the accursed 'Red Badge.' "

His belief that a true literary realist ought to write only about what he has experienced firsthand perhaps helps to explain his reluctance to write more war stories, which editors, with their eyes on the success of the novel, were bound to demand. In October 1895 he began a new novel, *The Third Violet*, published in 1897, a thin little comedy of manners based on personal experience which, though in accord with current realistic theory, was, as he realized almost from the beginning, not the kind of realism

his genius was best suited for. In November he reluctantly turned again to war stories. "I am writing a story—'The Little Regiment' for McClure," he complained. "It is awfully hard. I have invented the sum of my invention with regard to war and this story keeps me in internal despair." "The Little Regiment" became the title story of his collection of war stories published late in 1896, and he was still laboring over it in February 1896 when he wrote his friend Nellie Crouse, "I am engaged in rowing with people who wish me to write more war-stories. Hang all war-stories." He referred to "Three Miraculous Soldiers," another war story he was

writing at the time, as a "little" story in a note to McClure in January, warning him that the agreement they had made for Crane to write a series of war stories for the Phillip's-McClure Syndicate might not be altogether advantageous to the publisher. "I am perfectly satisfied with my end of it," he advised, "but your end somewhat worries me for I am often inexpressibly dull and uncreative and these periods often last for days"; and again, "I feel for you when I think of some of the things of mine which you will have to read or have read." But by the end of February he had written a total of five new war stories since the publication of *The Red Badge of Courage*: "Three Miraculous Soldiers," "An Indiana Campaign," "The Veteran," "An Episode of War," and "The Little Regiment." He sent at least three—"Three Miraculous Soldiers," "The Veteran," and "The Little Regiment"—to McClure, but only the last two appeared in *McClure's Magazine*. When he finished "The Little Regiment" at the end of that month he described it to the editor of the *Critic* as "a novelette which represents my work at its best," but he felt privately that it showed his failing inspiration as a war writer. He added emphatically that it was "positively my last thing dealing with battle."

The general tendency in these stories, published in late 1896 as *The Little Regiment*, is toward a more conventional realism. Although they draw heavily on the characteristic metaphors and images of *The Red Badge of Courage*, they tend toward a more conventional description, picturing the world not as a projection of the hero's anxieties and fantasies, as in the earlier fiction, but as a world objectively described by a disinterested narrator. The poignantly alienated little man, whose distressed psychological life provides a colorful and dramatic version of reality, appears in none of these stories, and the haunted landscape, though still invested with mystery and menace, is a landscape seen by the narrator, not by the fanciful hero. Thus the radical conflict between the hero and nature which accounts for the intensity and resonance of *The Red Badge of Courage* is abandoned in *The Little Regiment*. The heroes of these stories appear as more or less realistic social types. Unlike Henry Fleming, whose raw perceptions, fantasies, and mercurial emotions are the source of the poetry of the war novel, the heroes of *The Little Regiment* are more normally rational and judgmental. In "A Mystery of Heroism" Fred Collins charges across a field under heavy fire to fetch a bucket of water from a distant well, an action which recalls Henry's desperate charges under fire in the novel. But Collins, unlike Henry, is reflective and critical, conscious of his vanity and its ethical and social significance. The menace in the field is that of Confederate artillery, not a threat born of his guilt or fanciful expectations.

This tendency toward a more objective method and more discursive style is characteristic of the other stories as well. The hallucinatory imagery—the violent colors, the mystical air of menace and dread, the hyperbolic evocation of the monstrous which represents the hero's distraught moral sense—is notably subdued. "An Indiana Campaign" is a comedy of manners gently satirizing old Major Tom Boldin and the folks of Migglesville for their unsophisticated reaction to an idle rumor about a rebel soldier hiding in a cornfield. Although the heroine of "Three Miraculous Soldiers" has certain heroic ambitions, like her very distant fictional cousins Henry and the little man, her homely common sense protects her against fanciful schemes—"gorgeous contrivances and expedients of fiction"—to rescue three friendly soldiers imprisoned in her father's barn. The title story, "The Little Regiment," is an anecdote about two brothers whose deep mutual affection is concealed by their constant bickering, and the function of the war setting, which is profusely elaborated, is merely to provide the moment of danger which tests their true feelings. This story, three months in the writing, engaged Crane in a "daily battle with a tangle of facts and emotions," a difficulty which arose doubtless from his attempt to adapt the reflexive style of the novel to an inappropriate subject.

More successful is "The Veteran," a brief sequel to *The Red Badge of Courage* which tells how Henry Fleming as an old man sacrifices his life trying to rescue two colts from a burning barn, and points clearly toward the new style Crane was apparently seeking. The imagery of the familiar metaphysical landscape is much subdued and is largely external to old Henry's thought. The lean, disciplined prose moves the story rapidly from Henry's account of running away from his first battle at Chancellorsville to the narrator's sharp description of his final rush into the blazing barn, just before the roof falls in. The story begins with a brief glimpse of "three hickory trees placed irregularly in a meadow that was resplendent in spring-time green," a faint reminder of that spring long ago when young Henry found the idyllic landscape suddenly filled with "red and green dragons." In the distance, standing now invincible, is another version of the familiar little chapel, "the old, dismal belfry of the village church." Telling the story of his flight, old Henry can now appreciate "some comedy in this recital." The enemy, he recalls, appeared as a

"lot of flitting figures," and he remembers thinking at the moment of panic that "the sky was falling down," that "the world was coming to an end." Thus he describes in a serene latter-day recollection the "red and green dragons." The barn in which he meets his death is presented at first glance in "its usual appearance, solemn, rather mystic in the black night," but when he hurls aside the door, "a yellow flame leaped out at one corner and sped and wavered frantically up the old grey wall. It was glad, terrible, this single flame, like the wild banner of deadly and triumphant foes." This picture of satanic fire, "laden with tones of hate and death, a hymn of wonderful ferocity," crosses with the image of demonic war, and old Henry at last challenges the God of wrath he was permitted to evade at the end of *The Red Badge of Courage.* Thus the story skillfully adapts Crane's familiar symbolic materials to a new style, the style essentially of "The Open Boat," a story "after the fact," as the subtitle notes, but one which, like "The Veteran," is composed of elements drawn obliquely from his mythic imagination.

The Third Violet (1897), which he finished in December 1895, is a romantic comedy of courtship somewhat in the manner of Howells, though without his mentor's consummate mastery of the realism of specification or his grasp of the intricacies of social codes and conventions. Except in "The Pace of Youth," a charming 1893 story about the elopement of two merry-go-round attendants, Crane never wrote successfully about romantic love, and *The Third Violet*, which tells the story of an impressionist painter's wooing of a New York belle, is perhaps the most inconsequential of his efforts to deal with the subject, though his 1899 novel *Active Service* is also a notable failure. For the plot of *The Third Violet* he attempted to tie together two strands of autobiography: his unhappy summer romance with Helen Trent, whom he knew at Asbury Park in 1891, and his life in the gloomy old Art Students' League building he shared with other indigent bohemians in his early years in New York. The courtship begins when Billie Hawker meets Miss Grace Fanhall at a Sullivan County summer vacation hotel and continues in the city after the return of Hawker to his studio and Miss Fanhall to her elegant New York town house. The story ends when Hawker is permitted to understand at last that Miss Fanhall cares for him, an issue addressed somewhat esoterically in Miss Fanhall's manner when she makes her lover a gift, on three different occasions, of a single violet. Except for a vivid portrait of Hawker's awkward and endearing Irish setter, Stanley, and a few happy touches in the characterization of studio life, the novel could hardly be identified on the basis of its style as Crane's. He was aware himself that it was alien to his vision and method. When he mailed the manuscript to Appleton in December, he wrote a friend the same day, "It's pretty rotten work. I used myself up in the accursed 'Red Badge.' " *The Third Violet* is interesting chiefly as evidence of his literary uncertainty at this time and as an indication of the range of his experimentation under the pressure of his sudden recognition as a realist.

By mid-1896 he had arranged for the publication of all the books he had completed to date. Appleton accepted *The Third Violet* (though somewhat reluctantly, delaying its publication until the spring of 1897) and *The Little Regiment,* which appeared at the end of 1896. The publisher also scheduled a new edition of *Maggie,* which had languished in obscurity since its private publication in the spring of 1893, and Crane began revising it in March 1896, largely by smoothing out some of its doubtful grammar and deleting profanities. Another publisher, Edward Arnold, bought *George's Mother,* and in June both of these companion novels appeared. Although there was the usual carping among the reviewers about the ugliness of war and poverty, the books were on the whole well received, some reviewers finding *The Little Regiment* even better than *The Red Badge of Courage* because the stories admitted more of the spirit of romance. Very few denied the power and originality of the pictures of slum life in *Maggie* and *George's Mother,* evidence perhaps that readers were beginning to come to terms with Crane's innovative methods. He began no more big literary projects after finishing the war stories, though he considered and rejected McClure's earlier proposals that he write a novel about Washington politics and another book describing some of the major battles of the Civil War. Instead, he arranged with Hearst's *New York Journal* for a series of articles on New York low life and returned once again to the study of the Tenderloin which had been interrupted by his western excursion.

That fall (1896), while gathering material for a piece on New York police courts, he became involved in an incident which significantly affected the course of his life, since as a result of it he was never able to live in peace in New York City again. As he was leaving the Turkish Smoking Parlors late one September night with two women he had been talking to about their experiences in police courts, a prostitute named Dora Clark approached and joined the group. When Crane stepped aside for a

moment to escort one of the women to a cable car, a policeman suddenly appeared and arrested Dora Clark for soliciting. Crane protested, taking the matter as another indication of the notorious brutality and corruption of the police, the very subject he was investigating for his article. The officer threatened to arrest Crane, but the novelist followed him and his prisoner to the station and testified against him in the police-court hearing. Later, he sent a lengthy telegram of protest to Police Commissioner Theodore Roosevelt, and when Dora Clark's suit against the officer came up in court in October 1896, Crane testified again in her behalf. The affair was thoroughly aired in the newspapers, which hailed Crane as a hero for defending the abused Dora, though not without a good deal of sly humor at his expense. The affair cost him the friendship of Commissioner Roosevelt, who had been an early and enthusiastic admirer of *The Red Badge of Courage,* and earned him the lasting hatred of the New York police force, which, as a friend who was with him during the affair observed, "bent all its unscrupulous energies to discrediting him and making New York too hot for him." After he left New York in November 1896, he never lived in the city again; he was harrassed by the police as late as January 1899, when he paused there briefly to visit friends on his way home to England from Havana and the Spanish-American War. The policeman he testified against was Charles Becker, who was electrocuted in 1913 for hiring the murder of a gambler who threatened to expose his connections with the underworld.

In November, Irving Bacheller, convinced that Cuba's revolt against Spain would develop into a full-blown revolution, engaged Crane once more as a special correspondent, this time with an assignment far more dangerous and demanding than the one which sent him to the West and Mexico. He was now a war correspondent, a profession he would follow, off and on, for the rest of his life. Arriving in Jacksonville, Florida, in November 1896, with $700 in gold in his money belt, he began his search, in a tense atmosphere of international conspiracy and intrigue, for passage to Havana in one of the filibustering ships running arms and supplies to the Cuban insurgents. He met, fatefully, Cora Taylor, a colorful adventuress who had deserted her husband, a British army and foreign-service officer, to become the proprietress of a discreet brothel, the Hotel de Dream. She later accompanied Crane to Greece as the first woman war correspondent and still later to England as his common-law wife. In late December 1896 he signed

Cora Crane as war correspondent in 1897

on the crew of the filibuster ship *Commodore* as a seaman, and on New Year's Eve, carrying a cargo of cased guns and ammunition and a company of Cuban insurrectionists, the *Commodore* steamed down the St. Johns River, and finally, after delays caused by running aground twice on sandbars in the river, stood to the open sea.

His masterful dispatch to the *New York Press* on 6 January describes vividly the disaster which overtook the *Commodore*: the discovery on the night of 1 January that the groundings had opened her seams, the frantic and futile efforts of the crew to bail the flooded engine room when the pumps failed, the confusion in the management of the lifeboats which resulted ultimately in the stranding of seven crew members on the sinking ship, the horror of abandoning a terrified crewman in the water who threatened to swamp the heavily loaded dinghy Crane shared with the captain and two other crew members, the awesome plunge of the ship as it went down, and the death of the ship's oiler when the dinghy was swamped in the surf in the attempt to land it at Daytona Beach on 3 January. "The

history of life in an open boat for thirty hours," Crane wrote at the end of his report, "would no doubt be very instructive for the young, but none is to be told here now." Though physically exhausted and, according to one report, profoundly depressed for days after the ordeal, he must have begun "The Open Boat" almost immediately, for it was finished and in the hands of his literary agent by the end of February.

For this masterful story, Crane drew on literary resources he had been developing since the Sullivan County sketches of 1892. The metaphysical landscapes in these stories and in *The Red Badge of Courage* become in "The Open Boat" the ambiguous seascape which appears to the anxious correspondent, the protagonist of the story, in a bewildering variety of aspects. The sea is nature—"nature in the wind, and nature in the vision of men"—and it appears sometimes cruel, wrathful, and deadly; sometimes wildly beautiful and picturesque; and again merely stolidly indifferent. Like the hero of Crane's poems about God and the hero of his war novel, the correspondent feels that this problematic nature somehow holds the key to the mystery of existence, but unlike these earlier heroes, who confront nature's mystery in helpless and inarticulate confusion, the correspondent is fully conscious and introspective, aware of his egotistical presumptions and of the multifarious ironies in his shifting perceptions of his plight. He knows, as Henry does not, that uncertainty of perception is central to the whole issue. Speaking for himself and the men, he articulates through the narrator their anxiety in the face of uncertainty and mere seeming. To them, "the waves *seemed* thrust up in points like rocks." "Viewed from a balcony," their battle against the raging sea "would *doubtless* have been weirdly picturesque." It was "*probably* splendid" it was "*probably* glorious" (italics added). It merely *occurs* to a man that nature does not regard him as important, and for the correspondent the "high cold star on a winter's night" symbolizes nature's attitude toward the men in the boat. Sometimes the correspondent is in the boat, his vision exquisitely narrowed to the threat of the "slaty wall" of waves; sometimes he seems to observe their plight from afar, critically, sadly, even mockingly.

The structure of this powerful story is based on a number of such ironic contrasts, as in, for example, the dramatic antitheses in the exchange among the cook, the correspondent, and the oiler on the difference between a lifesaving station and a house of refuge. The cook's assertion that they will be rescued by the lifesaving crew at the house of refuge near Mosquito Inlet is like a propositon for a debate, challenged, after a balanced question and answer, by the correspondent's statement that houses of refuge have no lifesaving crews. The impasse is addressed by the oiler: "Well, we're not there yet"; but the cook, unwilling to abandon his hopeful illusion, restates his proposition, though allowing now for the correspondent's challenging discrimination between lifesaving stations and houses of refuge. The passage ends with the skeptical oiler's repeated "We're not there yet." The formal design of the colloquy, with its balance and contrast of assertion and the refrainlike comment of the oiler, emphasizes the cook's presumption, an ironic effect powerfully reinforced when the narrator intrudes to say almost casually: "It is fair to say here that there was not a life-saving station within twenty miles in either direction; but the men did not know this fact, and in consequence they made dark and approbrious remarks concerning the eyesight of the nation's life-savers."

Ironic tension is also sustained by the memorable imagery of the contradictory aspects of nature. To the men, the sea gulls seem at different times to be allies or agents of a hostile nature, for "the wrath of the sea was no more to them than it was to a covey of prairie chickens a thousand miles inland." The gull that attacks the captain and threatens to swamp the boat seems malicious. When the birds come close, they seem "uncanny and sinister" and "somehow gruesome and ominous" as they stare at the men with "black bead-like eyes." But later, when they are seen from afar "in slanting flight up the wind toward the gray desolate east," they seem to represent not nature's wrath but the beauty of her order and design.

This ambiguity is suggested also in such phrases as "the terrible grace of the waves," and memorably in the description of the shark, the unnameable "thing" whose "enormous fin" cuts "like a shadow through the water." Like the sea gulls, it strikes the correspondent as an agent of nature's inscrutable malice, and yet he can reflect, as he looks dully into the sea and swears, that "the speed and power of the thing was to be greatly admired."

But in the end, it is the "high cold star" and the desolate distant wind tower which seem to the correspondent to be the true correlatives of nature's significance. The wind tower, "standing with its back to the plight of ants," seems to represent "the serenity of nature amid the struggle of the individual. . . . She did not seem cruel to him then, nor beneficent, nor treacherous, nor wise. But she was indifferent, flatly indifferent." So much has the lit-

tle man changed since he strutted on the conquered mountain, oblivious to its unconscious neutrality, and since he forlornly, in one of the poems about God, addressed the sky and found it filled with armies.

In Jacksonville again, Crane regained his strength under Cora Taylor's care and set about trying once again to find his way to Cuba. After a month of wading the swamps south of the city, trying to elude U.S. Navy patrol boats, he gave up and signed on with the *New York Journal* to report the fighting between the Greeks and Turks. He was in New York in mid-March, where he was joined shortly by Cora Taylor, also going to Greece as a correspondent for the *Journal*. In London he arranged to report the war for the *Westminster Gazette* and then set out for Greece, arriving in Athens about mid-April 1897.

He then began a month of hectic chasing after battles and rumors of battles. He was in Arta briefly, then in Athens again to meet Cora Taylor when she arrived, under the name Imogene Carter. They joined the *Journal* staff and went north to Volo, where they heard on 4 May about the battle at

Crane in Athens, May 1897

Velestino. Crane arrived on the second day of the engagement, and from a mountain battery on a ridge overlooking Greek fortifications in the valley below, he witnessed real war for the first time. He followed the slow Greek retreat south, and eventually arrived in Athens from Chalcis with a transport of wounded soldiers two days before the armistice was declared on 20 May.

After the Florida experience Crane was never very strong again. He was ill and tired much of the time he was in Greece, and he stayed on until June, resting. He had found Greece and the war disappointing, complaining that observing the battle at Velestino was "like trying to see a bum vaudeville show from behind a fat man who wiggles," though he also told Joseph Conrad later that "The Red Badge is all right. I have found [war] as I imagined it." His fine story "Death and the Child," written that fall in England and the only significant fiction for which he drew on his Greek experience, shows that he described real war and imaginary war in much the same way, shifting events from the real world to the symbolic world of his vision. The hero of "Death and the Child," Peza, is an Italian war correspondent of Greek extraction moved by patriotic sentiment to join the fighting against the Turks. He approaches the front, excited by prospects of battle, and works his way finally to a rifle pit directly in the Turks' line of advance. His enthusiasm is momentarily checked when the officer in charge instructs him to take a rifle and bandolier from a dead soldier, but when he hesitates one of the soldiers performs the task for him and Peza takes his place, with misgivings now, at the parapet with the riflemen. He becomes aware of a rising panic, a sense of being pulled by the dead soldier's bandolier down "to some mystic chamber under the earth." Looking behind him he sees that the corpse's head is turned a little toward him, "as if to get a better opportunity for the scrutiny. Two liquid-looking eyes were staring into his face." Peza is suddenly overwhelmed by panic. Tearing madly at the bandolier—"the dead man's arms"—he bolts toward the rear. Later, a tiny child, deserted in the confusion of war, finds him far behind the lines where he has flung himself to the ground, exhausted and despairing. "Are you a man?" the child asks, and the correspondent, "confronting the primitive courage, the sovereign child, the brother of the mountains, the sky and the sea," knew that "the definition of his misery could be written on a wee grass blade." The story is clearly a version of *The Red Badge of Courage,* which it resembles in the incident of the panicky flight, in its implication of

Stephen Crane, 1899

nature in a drama of self-discovery, and in its imagery of the psychological distress that motivates the hero. But it is also like "The Open Boat" in that its protagonist is in a measure—up to the moment of panic—introspective and contemplative. "Death and the Child," "The Open Boat," and the two fine western stories which he also wrote that fall, "The Bride Comes to Yellow Sky" and "The Blue Hotel," show that Crane's powers were most formidable in works treating the crossing themes of man in war and man in nature, themes with which his more discursive, flexible, and reflective style, first developed in the sea story, discovered new and richer significance.

In London in June 1897 Crane decided to settle in England permanently to avoid gossip about his irregular relationship with Cora Taylor and the malice of the New York police, and after a few weeks in the city, moved to Ravensbrook House, Oxted, Surrey, where he plunged into work, writing with astonishing speed "The Monster," "Death and the Child," "The Bride Comes to Yellow Sky," and "The Blue Hotel." He was received cordially by prominent literary men, including Bernard Shaw, Ford Madox Ford, and Joseph Conrad. He discovered especially in Conrad, whose recently published *The Nigger of the Narcissus* (1897) he greatly admired, a kindred artistic spirit, and the mutual regard of the two men doubtless benefited them both. By the time he finished "The Blue Hotel" in February 1898, he was weary again, suffering poor health, as he had off and on ever since his ordeal in Florida, and the burden of debts he owed publishers and editors for advances. When the *Maine* exploded on 15 February, he seemed hardly to notice, but suddenly in April intimations of war touched his imagination, and "white-faced with excitement," he dragged Conrad about London to help him borrow passage money to New York, where he planned to join the navy. "Nothing could have held him back," Conrad wrote. "He was ready to swim the ocean." He sailed shortly, leaving Cora at Ravensbrook House to deal with their creditors as best she could.

It is regrettable, as John Berryman notes, that he drove himself at the expense of health and energy to those "boring false wars, away from the passionate private real war in his mind." In Cuba as a war correspondent, after failing the physical examination for the navy, he was ill and disconsolate, distracted and reckless. He exposed himself needlessly to Spanish fire at Guantánamo, where he landed with the marines in June, and again at San Juan in July, deliberately attempting suicide, some observers thought. Richard Harding Davis, the dean of war correspondents, who witnessed and reported the incident at San Juan, thought Crane was nevertheless the most successful war reporter in Cuba, citing Crane's "Marines Signalling Under Fire at Guantánamo" as one of the best dispatches of the war. After San Juan Crane was at Old Point Comfort, Virginia, resting, then in New York, where he learned at the *World* offices that he had been fired for filing a report for a wounded correspondent for a rival newspaper. He signed on with the *Journal* and immediately headed south to cover the Puerto Rican campaign, which ended when the armistice was signed in August. He then disappeared for months, burying himself in Havana to write most of the war stories for *Wounds in the Rain* (1900) and to finish his long, tedious novel about a correspondent's courtship in war-time Greece, *Active Service* (1899), begun at Ravensbrook House in 1898.

He was in New York six weeks at the end of the year, and then in England again in January, at Brede Place, an ancient manor house near Rye in Sussex which Cora had rented in his absence. He slowly recuperated from his Cuban adventure, writing little at first, reading mostly, and seeing his numerous literary friends. Henry James, who lived at Rye, was a frequent visitor, and Crane renewed his friendship with Conrad. H. G. Wells and Edward Garnett, both of whom wrote brilliant early critical studies of Crane, also came often, as did the journalist Robert Barr and other writers.

Three books appeared in 1899: *War is Kind,* his second volume of verse, whose title piece is the best, and the most complex, of all his poems; the Greek war novel, *Active Service;* and *The Monster,* whose title story, finished at Oxted in 1897, is a sharp study of community malice, written in a flattened, circumstantial style that moves toward conventional realism. The setting of "The Monster" and "His New Mittens," both in *The Monster,* is Whilomville, a fictional town modeled on Port Jervis, New York, where Crane lived as a young boy. This town is also the setting for the pieces he began writing later in the year, the amusing and often

Crane's grave in Hillside, New Jersey

astute anecdotal studies of child life later collected as the *Whilomville Stories* (1900). He also wrote more Cuban war stories to add to those he wrote in Havana, published posthumously as *Wounds in the Rain* (1900), and two, oddly, about an imaginary war, one of which, "The Upturned Face," a grim story about a military burial under sniper fire, is a six-page masterpiece.

There are flashes of his formidable powers in many of these new stories and in the long sketch "War Memories," but consumption gained rapidly on him in the early months of 1900, and he was too weak to undertake major work. In the spring he worked on his swashbuckling romance, *The O'Ruddy* (1903), which he was probably writing as insurance for Cora Crane, but when he became too ill to continue, he turned the manuscript over to Robert Barr, who wrote the last half according to Crane's plot outline. He was hemorrhaging regularly by May, and Cora took him to Dover, and then, desperately, to a sanitarium at Badenweiler, in the Black Forest. There he died on 5 June, five months short of his twenty-ninth birthday.

Letters:

Stephen Crane's Love Letters to Nellie Crouse, edited by Edwin H. Cady and Lester G. Wells (Syracuse: Syracuse University Press, 1954);

Stephen Crane: Letters, edited by R. W. Stallman and Lillian Gilkes (New York: New York University Press, 1960).

Bibliographies:

Joan H. Baum, *Stephen Crane* (New York: Columbia University Libraries, 1956);

Matthew J. Bruccoli, *Stephen Crane 1871-1971* (Columbia: Department of English, University of South Carolina, 1971);

R. W. Stallman, *Stephen Crane: A Critical Bibliography* (Ames: Iowa State University Press, 1972).

Biographies:

Thomas Beer, *Stephen Crane: A Study in American Letters* (New York: Knopf, 1923);

John Berryman, *Stephen Crane* (New York: Sloane, 1950);

R. W. Stallman, *Stephen Crane: A Biography* (New York: Brazillier, 1968).

References:

Frank Bergon, *Stephen Crane's Artistry* (New York & London: Columbia University Press, 1975);

Edwin H. Cady, *Stephen Crane* (Boston: Twayne, 1980);

Andrew Crosland, *A Concordance to the Complete Poetry of Stephen Crane* (Detroit: Gale Research/Bruccoli Clark, 1975);

Daniel Hoffman, *The Poetry of Stephen Crane* (New York: Columbia University Press, 1957);

Milne Holton, *Cylinder of Vision: The Fiction and Journalistic Writing of Stephen Crane* (Baton Rouge: Louisiana State University Press, 1972);

Marston LaFrance, *A Reading of Stephen Crane* (New York: Oxford University Press, 1971);

James Nagel, *Stephen Crane and Literary Impressionism* (University Park & London: Pennsylvania State University Press, 1980);

Eric Solomon, *Stephen Crane: From Parody to Realism* (Cambridge: Harvard University Press, 1966).

Papers:

Most of Crane's manuscripts and papers are in the Special Collection, Columbia University Libraries; the Stephen Crane Collection, Syracuse University Library; the Berg Collection, New York Public Library; and the Waller Barrett Collection, Alderman Library, University of Virginia.

Richard Harding Davis
(18 April 1864-11 April 1916)

Joseph R. McElrath, Jr.
Florida State University

SELECTED BOOKS: *The Adventures of My Freshman*
(Bethlehem, Pa.: Privately printed, 1884);
Gallegher and Other Stories (New York: Scribners,
1891; London: Osgood, McIlvaine, 1891);
Stories for Boys (New York: Scribners, 1891; London:
Osgood, McIlvaine, 1891);
Van Bibber and Others (New York: Harper, 1892;
London: Osgood, McIlvaine, 1892);
The West from a Car-Window (New York: Harper,
1892);
The Rulers of the Mediterranean (New York: Harper,
1894; London: Gay & Bird, 1894);
Our English Cousins (New York: Harper, 1894; London: Low, 1894);
The Exiles and Other Stories (New York: Harper,
1894; London: Osgood, McIlvaine, 1894);
The Princess Aline (New York: Harper, 1895; London: Macmillan, 1895);
About Paris (New York: Harper, 1895; London: Gay
& Bird, 1896);
Three Gringos in Venezuela and Central America (New
York: Harper, 1896; London: Gay & Bird,
1896);
Cinderella and Other Stories (New York: Scribners,
1896);
Dr. Jameson's Raiders vs. the Johannesburg Reformers
(New York: Russell, 1897);
A Year from a Reporter's Notebook (New York: Harper,
1897);
Cuba in War Time (New York: Russell, 1897; London: Heinemann, 1897);
Soldiers of Fortune (New York: Scribners, 1897; London: Heinemann, 1897);
The King's Jackal (New York & London: Scribners,
1898);
The Cuban and Porto Rican Campaigns (New York:
Scribners, 1898; London: Heinemann, 1899);
The Lion and the Unicorn (New York: Scribners,
1899; London: Heinemann, 1899);
With Both Armies in South Africa (New York: Scribners, 1900);
In the Fog (New York: Russell, 1901);
Ranson's Folly (New York: Scribners, 1902; London:
Heinemann, 1903);
Captain Macklin: His Memoirs (New York: Scribners,

1902; London: Heinemann, 1902);
"Miss Civilization": A Comedy in One Act (New York:
Scribners, 1905);
Farces: The Dictator, The Galloper, "Miss Civilization"
(New York: Scribners, 1906; London: Bird,
1906);
Real Soldiers of Fortune (New York: Scribners, 1906;
London: Heinemann, 1907);
The Scarlet Car (New York: Scribners, 1907);
The Congo and Coasts of Africa (New York: Scribners,
1907; London: Unwin, 1908);
Vera the Medium (New York: Scribners, 1908);
The White Mice (New York: Scribners, 1909);

Once Upon a Time (New York: Scribners, 1910; London: Duckworth, 1911);

The Consul (New York: Scribners, 1911);

The Man Who Could Not Lose (New York: Scribners, 1911; London: Duckworth, 1912);

The Red Cross Girl (New York: Scribners, 1912; London: Duckworth, 1913);

The Lost Road (New York: Scribners, 1913; London: Duckworth, 1914);

Peace Manoeuvres: A Play in One Act (New York & London: French, 1914);

The Zone Police: A Play in One Act (New York & London: French, 1914);

The Boy Scout (New York: Scribners, 1914);

With the Allies (New York: Scribners, 1914; London: Duckworth, 1914);

"Somewhere in France" (New York: Scribners, 1915; London: Duckworth, 1916);

With the French in France and Salonika (New York: Scribners, 1916; London: Duckworth, 1916);

Adventures and Letters of Richard Harding Davis, edited by Charles Belmont Davis (New York: Scribners, 1917).

COLLECTION: *The Novels and Stories of Richard Harding Davis*, Crossroads Edition, 12 volumes (New York: Scribners, 1916).

Richard Harding Davis is principally remembered as a popular romancer of the 1890s and early 1900s. The bulk of his writing was designed to please and titillate the popular readership, and, until his death in 1916, Davis regularly and rapidly wrote exactly what his large following wanted. True love, wrongs righted, vibrantly attractive heroines, manly heroes, and despicable villains were the familiar features of his short stories, novels, dramatic farces, and musical comedies. When he died he was receiving the highest fees paid for short fiction by American magazines. By 1916 he no longer resembled the bright, clever, and promising young artist who rose to national prominence in the early 1890s and seemed the American counterpart to Rudyard Kipling and Guy de Maupassant. Like others of his generation, the young Davis seemed an avant-garde figure who would help to shape the character and improve the quality of the nation's belles lettres in a period of cultural transition. At the end of his long and profitable career, though, it was difficult for eulogists to do more than reminisce about how he had stirred and charmed them long ago.

Born in 1864 to an equally promising writer, Rebecca Harding Davis, Richard was early intro-

duced to the literary environment in which he would spend his life. Rebecca Harding Davis had earned a permanent place in the publishing world three years earlier, when her novella *Life in the Iron Mills* had appeared in the *Atlantic Monthly*; and, because it was perceived as starkly realistic, she too enjoyed the image of an innovative fiction writer. With a mother who was a sought-after author, and with a father, Lemuel C. Davis, who was an inveterate theatergoer as well as a journalist, Richard and his brother Charles were virtually destined to enter the profession they later embraced. Luckily for Richard professional writers did not require college degrees in the 1880s; for, despite the genteel cultural environment in which he was reared, he failed to receive a degree from Lehigh University (1882-1885), and a year of studying political economy at John Hopkins (1885-1886) added little to his store of knowledge. His mother knew the New York and Boston publishers who would soon open doors to her son; and Mr. Davis, who knew every prominent actor of the day, held an editorial position at the *Philadelphia Public Ledger* and wielded some influence that would be used in his son's behalf. When Davis terminated his unsuccessful flirtation with higher education in 1886, he quite naturally turned

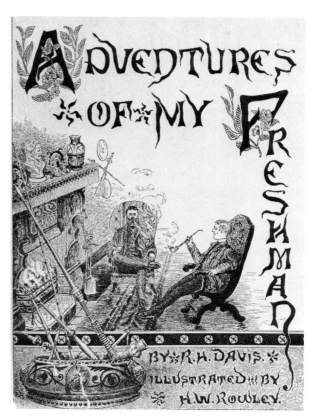

Front wrapper for Davis's first book, published when he was twenty

to writing for a living and, with his father's help, he enjoyed apprenticeships at two Philadelphia newspapers, the *Record* (1886) and the *Press* (1886-1889). His relationships with both papers were strained because Davis—whose egotism knew no bounds—balked at the idea of conventional news reporting. He insisted on seeing himself as an exceptional person; he demanded the opportunity to write special features; and by late 1889 he was granted the means to follow his bent. In Arthur Brisbane at the *New York Evening Sun* he found the indulgent superior that he needed. As Frank Norris later did when serving his journalistic apprenticeship in San Francisco, Davis specialized in sensationally describing the most colorful—and sometimes sordid—aspects of New York City life; and he was allowed to fictionalize the materials he found in his urban environment. This resulted in two developments in Davis's early career that were similar to those of many turn-of-the-century realists. As E. W. Townsend, Stephen Crane, Frank Norris, and Theodore Dreiser would do later, he turned to the lower socioeconomic urban environment for a setting and a cast of slum characters. In short stories such as "A Leander of the East River" (1890), Davis did not follow the method of Emile Zola. He was never fascinated by the horrific dimensions of the urban order; ever the gentleman, he never wrote a work like Crane's *Maggie* (1893). But he did venture among character types unfamiliar in the literature of genteel America; and he did contribute to the process of legitimizing new subjects having to do with low life that more radical realists would soon make their special province.

While working for the *Evening Sun*, he also produced a series of short stories that demonstrate his relationship to another literary tradition leading up to and becoming a part of the realistic movement then being championed by William Dean Howells. Davis, under the influence of his mother, had read widely during his youth. By 1889, he had been shaped by traditional favorites such as Fielding, Dickens, Thackeray, and Trollope. Davis had a comic and satiric sensibility, and in the novel-of-manners tradition he created for the *Evening Sun* readers the young New Yorker who was his most memorable character: Courtlandt Van Bibber. Even after he became the managing editor of *Harper's Weekly* in 1891, Davis continued in story after story to develop Van Bibber as the type of all that was both noble and silly in the life of Newport mansions, Long Island estates, and Manhattan's Park Avenue. When these stories were made available to a national readership in *Gallegher and Other*

Richard Harding Davis

Stories (1891), *Stories for Boys* (1891), and *Van Bibber and Others* (1892), Van Bibber became the medium through which the middle class saw, understood, and chuckled over the sometimes laudable but often preposterous antics of the rich. He was so well known that a "Van Bibber" brand of cigarettes was marketed; and Frank Norris repeatedly appropriated the figure for his magazine pieces of 1896-1898 and then modeled his heroes along the same lines in *Moran of the Lady Letty* (1898) and *Vandover and the Brute* (1914). As Norris admitted in *Blix* (1899), his most autobiographical novel, Davis was an irresistible influence on aspiring fiction writers of the mid-1890s; and the satirical view of polite society in Norris's novels may be easily traced to his experience of reading Davis.

In the early 1890s Davis also revealed promise in his travel writing, commissioned by *Harper's Weekly*. *The West from a Car-Window* (1892), a collection of the *Harper's Weekly* articles, allied Davis to the antiromantic sensibility best represented by Hamlin Garland in *Main-Travelled Roads* (1891). Davis approached a traditionally romantic subject, the American West, and in his travels he recorded the absence of any true romance, closing his account with the admission that he was glad to get back to New York City. *The West from a Car-Window* however, did not prove a spectacular success, and from then on Davis was more careful in his choice of topics. His readers and his publisher wanted something more colorful, and the success-oriented young author responded accordingly. He gravitated toward more exotic regions for several series of travel pieces, all republished in book form after magazine appearances: *The Rulers of the Mediterranean* (1894), *About Paris* (1895), *Three Gringos in Venezuela and Central America* (1896), *Cuba in War Time* (1897), and *A Year from a Reporter's Notebook* (1897)—all of which enhanced the physical and cultural landscapes and glamorized the role of the observer-writer whose experiences seemed the stuff out of which schoolboys' daydreams are made.

By the mid-1890s, Davis's career had become mainly a matter of conscious and deliberate grandstanding—of striking attractive poses in decadent Paris, on jungle trails in Central America, and on the battlefields of Cuba or any country in which war was being waged. He traveled to every available battle that occurred between 1897 and 1916. His image as the dashing journalist was quickly established, and he made himself the hero of eight travel books that read like adventure romances. In his fiction, a similar development took place. After the publication of his first and best novel, a successful synthesis of the features of the novel of manners and the romantic love story, *The Princess Aline* (1895), he began turning out romances in which the heroes closely resembled the adventurous narrators of his travel books. Robert Clay in *Soldiers of Fortune* (1897) is the quintessential Davis hero: brave, moral, sensitive, and all-capable. He wins the heroine—an embodiment of the "Gibson Girl" named Hope—after routing all of the villains bent against him in a "banana republic," one of Davis's favorite settings for dramatic intrigue. "Evil" is crushed when Clay triumphs over a group of South American revolutionaries; "Good" is restored as Clay eliminates all threats to the American-owned Valencia Mining Company; and the hero and heroine are able to look forward to a life of undying love. From 1897 to 1916 names and situations would change. Sometimes the heroes would battle against less formidable forces, but, in the end, morality and love would triumph. Davis's readers loved his many permutations of the same material, and they showered riches upon him, but reviewers

Col. Theodore Roosevelt and Davis in Cuba, 1898

would become increasingly irritated as the years passed and lament Davis's lack of literary maturation. As Rebecca Harding Davis had broken new ground in *Life in the Iron Mills* and then devoted herself to the composition of conventional sentimental fiction, so did her son.

Davis revealed his literary intelligence and good taste in his correspondence. He expressed his admiration for Henry James, and although he harbored an intense dislike for Stephen Crane, he appreciated *The Red Badge of Courage* (1895) as the novel that had most fully captured the war experience. Davis himself wanted to do something truly important, to write a serious novel, and over several years he labored over the work that was to be the masterpiece. The plot was to take the hero to another banana republic where the soldier of fortune scenario might be played out; but in the midst of flashing sabres and smoking gun barrels the real story was to be the psychological development of the protagonist, Royal Macklin. When *Captain Macklin*

(1902) finally appeared, it was judged an artistic failure, and Davis was crushed. He announced to his publishers that he would continue to write light drama and was available for journalistic assignments but he would never write fiction again. He explained that he respected fiction too much to do it badly, suggesting that he no longer had artistic resources from which he could draw.

He changed his mind within a short time. Because he lived in the grand manner of the independently wealthy friends he had made in England and America over the years, Davis had to return to the craft that paid so well. Once again, in 1907-1908, he decided to attempt a grandly meaningful novel. With a good deal of encouragement and advice from his mother, he composed *The White Mice* (1909), sending her letter upon letter assuring her that he would reveal a great truth about human nature. By the time he sent the manuscript to the *Saturday Evening Post* for serialization, though, he had changed his intentions, and he explained to his mother that he had settled for a rattling good yarn. It was his last novelistic effort, and from 1909 he wrote formula short stories, commercially designed plays, and journalistic reports.

When the short story "Gallegher" appeared in the August 1890 issue of *Scribner's Magazine*, Davis

at age twenty-six was an American "boy wonder." In his Van Bibber stories he provided what the *Westminster Review* described as "tales told with infectious gaiety," giving "a graphic and amusing picture of New York fashionable life and manners." *The Princess Aline* caused the *Saturday Review* and the *Critic* to make favorable comparisons between Davis and Henry James. In the early and mid-1890s Davis was a model for ambitious younger writers; by 1900 he was not only passe in the eyes of the progressive fiction writers of his generation but the symbol of that against which they were rebelling in their anti-romanticism.

References:

Clayton L. Eichelberger and Ann M. McDonald, "Richard Harding Davis (1864-1916): A Check List of Secondary Comment," *American Literary Realism*, 4 (Autumn 1971): 313-389;

Gerald Langford, *The Richard Harding Davis Years: A Biography of a Mother and Son* (New York: Holt, Rinehart & Winston, 1961);

Scott C. Osborn and Robert L. Phillips, Jr., *Richard Harding Davis* (Boston: Twayne, 1978);

Henry Cole Quinby, *Richard Harding Davis: A Bibliography* (New York: Dutton, 1924).

John William De Forest
(31 March 1826-17 July 1906)

Robert H. Woodward
San José State University

BOOKS: *History of the Indians of Connecticut from the Earliest Known Period to 1850* (Hartford, Conn.: Wm. Jas. Hamersley, 1851);

Oriental Acquaintance: Or, Letters from Syria (New York: Dix, Edwards, 1856);

European Acquaintance: Being Sketches of People in Europe (New York: Harper, 1858);

Seacliff or The Mystery of the Westervelts (Boston: Phillips, Sampson, 1859);

Miss Ravenel's Conversion from Secession to Loyalty (New York: Harper, 1867; revised edition, New York & London: Harper, 1939);

Overland (New York: Sheldon, 1871);

Kate Beaumont (Boston: Osgood, 1872);

The Wetherel Affair (New York: Sheldon, 1873);

Honest John Vane (New Haven: Richmond & Patten, 1875);

Playing the Mischief (New York: Harper, 1875);

Justine's Lovers, anonymously published (New York: Harper, 1878);

Irene the Missionary, anonymously published (Boston: Roberts, 1879);

The Bloody Chasm (New York: Appleton, 1881); republished as *The Oddest of Courtships* (New York: Appleton, 1882);

A Lover's Revolt (New York, London & Bombay: Longmans, Green, 1898);

The De Forests of Avesnes (and of New Netherland) a Huguenot Thread in American Colonial History, 1494 to the Present Time (New Haven: Tuttle,

Morehouse & Taylor, 1900);

The Downing Legends (New Haven: Tuttle, Morehouse & Taylor, 1901);

Poems: Medley and Palestina (New Haven: Tuttle, Morehouse & Taylor, 1902);

A Volunteer's Adventures, edited by James H. Croushore (New Haven: Yale University Press/London: Oxford University Press, 1946);

A Union Officer in the Reconstruction, edited by Croushore and David Morris Potter (New Haven: Yale University Press/London: Oxford University Press, 1948).

J W De Forest, 1868

During a literary career that spanned half a century John William De Forest wrote more than a dozen novels in which he recorded the breadth and diversity of the American scene, from the mansions of New England to the poverty-ridden hovels of South Carolina, and portrayed a varied cast of characters with attention to their human weaknesses as well as their strengths. At a time when readers sought sentimental or romantic stories, with an idealized view of life, he brought to the depiction of setting an eye for realistic detail and to his portrayal of character a conviction that it is often human folly rather than a propensity for vice or virtue that motivates mankind. His reputation rests largely on one novel, *Miss Ravenel's Conversion from Secession to Loyalty* (1867), which has been praised for its artful descriptions of battle during the Civil War, its analysis of the psychology of soldiers, and its realistic, though often unflattering, portrayal of women. Many of his other novels, frequently involving conventional plots, contain elements of realism that place him at the beginnings of literary realism in the United States. William Dean Howells, in fact, characterized *Miss Ravenel's Conversion* as "of an advanced realism, before realism was known by name."

The youngest of five sons, De Forest was born in Humphreysville (now Seymour), Connecticut, the son of John Hancock De Forest, a successful cotton manufacturer, and Dotha Woodward De Forest. Though study at Yale was a family tradition, poor health throughout his childhood and an attack of typhoid fever in his teens prevented De Forest from achieving a university education. Instead, in 1846, at the age of twenty, he began the first of his several extended periods abroad. The first trip was to Syria, where an elder brother, Henry, a missionary, was in charge of a girls' school in Beirut. For almost two years De Forest traveled in the Near East, visiting the Syrian ruins and Jerusalem, developing his understanding of racial differences, and writing letters home describing his observations.

Upon his return to America he busied himself at the Yale College Library with research for his first book, *History of the Indians of Connecticut from the Earliest Known Period to 1850*, which was published in 1851 with the approval of the Connecticut Historical Society. Though reviews were few, the book sold well and was republished twice in the following two years and a third time in Albany in 1871. The first work on the Connecticut tribes, De Forest's history is a remarkable work for a young man of twenty-three and has earned the praise of historians for its dispassionate and objective reporting. In the introduction to a new edition of the book in 1964, Wilcomb E. Washburn concluded about De Forest: "While American literature claims his mature years, American history can be proud of this proof of his youthful ambitions and talents."

Before the history appeared in book form, De Forest was abroad again, this time in Europe. For four years (1850-1855) he lived and traveled in England, Germany, Switzerland, France, and Italy, seeking a cure for his poor health, studying foreign languages, culture, and character, and, while in

Florence, even testing his Italian by beginning a translation of Hawthorne's *The House of the Seven Gables* (1851). He apparently went to Europe with the intention of educating himself to become a historian or biographer, but it was during this time that he became interested in foreign literature, including the French realists Honoré de Balzac, Stendahl, and George Sand.

De Forest's two sojourns abroad resulted in two travel books. The first, *Oriental Acquaintance* (1856), based upon his stay in Syria, is the work of an observant recorder but lacks the necessary sensitivity to the exotic to compel the reader's interest. The second, *European Acquaintance* (1858), suggests that the influence of De Forest's European period in giving him a cosmopolitan perspective unusual for American writers of his period may not have been as great as has been assumed. Of his travels in Italy he wrote that despite his "dutiful pilgrimages to countless classic shrines, I remained the same being that I had been in America, the spirit clogged by the body, the wings of the imagination as easily wearied as ever. . . ."

Back in the United States, he began his literary career in earnest and in 1856, the year of his marriage to Harriet Silliman Shepard of New Haven, produced his first novel, *Witching Times*, which was published serially and anonymously in *Putnam's Monthly Magazine* (1856-1857). This story of the Salem witchcraft trials combines the use of fictional and historical characters, Cotton Mather and Judge Hawthorne (to use De Forest's spelling) among the latter. The main fictional character, the English gentleman Henry More, opposes the witchcraft delusion but is himself hanged. The husband of his daughter Rachel, who is also condemned, rescues her from jail and escapes with her to Virginia. Through Mather, De Forest depicts how the clergy exploited the trials to retain their sovereignty in Massachusetts. In a number of authorial intrusions De Forest draws analogies between the world of Salem and the oppression of slaves and the tendency to superstition in the 1850s.

His second novel, *Seacliff* (1859), is a Gothic narrative with a contemporary setting near New Haven on Long Island Sound. The first of his realistically portrayed female characters, Ellen Westervelt, is involved in a plot to influence her uncle to change his will in her favor. The melodramatic story ends tragically after Ellen confesses her complicity, agonizes over charges that she has been unfaithful to her husband, and finally goes insane and commits suicide. Despite the unbelievable plot, the novel is redeemed by De Forest's accurate depiction of daily life and of setting and by his portrayal of several well-conceived and original minor characters.

Though his permanent home was in New Haven, De Forest spent much time in the South and became a close observer of Southern manners. His wife was the daughter of Charles Upham Shepard, a professor of chemistry at Amherst who regularly taught during the winter term at the Medical College in Charleston, South Carolina. De Forest had first visited Charleston early in 1855, when he was courting his future wife, who had accompanied her father. For most of the first two years of their marriage the De Forests lived in South Carolina. They visited it often after they returned to Connecticut in 1858 and in 1861 sailed north from Charleston not long before the fall of Fort Sumter in Charleston Harbor signaled the outbreak of the Civil War.

In New Haven De Forest organized a company of volunteers for the Twelfth Connecticut Volunteers, also known as the Charter Oak Regiment, Connecticut's contribution to a division consisting of one regiment from each New England state, and was commissioned as captain. After training at Camp Lyon, near Hartford, the unit left for New York in February 1862 and served in the Louisiana campaign in 1862 and in the Shenandoah Valley in 1864. From the beginning of his active service De Forest regularly wrote to his wife detailed descriptions of camp life and when in the field kept notes of the action in which he was involved.

Discharged from service in December 1864 because of poor health—he "went home," he said, "with what then seemed a totally ruined constitution"—he began writing the novel that has been his major literary contribution. The principal character of *Miss Ravenel's Conversion from Secession to Loyalty* (1867) is Lillie Ravenel, whose years in New Orleans have made her a Southern sympathizer despite the abolitionist views of her gentle father, the scholarly Dr. Ravenel. Back in New Boston (New Haven), she is courted by a young lawyer, Edward Colburne, and dashing John Carter, a Union army officer though a Southern aristocrat, whose reputation for dissipation leads her father to warn her against him. Colburne (like De Forest) raises a company of volunteers and, with Carter, participates in the New Orleans campaign. After New Orleans has been secured, the Ravenels return to that city. Lillie marries Carter, who has temporarily reformed but who eventually is engaged in an intrigue with Mrs. Larue, Lillie's aunt. Upon learning of his infidelity Lillie leaves him. Shortly thereafter he is killed in battle. Lillie's growing sympathy for the Northern cause throughout the story parallels her Christian development and ends in her conversion to abolitionism. At the end of the war she returns to New Boston and marries her faithful suitor, Colburne.

In the autumn of 1865, by which time he had been commissioned captain in the Veteran Reserve Corps and was stationed at Washington, De Forest completed writing the novel and sold it to Harper, who had already published in *Harper's New Monthly Magazine* several articles De Forest had written about his war experiences. It was the feeling of the publishers, however, despite their original plans to publish the story serially, that the harsh realism of the novel made it unsuitable for family readers, and in 1866 a new agreement called for book publication only. When it appeared, early in 1867, De Forest was serving with the Bureau of Freedmen and Refugees in Greenville, South Carolina. Neither he nor the publishers corrected proof, and the book appeared with numerous typographical errors. His later revision of the original manuscript was not published until 1939.

The first war novel in either English or American literature to be written by an author who could describe battle scenes from firsthand experience, *Miss Ravenel's Conversion* presents vivid accounts of the horrors of combat that were out of tune with the sentimentalized and romanticized conceptions of battle dear to the hearts of readers of conventional novels. De Forest did little to tone down the salty language of soldiers. He portrayed them as hard drinkers who were concerned as much with advancement and pay as with duty. He revealed his sympathy for the Northern cause but had an objective eye for the virtues of the South. He created in Mrs. Larue a woman with much charm and absolutely no moral standards. William Dean Howells could not think of her "without shuddering." Despite a number of reviews, including one by Howells in the *Atlantic*, that applauded De Forest's masterful characterizations and the realistic descriptions of war, the book did not enjoy good sales and, perhaps partly because of its large number of printing errors, was not reprinted. Seventeen years after the first printing of the book, over 1,600 copies were still in stock.

After his discharge from service on 1 January 1868, De Forest spent several months in New York City and began what proved to be an unsuccessful attempt to make a profitable living by writing. For the next thirteen years, first in New York City and then in New Haven, he wrote prolifically for the

MISS RAVENEL'S CONVERSION

FROM

SECESSION TO LOYALTY.

By J. W. DE FOREST,

AUTHOR OF "EUROPEAN ACQUAINTANCE," "SEACLIFF," ETC., ETC.

NEW YORK:
HARPER & BROTHERS, PUBLISHERS,
FRANKLIN SQUARE.
1867.

Title page for De Forest's best-known novel, which drew on his experiences as a captain in the Union army during the Civil War

magazines, contributing a large number of essays, short stories, and poems to major periodicals such as *Harper's*, the *Atlantic*, the *Nation*, and the *Galaxy*, as well as to popular periodicals like *Hearth and Home*. In one of his essays, "The Great American Novel," which appeared in the *Nation* in 1868, he contributed to American speech the familiar phrase of the title and suggested that among the reasons the great American novel had not been written and would not soon be written were the immature culture of the United States and the great diversity of the settings and subjects that constitute American life.

Two of the first three novels he wrote during his early years as a magazine contributor failed, like *Witching Times*, to find book publication. In *Della or The Wild Girl*, which appeared in *Hearth and Home* in 1870, the titular heroine is a young woman whose extreme feminist attitudes and attire are viewed as evidence of mental aberrations and whose deathbed marriage to a worthy young man signals her return to sanity and partially fulfills her proper feminine role. Similar in theme but different in treatment is *Annie Howard*, which also appeared in *Hearth and Home* in 1870. In this novel De Forest contrasts the stable Annie, who proposes to be financially self-reliant after losing a legacy, with her overtly feminist aunt, Mrs. Maria Stanley, whose feminism is depicted as both wildly foolish and hypocritical.

Mrs. Stanley reappears in De Forest's next novel, *Overland* (1871), which was serialized in the *Galaxy*. It is a melodramatic tale of the romance of an army lieutenant and a half-Spanish heroine. On their journey from Santa Fe to California they are beset by a pair of conscienceless villains but emerge unscathed, thanks to the bravery of the young lieutenant. The novel was praised for its effective descriptions of the Southwestern landscape, which De Forest, who had never been in the West, based solely upon his reading. Though pleased with his success in descriptive writing, De Forest had reservations about the story itself and later regarded it as "A Story for Boys."

With *Kate Beaumont* (1872), which was first serialized in the *Atlantic* in 1871, De Forest drew upon his experiences and observations in South Carolina, both before and after the Civil War, to produce what he considered "about the best thing I ever did." Despite the idealized portrayals of the two lovers, Kate Beaumont and Frank McAlister, whose families have been involved in a feud for so many years that their mutual enmity has become the center of their existence, and a melodramatic escape from a burning ship in the early chapters, the novel is rich in realistic portrayals of Southern types and effective in its condemnation of the *code duello* that defines the aristocratic conception of gentlemanly honor. Among the major characters are Kate's aunt, Mrs. Chester, an aging coquette with whom De Forest dramatizes his criticism of a way of life that has no better use for women than to idealize them, and Kate's sister Nellie Armitage, who is married to a handsome alcoholic. De Forest's harsh realism in the novel includes the depiction of a backwoods "cracker ball" attended by Nellie's husband, Randolph Armitage, and Randolph's violent attack upon Nellie when she hides his bottle. The portrayals of the members of the Huguenot Beaumonts and the Scotch-blooded McAlisters, other than the lovers Kate and Frank, are in keeping with De Forest's realistic conception of human nature as a mixture of good and evil. Though he

condones neither the dueling nor the feud, De Forest makes clear that it is human folly rather than depravity that has separated the two families until their traditional enmity is resolved through the marriage of Kate and Frank. Primary among the dramatic strengths of the novel is the portrait of Nellie, who, in Howells's words, is "absolute woman, and yet with rather more humor than is vouchsafed to most of her family. . . . She is pathetically, heroically, whimsically alive from the first moment. . . ."

With *The Wetherel Affair* (1873), serialized from 1872 to 1874 in the *Galaxy*, De Forest returned to the genre of the mystery story, this time involving an irresponsible young man, Edward Wetherel, whose wealthy uncle is murdered shortly after he revises his will to exclude his nephew. Although the will is not found and the uncle's fortune goes to Edward, the suspicion that falls upon Edward is sufficient to cause his fiancee, Nestoria Bernard, to leave him and go to New York City to make her own way. The lovers are reunited when Edward proves his innocence by finding his uncle's murderer. A weak novel, dependent upon coincidence, the book has little to justify Howells's assessment of it as a "superb sketch" or, on the strength of its authorship, of De Forest as "really the only American novelist."

In his next three novels De Forest turned his attention to the Washington political arena, the corruption of which he had suggested in *Miss Ravenel's Conversion*, and produced some of his strongest writing. Even though *Honest John Vane* (1875) is essentially allegory, peopled with characters with names such as Christian, Faithful, and Greatheart, it is an effective satire of the political immorality that undermined Congress in the 1860s and precipitated the Crédit Mobilier scandal. John Vane, whose basically untested reputation for honesty is his only qualification for Congressional office, succumbs to the complaints of his vain, ambitious, and childish wife about their poverty and sells his vote. Through a shrewd maneuver he is able to survive the storm created by disclosure of the illegal financing of the Great Subfluvial Tunnel (between Lake Superior and the Gulf of Mexico). Physically unattractive though somewhat likeable in his role as an ordinary man, Vane emblematizes the weakness of a political system whose representatives are elected upon the basis of their thin reputations rather than upon their demonstrated political effectiveness and wisdom.

Playing the Mischief (1875), which had first been serialized in 1874-1875 in a popular magazine, *Frank Leslie's Chimney Corner*, proved to be De

Forest's most popular novel, selling over 6,000 copies. It is also one of his most realistic works in its depiction of the varied contestants in the governmental arena in Washington. Reviewing the novel for the *Nation*, Henry James declared that as "the history of a fraudulent claim successfully carried through Congress, the book does well enough," though he added that De Forest carried realism too far, and James drew the line at finding any interest in the main character, Josephine Murray, whom he described as "a lying, thievish, totally heartless little jade without the faintest vestige of a moral nature." Whereas his previous novel had focused upon corruption within Congress, in this book De Forest allows a young widow to cheat the taxpayers of $100,000 by winning a damage award during the Grant administration for her father-in-law's barn that had been destroyed during the War of 1812. Not only does Mrs. Murray manage to dupe Congress, but she refuses to pay for the services of those who helped her, and at the end of the novel it is clear that she will herself be relieved of the money by an eminent though unscrupulous financier.

In 1875 or 1876 De Forest spent a few months in England and Scotland, hoping to write a history of the Huguenots, but returned to his quiet literary habits and to an unhealthy wife in New Haven when he found that he could not work in Europe. Although De Forest was familiar with political corruption and had explored it in two novels, he spent a few weeks in Washington in 1877, during the beginning of the Hayes administration, seeking a diplomatic or consular post. Unsuccessful in his attempts, and humiliated by the treatment he had received from bureaucrats, he incorporated his indignation in the third and last of his Washington novels, *Justine's Lovers* (1878). Published anonymously, the book was not associated with De Forest by reviewers and, so fully did he succeed in his intention, as he said, "to imitate the ordinary 'woman's novel,' " that one critic even assumed the author to be a "bright, clever, witty and wise woman." Basically a sentimental story, the novel traces the experiences of two women, Justine Vane and her widowed mother, as they are forced by circumstances to exchange their affluent Boston existence for a life of poverty in Washington. Justine's experiences in applying for a civil-service appointment allow De Forest opportunity to examine, and to find insufficient, the civil-service reforms under Hayes.

Now in his early fifties, with no great popular success to his credit, and with no prospects for literary reputation or financial independence, De

Forest turned to the Bible "as a home of healing and refuge" and, during those years, wrote a number of biblical translations that would later be published in his second volume of poems. After the death of his wife, on 29 March 1878, his creative productivity gradually lessened.

In 1879 he produced another anonymous novel, *Irene the Missionary*, which had first appeared serially in the *Atlantic* the same year. Drawing upon his observations in Syria during his young manhood, De Forest created an ideally virtuous and humanitarian heroine, Irene Grant, and installed her as a missionary in Syria during the time of the warfare of 1859 to 1860 that ended with the massacre of Christians in Damascus. The dramatic conflict in the story centers on the young missionary's choice among her three suitors—a dedicated but uncultivated medical missionary, a vulgar and politically ambitious consul, and a rich, young, and flirtatious archaeologist. The novel was not well received: the *Nation* observed that "There are a good many people connected with missionary life who are virtuous, but tedious, as is also much of the descriptive writing of the author."

With the publication of *The Bloody Chasm* (1881), the productive period of De Forest's career came to an end. The chasm of the title is the rift between the North and the South after the Civil War. De Forest uses the method of allegory to emblematize the two factions through the Northern Colonel Harry Underhill and the Southern Virginia Beaufort. Nephew and niece of an old Boston Puritan, Silas Mather, they must marry if Miss Beaufort is to inherit the fortune bequeathed to her by Mather. After their marriage, at which the bride wore black, the two separate, Miss Beaufort deliberately having never looked at her husband's face. Underhill, however, has fallen genuinely in love with Miss Beaufort, courts her under an assumed name, and wins her. Like Lillie Ravenel, Virginia Beaufort is converted to an understanding and acceptance of the North. She thus learns through love what she, as a Southerner, had not learned in defeat—respect for Northern virtues and values. The only realistic elements are the descriptions of a destroyed Charleston and the depiction of freed slaves. The novel was almost ignored by reviewers. Its republication the next year under a less colorful and more sentimental title, *The Oddest of Courtships*, met with similar silence.

During the remaining twenty-five years of his life De Forest had only a handful of short stories and poems published in periodicals. Except for scattered trips—to New York City in 1881, to Nova

Scotia in 1883, to Europe in 1884—he lived the uneventful and frustrated life of a disappointed author in New Haven. Following his return from Europe, where he had pursued his genealogical studies, he tried without success to find magazine publication for a new novel, "A Daughter of Toil," which he described to one editor as "the story of a poor and good girl, who by dint of worth and favoring chances, struggles up to—the best she can get."

Yet it was a period of continued literary activity. Beginning in the mid-1880s De Forest negotiated with at least two publishers for a uniform edition of his works, as a "small monument for myself," and even purchased the plates of his three novels published by Harper, but his hopes were never fulfilled. Nor did he manage to find a publisher for the two volumes of his "Military Life" that he put together from the letters and articles he had written during the Civil War and the Reconstruction. These two books, *A Volunteer's Adventures* and *A Union Officer in the Reconstruction*, did not appear until they were published in edited volumes by Yale University Press in the late 1940s.

Some measure of financial security came to De Forest in 1888, when a cousin left him $20,000, but money during his last years was always a problem. In 1904, more than a dozen years after his first application, he was granted a Civil War pension of $12 a month as a consequence of the heart disease that had plagued him for years and for which he had been hospitalized in 1903.

The popularity of the historical romance at the end of the century brought De Forest out of his literary retirement with his last novel, *A Lover's Revolt* (1898), set in the beginning days of the American Revolution. In this book, as in *Witching Times*, De Forest combines historical and fictional characters, and as in *Miss Ravenel's Conversion* he interweaves a love triangle with military action. The American heroine, Huldah Oakbridge, falls hopelessly in love with a British officer, Captain Moorcastle, who spurns her as an inferior. Like many of De Forest's foolish women, she becomes insane and dies. Her rejected suitor is an American soldier, Asahel Farnlee, with whom she could have found happiness. Like *The Bloody Chasm*, the novel equates characters too easily with their national or

"You ask a thought," verse message from De Forest

regional origins. Whereas the rift between the North and South could be bridged by love and understanding, what separated the colonials from England was the mother country's view of Americans as inferiors.

De Forest published at his own expense the only other of his books that appeared during his lifetime. In 1900 he brought out a genealogical study of the De Forest family, *The De Forests of Avesnes*. In 1901 he published the first of his books of poetry, *The Downing Legends*, four verse narratives that combine rustic verse reminiscent of James Russell Lowell's *The Biglow Papers* with the elevated diction and tone of the English romantic poets. His last volume, *Poems: Medley and Palestina* (1902), collects much of the verse that he had published in periodicals and the biblical translations he had written a score of years earlier. Neither of the volumes added to De Forest's reputation.

Still plagued by heart disease, De Forest lived at his son's home in New Haven during his last months. He died there on 17 July 1906 and was buried in the Grove Street Cemetery in New Haven.

Almost unknown as an author at the time of his death, De Forest has in the past forty years taken his place as a pioneer of American literary realism. The publication of De Forest's revised edition of *Miss Ravenel's Conversion* in 1939, with an introduction by Gordon S. Haight, brought critical attention to this novel. The 1867 version, with typographical errors corrected, was reprinted in a popular edition for students, again with an introduction by Haight, in 1955. In its portrayal of military psychology the novel has been favorably compared to Stephen Crane's *The Red Badge of Courage* (1895), which may have been influenced by De Forest's book. In his search for a popular audience with conventional tales of triangular love, however, De Forest never achieved success; and the often awkward admixture of sentimental and realistic elements in his novels worked against both his acceptance by readers and acclaim from critics. Before De Forest's death, but after the publication of his last novel, William Dean Howells placed De Forest among "the masters of American fiction," praised his "keen and accurate touch in character, his wide scope, and his unerring rendition of whatever he has attempted to report of American life," and expressed belief that it was De Forest's "certain scornful bluntness in dealing with the disguises in which women's natures reveal themselves" that prevented him from "winning a merited popularity"; but he also lamented that he could not "read many pages of his without wishing he had done this or that differently." Howells's

comparison of Henry James and De Forest—"Mr. De Forest's books are a part of our literary history; Mr. James's books are a part of our literature"—is by and large unchallenged. Haight has labeled De Forest "the first American writer to deserve the name of realist"; Van Wyck Brooks has written of De Forest's "breadth of understanding and . . . truth to actuality that were certainly unique at the moment"; and Albert Stone has rated *Miss Ravenel's Conversion* the best novel of the American Civil War. De Forest's place in American literary history, as a writer whose best work prepared the way for Crane, Norris, Dreiser, and those who followed, is firm.

Periodical Publications:
FICTION:
Witching Times, *Putnam's Monthly Magazine*, 8 (December 1856): 570-594; 9 (January 1857): 11-28; 9 (February 1857): 188-207; 9 (March 1857): 297-317; 9 (April 1857): 394-413; 9 (May 1857): 515-524; 9 (June 1857): 621-630; 10 (July 1857): 62-74; 10 (August 1857): 218-231; 10 (September 1857): 393-404;
Della, *Hearth and Home*, 2 (5 February-19 March 1870): 105-106, 121-122, 137-138, 153-155, 169-170, 185-186, 203;
Annie Howard, *Hearth and Home*, 2 (19 March-21 May 1870): 201-203, 217-219, 233-234, 249-251, 265-267, 281-282, 297-299, 313-314, 329-330, 347.
NONFICTION:
"The Great American Novel," *Nation*, 6 (9 January 1868): 27-29.

Bibliographies:
E. R. Hagemann, "A Checklist of the Writings of John William De Forest (1826-1906)," *Studies in Bibliography*, 8 (1956): 185-194;
"John William De Forest (1826-1906): A Critical Bibliography of Secondary Comment," *American Literary Realism*, 4 (1968): 1-56.

References:
Van Wyck Brooks, *New England: Indian Summer* (New York: Dutton, 1940), pp. 239-243;
Alexander Cowie, *The Rise of the American Novel* (New York: American Book Company, 1948), pp. 505-520;
Gordon S. Haight, "Realism Defined," in *Literary History of the United States: History*, Robert E. Spiller and others, third edition, revised (New York: Macmillan, 1963), pp. 878-898;
William Dean Howells, *Heroines of Fiction* (New York

& London: Harper, 1901), II: 152-163;
James F. Light, *John William De Forest* (New York: Twayne, 1965);
Thomas F. O'Donnell, "De Forest, Van Petten, and Stephen Crane," *American Literature*, 27 (January 1956): 575-580;
Arthur Hobson Quinn, *American Fiction* (New York: Appleton-Century, 1936), pp. 166-174;
Albert E. Stone, Jr., "Best Novel of the Civil War," *American Heritage*, 13 (June 1962): 84-88;
Edward Wagenknecht, *Cavalcade of the American Novel* (New York: Holt, 1952), pp. 104-108;
Edmund Wilson, *Patriotic Gore* (New York: Oxford

University Press, 1962), pp. 669-742.

Papers:

The major collection of manuscripts, including family letters and seventeen De Forest manuscripts, is the De Forest Collection, Yale Collection of American Literature, Yale University Library. The Houghton Library at Harvard University has thirteen letters from De Forest to Howells (1868-1890), and the W. C. Church Manuscript Collection of the New York Public Library has seventeen letters (1867-1877) related to De Forest's writings in the *Galaxy*.

Ignatius Donnelly

(3 November 1831 - 1 January 1901)

Stephen C. Brennan
Drexel University

SELECTED BOOKS: *The Mourner's Vision. A Poem* (Philadelphia: Privately printed, 1850);
Atlantis: The Antediluvian World (New York: Harper, 1882; London: Sampson, Low, 1882);
Ragnarok: The Age of Fire and Gravel (New York: Appleton, 1883; London: Sampson, Low, 1883);
The Great Cryptogram: Francis Bacon's Cipher in the So-called Shakespeare Plays (London: Sampson, Low, Marston, Searle & Rivington, 1888; Chicago, New York & London: Peale, 1888);
Caesar's Column, A Story of the Twentieth Century, as Edmund Boisgilbert, M.D. (Chicago: F. J. Schulte, 1890; London: Sampson, Low, 1891);
Doctor Huguet. A Novel (Chicago: F. J. Schulte, 1891; London: Sampson, Low, 1891);
The Golden Bottle or the Story of Ephraim Benezet of Kansas (New York & St. Paul: Merrill, 1892; London: Sampson, Low, 1893);
The American People's Money (Chicago: Laird & Lee, 1895);
The Cipher in the Plays, and On the Tombstone (Minneapolis: Verulam, 1899).

Ignatius Donnelly, "the Sage of Nininger," was a politician of mercurial temperament and shifting party allegiances who embraced nearly every radical reform movement of the post-Civil War period. Out of office as much as in, he at one

Donnelly during his tenure as a U.S. Representative from Minnesota (1863-1869)

time or another made a career as lawyer, farmer, lecturer, editor, and man of letters. As a writer, he is most often remembered for *Atlantis: The Antediluvian World* (1882), a pseudoscientific work still read by cultists; *The Great Cryptogram* (1888), one of the more sensational attempts to prove Francis Bacon's authorship of Shakespeare's plays; and *Caesar's Column* (1890), a futuristic anti-utopian novel expressing the hopes and fears of the American reform movement. In *Caesar's Column,* and in his other fiction as well, Donnelly attacks the evils of the American social and economic system. His novels are marred by didacticism, sentimentality, and fantastic plots, yet he at times projects a powerful and grotesque vision of a world gone mad. Although he offers some hope that man can direct his own destiny and establish a society based on a lost agrarian ideal, he creates a primarily naturalistic world in which man struggles weakly against the vast natural and social forces that threaten his destruction.

Donnelly was born in Philadelphia to Philip Carroll Donnelly, a physician, and Cathrine Gavin Donnelly. Deeply affected by the religious and racial conflicts that tore Philadelphia in his boyhood, Donnelly early rejected his Catholicism—even dropping his middle name, Loyola—but he always remained proud of his Irish heritage. He attended public schools and was especially fortunate in being sent to Philadelphia's Central High School, which had a curriculum equal to that of many colleges. In high school, he edited the school newspaper and began writing poetry. The year after graduation, he published *The Mourner's Vision. A Poem* (1850), a long poem about the suppression of freedom in Europe following the revolutions of 1848. Donnelly sent a copy of the poem to Oliver Wendell Holmes, who tactfully replied, "You have the inward adjustments which naturally produce melody of expression and incline you to rhythmical forms. . . . You are a bright scholar, who has read a good many books and perhaps have a little too much fondness of ornamenting your own composition with phrases borrowed from what you have read. . . ." Holmes's criticism, however, had little effect, and oratorical flourishes and pedantry were to be characteristic of all Donnelly's literary works.

After high school, Donnelly turned to law and studied for three years under Benjamin Harris Brewster, who later became attorney general of the United States. In late 1852, he started his own practice and by 1856 had proved an able orator for the local Democratic party. However, he began to realize that without capital and connections, his chances of success in the East were small.

Donnelly traveled west and, struck by the beauty of Minnesota and the boom-town prosperity of St. Paul, decided to move there with his bride, Katherine (Kate) McCaffrey Donnelly, whom he had married in September 1855 and with whom he was to raise three children. Hoping to make his fortune in land speculation, he formed a partnership with John Nininger to develop Nininger City, seventeen miles below St. Paul on the Mississippi, but the panic of 1857 ended the dream and nearly brought financial ruin. Undaunted, Donnelly made Nininger City his home and soon turned to politics.

By 1857, Donnelly had left the Democratic party over the slave question and had joined the newly formed Republican party. He quickly won the attention of "Bluff Alec" Ramsey, the state's Republican leader, and proved himself a tireless campaigner and stirring speaker for the abolitionist cause. In 1859, at age twenty-eight, Donnelly was elected lieutenant governor under Ramsey. He served two terms, often acting as governor in Ramsey's absence. He was elected to Congress as a radical Republican in 1863, serving three terms and winning a reputation as a reformer by uncovering abuses in the Indian Office. Donnelly, however, was prouder of the bills he introduced to establish a Bureau of Education and to plant forests on the Great Plains. Ironically, Donnelly the reformer was involved in some questionable deals: for a brief time he sold government secrets to a speculator, and, while serving on the Committee of Public Lands, he supported land grants for railroads from whom he received shares of stock.

Donnelly was strong-willed and made enemies easily. In 1868, a faction of the Republicans in his district opposed his candidacy and ran their own man, splitting the Republican vote and giving the election to the Democrats. Discouraged but hoping to profit from his Congressional ties, Donnelly returned to Washington as a lobbyist for Jay Cooke and the railroads. To mask his lobbying, he also served as correspondent for the *St. Paul Dispatch.* Donnelly worked hard to procure a large land grant for the Northern Pacific Railroad, knowing that his fifteen percent cut would make his fortune, but at the same time, he was beginning to understand the inner workings of monopolies and to realize their great cost to society. He also began to recognize the shallowness and greed of the moneyed classes. In one article for the *Dispatch,* he expressed his disgust at a Washington party, where "the great clatter, jangle and chatter goes on, a thousand interests, wishes, vanities, mingle together in one stupendous buzz and burr, while the mechanical host and hostess stand smiling away and working their pump handles, and the streams struggle in and out of the door."

Failing to get the land grant for Cooke, Donnelly returned to Minnesota in 1870 to run for Congress as an independent—with a Democratic endorsement. After his defeat, he turned briefly to farming, but the Fourth of July 1871 found him delivering a speech calling for a new unity of North and South. Surprisingly, especially for a recent ally of Jay Cooke, he also called for strong regulation of the railroads, which he now proclaimed "were created to transport the commerce of the country, not to rule its politics or corrupt its laws. If they can't behave themselves we must put them in irons."

The speech received little notice, even though several hundred copies were distributed to leading men in the state. Disappointed, Donnelly yielded to ambition and returned to the Republican party. Refusing to apologize for his alliance with the Democrats, he good-humoredly professed to the state convention that he had come back like a "drowned gopher" and offered as his only defense the story of "the boy who went fishing on Sunday": "A preacher saw him sitting on the river's bank. 'My son,' said he, 'don't you know you are committing a great sin fishing on the Sabbath day?' 'Wal,' said the boy, 'it can't be no great sin for I hain't ketched nuthin.' " Disarmed, the convention greeted Donnelly with laughter and cheers and welcomed his return. Donnelly, however, could not long put political expediency ahead of his beliefs. Although he knew that the surest way back to power lay in supporting Grant in the election of 1872, he toured the Midwest speaking for Horace Greeley and the Liberal Republicans. The election was a disastrous defeat, but it marked Donnelly's irrevocable turn down the road of reform.

The mid-1870s found Donnelly forming the state's Grangers into the Anti-Monopoly party and—when the Grangers' political enthusiasm waned—joining the Greenbacker crusade for plentiful paper currency. During two terms in the state senate, he led the radicals in exposing abuses in the state's timber contracts, in seeking to limit interest rates, and in working to regulate the railroads. But when he ran for Congress in 1878 on a Greenbacker-Democratic coalition ticket, he was again defeated. He traveled to Washington to file a suit charging his opponent, William Washburn, with election fraud, but the litigation was unsuccessful and he returned home heavily in debt. Convinced his political career was over, he wrote in his diary, "My life has been a failure and a mistake. My hopes have so often come to naught that I cease to hope. . . . Well. All I can do is to face the music and take my damnable future as it comes."

Donnelly devoted the next few years to his family, his farms, and his interest in science. Perhaps stimulated by Jules Verne's popular *Twenty Thousand Leagues under the Sea* (1870), he began reading everything he could find on the Atlantis legend. Ransacking scholarly works, folklore, myths, and religion, he attempted to prove that the continent of Atlantis had actually existed, that it had been the cradle of civilization, and that it had sunk beneath the sea in a natural cataclysm. *Atlantis: The Antediluvian World* was eagerly accepted by Harper and Brothers in 1882 and went through seven printings in its first year. By 1890, it had been through twenty-three American and twenty-six English printings. Although scholars never accepted his argument, Donnelly was gratified to receive an appreciative letter from Prime Minister William Ewart Gladstone and, in 1882, to be elected to the American Association for the Advancement of Science.

Encouraged by this success, Donnelly began a new book, *Ragnarok: The Age of Fire and Gravel* (1883). In this work, he argued that the earth's masses of sand, gravel, and clay had not been caused by glaciers, as was commonly believed, but by a comet that had collided, or nearly collided, with the earth. Although not nearly as successful as *Atlantis*, *Ragnarok* went through nineteen printings by 1899.

In both these works, Donnelly argued as a lawyer, not a scientist. He cared little for the reliability of his sources as long as they supported his thesis, and he had no qualms about ignoring contradictory evidence. Although *Atlantis* and *Ragnarok* are provocative arguments unifying masses of evidence culled from a wide variety of sources, they contributed little or nothing to the advancement of science. Nevertheless, they are important to an understanding of Donnelly's thought. In both works, he rejects the accepted belief in the uniform operation of natural laws and asserts that major changes are brought about through fearful and destructive cataclysms, a theme that would darken all his works of fiction.

Intent on a literary career, Donnelly resisted serious involvement with politics until 1884, when disenchanted Republicans began a movement to run him for Congress against their ineffective incumbent. After the People's party, Farmer's Alliance, and Democratic party all nominated him, Donnelly stumped the state speaking out against the

Donnelly's annotations to Henry the Fourth, Part 2, *in a facsimile of the 1623 Shakespeare folio. His argument for a cipher proving Francis Bacon wrote Shakespeare's plays is presented in* The Great Cryptogram.

railroads. National office was, however, never again to come within his grasp. Losing the election by less than 1,000 votes and failing to gain a patronage appointment from President Cleveland, he was once more near poverty.

During this period, Donnelly had not abandoned literary activity. Always ready to challenge authority, he had, in fact, been working off and on since 1878 to find the key to a cipher he believed he had uncovered in Shakespeare's plays. The cipher, he was convinced, would prove conclusively that Francis Bacon, whom he considered the greatest genius of his time, had written the plays attributed to the uneducated Shakespeare. By mid-1883, Donnelly felt he had the key. By mid-1887, his work had advanced so far that he had convinced R. S. Peale to publish *The Great Cryptogram* (1888). Prepublication publicity, however, stirred hostile attacks from both English and American critics, and cryptographers pointed out that the master key fitted much too loosely and that the system was hardly a system at all. In the spring of 1888, Donnelly traveled to England to defend his work and to debate its merits at both Oxford and Cambridge. He lost both debates but gave the Baconian argument its greatest public hearing. Controversy over the book continued for some time, and on his return to America, Donnelly was in great demand as a lecturer. But the book did not sell, and he was forced to give Peale several lots in St. Paul to pay back advance royalties. Donnelly, angry at what he considered mankind's stupidity, refused to give up his cause and continued to work on the cipher until his death.

After the Great Cryptogram debacle, Donnelly turned back to politics, but in late 1888 and early 1889, he suffered three defeats in close succession: he was forced to withdraw from the gubernatorial race because he lacked funds; he lost an election for the state legislature; and he was defeated in a campaign for the U.S. Senate. On 19 January 1889, the night after his third defeat, he began a novel projecting his fears for the future of an America he believed was fast becoming an oligarchy of the very rich.

Caesar's Column, undoubtedly exploiting the popularity of Edward Bellamy's *Looking Backward* (1888), is set in the New York of 1988. The story is narrated through the letters of Gabriel Weltstein, who is visiting America for the first time and writing home to his brother in their pastoral community in the mountains of Uganda. At first Gabriel is awed by the technological wonders of the city—airships, magnetic lights, marvelous communication

systems—but because he saves a beggar from a thrashing by an aristocrat's coachman, he finds himself hunted by the law and begins to realize the truth about America. The beggar turns out to be the disguised Maximilian Petion, a leader in the worldwide anarchist "Brotherhood of Destruction." Maximilian shows Gabriel the underworld of the working classes who, subjected to the "iron law of wages" of classical economists, have been starved into physical and moral degradation. The Oligarchy is run by Jews because centuries of Darwinian natural selection have produced in them the cunning to use deceit and bribery to win the struggle for existence. The state religion is a blend of hedonism and a ruthless Social Darwinism based on the assumption that "the plan of Nature necessarily involves cruelty, suffering, injustice, destruction, death."

In showing how America's industrial cities dehumanize the working classes, Donnelly anticipates Stephen Crane, whose *Maggie: A Girl of the Streets* was to appear three years later. Like Crane, Donnelly shows the urban poor "in the hands of some ruthless and unrelenting destiny." The workers live in a hellish environment that destroys their finer feelings, "the illusions of the imagination, which beckon all of us forward, even over the roughest paths and through the darkest valleys and shadows of life." Donnelly also anticipates Theodore Dreiser's *Sister Carrie* (1900), although the heroine of that novel manages eventually to escape a cold, repressive environment and to keep alive the illusion that she can find happiness. Unlike Crane and Dreiser, however, Donnelly presents the plight of the poor through the eyes of an outsider. He enables the reader to feel something of Gabriel's horror, but he does not create sympathetic characters whose degradation the reader can experience directly as he does Maggie's and Carrie's.

In the climax of the novel, airships called "The Demons" rain poisonous bombs on the armies of the Oligarchy as the Brotherhood unleashes its rage in a brutal slaughter of the upper classes. Civilization falls in a day, and an age of terror and rapine begins. In celebration, the drunken, bestial Brotherhood chieftain Caesar Lomellini erects a monument to the revolution, an enormous column filled with 250,000 bodies of murdered men, women, and children. But in the chaos, no authority is tolerated: Caesar's own followers butcher him and carry his head through the streets of New York on a pike. Only Gabriel, Maximilian, and their families escape in an airship to Uganda, where they set up a utopian community on Donnelly's reform principles: universal suffrage, no interest or tariffs, fair wages, and plentiful paper currency.

The novel has a clear didactic purpose in warning America of the consequences of failing to reform her social and political institutions. Although it ends with the creation of a utopia, the book is essentially pessimistic. Social and economic forces are, by 1988, beyond anyone's control. Gabriel and a few others may live out their lives "with linked hands" as "God smiles down upon them from his throne beyond the stars," but the rest of mankind is doomed to cyclic repetition of "the great human drama, which begins always with a tragedy, runs through a comedy, and terminates in a catastrophe."

Caesar's Column is not an artistic success. Donnelly, as might be expected of a natural orator, lards his work with long philosophic discussions, punctuated at every turn with literary quotations. At the most absurdly inopportune times, Gabriel risks his life to deliver bombastic speeches on true Christianity or brotherly love. Modern readers also have difficulty with the sentimental love plots that find both Gabriel and Maximilian rescuing impossibly virtuous girls from defilement. In addition, Donnelly has little regard for point of view, forgetting for long stretches to have Gabriel begin a new letter and letting Gabriel narrate sensational scenes he could not have witnessed.

At times, however, Donnelly's prose achieves a true nightmare quality fitting to his theme, as in his description of the crematoriums for the poor: "public safety and the demands of science had long ago decreed that they should be whisked off, as soon as dead, a score or two at a time, and swept on iron tram-cars into furnaces heated to such intense white heat that they dissolved, crackling, even as they entered the chamber, and rose in nameless gases through the high chimney. That towering structure was the sole memorial monument of millions of them. Their graveyard was the air." Similarly, Caesar Lomellini's macabre column is a powerful central image. As Walter Rideout puts it, the column "juts up hugely out of the city of the future like some fantastic detail from a painting by Hieronymus Bosch, grotesque, circumstantial, symbolic."

After several publishers rejected *Caesar's Column* as inflammatory, Donnelly managed to get it accepted by F. J. Schulte and Company of Chicago. Published in April 1890 under the pseudonym Edmund Boisgilbert, M.D., the book got little response from major newspapers and reviewers. However,

labor and rural newspapers gave it a hearing, and by December it was selling 1,000 copies a week. A popular, if not critical, success, it had sold 260,000 copies by 1906.

Caesar's Column was not just financial salvation; it was also a big boost for Donnelly's sagging political career. When his authorship was announced at the national convention of the Farmer's Alliance in December 1890, his immediate new popularity enabled him to win the presidency of Minnesota's Alliance and thrust him into national prominence in the union. At the 1891 convention in Cincinnati, Donnelly was so instrumental in turning the Farmer's Alliance into a new third party that he was acknowledged as the "father of the People's party."

When the Populists met in St. Louis, in February 1892, Donnelly's preamble to the platform became the party's manifesto. Calling for the return of government "to the hands of the 'plain people,' with whom it originated," Donnelly portrayed an America much like that of *Caesar's Column:* "The fruits of the toil of millions are boldly stolen to build up colossal fortunes, unprecedented in the history of the world, while their possessors despise the republic and endanger liberty. From the same prolific womb of governmental injustice we breed two great classes—paupers and millionaires. . . . A vast conspiracy against mankind has been organized on two continents and is taking possession of the world. If not met and overthrown at once it forbodes terrible social convulsions, the destruction of civilization, or the establishment of an absolute despotism." At the Populist nominating convention in July, Donnelly was again the party's spokesman and delivered the keynote address.

During this period, F. J. Schulte published Donnelly's second novel, *Doctor Huguet* (1891), which Donnelly had written in spare moments in the fall of 1890. The book's plot turns on a fantastic device. When Dr. Huguet, a young Southern aristocrat, decides to conceal his liberal feelings for Negroes in order to gain political favor, Jesus, surrounded by millions of supplicating black hands, appears to him in a vision. Huguet awakes the next morning to find that he has exchanged bodies with the most debased, thieving black man in the district. When he tries to assert his identity, he meets only ridicule and abuse and is hunted and nearly lynched for grasping the hand of a white woman, his fiancee, Mary Ruddiman. Huguet eventually vows to accept his lot and to inspire the Negro through example, but he finds himself locked out of any work except common labor. Always a believer in the value of education, Donnelly has Huguet set up a school,

where he teaches reading and writing to blacks and whites alike and delivers lectures on all manner of morally uplifting subjects—firmly warning blacks against hostility to whites.

But society will not permit an easy solution to the race problem. A white-hooded band of dissipated young aristocrats—led by Sam Johnsing, the Negro in Huguet's body—attacks the school and guns down all the blacks. Huguet himself is lynched, and Johnsing finishes him off with a pistol. But the joke is on Johnsing. As the pistol fires, the souls of Johnsing and Huguet are switched back to their proper bodies and Johnsing kills himself. The other hoodlums flee to the brothel where they habitually spend their nights in drunken fornication, but the responsible black and white citizens of the town trap them. Abigail, a beautiful and virtuous octaroon who has been raped by Johnsing, manages to set the brothel on fire before being killed, and the murderers and prostitutes are incinerated in a hellish blaze. In the aftermath, Huguet weds Mary and vows to devote his life to educating the blacks and raising them to equality.

Doctor Huguet is an admirable attempt to portray the plight of the Negro in the post-Reconstruction South. It shows that Donnelly had not forgotten the cause that had motivated him before and during the Civil War. Still, Donnelly has been charged with failing to break through racial stereotypes. The blacks in the novel are either viciously stupid or sentimentally childlike, and Huguet believes, with Donnelly's obvious concurrence, that blacks are intellectually inferior because they have evolved thick skulls to protect them from the harsh African sun. But if Donnelly could not overcome the prejudices of an age that smugly accepted such racist applications of Darwinism as scientific fact, he did see blacks as suffering human beings and did feel that changed circumstances and education could eventually raise them to the level of the white man. Although this attitude seems offensively paternalistic to the modern reader, for its time *Doctor Huguet* was a revolutionary portrayal of race relations.

Especially in its early chapters, the book looks forward to the works of Frank Norris and Theodore Dreiser. When Huguet, a respected member of society, awakes to find himself transformed into a black man, he faces a dilemma much like those of Norris's McTeague (*McTeague,* 1899) and Dreiser's Hurstwood (*Sister Carrie*). All three suddenly are cut off from their comfortable pasts and forced to struggle for existence on the fringes of a society that scarcely acknowledges their humanity.

Unfortunately, *Doctor Huguet* suffers from the same stylistic flaws as *Caesar's Column.* And what is for Norris and Dreiser material for powerful studies of degeneration with tragic overtones becomes for Donnelly the stuff of melodrama as Huguet strives to save the Ruddiman plantation from the clutches of an oily Northern lawyer. Even the catastrophe loses much of its social significance because it results as much from "a collision . . . between the respectable and profligate elements of society" as from racial hatred. However, America's indifference to the black man rather than flawed artistry is the likely reason for the failure of the book. Reviews were hostile and sales were slim.

When Donnelly returned from the Populist convention in 1892, he ran for governor of Minnesota. In the midst of a vigorous campaign, he dashed off another novel, *The Golden Bottle,* which, he proclaimed, was "intended to explain and defend in the thin guise of a story, some of the ideas put forth by the People's party."

The novel begins in realism akin to Hamlin Garland's, as foreclosure drives Ephraim Benezet and his family off their farm, and Ephraim, like heroes of Dreiser and Anderson, joins the influx to the city. At this point, the story becomes a fantastic parable. Ephraim receives from a mysterious stranger a bottle of liquid that turns iron into gold. Donnelly then uses Ephraim to illustrate the chief principle of populism: that a plentiful supply of money will save society. Ephraim eventually becomes president, saves America, conquers the world, and establishes a worldwide government similar to the utopia in *Caesar's Column*. Ephraim then wakes up to find that he has been dreaming and that his family faces destitution. In the future lies the possibility of a social cataclysm, but Ephraim eagerly sets out to prevent it. The book is thus more hopeful than Donnelly's others, but it had the least success, seeing only one small printing. It also did little for his campaign. In the November election, Donnelly was crushed and retreated to Nininger to work once more on his beloved cipher.

In the last years of his life, Donnelly sought to keep the Populist ideal alive and to maintain the party's autonomy as one after another of its principles were absorbed into the polical mainstream during the depression of the mid-1890s. In 1893, he began a weekly newspaper, the *St. Paul Representative*, which he used as a forum for discussion of Populist issues until his death.

In 1894, Donnelly's wife died of a stroke. For four years he lived alone, but in 1898, much to the distress of his children, he married his twenty-year-old secretary, Marian Hanson. Of this marriage, he wrote in his diary, "I am not moved by sensual considerations but by the hollowness of the heart—the yawning abyss of solitariness."

After the defeat of William Jennings Bryan in 1896, the power of the Populists waned rapidly. In 1900, the Mid-Road Populists chose Donnelly unanimously as their vice-presidential candidate, but by then he was merely a bystander on the political scene. On 4 July 1900 Donnelly suffered a mild stroke. Three days before the election, he wrote in his diary with deep regret, "My ill fortune pursues me. If I had not had a partial stroke of palsey [sic], I would have made the whole U. S. ring with my appeals. . . ." Shortly after midnight on 1 January 1901, Donnelly died of a heart attack.

In the years following his death, Ignatius Donnelly was, to many, a folk hero, the "Apostle of Discontent" defending the common man against the great and strong; to others, he was "The Prince of Cranks," an imperialistic, anti-Semitic dema-gogue. As Martin Ridge points out, both critics and supporters based their judgments on the flamboyant public figure and ignored the "highly sensitive, human, troubled man lost in the thicket of endless political intrigue." Once apparently headed for obscurity, Donnelly is now considered worth studying as representative of a significant phase of American political and literary history. His yearning for a lost agrarian ideal and his fear of the new industrialism are characteristic of the post-Civil War reform movement. His novels—though often didactic, sentimental, and fantastic—reveal the struggle for human dignity against terrible natural and social forces that links him with such naturalists as Crane, Norris, and Dreiser. In *Caesar's Column*, at least, Donnelly has achieved more than a curiosity of literary history. Like Aldous Huxley in *Brave New World* (1932) and George Orwell in *1984* (1949), Donnelly has given form to the chief neurosis of modern man, what Walter Rideout calls the "free-floating anxiety that afflicts our time even more than his, the ineradicable nervous fear that, despite one's hope for the future, civilization may already have made the wrong turning and is now moving inescapably toward world catastrophe." If Donnelly's Populist utopia now seems the quaint daydream of a simpler age, his nightmare is still very much our own.

Periodical Publications:
"The Shakespeare Myth," *North American Review*, 144 (July 1887): 57-68;
"Delia Bacon's Unhappy Story," *North American Review*, 148 (March 1889): 307-318.

References:
David D. Anderson, *Ignatius Donnelly* (Boston: Twayne, 1980);
Allan M. Axelrod, "Ideology and Utopia in the Works of Ignatius Donnelly," *American Studies*, 12 (Fall 1971):47-66;
Walter B. Rideout, Introduction to *Caesar's Column*, Donnelly (Cambridge: Harvard University Press, 1960);
Martin Ridge, *Ignatius Donnelly: Portrait of a Politician* (Chicago: University of Chicago Press, 1962).

Papers:
The Donnelly Papers, at the Minnesota Historical Society in St. Paul, Minnesota, are the most important repository of Donnelly materials, including many manuscripts of his books and articles.

Theodore Dreiser

Donald Pizer
Tulane University

See also the Dreiser entry in *DLB 9, American Novelists, 1910-1945* and *DLB Documentary Series 1.*

BIRTH: Terre Haute, Indiana, 27 August 1871, to John Paul and Sarah Schänäb Dreiser.

EDUCATION: Indiana University, 1889-1890.

MARRIAGE: 28 December 1898 to Sara Osborne White; 13 June 1944 to Helen Patges Richardson.

AWARD: American Academy of Arts and Letters Award of Merit, 1945.

DEATH: Los Angeles, California, 28 December 1945.

SELECTED BOOKS: *Sister Carrie* (New York: Doubleday, Page, 1900; abridged edition, London: Heinemann, 1901; Pennsylvania Edition, Philadelphia: University of Pennsylvania Press, 1981);

Jennie Gerhardt (New York & London: Harper, 1911);

The Financier (New York & London: Harper, 1912; revised edition, New York: Boni & Liveright, 1927; London: Constable, 1931);

A Traveler at Forty (New York: Century, 1913; London: Richards, 1914);

The Titan (New York: John Lane, 1914; London: John Lane, 1915);

The "Genius" (New York: John Lane, 1915; London: John Lane, 1915);

Plays of the Natural and the Supernatural (New York: John Lane, 1916; London: John Lane, 1916);

A Hoosier Holiday (New York: John Lane, 1916; London: John Lane, 1916);

Free and Other Stories (New York: Boni & Liveright, 1918);

Twelve Men (New York: Boni and Liveright, 1919; London: Constable, 1930);

The Hand of the Potter (New York: Boni & Liveright, 1919; revised, 1927);

Hey Rub-a-Dub-Dub (New York: Boni & Liveright, 1920; London: Constable, 1931);

A Book About Myself (New York: Boni & Liveright, 1922; London: Constable, 1929); republished as *Newspaper Days* (New York:Liveright, 1931);

The Color of a Great City (New York: Boni & Liveright, 1923; London: Constable, 1930);

An American Tragedy (New York: Boni & Liveright, 1925; London: Constable, 1926);

Moods: Cadenced and Declaimed (New York: Boni & Liveright, 1926; revised, 1928); revised and republished as *Moods Philosophic and Emotional, Cadenced and Declaimed* (New York: Simon & Schuster, 1935);

Chains (New York: Boni & Liveright, 1927; London: Constable, 1928);

Dreiser Looks at Russia (New York: Liveright, 1928; London: Constable, 1929);

A Gallery of Women (New York: Liveright, 1929; London: Constable, 1930);

Dawn (New York: Liveright, 1931; London: Constable, 1931);

Promotional photo of Dreiser, circa 1917

Tragic America (New York: Liveright, 1931; London: Constable, 1932);

America Is Worth Saving (New York: Modern Age, 1941);

The Bulwark (Garden City: Doubleday, 1946; London: Constable, 1947);

The Stoic (Garden City: Doubleday, 1947);

Notes on Life, edited by Marguerite Tjader and John J. McAleer (University: University of Alabama Press, 1974);

Theodore Dreiser: A Selection of Uncollected Prose, edited by Donald Pizer (Detroit: Wayne State University Press, 1977).

Theodore Dreiser is one of the most significant and most problematical of American writers. His place in American literary history is secure. The acknowledged "trailblazer" for a generation of early twentieth-century American writers, his rebellious commitment to the honest portrayal of American life and the vagaries of human nature placed him in the forefront of American literature about the time of World War I. The great popular and critical success of *An American Tragedy* in 1925 solidified his American and international reputations. But from the publication of *Sister Carrie* in 1900, Dreiser was also a byword for all that is inept in fiction and fuzzy in thinking. By the time Lionel Trilling launched his famous attack on him in 1950 (in Trilling's *The Liberal Imagination,* some five years after Dreiser's death), it was often assumed that Dreiser wrote like a journalist and thought like an adolescent. Yet somehow, despite continuous attack, Dreiser's best fiction continues to hold and move. In recent years, with the appearance of a major biography and a series of perceptive critical studies, the emphasis in Dreiser studies has shifted from defense or condemnation to an effort to come to grips with the elusive and complex nature of his temperament, ideas, and creative power.

It is difficult to overestimate the importance for American literary history of Dreiser's emergence as a major writer out of the special circumstances of his background. Until Dreiser, the typical American author was of Protestant Anglo-Saxon stock. And while not necessarily a college graduate (though many were), he nevertheless grew up either in a bookish setting or in one which permitted easy access to self-education. None of these conditions prevailed for Dreiser. His father, John Paul Dreiser, was a Catholic German immigrant who reached America in 1844 at the age of twenty-three. His mother, Sarah Schänäb, was of Bohemian Mennonite background (she became a Catho-lic on marrying John Paul Dreiser in 1851). The Dreiser family prospered for a time as John Dreiser pursued his career as a wool worker. But then—after the births of six children and after a business failure caused by the burning of an uninsured woolen mill—the Dreisers moved into their permanent condition of poverty and flight. It was into a family at the very bottom of the social scale—poor, large, Catholic, ignorant, and superstitious—that Dreiser was born in late August 1871 in Terre Haute, Indiana. Dreiser's ability to rise out of these conditions (at what cost to his psyche he himself would later document in his autobiography *Dawn*) not only reveals his innate talents and his powerful will to succeed but also anticipates the emergence in following generations of many writers out of similar immigrant stock (the Jewish, for example) and out of similar impoverished backgrounds (particularly the black ghetto).

The character and experiences of the Dreiser family in the years during which Theodore was growing up were later to supply the mature author with many of his themes. The underlying configuration of the family—the warm, forgiving, and loving mother; the narrow-minded, disciplinarian father; and the fun-loving, wayward, and seeking children—became that of Dreiser's fictional families from the Gerhardts of *Jennie Gerhardt* (1911) to the Barneses of *The Bulwark* (1946). And the constant movement of the Dreiser family in search of a better life—in Dreiser's youth from Terre Haute, Sullivan, and Evansville in Indiana, to Chicago, and then back to Warsaw, Indiana—was to suggest to him the centrality of the American life pattern (one pursued by Carrie and Frank Cowperwood and Clyde Griffiths) of pushing on to new worlds as an old world crashes behind one.

In Dreiser's early teens the family settled for some years in the pleasant central Indiana town of Warsaw. There Dreiser had the good fortune to be placed in public schools (he had hitherto been in parochial schools) and to receive the encouragement of sympathetic teachers. But with adolescence there also came—as Dreiser describes in *Dawn* (1931)—the first powerful stirrings of sex and the first sense of the wonder and beauty of life, a wonder and beauty which he could feel in nature, in poetry, and in the face of a girl, but which he as yet could neither understand nor articulate.

Anxious, like Clyde Griffiths, both to experience a wider range of life and to escape the repressive family atmosphere created by his father's religious dogmatism, Dreiser moved to Chicago in 1887, at the age of sixteen. There, living with several of his older sisters who had earlier made their way to the city, he eked out an existence. As Carrie was to be, he was enthralled by the exciting possibilities of the city, its theaters, restaurants, and mansions, but like Carrie on her arrival he was living precariously on the margin of life, with no prospects of change but downward. He was saved for a time by his high school English teacher from Warsaw, Miss Mildred Fielding, who sponsored him for a year at Indiana University. At Bloomington during 1889-90, he gained little from his classroom work but absorbed from the collegiate setting a drive to somehow achieve the assurance and elegance of the young collegiates around him.

At the end of his year at Indiana, Dreiser returned to Chicago and again held a series of miscellaneous jobs, including one as assistant to a real-estate agent and another as bill collector for an installment firm. During this period the Dreiser family, which had itself resettled in Chicago in the late 1880s, began to break up. Sarah Dreiser died in late 1890; Paul Dreiser (who was to adopt the professional name of Paul Dresser) had long since left the family for a career as an entertainer and songwriter; and Mame, Emma, and Claire Dreiser had found themselves a series of well-to-do lovers, the prototypes of the Hurstwoods and Lester Kanes who frequent Dreiser's early novels.

Dreiser during these years lacked direction, and the major foundation of his life, the family, was slipping away. And then, in the summer of 1892, at the age of twenty-one, he cut a thin wedge into the kind of life he had been dreaming about and to which he was to devote his life. Completely inexperienced as a newspaperman, he believed nevertheless that the worldliness and excitement of the reporter's life were for him. By dint of luck and perseverance, he was finally taken on by one of the poorer Chicago papers, the *Globe*. There, with the aid of an editor who took an interest in him, he began to learn the trade that was to lead to *Sister Carrie* some eight years later.

By November 1892 Dreiser felt confident enough in his journalistic skills to seek a position with the prestigious *St. Louis Globe-Democrat*. His sixteen months as a reporter in St. Louis, first on the *Globe-Democrat* and then on the *Republic*, played an extremely important role in his development. Assigned to almost every task on a metropolitan daily, he reported murders, robberies, and catastrophes, interviewed visiting personalities, and wrote drama reviews and paragraphs. He saw the life of a late nineteenth-century American city in all its fullness, and he encountered as well, in the journalistic con-

ventions of the day, the various subterfuges, hypocrisies, and shams present in the late Victorian representation of that life.

Another significant event of Dreiser's stay in St. Louis was his meeting, in the summer of 1893, Sara ("Sallie") Osborne White, a schoolteacher who was a few years older than himself. Dreiser's relationship to Sallie White (or Jug, as she was familiarly called) dramatized several paradoxes central both to American experience of the time and to Dreiser's own life, paradoxes which were to serve as major themes in his fiction. Although Dreiser and Sallie were passionately in love, her strict moralism prevented any consummation of their love through a six-year engagement. And Dreiser himself found that he was engaged to a girl he wished to possess rather than to marry. Out of these contradictions between the socially required and the felt were to emerge several of Dreiser's early fictional preoccupations.

Increasingly restless in St. Louis, Dreiser in early 1894 moved on to Pittsburgh and the *Dispatch*. A trip to New York during the summer of 1894 to visit his successful songwriting brother Paul convinced him that it was New York above all which offered a doorway to success, and he moved there in the fall of 1894 in search of a newspaper job. Dreiser's half-year in Pittsburgh, however, completed his education. His work for the *Dispatch* soon settled into the writing of a daily column, and he was therefore free much of the day. Reading deeply at the public library in the philosophical works of Herbert Spencer and the fiction of Balzac, he found in their writing a confirmation of the impressions of experience he had been acquiring the last several years. Spencer's "Synthetic Philosophy"—an amalgam of nineteenth-century social beliefs and evolutionary science—argues that there is no authority in supernaturally sanctioned moral codes, that only that which develops naturally through the struggle for existence, whether this struggle occurs in nature or society, is beneficial. And Balzac's novels in which "a young man from the provinces" seeks in the urban cockpit of Paris the glories of life reaffirmed Dreiser's own belief that the seeker will find in the great city not only struggle, degradation, and destruction but also wonder, beauty, and fulfillment.

New York during the winter of 1894-1895, however, offered Dreiser principally hardship and depression. Out of work and almost penniless, he wandered the city as an anonymous stranger in search of warmth, as Hurstwood was to do in his final phase. But in the spring there arose a wonderful opportunity. Paul Dresser had become part

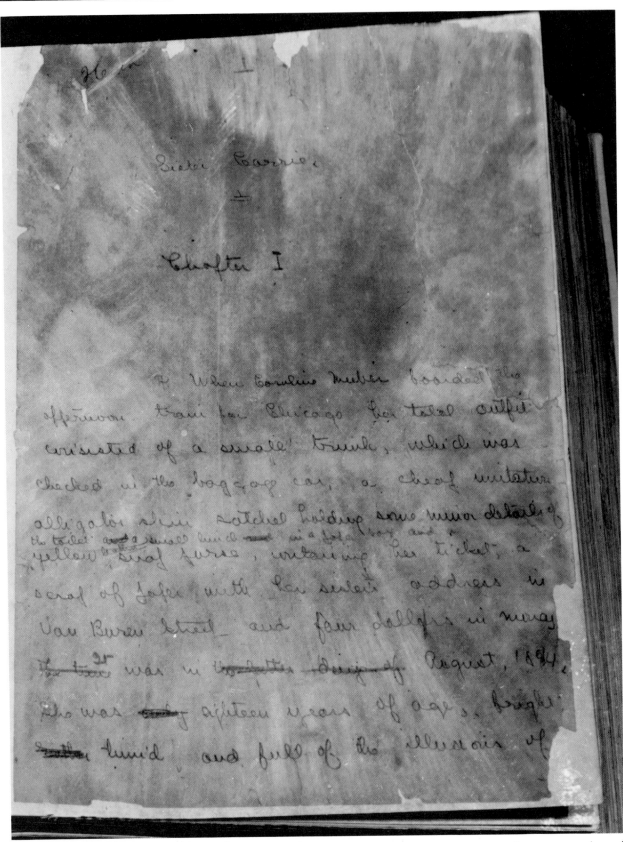

First page of the manuscript for Dreiser's first novel, unsupported by the publisher because of its frank treatment of a young woman's use of sex to advance herself

owner of a song-publishing firm and was seeking ways to popularize its songs. What better way to do this, Dreiser seems to have suggested to him, than to start a magazine, with Dreiser as editor, which would feature the firm's songs. *Ev'ry Month* appeared initially in October 1895. For two years Dreiser not only edited the magazine but contributed, frequently under a pseudonym, a wide variety of material to it. The most important of these miscellaneous contributions was a monthly column which he called "Reflections" and signed "The Prophet." In his column he tried out the ideas which he had been gathering both from his experience and his reading. (Many of the most significant of his "Reflections" columns are republished for the first time in *Theodore Dreiser: A Selection of Uncollected Prose*, edited by Donald Pizer.) A typical reflection would use a current event—an election, a winter storm, or a scandal—as an excuse for a disquisition on the nature of man and life. Dreiser's lifelong Balzacian custom of weaving philosophical commentary into his fiction received initial expression in the analogous form of the journalistic editorial.

After two years of editing *Ev'ry Month*, Dreiser appears to have desired broader and more fully rewarded opportunities. He resigned the editorship in the fall of 1897 and plunged into the expanding and competitive world of free-lance magazine writing. (The "ten-cent magazine revolution" of the 1890s had greatly increased the possibilities for a career as a free-lance journalist.) Writing on a wide variety of subjects (his favorites were accounts of artists and performers of all kinds, lavishly illustrated) and publishing in a large number of journals, Dreiser quickly made his mark in this field. One of the magazines he appeared in most frequently was *Success*, edited by Orison Swett Marden, a prominent promoter during the period of the American cult of success. Beneath the ingenuous optimism of the interviews Dreiser prepared for Marden, however, was his implicit understanding of the vast gulf that separates a Carnegie or a Field from a typical member of the audience of *Success*, a gulf which was to inform his depiction of both Frank Cowperwood and Clyde Griffiths.

Dreiser was aided in much of his free-lance writing by his close friend Arthur Henry. (They had met in Toledo in early 1894 and had cemented their friendship when Henry moved to New York later in the decade.) During the summer of 1899, Henry and his wife Maude Wood asked Dreiser and his wife (Dreiser and Sallie White had at last been married in late 1898) to visit them at their summer house on the Maumee River, near Toledo. It was

during this visit that Dreiser began in earnest, at the age of twenty-eight, his career as a writer of fiction. He had made several earlier attempts, notably during his first winter in New York in 1894-1895 and during his years on *Ev'ry Month*. These had all been aborted or had resulted in weak and derivative sketches. But now, encouraged by Henry, who also had aspirations for a career as a novelist, Dreiser wrote during that summer at Maumee four stories, each of which anticipates a major direction in his novels. The most important of these stories was "Nigger Jeff," later collected in Dreiser's *Free and Other Stories* (1918), in which a young reporter views and then comes to understand the lynching of a Negro accused of attacking a white girl. Based on an incident Dreiser had observed while a newspaperman in St. Louis, the story dramatizes Dreiser's realization that the tragic nature of man, whatever his station, lies in his capacity to feel pain, and that the tragic artist seeks to understand and express this capacity—to "get it all in," as the newspaperman exclaims at the end of "Nigger Jeff."

Although none of Dreiser's four Maumee stories was immediately accepted for publication, he was sufficiently stimulated by these new efforts in fiction to respond to Henry's suggestion, once they returned to New York in the fall, that he should undertake a novel. According to Dreiser's recollection, he began his first novel by taking a blank sheet of paper and writing on it, without further thought, its title, *Sister Carrie*. Be that as it may, the title *Sister Carrie* was immediately evocative to Dreiser for several reasons. Carrie in the role of sister has little importance in *Sister Carrie*. But in choosing this title Dreiser was signifying both that he was to tell a story, as did Balzac in his *Cousine Bette* (1846) and *Père Goriot* (1834), of individual failure and success in a great city, and more particularly for Dreiser, that the subject of this story was to be his own sister, Emma.

Emma Dreiser was one of several of Dreiser's sisters who had escaped the Dreiser family for a freer life in the city. In Chicago, she had had an affair initially with an architect and then, in 1885, with L. A. Hopkins, a chief clerk for Chapin and Gore, a firm which owned a number of Chicago saloons. Hopkins had a wife and family, and when his wife discovered his adultery in February 1886, he absconded to Canada with several thousand dollars from the firm's safe, taking a compliant Emma with him. Dreiser had met Emma and Hopkins in New York in 1894 and knew their story well. But for *Sister Carrie* he transformed it in several important ways, in particular by "refining" the characters of Carrie and Hurstwood and by giving their lives in New York a direction totally independent of that of Emma and Hopkins.

Dreiser began *Sister Carrie* in October 1899, and, aided by Henry and Jug at various times, completed it in March 1900. (One significant late revision was Dreiser's recasting of the conclusion to provide a Balzacian epilogue in which he effuses over the fate of Carrie.) It was with the completion of the novel that there occurred one of the most famous incidents in American literary history, the so-called suppression of *Sister Carrie* by Doubleday, Page, and Company, the publisher of the novel.

Doubleday, Page, a new firm, had on its staff as a reader the young novelist Frank Norris, whose own naturalistic *McTeague* had been published the previous year. Norris strongly endorsed *Sister Carrie,* and the firm agreed to publish it, even though its principal partner, Frank Doubleday, was in Europe at the time. On his return, however, Doubleday, Page, became much more hesitant about the book and also began to ask for revisions. Dreiser, his back up, refused most of the suggested changes and also refused to consider placing the novel elsewhere. At this point, Doubleday agreed to honor the earlier oral agreement and a formal contract was signed. But the firm failed to push or advertise the book, and it did not sell. In later years, and particularly in Dorothy Dudley's study of Dreiser's career, *Forgotten Frontiers* (1932), the actions of Doubleday, Page, became to Dreiser and his supporters a major symbol of control of American culture by a puritan ethic, and Dreiser was celebrated as a figure who both suffered from this control and persevered nevertheless. In particular, Mrs. Doubleday, who was rumored to have influenced her husband's attitude toward the novel but whose role is in fact unknown, became a figure epitomizing Victorian prudishness and narrowness. It is now known that the censorship of *Sister Carrie* by Doubleday, Page, was minimal (a few changes in profanity and proper names); that Doubleday did not have to agree to a contract after he found the book objectionable, but did so nevertheless; and that Dreiser and his supporters found it useful in later years to picture Dreiser as a martyr to American puritanism. But whatever the factual truth of "L'Affaire Doubleday" (as W. A. Swanberg calls it), the suppression of *Sister Carrie* has had a mythic truth of its own.

One can readily understand why Mrs. Doubleday, or any other proper American of the time, might have objected to *Sister Carrie.* Dreiser's novel begins with an archetypal American scene—the departure of a young girl from her home and family in a small town in order to make her way in the city. By the close of the novel, Carrie has risen, largely by the classic American combination of luck and pluck, to be a musical comedy star on Broadway. But within this traditional pattern of the American success story Dreiser is strikingly innovative. Carrie succeeds in part because at two crucial moments—when she is sick and exhausted after attempting to stay afloat in working-class Chicago, and after she has quarreled with her initial protector, Drouet—she accepts help from a man and then, almost casually and without a full crisis of conscience, sleeps with the man. The implication that sex for a young woman of Carrie's class and background was intimately linked to survival and success, and that a woman using her sex was not necessarily a fallen woman, ran counter to almost every conventional nineteenth-century belief about the nature of women and the inevitability of moral retribution.

Carrie's story is also one which Dreiser was to return to again in *The "Genius,"* that of the development of the artist. It is this aspect of Carrie—her "emotional greatness" and her capacity to seek "beauty"—which many readers have found less convincing than her career as a "soldier of fortune" armed only with her pertinacity and her sex. For many of these readers, the greater fictional figure in the novel—and for some the greatest in all of Dreiser's work—is Hurstwood, Carrie's second lover and the man with whom she runs away to New York after he has robbed his employers. In the character of Hurstwood Dreiser renders one of the basic fears of middle-class American life. A solid family man who nevertheless is bored by the graspingness and trivialities of his family, Hurstwood reaches out for something finer and richer in the person of Carrie, and in doing so sets the stage for his eventual tragic fall into the middle-class hell of disgrace and poverty. This, too, was one of Dreiser's deepest fears, just as Carrie's artistic success reflected his deepest hope. By informing both figures with his most intense personal feelings while maintaining their archetypal relevance to American life, Dreiser created a novel which has seldom failed to interest deeply even those who find major flaws in its form and style.

Dreiser's technical skills as novelist, even at their best, have almost always had their detractors. *Sister Carrie,* for example, like most of Dreiser's fiction, is marred by an inept prose style in which journalistic cliche, rank sentimentality (the chapter titles in particular), and clumsy syntax compete for attention. It is also a novel in which Dreiser's penchant for authorial philosophizing and commentary both impedes the flow of narrative and muddies characterization. Yet for all its weaknesses, the novel does hold, and in such sections as Carrie's seeking work in Chicago or Hurstwood down-and-out in New York it achieves the sublimity of expressing with a seeming inevitability the way we know life is.

Although Dreiser had begun a second novel, *Jennie Gerhardt,* even before the publication of *Sister Carrie* in November 1900, he made slow progress with the work. He was disturbed by the "suppression" of *Sister Carrie,* by money problems now that he was no longer writing for the magazines, and by the deterioration of his marriage. These worries soon began to take the form of frequent periods of depression, debility, and psychosomatic illness. Constant movement among various towns and cities in the Midwest and South in search of a cheap place to live and write did not help, and by early 1903 Dreiser was alone and penniless in New York, living in flophouses and afraid of meeting old friends, much like Hurstwood at the end of *Sister Carrie*. He was rescued by his brother Paul, who placed him in a health camp for overworked businessmen. This was followed by a period as a day laborer on the railroad, and in late 1903 Dreiser felt himself sufficiently recovered in body and spirit to return to his career as a writer. He began by again undertaking free-lance work; by the summer of 1905 he was installed as the editor of a popular monthly, *Smith's Magazine.* His success with *Smith's* and then, during 1906-1907, with the *Broadway Magazine* was capped in late 1907 when he was asked to become editor of Butterick's *Delineator,* the most popular magazine for women of its day.

Having reached this peak, Dreiser began to think of returning to fiction. The republication of *Sister Carrie* in 1907, to considerable critical acclaim, no doubt contributed to his belief that he had lain fallow too long. Another contributing factor was his establishment, also in 1907, of a lifelong relationship with H. L. Mencken. Mencken, who was himself just beginning his career as journalist and editor, shared with Dreiser a good-natured cynicism about the claims of popular taste on a magazine editor. By 1910, after three years at the *Delineator,* Dreiser had become extremely restless in his role as editor of a popular women's magazine while still relishing the power and wealth which the position entailed. Matters came to a head, as they were often to do for the remainder of Dreiser's life, on the crisis caused by a love affair. Dreiser had become infatuated with Thelma Cudlipp, the young daughter of a contributor to the *Delineator.* He pursued

Dreiser, circa 1908, when he was editor-in-chief at Butterick Publications

Thelma in a manner thought unfit for the married editor of a conservative journal and in October 1910 found himself fired. The affair itself soon collapsed, but it nevertheless had an important effect on Dreiser's life and work. It returned him perforce to writing—an effort to complete *Jennie Gerhardt* (1911)—and it was as an author that Dreiser was to spend the rest of his professional life. And it set the pattern for his personal life, a pattern of maintaining a shaky but long-term relationship with one woman (first Sallie White and later Helen Richardson) while pursuing as well many temporary affairs.

Dreiser completed *Jennie Gerhardt* in early 1911. This initial full version of the novel ended with the reconciliation of Jennie and her lover Lester Kane, but after several readers of the manuscript suggested the need for a tragic conclusion to the story, Dreiser revised its final chapters. *Jennie Gerhardt,* like *Sister Carrie,* has its origin in the life of one of Dreiser's sisters, in this instance Mame Dreiser. Jennie, like Mame, is seduced by a well-to-do benefactor of the impoverished Gerhardt family (a family modeled closely on the Dreisers) and has an illegitimate child by him. And again like Mame, Jennie then moves on to a far more satisfying relationship with the son of a prominent commercial family. *Sister Carrie* and *Jennie Gerhardt* are thus similar in centering on the sexual experience of a young girl and in intimating that such experience is not only inseparable from the texture of American life but that it can occur without blemishing the immortal soul of the girl. *Jennie Gerhardt* is dissimilar from *Sister Carrie*, however, in that the characters and fates of Jennie and Lester are considerably different from those of Carrie and Hurstwood.

Jennie is Dreiser's portrait of the woman as giver, of a spirit of feminine plentitude comparable to nature as mother. But as in Hardy's *Tess of the D'Urbervilles* (1891), a novel which influenced Dreiser deeply, Jennie's natural generosity runs counter both to the mercantile spirit of selling oneself dearly and to the religious spirit of offering oneself only within specific conditions. She gives herself in love, without marriage, and thus suffers rejection first by her family and then by the world at large. Yet despite this casting out, she continues to grow in spirit and mind—indeed, and somewhat like Carrie now, she seems to find in her difficulties a form of education of her inner nature.

Jennie's first relationship is with Senator Brander. After his death, she begins to live with Lester Kane, who bears a superficial resemblance to Hurstwood in that both men seek love outside of marriage despite prominence and success in their middle-class worlds. But Kane, unlike Hurstwood, is also an intellectual, and in his brooding, indecisive speculations about the nature of life Dreiser created one of his most moving characters. Loving Jennie deeply yet afraid to surrender the comforts of his position in the world, knowing from his reading the instability of the universe and of man himself, seemingly strong and assertive yet fundamentally insecure and weak, Kane attempts to have it both ways—to keep both Jennie and his "comforts"—and in the end has neither. He is forced to give up Jennie, and he eventually discovers that his old life has lost its savor. Bitterly disappointed, he can only tell Jennie, just before his death, that he has made a mistake. And for Jennie, at the close of the novel, there will only be "days after days in endless reiteration."

H. L. Mencken, who had a surprising weakness for sentiment, always believed that *Jennie Gerhardt* was Dreiser's best novel. Some readers have occasionally felt that Dreiser's earth-mother portrayal of Jennie, particularly in the early chapters, is too cloying. But other critics have found the novel to be a moving and significant portrayal of the nature of tragic pathos in human relations, of the failure of love less because of exceptional major flaws in character or because of extraordinary circumstances than through the steady pressure of social reality and the limitations of human nature upon so fragile a condition as a man and a woman in love.

On the whole, *Jennie Gerhardt* was both a critical and a popular success. Dreiser was encouraged sufficiently by its reception to believe that he should continue his literary career rather than return to editorial work. So, at the age of forty, Dreiser for the first time in his life determined that he would try not merely to make a living as a writer but would seek to combine that effort with an attempt to express himself as honestly as possible. Given both Dreiser's financial needs and his immense energy, the result over the next fifteen years (from *Jennie Gerhardt* in 1911 to *An American Tragedy* in 1925) of this full commitment to literature was an outpouring of creative energy seldom equaled in the history of American literature. Dreiser wrote during this period four very long novels (*The "Genius,"* 1915; *The Financier*, 1912; *The Titan*, 1914; and *An American Tragedy*, 1925); four equally lengthy works of travel narrative and autobiography (*A Traveler at Forty*, 1913; *A Hoosier Holiday*, 1916; *Dawn*, 1931; and *A Book About Myself*, 1922); two volumes of plays (*Plays of the Natural and the Supernatural*, 1916, and *The Hand of the Potter*, 1919); most of the contents of four collections of short stories and sketches (*Free and Other Stories*, 1918; *Twelve Men*, 1919; *Chains*, 1927; and *The Color of a Great City*, 1923); and a volume of philosophical essays (*Hey Rub-a-Dub-Dub*, 1920).

Dreiser's personal life was equally active during this period. After the turmoil caused by his affair with Thelma Cudlipp, he and Sallie Dreiser continued to live together in New York for occasional stretches until 1914, when they separated for the last time and Dreiser took up quarters in Greenwich Village. There he had a number of relationships, in particular with the youthful actress Kirah Markham—the Stephanie Platow of *The Titan*—until in 1919 he met an equally youthful and attractive distant cousin, Helen Patges Richardson. They fell in love, and though Dreiser was soon to pursue again his "varietistic" interests (his term for his constant need for different women), he and Helen were to live together for most of the remainder of his life. (They were not married, however, until 13 June 1944.) One immediate consequence of their meeting was Dreiser's move to Los Angeles with Helen in October 1919, since Helen wished to become a film actress. He was uncomfortable in Los Angeles, however, and after three years was happy to return to New York, where he was to live until 1938.

Two other major events of this period in Dreiser's life were the suppression of *The "Genius"* in 1916 and the long and important association with the publisher Horace Liveright which he established in 1918. Dreiser had come under increasing attack for his depiction of the sex drive in human experience—not for his portrayal of the physical aspect of sex (indeed, he was usually reticent in this matter) as for his amoral acknowledgment of its presence and power. Many reviewers had been scandalized by his depiction of Frank Cowperwood's sexual nature and values in *The Financier* and *The Titan*, and many were outraged even further by the sexual themes in *The "Genius"* on its publication in 1915. Among the most famous and influential attacks of this kind on Dreiser was Stuart P. Sherman's essay, "The Naturalism of Mr. Dreiser," in the 2 December 1915 issue of the *Nation*. Almost inevitably, given the cultural climate of the day, the New York Society for the Suppression of Vice (led by John S. Sumner) brought an action to have the novel banned. This led to a major literary skirmish. H. L. Mencken, who in fact thought the novel banal, organized a campaign in the name of artistic freedom to force the courts to void the censorship of *The "Genius,"* a campaign which a number of more conservative authors and critics supported. Although the case was not to be resolved for several years, it served to confirm in both the public mind and the literary scene the image of Dreiser as at once the champion of artistic freedom and the victim of cultural philistinism.

Of equal importance to Dreiser's career was his association with the flamboyant Horace Liveright. Dreiser had had a series of unsuccessful relationships with publishers—with Doubleday, Page, with Harper's, and finally with John Lane—all of whom, he felt, had failed him when they came under pressure from the forces of puritanism. In Liveright he found a publisher who was willing to take risks—who indeed was to publish in 1919 Dreiser's sympathetic treatment of a sex murderer in his play *The Hand of the Potter*. Although theirs was often a stormy association (Dreiser believed all publishers were dishonest), they remained together from 1918, when Boni and Liveright published *Free and Other Stories*, through the great success of *An American Tragedy* in 1925 to the dissolution of

Liveright's firm in 1932 after the publication of *Tragic America*.

Although *The "Genius"* was not published until 1915, Dreiser had completed a draft of the novel in the summer of 1911 after finishing *Jennie Gerhardt* and before beginning research on the Cowperwood trilogy. Publication of the novel was delayed because Harper's wished to publish *The Financier* and *The Titan* first. Thus, it was not until *The Titan* appeared in 1914 that the firm was ready to go on to *The "Genius"*. By this time, however, Dreiser had second thoughts about the conclusion of the work (as he did with almost all his novels, from *Sister Carrie* to *The Stoic*, 1947). In the original version of the novel, Dreiser's autobiographical protagonist Eugene Witla, in an act of fictional wish fulfillment by Dreiser, is reunited with Suzanne Dale, the Thelma Cudlipp of the novel. By 1915, Dreiser recognized the fatuousness of this conclusion and changed it to one in which Eugene has grown beyond the need for Suzanne and has turned fully to his philosophical musings and to his art.

Most readers of *The "Genius"* have held that it was not only the conclusion but the entire novel which reflected adversely Dreiser's excessive closeness to his material. Eugene Witla is Dreiser's most autobiographical fictional figure. Like Dreiser, he becomes an artist (a painter in Witla's case) after a midwestern boyhood, has a disastrous marriage to a woman who is at once sensual and puritanical, suffers a nervous breakdown, is restored to good health and to a career as an editor, and finally—after a love affair with a young girl—returns to his art. Literalness mars Dreiser's extremely long reprise of his life in *The "Genius"* from the beginning to the end of the novel—both the literalness of external detail and of the details of Eugene's emotional life. Although some sections—such as Eugene's working on the railroad—come to life, on the whole the entire work, in particular its last third, which concentrates on Eugene and Suzanne's affair, exaggerates the reader's interest in a figure as vapid, confused, and self-apologetic as Eugene. The only major area of the novel which still holds is that devoted to the marriage of Eugene and Angela Blue (the Sallie White of the novel). A study in a mismating of temperaments in which only a desperate sexuality and a jealous possessiveness bind the couple, these passages render the deceptions and torments of a destructive marriage with a power equal to that of Edward Albee's *Who's Afraid of Virginia Woolf?* (1962).

After completing *The "Genius"* in mid-1911, Dreiser plunged into research for the Cowperwood

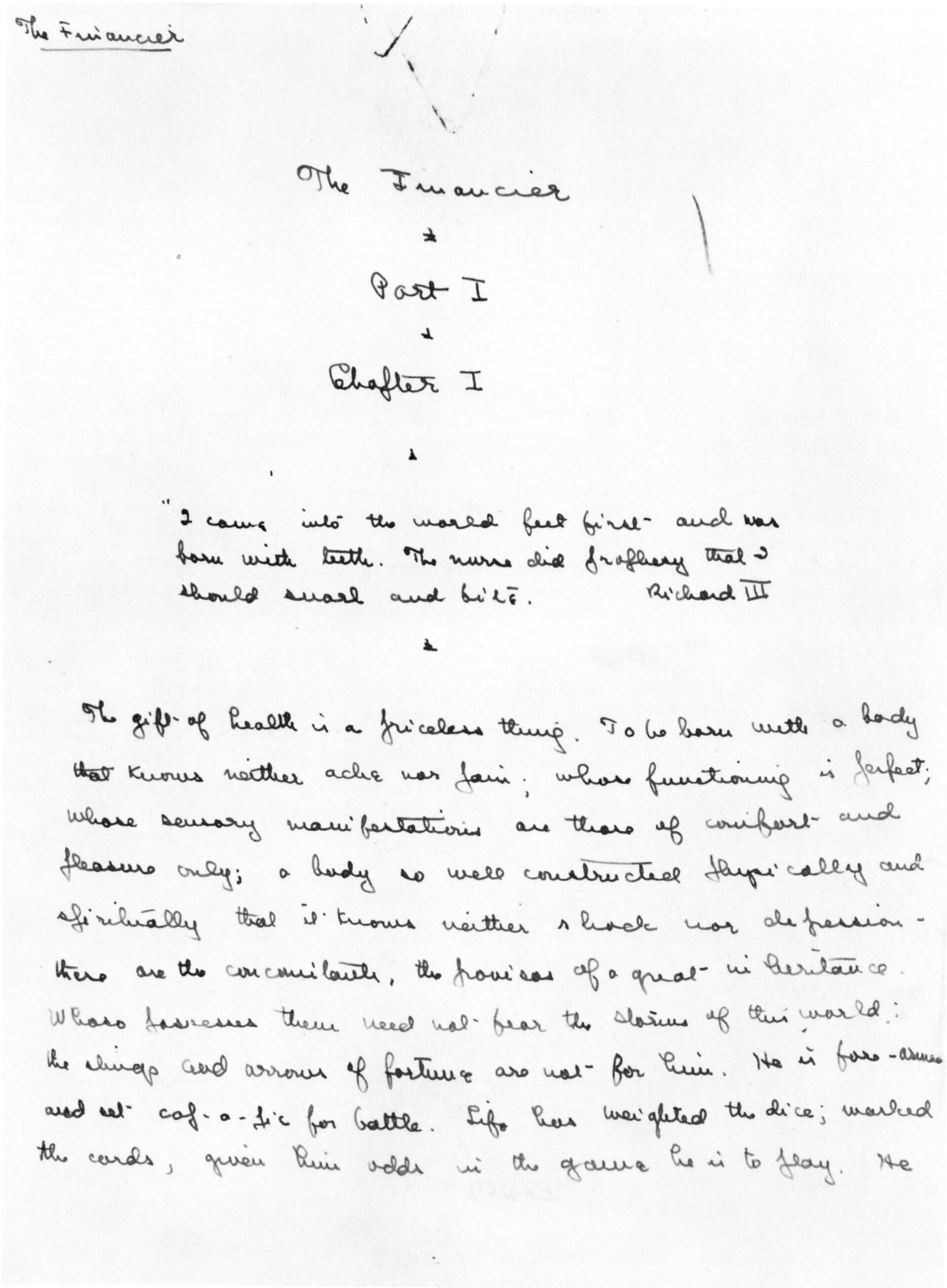

The Financier

The Financier

Part I

Chapter I

"I came into the world feet first and was born with teeth. The nurse did prophesy that I should snarl and bite. Richard III

The gift of health is a priceless thing. To be born with a body that knows neither ache nor pain; whose functioning is perfect; whose sensory manifestations are those of comfort and pleasure only; a body so well constructed physically and spiritually that it knows neither shock nor depression— these are the concomitants, the promises of a great inheritance. Whoso possesses them need not fear the storms of this world; the slings and arrows of fortune are not for him. He is fore-armed and set cap-a-pie for battle. Life has weighted the dice; marked the cards, given him odds in the game he is to play. He

Initial pages of the manuscript for first volume of the Cowperwood trilogy. The opening paragraph was omitted from the published book.

comes stamped with the tilka mark upon his brow. His pathway is cleared by armed outriders crying "make way". He is indeed the embodiment of that biblical legend — the phraseology of which is so perfect: "this is my beloved son in whom I am well pleased."

The Philadelphia into which Frank Algernon Cowperwood was born was at his very birth already a city of 250,000 and more. It was set with handsome parks, notable buildings, and crowded with historic memories. Many of the things that we and he knew later were not then in existence — the telegraph, telephone, express company, ocean steamers or city delivery of mails. There were no postage stamps or registered letters. The street car had not arrived and in their place were lines of omnibuses and for longer travel the slowly developing railroad system still largely connected with canals. Young Cowperwood's father was a bank clerk at his birth and his years later when young Cowperwood was turning a very sensible, vigorous eye on the world his father was still a clerk although he was a much more trusted

series. Now, after three works which had their source in his family or himself, he was to undertake a novel derived almost entirely from the life and times of a historical figure, the traction magnate Charles T. Yerkes. Yerkes had had a much-publicized career in Philadelphia, Chicago, and London as a traction company organizer, an art collector, and as a womanizer. Dreiser determined to describe Yerkes's life in all its phases through the character of Frank Cowperwood. His intent was to combine a study of the man of power with an epic account of the buccaneering period of American finance from the Civil War to the end of the nineteenth century.

Dreiser worked steadily on *The Financier* until late 1911, when he interrupted his writing for a five-month European tour. His reason for the trip was to gather material on Yerkes's London years, but he was also excited by the idea of going to Europe for the first time. In order to help finance the journey, he wrote for the *Century* magazine a series of travel essays and then, on his return, expanded these into a book. *A Traveler at Forty* is one of Dreiser's most engaging works. A kind of not-so-innocent-abroad travel narrative, the book combines Dreiser's often shrewd comments on European life and institutions with his ingenuous delight at the pleasures of the flesh and spirit (whether in French cafes or Italian galleries) which Europe so amply provided.

On his return from Europe, Dreiser completed *The Financier*. He had realized, by this time, that he would be unable to encompass Yerkes's life in one novel, and he and Harper's decided on a trilogy, with each novel to be separately published and titled. The first novel, dealing with Yerkes's early life in Philadelphia, was to be called *The Financier*; the second, with his great triumphs in Chicago, *The Titan*; and the last, with his London years and death, *The Stoic*. After completing *The Financier*, Dreiser went quickly ahead with *The Titan* and was able to have it published in 1914. He then put aside the trilogy until the early 1930s, when he worked on *The Stoic* but did not finish it. This he was unable to do until shortly before his death in 1945. For this reason it has become conventional to discuss the Cowperwood trilogy principally as *The Financier* and *The Titan* and to consider *The Stoic* as a novel of Dreiser's final years.

The Financier and *The Titan* can be described as anti-epics. That is, we follow Frank Cowperwood from his origins in conventional middle-class life to his climactic role as one of the titans of American economic life. Although he has several momentary

setbacks during this ascent, including a major one at the conclusion of *The Titan*, his shrewdness, strength, and ruthlessness always carry him on to fresh triumphs. Dreiser's celebration of Cowperwood as an American epic hero is thus inherently ironic, since Cowperwood's success derives principally from his ability to recognize and exploit the difference between the jungle amoralism of American life and the veneer of moral utterance which disguises that reality. What makes Cowperwood so powerful is his willingness to be consciously guided entirely by his own interests. "I satisfy myself," is his motto.

Theodore Dreiser

Dreiser also wished in the trilogy to dramatize his belief that the seeking spirit—whether it be a Carrie wishing happiness or a Cowperwood wanting power—almost always desires beauty as well. For Cowperwood, beauty is found in women and art, and much of *The Financier* and *The Titan* are devoted to his pursuit of these. Because Cowperwood has no respect for marriage, casual readers of the trilogy have often missed the "spiritual" nature of his pursuit of women, particularly in *The Titan,* where he has over a dozen affairs. For Cowperwood views sexual gratification not only as a fulfillment, through the "affections," of his desire to possess beauty, but also as communion with his lovers on a higher and higher scale of spirituality. By the close of *The Titan,* he finds in the ethereal and almost sexless Berenice a full expression of woman as spirit.

Neither *The Financier* nor *The Titan* is fully successful as fiction, though both have had their supporters. The two novels—and particularly *The Titan*—are frequently little more than narratives of Cowperwood's alternating successes in the board and bedroom, and for most readers they often contain too much detail of Cowperwood's financial transactions. Indeed, the most compelling portions of the two novels lie less in Cowperwood's epic struggles than in more intimate "family" material. In *The Financier,* Cowperwood, while married, falls in love with the young girl Aileen, whose father, Edward Butler, an Irish immigrant, has risen to power in the corrupt Philadelphia political world. The emotional permutations arising out of the "pagan" couple and the old-world protective father reveal Dreiser at his best. And in *The Titan* it is not the largely symbolic figure of Berenice which moves us but the now aging and discarded Aileen whose rages and bitterness have the ring of truth.

With Dreiser's completion of *The Titan* in 1914, and with his decision not to proceed with *The Stoic,* he was free to undertake new fictional projects. But though Dreiser worked sporadically on several long works of fiction during the next decade—principally on his novel of Quaker life, *The Bulwark*—it was not until 1925 that his next novel, *An American Tragedy,* appeared. A good deal of Dreiser's publications during this decade consisted of collections of the various sketches and short stories he had been writing since *Sister Carrie.* His major new writing was in the areas of autobiography, drama, and philosophy.

Dreiser's principal autobiographical works—*A Hoosier Holiday, A Book About Myself,* and *Dawn*—were written from approximately 1914 to 1920. *A Hoosier Holiday,* though superficially a record of Dreiser's automobile trip to Indiana in the summer of 1915 with his artist friend Franklin Booth, is more often an evocative account of Dreiser's Indiana boyhood laced with observations about American life. *Dawn* and *A Book About Myself* are more conventional autobiographies. (Although written before *A Book About Myself, Dawn* was not published until 1931 because of its frank depiction

of Dreiser's youthful sex experiences.) *Dawn* takes Dreiser up to about 1890, while *A Book About Myself* (which was entitled *Newspaper Days* on its republication in 1931) is devoted almost entirely to his career as a newspaperman in Chicago, St. Louis, Pittsburgh, and New York. Both works are not only invaluable accounts of Dreiser's early experiences, beliefs, and feelings but also have an aesthetic effect similar to that of Dreiser's best novels. Through a seemingly artless directness and fullness they engage us in the corporal and spiritual adventures of a frequently unattractive "hero" whose life and beliefs are nevertheless absorbing and moving.

Dreiser's plays and philosophical essays of this period—published in *Plays of the Natural and the Supernatural, The Hand of the Potter,* and *Hey Rub-a-Dub-Dub*—reveal his exploration in strikingly different forms of a similar concern. He was increasingly becoming absorbed in what he believed to be the tragic nature of the human condition and was seeking both to explain and dramatize this vision of life. In such realistic plays as *The Girl in the Coffin* (1917) and *The Hand of the Potter* (1919), he dealt with the theme by depicting man's inability to shape the direction of his life given his lack of control of his underlying makeup. *The Hand of the Potter,* in its sympathetic portrayal of a sex murderer, is a particularly sensationalistic rendering of this theme. And in a series of one-act plays of the "supernatural" which were heavily influenced by the contemporary expressionistic movement he sought to offer still further examples of the indeterminacy and waywardness of life. The essays of *Hey Rub-a-Dub-Dub*—a work subtitled *A Book of the Mystery and Terror and Wonder of Life*—deal discursively with these themes. Dreiser in his essays was heavily influenced by Herbert Spencer's ideas of "equation," in which individual fates are controlled by the evolutionary force which requires that such unequal conditions in life as poverty and wealth or weakness and strength constantly seek but never fully achieve a balance or equilibrium. The essays are plodding, repetitive, and on the whole unenlightening. Dreiser was the kind of speculative thinker who best expressed his ideas symbolically in the fictional reality of a novel.

The work which climaxed this productive decade and a half in Dreiser's career is *An American Tragedy.* Dreiser in the years after the publication of *An American Tragedy* frequently claimed that from the earliest days of his career as a newspaperman he had had an interest in a certain kind of crime which he believed was significantly expressive of American life. As he encountered this crime on various

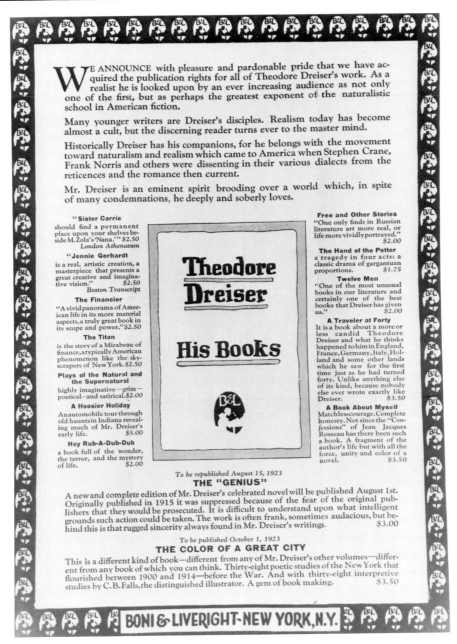

1923 advertisement by Boni & Liveright for Dreiser's works

occasions in St. Louis, Pittsburgh, and New York, it had a single underlying configuration beneath its superficial differences. A young man, poor but anxious to succeed, falls in love with a girl of his own class whom he makes pregnant. There then arrives on the scene a well-to-do young woman who is responsive to the young man and with whose aid he can rise. In one direction lie duty and poverty, in another wealth and power through love. When the young man seeks to solve his dilemma by disposing of "Miss Poor" so that he will be free to marry "Miss Rich," he is discovered and is ultimately punished.

Much of Dreiser's absorption in this kind of crime stemmed from the closeness of its basic characteristics to some of his own most deeply felt motives in life. He, too, as a poor, youthful outsider had dreamed of easily rising to great heights through the favors of a "Miss Rich." And he, too, had felt trapped in dutiful relationships—first with Sallie White (whom he did indeed "kill off" in *The "Genius"* by having Angela Blue die) and later, even while writing *An American Tragedy,* with Helen Richardson.

When Dreiser accompanied Helen to Los

Angeles in 1919, he ostensibly was at work on *The Bulwark,* his novel of Quaker life, which he had begun in 1914. But while in California he either discovered or became reinterested in a particular instance of this kind of crime, the famous Chester Gillette-Grace Brown murder case of 1906. In the summer of 1920 he put aside *The Bulwark* and began work on *An American Tragedy.* A lengthy false start, in which he depended too heavily on his own boyhood for the depiction of Clyde Griffiths's youth, delayed his efforts and it was not until his return to New York in late 1922 that he undertook the novel in earnest. Full use of the accounts of the Gillette trial in the *New York World,* a visit to the North Woods setting where Grace had been killed, and even attendance at a Sing Sing execution supplied some of the material for the million or so words of the novel which Dreiser wrote during the next several years. With the aid of friends and editors, more than half of this manuscript was cut, still leaving the substantial two-volume work which Liveright published in December 1925.

Chester Gillette had gone to the small upstate New York town of Cortland to work in his uncle's skirt factory. There he had seduced and made pregnant a girl from a neighboring village who also worked at the factory. Under pressure from her to marry, he killed her at an Adirondack lake by striking her with a tennis racket until she drowned. Although Dreiser used both the general outline and much specific detail from the Gillette case, he also made several significant changes which suggest the thematic direction he wished to give this material. For example, Clyde Griffiths comes out of a poorer and more limited background than did Gillette, and he is more interested in a specific upper-class girl—the Sondra of *An American Tragedy*—than was Gillette. And Clyde's involvement in the death of Roberta is far more ambiguous than was Gillette's in the murder of Grace Brown. Dreiser in these and similar changes revealed that his intent was less to render literally a sensational crime than to dramatize in fictional form a morally and culturally complex event.

Much of the success of *An American Tragedy* derives from Dreiser's ability to structure his very long novel into three distinctive parts, each with its own setting, pace, and climax, yet with each contributing as well to the powerful tragic effect at the center of the novel. The novel begins with Clyde as a young boy in Kansas City. His parents are ineffectual, self-deluded street evangelists, and Clyde is introduced early in life to the vast difference between their cloudy dreams and the riches and won-

ders of the metropolis. Although Clyde soon abandons their way of life, he remains—in his own weaknesses and mirages—their son. Clyde's principal initiation into experience occurs at the Green-Davidson Hotel where he works as a bellhop. There he falls in with a group of boys who come to represent all that he wishes in life—girls, clothes, a good time, and little responsibility. *An American Tragedy* thus has from its beginning the character of a simple dramatization of the parable of the prodigal son but for its developing theme that Clyde, because of both his limited equipment and the tawdry nature of the life he so desperately desires, also mirrors some of the essential flaws in the American Dream. Book one ends with an automobile accident which foreshadows the "accident" at the close of book two in which Roberta drowns. Off on a suspect escapade with his chums, Clyde is at once innocent and guilty of contributing to the accident, and he also hesitates in coming to the aid of his companions at a crucial moment.

In book two, Clyde makes his way to Lycurgus, in upstate New York, to take a position in his uncle's factory. In Lycurgus, he finds himself treated as a poor relation by the Griffithses, while the bulk of the town considers him a member of a wealthy and powerful family. Miserable and lonely, he finds comfort and love with Roberta Alden, who works with him in the factory and who is herself the daughter of poor local farmers. Despite her resistance, he persuades her to become his lover. Soon afterward, however, in a fulfillment of Clyde's wildest hopes, he is taken up by Sondra Finchley and her set. Sondra, the daughter of another Lycurgus manufacturer, is both attractive and rich, and she thus constitutes for Clyde an almost religious manifestation of his dreams. But first Clyde must get rid of Roberta, and as he works up courage to do so, she becomes pregnant. There then follows one of the most harrowing narratives in all of American fiction. Roberta is increasingly insistent that Clyde do something, but because of his ignorance, poverty, and fear, he is incapable of resolving the problem other than in the one way he refuses to accept—to marry Roberta. Sondra, in the meantime, is increasingly warm toward Clyde, and his prospect of marrying her is ever brighter. Driven to distraction, Clyde arranges a trip to the North Woods with Roberta. Ostensibly, they are to be married during the trip, but Clyde in fact plans to stage a mock accident at a lake, during which Roberta will drown and he will disappear. (He also plans to disguise his identity during this trip.) On the lake, Clyde's nerve fails him. He is so obviously overcome with emotion, however, that Roberta seeks to come to his aid. The boat tips over, and Roberta begins to drown. She calls for help, but Clyde swims away. Has he killed her or has he not?

Book three of *An American Tragedy* demonstrates that this question, as well as similar complex questions concerning moral responsibility and justice, is extraneous within the American legal system. Clyde is soon tracked down, captured, placed on trial, convicted, and sentenced to death. The jury is convinced of his guilt not only because he set out to murder Roberta but because the district attorney persuades them that Clyde, a wealthy Griffiths, seduced and then wished to abandon a poor country girl. Whatever ambiguities are attached to Roberta's death, the case is decided principally on the basis of the jury's class and sex prejudices. In prison, while awaiting execution, Clyde encounters a last dream, that offered by the Reverend McMillan, who promises forgiveness and salvation in return for confession and an acceptance of God. Clyde again reaches out, but at his death he wonders in his heart if he will find yet another mirage.

An American Tragedy has moved several generations of readers with its compelling power as a narrative of crime and punishment. It has had a more varied history, however, as a view of the tragic nature of experience. As a novel which seeks to dramatize an underlying flaw in American life, *An American Tragedy* reveals the terrible power of American national experience to convince even the weakest and most ineffectual that life is full of

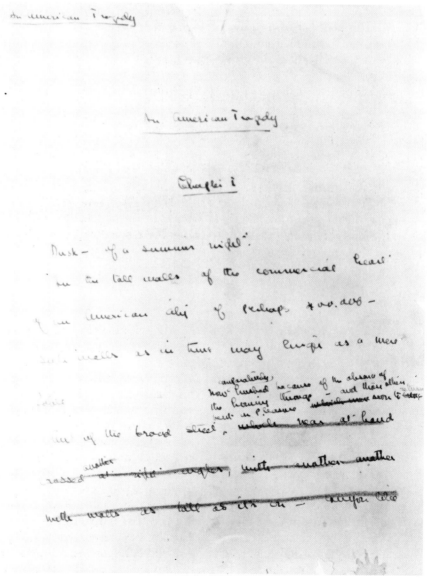

First page of the manuscript for Dreiser's best-known novel, based on the Chester Gillette murder case

promise and that the answer to our dreams lies in wealth. As a work of larger tragic dimensions, the novel forces the reader to share in the fall of a human being who, whatever his limitations, wishes to be understood and finds that he is merely condemned.

flurry of publication in the five years or so after the appearance of *An American Tragedy* to capitalize on the success of that work. Two editions of Dreiser's poems, a collection of short stories (*Chains*), and a two-volume collection of sketches (*A Gallery of Women*) all appeared between 1925 and 1930.

John Dos Passos, Theodore Dreiser, and Samuel Ornitz during their 1931 investigation of working conditions in Harlan County, Kentucky, coal mines

An American Tragedy was greeted as a great American novel on its publication. Even one of Dreiser's foremost detractors, Stuart P. Sherman, considered it a major work. The novel was also a financial success, with play and movie adaptations soon augmenting its earnings. So after twenty-five years of struggle for recognition and success as a writer of fiction, Dreiser had at last come into his own. Indeed, for some years it was believed that he would be the first American to be honored with the Nobel Prize.

With the completion of *An American Tragedy*, Dreiser did not turn immediately to another novel, as had been his habit earlier in his career, but rather permitted his increasing absorption in social and philosophical matters to occupy him, as they were to do for almost two decades. Not that there was not a

But for the most part Dreiser's interest during the late 1920's was focused on two fundamental problems—how to make America a better place in which to live, and how to describe the underlying truths of existence. The centrality of these concerns in Dreiser's thought and life of the time is suggested by two events of 1927 and 1928. In November 1927 Dreiser visited the Soviet Union and remained for several months, principally in Moscow. Like most American intellectuals of the day, he was fascinated by the Russian experiment, and like most, he was especially interested in its possible applicability to America. Then, during the summer of 1928, Dreiser spent several weeks visiting the Woods Hole experimental biology station in Massachusetts, where he talked with scientists and observed their work. His interest was less in the details of their experiments than in their beliefs about the fundamental processes of life.

These two personal ventures into knowledge in the late 1920s anticipate Dreiser's almost obsessive preoccupations of the 1930s. During that decade, despite several halfhearted and unsuccessful attempts to work on *The Bulwark* and *The Stoic*, Dreiser's interests were almost entirely limited to the support of left-wing causes and to his own philosophical studies. Out of the first came such volumes as *Dreiser Looks at Russia* (1928), *Harlan Miners Speak* (1932), a record of the investigation by Dreiser and others of the Harlan County miners strike in 1931 for which Dreiser wrote the introduction, and *Tragic America* (1931). Out of the second came a vast collection of notes and a number of muddy and diffuse essays. Several of these essays appeared in the 1930's, but the bulk of his philosophical writing remained unpublished until collected in Dreiser's posthumous *Notes on Life* in 1974.

As some observers have noted, and as Dreiser himself realized, there appears to be a contradiction between these two preoccupations. On the one hand, Dreiser's interest in American social problems, in the efforts of the poor and oppressed to gain a better life, posits a belief in man's ability to improve his condition through conscious effort. On the other, Dreiser's philosophical speculations had led him to reconfirm his earlier notion that the world was a machine in which the individual had no control over his destiny. To Dreiser, however, these positions were not irreconcilable. He had come increasingly to view the mechanistic foundations of life not so much as imprisoning but as a vast and intricate complex of beauty and wonder in which the destructive effects upon others of extremes in ability and fortune could be lessened through social change. The two positions were, in any case, to be reconciled in Dreiser's life and fiction in the last years of his life. In the period just before his death he was absorbed in the mystical aspects of Hinduism and joined the Communist party. And he sought in the final beliefs of his characters Solon Barnes in *The Bulwark* and Berenice in *The Stoic* to represent his own final equanimity in the face of both the world's pain and beauty.

Dreiser's personal fortunes suffered during the Depression, particularly after the collapse of his long-time publisher, Horace Liveright, in 1932. In 1938, he settled his affairs in New York, where at one time he had had both a country estate at Mt. Kisco and a luxurious apartment on Fifty-seventh Street in New York City, and moved with Helen to a small cottage in Los Angeles. There he became increasingly strident and single-minded in his party-line beliefs and public statements. Unlike most American writers, who had begun to drift away from the Communist party following the Stalinist purges of the mid-1930s and the Nazi-Soviet pact of 1939, Dreiser in the late 1930s and early 1940s became even more convinced that the capitalist countries of the world were engaged in a conspiracy to destroy the Soviet Union. He distributed from Los Angeles a series of privately printed broadsides (often enclosed in letters to friends) supporting his views. He also made these beliefs the center of the last book which he published during his lifetime, the polemic diatribe (largely ghostwritten by a party hack), *America is Worth Saving* (1941).

Dreiser's major creative effort during the last years of his life was the completion at long last of both *The Bulwark* and *The Stoic*. He had begun *The Bulwark* in 1914, after hearing from Anna Tatum, a young woman of Philadelphia Quaker background, the story of her father's tragic life, and had worked sporadically on the novel for the next several years. (Indeed, Liveright announced the imminent publication of the novel on several occasions during this period.) But though he made extensive notes for the novel, and wrote a lengthy draft of its early portion, he failed to complete it, and in 1920 put it aside to work on *An American Tragedy*.

The appeal to Dreiser of the story of Solon Barnes and his family was that it closely resembled both the shape of Dreiser's own family life and that of the families he was depicting in his fiction. A moralistic, disciplinarian father and a warmhearted, generous mother have children whose desire for a fuller, more exciting life breeds rebellion and anger toward the father despite his and their love. The father is thus a bulwark of faith and behavior who nevertheless cannot prevent the tragic consequences of family conflict. This was the kind of story which always moved Dreiser as he responded to its combination of love, blindness, and desire and enveloped the whole in his compassionate understanding.

When Dreiser returned to *The Bulwark* in 1942, he did so with interests which were to give this novel, as well as *The Stoic*, a significant new direction. As has been noted, Dreiser's studies in the 1930s had led him to view the mechanistic design of life as infinitely beautiful and awe-inspiring. He therefore found during these years that such traditional mystic faiths as Hinduism and Quakerism (as well as the transcendentalism of Thoreau, a collection of whose writings he edited in 1939) provided an accommodation of both his mechanistic and his religious beliefs. The world was a complex machine, but a machine so beautiful and complex must have a divine origin, and the man of intuitive insight could recognize the spiritual reality pervading all nature.

chronology are too expansive for Dreiser's almost chroniclelike treatment of character and event, and the central portion of the novel, much of which deals with Solon's business affairs, is out of key with the tone of the more "religious" sections of the

Theodore Dreiser in the last year of his life

It was with this vision of life that Dreiser began to revise *The Bulwark* in 1942, giving now much fuller attention at the beginning and close of the novel to Solon's Quaker beliefs and introducing at the close Solon's conversion to Dreiser's own mystical faith. Increasingly in poor health, however, Dreiser had great difficulty combining his old and new material. In the summer of 1944, he was joined in Los Angeles by Marguerite Tjader Harris, who worked closely with him on *The Bulwark* until the novel was finally completed in May 1945. Dreiser then sent the manuscript to his old friend and editor Louise Campbell, who cut it severely and also smoothed over Dreiser's prose. Although Dreiser's editor at Doubleday, Donald Elder, was later to restore some of Campbell's cuts, *The Bulwark* still reveals the effects of her editing in its uncharacteristic spare form and uncluttered prose.

The Bulwark bears several unfortunate consequences of its long genesis and of Dreiser's changing emphasis within the novel. Its cast and

novel. Yet the work also has a moving directness and simplicity in its account of a truly religious man who mistakes moralism and worldly success for God's word and who comes to see, at the end of his life, both the tragedy and beauty of all existence. *The Bulwark* lacks both the density of life and the Dreiserian presence of Dreiser's most characteristic fiction, but for many readers it has had a fictional quality and appeal distinctively its own.

Almost immediately after completing *The Bulwark*, Dreiser turned his attention to *The Stoic*. He had done most of the research for the volume thirty years earlier, at the time he was working on *The Financier* and *The Titan*. He had also made several attempts to write the novel in the late 1920s and early 1930s, and in 1932 had managed to complete a draft of about two-thirds of the book. It was to this draft that he returned in 1945. Now, ill and tired, but nevertheless anxious to bring the Cowperwood trilogy to a conclusion, he revised this draft by cutting a good deal of its financial detail and by adding a final section in which Cowperwood dies and Berenice becomes a convert to Yogaism. He had all but finished this task, leaving only the revision of the last two chapters incomplete, when he died in late December 1945.

Even more than *The Bulwark, The Stoic* is an anomalous joining of two widely different kinds of fiction. The first portion of the novel is a largely lifeless account of Cowperwood's efforts to win control of the London underground system and of his amorous affairs. The last portion, after his death, deals with the nature of Hindu mysticism and with Berenice's acceptance of its beliefs. Almost all readers have agreed that *The Stoic* is Dreiser's least successful novel. Interest in the work has therefore been confined to its concluding section, in which Berenice's conversion to Hindu mysticism offers a valuable parallel for the historian of Dreiser's ideas to Solon's return to Quaker mysticism at the conclusion of *The Bulwark*.

Dreiser's reputation was at a low ebb for some years after his death. A long period of fictional inactivity in which his political and philosophical ideas appeared either inane or muddy had been followed by the posthumous publication (in 1946 and 1947) of two uncharacteristic novels. No wonder that in 1950 Lionel Trilling viewed Dreiser's earlier stature as a historical aberration. During the past several decades, however, and particularly since the appearance of a number of major studies and appreciations of his work, Dreiser has increasingly been recognized as one of the principal figures in late nineteenth- and early twentieth-century American literature. His significance as the one major American naturalist who had a full career and who therefore best exemplifies the character of American naturalism is unchallenged. And the permanent worth and hold of his best fiction—in particular of *Sister Carrie, Jennie Gerhardt,* and *An American Tragedy*—is seen to reside not in some indefinable "power" but in a compelling vision of life expressed through an often brilliant craftsmanship.

Plays:

The Girl in the Coffin, New York, Comedy Theatre, 3 December 1917;

The Hand of the Potter, New York, Provincetown Playhouse, 5 December 1921.

Other:

Paul Dresser, *On the Banks of the Wabash Far Away,* first verse and chorus attributed to Dreiser (New York: Howley, Haviland, 1897);

Lieutenant Oswald Fritz Bilse, *Life in a Garrison Town,* introduction by Dreiser (New York: John Lane, London: John Lane/Bodley Head, 1914);

Dresser, *The Songs of Paul Dresser*, introduction by Dreiser (New York: Boni & Liveright, 1927);

Frank Norris, *McTeague,* introduction by Dreiser (Garden City: Doubleday, Doran, 1928);

Harlan Miners Speak: Report on Terrorism in the Kentucky Coal Fields, introduction by Dreiser (New York: Harcourt, Brace, 1932);

Henry David Thoreau, *Living Thoughts of Thoreau,* selected, with an introduction, by Dreiser (New York: Longmans, Green, 1938).

Letters:

Letters to Louise, edited by Louise Campbell (Philadelphia: University of Pennsylvania Press, 1959);

Letters of Theodore Dreiser, edited by Robert H. Elias, 3 volumes (Philadelphia: University of Pennsylvania Press, 1959).

Bibliography:

Donald Pizer, Richard W. Dowell, and Frederic E. Rusch, *Theodore Dreiser: A Primary and Secondary Bibliography* (Boston: G. K. Hall, 1975).

Biographies:

Dorothy Dudley, *Forgotten Frontiers: Dreiser and the Land of the Free* (New York: Harrison Smith, 1932);

Robert H. Elias, *Theodore Dreiser: Apostle of Nature* (New York: Knopf, 1949; emended edition, Ithaca: Cornell University Press, 1970);

Helen Dreiser, *My Life with Dreiser* (Cleveland: World, 1951);

W. A. Swanberg, *Dreiser* (New York: Scribners, 1965);

Marguerite Tjader, *Theodore Dreiser: A New Dimension* (Norwalk, Conn.: Silvermine, 1965).

References:

Richard W. Dowell, ed., *The Dreiser Newsletter*, 1970- ;

Philip L. Gerber, "Dreiser's *Stoic*: A Study in Literary Frustration," in *Literary Monograph*, no. 7 (Madison: University of Wisconsin, 1975);

Gerber, *Plots and Characters in the Fiction of Theodore Dreiser* (Hamden, Conn.: Archon, 1976);

Gerber, *Theodore Dreiser* (New York: Twayne, 1964);

Alfred Kazin and Charles Shapiro, eds., *The Stature of Theodore Dreiser* (Bloomington: University of Indiana Press, 1955);

Richard Lehan, *Theodore Dreiser: His World and His Novels* (Carbondale: Southern Illinois University Press, 1969);

John Lyndenberg, ed., *Dreiser: A Collection of Critical Essays* (Englewood Cliffs, N. J.: Prentice-Hall, 1971);

Kenneth Lynn, "Theodore Dreiser: The Man of Ice," in his *The Dream of Success* (Boston: Little, Brown, 1955), pp. 13-74;

F. O. Matthiessen, *Theodore Dreiser* (New York: Sloane, 1951);

H. L. Mencken, "Theodore Dreiser," in his *A Book of Prefaces* (New York: Knopf, 1917), pp. 67-148;

William E. Miller and Neda M. Westlake, eds., "Essays in Honor of Theodore Dreiser's *Sister Carrie*," *Library Chronicle* (University of Pennsylvania Library), 44 (Spring 1979);

Ellen Moers, *Two Dreisers* (New York: Viking, 1969);

Donald Pizer, ed., *Essays on Theodore Dreiser* (Boston: G. K. Hall, 1981);

Pizer, *The Novels of Theodore Dreiser: A Critical Study* (Minneapolis: University of Minnesota Press, 1976);

Jack Salzman, ed., special Dreiser issue, *Modern Fiction Studies*, 23 (Autumn 1977);

Salzman, ed., *Theodore Dreiser: The Critical Reception* (New York: David Lewis, 1972);

Charles Shapiro, *Theodore Dreiser: Our Bitter Patriot* (Carbondale: Southern Illinois University Press, 1962);

Robert Penn Warren, *Homage to Theodore Dreiser* (New York: Random House, 1971);

Neda M. Westlake, ed., special Dreiser issue, *Library Chronicle* (University of Pennsylvania Library), 38 (Winter 1972).

Papers:

The Theodore Dreiser Collection of the University of Pennsylvania Library is the principal repository of Dreiser papers. It contains manuscipts of published and unpublished works, including drafts and notes; letters to and by Dreiser; and clippings and scrapbooks. Other important collections of Dreiser papers are in the Cornell University Library, the Lilly Library of Indiana University, the New York Public Library, the University of Texas Library, and the University of Virginia Library.

Edward Eggleston

(10 December 1837-3 September 1902)

William Peirce Randel

SELECTED BOOKS: *Sunday School Conventions and Institutes, With Suggestions on County and Township Organization* (Chicago: Adams, Blackmer & Lyon, 1867);

The Manual: A Practical Guide to Sunday-School Work (Chicago: Adams, Blackmer & Lyon, 1869);

Mr. Blake's Walking-Stick: A Christmas Story for Boys and Girls (Chicago: Adams, Blackmer & Lyon/New York: Randolph, 1870);

The Book of Queer Stories, and Stories Told on a Cellar Door (Chicago: Adams, Blackmer & Lyon/New York: Randolph/Boston: Shute, 1871);

The Hoosier School-Master. A Novel (New York: Orange Judd, 1871);

The End of the World. A Love Story (London: Routledge, 1872; New York: Orange Judd, 1872);

The Mystery of Metropolisville (New York: Orange Judd, 1873; London: Routledge, 1873);

The Circuit Rider: A Tale of the Heroic Age (London: Routledge, 1874; New York: Ford, 1874);

The Schoolmaster's Stories, For Boys and Girls (Boston: Shepard, 1874);

Roxy (New York: Scribners, 1878; London: Chatto & Windus, 1878);

Tecumseh and the Shawnee Prophet, by Eggleston and Lillie Eggleston Seelye (New York: Dodd, Mead, 1878); republished as *The Shawnee Prophet; or the Story of Tecumseh* (London: Ward, Lock, 1880);

Pocahontas, by Eggleston and Seelye (New York: Dodd, Mead, 1879); republished as *The Indian Princess; or the Story of Pocahontas* (London: Ward, Lock, 1879);

Brant and Red Jacket, by Eggleston and Seelye (New

York: Dodd, Mead, 1879); republished as *The Rival Warriors, Chiefs of the Five Nations* (London: Ward, Lock, 1881);

Montezuma and the Conquest of Mexico, by Eggleston and Seelye (New York: Dodd, Mead, 1880); republished as *The Mexican Prince* (London: Ward, Lock, 1881);

The Hoosier School-Boy (London: Warne, 1882; New York: Scribners, 1883);

The Graysons: A Story of Illinois (New York: Century, 1888; Edinburgh: Douglas, 1888);

A History of the United States and Its People for the Use of Schools (New York: Appleton, 1888);

A First Book in American History (New York: Appleton, 1889);

The Faith Doctor: A Story of New York (New York: Appleton, 1891; London: Cassell, 1891);

Duffels (New York: Appleton, 1893);

The Beginners of a Nation (New York: Appleton, 1896; London: Longmans, Green, 1897);

The Transit of Civilization from England to America in the Seventeenth Century (New York: Appleton, 1901; London: Hirschfeld, 1901);

The New History (Washington, D.C.: U. S. Government Printing Office, 1901);

The New Century History of the United States (New York, Cincinnati & Chicago: American Book Company, 1904).

Best remembered as author of *The Hoosier School-Master* (1871), Edward Eggleston contributed significantly to the acceptance of realism by American readers and critics and, together with Mark Twain and William Dean Howells, to the emergence of the Middle West as a major literary region. But Eggleston did not keep pace with these two contemporaries either during his lifetime or later; although his novels are still in print, they attract relatively few readers and have little interest for literary historians. Eggleston's creative powers were not great. He showed little advance toward mastery of his craft, and he seldom departed from a formula that called for excessive reliance on local color, folk customs, and popular superstitions. Restless in nature, he changed course often: at different stages he was a successful preacher, an expert on Sunday schools, a Washington lobbyist (for copyright reforms), and the author of pioneering works in American social history.

Eggleston was born and spent his early boyhood in Vevay, Indiana, a quiet county seat on the Ohio River with a tradition of culture established by its Swiss settlers. In 1846 the early death of his father, Joseph Cary Eggleston, an honor graduate of the College of William and Mary and a lawyer of local prominence, left the family—Edward, age eight, three younger children, and their mother, Mary Jane Craig Eggleston—in somewhat reduced circumstances. Money was so limited that only one child could hope to attend college; and Edward, frail and often too ill to be in school, knew he would not be the one. But he had one teacher, a minor poet named Julia Dumont, who saw his potential and inspired in him a deep love of books and the ambition to become an author. He read avidly in the private library his father had collected, but few of the books were appropriate for very young readers, and some had harmful effects on a reader as literal-minded as Eggleston. Lindley Murray's *The English Reader* introduced him to many of the best of British writers but, as he wrote late in life, "made not the slightest concession to the immaturity of a child's mind." It was better, however, than the insipid moralizing of the Irish novelist Maria

Edgeworth and the strait-laced admonitions of a book titled Todd's *Hints to Young Men*, which led him to agonizing self-reproach and exhausting time schedules that produced not better character but physical breakdown.

A visit to a backcountry Indiana settlement in the summer of 1850 exposed young Eggleston to illiterate Hoosier speech and stimulated an interest in dialect that as late as 1894 resurfaced in two articles, "Wild Flowers of English Speech in America" and "Folk Speech in America." His horizons further broadened when he was sent, at age sixteen, to his father's relatives in Amelia, Virginia. But after thirteen months he decided he could not enjoy advantages based on slave labor and went back to Indiana. After a few weeks of grammar-school teaching, his only experience as a Hoosier schoolmaster, he left again, this time bound for Minnesota to regain his faltering health. He spent a decade there, working hard at one occupation after another, and gradually changed from a sickly, insecure adolescent to a successful, confident adult. By 1866 he was the pastor of one of the state's largest Methodist churches, a nationally recognized authority on Sunday schools, and the author of stories for children that appeared in the *Little Corporal*, a monthly magazine published in Chicago.

Sharing his happiness were his wife, Lizzie, whom he had married in 1858, and his three daughters, Lillie, Blanche, and Allegra.

In 1866 Eggleston abandoned both Methodism and Minnesota by moving to Evanston, Illinois, to begin a career in journalism as associate editor of the *Little Corporal* in Chicago. The job was no sinecure, for he was expected to write most of each issue, and did so with jokes, puzzles, bits of advice, and other fillers. What alone merit attention, however, are the stories that he continued to contribute—actually a series about Minnesota's Sioux and Chippewa, with an imagined audience of children who often interrupted with comments and questions. He had lived too close to the Indians, especially during the Sioux Outbreak of 1862, to endorse the "noble savage" concept popular with Easterners. At one point he observed, "the Indians the poets write about are very different from the wild and brutal savages themselves." His insistence that his "Round Table Stories" were all true to fact or to authentic Indian legend suggests his early leaning toward realism.

The *Little Corporal* proving an unreliable source of income, Eggleston soon branched out, writing topical essays for the *Chicago Evening Journal* in a column titled "Our Saturday Feuilleton"; prac-

Eggleston's birthplace in Vevey, Indiana

tical articles for the *Sunday School Teacher*, of which he became editor in 1867; and "Western Correspondence" for the *Independent* in New York. His success with this last activity led to his final move eastward in May 1870, to serve the *Independent* as literary editor and then as superintending editor. In 1871 he resigned from this prestigious journal to become editor-in-chief of a weekly family magazine, *Hearth and Home*, largely because it carried fiction and was a potential vehicle for his own short stories. He already had two books of fiction in print: the slender *Mr. Blake's Walking Stick* (1870) and a collection of short stories that he titled *The Book of Queer Stories and Stories Told on a Cellar Door* (1871). Unlike his earlier stories about Indians, these were sentimental, remote from ordinary life, and with little hint of the realism that would characterize his later fiction. Neither did his first contributions to *Scribner's Monthly*, "Huldah the Help. A Thanksgiving Story," and two feeble evocations of his Indiana boyhood. The fact that editors published and readers welcomed such fare is an indication of the literary taste of that period. In the late summer of 1871 he experimented with his first serial, a three-installment story in *Hearth and Home*, the extremely sentimental "Uncle Sim's Boy." Because readers liked the serial form he decided to try it again, with a story based on his brother George's experience as a teacher in rural Riker's Ridge, Indiana, and employing the uncouth dialect of that region. The first of the three installments he planned appeared in *Hearth and Home* on 30 September 1871 as *The Hoosier School-Master*.

The realism of this new story, so far removed from the sentimentality of its immediate predecessors, was largely the result of two main influences. One of the last books Eggleston reviewed for the *Independent*, in December 1870, was an English translation of Hippolyte Taine's *Philosophy of Art in the Netherlands*, in which Taine urged the use of common and familiar materials. And in a letter written earlier in 1870 James Russell Lowell thanked Eggleston for sending a list of Hoosier dialect terms and urged him to persevere and "give us a collection" for "it will soon be too late." In his new story Eggleston, for the first time, combined familiar commonplace materials, as Taine had advised, with the picturesque language of illiterate backcountry Hoosiers, in response to Lowell's encouragement. He acknowledged Lowell's influence in his dedication to the 1892 Library Edition of *The Hoosier School-Master*: "As a pebble cast upon a great cairn, this edition is inscribed to the memory of James Russell Lowell, whose cordial encouragement to my early dialect stories is gratefully remembered."

Nobody could have been more astonished than Eggleston by the success of the story. *Hearth and Home*'s circulation shot up sharply, and he was virtually forced to continue adding installments

Illustration by Frank Beard for The Hoosier School-Master, *depicting the new teacher's first meeting with Old Jack Means and his three children*

week by week until, by 30 December, there were fourteen in all. After exhausting George's reminiscences he mined his own memories of individuals and incidents he had observed in 1850, and for climax used the exposure of a leading citizen, Dr. Small (Smalley in the book), as the leader of a gang of night riders. Eggleston was soon caught up in a race with the printer, week after week, that made planning ahead barely possible. Compounding the difficulty was his almost total ignorance of novels or of how to write them. His early religious scruples had put reading fiction out of bounds because novels were viewed as lies, and his only knowledge of plot construction, he ruefully recalled in 1890, came from reading seventeenth-century French plays.

Public libraries are likely today to shelve *The Hoosier School-Master* (and any other Eggleston novels they may own) in the children's section. What skill in fiction he had already acquired was in stories for children, and although adults could enjoy *The Hoosier School-Master* in the 1870s, only unsophisticated modern readers can overlook the book's crudities. Characters tend to be stereotypes or caricatures. Ralph Hartsock, the new teacher in Flat Creek, is a sterling hero thrust into conflict with the school bully, hulking Bud Means, and Bud's father, Jack Means, whose surname suggests their consummate meanness. The local hard-shell preacher is Brother Sodom, and Squire Hawkins is an overdrawn caricature with his glass eye, false teeth, and dyed whiskers. Hannah, kept by Jack Means as an indentured servant, and her little brother Shocky are creatures of exaggerated pathos; Shocky's fear that God has forgotten them suggests Eggleston's flair for sentimentality. Readers could respond to the story's freshness; and the outcome is satisfactory: Hannah is proved to be of age and can be no longer legally bound to Jack Means; Bud Means repents and joins Ralph in a "Church of the Best Licks"; and Ralph is cleared of a criminal deed charged to him when the real villain is exposed. What gives the book its place as a pioneer in literary history is its starkly realistic setting in a raw, newly opened part of the nation, and its sharp contrast between educated speech and that of the illiterate Hoosier characters. Because nothing like it had ever been seen before, some reviewers were puzzled, but William Dean Howells in the *Atlantic Monthly* praised the book as "a picture of manners hitherto strange to literature," and one that acquainted readers "with the crudeness and ugliness of the intermediate West." Neither he nor any other reviewer faulted the book for the sentimentality obvi-

ous to most modern readers. A few Indianians voiced indignation, viewing the book as a slur on their state.

As soon as its serial run ended, *The Hoosier School-Master* was published as a book, without Eggleston's having a chance to revise the *Hearth and Home* text. Enjoying the instant popularity it brought him, he set about capitalizing on this first success by turning out more novels, three in rapid succession. All sold fairly well and won praise from reviewers; but they lacked the freshness of the first and did little to advance his reputation. *The End of the World* (1872) is a love story little different from hundreds of others except for its background, a sensational historic event that turned out to be a nonevent—the end of the world that the Millerites fully expected on the night of 11 August 1843. The colorless lovers, Julia Anderson and August Wehle, run the usual fictional gamut of family opposition, misunderstanding, estrangement, and eventual reconciliation. The German-American accent given

Front wrapper for Eggleston's second novel, based on boyhood memories of the Millerites, who believed that the world would end on 11 August 1843

to August's family is not very convincing. The folk customs that are part of Eggleston's formula—shivaree, egg supper, and telling fortunes by "turning the bible"—do much to enliven the story.

As a boy of five in 1843, Eggleston could have had no direct comprehension of the Millerite delusion to remember when writing *The End of the World*, but for his next two novels he had the advantage of a rich vein of experience and observation to draw upon. *The Mystery of Metropolisville* (1873) has little to recommend it, indeed, beyond its evocation of life in Minnesota as he knew it at the close of its frontier period. The central figure, Albert Charlton, somewhat resembles Eggleston upon his arrival there; but instead of advancing along the road to success as Eggleston did, Albert Charlton becomes a convict, serving a term in the state penitentiary in Stillwater for his part in the unsubstantial "mystery" introduced only late in the novel. In his preface Eggleston wrote, "I have wished to make my stories of value as a contribution to the history of civilization in America," but only to history-minded Minnesotans, perhaps, could *The Mystery of Metropolisville* provide any interesting details about life along the Cannon River, which he renames the Big Gun, or Faribault in Rice County, his Perritaut in Wheat County, or Red Wing, thinly disguised as Red Owl Landing. What emerges clearly, however, is a record of the historic boom-town phenomenon and the land-hunger of newcomers victimized by just such rascals as the land-shark Plausaby, who can make the most outrageous fraud sound plausible. The past is revived even more effectively in *The Circuit Rider* (1874), which Eggleston dedicated "To my Comrades of Other Years, The Brave and Self-Sacrificing men with whom I had the honor to be associated in a frontier ministry. . . ." While he used his own memories of the rigors of riding a Methodist circuit, for his main plot he turned to the autobiography of Jacob Young, a famous circuit rider of an earlier generation. Young was a wild, irreligious youth converted to Methodism out of remorse and despair, and so is Eggleston's fictional hero, Morton Goodwin. When Eggleston exhausted Young's memoir, and in turn his own remembered experience, he resorted to some of the stock situations of sentimental fiction. Sister Meacham, the "praying girl," is an attractive sinner who almost succeeds in snaring Morton. The deathbed marriage of Kike Lumsden, the most vividly portrayed character, is described with an excess of pathos, while the highwayman Burchard's revelation that he is Morton's brother would seem credible only to a lover of melodrama and coincidence.

In structure, *The Circuit Rider* is superior to its three predecessors, but reviewers were beginning to suggest that Eggleston's pace—four novels in less than four years—was too rapid; and Eggleston agreed. Uncertain what to turn to, he collected some of his early stories in a volume he titled *The Schoolmaster's Stories, for Boys and Girls* (1874), and in editing two elaborate religious books, *Christ in Art* (1875) and *Christ in Literature* (1875). The new course he could not decide for himself opened up for him in the final days of 1874, when he was offered the pulpit of a moribund Congregational church in Brooklyn that needed strong leadership for survival. He accepted, but insisted that the church dispense with any creed and any tie with an established denomination. He also provided a suitable name, Church of the Christian Endeavor, and almost at once attracted new members and considerable public attention. After two years, however, his enthusiasm began to wane, or rather it was diverted to other interests—helping launch his oldest daughter, Lillie Eggleston Seelye, on a literary career with a series of coauthored books (for which she did most of the writing) about famous American Indians; planning a permanent home on the shore of Lake George, and watching it rise; and seeing a fifth novel through the press. *Roxy*, published in the fall of 1878, was his first book to profit by careful planning and time for revision, which paid off, for it is now deemed to be his best.

The Church of Christian Endeavor, creedless and nondenominational, represents a midpoint in Eggleston's intellectual development, which so accelerated in the late 1870s that more and more each Sunday his sermons minimized, and finally eliminated, all trace of orthodox Christian dogma. *Roxy* manifests the same trend. The heroine, Roxy Adams, is presented as a lovely, lively girl admired by all who know her for her sterling religious character and behavior. Her perceptive best friend, Twonnet, suggests to her that she would welcome martyrdom; and after her marriage to Mark Bonamy and the birth of his illegitimate child to sultry Nancy Kirtley, Roxy undergoes something close to martyrdom in adopting the baby and forgiving Mark. Reviewers seized upon the novel's depiction of marital infidelity and its illegitimate product. Some praised Eggleston's handling of the theme, others thought it was too timid; but most cited the parallels to similar themes in George Eliot and Hawthorne, and Eggleston was pleased to be compared with such giants of fiction. Preoccupation with this theme, however, tended to lessen awareness of Eggleston's real purpose, specifically given in the final scene but rather understated: Roxy's advance from her lifelong religiosity to a genuine religious feeling. Not dogma, not conformity to outward forms of religious behavior, but redemption through suffering and complete forgiveness alone mark true religion. Eggleston once had accepted without question the forms and dogmas of orthodoxy; by 1878, in both his ministry and his writing, he was leaving them far behind.

Eggleston at the Century Club in New York, 1896

In the last weeks of 1879, he felt compelled to resign his pulpit; and it brought on, as earlier hard decisions had, an emotional and physical breakdown. With his wife and his two younger daughters he sailed at once for Europe, and did not return until the following August. By then he had decided to become a writer of American history. For someone who had never had a course of any kind in history, let alone a seminar in research methods, this decision might seem quixotic in the extreme.

But he had learned, while collecting facts for the Indian books, that research was exciting, and also that he enjoyed it. Having come to view his novels as contributions to the history of American civilization, it was easy to dispense with the fictional veneer and get to the factual heart of that history. His interest in local color and in the ordinary predisposed Eggleston to abandon the traditional stress on wars and politics and to emphasize social history instead. In November 1882 his first article, "The Beginners of a Nation," appeared in *Century* magazine. A dozen more articles followed by 1890, and before he died in 1902, two solid volumes were in print, *The Beginners of a Nation* (1896) and *The Transit of Civilization* (1901). A few established historians had deprecated his chances of success, but members of the American Historical Association, which he helped organize in 1884, thought well enough of him to elect him their president for 1900. His presidential address, *The New History*, though rambling and anecdotal, was a fitting valedictory to his final profession.

During his last two decades history did not preempt all other activity. A gregarious man with many friends, he was a cofounder of the Authors' Club in 1882 and the next year welcomed election to the Century Association. But if he dearly loved socializing with kindred spirits, he also had a strong sense of duty to fellow writers: he was a leader in the American Copyright League and was willing to devote long periods in Washington to the campaign for Congressional approval of international copyright, which came in 1891. He also took time out from history to write three more novels. *The Hoosier School-Boy* (1882), which he admitted was a potboiler to make money, is a pallid, virtually plotless story, written for children, of a poor boy struggling to get an education. Its chief interest lies in detailed descriptions of childhood games. Much better is *The Graysons* (1888), based on an anecdote about Lincoln's clearing a man charged with murder by referring to an almanac showing there was no moon on the fatal night. For this book, which was more than two years in the writing, Eggleston provided his usual quota of local customs and typical characters—a bound girl, a hero with little heroic about him, a dapper villain, a teacher with an East coast accent, and "citizens" itching to take part in a lynching party. The inclusion of Lincoln as the young rustic defense attorney guaranteed reader interest but also invited criticism—some people felt that Eggleston took too much freedom with Lincoln's personality, or with the anecdote itself.

His final novel, *The Faith Doctor* (1891), stands

Eggleston in Washington, D.C., 1901

alone in being set not in the Middle West but in Manhattan, and in the present rather than at some time in his remembered past. The characters are decidedly urban, whether the aristocratic Gouverneurs of Washington Square North; Charley Millard, who has recently gained social recognition and Mr. Hillbrough, a self-made man who has not; or Mrs. Frankland, a self-appointed "apostle to the genteel." The book's central figure, Phillida Callendar, under Mrs. Frankland's influence becomes a faith healer, only to be disillusioned when she contracts diphtheria from a patient and nearly dies. Eggleston may or may not have had Christian Science in mind; in his preface he insisted the book "was not written to depreciate anybody's valued delusions." What the book does demonstrate is that by 1891 Eggleston had completed his sometimes anguished journey from unquestioning orthodoxy to agnosticism and cheerful acceptance of scientific hypotheses. At one point he refers to Darwin as "the main source of all our metaphysical discomforts," and adds somewhat flippantly that "It is this same Charles Darwin who says that a man may be made

more unhappy by committing a breach of etiquette than by falling into sin."

No sooner was *The Faith Doctor* completed than Eggleston began making notes for yet another novel about metropolitan life, tentatively titled "The Agnostic," with faith healers replaced by the Salvation Army. His intention was to emulate Flaubert's technique in making the characters "flesh and blood." But he soon abandoned the project, and fiction altogether, and returned to the writing of the series of volumes on American history that he had projected; the two that were published did not carry the American story beyond 1700. Whether his fame would be more substantial had he devoted himself to fiction alone, or to history alone, is questionable; but to each he made a significant contribution.

Other:

Christ in Art, edited with a preface by Eggleston (New York: Ford, 1875);

Christ in Literature, edited with a preface by Eggleston (New York: Ford, 1875).

Bibliography:

William Randel, "Edward Eggleston, 1837-1902," *American Literary Realism*, 1 (Fall 1967).

Biographies:

George Cary Eggleston, *The First of the Hoosiers* (Philadelphia: Drexel Biddle, 1903);

William Peirce Randel, *Edward Eggleston: Author of The Hoosier School-Master* (New York: King's Crown Press, 1946).

References:

Ronald M. Benson, "Ignoble Savage: Edward Eggleston and the American Indian," *Illinois Quarterly*, 35 (1973): 41-51;

Bud T. Cochran, "The Indianas of Edward Eggleston's *The Hoosier School-Master*," *Old Northwest: A Journal of Regional Life and Letters*, 4 (1978): 385-390;

William Randel, *Edward Eggleston* (New York: Twayne, 1963);

Edward Stone, in his *Voices of Despair: Four Motifs in American Literature* (Athens, Ohio: Ohio University Press, 1966), pp. 137-178;

Gary N. Underwood, "Toward a Reassessment of Edward Eggleston's Literary Dialects," *Bulletin of the Rocky Mountain Language Association*, 28 (1974), 109-120;

Jack H. Wilson, "Eggleston's Indebtedness to George Eliot in *Roxy*," *American Literature*, 42 (March 1970): 38-49.

Papers:

The Eggleston Papers at the Cornell University Library include the bulk of primary material, in particular his prolific correspondence. Other important manuscript holdings are in the Indiana State Library, the Minnesota Historical Society, and the libraries of Harvard, Columbia, and the University of Virginia.

Harold Frederic

(19 August 1856-19 October 1898)

Robert H. Woodward
San José State University

BOOKS: *Seth's Brother's Wife; A Study of Life in the Greater New York* (New York: Scribners, 1887; London: Chatto & Windus, 1887);

The Lawton Girl (London: Chatto & Windus, 1890; New York: Scribners 1890);

In the Valley (New York: Scribners, 1890; London: Heinemann, 1890);

The Young Emperor William II of Germany; A Study in Character Development on a Throne (London: Unwin, 1891; New York: Putnam's 1891);

The New Exodus; A Study of Israel in Russia (London: Heinemann, 1892; New York: Putnam's, 1892);

The Return of the O'Mahony (New York: Bonner, 1892; London: Heinemann, 1893);

The Copperhead (New York: Scribners, 1893);

The Copperhead and Other Stories of the North During the American War (London: Heinemann, 1894);

Marsena and Other Stories of the Wartime (New York: Scribners, 1894);

Marsena (London: Unwin, 1896);

The Damnation of Theron Ware (Chicago: Stone &

Kimball, 1896); republished as *Illumination* (London: Heinemann, 1896);

Mrs. Albert Grundy; Observations in Philistia (London: John Lane/New York: Merriam, 1896);

March Hares, as George Forth (London: John Lane, 1896; New York: Appleton, 1896);

In the Sixties (New York: Scribners, 1897);

The Deserter and Other Stories; A Book of Two Wars (Boston: Lothrop, 1898);

Gloria Mundi (Chicago & New York: Stone, 1898; London: Heinemann, 1898);

The Market-Place (New York: Stokes, 1899; London: Heinemann, 1899);

Harold Frederic's Stories of York State, edited by Thomas F. O'Donnell (Syracuse: Syracuse University Press, 1966).

During his lifetime, and throughout the half century of neglect that followed his early death, Harold Frederic was classified variously as a regionalist, a realist, a naturalist, and a pioneer in the revival of American historical fiction. Though

Harold Frederic [signature]

ticularly history, and as a youngster developed his talent for writing and drawing. His graduation from the local advanced school in 1871 ended his formal education. He had worked for his stepfather as a youngster, delivering milk, but his first regular employment was with local photographers as a photographic printer and negative retoucher. His trade supported him marginally in Boston, where he went at the age of seventeen to live on the fringes of bohemianism and to try his hand at writing and painting. When he returned to Utica in 1875, he affected the role of the man of the world, smiling at the rusticities of Utica and sporting a long-tailed frock coat; but he settled for his old job of retouching negatives.

His career in journalism began later the same year, proofreading on the *Utica Morning Herald*. After a few months he joined the staff of the *Utica Daily Observer*, a Democratic newspaper, as proofreader but rose rapidly through the ranks, gaining a regional reputation as a reporter of sensational crimes and as an astute editorialist. These years were a period of dramatic growth. After a year with the *Observer* he published in its pages his first known short story, "The Two Rochards," with a Revolutionary War setting. This story was followed by sentimental stories. One of them, "The Blakelys of Poplar Place," although a story about the Revolution, has as heroine a young woman modeled after Frederic's neighbor Grace Williams. On 10 October 1877, three months after the story was published, Frederic married Grace Williams. Also in 1877, apparently ambitious to establish a name as a writer, he drew too heavily on William L. Stone's *Life of Joseph Brant* for his article on "The Mohawk Valley During the Revolution," published in *Harper's*, and was called a plagiarist in the pages of the rival local newspaper. During the next few years he and Grace Frederic began a family, and Frederic broadened his intellectual and cultural horizons through his intimacy with the liberal priest Edward A. Terry and Utica's Irish Catholic community. He would later draw heavily upon these associations for *The Damnation of Theron Ware*. In 1880, at the age of twenty-four, he became editor of the *Observer*.

In September 1882 Frederic accepted an offer to edit the *Albany Evening Journal*, a once influential Republican newspaper, and ignited an editorial barrage accusing him of political reversal and opportunism. Although ostensibly a Democrat, Frederic was essentially a political independent. From his new editorial chair he supported the nomination of the Democratic candidate for the governorship, Grover Cleveland. Under Frederic's hand the

criticized for employing newspaper standards, and hasty composition, as well as for leading an unconventional life, he eventually earned a firm place in literary history with *The Damnation of Theron Ware* (1896), the book for which he is best remembered and which has dominated the critical attention he has received in the past eighty years. Everett Carter, who sees Theron Ware's rise from ignorance to knowledge as both tragic and beneficent, views the novel as almost an allegory of the psychic fall of Americans and places it "among the four or five best novels written by an American during the nineteenth century."

Frederic was born in the Mohawk Valley city of Utica, New York, the only child of Henry Frederick, a freight conductor for the New York Central Railroad, and Frances Ramsdell Frederick, the daughter of a blacksmith. When Frederic was eighteen months old, his father was killed in a train wreck, and his resourceful mother, of sturdy, religious stock, opened a vest-making business. In 1861 she married William De Mott, who ran a milk and wood business.

Frederic had an early taste for reading, par-

newspaper again became a major political organ, and Frederic became a member of Cleveland's political faction in Albany. Among his intimates there was Father Terry, who had earlier been transferred to the diocesan headquarters.

Though a resourceful and successful journalist, Frederic was restless to devote his considerable energies to literature. For years he carried in his mind an outline of a novel about the Mohawk Valley in the Revolution; and other stories, vaguely autobiographical, were germinating. When the *Journal* changed hands, Frederic was invited to stay as editor if he would support the views of the new owner. Unable to do so, and unwilling to compromise his principles, he resigned in March 1884. After a few weeks of traveling to investigate possible new positions, he accepted a job as London correspondent for the *New York Times*.

When Frederic sailed for England—with his wife, two young daughters, and a letter of introduction from Cleveland—in June 1884, he dreamed of soon leaving what he called "this vile and hollow fool-rink" of journalism behind and of earning "a living by honest work in good humane literature, as the anchorite dreams of the day when he shall exchange his hair-shirt for the white robe." He was never to realize that dream. His outpouring of books, stories, essays, and reviews during the remaining fourteen years of his life would be in addition to his duties as correspondent. The psychological and physical drain upon his resources would take its toll.

During his first two years in England, Frederic established himself as a leading European correspondent. His weekly analyses of the news from Europe appeared on the front page of the Sunday edition of one of the most prestigious newspapers in America. He earned the applause of readers for his firsthand accounts of a cholera epidemic in southern Europe; and through his friendships with Irish members of Parliament and other leaders of the Irish struggle for Home Rule he became the principal shaper of the American attitude favoring the Irish cause. Gregarious, witty, a charming conversationalist, a generous host, he became an active member of the bohemian Savage Club and the politically centered National Liberal Club.

He was also able, during his first two years, to complete his first novel and to sell it to Scribners, who would run it as a serial in the new *Scribner's Magazine* from January through November 1887 before publishing it as a book. When Frederic returned home for his first vacation in 1886, therefore, it was with the hope that literary success was

imminent and that he would soon be free of journalism.

Set in upstate New York, *Seth's Brother's Wife* (1887) is remembered today primarily for its indictment of rural life as a narrowing, sterilizing influence upon human values and ideals. The complex plot, not perfectly integrated, follows the rise of young Seth Fairchild (whose career reflects Frederic's own early years in journalism) from proofreader to editor; the political ambitions of his opportunistic and unscrupulous elder brother and Seth's attraction to his brother's flirtatious wife; the

Front cover for Frederic's first novel, composed, he insisted, "purely as an experiment, to see what it was like to write a book"

desire of his ancient aunt to repair the decaying Fairchild name, farm, and fortune; and the machinations of state politics. The book is a strong first work, vivid in its depiction of the hardships of farm life and the often uncouth and ignorant inhabitants, but it also dramatizes an essentially optimistic message, in the words of Thomas F. O'Donnell and Hoyt C. Franchere, "that in spite of a certain drabness and apparent moral and spiritual laxity of life in upstate New York, the region could still produce from its own citizenry honest and devoted leaders who were capable of arousing the moral vigor of the public when such vigor was needed."

Frederic hoped that certain parallels in the book to Cleveland's political career would win the endorsement of his friend, whom Frederic visited in the White House in 1886, but Cleveland was not a reader of novels. Both the serial and the book appeared to good reviews—Hamlin Garland praised it for its "uncompromising . . . pictures of the barrenness and hopelessness of the average farmer's life," and William Dean Howells similarly praised its accurate depiction of rural life. But sales were poor. Nonetheless, Frederic worked first with Maurice Barrymore and then with Brandon Thomas to turn the novel into a play. Augustin Daly, a leading producer in both London and New York, bought the play and cast it, but apparently it was never produced.

After his stateside vacation, Frederic returned to England to draw upon his experience in writing his first novel to complete the work that had been his principal ambition. Although busy with journalistic work, Frederic finished the long book in only eight months. *In the Valley*, with illustrations by Howard Pyle, appeared as a serial in *Scribner's Magazine* from September 1889 through July 1890 before its book publication in October 1890. Set during the American Revolution, the story is narrated by Douw Mauverensen, a steady and sober Dutchman, whose rivalry with Philip Cross, an English aristocrat of his own age, for the hand of the orphaned Daisy parallels the conflict for the American continent by the colonials and the British. Douw tells the story as an old man, confessing that his impressions of events "come back slowly through the mist and darkness of nearly threescore years." The effect is that the characters are not fully realized. Frederic admitted they "always remained shadowy" in his mind.

The novel is nonetheless an accurate description of the several national groups in the valley, of the contrast between the Palatine farmers and the British landlords, and of the military action centered on the Battle of Oriskany in August 1777. Despite low critical regard for the historical novel at the time, the book received some fine notices. A major exception was the comment by Howells, who, always hostile to historical fiction, described Frederic's characters as "well trained, well costumed, but actors, and almost amateurs." In a later estimate of the book, Granville Hicks credited Frederic with

making his novel "far superior to its genre" by his realism, "by utilizing a solid knowledge of the economic and racial issues involved in the Revolution."

Following close upon the completion of *In the Valley* was work on *The Lawton Girl* (1890), the second of Frederic's novels about life in upstate New York. This work made clear Frederic's intentions of creating a single fictitious locale for his stories of New York state, with recurring characters, families, and place names. The mother of the two young Minster women in this novel, for example, is the granddaughter of *In the Valley*'s Douw Mauverensen, and several characters from *Seth's Brother's Wife* appear again. Although Jessica Lawton, a young woman who has been seduced by the rakish and dishonest Horace Boyce, is the titular heroine of the novel, the most engrossing aspect of the story is Boyce's attempt to swindle the young Minster women and their mother of ownership of the Minster Iron Works. Jessica is a strong character, who returns to the village that knows her shame and devotes herself to establishing a retreat for working girls, but Frederic allows her to die—"a false and cowardly thing to do," he later confessed, "since she . . . had not deserved or intended at all to die." The strength of the novel lies in its careful depiction of the squalor in which some residents of Thessaly live, in its portrayal of a variety of village types, and in its analysis of the economic and social problems of a country village as it becomes an industrialized town. Because of the novel's occasionally sordid subject matter, Frederic could find no magazine willing to serialize it. The book appeared to mixed notices, though more critical than commendatory. The *Independent*, which had warmly praised *Seth's Brother's Wife*, found the book pessimistic and, granting that Jessica's career had parallels in actuality, moralized that "no amount of art can dress up such a career to make it in the least interesting to a healthy mind."

While Frederic was successfully building a literary reputation with his first three books, he was not able to realize his dream of financial independence from journalism. Cleveland, whom Frederic again visited in 1888, failed to be reelected for a second term as president. Frederic's hope for a consular post came temporarily to an end. Nor was Frederic's personal life happy. In May 1887, the death of his first son, at the age of two, devastated him. He took his family on a trip through Europe in an effort to allay his grief. Another son, born a few months earlier, added to his ever-increasing expenses and his continual indebtedness. His relationship with his wife, a sickly, prudish woman who lagged behind him intellectually and socially, became strained. Sometime in late 1889 or in 1890 he met an American woman, Kate Lyon, whose companionship he found fulfilling. In 1891 he moved his family to a new home outside London and set up Kate Lyon as his mistress in the city. Henceforth, he would be supporting two families, for Kate Lyon (who began to call herself Kate Frederic) gave birth to three children in 1892, 1893, and 1894.

During the first half of the 1890s Frederic published only one novel, *The Return of the O'Mahony* (1892), in which he assessed the Irish temperament in a comic vein and, implausibly, transplanted to Ireland an American Civil War deserter as the inheritor of the O'Mahony estates. The novel is a boisterous tale of adventure, ranging in action from an episode in the Fenian rebellion of 1867 to the discovery of a hidden room, complete with skeleton, under a castle. But, as the resourceful American regenerates the small section of Ireland under his rule, Frederic dramatizes his belief that if Home Rule were ever to succeed it would be based upon "a political structure and a social economy which are distinctly national," inasmuch as Ireland had suffered from the attempt of the English "to make her something not Irish" (as Frederic stated in a later article, "The Ireland of Tomorrow").

His need for money to support his two households impelled Frederic to increased journalistic activity as well as to the production of a number of stories that added nothing to his reputation and little to his income. In 1890 he spent more than a month in Germany for a series of articles on the young Kaiser Wilhelm II that appeared in the *New York Times* in the summer and were published in 1891 as *The Young Emperor William II of Germany*. In July and August of that year he traveled in Russia, preparing a series of articles on the persecution and expulsion of Russian Jews. The resulting "Indictment of Russia" appeared in the *Times* that fall and in book form as *The New Exodus* in 1892. In consequence of his expose, he was permanently banned from Russia.

His fiction took many directions as he experimented with subject matter, form, and style and worked to perfect his craft. Four of his longer stories, two with settings during the Wars of the Roses and two during the American Civil War, were published as serials for juvenile readers, three of them in the *Youth's Companion*. "Where Avon into Severn Flows" (1891) has as hero a young scrivener of Tewkesbury Abbey. The story prompts young readers to learn their letters and dramatizes the danger of neglecting education. "How Dickon Came by His Name" (1892), subtitled "a tale of Christmas in the olden time," is ostensibly a retelling of a legend of how a lowborn smith, Dickon, became Sir Richard Tannibow, the surname a corruption of *tannenbaum*. The two American Civil War stories, "The Deserter" (1894) and "A Day in the Wilderness" (1895), were more successful. In the first, Frederic finds Mose Whipple, a paid substitute who left an aged and helpless father behind, morally justified in escaping from the idleness of winter quarters and going home to the assistance of his father. At the request of the *Youth's Companion*, Frederic revised the ending to make clear that in some circumstances moral right has precedence over legal right. The second story, though accurate in its military background, has as hero a young drummer boy and is marred by a sequence of implausible coincidences.

These two stories share only the war background with five other stories and novelettes that are among the best work Frederic accomplished—"a most notable achievement," in the opinion of Stephen Crane, "in writing times in America." Frederic's boyhood extended through the Civil War, and Crane felt that Frederic "was the only sensitive plate exposed to the sunlight" of those "supreme years." The longest novelette, *The Copperhead* (1893), dramatizes in a rural setting the clash of issues central to the war. Speaking for the majority is the abolitionist "Jee" Hagadorn, a scripture-quoting cooper; for the minority, Abner Beech, the copperhead, standing not for slavery but for states rights. Beech is one of the best of Frederic's creations, a man who stands firmly on principle despite popular opposition. The villagers' tentative acceptance of Beech renews his faith in America and underlines Frederic's message that the country is a unit, despite discords arising from mass hysteria at times of national crisis. The marriage of the children of the two adversaries presages a new generation with perspectives broader than those of their parents. Another novelette, *Marsena* (1894), is less hopeful in its analysis of the springs of human conduct. In it a beautiful young woman exerts her power over the male members of the community by enticing them to enlist as evidence of their affection. Vain, fickle, shallow, she counts among her admirers and converts a romantic young photographer, Marsena, who, in a patently ironic but unbelievable ending, dies clutching the hem of her skirt—she is now a nurse on the front—as she ignores him and tends a slightly wounded officer. "The War Widow"

3

of listening attention. If Murtogh heard, he gave no sign, but gazed again in meditation out upon the vast waste of waters, blackening now as the purple reflections of the twilight waned.

"Blind men have senses that others lack," he remarked at last. "Tell me, you — does the earth we stand on seem ever to you to be turning round?"

Owny shuddered a little at the thought which came to him. "When you led me out beyond here, and I felt the big round sea-pinks under my feet, and remembered they grew only on the very edge—" he began.

"Not that at all!" the chief broke in. "'Tis not my meaning. But at Rosbrin there was a book, writ by Fineen the son of Diarmaid, an uncle to my father's father, and my father heard it read from this book that the world turned round one way, like a duck on a spit, and the sun turned round the other way, and that was why we were apart all night. And often I come here, and I swear there is a movement under my feet. But elsewhere there is none, not in the bawn, or in the towers, or anywhere else but just here."

The old man turned his face, as if he could see the ground he stood upon, and shook his head after a moment's waiting. "It would not be true, Murty," he suggested. "Old Fineen had a mighty scholarship, as I have heard, and he made an end to edify the angels, but — but —."

Murtogh did not wait for the hesitating conclusion. "I saw his tomb when I was a lad, in the chapel at Rosbrin. He was laid at his own desire under a weight of stone like my wall here. I saw even then how foolish it was. These landsmen have no proper sense. How will they rise at the resurrection with all that burden of stone to hold them down? I have a better understanding than that. I buried my father, as he buried his father, out yonder in the sea. And I will be buried there too, and my son after me — and if I have other children—" he stole a swift glance at the old man's withered face as he spoke — "if I have others, I say, it will be my command that they shall follow me there when their time comes. I make you witness to that wish, Owny Hea."

The bard hung his head. "As if my time would not come first!" he said, for the mere sake of saying something. Then, gathering courage, he pulled upon the strong arm which was still locked in his and raised his head to speak softly in The O'Mahony's ear.

"If only the desire of your heart were given you, Murty," he murmured. "If only once I could hold a babe of yours to my breast, and put its pretty little hands in my beard — I'd be fit to pray for the men who tore my eyes from me. And Murty dear," his voice rose in tremulous entreaty as he went on — "tell me, Murty — I'm of an age to be your father's father, and have no eyesight to shame you — is she — is your holy wife coming to see her duty differently? Have you hope that — that —"

Murtogh turned abruptly on his heel, swinging his companion round with him. They walked a dozen paces toward the sea-gate of the castle wall before he spoke. "You have never seen her, Owny!" he said then, gravely. "You do not know at all how beautiful she is. It is not in the power of your mind to imagine it. There is no one like her in all the world. She is not human like us, Owny. I am a great lord among men, Owny, and I am not afraid of any man. I would put The MacCarthy, or even the Earl of Desmond, over my cliff like a rat if he came to me here and would not do me honour. But when even I come where she sits, I am like a little dirty boy, frightened before a great shrine of Our Blessed Lady, all with jewels and lights and incense. I take shame to myself, when she looks at me, that there are such things in my heart for her to see."

Owny sighed deeply. "The finest princess in the world might be proud to be mated to you, Murty," he urged.

"True enough," responded Murtogh, with candor. "But she is not a princess — or any mere woman at all. She is a saint. Perhaps she is more still. Listen, Owny! Do you remember how I took her — how I swam for her through the breakers — and snapped the bone of my arm to keep the mast of their wreck from crushing her when the wave flung it upon us, and still made land with her on my neck, and hung to the bare rock against all the devils of the sea seeking to pull me down —".

"Is it not all in my song!" said Owny, with gentle reproach.

Page from the manuscript for The Return of the O'Mahony

(1893), focusing again upon human vanity, is a sober study of mankind's misplaced allegiances to social status and education; but its ending, in the words of Stanton Garner, acknowledges "the democracy of suffering of the living and the awful equality of the dead."

The pervasive gloom of Frederic's backward glance at his boyhood was symptomatic of his own rapidly changing fortunes. The youthful optimism with which he had begun his literary career had disappeared. Though he remained a loving father of his children by Grace and spent weekends with them, his marriage was a shambles. He longed for divorce, but Grace refused. He was forced to resign from the Savage Club because of a dispute with another member, St. John Brenon, who sued him successfully for libel after Frederic assailed his character in print. The *New York Times* fell upon hard times under new owners. Another of his plays, on the theme of mesmerism, elicited no interest from prospective producers. His interest in the Irish cause waned when he lost the friendship of influential Irishmen over his comments repudiating the leadership of Parnell. And, all the while, he struggled to maintain two households—including seven children—and to carry his share of the expense of the good life with companions from the journalistic, literary, and artistic communities.

Among his dining companions was William Ernest Henley, editor of the *National Observer*, for which Frederic wrote a series of sketches entitled "Observations in Philistia" in 1892 and 1893. These observations, which he collected in 1896 under the title *Mrs. Albert Grundy*, are genially satirical. Frederic robes his Mrs. Grundy, a paragon of propriety, with the ample flesh of a British matron, makes her the wife of an executive and the mother of three nearly grown daughters, locates her in a villa in South Kensington, and good-naturedly describes her life and times in contemporary London. She has all the faults, and none of the virtues, of a well-to-do Englishwoman; but her little life is brimful of respectable adventure. Frederic began his vignettes with the intention of dissecting her petty motives, ridiculous ambitions, and dubious intellect. But he found more worthwhile subjects of ridicule in other members of her world—female journalists, male politicians, upstart ladies, and gentlemen with questionable business ethics. By the end of the sketches, Mrs. Grundy is more sinned against than sinning.

Perhaps encouraged by the support of Howells, whom he had visited on his third and last trip to the United States in 1890, Frederic had been working since that time on his major book, the third of his contemporary novels about upstate New York. With this work, the focus would be on fundamentalist Protestant religion (the kind he had learned from his mother) and the liberal religious views he had learned from Father Terry, who, as Father Forbes, would occupy a major role in the book. *The Damnation of Theron Ware* (1896) is both a character study and a sociological study. The principal character is Theron Ware, seminary educated and newly married, who is assigned to a backward Methodist church that opposes written sermons, choir singing, and any ornamentation of person or pulpit delivery. He is an initially likable young man, capable, to an extent, of standing up to the primitive trustees who control the church, but his fatal flaw is that he thinks well—too well—of himself and is ambitious for worldly success. Much like Frederic himself as a young journalist, Theron encounters in the town a number of persons who both challenge his simple faith and foster his self-image. Father Forbes is a scholarly Catholic priest who speaks of the "Christ-myth." His friend Dr. Ledsmar is an experimental scientist, an expert on Darwin and an atheist. Celia Madden, the beautiful red-haired organist at the Catholic church, is reminiscent of the fickle young woman in *Marsena*, though she is openly hedonistic, the daughter of a wealthy Irishman and thus able to indulge her aesthetic whims. As Theron falls under their subtle spell, he undergoes the spiritual and psychological change that gives the novel its title. He is saved—physically, if not spiritually—by Sister Soulsby, a pragmatist who uses her considerable knowledge of human nature as a religious vaudevillian in holding revivals for the purpose of raising money to pay off church debts. She teaches Theron to employ common sense—"the wisdom of the serpent," she calls it—to continue in the ministry despite his lapsed faith and to continue his marriage despite his superiority to his wife. Following her advice, Theron preaches brilliantly, but his rejection by his three new friends, whose motives he has misunderstood and who find him a bore, is nearly fatal. When he gives up the ministry to move to Seattle to work in real estate, he carries with him visions of success as a politician. In that profession, Frederic implies, his damnation would be complete.

Published in England as *Illumination*, the novel is both a critical self-appraisal of Frederic's own naivete and ambition and a searching assessment of the American character. A best-seller in its time, the book attracted readers because of its sensationalism, its supposed criticism of Methodism. The English

Front covers for American edition and retitled British edition of Frederic's most popular novel. By 1900, four years after publication, 75,000 copies of the book had been sold in the United States.

Spectator called it "one of the novels of the year" and placed Frederic "very near, if not quite at the head, of the newest American fiction"; William Morton Payne in the *Dial* termed it "one of the most striking and impressive novels of the year, or of several years." The novel has sustained Frederic's reputation and is read today as a portrait of the American Adam at the end of the century, an innocent who has lost his innocence. "It presents not only a brilliantly conceived and psychologically fascinating protagonist," according to Stanton Garner, "but a representative if unpromising man at the end of an era of confidence and simple faith and the beginning of a darker era of complexity and doubt."

Frederic, too, had lost his innocence. By the time the book appeared he had centered his life at Homefield, a large house in Surrey where he lived

with Kate Lyon, now using the name Frederic, and their children and to which he invited only a few chosen friends. What happiness he found during his final few years was in the company of Kate. Their romance is the subject of an inconsequential novel, *March Hares* (1896), which Frederic wrote hurriedly after completing *The Damnation of Theron Ware*.

The success of his best-selling novel gave Frederic financial relief for the first time in his life. He was able to give up a weekly stamp column he had conducted for two years and to cease sending additional articles to the *News York Times* to supplement his weekly salary of $80. He was also able to enjoy the respect and companionship of writers like Stephen Crane, who was in Frederic's debt because of Frederic's review of *The Red Badge of Courage*

(1895), which had called the attention of the American public to the merits of the book. When Crane arrived in England in 1897, he looked up Frederic, and the two became fast friends. With Kate Lyon and Cora Crane, they vacationed in Ireland, and they celebrated holidays together.

During Frederic's last two years he completed two more novels, both set in England. *Gloria Mundi* (1898) is the story of young Christian Tower, who inherits a dukedom and faces the problems of what to do with his money, how to adjust to his new life, and whom to marry. The story moves leisurely through quiet conversation and tedious exposition for nearly one hundred thousand words before any resolution is apparent.

The Market-Place (1899) has in recent years come to be regarded, by scholars such as Stanton Garner, as an important analysis of "the implications of the chaotic century which was about to arrive for the directionless people who must live in it." The American protagonist, Joel Stormont Thorpe, through his talent for underhanded, even illegal, financial negotiations, escalates a small amount of money into a fortune in less than a year. Like the Snopeses in Faulkner's *The Hamlet*, the amoral Thorpe is prepared to turn the venality of the decayed aristocracy to his own advantage. He marries into the aristocracy and plans to gain a seat

in Parliament, the first step on his rise to rule England.

Before the book publication of either of his last novels Frederic was dead, at the age of forty-two. In late 1897 he had experienced the first sign of the illness that was to take his life. Ignoring medical advice, he pursued his reckless schedule of work and social activities, smoking and eating to excess. He suffered a paralytic stroke in August 1898 and died two months later. The notoriety surrounding his death did much to popularize his last two books. A Christian Scientist, Kate Lyon had called in a faith healer to attend Frederic. The healer and Kate Lyon were charged with manslaughter after he died, and the account of their trial and acquittal was international news. His wife died of cancer the following March. Friends created a fund to aid her four orphaned children, and Cora Crane solicited help for Frederic's three children by Kate Lyon.

Frederic's reputation has grown steadily, particularly in the last thirty years. He was first regarded as a naturalist, rebelling against the constraints of rural and small-town life that shaped and narrowed his characters. A brief comment by Vernon Louis Parrington about *Seth's Brother's Wife*—"a drab tale of farm life in upper New York state, as bitter as any tale of the western border"—set the pattern of criticism for a generation. Now he stands

Harold Frederic in his study, circa 1897

The Coroner reading last week's depositions to Mrs. Mills.   Mrs. Mills, the Christian scientist.   Dr. Brown.

Mr. Stokes (Harold Frederic's executor.)   Dr. Freyberger, specialist.   Miss Frederic.   Miss Kate Lyon.

Courtroom sketches from the Daily Graphic *depicting the sensationalistic London trial of Frederic's mistress, Kate Lyons, and Christian Science healer Mrs. Athalie Mills for manslaughter after his death*

further from Hamlin Garland, Edgar Watson Howe, and Joseph Kirkland and closer to William Dean Howells, Frank Norris, and Theodore Dreiser—perhaps even Henry James—in his close studies of human psychology and social complexities. He is ranked with Stephen Crane, John William De Forest, and Ambrose Bierce in his studies of the Civil War, finding in it an emblem of national disunity rather than a background for romantic action and the sentimentalized portrayal of character. Most significantly, however, he is now read as a perceptive chronicler of the fortunes and misfortunes of the American Adam and the decay, in the closing years of the last century, of the American Dream.

Periodical Publications:
FICTION:
"The Blakelys of Poplar Place. A Legend of the Mohawk," *Utica Daily Observer*, 30 June 1877, p. 2;
"Brother Sebastian's Friendship," *Utica Daily Observer*, 6 September 1879, p. 2; republished in *Stories by American Authors* (New York: Scribners, 1884), VI: 145-164;
"The Editor and the Schoolma'am," *New York Times*, 9 September 1888, p. 14.

NONFICTION:
"The Mohawk Valley During the Revolution," *Harper's New Monthly Magazine*, 55 (July 1877): 171-183;
"The Ireland of Today," as X, *Fortnightly Review*, 60 (November 1893): 686-706;
"The Rhetoricians of Ireland," as X, *Fortnightly Review*, 60 (December 1893): 713-727;
"The Ireland of Tomorrow," as X, *Fortnightly Review*, 61 (January 1894): 1-18;
"Stephen Crane's Triumph," *New York Times*, 26 January 1896, p. 22.

Letters:
The Correspondence of Harold Frederic, edited by George Fortenberry, Stanton Garner, and Robert H. Woodward, text established by Charlyne Dodge (Fort Worth: Texas Christian University Press, 1977).

Bibliographies:
Thomas F. O'Donnell, Stanton Garner, and Robert H. Woodward, *A Bibliography of Writings by and about Harold Frederic* (Boston: G. K. Hall, 1975);
Noel Polk, *The Literary Manuscripts of Harold Frederic: A Catalogue* (New York & London: Garland, 1979).

References:
Austin Briggs, Jr., *The Novels of Harold Frederic* (Ithaca: Cornell University Press, 1969);

Everett Carter, *Howells and the Age of Realism* (Philadelphia: Lippincott, 1954), pp. 239-245;

Stanton Garner, *Harold Frederic*, University of Minnesota Pamphlets on American Writers (Minneapolis: University of Minnesota Press, 1969);

George W. Johnson, "Harold Frederic's Young Goodman Ware: The Ambiguities of Realistic Romance," *Modern Fiction Studies*, 8 (Winter 1962-1963): 361-374;

Thomas F. O'Donnell and Hoyt C. Franchere, *Harold Frederic* (New York: Twayne, 1961);

John Henry Raleigh, Introduction to *The Damnation of Theron Ware* (New York: Holt, Rinehart & Winston, 1960), pp. vii-xxviii;

Allen F. Stein, "Evasions of an American Adam: Structure and Theme in *The Damnation of Theron Ware*," *American Literary Realism*, 5 (Winter 1972): 23-36;

Edmund Wilson, *The Devils and Canon Barham* (New York: Farrar, Straus & Giroux, 1973), pp. 48-76;

Robert H. Woodward, "A Selection of Harold Frederic's Early Literary Criticism, 1877-1881," *American Literary Realism*, 5 (Winter 1972): 1-22;

Larzer Ziff, *The American 1890's* (New York: Viking, 1966), pp. 206-228.

Papers:
The Harold Frederic Papers at the Library of Congress is the major collection of manuscripts, including unpublished plays and notes for several incomplete stories. The New York Public Library has many letters, including transcripts, in the Berg Collection, the Ernest L. Oppenheim Papers, and the Paul Haines Papers. The Scribner Collection at Princeton University Library has copies of the correspondence between Frederic and Charles Scribner's Sons. The Stephen Crane Papers in the Butler Library at Columbia University has letters to Cora Crane in response to a request for contributions for Frederic's children by Kate Lyon after his death.

Mary Wilkins Freeman
(31 October 1852-13 March 1930)

Lynda S. Boren
Tulane University

SELECTED BOOKS: *Decorative Plaques: Designs by George F. Barnes and Mary E. Wilkins* (Boston: Lothrop, 1883);

Goody Two-Shoes and Other Famous Nursery Tales, by Freeman and Clara Doty Bates (Boston: Lothrop, 1883);

The Cow with Golden Horns and Other Stories (Boston: Lothrop, 1886?);

The Adventures of Ann: Stories of Colonial Times (Boston: Lothrop, 1886);

A Humble Romance and Other Stories (New York & London: Harper, 1887; London: Ward, Lock & Bowden, 1893);

A New England Nun and Other Stories (New York: Harper, 1891; London: Osgood, McIlvaine, 1891);

The Pot of Gold and Other Stories (Boston: Lothrop, 1892);

Young Lucretia and Other Stories (New York: Harper, 1892; London: Osgood, McIlvaine, 1892);

Jane Field (London: Osgood, McIlvaine, 1892; New York: Harper, 1893);

Giles Corey, Yeoman: A Play (New York: Harper, 1893);

Pembroke (New York: Harper, 1894; London: Osgood, McIlvaine, 1894);

Madelon (New York: Harper, 1896; London: Osgood, McIlvaine, 1896);

Jerome, A Poor Man (New York & London: Harper, 1897);

Silence and Other Stories (New York & London: Harper, 1898);

The People of Our Neighborhood (Philadelphia: Curtis / New York: Doubleday & McClure, 1898); republished as *Some of Our Neighbors* (London: Dent, 1898);

The Love of Parson Lord and Other Stories (New York & London: Harper, 1900);

The Heart's Highway: A Romance of Virginia in the Seventeenth Century (New York: Doubleday, Page, 1900; London: Murray, 1900);

Understudies (New York & London: Harper, 1901);

The Portion of Labor (New York & London: Harper, 1901);

Six Trees (New York & London: Harper, 1903);

The Wind in the Rose-bush and Other Stories of the Supernatural (New York: Doubleday, Page, 1903; London: Murray, 1903);

The Givers (New York & London: Harper, 1904);

The Debtor (New York & London: Harper, 1905);

"Doc." Gordon (New York & London: Authors and Newspaper Association, 1906); republished as *Doctor Gordon* (London: Unwin, 1907);

By the Light of the Soul (New York & London: Harper, 1907);

The Fair Lavinia and Others (New York & London: Harper, 1907);

The Shoulders of Atlas (New York & London: Harper, 1908);

The Winning Lady and Others (New York & London: Harper, 1909);

The Green Door (New York: Moffat, Yard, 1910; London: Gay & Hancock, 1912);

The Butterfly House (New York: Dodd, Mead, 1912);

The Yates Pride (New York & London: Harper, 1912);

The Copy-Cat & Other Stories (New York & London: Harper, 1914);

An Alabaster Box, by Freeman and Florence Morse Kingsley (New York & London: Appleton, 1917);

Edgewater People (New York & London: Harper, 1918).

A small doll-like woman, who never wished to grow old and yet came to resemble so many of her aging heroines, created in her fiction the heart of New England's life and ethos. Mary Wilkins Freeman created strong-willed characters, whose Yankee stoicism often led them into strange, single-minded paths of destructiveness or bizarre obsession. But she also analyzed her creations with loving kindness, supplying the leaven of humor and sympathy in works about family strife, delayed marriages, broken hearts, and small disappointments. In *Pembroke* (1894), as a father muses about his son, he conveys the painful differences between generations in New England villages: "There was no human being so strange and mysterious, such an unknown quantity, to Caleb Thayer as his own son. He had not one trait of character in common with him—at least, not one so translated into his own vernacular that he could comprehend it. It was to Caleb as if he looked in a glass expecting to see his own face and saw therein the face of a stranger." Such touches of empathy in Mary Wilkins Freeman's fiction caused readers to marvel and to delight in her creations. In 1926 Freeman received the William Dean Howells Medal of the American Academy of Arts and Letters for distinction in fiction. Presenting the medal, Hamlin Garland commended this woman, then in her seventies, for having created "unfaltering portraits of lorn widowhood, crabbed age, wistful youth, cheerful drudgery, patient poverty, defiant spinsterhood, and many other related and individual types of character . . . all making an unparalleled record of New England life. . . ." But she also expressed in her writing the beauty of the New England landscape that is never far removed as a solace to the suffering of the Calvinist soul. As Caleb's son, Barney, grieves for his lost love, he turns to New England earth for comfort: "Barney began sobbing and crying like a child as he lay there; he moved his arms convulsively and tore up handfuls of young grass and leaves and flung them away in the unconscious gesturing of grief. . . . He started off with a great stride, and then he stopped short and flung an arm around the slender trunk of a white birch tree and pulled it against him as if it were Charlotte and laid his cheek on the cool white bark and sobbed again like a girl. 'Oh, Charlotte, Charlotte!' he moaned, and his voice was drowned out by the manifold rustling of the young birch leaves, as a human grief is overborne and carried out of sight by the soft, resistless progress of nature."

Herself a product of the world of her fiction, Mary Wilkins's fragile beauty seemed at odds with the staunch Calvinist tone of her New England upbringing. Born into a respected family of the small town of Randolph, Massachusetts, Mary Eleanor Wilkins claimed ancestry dating back to Sir Thomas de Moulton (a knight who served Richard, Coeur de Lion) on her father's side and kinship to Lothrop Stoddard (well-known writer and lecturer) from her maternal branch. Her mother, Eleanor Lothrop, came from one of the founding families of East Randolph, Massachusetts, and Mary Wilkins inherited, along with her blue eyes and delicate features, a strong puritanical sense of moral rectitude.

Of the four children born to Warren and Eleanor Wilkins, Mary Eleanor alone survived beyond her teens, and her parents in their anxiety treated her with extravagant care. Her younger sister Nan died in 1876 at the age of seventeen. Mary's father was an accomplished housewright and carpenter; a proud man with a sharp wit, he seems to have passed on to Mary also his disturbing mood swings and extreme sensitivity. Staunch Congregationalists, Mary's parents observed the Sabbath regularly, taking the small child to church with them. At age seven Mary began school in a one-room schoolhouse where she learned "reading and spelling, repeating the Catechism, writing and arithmetic." Having been pampered by her family and reared practically as an only child, she had an air of aloof daintiness that caused the other children to dislike her. She was called the teacher's pet and that stuck up "little dolly-pinky-rosy." She survived the teasing by making friends with Mary John Wales, who was to remain a lifelong friend and supporter. They spent hours together playing at the Wales farm, an old house which had been built only twenty years after the Revolution. When she was not playing with Mary John, Mary Eleanor spent most of her time reading and daydreaming. She was a shy, imaginative child and became totally absorbed in fairy tales and adventure stories. In many respects her imaginative life provided an escape from the rigid Calvinism of her upbringing. Most forms of levity were condemned; the Ten Commandments, the Bible, and the Sabbath formed the backbone of her world. Her father's pride in one of the poems she wrote when she was in her early teens was deflated by Mary's puritanical Uncle Everett: "Lot of good that will do—letting that child write poetry!" All her life, Mary would feel the tension created by her Calvinist forebears.

When she reached high-school age, Mary's father moved the family to Brattleboro, Vermont, where he opened a dry-goods shop with a partner. At school there Mary studied Latin, natural philosophy, algebra, arithmetic, geometry, and rhetoric. She was a good student, and with her blue eyes and reddish-gold hair, she was an attractive young woman. Her social reticence remained with her, however, and she did not have a beau. Wanting the best for their daughter, the Wilkinses sent Mary to Mount Holyoke Female Seminary in fall 1870. She left at the end of the academic year a "nervous wreck," determined not to go back. The girls did all of the work at the school themselves, including the hard cleaning, and rules were rigidly enforced. Recording her memories of those days, Mary mused: "What I am sure of is that I ate so much beef in different forms and so many baked apples that I have never wanted much since. I have often wondered why they looked out so beautifully for our young morals, and did not vary our menu more. As I remember, I did not behave at all well at Mt. Holyoke, and I am inclined to attribute it to monotony of diet and too strenuous goadings of conscience." At nineteen Mary Wilkins had gone as far as she would go with her formal education. Still unmarried, still socially reticent, and still enamored of literature, she found companionship with another young woman, who, like Mary John, would remain a lifelong friend. Together Mary and Evelyn (Eve) Sawyer read Charles Dickens, Ralph Waldo Emerson, Edgar Allan Poe, Sarah Orne Jewett, and Harriet Beecher Stowe, among others, seeing in these writers the rebellion they too felt. In Eve's company Mary would mimic the village worthies they had visited during the day, displaying a wit she usually kept hidden from outsiders. When she was twenty-one, Mary Wilkins fell in love for the first time, when she met Hanson Tyler, a graduate of the U. S. Naval Academy and grandson of former Chief Justice Royall Tyler. Hanson Tyler was to embody a romantic ideal to which Mary Wilkins would always be drawn; hard drinking, handsome, and humorous, he was enormously popular but not altogether serious. Giving her a photo and promising to write, Hanson left for a cruise and never returned for her, eventually marrying someone else. After a series of financial disasters, Warren Wilkins gave up his shop and returned to carpentry but with little success. By 1877 the family fortune had so dwindled that Hanson Tyler's father, the Reverend Pickman Tyler, and his wife asked the Wilkinses to live with them, Mrs. Wilkins to act as housekeeper. After her mother's death in 1880, Mary, then twenty-eight, moved with her father (whose health was declining) to a house on North Street and there began to write for a living.

Mary Wilkins began her career with poetry for children; she received ten dollars for her first poem "The Beggar King," a long ballad published by *Wide Awake*, a magazine for children, in 1881. In 1882 her first adult story "A Shadow Family" won fifty dollars from the *Boston Sunday Budget*, and Wilkins was launched on her own. Most of her short stories grew out of the village gossip and legends she had heard so often, and she kept faithfully her edict that "a young writer should follow the safe course of writing only about those subjects she knows thoroughly, and concerning which she trusts her own convictions." In the autumn of 1882, Mary Wilkins's father left to take a construction job in Gainesville, Florida. He died of a fever after a severe chill on 10 April 1883, and his body was taken to Randolph for burial. With the death of her father, Wilkins was faced with loneliness. None of her immediate family remained. She was still unmarried and in need of support. After attending her father's funeral in Randolph she returned to Brattleboro to stay with the Wheeler family, friends who occupied a house built by her father. Her writing then provided Wilkins a means of support and gave her solace from grief. Out of the loss she must have felt so deeply, Mary Wilkins recreated the scenes and family stories of her youth with a strong desire to keep alive a sense of belonging to something. This longing was perhaps her motivation for returning to Randolph to live with the Wales family in 1884. By that time "A Humble Romance" had been accepted by *Harper's Bazar*, and her father's estate had been settled, leaving her $973. The Waleses treated her well, allowing her the afternoons in her own study for writing or reading. Mary John Wales, who never married, became Wilkins's manager of sorts. Strong, capable, and intelligent, Mary John, like so many of Wilkins's New England women, was not pretty enough to "catch a man,"

and never seemed to need one. Wilkins gained popularity as a writer of children's stories and poems before she was taken seriously as a writer of adult fiction. She was well known in Brattleboro for her delightful juvenile tales. With the appearance in 1887 of her first collection of adult short stories, *A Humble Romance and Other Stories*, Wilkins's reputation as a writer of note was established. American critics and the reading public alike received the stories warmly. "They are good through and through," William Dean Howells wrote in his "Editor's Study." "Whoever loves the common face of humanity will find pleasure in them." Wilkins's appeal lay in her benevolent use of what she knew best: her experiences and fantasies, the strife between husband and wife, village gossip, New England character types, and the suffering of younger generations caught between the rigid Calvinism of their parents and their hopes for a brighter future. No real-life story of human grief or heroism escaped Wilkins's keen observation. Remembering the plight of two aged spinsters of a good family of Brattleboro, Mary Wilkins incorporated them into "A Gala Dress," where, having only one black silk dress between them, the sisters take turns going to meeting. Their pride, in spite of their poverty, remains untouchable. Women, who often outnumber the men two to one in Wilkins's stories, are often (by necessity) stronger than the men. Although both women and men often fall victim to their own inordinate wills, by remaining true to their unrealistic ideals they are often metamorphosed into minor heroic beings worthy of respect. While she is generally classified as a local colorist, critics have compared Wilkins's technique to that of Tolstoy and Maupassant. Noting her similarity to these writers, but denying any direct comparison, Edward Foster writes that "technically, the most striking characteristic of the Wilkins story is its pace and directness—the short and wiry sentence; the short paragraph; concision in narrative, expository, and descriptive elements; boldness in moving fast to the scene developed in dialogue."

While the stories in *A Humble Romance* were intended primarily for a female audience, the themes and conflicts are universal. The title piece concerns a middle-aged tin peddler, Jake Russell, who awkwardly courts Miss Sally, a kitchen maid. She runs off with him, and they have three months of married bliss until Jake's wife, whom he thought dead, returns suddenly. Jake and Sally must separate and are reunited only after his first wife's death. The excellence of the story lies in Wilkins's depiction of character and her use of dialogue. "I

A HUMBLE ROMANCE

AND OTHER STORIES

BY

MARY E. WILKINS

NEW YORK
HARPER & BROTHERS, FRANKLIN SQUARE
LONDON: 30 FLEET STREET
1887

A NEW ENGLAND NUN

AND OTHER STORIES

BY

MARY E. WILKINS
AUTHOR OF "A HUMBLE ROMANCE" ETC.

NEW YORK
HARPER & BROTHERS, FRANKLIN SQUARE
1891

Title pages for the two books that established Freeman's reputation as a New England local-color writer

wouldn't go with the King, if it wan't to—go—honest—," Sally warns Jake before their elopement. Something of the dignity of Dickens's characters in *Hard Times* can be felt in Wilkins's portrayal of small-town integrity. The remaining stories in this collection concern themselves with similar themes. Caroline Munson of "A Symphony in Lavender" rejects, in her late forties, the "man of her dreams" because he is, indeed, the embodiment of the beautiful but evil youth she dreamed of, with ambivalent feelings, in her girlhood. In "Gentian" we are introduced to one of Wilkins's multitude of absurdly unbending male characters. "Alferd" Tollett, refusing to accept advice or medication, stoically faces his inevitable death. His wife, Lucy, finally transcends her subordinate role as obedient wife and slips gentian into his tea. When he improves, Lucy confesses, and Alferd, in a rage, refuses to allow her to cook for him. After a period of separation, they are reconciled. The humor and whimsy beneath the tales is so closely interwoven with Wilkins's feeling for human nature that after reading a story like "Gentian" the reader is left with a rather gratifying sense of benediction. At her best,

Wilkins answers her readers' demands and her own that a good story be, above all, honest.

Her second collection of adult stories, *A New England Nun and Other Stories* (1891), was also well received. In the title piece, Louisa Ellis breaks her fourteen-year engagement to Joe Daggett, who has been in Australia making his fortune, because the lengthy separation has forced her into a life "full of a pleasant peace." Reentering her orderly world of "long sweet afternoons," Joe destroys her illusions of permanence. Later, she overhears by accident Joe's declaration of love to another woman, and, although Joe still plans to marry her out of a sense of honor, Louisa turns him away. Resigned to her condition "she gazed ahead through a long reach of future days strung together like pearls in a rosary, every one like the others, and all smooth and flawless and innocent, and her heart went up in thankfulness."

With *Pembroke* (1894), her best novel, Wilkins achieved a tour de force in grim dramatic portrayal of New England's Old Testament ethos. Drawn on classical lines, the story evolves from Wilkins's family history and centers around the house in which

Doc. Gordon

Chapter 1

It was very early in the morning, it was scarcely dawn when the young man started upon a walk of twenty-five miles in order to reach Allen, where he was to be assistant to the one physician in the place: Doctor Thomas Gordon, or Doc Gordon as he was familiarly called.

Mary E. Wilkins Freeman.

First page of manuscript for Doc Gordon

she had lived with her family in Randolph. The house had been built in the 1830s by Barnabas Lothrop for his son Barnabas Junior, who was engaged to Mary Thayer, a local belle. Mr. Thayer and Barnabas Junior disagreed violently on political issues. After a heated argument, Mr. Thayer threw Barnabas out of his house, refusing to allow the marriage to take place. In *Pembroke* Wilkins alters the name slightly. Barney Thayer is thrown out by Charlotte Barnard's father, and because of his immense pride, Barney cannot humble himself to apologize, even if it means losing Charlotte. Both families, the Thayers and the Barnards, are locked in a clash of wills that all but destroys the younger generation. The house that Barney built in anticipation of his marriage to Charlotte becomes his hermitage. That and the death of his invalid brother cast a pall on the life of Pembroke. While the real-life Barnabas and Mary never reunited, Wilkins brings her novel to a bittersweet conclusion, by reuniting the lovers in middle age. Barnabas "entered the house with his old sweetheart and his old self." The bitterness in the story is mingled with the pathos found in classical tragedy. Pride is the hamartia of Wilkins's self-righteous elect, and the village gossips function as a Greek chorus to the tragic events: " 'Do you see that house?' a woman bent on hospitable entertainment said as she drove a matronly cousin from another village down the street. 'The one with the front windows boarded up, without any step to the front door? Well, Barney Thayer lives there all alone. He's old Caleb Thayer's son, all the son that's left; the other one died. There was some talk of his mother's whippin' him to death. She died right after, but they said afterwards that she didn't, that she run away one night an' had heart trouble.' " Within the darkness of tragedy, however, Barnabas Thayer and Charlotte Barnard triumph through humility as both eventually cast aside their pride and seek reunion. Echoes of Milton's recovered paradise and Hawthorne's qualified innocence reverberate in the denouement of Wilkins's finest achievement. Although she produced over a dozen novels, *Pembroke* remains by general consent Wilkins's best.

In 1892 on a visit to friends in Metuchen, New Jersey, Wilkins met a man seven years her junior who seemed cast in the mold of her idealized Lieutenant Tyler. Kate Upson Clarke, who introduced the two, described Dr. Charles Manning Freeman as a man who "drank too much, drove fast horses, courted all the girls, [and] skillfully eluded marriage." Attracted, but cautious, Wilkins prepared for her eventual marriage to the doctor. On

Portrait of Freeman by W. D. Stevens for Harper's Weekly, *30 December 1905*

1 January 1902, ten years, six announcements, and six denials later, Miss Wilkins and Dr. Freeman were at last married. "At this extremely late hour of the day," she wrote to Eve Severance, "I am about to be married. . . . The unfortunate man is Dr. Chas. M. Freeman. . . . We are very old friends, but have not been engaged as long as the newspapers state. They have married and postponed at their own discretion." After the marriage, Dr. Freeman proved a temperate, loving husband. It was Mary Freeman who proved difficult. Addicted to sedatives for her insomnia, she could not sleep without them. Shocked by this discovery and disturbed by his wife's moodiness, Freeman wrote to Mary John Wales for advice. Devoted to his wife, however, Charles Freeman regulated her activities so that she could continue her writing in a placid setting. As she grew older, Mary Freeman began more and more to sink into domesticity. Finding less time for writing, she was also handicapped by her gradual loss of hearing. After the publication of her last collection of short fiction, *Edgewater People*, in 1918, she did little writing. Her husband had once again begun to drink heavily, and he was committed in the last

NELLY EMERGED FROM THE FRONT DOOR AND MOVED TO
MEET HIM

EDGEWATER
PEOPLE

BY
MARY E. WILKINS FREEMAN
Author of "THE PORTION OF LABOR",
"JEROME", "A NEW ENGLAND NUN" ETC.

HARPER *&* BROTHERS PUBLISHERS
NEW YORK AND LONDON

Frontispiece and title page for Freeman's last book, published twelve years before her death

stages of alcoholism to the New Jersey State Hospital for the Insane at Trenton in 1920. In a letter to a friend after the death of her husband in 1923, Mary Freeman wrote: "Sometimes I think the Volstead Act was what really finished him. If he could have had good whiskey he might have weathered the gale." On his deathbed he had in his derangement left only one dollar to Mary Freeman, bequeathing the majority of the estate to the chauffeur and his wife. The will was finally broken after tedious litigation, and Mary Freeman secured his estate of over $200,000. Until her own death in 1930, Mary Freeman continued to live a rather lonely existence, but she never lost her marvelous wit. After receiving the Howells medal, she wrote, "My gold medal weighs a ton and I don't know what to do with it. Hamlin Garland told me I could hock it."

If Mary Wilkins Freeman's gold medal made little impression on her, it nevertheless remains a tribute to her mastery. Although her reputation fell into decline in this country until the 1930s, she was highly regarded by the writers and readers of her day (among them Henry James). F. O. Matthiessen felt that Freeman was "unsurpassed . . . in her ability to give the breathless intensity of a moment." Most anthologies of American literature now include Freeman's work; Fred Lewis Pattee and Van Wyck Brooks, among others, have established her place in American culture. Perhaps she is described best by Hamlin Garland, who recorded in his diaries that "Mary was quietly, almost roguishly humorous. She was 'an old maid' in appearance and movement, but her keen laughing blue eyes and quizzical smile denoted the novelist who saw everything and remembered what was of value to her."

Other:

The Whole Family, A Novel by Twelve Authors, includes a chapter by Freeman (New York & London: Harper, 1908).

References:

Van Wyck Brooks, *New England: Indian Summer* (New York: Dutton, 1940);

Edward Foster, *Mary E. Wilkins Freeman* (New York: Hendricks House, 1956);

F. O. Matthiessen, "New England Stories," in *American Writers on American Literature*, edited by John Macy (New York: Liveright, 1931);

Paul Elmer More, "Hawthorne: Looking Before and After," in *The Shelburne Essays*, Second Series (Boston: Houghton, Mifflin, 1905), pp. 173-187;

Vernon L. Parrington, *The Beginnings of Critical Realism in America* (New York: Harcourt, Brace, 1930);

F. L. Pattee, *A History of American Literature Since 1870* (New York: Century, 1915);

Arthur H. Quinn, *American Fiction: A Historical Survey* (New York: Appleton, 1936);

Perry D. Westbrook, *Acres of Flint: Writers of Rural New England* (Washington, D. C.: Scarecrow Press, 1951);

Westbrook, *Mary Wilkins Freeman* (New York: Twayne, 1967).

Henry Blake Fuller
(9 January 1857-28 July 1929)

John Pilkington, Jr.
University of Mississippi

BOOKS: *The Chevalier of Pensieri-Vani together with Frequent References to the Prorege of Arcopia*, as Stanton Page (Boston: J. G. Cupples, 1890; London: Osgood, McIlvaine, 1891); revised and enlarged as *The Chevalier of Pensieri-Vani* (New York: Century, 1892; London: Osgood, McIlvaine, 1892);

The Chatelaine of La Trinité (New York: Century, 1892; London: Osgood, McIlvaine, 1892);

The Cliff-Dwellers: A Novel (New York: Harper, 1893);

With the Procession: A Novel (New York: Harper, 1895);

The Puppet-Booth: Twelve Plays (New York: Century, 1896; London: John Lane, 1896);

From the Other Side: Stories of Transatlantic Travel (Boston & New York: Houghton, Mifflin, 1898);

The New Flag: Satires (Chicago: Privately printed, 1899);

The Last Refuge: A Sicilian Romance (Boston & New York: Houghton, Mifflin, 1900);

Under the Skylights (New York: Appleton, 1901);

Waldo Trench and Others: Stories of Americans in Italy (New York: Scribners Sons, 1908);

Lines Long and Short: Biographical Sketches in Various Rhythms (Boston & New York: Houghton Mifflin, 1917);

On the Stairs (Boston & New York: Houghton Mifflin, 1918);

Bertram Cope's Year: A Novel (Chicago: Seymour, 1919);
Gardens of This World (New York: Knopf, 1929; London: Knopf, 1930);
Not on the Screen (New York: Knopf, 1930; London: Knopf, 1930).

In his essay, "The Great American Novel" (1932), Theodore Dreiser remarked that "if there is such a person as the father of American realism, Henry B. Fuller is that man." In *With the Procession* (1895), Dreiser said, Fuller "introduced for the first time the purely American realistic novel" in which "we are permitted to glimpse the true Chicago American scene of the day." While making these assertions, Dreiser rejected Henry James as "too narrowly and thinly class-conscious" and William Dean Howells as "too socially indifferent and worse, uninformed." Although these judgments on Howells and James may be questioned and that of Fuller understood as applicable to only a portion of his work, Dreiser properly placed Fuller among the pioneers of realism in American literature and, perhaps unknowingly, raised issues which lie at the center of Fuller's relationship to life and to literature.

"I was born and brought up in Chicago," Fuller often remarked, "and there I belong." The comment should not be taken to imply that he found it a comfortable environment. His grandfather, Judge Henry Fuller, a cousin of Margaret Fuller's, had brought his family, which included Henry Blake Fuller's father, George Wood Fuller, to Chicago in 1848. Henry Fuller's mother, Mary Josephine Sanford Fuller, was also from an old New England family, and the Fullers' outlook reflected that heritage. The Fullers were part of a group that would come to be known as "old settlers," the more conservative people who had settled in Chicago before the great fire of 1871, and Fuller gave his allegiance to the America of James Russell Lowell, Henry Wadsworth Longfellow, and Charles Eliot Norton. As a high-school student, he found refuge from the commercialism of Chicago in the Allison Classical Academy in Oconomowoc, Wisconsin. The escape was only temporary, however, for by 1875 he was back in Chicago working in a crockery store and later in a bank. Increasingly, he found Chicago repugnant and antithetical to every value he cherished. Longing to enjoy the civilization, especially the architecture, of the Old World, Fuller saved his money until he had sufficient funds to make his pilgrimage.

On 17 August 1879, Fuller left Chicago for Europe; he would be gone a year to the day, probably the most important year in his life. He visited England, France, Italy (spending three months in Rome), Switzerland, Germany, and Holland. Each night in his journal he wrote meticulous accounts of the architecture, painting, sculpture, and natural scenery he had seen during the day; and he brought back with him a manuscript which could serve as the basis for a book about Europe. His pilgrimage had confirmed his distaste for the raw ugliness of Chicago and the material values of its businessmen. He could never again work in a crockery store, a bank, or any other business firm. He was committed to a writing career.

Fuller had scarcely returned to Chicago before he longed to get back to Europe. In September 1883 he again fled the philistinism of the city. This time his primary destination was Rome. Again he kept a notebook; but instead of merely recounting the day's travels, he wrote about incidents and anecdotes that he could later use as the basis of essays, sketches, and stories. Perhaps more important for his personal development, the trip gave him a second look at Europe, and his comparisons raised doubts about the attractiveness of the expatriate's life and even of the superiority of the Old World to the New. Instead of returning to Chicago, Fuller went to Boston, which, he felt, represented something of a compromise between the beauty of Europe and the ugliness of Chicago. Boston, moreover, was the home of William Dean Howells, whose *Venetian Life* (1866), blending personal observation with fact and criticism, represented the kind of travel sketches which Fuller desired to write.

The illness and death of his father in 1885, however, forced Fuller to return to Chicago; Judge Fuller had made money in the railroad business, but after the judge died, George Fuller suffered financial difficulties, and by the time of his death, the family fortunes had declined noticeably. Subsequently, the management of his father's rental properties kept Fuller in the city. Meanwhile, Fuller had written a number of sketches, short stories, and poems. Although they are apprentice pieces, they show how deeply Fuller was thinking about the differences between Europe and America. Nowhere did Fuller see this comparison more vividly dramatized than in the persons of Howells and Henry James. In 1885 he wrote the important essay, "Howells or James?," which, for some reason, was never published in his lifetime. In it, he came to grips with the issue which troubled him throughout his life.

Fuller knew that Howells, after spending four

years in Venice, had resisted the pleasures of the expatriate life in Europe, returned to America determined to live here permanently, and committed himself to American subjects. Howells had, as Fuller wrote, "a clear perception of the direction in which the cat . . . was about to jump" and "crossed over" to America, where "the writer who is most thoroughly permeated with the realistic spirit may confidently expect the widest hearing and the securest place." Increasingly, Howells, writing about the commonplace activities of businessmen, reporters, housewives, and other people one would meet in everyday life, had adopted the realistic technique for his fiction. Henry James, on the other hand, had decided to remain in Europe and to write about exceptional persons in a European setting; and even though James ultimately dealt in realities, "a realism," said Fuller, "made up of select actualities is pretty apt to come out idealistically in the end." For himself, Fuller felt torn between the two poles. Howells came to represent America and James Europe. The dichotomy could be expressed in various ways: Howells or James, America or Europe, American subjects or European, Chicago or Rome, the commonplace or the exceptional, realism or romanticism. Basically, he felt that Howells was right, but Fuller could not put aside his longing for Italy.

The conflict between Europe or Italy and America or Chicago underlies Fuller's first published book. During a period of considerable personal depression in 1886, Fuller began to write about his Italian experiences. At first he had no intention of having his book published, but as the manuscript slowly developed in his small business office on Lake Street, he decided to call it *The Chevalier of Pensieri-Vani* (1890), to use the pseudonym Stanton Page, and to seek a publisher. But after the work was finished in 1887, Fuller had trouble finding a firm willing to bring it out. Finally, the J. G. Cupples Company of Boston agreed to publish it at Fuller's expense, and, late in 1890, Fuller had the thin volume in his hands. The book might have gone entirely unnoticed had not someone sent a copy to Charles Eliot Norton. Norton immediately acclaimed it as a work of genius and sent a copy to James Russell Lowell, who also found the work impressive. Through the sponsorship of Norton and Lowell, *The Chevalier of Pensieri-Vani* became widely known in Boston and began to be reviewed in the best literary periodicals. Overnight, Fuller emerged as the most prominent writer in Chicago. By the end of 1891, the Cupples Company had reprinted the book twice; and in the spring of

1892, the Century Company brought out under the direction of Richard Watson Gilder a splendid new edition with a dedication to Norton and an added chapter. This edition, advertised by the Century Company as if it were an entirely new book, prompted additional reviews. Uniformly the critics failed to grasp the essential meaning of the book.

The Chevalier of Pensieri-Vani is a poor young gentleman who loves "the post-roads of Tuscany . . . and every antique stone of the fair Italian land." As the chevalier, who represents Fuller himself, leisurely travels around the country, he encounters a variety of personages and participates in a series of incidents loosely connected to each other. Each episode in the chevalier's adventures is complete in itself and makes an independent, humorous, and satirical point, though the incidents themselves are much less significant than the opinions of the characters. With the possible exception of the Prorege of Arcopia (the name suggests a combination of Arcadia and Utopia) each character has traveled to Italy because he believes that life there will be "better worth living than he could make it seem in the region where he had had the misfortune to be born"—a purpose that recalls the motivations of many of Henry James's characters. The primary characters include the Prorege of Arcopia, his pupil George W. Occident, and the chevalier. They are well supported by the secondary characters whose names may have been intended to suggest either position or character: the Duke of Avon and Severn; Hors-Concours, the Contessa Nullaniuna, the Margravine of Schwahlbach-Schreckenstein, and the expatriate medievalist Gregorianius.

At the conclusion of the volume, after the characters have gone their separate ways, the chevalier laments: "how much he had left unseen. . . . How many masterpieces remained unviewed, . . . how many memorable spots he had left unvisited! Such are some of the *pensieri vani* ["vain thoughts"] that torment the home-come voyager." The chevalier voices Fuller's own feelings: his love for Italy, his admiration for the past over the present, his need for privacy, his taste for architecture and music, and his love of rural landscapes. At the same time, the chevalier also reflects Fuller's self-doubts, his fears of failure, and his bleak outlook on the future.

Fuller sought to make the fictional chevalier a mean between the extreme positions taken by the Prorege of Arcopia and George W. Occident. The prorege, a sensitive and compassionate man, firmly believes in an enlightened despotism as the best form of government. In his agrarian Arcopia, the arts are protected, encouraged, and rewarded. Architecture and music are the special glories of the country. Life in this paternalistic kingdom is much like that during the periods in Italian history when the arts reached their highest level of achievement. Yet the chevalier (and Fuller) cannot wholly approve of the prorege because of the innate selfishness and vanity that seem the necessary accompaniment of his political theories. The prorege has as his pupil, the immensely wealthy and "promising young barbarian," George W. Occident, who has left his native Shelby County (Chicago) to seek a richer, fuller life abroad. In his "uninstructed state" Occident has no appreciation of art, but he is "extremely bright" and has "picked up ideas with the utmost readiness." Occident does have strong convictions about the nature of government, the value of action for action's sake, and the democratic structure of society. He voices precisely the attitudes and opinions that one would expect a young man from Chicago to hold and becomes the antithesis of the Prorege of Arcopia. Occident appears to take the aesthetic position of Howells, while the prorege seems to voice that of James.

Throughout *The Chevalier of Pensieri-Vani*, Fuller displays his preference for the Italian past. The crown of Old Lucumo, the Etruscan warrior, for example, has remained intact for centuries, but in modern times "there was no head on which to place it." Chicago, Fuller thought, was full of men like Occident, who, despite their millions, had no real purpose in life and who lived in woeful ignorance of the things that could make life both beautiful and meaningful. Italy, by contrast, was full of artistic monuments that proved that in the past men "could dare and do." Modern man has failed to build upon the achievements of the past; all too often he has merely turned the lovely garden of the ancients into a hideous wasteland.

The brunt of Fuller's attack falls upon modern industrialism, which, in the words of the prorege, has made it "more and more difficult to discriminate between a man and a highly specialized machine." Prodded by Occident, the prorege adds that if it were necessary to distinguish between a man and a machine, it would be "doubly, trebly necessary to discriminate between a man and a mere money-machine." Fuller held that the growth of industrialism in Chicago (and elsewhere in America), the passion for bigness, and the lack of integrity in government left little for the individual who would not live the life of a "money-machine." Essentially, his book was an indictment of Chicago; he poured out his hatred and frustration at its false

values, its emptiness, and its intoxication with material good. Outwardly, *The Chevalier of Pensieri-Vani* appears to be a gentle, romantic fantasy featuring the adventures of a kindly little man along the post roads of Tuscany; but embedded in Fuller's polished prose is a hard, tough, biting satire upon the worship of success in Chicago.

Although Fuller had no doubts about the realities of Chicago, he had not yet settled the issue of "crossing over" permanently to America. Through the expatriate medievalist Gregorianius, for whom Italy had been the great experience of his life, Fuller warned others not to become alienated from their own country. Gregorianius, in Fuller's words, shows the futility of "living through other lives, and making but a thin blood by dieting on the unnutritious husks of a dead-and-gone past." Eventually, Fuller made the decision to cross over to his own country, but increasingly during his later years Fuller, like his fictional character, lived vicariously through the lives of his friends. Like the chevalier too, in some ways Fuller was always "too inveterate a 'looker-on.' "

Expressing, as it did, Fuller's strong feelings about Chicago and Italy, *The Chevalier of Pensieri-Vani* was an intensely personal book. In writing it, however, Fuller had neither wholly relieved his personal tensions nor fully voiced his thoughts about modern times. During the summer of 1891, he wrote a sequel, *The Chatelaine of La Trinité*, which Gilder serialized in the *Century* magazine before its publication as a book in 1892. The sequel readily exhibited resemblances to its predecessor in the title, the obscure place names (in Switzerland instead of Italy), and the allegories suggested by the names of such characters as Aurelia West, Fin-de-Siècle, Tempo-Rubato, Baron Zeitgeist, Professor Saitoutetplus, and Mdlle. Pasdenom. *The Chatelaine of La Trinité* was in every respect a polished, even elegant, successor.

What was not so apparent to contemporary readers was that *The Chatelaine of La Trinité* was actually a very different book. Instead of the "idealistic travel-fiction" of *The Chevalier of Pensieri-Vani*, Fuller now offered a work much closer to the conventional novel in suspenseful plot and firmly drawn characters. If it lacked the romantic charm of the earlier work, it was much closer to Howells's realism. Essentially, Fuller told the story of the efforts of Aurelia ("Gold") West, from Rochester, New York, to transform a modest Swiss country girl with an aristocratic background, Bertha, the Chatelaine of La Trinité (a courtesy title), into Miss West's conception of a modern (Americanized) European noblewoman.

In many respects, Aurelia West occupies the place held by George W. Occident in the earlier volume. Aurelia, however, is not a passive figure; rather, she is a vicious, militant female, whose goal is to make Bertha over into an American woman in a European setting. Her most vocal opponent is the Baron Zeitgeist, who speaks for Fuller. Zeitgeist believes that modern industrial and urban America could hardly fail to develop an aristocracy of privilege that has at its topmost peak an "incredibly widespread, close-knit, firm-rooted, all-pervasive, and ultra-tyrannical . . . aristocracy of sex." Much that Fuller would later elaborate and illustrate in *The Cliff-Dwellers* and *With the Procession* is anticipated when Zeitgeist is reported as saying, "What was American society . . . but a magnificent galley in which husbands and fathers toiled at the oars, while wives and daughters sat above in perfumed idleness? He had met a gentleman in New York, the possessor of twenty millions of florins, who told him that he was working for his board and clothes. . . . This unfortunate . . . had absolutely not a single pleasure; but his wife and daughters . . . resided in a great hotel, without duties, insensible of any obligations, and unoccupied except by their own diversions."

Fuller, circa 1900

Aurelia West's opinions and actions document the validity of Zeitgeist's assertions. "It was her fundamental belief," wrote Fuller, "that the young woman was the corner-stone of the social edifice—the *raison d'être* of society—almost its be-all and end-all. . . ." Ultimately, in Fuller's book, Aurelia, and what she represents, is defeated, at least temporarily, by the male characters who refuse to risk their lives to satisfy the momentary whims of the chatelaine and Aurelia.

For Fuller, perhaps the most unhappy implication of *The Chatelaine of La Trinité* is the realization that inevitably "Americanization was the impending fate of Europe" because Europe, like the chatelaine, is all too eager to be Americanized. Nowhere did he make the point more forcefully than in the paragraphs that serve as an epilogue to the book. A wayfarer is descending from the mountains into the valley below the chateau of La Trinité. He passes a group of clever young engineers making a survey; soon he meets some laborers constructing a dam. "A mile lower the gaunt form of a great iron truss spanned the river, and from beyond the jutting crag that closed the view came the muffled shriek of a steam-whistle." The modern industrial order is steadily eroding the beauty and charm of Europe. Meanwhile, the chatelaine has left her birthplace for Paris. Europe is rapidly becoming like America, Chicago.

After completing *The Chatelaine of La Trinité*, Fuller returned to Europe for six months of travel. By the end of June 1892, he was back in Chicago, surprised at the considerable progress made during his absence in the planning and construction of the World's Columbian Exposition. Fuller admired the work of Daniel H. Burnham and John W. Root, who conceived the basic architectural design for the fair. Shortly before the dedication services on 20 October 1892, Fuller wrote a series of articles about the architecture of the exposition for the *Chicago Record*. In them he praised the choice of the classical style for the buildings and declared that the advances in them "should be sufficient to show that artistic America is moving along at an equal pace with industrial America." Fuller found the buildings in the Court of Honor, the southern section designed by Richard W. Hunt and his associates from Boston and New York, much more admirable than those in the northern section designed by Chicago men. He tended to associate their work with the skyscraper architecture created by William Le Baron Jenney and Louis J. Sullivan. Expressing an attitude that revealed his affinities with an earlier America, Fuller did not agree with the more mod-

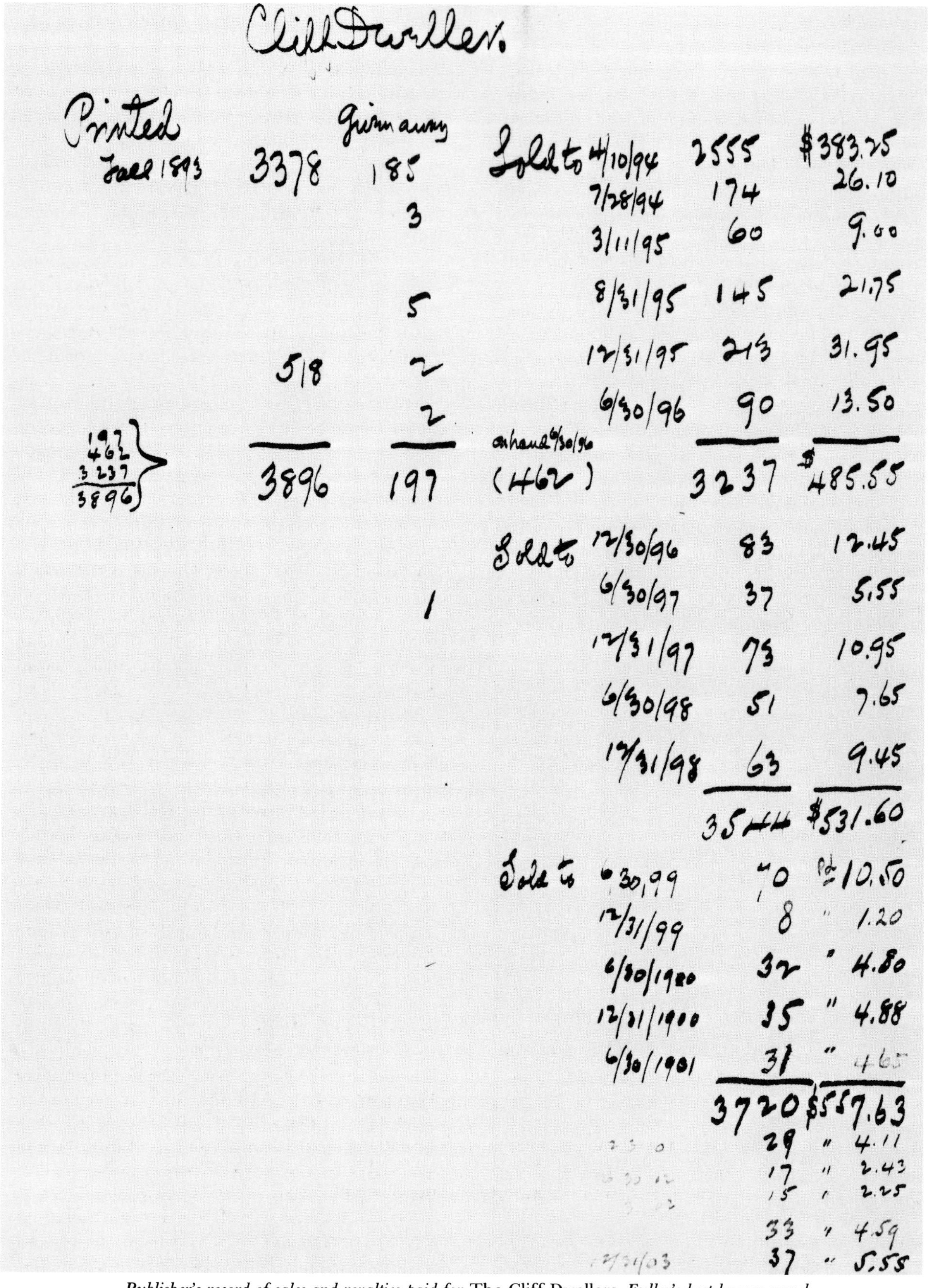

Cliff Dwellers.

Printed		Given away				
Fall 1893	3378	185	Sold to	4/10/94	2555	$383.25
				7/28/94	174	26.10
		3		3/11/95	60	9.00
		5		8/31/95	145	21.75
	518	2		12/31/95	213	31.95
		2		6/30/96	90	13.50
197 / 462 / 3237 / 3896	3896	197	on hand 6/30/96 (462)		3237	$485.55
			Sold to	12/30/96	83	12.45
		1		6/30/97	37	5.55
				12/31/97	73	10.95
				6/30/98	51	7.65
				12/31/98	63	9.45
					3544	$531.60
			Sold to	6/30/99	70	Pd 10.50
				12/31/99	8	" 1.20
				6/30/1900	32	" 4.80
				12/31/1900	35	" 4.88
				6/30/1901	31	" 4.65
					3720	$557.63
				12/31/01	29	" 4.11
				6/30/02	17	" 2.43
				12/31/02	15	" 2.25
					33	" 4.59
				12/31/03	37	" 5.55

Publisher's record of sales and royalties paid for The Cliff Dwellers, *Fuller's best-known novel*

ern view that the classical style was not suitable for urban office buildings.

Fuller's study of the significance of the architectural features of the World's Columbian Exposition brought him back to the realities of Chicago and provided the stimulus for his first novel wholly set in Chicago. In many respects, *The Cliff-Dwellers* (1893) was his response to the great exposition. While builders were putting the final touches upon the exposition in preparation for its opening on 1 May 1893, Fuller wrote *The Cliff-Dwellers*, one of the most celebrated novels about Chicago ever published. The opening chapter was brilliantly written. In it Fuller imaged Chicago as a "tumultuous territory" pitted by great chasms produced by the eroding action of "rushing streams of commerce" and closed in "by a long frontage of towering cliffs," which rose higher and higher each year because of the onrush of "an ever-increasing prosperity" at the bottom. All around the area was the treeless, shrubless, rugged, and erratic plateau of Bad Lands. Amid these monstrous cliffs, wrote Fuller, towered the eighteen-story Clifton with its glittering windows and ten elevators which "ameliorate the daily cliff-climbing for the frail of physique and the pressed for time." Its 4,000 inhabitants—including bankers, capitalists, lawyers, promoters, brokers, clerks, stenographers, errand boys, janitors, and scrubwomen—could find within its walls every item needed in the pursuit of wealth, the sole end of their activity. The Clifton, Fuller's fictional skyscraper, becomes a microcosm of Chicago's multilevel society.

The central figure of the novel, George Ogden, a newcomer to Chicago, seeks, like everyone else in the Clifton, only to advance himself. A man of mediocre ability, Ogden moves upward socially and financially until the pressure of the competition prompts him to steal money from the bank. During his upward movement, Ogden meets various types of persons through whom Fuller documents his case against the materialistic values of Chicago. Among them are Erastus M. Brainard, president of the Underground National Bank, and Cornelia McNabb, a female version of Ogden.

Brainard, who has sacrificed his humanity for business success and thereby ruined his family, represents what Fuller saw as the single-minded obsession of Chicago men of his generation with the making of enormous fortunes. Brainard has reached the top. Far below him but steadily climbing upward with great energy, resourcefulness, and opportunism, Cornelia McNabb, like Ogden a new-

comer, struggles to achieve her ambition to rival the acknowledged leader of Chicago society, Mrs. Arthur J. Ingles, wife of the owner of the Clifton. Cornelia begins as a waitress in Ogden's West Side boardinghouse, but by the end of the novel she has married Brainard's son Burton and begun to "cut a pretty wide swath" in the highest circles of society. When her husband suddenly meets financial disaster, she determines to rise again. "Just you wait," she says to herself; "Burt's smart and I'm careful, and we shall catch up . . . yet!"

Fuller could endow Ogden, Brainard, Cornelia McNabb, and other Chicagoans with unusual plausibility because he had seen their counterparts in real life. Although he respected and, perhaps, even admired their dedication to a single goal, he was fully convinced that they were engaged in a mad competition for a worthless prize. He saw that the philosophy of "I satisfy myself" only prompted the individual to take from society. Fuller could not admit that such persons contributed anything worthwhile to society. The race upward stifled the values of family relationships, community service, religion, and art, which he thought contributed most to the meaning of life. The intensity of his convictions and the clarity of his insight helped to give reality to his fiction. As Howells said, Fuller had done for Chicago what no one—Howells might have excepted his own *The Rise of Silas Lapham*—had done for any other major American city.

Fuller wrote Howells that *The Cliff-Dwellers* was "not definitive"; rather, he said, it was "the wrist-and-elbow exercise of a new man who hopes to 'get his hand in' for better things." Undoubtedly, Fuller realized that in *The Cliff-Dwellers* he had allowed subordinate actions that take place outside the Clifton, a host of minor characters, and a multiplicity of themes to weaken or at least blur the focus of his main attack. In the winter of 1893, when he began to write *With the Procession*, he determined to confine himself to characters to whom the unprecedented commercial prosperity of Chicago since the fire of 1871 had brought unresolved tensions and often deep unhappiness. He could show what happened to those who refused to "keep up with the procession" (the Marshall family) and to those who compromised with the new order (Mrs. Granger Bates). By thus narrowing the point of his criticism, he could give *With the Procession* an organic unity of form not possessed by his earlier work.

The Marshall family, David, his wife Eliza, and their five children, have refused to keep up with the Chicago procession. David and Eliza, "old settlers" who resemble Fuller's parents, built their house before the Civil War and have remained in it long after their contemporaries moved to more fashionable areas. David, who made his fortune for the most part honestly in the wholesale grocery business, has always been a rather dull, plodding "dray horse." Though a kindly man, he feels no responsibility to the community; but both he and Eliza feel slighted when they are left out of community activities and their children ignore them. The main plot of the novel deals with the efforts of their eldest daughter, Jane, to get the Marshalls to "catch up."

Jane, admittedly not very attractive, exhibits a good measure of intellectual honesty and clear-sightedness. She determines to advance the social fortunes of her younger sister, Rosamund or Rosy, a rather selfish, inconsiderate, and vain girl with sufficient beauty and youthful charm to make her socially attractive. Jane finds a strong ally in Mrs. Granger Bates, whose attachment to David Marshall has persisted from youth to advanced middle age. Mrs. Bates, an "old settler," has kept up with the procession and now marches in its vanguard. With her help, Jane endeavors to make Rosy a social success, to persuade her father to assume a place of leadership in the community, and to get her parents to build a new home in a socially desirable district. Guided by Mrs. Bates, Jane launches Rosy in society by showing Rosy "for five minutes to Mrs. Cecilia Ingles," the acknowledged arbiter of Chicago society.

Jane achieves a modest success with her father. He delivers the speeches she writes for him, but he resists many of her suggestions. In particular, he balks at giving a huge sum for a philanthropic or community project. Mrs. Bates suggests a dormitory at the university—she and her husband are giving Susan Lathrop Bates Hall for women—or a hospital, or even an endowment for a symphony orchestra. Marshall does make a provision in his will for an academic building, but at the last minute he leaves all of his wealth to Jane. Near the end of his life, he also consents to the construction of a new home; and a few days before he dies, he and his family move into a chilly, inhospitable, unfinished and underfurnished new house.

Howells considered Mrs. Bates "the chief triumph of the book" and added that she possessed "a mass of good sense, and good will, and good principle," but he and other reviewers failed to see that she has lost a good deal of integrity. Outwardly she seems to have admirable qualities. Ambitious, energetic, and practical, she has begun life as the daughter of a carpenter but has rapidly risen to the uppermost financial and social strata. She considers herself a success, but her goals have been achieved through actions that arise from the wrong motives. She collects paintings, not because she enjoys them but because, as she says, "people of our position would naturally be expected" to have them. She learns to play the music of Grieg and Chopin only because the skill will admit her to the Amateur Musical Club. She furnishes her home in the latest fashion, which she dislikes, and lives in a small upstairs bedroom furnished in the old style. When she advises David Marshall to give a building, she emphasizes the importance of making it "something that people can *see*." From Fuller's point of view, Mrs. Bates's energies are misdirected; she has compromised her integrity; and she has allowed her desire to keep up with the Chicago procession to make her, outwardly at least, a living deception. Essentially, she is a shallow person.

Of all the characters in *With the Procession* (1895), Truesdale Marshall, the youngest son in the family, most nearly voices Fuller's own criticism of the city. By Chicago's standards, Truesdale is a hopeless failure. He returns from travel in Europe unwilling to enter his father's grocery business and a sharp critic of the values of the marketplace. He feels engulfed by the life of Chicago. "The great town, in fact," wrote Fuller, "sprawled and coiled about him like a hideous monster—a piteous, floundering monster, too." Everywhere he saw tireless activity, a "determined striving after the ornate," and a relentless endeavor toward success, yet "nowhere a result so pitifully grotesque, gruesome, appalling." Truesdale concludes, "So little training, so little education, so total an absence of any collective sense of the fit and the proper!"

In every respect, the plot of *With the Procession* meets the tenets of Howells's realism. The novel deals exclusively with the lives of ordinary people and chronicles the commonplace events of their lives. Fuller's plot is all the more realistic because he avoids even the slightest hint of melodrama, while at the same time his work has an organic unity. The dialogue bears the stamp of ordinary speech without being a literal transcription of speech. For his work, Fuller won the enthusiastic endorsement of his master; Howells wrote in a review of the book, "at present, we have no one to compare with him in the East, in scale and quality of work."

In both *The Cliff-Dwellers* and *With the Procession*, Fuller struck hard at the absence of worthwhile goals in the lives of Chicago's citizens. Although he did not make the point in so many words, he saw American life in Chicago as fundamentally a struggle to obtain material goods, without reference to

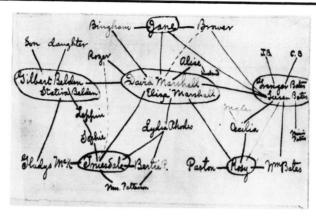

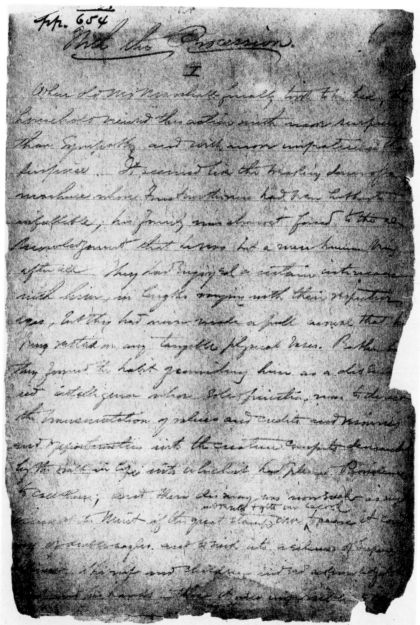

Diagram of characters and first page of manuscript for Fuller's 1895 novel about social self-consciousness in Chicago

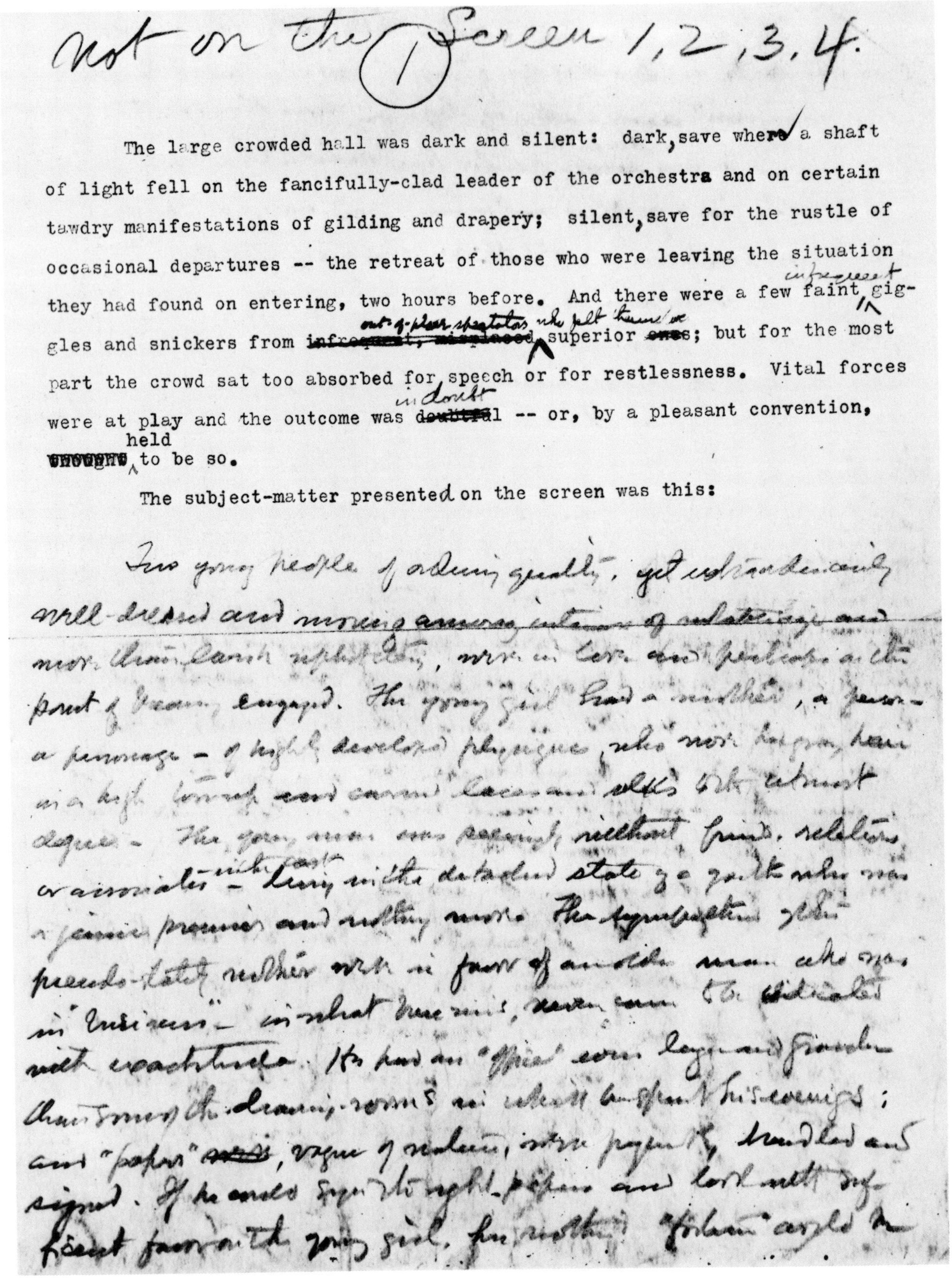

Not on the Screen 1, 2, 3, 4.

(1)

The large crowded hall was dark and silent: dark, save where a shaft of light fell on the fancifully-clad leader of the orchestra and on certain tawdry manifestations of gilding and drapery; silent, save for the rustle of occasional departures -- the retreat of those who were leaving the situation they had found on entering, two hours before. And there were a few infrequent gig-gles and snickers from out-of-place spectators who felt themselves superior; but for the most part the crowd sat too absorbed for speech or for restlessness. Vital forces were at play and the outcome was in doubt -- or, by a pleasant convention, held to be so.

The subject-matter presented on the screen was this:

First page of the working draft for Fuller's last published novel, a satire, set in Chicago, about motion pictures

spiritual qualities. Basically urban life was a struggle for survival; and such matters as art, beauty, religion, and the individual's enjoyment of art or adherence to meaningful ideals had no place in it.

The decade of the 1890s was the happiest period of Fuller's life. Although a shy person, he made friends with a large circle of Chicago artists. For years he was a "regular" at their Friday afternoon gatherings in the Little Room. As time passed, he seemed to live an increasingly vicarious life through the careers of such friends as Hamlin Garland, sculptors Lorado Taft and Bessie Potter, dramatic coach and theater director Anna Morgan, and writers Harriet Monroe and Hobart Chatfield-Taylor. Painstakingly, he proofread the work of Garland (in whose home he frequently stayed), Taft, and, later, the contributors to Harriet Monroe's *Poetry: A Magazine of Verse*. The quality of his own writing, however, declined. *The Puppet-Booth* (plays, 1896), *From the Other Side* (short stories, 1898), *The New Flag* (bitter satires against American imperialism, 1899), and *The Last Refuge* (a romance set in Sicily, 1900) added little to his reputation. After 1900, Garland thought Fuller looked worn-out and haggard, his clothes seedy, and his eccentricities increasingly pronounced. Intellectually, Garland conceded, Fuller remained as sharp as ever.

In 1901, Fuller brought out *Under the Skylights*, three satirical novelettes portraying himself, Garland, and the artists of the Little Room coterie. Although their appeal is limited by the immediacy of the satire, Fuller's friends recognized their merit. Implicit in these stories is Fuller's defense of his own career and his methods of writing. He attacked Garland's veritism, a version of realism that Garland defined as "the truthful statement of an individual impression corrected by reference to fact," on the ground that it made the writer a "reporter sublimated" instead of an artist. He criticized the Little Room painters, sculptors, architects, and poets for selling out to the desire of businessmen for commercial advertising. Beneath his playfulness, Fuller was again dramatizing his case against the false values of Chicago. With this volume, Fuller concluded that he was fighting a losing battle and determined to withdraw from further competition in the arts.

For more than fifteen years after *Under the Skylights*, Fuller produced no more novels or novelettes. In 1918, however, he wrote another novel about Chicago, *On the Stairs*, a remarkably well-plotted novel, dealing with the careers of two boys, one of whom is Fuller himself. Their lives pass

Fuller at age sixty-seven

"on the stairs" as one goes "upward" to business success and the other (Fuller) "descends" into the world of art. Both careers lead to futility, loneliness, and bitterness. Garland read it and felt "a gray desolation in my spirit." In 1919, Fuller tried to deal with homosexuality in *Bertram Cope's Year*. The book was a failure, probably because of his inability to objectify his experiences and his delicacy, almost prudishness, in handling the subject. To Garland, Fuller announced that he was going to stop writing. Actually, he continued to write for periodicals and to promote the literary fortunes of his friends; and at the age of seventy-two, in the last year of his life, he produced two additional novels, *Gardens of This World* (1929) and *Not on the Screen* (1930). Neither work was well received. One finds in them, however, echoes of Fuller's lifelong quarrel with Chicago and beyond it, America. In *Gardens of This World*, expatriate life in Europe is no longer a temptation, though one may find abroad occasional surcease from the turmoil of urban life; in *Not on the Screen*, Fuller explored the dullness and absence of purpose that he saw in the lives of young American businessmen. Fuller had finally returned to the realism of *With the Procession*.

Fuller's own evaluation of his contribution to

American literature can be seen in a remark he made a few weeks before he died. Garland had said that Fuller would rank close to Howells, and Fuller replied, "Yes, I'll fall in somewhere behind . . . Howells, and be glad to." In calling him "the father of American realism," Dreiser may have only slightly overstated Fuller's position in American literature. For his rendering of the American urban middle class, for his protest against the lack of beauty and spiritual values in American life, and for his skill as realist and as satirist, Fuller must be accorded the admiration of literary historians.

Periodical Publications:

"World's Fair Architecture," *Chicago News Record*, 14 September 1892, p. 4;

"Second Paper," *Chicago News Record*, 16 September 1892, p. 4;

"The Upward Movement in Chicago," *Atlantic Monthly*, 80 (October 1897): 534-547;

"Art in America," *Bookman*, 10 (November 1899): 218-224;

"A Plea for Shorter Novels," *Dial*, 63 (30 August 1917): 139-141;

"Howells or James?," edited by Darrel Abel, *Modern Fiction*, 3 (Summer 1957): 159-164.

References:

Bernard R. Bowron, Jr., *Henry B. Fuller of Chicago: The Ordeal of a Genteel Realist in Ungenteel America*, Contributions in American Studies, No. 11 (Westport, Conn.: Greenwood Press, 1974);

Van Wyck Brooks, *The Dream of Arcadia: American Writers and Artists in Italy 1760-1915* (New York: Dutton, 1958);

Bernard Duffey, *The Chicago Renaissance in American Letters: A Critical History* (East Lansing: Michigan State University Press, 1956);

John Farrar, "The Literary Spotlight," *Bookman*, 58 (February 1924): 645-649;

Hamlin Garland, *Afternoon Neighbors* (New York: Macmillan, 1934);

Garland, *Back-Trailers from the Middle Border* (New York: Macmillan, 1928);

Garland, *Companions on the Trail* (New York: Macmillan, 1931);

Garland, *A Daughter of the Middle Border* (New York: Macmillan, 1921);

Garland, *My Friendly Contemporaries* (New York: Macmillan, 1932);

Garland, *Roadside Meetings* (New York: Macmillan, 1931);

Mark Harris, Introduction to *With the Procession: A Novel* (Chicago: University of Chicago Press, 1965);

James Huneker, "The Seven Arts. Mr. Fuller's Masterpiece," *Puck*, 78 (11 September 1915): 10, 21;

Kenny Jackson, "An Evolution of the New Chicago from the Old: A Study of Henry Blake Fuller's Chicago Novels," Ph.D. dissertation, University of Pennsylvania, 1961;

Elwood P. Lawrence, "Fuller of Chicago: A Study in Frustration," *American Quarterly*, 6 (Summer 1954): 137-146;

Robert Morss Lovett, "Fuller of Chicago," *New Republic*, 60 (21 August 1929): 16-18;

Harriet Monroe, "Henry B. Fuller," *Poetry*, 35 (October 1929): 34-41;

Anna Morgan, ed., *Tributes to Henry B.* (Chicago: Seymour, 1929);

Donald M. Murray, "Henry B. Fuller, Friend of Howells," *South Atlantic Quarterly*, 52 (1953): 431-444;

Richard A. Pearce, "Chicago in the Fiction of the 1890's as Illustrated in the Novels of Henry B. Fuller and Robert Herrick," Ph.D. dissertation, Columbia University, 1963;

Donald Culross Peattie, "Henry Blake Fuller," *Reading and Collecting*, 2 (January 1938): 19-20;

John Pilkington, Jr., *Henry Blake Fuller* (New York: Twayne, 1970);

Agnes Repplier, "A By-Way in Fiction," *Lippincott's Monthly Magazine*, 47 (June 1891): 760-765;

Paul Rosenblatt, "The Image of Civilization in the Novels of Henry Blake Fuller," Ph.D. dissertation, Columbia University, 1960;

Victor Shultz, "Henry Blake Fuller: Civilized Chicagoan," *Bookman*, 70 (September 1929): 34-38.

Papers:

The Henry B. Fuller Collection of the Newberry Library, Chicago, is the largest single repository of Fuller manuscripts. The University of Southern California Library, Los Angeles, holds Fuller's letters to Hamlin Garland and other material relating to Fuller. The Henry E. Huntington Library, San Marino, California, holds the diaries of Hamlin Garland, a major source for information about Fuller. The Houghton Library of Harvard University, Cambridge, Massachusetts, has Fuller's letters to Howells. The Chicago Historical Society, Chicago, has considerable material relating to Fuller and his contemporaries.

Hamlin Garland

(14 September 1860-5 March 1940)

James B. Stronks
University of Illinois at Chicago Circle

SELECTED BOOKS: *Under the Wheel: A Modern Play in Six Scenes* (Boston: Barta Press, 1890);

Main-Travelled Roads (Boston: Arena Publishing Co., 1891; London: T. Fisher Unwin, 1892; enlarged, New York & London: Macmillan, 1899; enlarged again, New York & London: Harper, 1922; enlarged again, New York & London: Harper, 1930);

Jason Edwards (Boston: Arena Publishing Co., 1892);

A Member of the Third House (Chicago: Schulte, 1892);

A Little Norsk; or Ol' Pap's Flaxen (New York: Appleton, 1892; London: T. Fisher Unwin, 1892);

A Spoil of Office (Boston: Arena Publishing Co., 1892);

Prairie Songs (Cambridge, Mass., & Chicago: Stone & Kimball, 1893);

Prairie Folks (Chicago: Schulte, 1893; London: Sampson Low, 1893);

Crumbling Idols: Twelve Essays on Art Dealing Chiefly with Literature, Painting and the Drama (Chicago & Cambridge, Mass.: Stone & Kimball, 1894);

Rose of Dutcher's Coolly (Chicago: Stone & Kimball, 1895; London: Beeman, 1896; revised edition, New York & London: Macmillan, 1899);

Wayside Courtships (New York: Appleton, 1897; London: N. Beeman, 1898);

Ulysses S. Grant: His Life and Character (New York: Doubleday & McClure, 1898);

The Spirit of Sweetwater (Philadelphia: Curtis / New York: Doubleday & McClure, 1898; London: Service & Paton, 1898); revised and enlarged as *Witch's Gold* (New York: Doubleday, Page, 1906);

Boy Life on the Prairie (New York & London: Macmillan, 1899);

The Trail of the Goldseekers (New York & London: Macmillan, 1899);

The Eagle's Heart (New York: Appleton, 1900; London: Heinemann, 1900);

Her Mountain Lover (New York: Century, 1901; London: Dollar Library, 1901);

The Captain of the Gray-Horse Troop (New York &

London: Harper, 1902; London: Grant Richards, 1902);

Hesper (New York & London: Harper, 1903);

The Light of the Star (New York & London: Harper, 1904);

The Tyranny of the Dark (New York & London: Harper, 1905);

Money Magic (New York & London: Harper, 1907);

The Shadow World (New York & London: Harper, 1908);

The Moccasin Ranch (New York & London: Harper, 1909);

Cavanagh, Forest Ranger (New York & London: Harper, 1910);

Other Main-Travelled Roads (New York & London: Harper, 1910);

Victor Ollnee's Discipline (New York & London: Harper, 1911);

The Forester's Daughter (New York & London: Harper, 1914);

They of the High Trails (New York & London: Harper, 1916);

A Son of the Middle Border (New York: Macmillan, 1917);

A Daughter of the Middle Border (New York: Macmillan, 1921);

A Son of the Middle Border [and *A Daughter of the Middle Border*] (London: John Lane, 1921);

The Book of the American Indian (New York & London: Harper, 1923);

Trail-Makers of the Middle Border (New York: Macmillan, 1926; London: John Lane, 1926);

Back-Trailers from the Middle Border (New York: Macmillan, 1928);

Roadside Meetings (New York: Macmillan, 1930; London: John Lane, 1931);

Companions on the Trail (New York: Macmillan, 1931);

My Friendly Contemporaries (New York: Macmillan, 1932);

Afternoon Neighbors (New York: Macmillan, 1934);

Forty Years of Psychic Research (New York: Macmillan, 1936);

The Mystery of the Buried Crosses (New York: Dutton, 1939);

Hamlin Garland's Diaries, edited by Donald Pizer (San Marino, Cal.: Huntington Library, 1968);

Hamlin Garland's Observations on the American Indian, 1895-1905, edited by Lonnie E. Underhill and Daniel F. Littlefield (Tucson: University of Arizona Press, 1976).

Hamlin Garland wrote over forty books, two of which remain important today. One of these is *Main-Travelled Roads* (1891), realistic short stories about midwestern farmers, while the other is Garland's autobiography, *A Son of the Middle Border* (1917), a definitive portrait of American character. Both books are respected more for their historical value than for their literary merit. Because much of his work was mediocre and has faded in interest, Garland is recognized, not as an artist, but rather as a representative mind and career.

Garland's writing divides quite clearly into three periods. Until 1895 (when he was thirty-five), he wrote reform journalism and realistic fiction set in the recently settled areas of the Middle West, and it is for this early work that he has always been most admired. From about 1896 to 1916 he wrote popu-

lar romantic novels set in the Rocky Mountains. And from 1917 (when he was fifty-seven) to his death in 1940, the aging Garland produced volume after volume of autobiography.

Hannibal Hamlin Garland was born to Richard H. and Isabelle McClintock Garland in 1860 on a farm near New Salem, Wisconsin, not far from the Mississippi River. (He dropped his first name early in his life.) One of his earliest memories was of his soldier father returning home to the farm in 1865 at the end of the Civil War, an event he later put into one of his best-known stories, "The Return of a Private." Garland's best stories, indeed, would always draw heavily on his own life, for he lacked skill at invention and plotting. He was an excellent writer of description, however, and what he described best was the rural landscape of the Middle Border. By "Middle Border" Garland meant that recently settled region, not on the very edge of the frontier, where he had lived as a boy on the Garland family farms, in southwestern Wisconsin in the 1860s, in northern Iowa in the 1870s, and in eastern South Dakota (then Dakota Territory) in the 1880s.

Young Hamlin also knew town life during the five years he attended Cedar Valley Seminary in Osage, Iowa. Graduating in June 1881, when he was twenty-one, he tramped through eastern states, supporting himself by odd jobs and carpentry. He tried a year of school teaching in Illinois in 1882-1883 and in 1883 "staked a claim" on virgin prairie in McPherson County, Dakota Territory.

Always an eager reader, Garland spent that winter tending store while reading the works of Henry George and Hippolyte Taine's history of English literature. One winter on the treeless Dakota plain was enough, and in late 1884, when he was twenty-four, Garland obeyed a deep urge to go east and study in Boston, which he revered as the intellectual and cultural capital of the country. In Boston, friendless and living penuriously on his scant savings, Garland read twelve hours a day in the public library, most notably in Darwin, Herbert Spencer, and Eugene Veron. His one indulgence was spending an occasional thirty-five cents to stand in the balcony and see Edwin Booth play Shakespeare. Gradually, over the next few years, Garland edged his way into book reviewing for Boston newspapers. He also taught at The Boston School of Oratory and lectured on modern literature to adult study groups.

In the summer of 1887 Garland made a trip back to Iowa and Dakota. The experience was a turning point in his career. He was now nearly twenty-seven, and two and a half years in civilized

Garland family home in Ordway, Dakota Territory

Boston had given him a fresh eye for seeing his home neighborhoods in the West. In a notebook he jotted down trenchant impressions of farm life as he now saw it at that specific time and place: rural Mitchell County, Iowa, settled only ten years, and Brown County, in what was soon to become South Dakota, even newer and rawer. Garland was dismayed at the hard lives of many of the farmers and farm women, and angered by their plight. He also saw that it could be literary material, and after a second trip west in 1888 he began to shape this unlovely subject matter into the short stories which would make his reputation. He collected six of these into the best book he would ever produce, *Main-Travelled Roads* (1891), and put others into a companion volume, *Prairie Folks* (1893).

The 1891 edition of *Main-Travelled Roads* (so many stories were added to later editions of *Main-Travelled Roads* that the original character of the book became changed) is an important example of what was called "realism" in the 1880s and 1890s. Garland himself, however, liked to call it "veritism" and to call himself a "veritist," terms he adapted from his reading of Veron's *Aesthetics*. "My own conception," he explained in 1894, "is that realism (or veritism) is the truthful statement of an individual impression corrected by reference to the fact." In itself this definition is not very helpful, but when applied to Garland's own fiction it becomes clearer. To Howells's kind of realism, which was a self-effacing recording of objective facts, Garland would add an infusion of impressionism, to make the results less passive and more personal.

By whatever name, Garland's view in *Main-Travelled Roads* emphasized the unending toil and the narrow, monotonous lives of many Middle Border farmers and their lonely, worn-out wives. A whole region and people were involved—his region and his people—and Garland felt their way of life to be a tragedy and was resentful of the underlying causes. Not long escaped from the reeking barnyard himself, he was determined, he said, to include a "proper proportion of the sweat, flies, heat, dirt, and drudgery" in his farm scenes. As a local-color realist, he was accurate with setting and its effect on character and behavior. He was specific in describing fieldwork the farmer performed, often in severe weather, the ugly farmhouse interiors, the rough clothing and food, and the physical wear on the people. And in his dialogue he tried to catch their actual talk, banal or coarsely pronounced though it might be.

Main-Travelled Roads was not all negative. Occasionally his farm people are uplifted by the beauty of the countryside, and his farm youths abound with hearty high spirits. But on balance the book presents a depressing picture. Some of Garland's readers in Iowa—mainly townspeople rather than working farmers—were indignant, and protested that his view was too grim. Obviously Garland's refusal to prettify, to write happy endings, to be romantic or charming or gracious, ran counter to the popular taste in fiction in the 1890s. Magazines often rejected his stories for being blunt, crude, and unpleasant. They believed that the genteel readers of their fiction would feel an aversion for stories

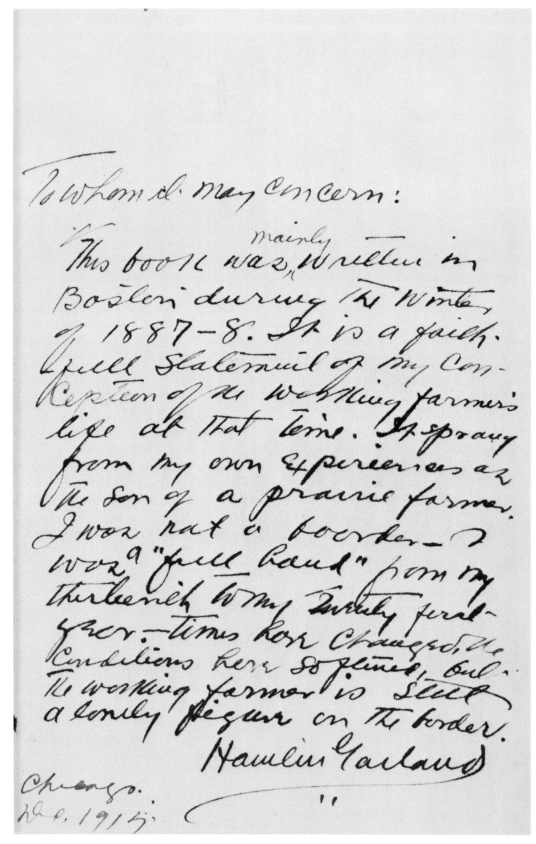

Garland's account of how he wrote Main-Travelled Roads, *written twenty-six years after first publication of the book*

such as those in *Main-Travelled Roads* on the grounds that they expressed a vulgar materialism, lacked an uplifting sense of the ideal, forced the reader into the company of underbred common people in sordid circumstances, and were written in an ungraceful literary style.

Professional critics, however, received *Main-Travelled Roads* with respect for Garland's sincerity, if regret for his rough craft. Chief among these were Brander Matthews, C. T. Copeland, and his good friend William Dean Howells, whose praise of *Main-Travelled Roads* was the most valuable critical event in Garland's early career.

His mentor Howells was always important to Garland, and their close, affectionate relationship would last until Howells's death in 1920. The unknown Garland had first introduced himself to Howells in 1887, when Howells, then fifty, was probably the most respected novelist and critic in America. Thereafter, Garland visited Howells whenever he could, wrote to him when he could not, became a loyal disciple, and exploited the connection whenever possible. It was a sincere friendship, however, one of the longest and closest in American letters, and in the 1890s it was cemented not only by their mutual literary ideals but by their economic and social convictions as well.

As the recognized leader of the new realists in fiction, Howells defended them against an often hostile public in "The Editor's Study," his monthly department in *Harper's*. His review of *Main-Travelled Roads* conceded Garland's "harshness and bluntness, an indifference to the more delicate charms of style." But he admired Garland's courage in setting out unpalatable truths, by his seriousness, and by the relevance of his subject matter: "If anyone is still at a loss to account for that uprising of the farmers in the West," wrote Howells, "let him read *Main-Travelled Roads*."

Howells was referring to what the textbooks have called agrarian discontent. By 1891, the classic American optimism about the promise of "free land" in "The Garden of the West" had collapsed. Garland, well aware of the myth (and surely his book was one of the causes for its collapse), showed in his fiction that, far from free, the land was now largely controlled by landlord-speculators, or was in corporate hands. Economic conditions were unfavorable to farmers, especially renters, whose cash crops were selling at low prices while their bank loans carried high interest rates. Even Nature herself brought about periodic failures by sending grasshoppers, army worms, cinch bugs, hail, drought, dust storms, and cyclones—all of which

appear in Garland's stories. Garland's father, farming one thousand acres of wheat, was better off than many, yet sometimes he could not earn enough to pay even his taxes; and two of his neighbors had gone insane over their failure.

But economic conditions could be improved. Garland had devoured Henry George's *Progress and Poverty* (1879) in winter 1883, when it was still an exciting new book; and when George a few years later advanced his Single Tax theory, Garland became its eager publicist. By the time he was hammering out his Middle Border stories, Garland was an ardent Single Tax advocate. In George's philosophy, the root of poverty was land monopolization. Under his Single Tax plan, *all* taxation would be discontinued and replaced by a *single* tax on the annual value of the land. The Single Tax would absorb the "unearned increment" (i.e., the "undeserved" appreciation in value) reaped by owners of real estate. George saw unearned increment as the basic cause of myriad economic and class inequities and social ills—which accounted for his appeal to such adherents as Garland, Clarence Darrow, and George Bernard Shaw.

The Single Tax was a radical plan, and simplistic, but "I was of an age to be extreme," said Garland later. As a personal friend of George's, and later often in his home, Garland's zeal was fed at the source, and he threw himself into the Single Tax cause by delivering lectures and writing articles for George's weekly *Standard*. These energies overlapped his western campaigning for the People's Party (the "Populists") in 1892, an election year. In addition to making speeches, Garland read aloud one of the stories in *Main-Travelled Roads* to the Populist national convention in July 1892. The story was "Under the Lion's Paw," a heavy-handed Single Tax story turning on the injustice that unearned increment and a hard landlord wreak upon an Iowa farmer's family.

As a practical reformer who was basically a fiction writer, young Garland now held "two great literary concepts," as he called them: "that truth was a higher quality than beauty, and that to spread the reign of justice should everywhere be the design and intent of the artist." Much of his early writing went into the *Arena*, a liberal new Boston monthly whose motto was "Art for Truth's Sake," and whose editor, Benjamin Orange Flower, encouraged Garland, the engaged artist, to write his harsh farm stories and to continue his third-party activism.

In 1892, the year following *Main-Travelled Roads*, Garland excitedly rushed into print four books, three of which were novels of politics and reform. *Jason Edwards* was a propagandistic novelette (largely based on his bitter 1890 play *Under the Wheel*) about the cruel economic determinism in the farming West and the dearth of free land. Garland later called the book too sour, drab, and preachy, and it went virtually unnoticed by critics. *A Member of the Third House* (based on another of his plays of 1890) was a story about the power of the lobby, and was suggested to Garland by an actual scandal in the Massachusetts state house. Unfortunately he was more interested in his theme than in developing his characters or in managing his plot. *A Spoil of Office*, subsidized by the ever-supportive Flower, was Garland's first full-length novel. It concerns a young Iowan who goes to Congress and becomes disheartened by political immorality, but is reinspired by the love and ideals of a feminist reformer who nicely combines brains and sex appeal. Garland said he tried to make *A Spoil of Office* a "panorama" of Populist arguments; indeed, the book argues too many issues. The critics, as they usually did in those years, pronounced Garland's social history authentic and his intentions sincere, but they found his art crude and slapdash. "Too much of it was written on the train," admitted Garland later, remembering how his political activism had kept him in constant motion.

A Little Norsk of 1892 was unlike the others, a novelette about two homesteading Dakota bachelors who adopt an orphaned immigrant child and lovingly rear her. Compared to *Jason Edwards*, it is a soft and sentimental story, and realistic only in its description of farm work and plains scenery. Tailored for the genteel readers of the *Century*, a quality magazine that paid well, *A Little Norsk* is an anomaly in this phase of Garland's career. But its success was a lesson not lost on Garland, the free-lance writer who was earning very little from his high-minded realistic fiction.

A constant traveller, Garland had been shuttling from East to West and back again, but in 1893 he settled in Chicago for a few months in order to share in the excitement of its world's fair, the Columbian Exposition. At a literary congress there he read a paper on "Local Color in Fiction," always one of his favorite themes as a literary critic. And in a floor debate he argued for the new realism with his "accustomed intensity of manner," as a local reporter put it, "ardent, partisan, and uncompromising." Garland's handsome photographs of this period suggest that his beard and broad shoulders enhanced his public-speaking impact. He looked, as Stephen Crane confided to a friend, "like a nice Jesus Christ."

In Chicago in 1893 Garland produced *Prairie Songs*, which was a collection of his mediocre nature poetry, and *Prairie Folks*, Middle Border stories. While in Chicago he was in easy visiting distance of his parents in Wisconsin, a fact which relates to his fiction. His stories sometimes show a young man who (like Garland himself) had escaped the family farm and made a success elsewhere, returning some years later to feel both superior and guilty: superior to his family's rusticity and guilty at having "abandoned" them in their hard grind to survive. (Actually, the Garland family was not poor.) In his autobiography Garland frequently, even tediously, berates himself, not for having left his stern disciplinarian father, but for "abandoning" his mother, a more passive and pitiable victim of farm hardships and the prototype for Garland's gallery of tragically wasted farm women. Hence his satisfaction in 1893 at being able to transplant his aging parents, his mother now in poor health, from their arid Dakota plain back to a snug home in sheltered Wisconsin.

Deciding to settle in Chicago "permanently" in 1894 (he would live there, off and on, until 1916), Garland was conspicuous for the variety of his interests. This was the Chicago of Eugene Field, George Ade, and Finley Peter Dunne, of Joseph Kirkland, Will Payne, Robert Herrick, and Thorstein Veblen, of the publishers Stone & Kimball and their chic *Chap-Book* magazine, of the *Dial*, of the new University of Chicago, the new Newberry Library, the new symphony orchestra and Art Institute—and with most of these writers and institutions Garland was closely involved. His political reform phase might be cooling, but there was no shortage of other causes. Whether in Boston or Chicago, Garland led in the push for women's rights, for an American theater, for research in spiritualism, for the Single Tax and the People's party, for impressionism in art, for regional western painting, for conservation of natural resources, and an enlightened Indian policy. Among other enthusiasms, he now organized the Central Art Association, which sent traveling exhibits of new paintings from the Art Institute to small midwest cities. Not only did Garland write commentaries to accompany the exhibits, but he made the boxes in which the paintings were shipped. Socially, he was a familiar figure among Chicago artists and writers of the Little Room circle, two of whom became his close friends for life: Henry Blake Fuller the novelist (who would satirize Garland in "The Downfall of Abner Joyce") and Lorado Taft the sculptor, whose sister Zulime would marry Garland in November 1899. Always an organizer of authors' committees, benefit readings, and the like, Garland would also found and lead The Cliff-Dwellers Club in Chicago, which is still in existence.

At this stage, in the mid-1890s, Garland's reputation was that of a morally earnest, self-confident (and perhaps humorless) reformer and realist. In this character he now produced a self-important little book which he called *Crumbling Idols: Twelve Essays on Art Dealing Chiefly with Literature, Painting and the Drama* (1894). A provocative manifesto which could have been written by no one but Hamlin Garland, *Crumbling Idols* owed something to Emerson's "The American Scholar" and Whitman's preface to *Leaves of Grass*, but most to Howells's similar book, *Criticism and Fiction* (1891).

By "crumbling idols," Garland meant that the classics and the conservative tradition in the arts were losing, or ought to be losing, their authority and must give way before the greater relevance of the native and the contemporary in art. Like Howells, he denounced romanticism in fiction, asserted the superiority of realism, and argued for "Local Color in Art." In essays which presented ideas advanced for their day, he praised Ibsen and also Impressionist painting. He tended to equate the East with conservative and the West with liberal values, and, as a professional westerner, he prophesied the emergence of Chicago and the new young democratic Midwest as the coming cultural center of the country.

The critics fell upon Garland from every direction, even in Chicago. According to the estimate of a veteran editor, *Crumbling Idols* provoked over a thousand editorials—hostile, indignant, or amused. Scoffing at Garland as "the cowboy as artist," many called his viewpoint provincial, his ideas sophomoric, and his rhetoric overheated. While these charges are partly true, *Crumbling Idols* must yet be weighed seriously by anyone who would understand Garland during his most significant period.

Garland now wrote his best novel, *Rose of Dutcher's Coolly* (1895). Its first half, especially, reveals an imagination and subtlety for which Garland seldom gets credit because he seldom exhibited it anywhere else. Rose Dutcher is a motherless, unchaperoned, Wisconsin farm girl who grows up a tomboy and free spirit at the country school, then attends the state university and ripens into a magnetic beauty with talent as a poet. Upon graduation, she goes to Chicago to make a career and becomes part of a cultivated circle which includes an interesting newspaperman-novelist, Mason. He eventually proposes to her in a cool letter—a kind of

proferred contract—and at the end of the story Rose accepts.

In this, his most painstaking fiction to date, Garland's frankness about Rose's adolescent awakening to sex met with widespread critical disapproval. (For a new edition in 1899, he revised the text into the version usually read today.) The critics punished Garland for his insistence upon his heroine's latent sexuality in 1895. Though the book was sexually candid for its time, it is but an interesting museum piece today. Garland's emphasis upon Rose's sexuality should be remembered, however, because by the 1920s he would be perceived by younger writers as a reactionary critic of what he then called indecency in the American novel.

During 1896 and 1897, Garland traveled 30,000 miles, researching and writing *Ulysses S. Grant: His Life and Character* (1898). And in 1898, hungering for a wilderness adventure, he rode 750 miles overland from British Columbia to Alaska, hoping to see the Klondike gold rush. All he saw was drizzle and caribou flies, but he got a book out of it, *The Trail of the Goldseekers* (1899). With such miscellaneous and time-consuming projects as these, Garland had entered a period of "confused, wavering, experimental" aims, as he put it later. It was the beginning of his "decline."

By "Hamlin Garland's decline," as critics have come to call it, is meant his disappointing change about 1896 from an uncompromising critical realist committed to social justice and harsh but necessary truths about Middle Border farm life into a carpenter of conventional romantic novels laid in the Far West and intended mainly as entertainments for a large popular audience.

This change is not hard to account for. By the later 1890s Garland's reform ardor was on the wane, as was the Populist revolt which had fueled it; indeed, the Populist party itself was extinct. Over the years, his realistic fiction had earned him little money but a great deal of criticism for his depressing subject matter and crude art. He wished to be more widely read and liked, and by 1899, as a newly married man, he needed to be better paid. The best-sellers in 1900 were historical romances laid in a colorful past, and Garland decided that perhaps the colorful present would please as well. Garland had begun to travel a great deal in the western mountains, a region which he found exciting. He now saw it as a fresh province for a local-color storyteller who had used up his midwestern material. After 1895, therefore, when his Middle Border writing was finished and when indeed the Middle Border itself no longer existed, Hamlin Garland began his second phase, or middle period, as the author of popular romances laid in the Rocky Mountains.

His industry, at least, can hardly be faulted. His Far West fiction includes *The Spirit of Sweetwater* (1898), *The Eagle's Heart* (1900), *Her Mountain Lover* (1901), *The Captain of the Gray-Horse Troop* (1902)— his most popular book, *Hesper* (1903), *The Light of the Star* (1904), *Money Magic* (1907), *Cavanagh, Forest Ranger* (1910), and *The Forester's Daughter* (1914). In 1916 he collected short stories about the region into *They of the High Trails*, and in 1923 other pieces from this second phase appeared in *The Book of the American Indian*.

Because they are written by Hamlin Garland, these mountain novels contain excellent pictorial sketching of scenery and weather and local-color details. These things Garland had recorded in his travel notebooks on the spot, but his characterization is shallow, and his point of view and plotting poorly managed. In general, Garland is an able narrator when events are strictly masculine; but when a well-bred heroine is present (she is often a wealthy Easterner), or courtship even thought of, his story at once becomes false.

Garland's romances of the Rockies frequently remind one of old western movies (in fact Vitagraph made two or three of them out of Garland novels in 1916) in their stock plots and sentimentality. But Garland's chief failure is in his stereotyped heroes. Their noble, stagey posturing and stilted speeches often sound like juvenile fiction, or as if influenced by the best-sellers of Richard Harding Davis, which they may have been.

Garland protested, defensively, that he wrote his romantic western fiction in much the same truth-telling spirit as had given *Main-Travelled Roads* its realism and integrity. If he really believed this, he was mistaken. Some of his western novels sold well, but even Howells, his most generous critic, cautioned him privately in a letter of 1910: "One day, I hope you will revert to the temper of your first work and give us a picture of [the Far West] along the lines of *Main-Travelled Roads*. You have in you greater things than you have done, and you owe the world which has welcomed you the best you have in you. 'Be true to the dream of thy youth'— the dream of an absolute and unsparing 'veritism'; the word is yours."

But Garland's western writings were realistic about the Indian. Garland traveled in the Far West a great deal between 1892 and 1900 to gather material for articles and stories. With notebook and cam-

Hamlin Garland, circa 1885

era, sometimes on horseback and with an interpreter, he visited a dozen or more reservations at that moment in history when the Indian was between his ancient way of life and the new. Garland's friend President Theodore Roosevelt, who had a special interest in the West and Western writers, brought Garland to the White House as consultant on how the Indian and the government could best steer between the primitive and the white man's way. Garland might unblushingly incorporate a cavalry-to-the-rescue climax in *The Captain of the Gray-Horse Troop*, but the book was otherwise practically a sociological tract on the Indian question. And his article "The Red Man's Present Needs," published in the *North American Review* in 1902, was a solid, well-written criticism of conditions on the reservations, full of practical proposals which reveal his sensitive concern for the native American.

The main discovery of Garland critics in recent years has been that, whatever the shortcomings of his mountain romances, some of Garland's best work is his fiction about Indians, written at the same time. The best of these stories, such as "The New Medicine House" and a novelette, "The Silent Eaters," were collected in *The Book of the American Indian* (1923). The publisher illustrated the book with pictures by Frederic Remington, and it is significant that Garland objected to them as contemptuous stereotypes.

By 1916, when Garland left Chicago and moved to New York to be close to his market, his Far West writing was at an end. His third and last phase as an author began. In his middle fifties, with creative powers flagging, Garland had suffered through a period of depressing ineffectuality as a writer. But now, laboriously writing and rewriting, he worked out a successful book-making formula which he would use for the rest of his life: he would depend heavily on the diaries he had kept since 1898 to create volumes of autobiography. In the next eighteen years, Garland produced eight large volumes of family history and personal memoirs.

The first and best of these books was *A Son of the Middle Border* (1917), an important American autobiography. Garland covers only the first thirty-four years of his life, but he seems to have nearly total recall of Middle Borders manners and social history. It is an interesting American life story: his shocking labor ten hours a day steering a plow and a team of horses when he was ten years old, his insistence on further schooling after the eighth grade, his duel of will, as he matured, with a none too sympathetic father, his breaking away to study in Boston, and his exciting growth as a militant young author-reformer.

A Son of the Middle Border was praised by the critics, even by critics who disliked Garland, not for being a graceful literary performance, which it was not, but for its sincerity and historical value. The writing is direct, simple, and naive in manner, and Garland's sentimentality about his failing old mother makes the final chapters tiresome to many readers. The book's very artlessness, however, is part of its authenticity as an American social document.

Its sequel, *A Daughter of the Middle Border* (1921), lacks the density, the richness, and emotion of the first book. The "daughter" in the title refers to both his mother and his wife, but principally the book is the continuation of Garland's autobiography from 1899 to about 1915. When it won the Pulitzer Prize for biography in 1922, the Pulitzer committee told Garland privately the prize was actually for *A Son of the Middle Border*. The third book in the series, *Trail-Makers of the Middle Border* (1926), was the story of his father's early life, told much in the form of a novel. It traces the elder Garland's migrations from Maine to Boston to border Wisconsin, his lumber rafting there and his soldiering

under Grant at Vicksburg. Finally, *Back-Trailers from the Middle Border* (1928) completed the family chronicle, or more accurately the Hamlin Garland autobiography, by telling of his own return to New York, and his life there with his wife and two daughters into the 1920s. By this fourth volume Garland's is no longer a typical American career nor a significant story. It is merely personal and prosaic. Repetitious, humorless, and platitudinous, the book is saturated with his sense of failure in later life. He grumbles much about deterioration in 1920s American manners, morality, literary magazines, popular arts, and Anglo-Saxon purity (an attitude he shared with many of his generation and class).

Garland now began writing his literary memoirs. These were *Roadside Meetings* (1930), which recounted his literary life to 1899, thus duplicating much of *A Son of the Middle Border*; *Companions on the Trail* (1931), which covered 1900-1913; *My Friendly Contemporaries* (1932), covering 1913-1923; and *Afternoon Neighbors* (1934), covering the 1920s.

The earlier Middle Border series had emphasized his family life and personal fortunes. These new books, though they covered the same years and mentioned again many of the same incidents, were given mainly to anecdotes and portraits of prominent people Garland had known, aggressively cultivated, and visited in America and Europe. In Britain, alone, these included Barrie, Bennett, Conrad, Doyle, Galsworthy, Gosse, Kipling, and Shaw. Garland emphasized that these four books of memoirs were accurate because they were based on his dated diaries. Ground out during the gray Depression years when Garland was in his seventies, the memoirs, totalling 2,146 pages, are sometimes little more than garrulous calendars of his goings and comings, of letters written and conversations reconstructed to flatter himself. But here and there are truly valuable portraits: old Walt Whitman creeping about his room in Camden, young Stephen Crane in New York on the threshold of fame, Henry James happy at home in Rye. These memoirs are public—Hamlin Garland as he wished to be seen—and should be supplemented by a reading of *Hamlin Garland's Diaries* (1968), excerpts from his unrevised private daily notes over the decades.

His memoirs concluded, the aging Garland returned to his study of what he called occult phenomena. However improbable in a man of his stamp, Garland had organized seances and experimented with mediums ever since his Boston days and had written three novels on the subject, *The Tyranny of the Dark* (1905), *The Shadow World* (1908), and *Victor Ollnee's Discipline* (1911). In 1936 he summarized his studies in *Forty Years of Psychic Research* and in 1939 he produced another book about spiritualism, *The Mystery of the Buried Crosses*. Unfriendly critics have been severe on the subject of Garland's psychic investigations. Friendly critics have chosen to remain silent.

More deserving of study is Garland's magazine writing. As a free-lance writer, he was always a busy journalist. The best of Garland's articles are better written than his novels and are more interesting today.

A member of the Century Club and The Players when he lived in New York, and a vice president of the National Institute of Arts and Letters, Garland was elected into the more exclusive American Academy in 1918, again on the strength of *A Son of the Middle Border*, and he helped to manage academy affairs for years. Besides his 1922 Pulitzer Prize, he was awarded honorary Doctor of Letters degrees from the University of Wisconsin (1926) and Northwestern University (1933). After 1930 he lived in Hollywood, California, near his married daughter. He died of a cerebral hemorrhage in 1940 at the age of seventy-nine and is buried near West Salem, Wisconsin.

When Garland published his brash, antiestablishment *Crumbling Idols* at thirty-four, it would have seemed impossible that his final chapter would be as devoted clubman and academician and then a resident of movie town. Long before he was dead there were critics, especially young men on liberal magazines, who censured him as an opportunist who had dropped honest fiction on reform themes in order to try for popular success—and eventually to fossilize into a reactionary figurehead. Garland's views had really stayed much the same while American society and its values changed rapidly, especially after World War I. As for his fiction, as early as 1900 the work of Stephen Crane and Theodore Dreiser, among others, had made Garland's veritism obsolete. His moment was the late nineteenth century.

At his prime, graceless but sincere, Garland produced in five or six years a small amount of fiction which will always be respected. But more important than his writing, finally, is the representativeness of the man and his mind, and what he himself came to see as "the typical character of my career." In the subject matter of his books, in his literary style and creed, in his personality and private values, in the things he was radical about when he was young and conservative about when he was

old—in all of these ways Hamlin Garland's life was definitive, nothing less than symbolic, for his class, in his time, in his native region.

Periodical Publications:
"Homestead and Its Perilous Trades: Impressions of a Visit," *McClure's*, 3 (June 1894): 3-20;
"The Productive Conditions of American Literature," *Forum*, 17 (August 1894): 690-698;
"The Red Man's Present Needs," *North American Review*, 174 (April 1902): 476-488.

Bibliographies:
Lloyd A. Arvidson, "A Bibliography of the Published Writings of Hamlin Garland," M.A. thesis, University of Southern California, 1952;
Arvidson, *Hamlin Garland: Centennial Tributes and A Checklist of the Hamlin Garland Papers in the University of Southern California Library*, Bulletin no. 9 (Los Angeles: University of Southern California Library, 1962);
Jackson R. Bryer and Eugene Harding, *Hamlin Garland and the Critics, An Annotated Bibliography* (Troy, N.Y.: Whitston, 1973);
Charles L. P. Silet, *Henry Blake Fuller and Hamlin Garland: A Reference Guide* (Boston: G. K. Hall, 1977).

Biographies:
Jean Holloway, *Hamlin Garland, A Biography* (Austin: University of Texas Press, 1960);
Donald Pizer, *Hamlin Garland's Early Work and Career* (Berkeley: University of California Press, 1960).

References:
Lars Ahnebrink, *The Beginnings of Naturalism in American Fiction* (Upsala: University of Upsala, 1950), pp. 63-89;
Donald Pizer, "Hamlin Garland," *American Literary Realism*, 1 (Fall 1967): 45-51;
Lonnie E. Underhill and Daniel F. Littlefield, Introduction to *Hamlin Garland's Observations on the American Indian, 1895-1905* (Tucson: University of Arizona Press, 1976).

Papers:
The Hamlin Garland Collection in the Doheny Library, University of Southern California, contains some 10,000 letters, Garland's personal library, his notebooks, journals, manuscripts, speeches, records, and memorabilia. Garland's forty-three annual diaries, 1898 to 1940, are at the Huntington Library in San Marino, California.

Ellen Glasgow

(22 April 1873–21 November 1945)

Linda W. Wagner
Michigan State University

See also the Glasgow entry in *DLB 9, American Novelists, 1910-1945*.

BOOKS: *The Descendant* (New York: Harper, 1897; London: Harper, 1897);

Phases of an Inferior Planet (New York & London: Harper and Brothers, 1898);

The Voice of the People (New York: Doubleday, Page, 1900; London: Heinemann, 1900);

The Battle-Ground (New York: Doubleday, Page, 1902; London: Constable, 1902);

The Deliverance (New York: Doubleday, Page, 1904; Westminster: Constable, 1904);

The Wheel of Life (New York: Doubleday, Page, 1906; London: Constable, 1906);

The Ancient Law (New York: Doubleday, Page, 1908; London: Constable, 1908);

The Romance of a Plain Man (New York: Macmillan, 1909; London: Murray, 1909);

The Miller of Old Church (Garden City: Doubleday, Page, 1911; London: Murray, 1911);

Virginia (Garden City: Doubleday, Page, 1913; London: Heinemann, 1913);

Life and Gabriella (Garden City: Doubleday, Page, 1916; London: Murray, 1916);

The Builders (Garden City: Doubleday, Page, 1919; London: Murray, 1919);

One Man in His Time (Garden City: Doubleday, Page, 1922; London: Murray, 1922);

The Shadowy Third and Other Stories (Garden City: Doubleday, Page, 1923); republished as *Dare's Gift and Other Stories* (London: Murray, 1924);

Barren Ground (Garden City: Doubleday, Page, 1925; London: Murray, 1925);

The Romantic Comedians (Garden City: Doubleday, Page, 1926; London: Murray, 1926);

They Stooped to Folly (New York: The Literary Guild, 1929; Garden City: Doubleday, Doran, 1929; London: Heinemann, 1929);

The Sheltered Life (Garden City: Doubleday, Doran, 1932; London: Heinemann, 1933);

Vein of Iron (New York: Harcourt, Brace, 1935; London: Cape, 1936);

In This Our Life (New York: Harcourt, Brace, 1941; London: Cape, 1941);

A Certain Measure (New York: Harcourt, Brace, 1943);

The Woman Within (New York: Harcourt, Brace, 1954; London: Eyre & Spottiswoode, 1955);

The Collected Stories of Ellen Glasgow, edited by Richard K. Meeker (Baton Rouge: Louisiana State University Press, 1963);

Beyond Defeat: An Epilogue to an Era, edited by Luther Y. Gore (Charlottesville: The University Press of Virginia, 1966).

Ellen Anderson Gholson Glasgow wrote nineteen novels, many of which were best-sellers. She was known as one of the first realists in American letters, and as an important ironist. Like Willa Cather, Glasgow was one of the most widely read of America's novelists in this century. Yet her critical acclaim falls somewhat behind her popular reputa-

Ellen Glasgow, circa 1900

213

tion. She also wrote short stories and a series of prefaces about the art of fiction, which were collected and published in 1943 as *A Certain Measure*. Another important book was *The Woman Within* (1954), Glasgow's autobiography, which recounted with both candor and style the problems of being a woman writer.

Whether consciously or not, much of Glasgow's fiction also dealt truthfully with the theme of women finding achievement, success, in their daily lives. At the turn of the century, women usually married and subordinated their interests and personalities to those of their husbands. By never marrying as well as by becoming a highly successful author, Glasgow lived out the existence of many of her female characters. In her earlier novels (*The Descendant*, 1897; *Phases of an Inferior Planet*, 1898; *The Wheel of Life*, 1906) women characters often led unhappy lives as they searched for careers as artists, singers, poets. Given the Southern culture in which she lived, Glasgow found it difficult to imagine women breaking from accepted social patterns. *Virginia* (1913), one of her best novels, showed the tragedy of a woman's believing that self-sacrifice was all that marriage should mean to women.

By the time of her middle novels, however (*Life and Gabriella*, 1916, and *One Man in His Time*, 1922), Glasgow was drawing women who chose to live independently and to have careers rather than marry unsuitable men. The culmination of this theme came with her masterful novel of 1925, *Barren Ground*, a book which still provokes critical controversy. Is Dorinda Oakley, a successful farmer, neurotic and barren, or is she a self-achieving female character? Glasgow's tendency to criticize male characters while praising her feminine creations continued in the three satiric novels which followed (*The Romantic Comedians*, 1926; *They Stooped to Folly*, 1929; and *The Sheltered Life*, 1932). *The Sheltered Life*, a bitter treatment of sheltered womanhood, parallels Edith Wharton's *The Age of Innocence* (1920) and completes Glasgow's portrayal of miseducated women. These books are among Glasgow's best. She was not only writing at the top of her ability during the 1920s and 1930s; she had also begun to be recognized as an important novelist, not simply as a writer of best-sellers for women readers.

Critical acceptance was important for Glasgow. She began writing with very little encouragement. Born into a large, well-established Richmond, Virginia, family, she was too fragile in health to attend school often. She was largely self-educated, being guided in her reading in philosophy and science by an attentive brother-in-law. Her fragility

was also psychological. While Ellen was still a child, her beloved mother suffered a nervous breakdown for which the child blamed her father. She never forgave him for that injury to her mother, whether real or imaginary.

Glasgow's attempts to write were viewed as inappropriate for a young Southern woman. When her first book, *The Descendant*, was published anonymously, it created a mild sensation as a daring social statement. The book was attributed to the popular Harold Frederic; Glasgow felt it the highest compliment to be read as a male writer. Not only was she apologetic about her literary ambition, she was also content to be judged by established (and usually male) literary standards. Few members of her family, few friends, read her early work. Among her books, *The Descendant* holds a special place because, as the author herself admitted, it contained "the germ" of her future work.

After her mother's death in 1893, Glasgow suffered severe depression and a partial loss of her hearing. That handicap made traveling and living

Title page for Glasgow's anonymous first novel, which some critics falsely attributed to Harold Frederic

as an independent woman almost impossible. Glasgow began to rely on her sisters, Rebe and Cary, and on certain of her Richmond friends who became her traveling companions. She enjoyed trips to New York, the West, Maine, and abroad for much of the rest of her life. Through her travels, she met other writers—Joseph Conrad, Thomas Hardy, Henry James—and learned to feel less isolated in the real work of her life.

issues in her fiction long before the country was aware of women's rights.

Critical attitudes early in this century were such that writing truthfully about the problems of women was less acceptable than writing fiction about the problems of the post-Civil War South. Glasgow's novels were set in the South; her chief characters were Southern. Several of her books dealt with the Civil War. Glasgow's acceptance as a

The study in Ellen Glasgow's Richmond house

Except for a few years in New York (1911 to 1916), Glasgow lived in the family home at One West Main in Richmond. In her forties, she nearly married a Southern lawyer, Henry Anderson, who lived nearby; but that engagement changed into a friendship that lasted—with interruptions—until her death. Glasgow had earlier been engaged to the Reverend Frank Paradise; according to *The Woman Within*, she also had at least one romance with a man who was not free to marry her. She was an attractive woman. Her autobiography suggests that she experienced many of the dilemmas that her women characters face in her fiction: whether or not to marry; whether or not to relinquish a career for marriage; whether or not to maintain independence. Glasgow was dealing realistically with these

serious writer, then, came because critics felt she was writing a chronicle of Southern history in the past century. Following the suggestion of her fellow author James Branch Cabell, Glasgow encouraged readers to see her novels as explorations of life in the South at various periods and in various social strata. Her prefaces to the novels emphasize this theme. Probably because of that emphasis, Glasgow began to achieve formal critical recognition as well as general popularity during the 1920s. Her 1926 novel, *The Romantic Comedians,* was a Book-of-the-Month Club selection; in 1929 *They Stooped to Folly* was purchased by the Literary Guild. In recognition of her status as an important writer of fiction, Glasgow was chosen the sixth woman member of the Academy of Arts and Letters and awarded the

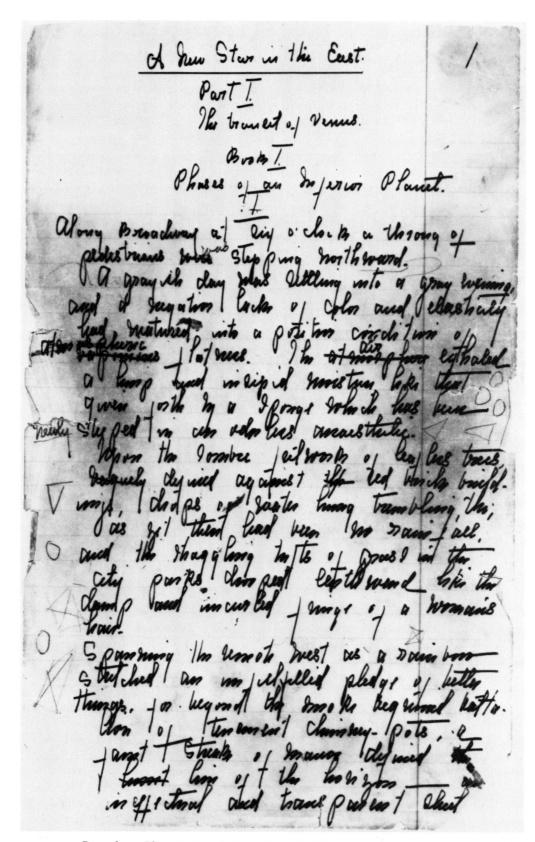

Pages from "Phase First" and "Phase Second" of Glasgow's second novel, Phases of an Inferior Planet

"and not even here do all agree, no. 9
with himself." Marcus Aurelius
Chapter 1.

1

Phases of an Inferior Planet.

Phase Second.

"Woe unto you when all men, I speak well of
you! for did their fathers to the false
Prophets-" ―― Luke VII. 26.-

Chapter 1.

Two men passed the Church of the Immaculate
Conception, which suddenly turned and came
back.

"By Jove, Driscoll, you have been eat dish of
Civilization," said one who was fat
and florid with a general suggestion of
potential apoplexy. Polished by the art of
indulgence. "What, you haven't
heard the Reverend Algarcio? Why,
in its popularity
the Brackenhurst Scandal and his
power is only equalled by that of ―――
of Tammany."

John Driscoll laughed cynically.

"Let's have the Scandal, by all means,"
he returned. "Spare me the guiding priests ―
Bless my soul, man, don't tell me the
Brackenhurst hasn't reached the
Pacific Slope. What a hole of a place!
Mell Ilerskey was named Co-respondent, you
know. You remember Ilerskey, the
fellow who nosed in Lady Jawes.

prestigious Howells Medal for Fiction in 1940. She also received a special award from the *Saturday Review of Literature* and, in 1942, the Pulitzer Prize for *In This Our Life* (1941). Since World War II, however, and almost since the moment of her Pulitzer Prize, Glasgow's critical reputation has been in decline. More talked about than read, the impressive list of her titles has become familiar to a select—rather than a mass—audience.

Glasgow found great satisfaction in being able to effect change in the turn-of-the-century novel. As she recalled in *A Certain Measure*, "I was, in my humble place and way, beginning a solitary revolt against the formal, the false and affected, the sentimental, and the pretentious, in Southern writing. I had no guide. I was, so far as I was then aware, alone in my rejection of a prescribed and moribund convention of letters. But I felt, 'Life is not like this.' I thought, 'Why must novels be false to experience?'" Glasgow was not to know the work of Henry James or William Dean Howells until fairly late in her career, but she learned a great deal from European and Russian novelists, and wrote largely from her personal knowledge of reality. Only near the end of her career, when a sometimes oppressive "message" became obvious in her fiction, could she be criticized for leaving behind her realist intention that her fiction be true to experience.

Glasgow's first novel, *The Descendant*, appeared in 1897 to mixed reviews. The book could be said to be the story of Michael Akershem, an educated liberal trying to overcome the stigma of his illegitimate birth. It could also be said to be the story of his lover, Rachel Gavin, an aspiring and talented painter. Once Rachel meets Michael, she gives up the very independence he admires, convinced as she is that he is a superman, someone to worship. As she abandons her own work, he comes to value her less and eventually leaves her for "a pure woman." Even though Michael later comes to realize "the wealth of her nature, the immensity of the love with which she had loved him," that realization does little to counter the irony of Glasgow's theme—that Rachel had pushed herself to her destruction through an unnecessary self-sacrifice.

Published one year later, Glasgow's second novel, *Phases of an Inferior Planet* (1898), continues the theme but the indictment here falls more directly on conventional male attitudes as being responsible for women's difficulties. Still relying on Glasgow's interest in economics and skepticism, this book is almost a casebook for the attitudes Glasgow is trying to break with. The novel opens with the story of Mariana Musin, "graceful and feminine

and fragile." Mariana studies voice but, chameleon-like, she adapts to cultural expectations. Once she meets the restless agnostic Anthony Algarcife (who later becomes an Episcopalian priest), she too relinquishes her career to become a wife. "She threw herself into the worship of him with absolute disregard of all retarding interests. When he was near, she lavished demonstrations upon him; when he was away, she sat with folded hands and dreamed day dreams. She had given up her music. . . ." A central issue in this novel is the concept that Anthony owns Mariana: "He possessed her, this was sufficient. She was to be his forever, come what would." Glasgow's attempt to set the Mariana-Anthony story in a larger context is partly responsible for the clumsy denouement and for the equally clumsy title. The most naturalistic of her novels, *Phases of an Inferior Planet* proposes that passion is inexplicable, that love is fated, and that fate also controls the destinies of those who live on this planet. The susceptibility to passion *is* the human quality, Glasgow states. It is only when Anthony denounces his love for Mariana and leads an ascetic life that he becomes alien. The contradictions in Anthony's religious life are set against the clear bond of love that exists between Mariana and Mrs. Ryder in an episode involving the latter's child. This relationship between women is the first of many Glasgow was to articulate, repeating again and again that women have no need for verbal strategy, lies, hypocrisy. Women understand each other's needs.

With the publication of *The Voice of the People* in 1900, Glasgow found her Southern subject and setting, but the characters of this novel lack the sense of reality evident in the earlier two novels. The young Nicholas Burr, a farmer's child who aspires to be a judge, and the wealthy Eugenia Battle are playmates throughout their childhood. Briefly engaged, they soon follow the direction of class lines, and Eugenia marries a man who eventually becomes Nicholas's political rival. Interest in the novel must follow Nicholas, who becomes the spokesman for Glasgow's recurring theme that people shape their own destinies. The poor boy who succeeds despite a less-than-noble birth was one of her favorite characters, especially early in her career. That Nicholas can state, "Men make their stations, madam" sets the distinction between women and men clearly. Eugenia must marry a "suitable" mate; her decisions are limited from the start. Nicholas chooses an active political career and, even though he dies at the hands of a lynch mob early in his life, his spirit has been of real value to his culture.

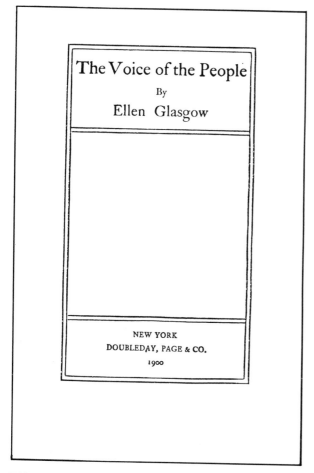

The Voice of the People

By

Ellen Glasgow

NEW YORK
DOUBLEDAY, PAGE & CO.
1900

Title page for the first of a series of novels in which Glasgow explores the cultural history of Virginia

Eugenia's life remains pale beside Nicholas's.

Such was not the case with the female protagonist of Glasgow's 1902 novel, *The Battle-Ground*. Betty Ambler, fiery redhead, foreshadows Scarlett O'Hara of *Gone With the Wind* in her intemperate love for Dan Lightfoot. She is indomitable, waiting throughout the Civil War for his return; no circumstances defeat her spirit. Winsome, impractical, courageous to a fault, Ambler forestalls despair and convincingly creates an optimistic romantic atmosphere. The novel ends with her words, "We will begin again . . . and this time, my dear, we will begin together."

Whereas attention in *The Battle-Ground* is consistently given to Betty Ambler, Glasgow works hard in *The Deliverance* (1904) to keep Christopher Blake, another superhero, central. In this book Glasgow reverses the strengths of hero and heroine. Blake is no ascetic; his life is ruled not by a denial of emotion but by an immersion in hatred. He exists only to avenge his family's honor against Bill Fletcher, who has stolen the Blake land and home. Ironically, Blake's salvation as a human being occurs through his love for Maria Fletcher, the granddaughter of his enemy, whose balanced view of life sets the moralistic tone of the novel. Maria's knowledge stems from both education and experience.

Unlike Maria, Blake remains the romantic: "I want the excitement that makes one's blood run like wine. . . . War, and fame, and love." In his lack of awareness, Christopher joins the number of Glasgow's heroes who continually flee reality. Glasgow's 1938 preface to *The Battle-Ground* also states that the novel "is not a romance"; "it is, nevertheless, the work of romantic youth. The person who conceived it is nowadays a dead person." In the corresponding preface to *The Deliverance*, Glasgow speaks of Maria's love as being able to change her lover's character and admits, "Had I written this book at the present time, it is probable that I should have subdued the romantic note to an ending of stark tragedy. . . . I have doubted, in later years, whether any love, however exalted, could have conquered the triumphant hatred in Christopher's heart and mind." As *The Deliverance* ends, however, Maria's love has changed Blake's character, and she goes to welcome him as he returns from prison "across the sunbeams."

Easily the most affirmative and romantic of her novels, *The Battle-Ground* and *The Deliverance* mark a period in Glasgow's life when she was experiencing the long romance with the man identified only as "Gerald B." in her memoir. To believe that women might wait for their beloveds, despite personal feuds or the Civil War, and be rewarded for their endurance was an attitude quickly passed. The despair of her 1906 novel, *The Wheel of Life*, with its reliance on Eastern thought and mysticism, came in rapid sequence and, one presumes, with the end of her personal romance.

Laura Wilde, a beautiful otherworldly poetess, nearly marries the wrong man, but ends with an understanding older lover. The romance of Laura and Roger constitutes the plot of the book which, for all its happy ending, treats romantic conventions with refreshing irony. The chapter titles, for example, suggest that Glasgow is mocking prescriptive fiction ("Ch. I, In Which the Romantic Hero Is Conspicuous by His Absence"; "Ch. VI, Shows That Mr. Worldly-Wise Man May Belong to Either Sex"; "Ch. X, Shows the Hero To Be Lacking in Heroic Qualities"). *The Wheel of Life*, once again, turns out to be a treatise on the *unreality* of feminine expectations about romance. Glasgow structures the novel in four sections that reflect the wisdom Laura will have to gain: "Impulse," in which Laura yearns for an ideal love; "Illusion," in which she falls in love with Kemper; "Disenchantment," the demise of the romance; and most important, "Reconciliation," which Glasgow defines as Laura's reunion with herself, not with a lover. Significantly, when Laura is most bereft, it is to her woman friend Gerty that she turns; and to the poor of her parish that she gives her full sympathy.

In this 1906 novel, Glasgow shows that she has learned not only to attack romantic myths but also to provide alternatives for them. In Laura's final conception of the word *love* ("all emotion is but the blind striving of love after the consciousness of itself"), she is able to give up language and trust her feeling for people. Serving others less fortunate than she leads Laura to a moment of transcendence. Only after she has moved past her own personal needs and pain, will she be ready to love again.

Even though Glasgow regarded *The Wheel of Life* a failure, she repeated its theme—love as transcendent of selfish passion—in her next several novels. In 1908 *The Ancient Law* explored the possibility of a man's living a fulfilled life, beyond all physical passion. It chronicles what might have been an absorbing love between Daniel Ordway Smith and Emily Brooks, a love which culminates instead with all personal romance relinquished to a larger love for mankind.

The characters of Glasgow's next novels, *The Romance of a Plain Man* (1909) and *The Miller of Old Church*, published in 1911, may have been reflections of her personal need to escape from reality. Each novel, despite its title, includes strong female characters and somewhat atypical social situations. In both books, Glasgow appears to be investigating the conventions of most interest to women at the turn of the century.

The Romance of a Plain Man opens with an abused wife, Sarah Mickleborough, running away from her drunken husband. Paralleling *The Voice of the People*, this novel follows the lives of Sarah's daughter, Sally, and Ben Starr as Ben educates himself and then claims Sally's love. Unfortunately for the couple's happiness, Ben is as adamant about financial success as he was about winning Sally. But keeping their marriage intact finally demands that Ben give up his business. Meanwhile, Sally has made her own choices in life; she refuses to be bound by conventional concerns about social position or money. *The Miller of Old Church* develops similar themes. Here, both Molly Merryweather, the illegitimate daughter of Jonathan Gay, and the mil-

ler, Abel Revercomb, rise into higher social positions through their own merits. In this novel, Glasgow uses subplots to emphasize the conflict between traditionally acceptable roles for women and the reality of women's emotional lives. *The Miller of Old Church* was especially important for Glasgow's development as novelist because it allowed her to combine an examination of class change with the study of woman's role in the custom-bound South.

Typical female characters in the book include: the maiden lady too late freed from family obligations (Kesiah); the protected genteel mother, whose ignorance of life enervates and eventually destroys her family (Mrs. Gay); and the young women whose lives exist only for romantic fulfillment (Judy Hatch, Blossom Revercomb). Molly stands apart; her difference from most adolescent girls is established early. Yet *The Miller of Old Church* also emphasizes friendships among women to a greater extent than anything in Glasgow's previous fiction.

In one climactic scene, as Molly is comforting the disillusioned Blossom, Glasgow propounds, "The relation of woman to man was dwarfed suddenly by an understanding of the relation of woman to woman. Deeper than the dependence of sex, simpler, more natural, closer to the earth, as if it still drew its strength from the soil, he realized that the need of woman for woman was not written in the songs and the histories of men, but in the neglected and frustrated lives which the songs and the histories of men had ignored."

Much of Glasgow's later fiction was an effort to present and illuminate those "neglected and frustrated lives," and in that respect *Virginia* is one of her most important novels. Its title was meant to be suggestive. By 1913, the year of its publication, Glasgow had developed some concept of using fiction to trace a history of her native state. The title relates to that location, complete with its Southern attitudes and mores. More important, the title also implies an ideal female, a woman named reverentially after the land, serving the expected female functions of earth-mother, child-bearer, mythic and actual home. The tragic ending of *Virginia* can only show Glasgow's personal view of the pathos of her title character, "cut out for happiness" yet fated to live so unhappily, subordinated to her husband; the woman who embodied "the Victorian ideal for whom love was enough."

This novel convincingly ties women's attitudes about love to their religious beliefs. Virginia's father is a minister; her mother leads a life of complete self-abnegation. When Virginia asks her mother, "Love is the only thing that really matters, isn't it, mother" and is answered, "A pure and noble love, darling. It is a woman's life. God meant it so," the die is cast for tragedy. The liberal Oliver Treadwell, attracted to Virginia's submission, cannot long remain sympathetic with it; and he eventually leaves her. Once alone, Virginia has no identity, no resources, no life. Yet, Glasgow does not draw Virginia as pathetic. As she explained, "The pathos of it was that neither in life nor in my novel was she a weak character, as some undiscerning readers have called her. On the contrary, she was a woman whose vital energy had been deflected, by precept and example, into a single emotional centre. She was, indeed, as I had known her prototype in one I loved and pitied, the logical result of an inordinate sense of duty, the crowning achievement of the code of beautiful behaviour and the Episcopal Church." As warning of the fate of this "single dream of identity," the title character of *Virginia* stands clearly defined in American letters. To prevent misread-

ing, Glasgow creates a foil to her, the girlhood friend Susan Treadwell, whose clear-headed independence makes her atypical. That the novel is less her story than Virginia's is a tribute to Glasgow's power of characterization, but she would return soon to a Susan-like creation.

Glasgow's progression of Southern women characters continued in 1916 with Gabriella Carr in *Life and Gabriella*. As Glasgow commented, "Gabriella was the product of the same school, but instead of being used by circumstances, she used them to create her own destiny. . . . Gabriella had the courage of action and through molding circumstances wrested from life her happiness and success." The traits given to Susan Treadwell in *Virginia* here make possible Gabriella's accomplishment—the development of independence, an independence with direction—but Glasgow as late as 1916 seemed to realize that even Gabriella was not the epitome of emancipation. Yet, Glasgow created a comparatively believable Gabriella. She may have sacrificed a bit to make her point, urged on the reader by the title: that the battle is between woman and "circumstances," the sum total of cultural and religious attitudes and social expectations. The positive result is that Gabriella does have life at the end of the novel, rather than the death that awaits Virginia Treadwell. Fittingly, *Life and Gabriella* was subtitled *The Story of a Woman's Courage*.

One of the more interesting points to be made about *Life and Gabriella*, especially in light of its great popularity with the reading public, is that it foreshadowed Glasgow's own life to come. From 1911 to 1916, she had lived alone in New York. Many of the siblings she cared most about had died and, until her father's death in 1916, Glasgow had no thought of returning to Richmond. But in the spring of 1916 she did return to One West Main, and soon met Henry Anderson, the bachelor politician who courted her enthusiastically. Glasgow and Gabriella were both in their early forties, successful examples of independent women. Yet both felt that the urgency to be totally involved in their work had passed; they were in need of human companionship. That Glasgow nearly married Henry Anderson is clear from their correspondence; that her engagement to him, never formally broken, brought her much unhappiness is also clear. To be an unmarried woman—even though a talented and acclaimed professional—continued to carry a stigma which Glasgow found hard to ignore. Her writing of the next decade was to reflect this personal quandary.

The fondest portrait of an Anderson-like

character occurred in Glasgow's 1919 novel, *The Builders*. David Blackburn, an "idealist, literally on fire with ideas," survives an unfortunate marriage and comes to love Caroline Meade, the nurse-tutor in his household, whose life has ended with a broken engagement. Blackburn is a complete idealist, firmly committed to political salvation and willing to sacrifice any personal happiness for the good of his country. Caroline "understands" when Blackburn goes back to his villainous wife and leaves her; she explains his desertion as being motivated by "unselfish patriotism" and "sacrifice for the general good."

One Man in His Time (1922) reads as a sequel to *The Builders*, although here Glasgow has used three male characters rather than one. Her attention rests primarily with Corinna Page, a beautiful, independent woman in her late forties (as Glasgow was at that time), whose aim in life is to make existence pleasant for others, regardless of her personal situation. Corinna is engaged to one of the male protagonists, but in the course of the book, she breaks that engagement and stands once again on her own joy of life. The novel had shown her sadness over her life (imaged as "a gray lane without a turning that stretched on into nothingness!"), her feeling that living alone was unsatisfying; yet once she had the option of marrying again, she refused it. Her philosophy is conveyed effectively as she watches over the young Patty Vetch, a rebel amid the effete Southern belles. Corinna's warning to Patty, then in the throes of a love affair, echoes Glasgow's statements elsewhere: "Just so much and no more. . . . Give with the mind and the heart; but keep always one inviolable sanctity of the spirit—of the buried self beneath the self." Self-assurance, self-knowledge—Corinna is the character truest to Glasgow's own self-image during these years. Never saccharine, Corinna impresses the reader with her poise and capacity to know sorrow. This novel introduces the image of the "vein of iron" that was to recur in much of Glasgow's late fiction. As the author describes Corinna, "Her destiny was the destiny of the strong who must give until they have nothing left, until their souls are stripped bare."

No longer apologetic for a woman's sensibility, Glasgow does not hesitate to criticize male characters, to criticize them in that most undignified way, through satire. She continues this tendency through a series of short stories, written largely during the 1920s, stories in which women characters are independent, obviously female (instead of copying male traits in order to succeed in male worlds), and often paired with male characters who are either vapid and insensitive, or downright traitorous.

Several stories are illustrative. "Thinking Makes It So" is the story of aging poetess Margaret French, who comes to life when an unknown admirer writes to her and falls in love with her poetry. The change in her physical appearance mirrors that in her mental outlook. That Margaret is a middle-aged writer waiting to be brought to life through a man's love suggests Glasgow's personal situation when she had just become engaged to Henry Anderson. Most of the stories are definitely unromantic, however. In "The Professional Instinct" the successful Judith Campbell relinquishes her chance to become a college president in order to run away with a frustrated professor whose career seems at an end. When Estbridge hears that he has been chosen for a coveted appointment, he fails to meet Judith at the station and leaves her romantic hopes in ashes. His instincts are entirely self-serving. Even more bitter are such stories as "The Difference" and "Romance and Sally Byrd."

Writing about Corinna Page in *One Man in His Time* and creating various characters in the short stories gave Glasgow a greatly expanded range of experience with women characters. By the time she approached the rich Dorinda Oakley in *Barren Ground* (1925), she was in command of her craft. In that novel, Glasgow wove the imagery of natural landscape into Dorinda's battle to become a successful farmer (as well as a successful woman) and created a character that stands against her setting in dramatic relief. No simple Virginia farm girl, Dorinda showed the toughest "vein of iron" as she came back to the farm after being impregnated and betrayed by her lover, Jason Greylock. She has forced her culture to accept her, by becoming successful in that culture's own terms. In reversing Dorinda's Cinderella-story expectations, Glasgow robs her of the only cultural information she has been given. Moreover, no other woman in this novel understands Dorinda's dilemma; all the other women characters are traditional earth-mothers. In its bleakness, *Barren Ground* illustrates the scarcity of options for women who choose to avoid marriage.

The strength of Glasgow's novel is not that Dorinda succeeds as a farmer, but rather that we do not like her during much of the book. Her conquest of the land is motivated by vengeance. She cannot forget Jason's betrayal. She intends to make him aware that she is a survivor (unlike his wife, who goes mad living with him). It is only late in the novel that Dorinda begins to feel compassion for other human beings; only then does the reader feel that her life has been exonerated. The ambivalence with which Glasgow presents her heroine is an unexpected departure for a novelist whose sympathies would clearly be with such a woman. The great writing which *Barren Ground* contains is a tribute to psychological realism. The whole impact of the book hinges upon the reader's definition of the word "barren," with its various levels of irony. Childless after an accident, Dorinda might be termed "barren"; but Glasgow shows clearly that Dorinda has never been a barren woman: she has known passion, she has conceived. And what she wrests from the generally unyielding land is fruit, success, promise for the future—the opposite of barrenness. The title phrase is used early in the book: "Almost everybody is poor at Pedlar's Mill. The Ellgoods are the only people who have prospered. The rest of us have had to wring whatever we've had out of barren ground," and Dorinda ob-

Title page for one in the series of Glasgow's "vein of iron" novels about self-sufficient women

serves as she runs away to New York, "That's what life is for most people, I reckon. . . . Just barren ground where they have to struggle to make anything grow."

That Dorinda will not be content with a minimal existence prefigures the kind of constancy and ambition Glasgow was to illustrate in her later novels. The writing of *Barren Ground* served to open new narrative possibilities. As she said of the novel, "It is the best book I have written"; "the one of my books I like best." In view of her personal circumstances, Glasgow's comment that *Barren Ground* had also been a "vehicle of liberation" might suggest that the independent woman, even if alone, could become a reality. The message was well accepted, as the book received acclaim in both America and England. It has remained the most popular of her titles.

In 1926 Glasgow published the first of her ironic comedies, *The Romantic Comedians*. She called this novel "a tragicomedy of a happiness-hunter," Judge Honeywell, an aging man who resembles Henry Anderson in his propensity for young and beautiful women. The theme is the eternal foolishness of men searching for romantic love; running parallel with her expose of male foibles is a similar expose of the foolishness of the waiting woman. Glasgow's irony is, of course, that Honeywell himself does not realize the falsity of possession. Even married to young Annabel Upchurch, he enjoys no genuine love. She, in fact, runs away with another man. At the end of the novel, however, Honeywell remains as blind as he has been throughout his life, finding himself interested—even on his deathbed—in the young nurse that cares for him.

Mr. Virginius Littlepage, hero of *They Stooped to Folly*, published in 1929, resembles Honeywell. Happily married to the regal and loving Victoria, Littlepage spends much of his life dreaming about a fantasy liaison with Amy Dalrymple, the town tramp. Glasgow's positive characterization of his wife, however, undermines the comedy of Littlepage's obsession. *They Stooped to Folly* does not hesitate to praise characters who love truly and selflessly. Such people as Louisa Goddard, Milly Burden, Marmaduke Littlepage, and Aunt Agatha are treated with tenderness instead of ridicule. They are the seekers, people looking not simply for love but rather for "something worth loving."

Glasgow's satire in these three novels of manners (*The Romantic Comedians, They Stooped to Folly,* and *The Sheltered Life*) gradually modifies into bitter commentary. Each book explores the basic

Ellen Glasgow at about the time of Barren Ground

foible—man's constant desire to find romance, to make conquests—but with increasing condemnation of that male impulse. In this second novel, Littlepage is brought to fidelity through his wife's martyrlike death; he finally realizes that he has been blessed with a great love. A stronger condemnation occurs in Glasgow's *The Sheltered Life* (1932), where the male evil taints the innocence of an adolescent girl. By this time, the author saw that her satire had become a "serious study, with ironic overtones . . . of contemporary society."

In *The Sheltered Life,* Glasgow creates female characters who have been reared in the unrealistic innocence the South provides for its womenfolk. Jenny Blair Archbald, the child, learns her role from the most beautiful woman in Queenborough, Eva Birdsong. Eva, wife of an unfaithful husband, becomes the epitome of the wasted woman, modeled to an image of perfection in order to hold the man who is consistently betraying her. Early in the novel, Eva says to the admiring Jenny, "You will understand still better when you are older. You will know then that a great love doesn't leave room for anything else in a woman's life. It is everything. . . . you can never give up too much for happiness."

That she must define happiness in these terms points again to the falsehood in her life, and in the lives of similar women.

Tightly and brilliantly written to its unexpected ending, *The Sheltered Life* may be Glasgow's best novel. In sales, it did well, rising high among the year's best-sellers. That it was so intimately connected with her own life experience creates once again that inexplicable bond between a writer's knowledge and narrative craft.

When she was past sixty, Glasgow began the novel that became, for her, the culmination of a personal philosophy. *Vein of Iron* was in many ways a sequel to *Barren Ground*. No longer satiric, Glasgow's narrative here seems almost heavy-handed in contrast to the three comedies of manners, which had been well received critically and commercially. Published in 1935, *Vein of Iron* brought forward many of the themes from the writer's earlier fiction—individual determination in conflict with social pressure; romantic love and love beyond romance; family traditions; and the artistic (or feminine) struggle for fruition. Above all, Glasgow was studying the power of endurance, the importance in her characters of the "vein of iron."

Protagonists in the novel are Ada Fincastle and her father, John. Through the thirty years of the story, Glasgow traces the Scots-Presbyterian family (John is a former minister turned philosopher and agnostic). The ostensible plot involves Ada's lost love and her resulting pregnancy. In *Vein of Iron* she bears and rears the child. Finally married to Ralph McBride, Ada comes to realize that her conception of romantic love is false. To maintain the family, she endures his infidelity and his depression. They finally return to the family home and vow to begin their lives again—if only for their descendants.

Yet the center of *Vein of Iron* is not Ada so much as it is John Fincastle. Having lived his life as a maverick, he sacrifices his final days traveling back to the manse to save his family burial expenses. His death, alone, with the well-being of others at the forefront of his consciousness, marks Fincastle as the true altruist. Here Glasgow seems to have used the character of the older man to represent the divided consciousness of the artist in an unfriendly culture. Ada Fincastle is a characteristic portrayal of the passionate woman who loves with "a single heart." John Fincastle is the other worldly person whose life moves past the merely personal into the spiritual. The novel needed both characters to be convincing. In *Vein of Iron,* nevertheless, Glasgow came closest to those panoramic Russian novels she so admired—with a wide span of time, many characters, many experiences, and with themes that carry import to any reader, regardless of generation. Critics praised the book, and the public rushed to buy it; in all more that 100,000 copies were printed in 1935.

Between 1935, when *Vein of Iron* appeared, and 1945, when Glasgow died in her sleep after a heart attack, she wrote two more novels (*In This Our Life,* published in 1941, and *Beyond Defeat,* not published until 1966), her autobiography (*The Woman Within*, 1954, by her choice, not published in her lifetime), and the prefaces to those novels included in The Virginia Edition of 1938. (These prefaces were collected and published in 1943 as *A Certain Measure*.) Each of these books holds a place of some importance; together they constitute a tribute to her persistence in the face of illness and increasing weakness, that she could write so well even though she was, in some years, limited to working fifteen minutes a day. Critics found something to praise in each, but sales fell well below the heights achieved by *Vein of Iron* and earlier novels. Yet there were new opportunities and rewards.

In This Our Life was made into a film, starring Bette Davis, Olivia de Havilland, and Dennis Morgan. It also won for Glasgow her first Pulitzer Prize for Fiction (1942). More of Glasgow's energy during her last decade went into the prefaces of *A Certain Measure* and her autobiography than into her fiction. She saw her study of narrative in some ways as personal as her autobiography; indeed, some very personal statements occur in the prefaces, and help to expand the significance of *The Woman Within*. For Glasgow to write about her life, to let down those barriers of the proud, successful woman, so that others might understand her pain as well as joy, was in itself unusual. Her secrecy as she worked on the manuscript can well be understood.

Glasgow, during these later years, depended more and more on her companion, Anne Virginia Bennett, who lived with her at One West Main in Richmond, and on her literary friends. Such writers and critics as Carl Van Doren, Howard Mumford Jones, Allen Tate, Stark Young, Marjorie Kinnan Rawlings, James Branch Cabell, and others were supportive of and interested in her well-being. As the writer of *A Certain Measure* and *The Woman Within*, Glasgow had a clear, important public identity. Late in her life, she became especially sensitive about being described as only a "Southern" writer, or, worse, a "maiden lady." She viewed herself as a distinguished writer, not limited to local-color excellence; a well-traveled woman, rich in experience and study. In 1941 she took offense at an anonymous reviewer's claim in *Time*, that she had lived "a thoroughly conventional spinster's life." Glasgow's asperity is obvious: "as a matter of verity, the one experience I have never had is the life of a conventional spinster, whatever that is. Or a conventional life of any other nature."

That Glasgow succeeded as a writer can be partly attributed to her unwillingness to be conventional in any role. From the beginning, her stubbornness in attempting to become a writer kept her from becoming discouraged when even her family tried to dissuade her. To read *The Woman Within,* with its account of her arduous work, her personal griefs, her family's problems, is to know how difficult her life as a writer must have been. But Glasgow's career offers much more than the usual success story, for her fiction gives each reader a number of important insights. Thematically, her novels show the verities and virtues of American culture from the Civil War through World War II. They also show a shifting technique which leaves more and more to the reader's own participation (until her last, more didactic novels). But primarily, they show a panorama of believable women characters—from the self-effacing to the aggressive, the puritanical to the demonic—unmatched in American fiction before her time. Glasgow's characterizations gave flesh to the complexity of the female mind and heart, even as she herself grew from being a "philosophical" novelist whose first book was credited to a male writer, into a woman writer whose greatest work came from her own responses to her thoroughly feminine identity.

Periodical Publications:

"Feminism," *New York Times Book Review*, 30 November 1913, pp. 656-657;

"Feminism, a Definition," *Good Housekeeping*, 58 (May 1914): 683;

"Evasive Idealism in Literature," *New York Times*, 5 March 1916, VI: 10;

"The Dynamic Past," *Reviewer*, 1 (15 March 1921): 73-80;

"Impressions of the Novel," *New York Herald Tribune Books*, 20 May 1928, pp. 1, 5-6;

"Some Literary Woman Myths," *New York Herald Tribune Books*, 27 May 1928, pp. 1, 5-6;

"What I Believe," *Nation*, 136 (12 April 1933): 404-406;

" 'Nominalism and Reality' by Ellen Glasgow: An Unpublished Essay," edited by Luther Y. Gore, *American Literature*, 34 (March 1962): 72-79.

References:

Louis Auchincloss, *Ellen Glasgow* (Minneapolis: University of Minnesota Press, 1964);

E. Stanly Godbold, Jr., *Ellen Glasgow and the Woman Within* (Baton Rouge: Louisiana State University Press, 1972);

C. Hugh Holman, *Three Modes of Southern Fiction* (Athens: University of Georgia Press, 1966);

M. Thomas Inge, ed., *Ellen Glasgow, Centennial Essays* (Charlottesville: University Press of Virginia, 1976);

William W. Kelly, *Ellen Glasgow: A Bibliography* (Charlottesville: University Press of Virginia, 1964);

Frederick P. W. McDowell, *Ellen Glasgow and the Ironic Art of Fiction* (Madison: University of Wisconsin Press, 1963);

Monique Parent, *Ellen Glasgow, Romancière* (Paris: A. B. Nizet, 1962);

Julius Rowan Raper, *From the Sunken Garden, The Fiction of Ellen Glasgow, 1916-1945* (Baton Rouge: Louisiana State University Press, 1980);

Raper, *Without Shelter: The Early Career of Ellen Glasgow* (Baton Rouge: Louisiana State University Press, 1971);

Blair Rouse, *Ellen Glasgow* (New York: Twayne, 1962);

Rouse, ed., *Letters of Ellen Glasgow* (New York: Harcourt, Brace, & World, 1958);

Dorothy McInnis Scura, "The Southern Lady in the Early Novels of Ellen Glasgow," *Mississippi Quarterly*, 31 (Winter 1977-1978): 17-31;

Oliver Steele, "Ellen Glasgow's *Virginia*: Preliminary Notes," *Studies in Bibliography* (1974): 265-289;

James Southall Wilson, "Ellen Glasgow: Ironic Idealist," *Virginia Quarterly Review*, 15 (January 1939): 121-126;

Stark Young, "Prefaces to Distinction," *New Republic*, 125 (7 June 1933): 101-102.

Papers:

Glasgow's papers are in the Alderman Library, University of Virginia and in the University of Florida library.

Bret Harte

Ben Merchant Vorpahl
University of Georgia

BIRTH: Albany, New York, 25 August 1836, to Henry and Elizabeth Ostrander Harte.

MARRIAGE: 11 August 1862 to Anna Griswold; children: Griswold, Francis King, Jessamy, Ethel.

DEATH: Surrey, England, 5 May 1902.

SELECTED BOOKS: *Condensed Novels, and Other Papers* (New York: Carlton/London: Low, 1867; enlarged edition, Boston: Osgood, 1871);

The Lost Galleon and Other Tales (San Francisco: Towne & Bacon, 1867);

The Luck of Roaring Camp, and Other Sketches (Boston: Fields, Osgood, 1870; enlarged, 1870);

Poems (Boston: Fields, Osgood, 1871);

East and West Poems (Boston: Osgood, 1871; London: Hotten, 1871);

Mrs. Skaggs's Husbands, and Other Sketches (London: Hotten, 1872; Boston: Osgood, 1873);

An Episode of Fiddletown and Other Sketches (London: Routledge, 1873);

M'liss. An Idyl of Red Mountain (New York: DeWitt, 1873);

Echoes of the Foot-hills (Boston: Osgood, 1875);

Tales of the Argonauts, and Other Sketches (Boston: Osgood, 1875);

Gabriel Conroy (London: Warne, 1876; Hartford, Conn.: American Publishing Company, 1876);

Two Men of Sandy Bar: A Drama (Boston: Osgood, 1876);

Thankful Blossom, a Romance of the Jerseys, 1779 (Boston: Osgood, 1877; London & New York: Routledge, 1877);

The Story of a Mine (London: Routledge, 1877; Boston: Osgood, 1878);

The Man on the Beach (London: Routledge, 1878);

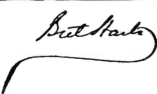

"Jinny" (London: Routledge, 1878);

Drift from Two Shores (Boston: Houghton, Osgood, 1878);

The Twins of Table Mountain (London: Chatto & Windus, 1879);

The Twins of Table Mountain and Other Stories (Boston: Houghton, Osgood, 1879);

Flip and Other Stories (London: Chatto & Windus, 1882);

Flip and Found at Blazing Star (Boston: Houghton, Mifflin, 1882);

In the Carquinez Woods (London: Longmans, Green, 1883; Boston: Houghton, Mifflin, 1884);

On the Frontier (London: Longmans, Green, 1884; Boston: Houghton, Mifflin, 1884);

By Shore and Sedge (Boston: Houghton, Mifflin, 1885; London: Longmans, Green, 1885);

Maruja (London: Chatto & Windus, 1885; Boston & New York: Houghton, Mifflin, 1885);

Snow-Bound at Eagle's (Boston & New York: Houghton, Mifflin, 1886; London: Ward & Downey, 1886);

The Queen of the Pirate Isle (London: Chatto & Windus, 1886; Boston & New York: Houghton, Mifflin, 1887);

A Millionaire of Rough-and-Ready and *Devil's Ford* (Boston & New York: Houghton, Mifflin, 1887);

Devil's Ford (London: White, 1887);

A Millionaire of Rough-and-Ready (London: White, 1887);

The Crusade of the Excelsior (Boston & New York: Houghton, Mifflin, 1887; London: White, 1887);

A Phyllis of the Sierras and A Drift from Redwood Camp (Boston & New York: Houghton, Mifflin, 1888);

The Argonauts of North Liberty (Boston & New York: Houghton, Mifflin, 1888; London: Blackett, 1888);

Cressy (London & New York: Macmillan, 1889; Boston & New York: Houghton, Mifflin, 1889);

The Heritage of Dedlow Marsh and Other Tales (Boston & New York: Houghton, Mifflin, 1889; London: Macmillan, 1889);

A Waif of the Plains (London: Chatto & Windus, 1890; Boston & New York: Houghton, Mifflin, 1890);

A Ward of the Golden Gate (London: Chatto & Windus, 1890; Boston & New York: Houghton, Mifflin, 1890);

A Sappho of Green Springs and Other Stories (London: Chatto & Windus, 1891; Boston & New York: Houghton, Mifflin, 1891);

A First Family of Tasajara (London & New York: Macmillan, 1891; Boston & New York: Houghton, Mifflin, 1892);

Colonel Starbottle's Client and Some Other People (London: Chatto & Windus, 1892; Boston & New York: Houghton, Mifflin, 1892);

Susy: A Story of the Plains (Boston & New York: Houghton, Mifflin, 1893; London: Chatto & Windus, 1893);

Sally Dows, Etc. (London: Chatto & Windus, 1893); republished as *Sally Dows and Other Stories* (Boston & New York: Houghton, Mifflin, 1893);

A Protegee of Jack Hamlin's and Other Stories (Boston & New York: Houghton, Mifflin, 1894; enlarged edition, London: Chatto & Windus, 1894);

The Bell-Ringer of Angel's and Other Stories (Boston &

New York: Houghton, Mifflin, 1894; London: Chatto & Windus, 1894);

Clarence (London: Chatto & Windus, 1895; Boston & New York: Houghton, Mifflin, 1895);

In a Hollow of the Hills (London: Chapman & Hall, 1895; Boston: Houghton, Mifflin, 1895);

Barker's Luck and Other Stories (Boston & New York: Houghton, Mifflin, 1896; London: Chatto & Windus, 1896);

Three Partners or The Big Strike on Heavy Tree Hill (Boston & New York: Houghton, Mifflin, 1897; London: Chatto & Windus, 1897);

Tales of Trail and Town (Boston & New York: Houghton, Mifflin, 1898; London: Chatto & Windus, 1898);

Stories in Light and Shadow (London: Pearson, 1898; Boston & New York: Houghton, Mifflin, 1898);

Mr. Jack Hamlin's Mediation and Other Stories (Boston & New York: Houghton, Mifflin, 1899; London: Pearson, 1899);

From Sand Hill to Pine (Boston & New York: Houghton, Mifflin, 1900; London: Pearson, 1900);

Under the Redwoods (Boston & New York: Houghton, Mifflin, 1901; London: Pearson, 1901);

On the Old Trail (London: Pearson, 1902); republished as *Openings in the Old Trail* (Boston & New York: Houghton, Mifflin, 1902);

Condensed Novels, Second Series: New Burlesques (Boston & New York: Houghton, Mifflin, 1902; London: Chatto & Windus, 1902);

Sue: A Play in Three Acts, by Harte and T. Edgar Pemberton (London: Greening, 1902);

Trent's Trust and Other Stories (London: Nash, 1903; Boston & New York: Houghton, Mifflin, 1903);

Stories and Poems and Other Uncollected Writings, compiled by Charles Meeker Kozlay (Boston & New York: Houghton, Mifflin, 1914).

COLLECTION: *The Writings of Bret Harte*, 20 volumes (Boston: Houghton, Mifflin, 1896-1914).

Bret Harte was the first Pacific slope writer to gain an international reputation for his work. As a deft observer of character and conditions, he introduced to a worldwide audience the picturesque life of mid-nineteenth-century northern California. Yet his best stories and sketches contain much more than local color. The spectacular settings, the accurate costumes and dialects, even the realistic depictions of character types—ranging from aristocratic hidalgos to scheming women, whores, and bumptious Missourians—are finally subordinate to the questions of courage, cowardice, and moral ambiguity that fascinated Harte as a writer and plagued him as a man. These are also the questions that have occupied literature about the American West throughout the nineteenth and twentieth centuries. Harte did not discover them first, but he did address them with intelligence, insight, and wit during the four decades of his active writing career. As a writer of short stories, a novelist, an editor, and a critic, he gave the world an image of the West that still prevails.

Francis Brett Harte, as he was christened, was born to Henry Harte and Elizabeth Ostrander Harte at Albany, New York, on 25 August 1836. There were two older children, Eliza, born in 1831, and Henry, born in 1835. A fourth, Margaret, would be born in 1838. Henry Harte operated a private school in the modest family home on Columbia Street. However, the financial panic of 1837 forced the school to close, and the Hartes were plunged into serious financial difficulty. For the next eight years they moved from town to town, setting up a household wherever Henry could find work as a teacher. The lack of permanence, and the anxiety about money and employment, must have been hard on young Frank. He was a quiet, withdrawn child, ill much of the time, who soon took refuge in books. At six, he was reading Shakespeare. By the time he was ten, he had familiarized himself with most of the major British novelists, but Alexandre Dumas's *The Count of Monte Cristo*, which he read at about this time in a translation from the French, remained his favorite novel throughout his life.

Frank was nine years old when his father's death in 1845 left the family destitute. Neither he, his mother, nor his brother and sisters were qualified to earn money. It therefore became necessary for Elizabeth Harte—from all indications a proud woman—to request aid from relatives. Her own family supplied some help, but not enough. Fortunately, her late husband's eighty-one-year-old father, Bernard Hart, was wealthy enough to provide more, but asking him for it must have been difficult. He had secretly married Catherine Brett, Henry's mother, in 1799, but their marriage was dissolved in 1800, just after Henry's birth. Henry's chief reason for adding the *e* to the family name had probably been to dissociate himself from the father for whom he felt only bitterness. However, Bernard Hart did provide Elizabeth and her offspring with the means for staying together, at least for a time.

They settled in New York City in 1845, where Frank was able to continue school until he was thirteen years old. At eleven he had his first work, a sentimental poem called "Autumn Musings," published in the *Sunday Morning Atlas*. On leaving school he worked briefly in a law office and then a counting-house. Meanwhile, the little family began to break up. Henry Harte went to fight in the Mexican War in 1846, later showing up as an argonaut at San Francisco in 1849. Eliza Harte married in 1851. In 1853, their mother became engaged to Andrew Williams, a California businessman, whom she married at San Francisco early the next year. Sixteen-year-old Bret, as Frank now began to be called, and his younger sister, Margaret, joined Elizabeth and her new husband in March 1854, after a harrowing passage down the East Coast to Nicaragua, across the isthmus, and up the West Coast to San Francisco. The family settled in Oakland, where Williams enjoyed modest success and prosperity, but Bret was apparently dissatisfied. Late in 1854, he left home to wander in the foothills and valleys about which he would soon begin to write.

Harte probably taught school for a time at LaGrange, on the bank of the Toulumne River, a community that appears as Smith's Pocket in his early short story, "M'liss." He then seems to have drifted north, looking for gold. Acquaintances from this period remember him as a tenderfoot, who came into the country ill-prepared for its rigors of climate and terrain. He wore patent leather shoes and a suit of city clothes. Early in 1856, he borrowed an overcoat and money from a friend, returned to his stepfather's house in Oakland, and announced to his family that he intended to become a writer.

He approached his newly chosen line of work in the characteristically calculated and methodical fashion that would be one of his trademarks throughout life. Dickens, he decided, would be his mentor. A recently purchased complete set of Dickens's novels occupied him during the summer of 1856 while he worked at an Oakland drugstore. In the fall, he left for a ranch in the Sycamore Valley, at the foot of Mount Diablo, where he tutored the four sons of Abner Bryan, a local rancher and religious enthusiast. In 1857, he briefly took the unlikely position of a Wells Fargo guard on a stagecoach before becoming an apprentice printer on the Humboldt County *Northern Californian* in Arcata the following year. While such meanderings might have led nowhere for someone with less thrifty habits of mind, Harte made them count, drawing from them materials for his writing. From his experience on the Bryan ranch, he wove "A Legend of Monte del Diablo," the story of how a pious Spanish padre is tutored in history by a gentlemanly devil. Out of his experience as a stagecoach "shotgun" comes Yuba Bill, the wryly laconic driver in such tales as "Miggles," "M'liss," "Snow-Bound at Eagle's," and "A Niece of Snapshot Harry's." The job on the weekly *Northern Californian*, of course, was a humble beginning at the enterprise that would make him a momentary celebrity, promise him riches, and actually provide him with a competent living over the long term.

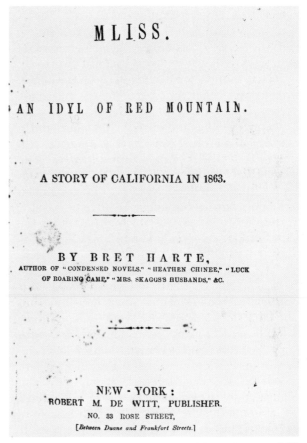

MLISS.

AN IDYL OF RED MOUNTAIN.

A STORY OF CALIFORNIA IN 1863.

BY BRET HARTE,
AUTHOR OF "CONDENSED NOVELS," "HEATHEN CHINEE," "LUCK OF ROARING CAMP," "MRS. SKAGGS'S HUSBANDS," &C.

NEW - YORK:
ROBERT M. DE WITT, PUBLISHER.
NO. 33 ROSE STREET,
[*Between Duane and Frankfort Streets.*]

Pirated publication of Harte's story with his revisions and fifty chapters, added without Harte's authorization, by R. G. Densmore

Although working in a frontier print shop was probably not what Harte had in mind when he announced in 1856 that he intended to be a writer, newspaper work agreed with him, and he was good at it. He soon found his way out of the back room and into the community, where he covered local news stories with a flair that did him credit. In 1859, Harte was routinely left in charge of the paper whenever S. G. Whipple, the editor, went to San Francisco. Early in 1860, however, he learned for the first time that to have one's work published was not necessarily to be admired, a lesson he would later have many occasions to ponder. On 26 February—a Sunday—a group of whites armed with guns, knives, and axes surprised an Indian camp on Gunther's Island in nearby Humboldt Bay and butchered some sixty inhabitants, mostly women and children. As it happened, Whipple was away. Harte not only reported the incident with outrage; he wrote a stingingly indignant editorial. Not surprisingly, his popularity in Humboldt County evaporated at once. He was probably not seriously threatened with physical violence, but he was certainly made to feel unwelcome. Accordingly, he left the *Northern Californian* the next month and took a steamer down the coast to San Francisco.

Harte found a job as a printer with the *Golden Era*, a respected San Francisco literary magazine, and contributed a number of lively—if somewhat derivative—sketches and stories to that journal. He also completed his first considerable literary effort, the story first published in abridged form as "The Work on Red Mountain." This work created a considerable stir when the *Golden Era* printed it in two installments during December 1860. Superficially, it is the rags-to-riches story of Melissa Smith, the daughter of an indigent gold miner whose claim is discovered, after his death, to be fabulously rich. Even this version raises questions concerning the effects of wealth on M'liss and those around her. However, Harte had written a much longer version of the same story before "The Work on Red Mountain" appeared in print. The longer version, subsequently revised and renamed "M'liss," lacks the economy and easy grace of later tales such as "The Outcasts of Poker Flat," but it is certainly one of the most important stories Harte ever wrote. This dark fable, written when the author was only twenty-four years old, is Harte's prototypical tale of the West. It expresses the wryly bemused attitude that characterizes Harte's realism as a whole; it even roughs out the four roles which Harte would spend the rest of his career refining and rearranging. Its lack of artistic finish only emphasizes the quality that would become Harte's trademark—a sense that the play of surface appearances, fascinating in itself, hides some meaning which can never be known.

Harte later wrote that he regarded American life and literature as essentially comic, and "M'liss" is probably a good example of what he meant by comedy. The northern California setting and its rough-hewn but crafty inhabitants express the raffish, accidental grace he could not help recognizing in both himself and his country. Even more

important, deceit, surprise, and a peculiar but insistent vitality—qualities in which he delighted, but which he surely knew would get him into trouble—characterize the story and govern the conduct of its four basic roles. One role, played by M'liss herself, is that of the youthful innocent. A second, played by a frontier schoolmaster (whose name, appropriately not revealed until the final chapters, is Gray) is that of the ambivalent observer. A third is that of the attractive but mysterious female, portrayed as a "stunner" who may or may not be M'liss's mother, but who shows up at the close to claim the girl as her daughter, invites schoolmaster Gray to be her lover, transforms the settlement, and acquires a gold mine. The fourth role is that of the physical environment, which continues to assert its manifold and unpredictable powers, despite whatever depredations may be performed against it by settlers, speculators, and others. Murder, lust, greed, suicide and madness fill out the plot. The action is more or less continuously commented upon by a polyglot chorus, which includes the hypocritical Reverend Mr. McSnagley, the Morpher family—all of whose children bear names drawn from classical lore—and various miners and townspeople. The focus of "M'liss" is on arresting but inscrutable surfaces.

The story opens with a brief description of Smith's Pocket, a settlement located at the base of Red Mountain and named for "Bummer" Smith—presently the town drunk, but formerly a prospector who discovered a small pocket of gold ore near the present townsite and triggered a flurry of speculation. The town soon flaunted "its two fancy stores, its two hotels, its one express office, and its two first families." More recent additions include "a Methodist church, and hard by a monte bank, and a little beyond, on the mountain side, a graveyard; and then a little schoolhouse." Melissa Smith, Bummer's only offspring, has grown into a preadolescent ragamuffin with a reputation for incorrigibility, but she shows up one evening at the schoolhouse to request that the master admit her as a student. Shortly after she enters the school, proving herself to be intelligent, eccentric, and darkly attractive, her father is found dead on the site of his former claim, presumably a victim of suicide. M'liss is placed as a foster child in the Morpher home, near town, and soon comes to regard herself as a rival of Clytie (Clytemnestra) Morpher, a classmate, for the young schoolmaster's affections. Meanwhile, Aristides Morpher, Clytie's younger brother, discovers that the long abandoned Smith claim is being worked in secret. At about the same time, the schoolmaster begins to suspect that Bummer Smith may have been murdered to keep him from developing the claim. A sinister-looking prospector named Waters also appears, and stories are told at the hotels and express office about his having been seen elsewhere in company with a stunningly beautiful woman. The schoolmaster then learns that Dr. Dusquene, the local physician, has evidence that M'liss has murdered her own father.

Waters is eventually arrested—not for the murder of Smith, but for the murder of the Reverend Mr. McSnagley—and is threatened with lynching, but M'liss, who visits him at the jail on the night of his arrest, bringing him a bottle of brandy, mysteriously frees him, and in the process sets the town on fire. She then discovers that he has gone mad, and he wanders off into the mountains. On the night of McSnagley's murder, the burning of the town and the disappearance of Waters, the schoolmaster visits the Smith claim and discovers that what everyone has supposed to be a pocket is actually a lode, studded with huge nuggets. Although Waters (or someone) has been secretly removing large quantities of ore, incalculable riches remain. The schoolmaster stakes the claim out in M'liss's name and the next evening consults with Judge Plunkett, the town lawyer, about establishing the girl's ownership of the mine. However, a "handsome woman" of undetermined age is already there in Plunkett's parlor, claiming to be M'liss's mother—the estranged but undivorced wife of Bummer Smith's youth. She, rather than M'liss, will presumably be the heiress. She loses no time in staking her claim to young schoolmaster Gray, as well, who finds himself wondering whether she has been an actress. With a "very vivid disclosure of eyes and teeth," she takes his arm and passes into the night.

Only four weeks later, the town is well along toward being rebuilt on a grander scale, as adventurers and developers pour in to take advantage of the newly discovered wealth. M'liss has joined the "handsome woman," who waits in town for the settlement of her claim to the mine. The girl's former boisterousness has been replaced by what seems a guarded stoicism. Schoolmaster Gray has decided to quit his job, gather his small assets of some thirty dollars, and see the world. On the morning of his departure, he first calls on Clytie Morpher, who, still smitten, insists that he accept from her a gift he must promise not to open until his marriage. He then makes his way to the quarters of M'liss and Mrs. Smith, where he kisses M'liss goodbye. As Gray leaves town, Aristides Morpher stops the stagecoach to deliver to him a note from Mrs. Smith informing him that her legal claim to the mine has been confirmed and inviting him to visit her in San Francisco.

There have been two supposed murders—not counting a jailhouse guard killed in the fire M'liss sets as she frees Waters. Neither murder is solved. Further, each of the fable's four roles has written into it a large measure of guilt. M'liss, the youthful innocent, is clearly not innocent at all—or, if she is, her innocence is catastrophic. Whether accidentally or not, she does kill the jailhouse guard and set fire to the town. Strands of her hair are found on the revolver that killed her father. Concerning McSnagley's murder, she tells schoolmaster Gray that the minister "ought to have been killed long ago." She may, indeed, have conspired with Waters and the "handsome woman" in *both* murders—perhaps to acquire the wealth and respectability she felt might make her more attractive to schoolmaster Gray. Gray, in his turn, cannot observe the events of the community without becoming involved with them. He neither quite succumbs to nor quite resists the charms of adoring Clytie Morpher, an "early bloomer." M'liss, with her "great dark eyes," her fierce passions, her secrets and her promise of wealth, attracts him in more complicated ways. The "handsome woman" whose looks he cannot fathom, whose age he cannot guess, and whose identity he can never be sure of, affects him in ways that are more complicated still. It is suggested not only that she has been an actress, but that she is the same "stunner" who has been seen consorting with Waters. She may be mother, murderess, mistress, or redeemer—or she may be all of these. As the nexus of feminine sexuality she is both attractive and inscrutable, traits Harte often gave his female characters. The landscape shares these same traits. On one hand it seems to promise gratification of various kinds—from aesthetic enjoyment to treasure. On the other, it yields disfigurement and misery as shafts are sunk into Red Mountain and prospectors suffer agonies of speculation about the direction of "Smith's lead." The fable seems to demonstrate that all appearances are deceptive, all motives questionable, and all speculations fruitless.

Yet "M'liss" is no tale of irrational horror or psychological breakdown, although Harte had read the works of Edgar Allan Poe, and admired especially "Ligeia"—which contains, in the title character and Lady Rowena, two women who resemble adult versions of M'liss and Clytie Morpher, respectively. It is told with charm, even gaity, a characteristic of Harte's realism. Treating dark subjects in a light manner was a trick of frontier journalism that might, had Harte practiced it in his reports of the Humboldt Bay Indian massacre, have kept him his job on the *Northern Californian*. Harte's fiction had a tone of bantering nonchalance many San Franciscans found attractive, enjoying parodies of their own sentimentalism and chauvinism—as well as their numerous other gaucheries. Harte had a schoolboy's reckless talent for this kind of showing off—but one that was also attached to an adult intelligence. He soon attracted a following of distinguished admirers who involved him in a busy social life. Secession and the outbreak of the Civil War did not diminish his newfound popularity as a regional court jester who often told his jokes without announcing that they were funny, and, just as often, shrouded his oracular pronouncements about history and humanity in a veil of farce or melodrama. He had a knack for stating his clear, ironic vision in prophetic terms.

Harte married Anna Griswold on 11 August 1862, just short of his twenty-sixth birthday. She was four years his senior and had been reared in New York City. When Harte met her, she was living with her married sister in San Francisco. Money was a problem for the newlyweds from the beginning. Harte had left his job as a printer for the *Golden Era* in 1861 and accepted the steadier but less exciting position of a clerk in the Surveyor General's office, where he earned $100 per month. He continued to contribute sketches, essays, and verse to the magazine, and to participate in the city's increasingly active literary community—enlivened, now, by such people as Charles Warren Stoddard, Robert Newell (Orpheus C. Kerr), Albert Bierstadt, Charles Farrar Browne (Artemus Ward), and later, Samuel Clemens (Mark Twain)—but he was continually short of cash. In 1863, just before the birth of his first child, Griswold, he left the Surveyor General's office for a job in the U.S. Mint, which paid considerably more and required little work. In late 1864 he and Clemens became good friends. He also began having his work published in the *Californian*, a magazine started by Charles H. Webb, a former associate editor on the *Golden Era*. He took an active, if mostly informal, editorial role in the new magazine, leading, more or less directly, to his editorship in 1865 (the year his second child, Francis King Harte, was born) of *Outcroppings*, a volume of verse by California authors. Although the volume was not a success, assembling it probably put Harte in the mood for composing the fifteen "Condensed Novels" he published in the *Golden Era* and the *Californian* and then brought out as a book in 1867. These are witty and perceptive parodies of

novelists such as Charles Dickens, Charlotte Brontë, James Fenimore Cooper, and T. S. Arthur, and exhibit Harte's surprising skill as a critic and editor. His big break came the next year, in 1868, when he was appointed editor of the newly established *Overland Monthly*.

Anton Roman, the publisher, started the *Overland Monthly* as a regional magazine with national aspirations. He aimed to capture a large audience by emphasizing a positive and sympathetic approach to interests of California and the Pacific slope. Harte, on the other hand, envisioned a more literary magazine, one with less of a tilt toward the local boosterism Roman advocated. The go-between who brought Roman and Harte together on the project was Charles Warren Stoddard, a mutual friend. The first issue of the magazine, which appeared in July, gave little indication that the uneasy alliance of Harte and Roman would succeed, but the second issue, printed in August, carried "The Luck of Roaring Camp," now Harte's most widely acclaimed work, and a major step in exploring the dark fable he had begun to compose eight years earlier, in 1860. "The Luck of Roaring Camp" surprised everybody, including even the

THE

LUCK OF ROARING CAMP,

AND

OTHER SKETCHES.

BY

FRANCIS BRET HARTE.

BOSTON:
FIELDS, OSGOOD, & CO.
1870.

Title page for the collection that established Harte's popularity

author. At a single stroke, the story fulfilled the *Overland Monthly*'s aspirations for a national audience. It also brought Harte instant fame as a master storyteller. Some San Francisco readers were dubious at first—suspecting, perhaps, that the tale made fun of them—but the *Atlantic Monthly* wrote to Harte from Boston requesting a story like "The Luck of Roaring Camp" for its own pages as soon as possible. Some eastern critics even hailed Harte as an American Dickens, doubtless recalling for the thirty-one-year-old author that Dickens had been his model from the beginning.

"The Luck of Roaring Camp" takes place in 1850-1851 at an isolated mining settlement in the California foothills with the self-explanatory name of Roaring Camp. A prostitute known as Cherokee Sal, the camp's only female, dies in childbirth, much to the grief of the miners. But Sal's infant son survives, presenting the camp with an immediate and pressing problem. An impromptu town meeting is called after Sal's slapdash funeral, and the miners arrive at a consensus: they will contrive to somehow raise the child themselves, rather than sending him elsewhere or bringing in a female nursemaid. The child thrives, suckled on ass's milk. John Oakhurst, a dapper gambler, remarks one day that his birth has "brought 'the luck' to Roaring Camp." The name sticks and is made official at a makeshift christening where a motherly miner named Stumpy announces that "I proclaim you Thomas Luck, according to the laws of the United States and the State of California, so help me God."

Like Cherokee Sal, the miners all bear names that tell something about them—Stumpy and Kentuck, for instance. Tommy thus goes by "The Luck." When the miners bring in a rosewood cradle from Sacramento, they discover that it makes the rest of their furniture—and the rest of the settlement— look crude. They therefore begin a program of general improvement, painting, repairing, and even planting flowers. They wear clean clothes and wash before meals. Profanity and vice are abandoned. The camp no longer roars. As stories about the transformation begin to circulate, mythic elements are added: "They've a street up there in 'Roaring' that would lay over any street in Red Dog. They've got vines and flowers round their houses, and they wash themselves twice a day. But they're mighty rough on strangers, and they worship an Ingin baby." The Luck survives a single "golden summer." The winter of 1851 brings snow to the mountains and torrential rains to the foothills. One night, a flash flood inundates Roaring Camp, and sweeps away the cabin where The Luck is sleeping.

The miner known as Kentuck is found the next morning, barely alive, with The Luck in his arms. Ironically, however, the child is dead, and Kentuck dies as well, proclaiming, "he's a taking me with him. Tell the boys I've got The Luck with me now."

"The Luck of Roaring Camp" is strongly flavored with sentimentalism, but to account thus for its popularity does not do justice to either Harte or his reading public. The story is funny but not laughable, sad but not tearful, palatable but certainly not sweet. That Harte could use sentimentality without succumbing to it is a tribute to his finely calibrated skill. Examining the recurrence in "The Luck of Roaring Camp" of the four roles Harte first identified in "M'liss" shows not so much that he had begun to develop a successful formula for capturing the public imagination as it does that he had discovered a real subject which was worthy of extensive development. The youthful innocent in "The Luck of Roaring Camp" is of course Tommy Luck himself; the female principle is embodied in Cherokee Sal; the physical environment is still the California foothills. However, the ambivalent observer has shifted positions. No longer a character in the story, he has become the narrator who tells the story from the outside. The youthful innocent, the female, and the land are not parts of his direct experience, as they are for schoolmaster Gray in "M'liss," but elements in a story he has heard and which he relates. The difference is subtle but important. The Luck, Cherokee Sal, and Roaring Camp are one step further removed from conventional history than are M'liss, the putative Mrs. Smith, and Smith's Pocket. The story's emphasis is thus shifted away from the events which are said to have happened and toward the processes through which the story is told. The events in "The Luck of Roaring Camp" have relatively little importance, except as they are shown to have become legendary. With "The Luck of Roaring Camp" Harte's dark fable of the West became more fabulous and less historical, which is another way of saying that it came closer to addressing universal themes rather than personal or regional peculiarities. Harte was imprinting the fable with the stamp of his own brand of realism.

"The Outcasts of Poker Flat," published in the *Overland Monthly* for January 1869, some five months after the publication of "The Luck of Roaring Camp," carries forward the development of Harte's realism. Significantly, the mystery of luck again provides a major theme, and even John Oakhurst, the gambler whose comment led to Tommy Luck's naming at Roaring Camp, makes a reappearance. The story opens on the morning of

23 November 1850—late in the fall that preceded Roaring Camp's catastrophic flood. Poker Flat, a more pretentious settlement than nearby Roaring Camp, has "lately suffered the loss of several thousand dollars, two valuable horses, and a prominent citizen." Although Oakhurst has not committed a crime, he is victimized by a local "spasm of virtuous reaction quite as lawless and ungovernable as any of the acts that had provoked it." Also caught in the spasm are three other "outcasts": a young prostitute known as The Duchess, an elder prostitute called Mother Shipton, and a profane drunk called Uncle Billy. The four are escorted to the edge of town and told by a member of the vigilance committee that if they return they will be killed.

Sandy Bar, the nearest settlement that might receive them, is a day's journey off, across a high mountain pass, but The Duchess tires by noon and dismounts, refusing to go any farther. Oakhurst protests that they have no food. Uncle Billy produces whiskey instead, and they make an early camp. Meanwhile, they are joined by a pair of lovers on their way from Sandy Bar to Poker Flat. Young Tom Simson—whom Oakhurst has earlier made a "devoted slave" by returning to him money he lost in a poker game—is known as " 'The Innocent' of Sandy Bar." The former waitress at a temperance restaurant with whom he is eloping to Poker Flat is a "stout, comely damsel of fifteen" named Piney Woods. Tom and Piney, who have a mule laden with provisions, sociably decide to join the camp for the night. Piney, says Tom, can sleep with "Mrs. Oakhurst" (The Duchess) and Mother Shipton in a ruined cabin he has discovered nearby. The lovers, who never think to inquire why Oakhurst and the others happen to be camped on the mountainside without provisions, seem to exert a benign influence on the outcasts—one much like the influence of The Luck on Roaring Camp—but Oakhurst awakens toward morning to find that a blizzard has begun, and that Uncle Billy has stolen the mules and departed for Sandy Bar.

Innocence prevails, even in the face of terrible ill fortune. Oakhurst has hidden the cards and whiskey; The Duchess and Mother Shipton devote themselves to amusing Piney; Tom produces an old accordion. The evening of the second day is spent singing hymns around the blazing fire. The third day is successfully passed by telling stories—chiefly Alexander Pope's translation of the *Iliad* as remembered by Tom, who has read a copy not long before. However, food soon begins to run out, and the camp is increasingly hemmed in by snowdrifts. Late on the tenth night, Mother Shipton quietly dies,

after revealing to Oakhurst that she has been starving herself for the benefit of the others. On the following day, Oakhurst fashions a pair of snowshoes from an old pack saddle left behind by Uncle Billy and instructs Tom to go down the mountain to Poker Flat for help. As Tom and Piney part with a kiss, The Duchess anxiously asks Oakhurst whether he is leaving too. The gambler replies, "as far as the cañon," then suddenly kisses her with a passion that leaves her trembling. That night, the blizzard returns, but Oakhurst does not. Piney and the Duchess gradually weaken, die, and are covered over by the drifting snow, where rescuers later find them clasped in each other's arms. Oakhurst has not deserted—at least not in the manner of Uncle Billy. The rescue party finds him—also buried in the snow—at the edge of the canyon, "pulseless and cold, with a Derringer by his side and a bullet in his heart." Pinned with a bowie knife to the trunk of a pine tree above his body is a deuce of clubs bearing his penciled inscription:

> Beneath This Tree
> Lies the Body
> of
> JOHN OAKHURST,
> Who Struck A Streak of Bad Luck
> On the 23D of November, 1850,
> And
> Handed In His Checks
> On The 7TH December, 1850

Clearly, there are significant differences between "The Outcasts of Poker Flat" and "The Luck of Roaring Camp," even though the two stories run parallel in some ways. The role of youthful innocent is played in the later story by Tom Simson and Piney Woods; that of the female principle is similarly shared by The Duchess and Mother Shipton. However, the role of the physical environment is considerably enlarged, and that of the ambivalent observer is rendered both more diffuse and more self-conscious. Harte's realism tends to focus on relationships between the observer and the landscape.

Harte increased the landscape's importance by reducing its scope in "The Outcasts of Poker Flat." Nearly all the events of the story occur at the outcasts' camp on the mountainside—a severely limited scene in which prospect, refuge, and hazard are mingled: "The spot was singularly wild and impressive. A wooded amphitheatre, surrounded on three sides by precipitous cliffs of naked granite, sloped gently toward the crest of another precipice that overlooked the valley." Described as "the most suitable spot for a camp, had camping been advisable," this locale offers the outcasts shelter from the blizzard. Yet it also traps them in the drifts of snow that eddy into the three-sided amphitheater from the summits of the upper cliffs. Similarly, it insulates them from hostile Poker Flat and also provides them with a clear view of the valley, where—seen from the "remote pinnacle of . . . rocky fastness"—the hypocritical town seems a "pastoral village." Finally, the environment's threat to life and its nurturing of the humane values of courage, wisdom, and love are curiously intertwined, even to the point of being indistinguishable from each other. Tom's recitations of Homer, Oakhurst's discourses on luck, Mother Shipton's sacrificial fasting, and the final embrace of The Duchess and Piney Woods are all direct consequences of the environment. Just as the "virgin breast" of appropriately named Piney Woods finally cradles the head of the "soiled" Duchess in death, the fatal landscape brings out the best in the flawed outcasts before also bringing about their destruction. "The Outcasts of Poker Flat" is Harte's most skillfully staged story—one in which the physical setting contributes importantly to the action.

It may also be his most carefully directed story—one in which a reader's point of view is carefully and effectively controlled. In the first sentence John Oakhurst is stepping into the street of Poker Flat in the morning, "conscious of a change in . . . moral atmosphere since the preceeding night." The last sentence finds him dead beneath his self-composed epitaph, and calls him "at once the strongest and yet the weakest of the outcasts of Poker Flat." Throughout, Oakhurst seems the story's prescient center. While his companions are more or less consistently befuddled, he alone is said to be "aware," to "recognize," to "listen," and "look." When he is resurrected in later stories such as "The Poet of Sierra Flat," or "A Passage in the Life of Mr. John Oakhurst," he seems unrealistic. He is too exotic to be believable save in the spectacular surroundings and among the colorful companions of the outcast camp on the mountain. Although he unquestionably plays the role of ambivalent observer in "The Outcasts of Poker Flat," his bizarre perceptions and insights must be interpreted by an anonymous narrator—the one who glosses the gambler's cryptic epitaph. The paradox framed in this designation deftly sums up the governing mystery of Harte's dark fable of the West: whoever he may be, and wherever he turns his attention, the observer cannot discover any intelligible certainty.

Because the face of the world is truly blank, the most a storyteller can hope for is to beguile his audience with some "new diversion" like Tom Simson's rendition of the *Iliad*—which, of course, is both new and old, another paradox. Harte's realism brings this paradox into view and examines it.

Charles Dickens, who read "The Outcasts of Poker Flat" in England, was deeply moved. But Harte's bleak theory of fiction, and of life, was perilous for Harte as editor of the *Overland Monthly*. Many of those whose manuscripts were rejected thought Harte's manner aloof, overbearing, and arrogant. Anton Roman found his initial plans for the magazine derailed by Harte's abrupt editorial style and by the colorful stories he peopled with attractive but unsavory characters. Both the editorial style and the stories brought attention to San Francisco and the Pacific slope, but not attention of the variety Roman had anticipated. He sold the magazine to John H. Carmany in 1869, before it was quite a year old. Meanwhile, Fields, Osgood and Company of Boston contracted with Harte to publish his early stories as a book which appeared in 1870 as *The Luck of Roaring Camp and Other Sketches*. This was his first (and last) major collection of short fiction. September 1870 saw publication in the *Overland Monthly* of Harte's humorous dialect verse, "Plain Language from Truthful James," which caught on immediately, nearly everywhere. Popularly known as "The Heathen Chinee," this jingling account of how two white frontier card sharks are outwitted at euchre by a wily Chinese adversary was pirated, recited, quoted, dramatized, and set to music until it seemed that everyone in the country knew it by rote. Harte, who disliked the poem, was astonished. He should not have been. Its immediate and unpredictable popularity proved the theory of uncertainty he had advanced in "The Outcasts of Poker Flat."

In January 1871, when Harte announced that he was resigning his post on the *Overland Monthly* and leaving San Francisco for the East, he was one of America's most famous writers, a condition to which he could not very well object, but also one with which he was not prepared to deal wisely. The *Atlantic Monthly* had offered him a lucrative one-year contract, which he soon accepted, just to write stories. Representatives of the *Lakeside Monthly*, a new journal being started at Chicago, pressed him with attractive offers to become the first editor. John Carmany proposed to double his salary if he would stay on with the *Overland Monthly* at San Francisco. Friends and admirers suddenly seemed to surround him, each promising some opportunity

First page of the manuscript for "Captain Jim's Friend"

to which (of course) requirements were attached, and Harte—shy, bookish, and withdrawn, as ever—began almost at once to confuse and dismay his new supporters with the same brusque unpredictability of manner that had earned him the dislike of would-be contributors to the *Overland Monthly*. Negotiations with the *Lakeside Monthly* abruptly broke down when he failed to show up at a lavish luncheon in Chicago where the journal's publishers had planned to present him with a $14,000 bonus in advance. He was slow in meeting his obligations to the *Atlantic Monthly*, and his contract was not renewed after the first year. When he and his family were houseguests of William Dean Howells in Boston for a week, before moving into a country place called The Willows at Morristown, New Jersey, he affected a totally uncharacteristic breeziness that managed to offend such luminaries as Emerson, Longfellow, Oliver Wendell Holmes, and Richard Henry Dana. Howells remained unflappable, later declaring that Harte was one of the most charming personalities he had ever met.

For whatever reasons, Harte's output for the *Atlantic Monthly* fell considerably below the standard set by his earlier work for the *Golden Era* and the *Overland Monthly*. Late in 1872, chronic money problems forced him to embark on a lecture tour that took him down the eastern seaboard to Washington, across the American Midwest, and into Canada. Predictably, he found the experience exhausting, depressing, and less rewarding than he had hoped, but he undertook a similar tour the following year, in the fall and winter of 1873-1874, this time into the American South. Collections of his poems and sketches now appeared often, but were not distinguished. Between the two lecture tours, he began his first novel, *Gabriel Conroy*, which would be published as a book in 1876, after serialization in *Scribner's* magazine. In many ways, this curious work resembles an expanded version of "M'liss," complete with innocence, sex, violence, and the promise of vast wealth, but it is "M'liss" rehashed and warmed over, lacking the vitality and precision that characterized Harte's earlier explorations of his fable of the West in tales such as "The Luck of Roaring Camp" and "The Outcasts of Poker Flat." Criticism of the novel was mostly unfavorable, and—even though it sold moderately well—the royalties were not enough to extricate Harte from his financial difficulties. What had been hailed as new only seven years earlier, when "The Luck of Roaring Camp" appeared in the *Overland Monthly*, had become old hat.

Yet Harte, far from old at the age of forty, and, with a family to support, could not afford to stop writing. He had fathered two more children—Jessamy, born in 1873, and Ethel, born in 1875.

Bret Harte, circa 1890

Since he had been fascinated with the theater since childhood, it was perhaps natural that he should turn to writing plays. *Two Men of Sandy Bar*, his first effort, opened at New York in May 1876 to a mixed, but mostly favorable, audience response. Critics, however, were quick to attack Harte for having the temerity to try palming himself off on the public as a playwright. *Ah Sin*, a second play, written in collaboration with Clemens, opened in July of the following year (1877). Critics were generally somewhat kinder—probably because of Clemens's part in the project—but the play fell short of real success. It also brought to an end the friendship between Clemens and Harte. Neither man ever revealed the cause of the falling out, but it probably had something to do with Harte's cavalier attitudes toward money, women, and society. Ironically, these attitudes were much like the ones Clemens had celebrated in *Roughing It* (1872), but Clemens had become respectable while Harte remained as boyishly irresponsible as ever. Which of the two former friends remained truer to his own vision is problematical, but Clemens kept his place as America's literary spokesman while Harte came to resemble the outcasts he had written about in 1869. The mass culture of the Gilded Age, with its casual morality, its technology, its gaudy, shifting enthusiasms, and its taste for new diversions was closing in on the thoughtful, serious clown who had nearly twenty years before begun to publish his observations in San Francisco's *Golden Era*.

When prospective arrangements for him to coedit a new Washington magazine to be called the *Capitol* broke down in 1878, Harte sought and obtained from the Hayes administration an appointment as U.S. Consul at Crefeld, in Germany. After a brief visit with his family at Morristown he sailed on 28 June never to return to the United States again. Anna Harte, with whom his relationship had been strained for some time, remained in Morristown. Harte would continue to write her letters, and to send money, but he would not see his wife again until she arrived at London, unbidden, in 1898. Meanwhile, he disliked Crefeld, and spent as little time there as he could manage, making trips to Switzerland and England. London, he found, was more hospitable and less fickle than San Francisco or New York. He managed to be transferred to Scotland in April 1880, where he was assigned the consulate at Glasgow, a post he held until 1885 when Grover Cleveland, a Democrat, ordered his dismissal. He circulated freely in literary circles, creating something of a scandal by his relations with Marguerite Van de Veldes, the wife of a Belgian diplomat and the mother of nine children. When he lost his consulship in 1885, he elected to stay in England, where he wrote steadily and voluminously, on a free-lance basis, until his death from cancer of the throat on 5 May 1902.

Harte's career as a writer spans a full forty-two years, but his status as a major American realist depends upon the work he completed before leaving San Francisco in 1871. Harte had not exhausted his subject matter. Most of the stories he wrote in England after 1885 concern deserts and mountains, frontiersmen, and bittersweet human relationships—all much like those in the stories he wrote at San Francisco before 1871. Nor had readers lost interest in him. The audience for his later works, especially in England, was steadier and more affectionate than the American Easterners who had earlier received works like "The Luck of Roaring Camp" with surprised excitement. The problem is in Harte's own reluctance to probe the depths of his vision as Clemens and Howells did. He merely rearranged the parts of his initial vision in different combinations. In *The Crusade of the Excelsior* (1887), for instance, contemporary middle-class Americans stranded in a remote Mexican settlement must deal with frontier conditions resembling those of Poker Flat and Sandy Bar. Similarly, Jack Hamlin, Colonel Starbottle, John Oakhurst, and other characters from the early tales, turn up repeatedly in later works—usually unchanged. While Harte's later works satisfied the tastes of readers who liked knowing what to expect, they neither invite nor bear sustained critical attention.

The early works, however, are quite another matter, because they show—in deft, quick strokes—what Harte's realism is about, and how it works. Here are no siftings and winnowings of fact to find some kernel of precious speculation about "truth." Here are no moralizings, ironic or otherwise. Above all, here are no attempted explanations. Here, rather, is an array of opaque surfaces arranged to show (rather than tell) the relationships among planes of experience—Mother Shipton's obscurely motivated sacrifice of herself, John Oakhurst's ambivalent suicide, Tom Simson's dubious rendition of the *Iliad*. Harte's greatest achievement was not to indicate how communication among such people might be possible, but to demonstrate that it actually occurs. He did so not by establishing and examining philosophical principles, but by building into his works figurations which paralleled the experience of his readers. For Harte's realism—founded so much more thoroughly in the vernacular and the current than that of Clemens, Howells or his other contemporaries—to have remained viable and attractive for as long as it has is itself a delightful and instructive surprise.

Letters:

The Letters of Bret Harte, edited by Geoffrey Harte (Boston & New York: Houghton Mifflin, 1926).

Bibliography:

Joseph Gaer, ed., *Bret Harte: Bibliography and Biographical Data* (1935; New York: Burt Franklin, 1968).

Biographies:

Henry W. Boynton, *Bret Harte* (New York: McClure, Phillips, 1903);

Henry Childs Merwin, *The Life of Bret Harte* (Boston

& New York: Houghton, Mifflin, 1911);

George R. Stewart, Jr., *Bret Harte: Argonaut and Exile* (Boston & New York: Houghton Mifflin, 1931);

Richard O'Connor, *Bret Harte: A Biography* (Boston & Toronto: Little, Brown, 1966).

References:

Linda D. Barnett, *Bret Harte: A Reference Guide* (Boston: G. K. Hall, 1980);

Margaret Duckett, *Mark Twain and Bret Harte* (Norman: University of Oklahoma Press, 1964);

Patrick D. Morrow, *Bret Harte Literary Critic* (Bowling Green, Ohio: Bowling Green University Popular Press, 1979);

Arthur H. Quinn, *American Fiction* (New York: Appleton-Century, 1936);

Franklin Walker, *San Francisco's Literary Frontier* (New York: Knopf, 1934).

John Hay

(8 October 1838-1 July 1905)

George Monteiro
Brown University

SELECTED BOOKS: *Jim Bludso of the Prairie Belle, and Little Breeches* (Boston: Osgood, 1871);

Pike County Ballads and Other Pieces (Boston: Osgood, 1871);

Castilian Days (Boston: Osgood, 1871; revised edition, Boston & New York: Houghton, Mifflin, 1890; revised again, Boston & New York: Houghton, Mifflin, 1903; London: Heinemann, 1903);

The Bread-winners: A Social Study, anonymous (New York: Harper, 1884; London: Warne, 1884);

Poems (Boston & New York: Houghton, Mifflin, 1890);

Abraham Lincoln: A History, by Hay and John G. Nicolay, 10 volumes (New York: Century, 1890);

Addresses of John Hay (New York: Century, 1906);

The Complete Poetical Works of John Hay (Boston & New York: Houghton Mifflin, 1916);

Lincoln and the Civil War in the Diaries and Letters of John Hay, selected with an introduction by Tyler Dennett (New York: Dodd, Mead, 1939);

The Blood Seedling and Other Tales: The Uncollected Fiction of John Hay, edited by George Monteiro (Providence: Cut Flower Press, 1972).

John Hay died in high office. He was at the time, as he had been since 1898, U. S. secretary of state. As Henry Adams declared in *The Education of Henry Adams*, Hay "had solved nearly every old problem of American statesmanship. . . . For the first time in fifteen hundred years a true Roman *pax*

was in sight, and would, if it succeeded, owe its virtues to him." Under Presidents William McKinley and Theodore Roosevelt, Hay had become one of the nation's great heroes. But John Hay had also been a poet and historian of considerable fame. As William Dean Howells wrote in the *North American Review* in the year of Hay's death, "He lived to be recognized as the ablest public man of his time, the inventor of a diplomacy that was sincere, coura-

John Hay

geous and generous, and it has seemed to me, in reviewing what he wrote, that he might have had an equal and a kindred fame in literature." At some point Hay had made a choice of public service over literature. And yet, although he had, intermittently at first and then predominantly, chosen the political life of a public servant, in 1904 Hay's literary fame was handsome enough to have him numbered among the very first seven individuals elected to the American Academy of Arts and Letters, and although Howells also numbered among the first seven, Henry James and Henry Adams did not.

John Milton Hay was born on 8 October 1838 in Salem, Indiana, the fourth child of Dr. Charles Hay and Helen Leonard Hay, who were transplanted New Englanders. Three years later the Hay family, which ultimately included six children, moved to Spunky Point, later called Warsaw, Illinois. Hay was educated in Pittsfield, Illinois, at a private classical school, and later, in 1852-1855, he attended college at Springfield, Illinois. In September 1855, Hay went east, to matriculate at Brown University with advanced standing as a member of the sophomore class. During his stay at Brown (he graduated, in June 1858, the class poet), he distinguished himself as much for his poetry as for his studies, meeting in the course of those years, the poet Sarah Helen Whitman, once Edgar Allan Poe's fiancee. He formed closer friendships with Nora Perry and Hannah Angell, to both of whom he addressed his poet's letters from Warsaw after his departure from Providence. In a letter to Nora Perry, the young poet wrote in October 1858: "In spite of the praise which you continuously lavish upon the West, I must respectfully assert that I find only a dreary waste of heartless materialism, where great and heroic qualities may indeed bully their way up into the glare, but the flowers of existence invariably droop and wither. So in time I shall change. I shall turn from 'the rose and the rainbow' to corner-lots and tax-titles, and a few years will find my eye not rolling in a fine frenzy, but steadily fixed on the pole-star of humanity, $!"

After some floundering, Hay finally decided to read law in his uncle Milton Hay's office in Springfield, Illinois, where he met John G. Nicolay, who was a clerk in the Illinois secretary of state's office. He also became acquainted with the partners in the law firm of Abraham Lincoln and William Herndon, located next door to his uncle's office. In 1860 when Abraham Lincoln won the Republican nomination and ran for president, Hay campaigned for him both personally and through reports to the

Providence Journal and the *Missouri Democrat*. Upon Lincoln's election, he and Nicolay were rewarded with appointments as White House secretaries to the president himself. During his four years in the White House, Hay dispatched his duties with competence, spirit, and intelligence. Despite the pressing duties of assisting a president who was conducting a major civil war, Hay found time to write and have published poetry in periodicals, essays, and at least one patriotic story, "Red, White, and Blue," dealing with the duties of those who would be faithful and responsible to the Union. It was published, fittingly, amid engravings of war scenes and national heroes in *Harper's Weekly* in 1861. Early in 1865, with the end of the war imminent, Hay made plans to change careers. Sporting the recently acquired rank of colonel (by which he would be known, off and on, for the rest of his life), Hay secured a consular post in Europe, serving over the next five years initially as first secretary of the United States legation in Paris (1865-1867), then as charge d' affaires at Vienna (1867-1868), and finally as secretary of the legation at Madrid (1868-1870). During this period he continued to write for American journals. He prepared essays on inevitable topics for the American interested in Europe (such as "Down the Danube") and for an America reaching back into the nexus of parochial and national history ("The Mormon Prophet's Tragedy"). He wrote stories drawing upon his Parisian experiences (such as "Shelby Cabell" and "Kane and Abel") as well as on regional boyhood experiences ("The Foster-Brothers" and "The Blood Seedling"). In the stories set in Paris, Hay emphasizes the early international notion that grave dangers await innocent and not-so-innocent Americans trying to make their way in Paris, while in the midwestern stories he concerns himself, respectively, with the bitter wages of love and miscegenation and the murderous proclivities in the heart of the midwestern farmer (the dark side of the Pike County Golyers in his humorous poems). While still a member of the legation at Madrid, he began to write essays about his experiences there that, after his return to the United States in 1870, would become part of *Castilian Days* (1871), which brought him considerable acclaim.

Calling an end to his consular career in 1870, he decided to accept an offer to write editorials on a daily basis for the *New York Tribune*. In the years he spent with the *Tribune*, he earned the highest praise from the newspaper's senior editor, Horace Greeley, who once called Hay "The best newspaper writer in the United States." Within months of

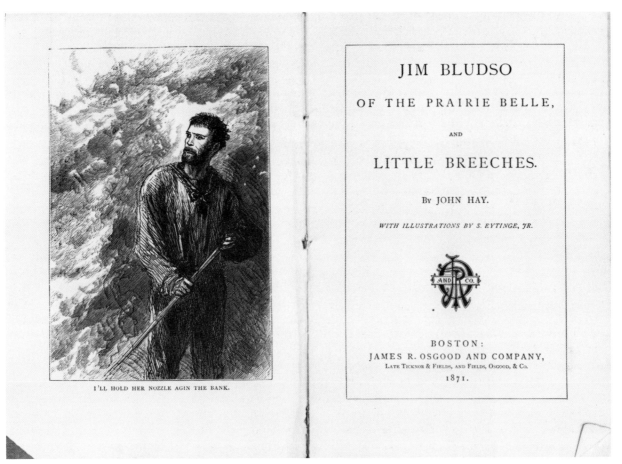

I'LL HOLD HER NOZZLE AGIN THE BANK.

JIM BLUDSO

OF THE PRAIRIE BELLE,

AND

LITTLE BREECHES.

By JOHN HAY.

WITH ILLUSTRATIONS BY S. EYTINGE, JR.

BOSTON:
JAMES R. OSGOOD AND COMPANY,
LATE TICKNOR & FIELDS, AND FIELDS, OSGOOD, & CO.
1871.

Frontispiece and title page for the first of Hay's Pike County ballads, noted for their skillful use of midwestern dialect

joining the *Tribune*, however, Hay had achieved another kind of fame. In the pages of the *Tribune* were published the first of his regional poems, "Little Breeches" (19 November 1870) and "Jim Bludso (of the Prairie Belle)" (5 January 1871). The poems caught on and, like wildfire, spread across the newspapers and journals of the nation.

Dealing with "Western" subjects and adopting the regional dialect of Pike County, the success of these poems encouraged the writing of others, "Banty Tim" and "The Mystery of Gilgal." Their success also made it possible for Hay to establish himself as a poet with the publication of *Pike County Ballads and Other Pieces* (1871), including 16 pages of the ballads and 137 pages of the other kinds of poetry Hay had been writing since his university days.

On 4 February 1874, he married Clara Louise Stone, the daughter of the wealthy Amasa Stone of Cleveland, Ohio. In less than seventeen months, Hay had resigned from the *Tribune* and removed himself to Cleveland to participate in Amasa Stone's financial affairs. He also assumed an active role in Ohio politics, a role that in 1879 resulted in his appointment as assistant secretary of state by President Rutherford B. Hayes. He served until March 1881, when he agreed to return to New York to edit the *Tribune* for six months while his friend Whitelaw Reid honeymooned in Europe.

Hay's public literary career between the end of his duty with the *Tribune* in 1875 and his return to the paper in 1881 was hardly auspicious. In 1881-1882, however, he wrote anonymous reviews of novels for the *Tribune* (only one, of Henry James's *The Portrait of a Lady*, has been identified for certain) and of several books relating to the Union generals in the Civil War. The latter reviews lead us to Hay's major literary work of this period and of the next decade as well—his researching and writing of the monumental *Abraham Lincoln: A History*, done in collaboration with his friend and former fellow worker in the White House, John G. Nicolay. Announced intermittently over more than a decade, *Abraham Lincoln* was serialized by the *Century* (which paid the authors $50,000) over the period November 1886-February 1890, before appearing in ten volumes in 1890.

But his work on Lincoln was not Hay's only literary work in the 1880s. In August 1883 appeared the first installment of *The Bread-winners*, a

high-school graduate who brazenly challenges her betters. She represented a new type of woman, and John Hay was the first to depict that type in a novel. Something of the author's attitude toward such social self-starters, though, is revealed in his not-so-jocular motto, "Love your neighbor, but be careful of your neighborhood."

The Bread-winners also includes something of a

John G. Nicolay and Hay with President Abraham Lincoln. After Lincoln's assassination, Hay and Nicolay, who had served as the president's secretaries, collaborated on a ten-volume historical biography of Lincoln.

novel that was published anonymously in the *Century* through January 1884 before appearing as a book later that year. An early antilabor novel reflecting the establishment's alarm over the growing threats to the social, political, and economic status quo exemplified in the violent strikes of 1877 and their fallout, *The Bread-winners* is a serious, intelligent work marked by a sprightly, engaged style.

If for no other reason, the book deserves to be read for its portrait of Maud Matchin, the self-made

self-portrait in the character Arthur Farnham, who presents John Hay's own sense of himself as a member of beleaguered society. Like Farnham, when things public began to upset Hay, he would take himself off to Europe. And for two decades that is exactly what Hay did, as he enjoyed his wife's wealth, indulged his hypochondria, and cultivated friends and acquaintances on both sides of the Atlantic. And indeed while he so traveled and rested, he did less and less in the literary line. It is true that the reverent reception of the serialization of *Abraham Lincoln* fostered the publication of a collective volume of his *Poems* (1890).

Yet, with the exception of a handful of poems published in periodicals, there would be no more literature from Hay's pen. That is not to say, however, that his fame as a writer diminished after 1890. On the contrary. Hay's politics, in the 1890s, were entirely national, and, in 1897, he secured the ambassadorial appointment to the Court of St. James. In the course of his spectacularly successful tenure in England, his poems were rediscovered by the English and reprinted in London. Although he would claim that the call back to Washington marked an end to his long-desired peace and equanimity, he agreed to assume the position of secretary of state and arrived in the capital on 1 October 1898. Even had Hay wanted to resume his literary career (he wrote a poem now and then, including a sonnet to Theodore Roosevelt), he no longer had the time, energy, or spirit to do so. Ironically, this period was the time for the fullest recognition of his literary accomplishments.

Hay's literary fame began to wane almost, it seems, from the moment of his death. There were, in 1905, obligatory reprintings in journals of his poems, of the story "The Blood Seedling," and even—though his authorship still had not been publicly acknowledged—of *The Bread-winners*. In 1906 his *Addresses* were published, but collected therein were only the statements of an official known for his tact and his politics (not, it should be noted, the pieces he wrote in the 1870s for the *Tribune* on the Chicago fire or on the down-and-out politics of the 1880s). *Pike County Ballads*, with fine illustrations by N. C. Wyeth, was republished in 1912, and after it had become public knowledge that Hay was its author, there appeared an edition in 1916, with an introduction by Clarence L. Hay, Hay's son, of *The Bread-winners*. These were followed, in 1916, by the publication of Hay's *Complete Poetical Works*. After 1916 very little of his work appeared in print, with the important exception of the appearance in 1939 of *Lincoln and the Civil War in the Diaries and Letters of John Hay*, a selection culled from the material of the 1860s left in manuscript for seven decades.

It may well be, as Howells concluded, that Hay, after the mid-1880s, decided not to turn again to literature, thereby renouncing what was still possible for him, to "be one of our first poets, one of our first novelists, one of our first essayists, as he certainly became one of our first historians." But if

THE BREAD-WINNERS

A Social Study

NEW YORK
HARPER & BROTHERS, FRANKLIN SQUARE
1884

Title page for Hay's only novel, published anonymously

there were lost opportunities, there were accomplishments: the Spanish essays, the realistically detailed short stories (admired by F. L. Pattee), the socioeconomic novel with its brilliant portrait of the "self-made" girl and its hard-line treatment of organized labor, the poems of narrative and statement, the biography of Lincoln, and the letters written by, in the words of Theodore Roosevelt, "The best letter-writer of his age."

Perhaps the way in which John Hay understood his successful life in letters and politics, best expressed in a "distich" he included in *Poems*, offers a way to measure it: "Try not to beat back the current, yet be not drowned in its waters; / Speak with the speech of the world, think with the thoughts of the few."

Periodical Publications:
FICTION:
"Red, White, and Blue," *Harper's Weekly*, 5 (19 October 1861): 666-667;

"Shelby Cabell," *Harper's New Monthly Magazine*, 33 (October 1866): 601-611;

"The Foster-Brothers," *Harper's New Monthly Magazine*, 39 (September 1869): 535-544;

"The Blood Seedling," *Lippincott's Magazine*, 7 (March 1871): 281-293;

"Kane and Abel," *Frank Leslie's Illustrated Newspaper*, 22 April 1871, pp. 85-87; 29 April 1871, pp. 106-107;

" 'The Minstrel.' An Unpublished Story by John Hay," edited by George Monteiro, *Books at Brown*, 25 (1977): 27-42.

NONFICTION:

"The Mormon Prophet's Tragedy," *Atlantic Monthly*, 24 (December 1869): 669-678;

"Down the Danube," *Putnam's Magazine*, new series, 5 (June 1870): 625-635;

"John Hay as Reporter: Special Correspondence on the Great Chicago Fire," edited by Monteiro, *Books at Brown*, 22 (1968): 81-94;

"John Hay and the Union Generals," edited by Monteiro, *Journal of the Illinois State Historical Society*, 69 (February 1976): 46-66.

Letters:

Letters of John Hay and Extracts from Diary, edited by Clara Stone Hay and Henry Adams, 3 volumes (Washington, D.C.: Privately printed, 1908);

A Poet in Exile: Early Letters of John Hay, edited by Caroline Ticknor (Boston & New York: Houghton Mifflin, 1910);

A College Friendship: A Series of Letters from John Hay to Hannah Angell (Boston: Privately printed, 1938);

John Hay-Howells Letters: The Correspondence of John Milton Hay and William Dean Howells 1861-1905, edited by George Monteiro and Brenda Murphy (Boston: Twayne, 1980).

Bibliographies:

The Life and Works of John Hay 1838-1905: A Commemorative Catalogue of the Exhibition Shown at the John Hay Library of Brown University in Honor of the Centennial of his Graduation at the Commencement of 1858 (Providence, R.I.: Brown University Library, 1961);

David E. E. Sloane, "John Hay (1838-1905)," *American Literary Realism 1870-1910*, 3 (Spring 1970): 178-188;

Sloane, "John Hay" [guide to dissertations], *American Literary Realism 1870-1910*, 8 (Summer 1975): 270-271.

Biographies:

William Roscoe Thayer, *The Life and Letters of John Hay* (Boston & New York: Houghton Mifflin, 1915);

Tyler Dennett, *John Hay: From Poetry to Politics* (New York: Dodd, Mead, 1933);

Kenton J. Clymer, *John Hay: The Gentleman as Diplomat* (Ann Arbor: University of Michigan Press, 1975).

References:

Robert L. Gale, *John Hay* (Boston: Twayne, 1978);

William Dean Howells, "John Hay in Literature," *North American Review*, 181 (September 1905): 343-351;

Frederic Cople Jaher, "Industrialism and the American Aristocrat: A Social Study of John Hay and His Novel, *The Bread-winners*," *Journal of the Illinois State Historical Society*, 65 (Spring 1972): 69-93;

Howard I. Kushner and Anne Hummel Sherrill, *John Milton Hay: The Union of Poetry and Politics* (Boston: Twayne, 1977);

George Monteiro, *Henry James and John Hay: The Record of a Friendship* (Providence, R.I.: Brown University Press, 1965);

Monteiro, "John Hay's Short Fiction," *Studies in Short Fiction*, 8 (Fall 1971): 543-552;

Lorenzo Sears, *John Hay: Author and Statesman* (New York: Dodd, Mead, 1914);

David E. E. Sloane, "John Hay's *The Bread-winners* as Literary Realism," *American Literary Realism 1870-1910*, 2 (Fall 1969): 276-279;

Kelly Thurman, *John Hay as a Man of Letters* (Reseda, Cal.: Mojave Books, 1974);

Charles Vandersee, "The Great Literary Mystery of The Gilded Age," *American Literary Realism 1870-1910*, 7 (Summer 1974): 245-272;

Vandersee, Introduction to *The Bread-winners* (New Haven, Conn.: College and University Press, 1973), pp. 7-54;

Sister Saint Ignatius Ward, *The Poetry of John Hay* (Washington, D.C.: Catholic University of America, 1930).

Papers:

The bulk of John Hay's papers are divided between Brown University Libraries, Providence, Rhode Island, and the Library of Congress. There are also significant materials at the Massachusetts Historical Society and the Illinois Historical Society.

Lafcadio Hearn

(27 June 1850 - 26 September 1904)

Michael Kreyling
Tulane University

SELECTED BOOKS: *Stray Leaves from Strange Literature: Stories Reconstructed from the Anvar-isoheili, Baitál, Pachísi, Mahabharata, Pantchatantra, Gulistan, Talmud, Kalewala, Etc.* (Boston: Osgood, 1884; London: Paul, Trench, Trübner, 1889);

Some Chinese Ghosts (Boston: Roberts, 1887);

Chita: A Memory of Last Island (New York: Harper, 1889);

Two Years in the French West Indies (New York: Harper, 1890);

Youma: The Story of a West-Indian Slave (New York: Harper, 1890);

Glimpses of Unfamiliar Japan, 2 volumes (Boston & New York: Houghton, Mifflin, 1894; London: Osgood, McIlvaine, 1894);

"Out of the East": Reveries and Studies in New Japan (Boston & New York: Houghton, Mifflin, 1895; London: Osgood, McIlvaine, 1895);

Kokoro: Hints and Echoes of Japanese Inner Life (Boston & New York: Houghton, Mifflin, 1896; London: Osgood, McIlvaine, 1896);

Gleanings in Buddha–Fields: Studies of Hand and Soul in the Far East (Boston & New York: Houghton, Mifflin, 1897; London: Harper, 1897);

Exotics and Retrospectives (Boston: Little, Brown, 1898; London: Low, 1899);

In Ghostly Japan (Boston: Little, Brown, 1899; London: Low, 1899);

Shadowings (Boston: Little, Brown, 1900; London: Low, 1900);

A Japanese Miscellany (Boston: Little, Brown, 1901; London: Low, 1901);

Kottō: Being Japanese Curios, with Sundry Cobwebs (New York & London: Macmillan, 1902);

Kwaidan: Stories and Studies of Strange Things (Boston & New York: Houghton, Mifflin, 1904; London: Kegan Paul, 1904);

Japan. An Attempt at Interpretation (New York & London: Macmillan, 1904);

The Romance of the Milky Way and Other Studies & Stories (Boston & New York: Houghton Mifflin, 1905; London: Constable, 1905);

Leaves from the Diary of an Impressionist: Early Writings (Boston & New York: Houghton Mifflin, 1911);

Fantastics and Other Fantasies, edited by Charles Woodward Hutson (Boston & New York: Houghton Mifflin, 1914);

Karma, edited by Albert Mordell (New York: Boni & Liveright, 1918; London: Harrap, 1921);

Essays in European and Oriental Literature, edited by Mordell (New York: Dodd, Mead, 1923; London: Heinemann, 1923);

Creole Sketches, edited by Hutson (Boston & New York: Houghton Mifflin, 1924);

An American Miscellany: Articles and Stories, edited by Mordell, 2 volumes (New York: Dodd, Mead, 1924); republished as *Miscellanies: Articles and Stories* (London: Heinemann, 1924);

Occidental Gleanings: Sketches and Essays, edited by

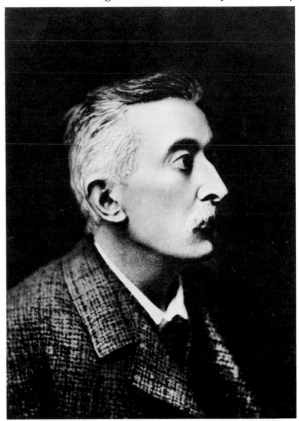

Lafcadio Hearn

Mordell, 2 volumes (New York: Dodd, Mead, 1925; London: Heinemann, 1925);

Editorials, edited by Hutson (Boston & New York: Houghton Mifflin, 1926);

Essays on American Literature, edited by Sanki Ichikawa (Tokyo: Hokuseido Press, 1929);

Barbarous Barbers and Other Stories, edited by Ichiro Nishizaki (Tokyo: Hokuseido Press, 1939);

Buying Christmas Toys and Other Essays, edited by Nishizaki (Tokyo: Hokuseido Press, 1939);

Literary Essays, edited by Nishizaki (Tokyo: Hokuseido Press, 1939);

The New Radiance and Other Scientific Sketches, edited by Nishizaki (Tokyo: Hokuseido Press 1939);

Oriental Articles, edited by Nishizaki (Tokyo: Hokuseido Press, 1939);

The Buddhist Writings of Lafcadio Hearn, edited by Kenneth Rexroth (Santa Barbara: Ross-Erikson, 1977).

COLLECTION: *The Writings of Lafcadio Hearn,* 16 volumes (Boston & New York: Houghton Mifflin, 1922).

Patricio Lafcadio Tessima Carlos Hearn led an exotic and restless life from his birth on an island off the coast of Greece until his death in Japan fifty-four years later. He lived in loneliness in Ireland, England, and France as a child. He spent two years in obscurity in New York City, six years in turmoil and creative growth in Cincinnati, and eight years in sickness, desperation, and the beginnings of literary renown in New Orleans. Then he wandered from Martinique in the West Indies to New York and Philadelphia anxiously striving to keep his literary success from dying out. Finally he journeyed across North America, sailed for Japan, there to spend the last twelve years of his life in the only measure of stability and domestic calm he seems to have found: husband and father, professor of literature, and interpreter of Japanese culture for the Occidental audience he had fled. Even in Japan, however, Hearn wandered: from one university post to another, from one house to another.

He tried newspaper reporting, satires and opinion columns, a cookbook (perhaps part of an ill-starred venture as partner in a New Orleans eatery), and collected Creole proverbs in dialect for a little book he titled *"Gombo Zhèbes"* (1885). His translations of Théophile Gautier and Anatole France are still respected after nearly a century. He wrote travel literature, fiction, and essays on literary criticism and literary history to be used by his Japanese students. And, in his last years in Japan,

his retellings in English of Japanese folktales became more than simple translations. Such works as *Kokoro* (1896) and *Kwaidan* (1904), which has had thirty editions, are treasured by the Japanese because they retrieve a medieval past that was quickly being lost at the turn of the twentieth century. Hearn's *Japan. An Attempt at Interpretation* (1904) is a significant attempt to introduce the Orient to Western audiences in the years when Ernest Fenellosa and Ezra Pound were attempting the same thing on a more scholarly level.

Restlessness and a taste for the exotic were bred into Hearn. His father was an Anglo-Irish surgeon-major, Charles Bush Hearn, who bore, according to family legend, the blood of gypsies in his veins. His mother, Rosa Tessima, was an exotic Ionian beauty, who had never seen the world beyond her island. From mother and father Hearn inherited a past that would be difficult for any imaginative youth to ignore.

Hearn's early life left him with more than the parental heritage to reinforce his leanings toward exoticism and restlessness. When he was two years old, his father was ordered to the West Indies. The elder Hearn, in true gypsy fashion, did not hesitate to go—but without his wife and two sons, whom he dispatched to his aunt in Dublin. The dreary Irish climate, and the news that her husband had taken another "wife" in the West Indies, soon exhausted Hearn's mother physically and emotionally. In 1857 a cousin came to rescue her, and she fled with him back to Greece. After she and Dr. Hearn were divorced, Lafcadio's mother and her rescuer were eventually married.

Lafcadio and his brother were left with their great-aunt Sarah Brenane, a stern Catholic convert who sent Lafcadio to Jesuit schools. Hearn found no comfort in the hands of the Society of Jesus. He developed theories of a pantheistic divinity to confound the orthodox religious dogma the Jesuits tried to teach him. As if theological and familial upheavals were not enough, Hearn, at the age of thirteen, suffered an injury to his left eye. The eye, improperly treated, atrophied and developed an ugly milky film. Hearn's right eye enlarged to compensate for the loss of sight in the left. Reading, Hearn's lifelong passion, became for him a race against blindness. His frequently fierce opinions about literature can be traced at least partially to his conviction that the pleasure of literature had been minutely rationed to him.

The vision in his good eye, moreover, was far from perfect and did not grow any stronger from his habit of reading for hours in poor light. At least one biographer, Edward Larocque Tinker, has wondered if the strained vision of the "good" eye were not responsible for the impressionistic colors and lights that mark Hearn's prose style. To place such a burden as this on a single event in any writer's life is risky, but Hearn seems to have cultivated a fetish about his eye.

He became morbidly sensitive about his appearance, developed a tremendous shyness, affected wide-brimmed hats to conceal the left side of his face, and never allowed himself to be sketched or photographed from that side. He was thus convinced early in his life that his physical appearance had become freakish and accordingly felt most comfortable on the fringes of polite society. In his own cartoons of himself, in letters, in conversations and social situations reported by those who knew him, Hearn seems to have consistently called attention to his extraordinary appearance.

After Jesuit schools in England, Hearn, in his later teens, was sent to Rouen, France, to the school that one of his future literary idols, Maupassant, was to enter a year later. But Hearn did not remain to meet Maupassant. Before his first year at Rouen was completed, he had decamped for the more exotic life of the Parisian Latin Quarter. When his great-aunt learned of the defection, she stopped his allowance and, to purge the wanderlust from young Hearn's soul, she sent him to live with a former parlor maid of hers. Hearn lived only a short time in this dreary household near the London docks. He left when his great-aunt's wealth, on which he more or less depended, was lost through unwise investments. Hearn blamed the Jesuits for the wreck of his fortunes, for the old woman's major friend and counsellor was a Jesuit. There was only enough money left to purchase for Hearn a one-way ticket to Cincinnati where there were relatives willing to take him in. In 1869, at the age of nineteen, Hearn left Europe forever, on his way to Ohio via New York.

For the first two years of his American sojourn, 1869-1871, Hearn lived in New York City. Not much is known of what he did or how he survived. He was frail and small and was soon convinced that his blood was too thin for Northern climates. His biographers believe that he found work with a typesetter where his passion for accuracy in spelling and punctuation could be used. In two years Hearn tired of the big city and resumed the interrupted journey to Cincinnati.

Because of his accurate note taking, spelling, and punctuation, Hearn found work as a reporter for the *Cincinnati Enquirer*. He was too shy to inter-

view anyone, but at recording meetings and the scenes of crimes, brawls, and riots he was superb. He soon made friends with the artist Henry Farney, with whom he started *Ye Giglampz*, a journal of satire, parodies, and witty debunking of bourgeois pieties. The title of the journal testifies to Hearn's willingness to make fun of his appearance, for Farney came up with the title because Hearn's large

Vol. 1, No. 1 of Ye Giglampz, *the satirical journal Hearn edited*

right eye, amplified by a monocle, reminded him of a carriage lamp. *Ye Giglampz* survived for only a few months, but it afforded Hearn an outlet for expressing his growing interest in art and literature.

Another Cincinnati friend was E. H. Krehbiel, with whom Hearn prowled the city in search of lurid and interesting "news" items. Krehbiel, a music critic and scholarly authority on exotic musical instruments, seems to have possessed more patience and indulgence of Hearn's temperament than other friends. A few years later in New Orleans, for example, Hearn's friendship with George Washington Cable would cool over Hearn's use of the story of the great hurricane at L'Isle Dernier (Last

Island) as the basis for *Chita* (1889), his first novel. Cable, from whom Hearn had first heard the story of the storm, had planned to use it himself.

Hearn's name as a journalist was made by a piece he wrote for the *Enquirer* about a grisly murder and dismemberment known as the Tan-Yard Case. Hearn recreated so vividly the mind of the murderer as he perpetrated the deed that the *Enquirer's* readers were horrified and could hardly wait for more. Hearn obliged with stories about exhumation, city riots, hunters who froze to death while adrift on a skiff in the Ohio River. Once he had himself hoisted to the top of the steeple of St. Peter-in-Chains cathedral so that he could recreate the sensations for his readers.

After six years of newspaper work in Cincinnati, Hearn became restless for something more exotic. He proposed to his editors that he be sent to New Orleans to report on the electoral recount in the disputed Tilden-Hayes election of 1876. He never wrote a word of political news, but instead sent back impressionistic travel pieces about the most exotic city in America. Several years later, in 1883, he was to write of his first sighting of New Orleans that coming from "gray northwestern mists into the tepid and orange-scented air of the South, my impressions of the city drowsing under the violet and gold of a November morning, were oddly connected with memories of [George Washington Cable's] 'Jean-ah Poquelin.' That strange little tale had appeared previously in the *Century*; and its exotic picturesqueness had considerably influenced my anticipations of the Southern metropolis, and prepared me to idealize everything peculiar and semi-tropical that I might see." Hearn sent pieces in this vein until his *Enquirer* editors stopped his salary. Then he wandered around New Orleans, contracted fevers, contemplated suicide, came close to starvation, worshipped the exotic women he met in the brothels of the Vieux Carré, and stored up a myriad of impressions. After nearly a year of this desperate living Hearn found a job on a fledgling newspaper, the *New Orleans Item*. He became columnist, cartoonist, book reviewer, and, because of his excellent knowledge of French, compiler of news from the French-language weeklies that came into his New Orleans office from the surrounding parishes.

Hearn haunted the French Quarter every day after his eye could no longer take the strain of translating and proofreading. He became a member of the fringe, counting among his friends the ladies of several brothels, a 300-pound muscleman-for-hire who had committed at least one murder, a bookseller by the name of Armand Hawkins who was rumored to sleep in his beaver stovepipe hat, and the reputed voodoo priestess Marie Laveau.

Hearn also discovered the people and scenes that George Washington Cable was writing about, and soon met Cable himself. Through Cable Hearn moved into polite literary circles and came to the attention of national editors. In 1882 Cable arranged with his *Century* magazine connections for Hearn to write "The Scenes of Cable's Romances," in which Hearn tours the settings of several of the stories in *Old Creole Days* (1879), commenting on the criminal neglect of old architecture. Hearn became one of Cable's staunchest defenders when Creole New Orleans buzzed with anger over *The Grandissimes* (1880). And he continued to review Cable's work favorably, albeit with growing disapproval of Cable's themes of social reform. Hearn had found in Cable a fellow artist who, he thought, shared his tastes for the finer points of European realism. Cable's direct or polemical comments upon prevailing social and economic conditions and their causes struck Hearn as beneath the talent of the genuine realistic artist. For Hearn the true realist was concerned with the forms and processes of perception; he ought to have no time for preconceived notions of experience.

At this juncture in his career Hearn's own literary tastes came into focus. He became fundamentally a creator of atmosphere, mood, feeling. His early work on newspapers had drawn him in this direction, for he selected detail for its evocative or sensory power, not for its fixed place in a narrative. To Hearn, New Orleans—with its polyglot denizens, sounds, aromas, sights—was a carnival of sensations and moods. In his own writing he tried to evoke this sense of New Orleans. As Cable gradually departed from his exotic treatment of the city, Hearn took up the cause. For Hearn realism in art was a matter closely linked with perception of the world. It had less to do with what Howells would have termed the average and more to do with the above average perceiver.

Hearn's literary heroes were the mid-century French romantics; he was one of the few Americans with sufficient knowledge of French language and literature to translate the works of Loti, Maupassant, and Gautier. Hearn's readers in New Orleans were among the few Americans even to hear about these writers, for he supplied them with translations in the pages of the *Item* and *Times-Democrat*.

The attention of Henry Mills Alden and *Harper's* magazine provided Hearn with the opportunity, in the middle 1880s, to have his impressionistic evocations of New Orleans published in a national journal. Although the vogue for Southern literature, local color, and the picturesque gave Hearn his chance to be read by a national audience, he was not really a Southern local-color writer. For Hearn *south* meant south of the equator; the division between North and South was for him not political but mythic and was rooted in his memory of the opposites brought together in the marriage of his parents. Hearn possessed a global imagination, and American literature often struck him as parochial. Howells, for instance, bored him; in a column headed "Sins of Genius" (6 July 1886) Hearn pilloried Howells, the leading proponent of the American realistic movement, as a man whose "philosophy seems to be that of a schoolboy, and his power of criticism limited to Sunday-school standards." Howellsian realism Hearn saw as neo-Puritanism, and it was not long before Hearn found himself at odds with the critics who upheld Howellsian values in literature and in life.

Chita (1889) was to be the work that would make Hearn's mark among American writers. Into it he poured research, care, and all the creative energy he could muster. He had begun work on *Chita* as early as 1884. Sometime before that Cable had told him the story of the great storm of August 1856 that had wiped out Last Island and many of the wealthy Creoles vacationing there. Arlin Turner, in his introduction to the 1969 University of North Carolina Press edition of *Chita*, traces Hearn's research in the files of the *New Orleans Picayune* which carried many accounts of the storm from survivors and from those who went on missions of rescue and burial of the dead. But Hearn went beyond the journalistic novel. He used *Chita* to experiment with his type of evocative romanticism. The early pages are thick with botanical and climatic description as the narrator leads the reader on a tour through the bayous south of the city, toward Last Island in the Gulf of Mexico. Hearn establishes an opposition of mythic proportions between the land and the sea: the sea is devouring the land in their eternal antipathy. Over all he places his pantheistic deity, not personally present but nevertheless indwelling: "There is something unutterable in this bright Gulf-air that compels awe—something vital, something holy, something pantheistic; and reverentially the mind asks itself if what the eye beholds is not the πνεῦμα indeed, the Infinite Breath, the Divine ghost, the Great Blue Soul of the Unknown." In this and in similar passages Hearn strives to transcend the realism of the neo-Puritans

who, he thought, bound American literature to the earth. Later in the novel he says that the individual is but a drop in the "vast and complex Stream of Being." In such philosophical asides Hearn strains for release from traditional Western theories of personality. His movement away from Western philosophical bases was paralleled a few years later by his physical movement to the East.

Chita is, finally, more than a philosophical dissertation. Hearn's ability to accelerate the pace of his prose as the fatal storm approaches, for instance, is proof of his expertise in the craft of writing. His unflinching descriptions of death and decomposition in the sea, and the gruesome scavenging of jewelry from bloated corpses, show that the lessons in horrifyingly realistic prose were well learned. But, in the last analysis, Hearn's powers—evocation of atmosphere, poetic description, the gruesome instant of facing a rotting corpse—are not sufficient to sustain a novel.

The plot of *Chita* depends upon coincidence and contrivance and does not bear too much critical attention. The only survivor of the terrible hurricane that swept the resort hotel into the Gulf is a little girl, called Chita by her rescuers, a Spanish fisherman and his wife. From hints dropped in the text we know that Chita is the daughter of a New Orleans doctor, Julien LaBrierre, who had been in the city when the storm killed his wife and, he thinks, his only daughter. Several years later, when Chita is fifteen and has taken on the physical beauty of her dead mother, LaBrierre comes to treat Chita's foster-father. He also brings yellow fever. His death, described in gruesomely effective detail, does not come before he and Chita exchange looks of mutual recognition.

Chita was a success when it appeared in *Harper's Magazine*. On the strength of it Hearn left New Orleans for New York, where he obtained a commission for some articles on the West Indies. Soon Hearn was adrift in Martinique as he had been in New Orleans. But he was in the genuine tropics, the heart of the "nude, warm, savage, amorous Southern Nature" that he preferred to the vigorous "Germanic North." *Two Years in the French West Indies* (1890), a collection of travel pieces that had appeared in *Harper's* and a novel, *Youma: The Story of a West-Indian Slave* (1890), are the products of his stay in Martinique. This work did not, however, bring him the audience that he desired and needed, and *Youma* did not receive the critical approval that *Chita* had won.

Hearn made Japan his next assignment. Obtaining a loosely defined agreement with *Harper's*,

Note from Hearn expressing his debt to George M. Gould in 1889, while he was writing Karma

Hearn sailed for the Orient. He quickly repudiated the deal with the magazine, and became instead a teacher of Western literature to Japanese students at several schools, rising eventually to the post of professor at the University of Tokyo. He married Setsuko Koizumi in 1891, and they had three sons.

sence. Both setbacks caused the shy and insecure Hearn much anguish. He died of a stroke on 26 September 1904, never completely convinced that he had not been snubbed.

Since his death Hearn has been more revered in Japan than in America. His labors in saving and

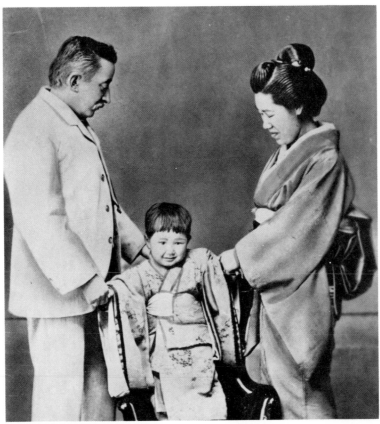

Hearn, his wife, and their son Kazuo

His creative work was devoted to interpreting Japanese folktales and culture for a Western audience. *Kokoro* (1896), *Kottō* (1902), and *Kwaidan* (1904) are but three of his many volumes of Japanese folktales, anecdotes, and contemplations. His teaching produced lectures on English and American literature, published posthumously from transcripts made by his students, and equipped a generation of Japanese students with most of what they knew about literature and ideas in the West.

As happy as he seemed, Hearn was still restless. He and his family wandered from one end of Japan to the other in search of permanent peace. Two years before his death Hearn negotiated for a visiting lectureship at Cornell University, but the offer was withdrawn for reasons that are not clear, and the administration of the University of Tokyo refused to grant Hearn the necessary leave of ab-

retrieving old Japanese tales have come to be highly valued by Japanese who were themselves surprised at how quickly they lost their past to the fast pace of change in the twentieth century. Hearn's books are still used in the teaching of English to Japanese students, and the collection of his works in the Howard-Tilton Memorial Library of Tulane University is frequently visited by Japanese scholars.

In the history of American literature Hearn's place is more difficult to assess. Kenneth Rexroth, introducing *The Buddhist Writings of Lafcadio Hearn* (1977), claims that Hearn was instrumental in bringing Oriental art and philosophy to the attention of American writers of the 1950s. Hearn's translations of French writers such as Gautier, Maupassant, Flaubert, and Anatole France played an important role in introducing this type of European realism to the American audience. His translation of France's *The Crime of Sylvester Bonnard* (1890), for example, has gone through seven editions, one of which has been published by the Modern Library.

In 1891 Hearn became a Japanese citizen and took the name Koizumi Yakumo

Hearn's place in the age of American realism must be that of an outsider of stubborn, if inconsistent, dissent. The world of which Howells was the chief priest and doctor was not Hearn's world, nor did he see the artist's role as Howells did. Yet as early as 1882 he had pronounced romance as a philosophical and fictional form "blasé." For Hearn the artist was one who penetrated the drab world of appearance, who showed the way toward transcendence of the dull and mundane, who could breathe the "Infinite Breath" and share it with the rest of mortal men. In spite of his aims as a man of letters,

Hearn has become identified with the school of Southern local color that surrounds Cable—a minor and flickering light in the group pursuing the picturesque.

Had Hearn remained in America or Europe he might easily have adopted the art-for-art's-sake aesthetic of Walter Pater and Oscar Wilde, for Hearn believed in the artistic object as its own reason for being and fought for style over material or moral usefulness in literature. The theory that art is an instrument for social change was heresy to Hearn. He fought against it passionately all his life. That life was lived on the fringes of major movements and circles, on the brink of influence and renown. In spite of obscurity and defeat, Hearn remained passionately committed to literature and art. For him reading and writing were not merely a living; they were life itself.

Other:

Théophile Gautier, *One of Cleopatra's Nights and Other Fantastic Romances*, translated by Hearn (New York: Worthington, 1882);

La Cuisine Creole. A Collection of Culinary Recipes from Leading Chefs and Noted Creole Housewives, Who Have Made New Orleans Famous for Its Cuisine, compiled by Hearn (New York: Coleman, 1885);

"*Gombo Zhèbes*." *Little Dictionary of Créole Proverbs, Selected from Six Créole Dialects*, compiled and translated by Hearn (New York: Coleman, 1885);

Anatole France, *The Crime of Sylvestre Bonnard*, translated by Hearn (New York: Harper, 1890).

Letters:

Letters from the Raven, Being the Correspondence of Lafcadio Hearn with Henry Watkin, edited by Milton Bronner (New York: Brentano's, 1907; London: Constable, 1908);

The Japanese Letters of Lafcadio Hearn, edited by Elizabeth Bisland (Boston & New York: Houghton Mifflin, 1910; London: Constable, 1911);

Some New Letters and Writings of Lafcadio Hearn, edited by Sanki Ichikawa (Tokyo: Kenkyusha, 1925).

Biography:

Elizabeth Bisland, *The Life and Letters of Lafcadio*

Hearn, 2 volumes (Boston & New York: Houghton, Mifflin, 1906);

Edward Larocque Tinker, *Lafcadio Hearn's American Days* (New York: Dodd, Mead, 1924).

References:

Charles Coleman, "The Recent Movement in Southern Literature," *Harper's Monthly*, 74 (May 1887): 837;

George M. Gould, *Concerning Lafcadio Hearn* (Philadelphia: Jacobs, 1890);

Arthur E. Kunst, *Lafcadio Hearn* (New York: Twayne, 1969);

Elizabeth Stevenson, *Lafcadio Hearn* (New York: Macmillan, 1961);

Beong-cheon Yu, *An Ape of Gods: The Art and Thought of Lafcadio Hearn* (Detroit: Wayne State University Press, 1964).

Robert Herrick
(26 April 1868 - 23 December 1938)

Tom H. Towers
University of Rhode Island

SELECTED BOOKS: *The Man Who Wins: A Novel* (New York: Scribners, 1897);

Literary Love Letters, and Other Stories (New York: Scribners, 1897);

The Gospel of Freedom (New York & London: Macmillan, 1898);

Love's Dilemmas (Chicago: Stone, 1898);

Composition and Rhetoric for Schools, by Herrick and Lindsay Todd Damon (Chicago: Scott, Foresman, 1899; revised, 1902); revised again as *New Composition and Rhetoric for Schools* (Chicago: Scott, Foresman, 1911; revised again, 1922);

The Web of Life (New York & London: Macmillan, 1900; London: Mills & Boon, 1900);

The Real World (New York & London: Macmillan, 1901);

Their Child (New York & London: Macmillan, 1903);

The Common Lot (New York & London: Macmillan, 1904);

The Memoirs of an American Citizen (New York & London: Macmillan, 1905);

The Master of the Inn (New York: Scribners, 1908);

Together (New York & London: Macmillan, 1908);

A Life for a Life (New York: Macmillan, 1910);

The Healer (New York: Macmillan, 1911);

One Woman's Life (New York: Macmillan, 1913; London: Mills & Boon, 1913);

His Great Adventure (New York: Macmillan, 1913; London: Mills & Boon, 1914);

Clark's Field (Boston & New York: Houghton Mifflin, 1914);

The World Decision (Boston & New York: Houghton Mifflin, 1916);

The Conscript Mother (New York: Scribners, 1916; London: Bickers, 1916);

Robert Herrick

Homely Lilla (New York: Harcourt, Brace, 1923);
Waste (New York: Harcourt, Brace, 1924);
Wanderings (New York: Harcourt, Brace, 1925;
　　London: Cape, 1926);
Chimes (New York: Macmillan, 1926);
Little Black Dog (Chicago: Rockwell, 1931);
The End of Desire (New York: Farrar & Rinehart,
　　1932);
Sometime (New York: Farrar & Rinehart, 1933).

Although he is largely forgotten today, Robert Herrick was regarded in the decade before World War I as an important inheritor of the realist tradition and a controversial critic of American materialism. Herrick was one of a number of middle-class, generally "progressive" novelists, frequently midwestern by birth or adoption, whose indictments of American society were more detailed and comprehensive than those of Howells, but whose tentative, usually nostalgic analyses of social and economic causation were overwhelmed in their own time by such writers as Dreiser, and who were later eclipsed by the writers of the 1920's.

Robert Welch Herrick was born in Cambridge, Massachusetts, the fourth of six children and third son of William Augustus and Harriet Peabody Emory Herrick. He was descended through both parents from old, established New England families. Herrick characterized the New England of his childhood as "strenuously intellectual," a culture in which traditional values reflected a "belief that human life meant more than money getting and money spending, that about the poorest claim to respect was that based upon a bank book. . . . It was a spirit that counted not the flesh."

Herrick perceived the progress of his immediate family as a metaphor for the general and calamitous defection from that tradition. Motivated by a desire to rise higher than his rural beginnings, William Herrick undertook the study of law but never managed to establish a truly successful practice, although he made a modest reputation for his academic publications. Herrick's mother, Harriet Peabody Emory Herrick, was driven all her life by the desire for money and status. She constantly berated her husband for what she regarded as his failure. She persistently tried to force her children into ever higher reaches of Cambridge society, enrolling them in private schools. Herrick remembered spending his childhood always in "the worst house in the best neighborhood." He thought of himself as the spiritual heir of his more distant forebears, oppressed by his worldly mother, vic-

timized by more aggressive brothers and sisters, and betrayed by a father too defeated to resist his wife's "squalid" ambitions. Throughout his life, Herrick felt guilty for his father's—and his own—"failure" to live up to Harriet Herrick's expectations, and at the same time experienced recurrent self-contempt for acquiescing, however sporadically, in her materialistic aspirations.

In 1890 Herrick graduated from Harvard, where he had contributed to both the *Monthly* and the *Advocate*, and became editor of the *Monthly* in 1888. He taught writing for three years at MIT, and in 1893 joined the English faculty of the newly founded University of Chicago. On 9 June 1894 he married his first cousin, Harriet Peabody Emory. Of their three children, only one, Philip Abbot Herrick, lived to adulthood.

Like many of his contemporaries, Herrick found in the reckless expansiveness of Chicago the embodiment of a headlong materialism and nagging spiritual malaise that seemed to him symptomatic of what he came to call "the American sickness." Chicago became the setting for most of Herrick's fiction, and the resentment, frustration, and sense of cultural dispossession that informed his own past provided the base for Herrick's understanding of the new America.

Herrick's first three full-length novels, *The Gospel of Freedom* (1898), *The Web of Life* (1900), and *The Real World* (1901), are concerned with characters who, in fundamental ways, resemble Herrick himself. That is, they are all products of a more traditional culture who seek to make their way in a morally disordered modern world. Adela Anthon, the heroine of *The Gospel of Freedom*, inherits a fortune from her father, a pioneer manufacturer, but finds her father's style and values no longer viable. Under the direction of the art critic Simeon Erard (a transparent and vicious rendering of Herrick's Harvard friend Bernard Berenson), she dabbles in the bohemian world of Paris but ultimately rejects that life as a "bloodless, toady existence." She then marries a rising Chicago businessman, hoping to find fulfillment through his pursuit of wealth and power. But she finds his merely plutocratic values equally unsatisfying. At last she renounces both aesthetic and entreprenurial values, divorcing her husband and settling into a life of carefully calculated devotion to private charities—a later version of her father's "gaunt ideal." She has renounced the modern, finding in the traditional the truest means of self-realization.

In *The Web of Life* Herrick attempts to bring the struggle for selfhood into closer relation with the facts of modern life by playing the drama of his hero, Howard Sommers, against such major public events as the destruction by fire of the neoclassic buildings of the 1893 Columbian Exposition, the great rail strike of 1894, and the Spanish-American War. But in the end, the novel turns away from its analysis of contemporary life and offers another traditional, nostalgic solution. Sommers is a young Ohio physician who goes into practice with a fashionable Chicago society doctor. The suffering and violence brought about by the strike persuade him of the moral irrelevance of that life, and he first takes up a slum practice, and then goes into romantic withdrawal from society with Herrick's first rendering of the "new woman," living in what he refers to as a "Greek temple," really an abandoned ticket booth from the fair. The poor of Chicago's West Side reject both Sommers's condescending self-sacrifice and his medicine, and his life with Alves Preston denies him the fulfillment of meaningful social engagement. After Alves commits suicide because she feels she is holding Sommers back from a successful career, Sommers serves a purgative tour in the field hospitals of Cuba and returns at last to marry heiress Louise Hitchcock and take up an established middle-class medical practice. Like Adela Anthon he returns to the traditions of his father and can offer no better solution to the modern problem than the complacent view that "Most people are best off in the struggle for bread." He goes on to explain that a few understand how unsatisfying work for profit is. By renouncing "profits" Sommers has separated the moral and material aspects of traditional striving and has created for himself an insulated, private version of old-fashioned selfhood.

These first two full-length novels are essentially realistic works, particularly in their acceptance of the material society as the locus of reality and in their relatively unadorned objective style and avoidance of labored symbolism and melodramatic plotting. *The Real World* is the first of what Herrick thought of as his "idealistic" works. Like his later "idealistic" novels—*A Life for a Life* (1910) and *The Healer* (1911)—*The Real World* resembles Herrick's realist fictions in its preoccupation with individual self-realization but differs from them in its use of often pretentiously symbolic language and allegorical plot. His purpose in all these novels is to tell "the story of a man's inner perception of living," and for him that means shifting the location of "reality" from the social, institutionalized world to the inner world of the hero's consciousness.

Jack Pemberton, the hero of *The Real World*, grows up in a home similar to Herrick's and like the young Herrick is intuitively aware of the moral and spiritual insufficiency of that life. When his father dies, Jack gives up the chance for a place in an uncle's business and removes to a Maine farm where he comes under the influence of romantically benevolent nature. But as restorative as nature is, Jack is also stultified by the meanness of farm labor and village life and is receptive to the seductive advice of a beautiful, social-climbing summer visitor, Elsie Mason, who urges him to go to the city to struggle in "the big rings." He prepares himself at Harvard and takes a place in a large New York law firm. The sordidness of corporate life and the discovery that Elsie is engaged in a series of tawdry adulteries causes him to flee to Iowa where he devotes himself to saving a family-owned railroad from the grasp of speculators who would liquidate the road and ruin the farmers and merchants who are dependent on it. His efforts succeed; he marries an heiress very much like Louise Hitchcock of *The Web of Life* and takes up a life of making "life better and easier for others." Like Adela Anthon and Howard Sommers, Pemberton has retreated from the new America and sought fulfillment in the nostalgic dedication to older values. However, despite its similarity to *The Gospel of Freedom* and *The Web of Life*, *The Real World* is a more unified work than either of them, mainly because Herrick here makes no serious analysis of society. This absence of social analysis obviates the difficulties Herrick encountered earlier in relating such analysis to the asocial romantic progress of his characters. The world's ills are seen here not as systemic, but as merely the consequence of individual greed and sensuality.

The Common Lot (1904), *The Memoirs of an American Citizen* (1905), and *Together* (1908) are generally acknowledged to be Herrick's best and most important novels. Their themes are much the same as those of his first novels, but the protagonists instead of being "tourists from an older America" are unmistakably products of the modern world and its values, and for them there can be no self-realization which is not at the same time a step toward the transformation of the modern world characterized by Chicago. Jackson Hart of *The Common Lot* is an architect, who, unlike Howard Sommers or Jack Pemberton, has no allegiance to any puritan past. He is admittedly and exclusively devoted to the pursuit of money, and when he finds himself disinherited by his wealthy uncle, he sets out to become rich in any way he can—first by designing houses that look like fake chateaus for his society clients, then by becoming a partner to a shady con-

First pages from an early draft of Herrick's first full-length novel, The Gospel of Freedom

for was American like. He amuses her, she never regards him as a possible husband. She forces him down Wilbur's throat. Wilbur gets to like him, has him at their house in the country. Erard runs in London a little. His matter is "cultivate your sensations." His conceit, his boundless faith in himself,— wh. he makes into a faith in others. His belief in the propriety of others supporting him. His apartments in Paris. His first picture.

1. Adela Linthoss sees the picture. First scene in Erard's rooms in Paris. Erard talks to Adela who comes with her mother and uncle Sebastian to see his protégé's work. She brings John Foster Wilbur with her. His remarks. They have dinner together.

2. Why she accepts John Wilbur / Foster. The ennui of a minute in St. Louis. Brother John's wife; brother Harry's eldest child; the fallacy of a studio at home the impossibility of doing anything in Paris. The freedom of marriage.

3. Wilbur begins his life in Chicago. Success as he sees it. Her child. Her sense of bondage. Her inability to read. Erard's Chicago patrons. The sphere of a woman in Chicago. Erard's attentions to Mrs. Wilbur. Scene, vulgar, where Wilbur finds himself in the wrong, and throws Erard out of the house. This completes Erard's control over Mrs. Wilbur's imagination. She makes an arrangement with her husband. Erard

tractor. Hart designs an apartment house to be built by his new partner and, preoccupied by his own greed, blinks at the shoddy materials and irresponsible shortcuts employed by the builder. When the apartment house burns, causing the deaths of dozens of residents, Hart is shocked out of degeneracy and gropes after a morally better life. The answer is to "return to the ranks" and slowly build for himself an "honest" career designing sound, useful buildings and thus literally rebuilding—and symbolically redeeming—Chicago. Jack's eventual self-realization is not a consequence of an easy decision to return to an older and better America. If that America ever existed it is irretrievably lost. Instead he must accept the new and shape a life within it.

Robert Herrick

In the course of the novel, Herrick, through minor characters, explores both Darwinist and Marxist solutions to the predicament of industrial society but rejects them because they fail to take sufficient account of the individual. Herrick places the responsibility for social change upon the moralizing individual will but insists that the individual must accept the irreversibility of history. The new America here has an incontrovertible reality denied in the nostalgia of the first three full-length novels.

The Memoirs of an American Citizen is unique among Herrick's works partly because it is his only

attempt at first-person narrative and partly because Van Harrington is, for all of Herrick's concern with modern materialism, his only businessman protagonist. Narrated by Van, the novel is in many ways a self-told success story. Van arrives penniless in the Chicago of the 1880s. Hard work and an eye for the main chance allow him to rise from grocery clerk to packinghouse operator to railroad owner and at last to a seat in the U. S. Senate. His progress is marked by shady deals, bribes of public officials, betrayals of sometime allies, and stock manipulations—the kinds of things Herrick usually sees as symptomatic of moral and social deterioration. Harrington is, however, even more intimately a part and product of the new America than Jackson Hart. He justifies his acts by explaining that to function in the world one must have the necessary "fingers and toes," and he consoles himself over moralistic attacks from more traditional characters with the knowledge that men like him have built America and made possible the fulfillment of manifest destiny—the belief that man's exploration and development of the American wilderness for his own use were divinely ordained. What is striking in the book is that Van's critics are for the most part feeble and often hypocritical. At the end, in the comfort of the Senate cloakroom, Van contemplates his rise. He is uncontested in his claim that he has at least made "good sausage" and that the world is the better for his efforts. Unlike most of Herrick's novels, *The Memoirs of an American Citizen* ends ambiguously. On the one hand Herrick seems tacitly to accept Van's notion that his acts have been inevitable. On the other, he makes it clear that despite Van's often good intentions, his wholehearted participation in the modern system makes it impossible for him to reform that system or to use it for other than self-perpetuating ends. Van's wealth provides the basis for social and political power, but the system mandates that such power can only be used to gain more money and more power, never to break the hold of materialistic values. The strength of the novel resides in the complexity of Herrick's final vision and in his refraining from his more customary moralizing.

With the possible exceptions of *A Life for a Life* (1910) and *Waste* (1924), *Together* (1908) is the most ambitious of Herrick's works, a conscious effort to render the social panorama he associated with Tolstoy. A partial inventory of topics treated in *Together* would include the rise of the business conglomerate, the intrusion of business into politics, corporate corruption, the development of the Southwest, the Europeanizing of American taste,

Page from the first draft of Herrick's only first-person novel, The Memoirs of an American Citizen

the psychological costs of conspicuous consumption, and a host of issues relating to marriage and the transformation of women's traditional roles. Although the book abounds in subplots and minor characters who dominate the action for many pages, the controlling story is that of John and Isabelle Lane. Herrick begins with their marriage and follows them as John's career takes them to the coal town of Torso, Indiana, to St. Louis, and at last to New York. As John rises from division superintendent to vice-president of the great Atlantic and Pacific railroad, Isabelle is transformed from an idealistic young bride to a "new woman" dedicated to the conspicuous consumption of her husband's growing wealth and to the gratification of her own increasingly depraved appetites. Isabelle's story reaches a climax when her brother, Vickers, is shot and killed as he confronts Isabelle's latest lover. The shock of Vickers's death turns Isabelle away from the false values she has embraced, and under the tutelage of Dr. Renault, a physician whose therapy seems based more on Emersonian notions of self-reliance than on conventional medicine, she renounces the egoism Renault identifies as the curse of the modern age and commits herself to the proposition that "Life is GOOD—all of it—for everyone." Her new faith causes her for the first time genuinely to involve herself in her husband's career, and after he is convicted and fined in a rate-fixing scandal, she can lend him her new strength and support him in their joint effort to begin a new life in the Southwest. But, as in *The Common Lot*, the Lanes' spiritual enlightenment must be worked out in the context of the world as it is. They must reenter "the game of life," not retreat from it in the manner of Howard Sommers. John and Isabelle reach selfhood only after they free themselves from the egoistic isolation that is the public and private "pestilence" of the new America and in mutual self-sacrifice pledge themselves to the ideal of modern pioneers as Lane assumes the management of a struggling railroad in the still developing Southwest. This resolve is depicted as wholly the product of personal will—Renault is really a doctor of the will and preaches that "life is plastic."

Thus in the end Herrick has things both ways. He spends much of the novel analyzing the systemic failures of America but in the end can hold out the promise that the enlightened individual can break the power of the system and through his actions redeem it. Aesthetically *Together* is less impressive than either *The Common Lot* or *The Memoirs of an*

American Citizen. Herrick often cannot control the proliferation of plots and characters. The Renault sections especially are an unassimilated idealistic intrusion on the generally realistic quality of the novel. And the complacency of the ending seems somewhat inconsistent with the vaguely naturalistic sense of a complex determinism that emerges from much of the rest of the book. Despite such weaknesses, however, Herrick often deals perceptively and provocatively with isolated issues, especially sexual ones which he treats with a candor unusual for his times. Furthermore, the "philosophy" of Renault provides some theoretical underpinning for the personal and social "solutions" put forward here and earlier in *The Common Lot*.

After *Together* Herrick's career steadily declined. His next novels, *A Life for a Life* and *The Healer*, are idealistic novels much less successful on all counts than *The Real World*. *A Life for a Life* traces the progress of Hugh Grant through a world dominated by the twin forces of greed and sensuality. Hugh, who is an only slightly revised version of Jack Pemberton, is victim of his own financial ambition and of his sexual appetites. He "breaks the circle" of subjugation only when a great earthquake destroys New York and the society it embodies. The survivors, including Hugh, are thus allowed to start society over again in a primitivistic utopia of shared effort. But Herrick resignedly admits, "When the banks are open and the saloons, THIS will cease." Herrick's bitterness obtrudes at every point, and the novel quickly degenerates into diatribe; characters are seldom more than flimsy masks; and what plot there is is dependent upon such forced events as the climactic but incredible earthquake. The central failure of the novel is perhaps suggested by its subtitle—*An Allegory for Today*.

The Healer is also a weak novel, though somewhat more unified and controlled than *A Life for a Life*. The hero, Eric Holden, derives directly from Renault of *Together*. He is the embodiment of the supreme will of the romantic and literally performs miracles on the patients who flock to his wilderness sanatorium as he revitalizes their dead souls, the real seat of their physical maladies. His spirit and his power are passingly threatened as his fame spreads and he becomes lionized by the enervated plutocrats who flock to him. But he recovers, symbolically liberating himself by burning his hospital, abandons his materialistic wife, and emerges at last to preside over a great research hospital. There is nothing to commend either *A Life for a Life* or *The Healer*. Both suggest an angry and tired author unable or unwilling to do more than assert increasingly despairing and embittered ideas which he does not imaginatively develop.

One Woman's Life (1913) and *Clark's Field* (1914) mark a return to what Herrick thought of as realism, as distinct from what he called "idealism." *One Woman's Life*, in some ways a feminine version of *The Memoirs of an American Citizen*, is in its conception perhaps the simplest and most straightforward of all Herrick's works. Milly Ridge, the heroine, rises from humble origins, impelled by an inarticulate expectation of a somehow grander future for herself. She desires, successively, social status, transcendent love, and career and is made to serve a double allegorical role—as typical American and as representative woman—that denies to her any intrinsic interest. Herrick's obvious intention is to analyze the decline of woman from helpmate to mere consumer, from creative humanity to destructive egoism, and he promises that to understand Millie will also be to understand America. The novel begins engagingly enough but founders at last on its quasi-allegorical characterization and action. It ends without extending any hope or possibility of escape or transcendence for Millie, who like Van Harrington seems inevitably a product and to some extent a victim of the modern world.

Clark's Field is arguably Herrick's best novel, certainly deserving of comparison with *The Common Lot* and *The Memoirs of an American Citizen*. As with *One Woman's Life* the basic story is quite simple. The field of the title is what remains of a once substantial and prosperous farm, steadily encroached upon by the growing industrial suburb of Alton, Massachusetts. For generations the Clarks, owners of the land, have counted on the annexation and development of their land to bring them wealth and status. The Clarks have been corrupted by their dream of eventual and unearned riches, and the family history is one of impossible expectation and increasing irresponsibility. Title at last devolves upon the humble orphan Adelle Clark just when the long anticipated development is finally initiated. The central concern of the novel is Adelle's painful moral education. When she comes of age and into the posssession of what is now an estate valued in the millions, she embarks on a career of hedonistic self-indulgence. But she learns at last that the only truly satisfying life is a spiritual recommitment to the ancestral land. She takes personal charge of her money, and returning to the land, she uses her fortune to implement modernized forms of the first Clarks' careful husbandry. She causes the erection of clean, solid housing in place of the shamble of tenements that has grown up. She oversees the creation of centers for community life and in general enhances both the value of the land and its social productiveness. In some ways this resolution is reminiscent of Jackson Hart's "return to the ranks" or the latter-day "pioneering" of John and Isabelle Lane. However there is no suggestion that Adelle breaks through to romantic selfhood like Hart or that she achieves an equally romantic triumph of the will like the Lanes. For Adelle the problem is how to use her money in a world she cannot escape; more generally the question is how to adapt the materials and uses of irreversible modernism to moral ends. Along with *The Memoirs of an American Citizen*, *Clark's Field* constitutes Herrick's fullest acknowledgment of social and economic reality, and for that reason ranks with *The Memoirs of an American Citizen* as his best and most complex work.

By the time he produced *Clark's Field*, Herrick felt he had reached a dead end. His always troubled marriage had ended in 1913 when his wife, who had recognized an unflattering portrait of herself in Millie Ridge, initiated what became a permanent separation. An intense love affair of several years' duration had been broken off. Herrick had become increasingly impatient with the demands of his academic appointment, and sales of his novels after the very popular *Together* had been disappointing. Under the influence of Robert Morss Lovett, his friend and fellow professor at the University of Chicago, Herrick had become increasingly interested in politics, and the beginning of World War I in Europe provided the opportunity to break from his accustomed life while pursuing his growing involvement in larger public matters. He was hired as a correspondent by the *Chicago Tribune* and began writing on behalf of the allied cause. His initial response to the war was to cast Germany as the representative of modern rationalism and industrialism, and the allies, especially Italy, as defenders of the humanist tradition. Those sentiments were developed in his novella, *The Conscript Mother* (1916), and his journalistic nonfiction volume, *The World Decision* (1916). However, by the time America entered the war, he had begun to see the war as the product of comprehensive cynicism, a view that pervades his postwar fiction.

Herrick returned to novel writing in 1923 with *Homely Lilla*, in its subject matter at least, a return to "the woman question" that helped make *Together* a best-seller. The novel traces the heroine's progress from a Wyoming ranch, through a disastrous middle-class marriage in Chicago, to her emergence as a spiritually independent woman who rejects the influence of society and its values. As it develops the idea of a romantic selfhood at odds with modern society, *Homely Lilla* marks a turning away from the more complex vision of *Clark's Field* toward the themes of Herrick's earliest work.

and ends as a teacher at MIT. Thornton marries, is divorced, takes two mistresses, fathers one child, and adopts another. He lives in Boston, Chicago, Idaho, Mexico, Maine, and Europe. He makes a killing in the stock market and becomes involved in the study of anthropology and the practice of primitive religions. All of his careers and en-

Herrick in his office at Government House, St. Thomas, 1935

All of Herrick's postwar novels are informed by rejection of the present and by escape to versions of romantic isolation. Except for *Waste*, they are the works of a writer who has lost not only his audience, but his own artistic conviction. *Waste* itself is notable only for its comprehensiveness and for its place as a kind of valedictory to Herrick's literary career. Its hero, Jarvis Thornton, is the direct descendant of Jack Pemberton of *The Real World*, and Herrick here reworks the same autobiographical episodes used in the earlier novel. *Waste*, like Herrick's other "big" novels *Together* and *A Life for a Life*, undertakes to chronicle not only the life of its hero, but also America's historical decline from "puritanism" to plutocracy. Thornton thus becomes a participant in or observer of the construction of the Columbian Exposition, Theodore Roosevelt's conservationism, World War I, and the postwar Red scares. He begins as a physicist, becomes an engineer and architect,

thusiasms are strategies intended to overcome the "squalor" of the modern, but at last he is defeated. He perceives that all his aspirations have been merely "poetic illusion" and despairingly concludes that "detachment, poverty, and suffering" constitute the unavoidable human condition. Although he wrote three more novels, Herrick by the mid-1920s had given up any faith that art could bring about America's spiritual redemption or affect either the general, or even the personal, aspects of universal squalor.

For a number of years Herrick, under Lovett's sponsorship, had been writing political pieces, most notably for the *New Republic*, with which Lovett had been associated since 1921, and had become more and more active in reformist politics. In 1935, again through the offices of Lovett, Herrick was appointed by Secretary of the Interior Harold Ickes to be government secretary of the Virgin Islands. He had earlier traveled a good deal in the Caribbean and found its culture a welcome relief from American materialism. At the same time, he took genuine satisfaction in the bureaucratic position that enabled him to create limited but real improvements for the islanders. His letters and occasional articles from these last years suggest that he was able to put behind him the bitterness of the previous twenty years, and he said that his years in government were the happiest of his life. Herrick died in the Virgin Islands on 23 December 1938.

References:

Daniel Aaron, Introduction to *Memoirs of an American Citizen* (Cambridge: Harvard University Press, 1963);

Louis J. Budd, *Robert Herrick* (New York: Twayne, 1971);

Phyllis Franklin, "Robert Herrick's Postwar Literary Theories and *Waste*," *American Literary Realism, 1870-1910*, 11 (1978): 275-283;

William Dean Howells, "The Novels of Robert Herrick," *North American Review*, 189 (June 1909): 812-820;

Alfred Kazin, *On Native Grounds* (New York: Reynal & Hitchcock, 1942);

Kenneth S. Lynn, *The Dream of Success: A Study of the Modern Imagination* (Boston: Atlantic/Little, Brown, 1955), pp. 208-240;

Blake Nevius, *Robert Herrick: The Development of a Novelist* (Berkeley: University of California Press, 1962);

Tom H. Towers, "Self and Society in the Novels of Robert Herrick," *Journal of Popular Culture*, 1 (Fall 1967): 141-157;

Charles Child Walcutt, "Naturalism and Robert Herrick: A Test Case," in *American Literary Naturalism: A Reassessment*, edited by Yoshinobe Hakutani and Lewis Fried (Heidelberg: Winter, 1975), pp. 75-89.

Papers:

Almost all of Herrick's papers, including manuscripts, journals, letters, memoirs, and contemporary reviews, are held by the Division of Archives and Manuscripts, University of Chicago Library, Chicago, Illinois.

E. W. Howe
(3 May 1853-3 October 1937)

Martin Bucco
Colorado State University

BOOKS: *The Story of a Country Town* (Atchison, Kans.: Howe, 1883; London: Cape, 1933);

The Mystery of The Locks (Boston: Osgood, 1885);

A Moonlight Boy (Boston: Ticknor, 1886; London: Trübner, 1886);

A Man Story (Boston: Ticknor, 1889);

An Ante-Mortem Statement (Atchison, Kans.: Globe Publishing, 1891);

The Confession of John Whitlock, Late Preacher of the Gospel (Atchison, Kans.: Globe Publishing, 1891);

Daily Notes of a Trip Around the World (Topeka, Kans.: Crane, 1907);

The Trip to the West Indies (Topeka, Kans.: Crane, 1910);

Country Town Sayings (Topeka, Kans.: Crane, 1911);

Travel Letters from New Zealand, Australia and Africa (Topeka, Kans.: Crane, 1913);

Success Easier than Failure (Topeka, Kans.: Crane, 1917);

The Blessing of Business (Topeka, Kans.: Crane, 1918);

Ventures in Common Sense (Topeka, Kans.: Crane, 1919); republished as *Adventures in Common Sense* (London: Melrose, 1922);

The Anthology of Another Town (New York: Knopf, 1920);

Notes for My Biographer (Girard, Kans.: Haldeman-Julius, 1926);

Sinner Sermons (Girard, Kans.: Haldeman-Julius, 1926);

Preaching from the Audience (Girard, Kans.: Haldeman-Julius, 1926);

Dying like a Gentleman and Other Stories (Girard, Kans.: Haldeman-Julius, 1926);

When a Woman Enjoys Herself and Other Tales of a

Small Town (Girard, Kans.: Haldeman-Julius, 1928);

The Covered Wagon and the West (with Other Stories) (Girard, Kans.: Haldeman-Julius, 1928);

Her Fifth Marriage, and Other Stories (Girard, Kans.: Haldeman-Julius, 1928);

Plain People (New York: Dodd, Mead, 1929);

The Indignations of E. W. Howe (Girard, Kans.: Haldeman-Julius, 1933).

E. W. Howe's importance in the development of American realism rests on his first and best book, *The Story of a Country Town* (1883). Howe's autobiographical novel, depicting midwestern drabness and neurotic failure, anticipates the early work of Hamlin Garland (which with the writings of Harold Frederic, Stephen Crane, and Frank Norris paved the way for Theodore Dreiser). S. J. Sackett suggests in his critical study, *E. W. Howe* (1972), that Howe's early lessons in survival and his awareness of Charles Darwin and Emile Zola led him toward determinism. Because eastern publishers initially rejected his manuscript, Howe first printed *The Story of a Country Town* in his *Atchison Globe* newspaper shop. During the 1880s and 1890s Howe, a hardworking country newspaper editor, wrote five more novels, all inferior to the deeply experienced *Story of a Country Town*. Many readers have called it the great American novel, and newspapers all over America quoted Howe's aphorisms from the *Atchison Globe*, which he edited from 1877 to 1910. In "retirement" at his country home, Potato Hill, the crusty editor-novelist published single-handedly his *E. W. Howe's Monthly* (1911-1933), wrote articles and stories for mass-circulation magazines, and compiled many books of perceptive comments on his travels and his commonsense philosophy. During this time, H. L. Mencken and others hailed the aphoristic Atchisonian as the "Country Town Philosopher," the "Kansas Diogenes," and the "Sage of Potato Hill."

Howe's engaging autobiography, *Plain People* (1929), is not always factually reliable. Edgar Watson Howe was born on a farm in Wabash County, Indiana, on a site that later became Treaty, Indiana. According to biographer Calder M. Pickett, three years later Henry and Elizabeth Irwin Howe, with their infant son and two children from Elizabeth's first marriage, trekked west to Fairview, Harrison County, Missouri. Henry and Elizabeth Howe had four more children. Later, E. W. Howe claimed that, from sheer boredom, he learned to read before starting school; he grew up knowing not only unremitting toil but whippings conferred by his

father, a Methodist preacher and abolitionist. After serving briefly in the Civil War, Henry Howe bought a newspaper in the county seat, Bethany, Missouri, where, as a printer on this newspaper, the *Union of States*, young Edgar learned to compose sentences. A fundamental influence on his later writings on religion and marriage was his father's desertion of his family in 1865 to run off with a widowed relative. Economic necessity soon forced Howe to leave his mother in Bethany and go to work as a printer—first in Missouri, Iowa, and Illinois and later in Nebraska, Wyoming, and Utah. Returning to Nebraska in 1870, he found work in Falls City, on the *Nemaha Valley Journal*; here Howe fell in love with Clara Frank (1847-1937), fresh from an eastern boarding school and six years his senior, but he fled west again after a spat with his boss. In Colorado, Howe and a former sidekick, William Dorsey, bought the *Golden Eagle*, but Dorsey's intemperance soon left Howe the sole owner of the newspaper, renamed the *Golden Globe*. Howe returned to Falls City to marry Clara Frank, only to learn on his honeymoon in nearby Atchison, Kansas, that he was not his bride's first lover; embittered, Howe returned to Colorado with his wife, who was to bear him five children. In 1877, soon after the Howes returned to Atchison, their first two children died of diphtheria. On 8 December the first issue of the *Atchison Globe* appeared—the true beginning of Edgar and his half-brother Jim's dream of a newspaper that would prosper. E. W. Howe seized on pithy items, on "the small affairs of humanity not ordinarily noticed by newspapers." Although the *Globe* printed details of scandal and hypocrisy, it generally boosted the region and reflected material progress.

A New Year's visit from his father in 1882 set Howe to brooding on his bleak frontier boyhood. The editor spent night after night writing at the kitchen table, recreating the characters and scenes of his youth and recording his contradictory feelings about marriage and country-town life on the blank pages of a country-store daybook. Toward year's end, he wrote the last paragraph. Howe wrote in his preface: "I do not think a line of it was written while the sun was shining, but in almost every chapter there are recollections of the midnight bell." After a half-dozen eastern publishers rejected his nearly 200,000-word novel, Howe resolved to print 1500 copies at the *Globe*, on a Gordon job press.

"Ours was the prairie district, out West," says the narrator of *The Story of a Country Town*, "where we had gone to grow up with the country." Ned Westlock describes his unhappy childhood in the Missouri farm settlement of Fairview, where his father preaches, and, later, his youth in the nearby country town of Twin Mounds, where he works first as a printer and later as an editor on his father's newspaper. He also details his father's desertion of his wife for another woman, his young Uncle Jo's marriage to Mateel Shepherd from the east, his mother's death, and, finally, Jo's divorce from Mateel, which is followed by Jo's murder of her second husband and his suicide in prison. Jo's murder of Clinton Bragg seems to suggest Ned's symbolic murder of his father, as, on her deathbed, Mateel mistakes Ned for Jo. The two triangles—Ned, his mother, and his father; Jo, his wife and her suitor—pull the realistic first half and the romantic second half of the novel into a strange unity. Most early reviewers praised Howe's realistic depiction of prairie, home, school, church, and local character. Often quoted is the cynical remark of a minor

character who undercuts Jo's early vision of eastern refinement coming to turn the empty west into a cultural garden: "Men who are prosperous, or men who live in elegant houses, do not come west, but it is the unfortunate, the poor, the indigent, the sick— the lower classes, in short—who come here to grow up with the country, having failed to grow up with the country where they came from."

Howe's portrait of general failure was a great success. Samuel Clemens wrote to the young author: "Your style is so simple, sincere, and direct, and at the same time so strong that I think it must have been born to you, not made." William Dean Howells acknowledged the writer's "honesty and nerve in putting squarely before the reader some unpalatable truths about human nature and the Western village." Eastern publishers now sought out the midwestern editor.

Though Clemens and Howells privately warned Howe against rushing once more into print, he resolutely continued his daily newspaper grind and his nightly composition, taking nine months to complete his second narrative, accepted by Osgood and Company of Boston, publishers also of the second edition of *The Story of a Country Town*. *The Mystery of The Locks* (1885) depicts the decaying western river town of Davy's Bend, where Dr. Allan Dorris buys an eerie mansion, the Locks, and in time weds the town's angelic organist. But his murder by the skulking brother of his vengeful former wife cuts short his marital bliss. Howe peppers his story of civic and marital degeneration with antireligious sentiments. The author intended his second novel to be "smoother" than his first, but the action is melodramatic, the dialogue wooden. Windy debates on love and marriage alternate with village shenanigans. An unwieldy omniscient narration replaces *The Story of a Country Town*'s effective first-person narrator, and, despite graphic asides on river-town life, it contributes to this novel's conspicuous falling off from Howe's maiden effort. It received little notice.

Although Howe's depiction of country towns is gloomy, he still believed that people living in small communities had civilization's best values. After spending the summer of 1885 in Europe, Howe started his third novel for his new Boston publisher, Ticknor. Written in five months—at night—*A Moonlight Boy* (1886) is narrated by King Cole, the "moonlight boy" or foundling. Cole tells an implausible tale of his development from raw western youth to sophisticated New Yorker back to reaffirmed westerner. Character, the reader learns, is more important than origin, and the best of both

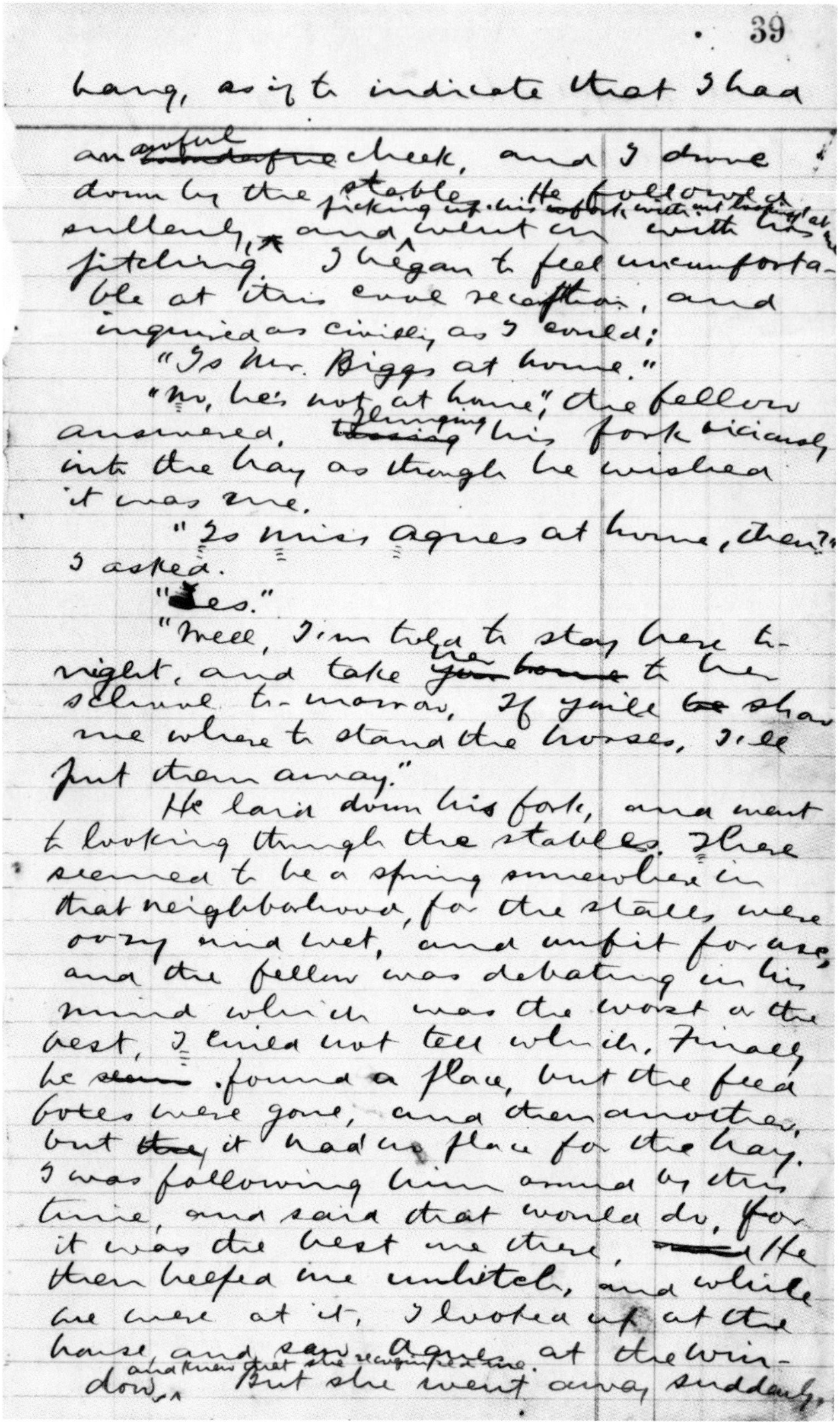

39

hang, as if to indicate that I had an awful cheek, and I drove down by the stable. He followed sullenly, and went on with his pitching, picking up his fork without looking at me. I began to feel uncomfortable at this cool reception, and inquired as civilly as I could:

"Is Mr. Biggs at home."

"No, he's not at home," the fellow answered, flinging his fork viciously into the hay as though he wished it was me.

"Is Miss Agnes at home, then?" I asked.

"Yes."

"Well, I'm told to stay here to-night, and take the to the school to-morrow. If you'll show me where to stand the horses, I'll put them away."

He laid down his fork, and went to looking through the stables. There seemed to be a spring somewhere in that neighborhood, for the stalls were oozy and wet, and unfit for use, and the fellow was debating in his mind which was the worst or the best, I could not tell which. Finally he found a place, but the feed boxes were gone, and then another, but it had no place for the hay. I was following him around by this time, and said that would do, for it was the best one there. He then helped me unhitch, and while we were at it, I looked up at the house, and saw Agnes at the window, and knew that she recognized me. But she went away suddenly,

Pages of the manuscript for The Story of a Country Town

40

and I expected her down to greet me.

She didn't come, however, and I began to feel very uncomfortable. The man had treated me rudely enough, but I had expected that he would be ashamed of it, repent when he found that I was a friend of Agnes from Fairview, and even pictured his regrets when he saw Agnes run down to welcome me. But she didn't come, and kept away from the window, and I was uncertain whether to go home or seek lodging for the night at another house. In the meantime I noticed that the fellow helping me was a giant in stature, and that he had a very little head, on which perched a hat evidently bought for one of the children, of a brindle color, and the band and shape being fine, it looked very much like the letter A upside down.

"I suppose you are the preacher's boy," he said, finally, as though that were a very good reason why he should dislike me.

I answered that I was, wondering what he intended to do about it.

"I have heard of you. Frequent," he went on, apparently better humored. "I live here. I am the hired man. My name is Casebolt, Ben Casebolt they calls me. She owns the farm, but Biggs here one in a long while and pretends to own it. I do all the work that's done. Perhaps you think I am not very busy. But I am. There are four hundred acres here, and she

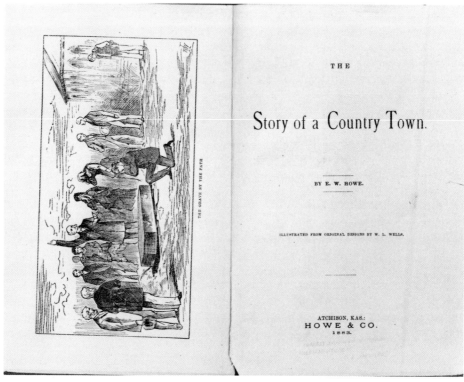

Frontispiece and title page for Howe's first novel. When he could not find a publisher, Howe, who owned the Atchison Globe, *printed the book himself.*

worlds—West and East—shapes King Cole's character. Howe achieved a smoother style in his third novel, but *A Moonlight Boy* is marred by feeble plotting. Still, Hamlin Garland, reviewing the book in the *Boston Transcript*, liked its naturalness and humor.

Howe's fourth novel, *A Man Story* (1889), seems less a novel than an inflated marital anecdote. A traveling salesman, Barnaby, leaves his shrewish city wife; under the name Saulsbury, he marries a saintly country girl. When city wife confronts country wife, the traveling bigamist flees both. Finally, after he falls ill, his second wife nurses him back to health and the first relinquishes her claims. The narrator, Chance Bennington (agent of risk), succeeds in reuniting pigheaded Barnaby and his country wife, whereas Ned Westlock failed to reunite Jo and Mateel. Chance's story is full of artless happenings and Howe's compulsive didacticism on love and marriage, both of which detract from surface realism. A dreary chapter-long letter points to the heavy-handed documentation of Howe's last novels. Garland thought the novel too remote from actual life, and William Allen White saw no connection between the minor characters and the plot.

Among regional newspapermen Howe the editor was becoming a legend; among the literati, however, the country novelist who brooded on problems of marriage and religion did not fare so well. Howe printed his last two novels at the *Globe*. For several years he struggled with the confessional *An Ante-Mortem Statement* (1891). Unable to give his second wife a "second-hand love," the widower Judge Will passes sentence upon himself: "As soon as I complete this statement, I intend to kill myself." Poorly structured, the essayistic narrative boils down to a long series of meditations and precepts on love and wedlock.

The Confession of John Whitlock, Late Preacher of the Gospel (1891), Howe's last novel, is all testimony. Whitlock's confession rests on a paradox: for forty years he had successfully preached a faith in which he himself has no belief. Renouncing his hypocrisy, Whitlock now admits only the reality of reason and the natural world. The confessor's inspired revelations seem at times closer to interior monologue than to realistic documentation. Reviewers rightly dismissed Howe's last novels.

Ironically, in 1901 the moody Howe, by moving into a cottage in his backyard, intentionally gave his wife of thirty-seven years grounds for divorce—desertion. He continued to be luckier in journalism than in love. So popular were his cracker-barrel maxims on women, politics, religion, business, newspapers, and human nature ("The pot of gold is not found at the end of a rainbow, but at the end of a good day's work." "A good scare is worth more to a man than good advice." "If you have sense enough to realize why flies gather around a restaurant, you should be able to appreciate why men run for office.") that five collections appeared between 1917 and 1926. In the 1920s Howe's inconsequential shorter fiction and some of his witty paragraphs appeared in Haldeman-Julius's Little Blue Books. As a globe-trotter in 1905-1906, 1909, 1910, and 1912-1913, he capitalized on his travel reportage by having three collections published by Crane and Company of Topeka. More important, the *Saturday Evening Post* serialized Howe's autobiography, *Plain People*, in 1928, and a year later Dodd, Mead published it as a book. The Sage of Potato Hill died of "partial paralysis and infirmities" in Atchison at age eighty-four.

Extolled in its day, *The Story of a Country Town* received relatively little scholarly attention during the early decades of the twentieth century. In 1930, however, Hamlin Garland, in *Roadside Meetings*, declared his debt to the prairie novelist. Critics have argued over the nature of Howe's realism, but all saw *The Story of a Country Town* as an early "revolt-from-the-village" novel. In the 1960's four new editions of *The Story of a Country Town*, with introductions by well-known scholars, and Calder M. Pickett's biography signaled a small Howe revival. Two surveys of Howe's literary work and several articles on *The Story of a Country Town* have appeared since. Doubtlessly, E. W. Howe's pastoral melodrama, a volatile mix of midwestern verisimilitude and psychological symbolism, will attract further attention and make secure its author's place in any history of American realism and naturalism.

Bibliography:

Clayton L. Eichelberger, "Edgar Watson Howe: Critical Bibliography of Secondary Comment," *American Literary Realism*, 2 (Spring 1969):1-49.

Biography:

Calder M. Pickett, *Ed Howe: Country Town Philosopher* (Lawrence: University of Kansas, 1968).

References:

Virgil Albertini, "Edgar Watson Howe and *The Story of a Country Town*," *Northwest Missouri State University Studies*, 25 (Fall 1975): 19-29;

Sylvia E. Bowman, Introduction to *The Story of a Country Town* (New York: Twayne, 1962);

Percy H. Boynton, "Some Expounders of the Middle Border," *English Journal*, 19 (June 1930): 431-440;

Martin Bucco, *E. W. Howe* (Boise: Boise State University Western Writers Series, 1977);

Eugene A. Howe, "My Father Was the Most Wretchedly Unhappy Man I Ever Knew," *Saturday Evening Post*, 21 (25 October 1941): 25, 44-46, 49;

Russel Lord, "The Indignant Kansan," *Country Home*, 57 (September 1934): 7-9, 30-31;

Charles W. Mayer, "Realizing 'A Whole Order of Things,' " *Western American Literature*, 11 (May 1979): 23-36;

S. J. Sackett, *E. W. Howe* (New York: Twayne, 1972);

C. E. Schorer, "Growing Up With the Country," *Midwest Journal*, 6 (Fall 1954):12-26;

Schorer, "Mark Twain's Criticism of *The Story of a Country Town*,"*American Literature*, 27 (March 1955): 109-112;

Claude M. Simpson, Introduction to *The Story of a Country Town* (Cambridge: Harvard University Press, 1961);

James B. Stronks, "William Dean Howells, Ed Howe, and *The Story of a Country Town*," *American Literature*, 29 (January 1958): 473-478;

Carl Van Doren, Introduction to *The Story of a Country Town* (New York: A. & C. Boni, 1926);

Van Doren, "Prudence Militant," *Century*, 106 (May 1923): 151-156;

John William Ward, Introduction to *The Story of a Country Town* (New York: New American Library, 1964);

Brom Weber, Introduction to *The Story of a Country Town* (New York: Rinehart, 1964);

Brand Whitlock, Introduction to *The Story of a Country Town* (London: Cape, 1933).

Papers:

The University of Kansas has clippings and letters; Indiana University has the Howe-Upton Sinclair correspondence; and the University of Southern California has the Howe-Hamlin Garland correspondence.

William Dean Howells

James Woodress
University of California, Davis

BIRTH: Martin's Ferry, Ohio, 1 March 1837 to William Cooper and Mary Dean Howells.

MARRIAGE: 24 December 1862 to Elinor Gertrude Mead; children: Winifred, John Mead, Mildred.

AWARDS: Honorary M.A., Harvard University, 1867; Litt. D., Yale University, 1901; Litt. D., Oxford University, 1904; Litt. D., Columbia University 1905; Litt. D., Princeton University, 1912; Academy of Arts and Letters Gold Medal for fiction, 1915.

DEATH: New York, New York, 11 May 1920.

SELECTED BOOKS: *Poems of Two Friends*, by Howells and John J. Piatt (Columbus: Follett, Foster, 1860);

Lives and Speeches of Abraham Lincoln and Hannibal Hamlin, life of Lincoln by Howells and life of Hamlin by J. L. Hayes (Columbus: Follett, Foster, 1860);

Venetian Life (London: Trübner, 1866; New York: Hurd & Houghton, 1866; expanded, New York: Hurd & Houghton, 1867; London: Trübner, 1867; expanded again, Boston: Osgood, 1872; revised and expanded again, Boston & New York: Houghton, Mifflin, 1907; London: Constable, 1907);

Italian Journeys (New York: Hurd & Houghton, 1867; London: Low, 1868; enlarged, Boston: Osgood, 1872; revised, London: Heinemann, 1901; Boston & New York: Houghton, Mifflin, 1901);

No Love Lost (New York: Putnam, 1869);

Suburban Sketches (New York: Hurd & Houghton, 1871; London: Low, 1871; enlarged, Boston: Osgood, 1872);

Their Wedding Journey (Boston: Osgood, 1872; Edinburgh: Douglas, 1882);

A Chance Acquaintance (Boston: Osgood, 1873; Edinburgh: Douglas, 1882);

Poems (Boston: Osgood, 1873; enlarged, Boston: Ticknor, 1886);

A Foregone Conclusion (Boston: Osgood, 1874; London: Low, 1874);

Sketch of the Life and Character of Rutherford B. Hayes . . . also a Biographical Sketch of William A. Wheeler (New York: Hurd & Houghton/ Boston: Houghton, 1876);

The Parlor Car. Farce (Boston: Osgood, 1876);

Out of the Question. A Comedy (Boston: Osgood, 1877; Edinburgh: Douglas, 1882);

A Counterfeit Presentment. Comedy (Boston: Osgood, 1877);

The Lady of the Aroostook (Boston: Houghton, Osgood, 1879; Edinburgh: Douglas, 1882);

The Undiscovered Country (Boston: Houghton, Mifflin, 1880; London: Low, 1880);

A Fearful Responsibility and Other Stories (Boston: Osgood, 1881); republished as *A Fearful Responsibility and "Tonelli's Marriage"* (Edinburgh: Douglas, 1882);

Dr. Breen's Practice (Boston: Osgood, 1881; London: Trübner, 1881);

A Modern Instance (1 volume, Boston: Osgood, 1882; 2 volumes, Edinburgh: Douglas, 1882);

William Dean Howells, circa 1865

270

A Woman's Reason (Boston: Osgood, 1883; Edinburgh: Douglas, 1883);

The Register, Farce (Boston: Osgood, 1884);

Three Villages (Boston: Osgood, 1884);

The Elevator, Farce (Boston: Osgood, 1885);

The Rise of Silas Lapham (1 volume, Boston: Ticknor, 1885; 2 volumes, Edinburgh: Douglas, 1894);

Tuscan Cities (Boston: Ticknor, 1886; Edinburgh: Douglas, 1886);

The Garroters, Farce (New York: Harper, 1886; Edinburgh: Douglas, 1887);

Indian Summer (Boston: Ticknor, 1886; Edinburgh: Douglas, 1886;

The Minister's Charge (Edinburgh: Douglas, 1886; Boston: Ticknor, 1887);

Modern Italian Poets (New York: Harper, 1887; Edinburgh: Douglas, 1887);

April Hopes (Edinburgh: Douglas, 1887; New York: Harper, 1888);

A Sea-Change, or Love's Stowaway: A Lyricated Farce (Boston: Ticknor, 1888; London: Trübner, 1888);

Annie Kilburn (Edinburgh: Douglas, 1888; New York: Harper, 1889);

The Mouse-Trap and Other Farces (New York: Harper, 1889; Edinburgh: Douglas, 1897);

A Hazard of New Fortunes (2 volumes, Edinburgh: Douglas, 1889; 1 volume, New York: Harper, 1890);

The Shadow of a Dream (Edinburgh: Douglas, 1890; New York: Harper, 1890);

A Boy's Town (New York: Harper, 1890);

Criticism and Fiction (New York: Harper, 1891; London: Osgood, McIlvaine, 1891);

The Albany Depot (New York: Harper, 1891; Edinburgh: Douglas, 1897);

An Imperative Duty (New York: Harper, 1891; Edinburgh: Douglas, 1891);

Mercy (Edinburgh: Douglas, 1892); republished as *The Quality of Mercy* (New York: Harper, 1892);

A Letter of Introduction, Farce (New York: Harper 1892; Edinburgh: Douglas, 1897);

A Little Swiss Sojourn (New York: Harper, 1892);

Christmas Every Day and Other Stories (New York: Harper, 1893);

The World of Chance (Edinburgh: Douglas, 1893; New York: Harper, 1893);

The Unexpected Guests, A Farce (New York: Harper, 1893; Edinburgh: Douglas, 1897);

My Year in a Log Cabin (New York: Harper, 1893);

Evening Dress, Farce (New York: Harper, 1893; Edinburgh: Douglas, 1893);

The Coast of Bohemia (New York: Harper, 1893; New York & London: Harper, 1899);

A Traveler from Altruria (New York: Harper, 1894; Edinburgh: Douglas, 1894);

My Literary Passions (New York: Harper, 1895);

Stops of Various Quills (New York: Harper, 1895);

The Day of Their Wedding (New York: Harper, 1896); republished in *Idyls in Drab* (Edinburgh: Douglas, 1896);

A Parting and a Meeting (New York: Harper, 1896); republished in *Idyls in Drab*;

Impressions and Experiences (New York: Harper, 1896; Edinburgh: Douglas, 1896);

A Previous Engagement, Comedy (New York: Harper, 1897);

The Landlord at Lion's Head (Edinburgh: Douglas, 1897; New York: Harper, 1897);

An Open-Eyed Conspiracy (New York & London: Harper, 1897; Edinburgh: Douglas, 1897);

Stories of Ohio (New York, Cincinnati & Chicago: American Book Company, 1897);

The Story of a Play (New York & London: Harper, 1898);

Ragged Lady (New York & London: Harper, 1899);

Their Silver Wedding Journey, 2 volumes (New York & London: Harper, 1899);

Bride Roses, A Scene (Boston & New York: Houghton, Mifflin, 1900);

Room Forty-Five, A Farce (Boston & New York: Houghton, Mifflin, 1900);

An Indian Giver, A Comedy (Boston & New York: Houghton, Mifflin, 1900);

The Smoking Car, A Farce (Boston & New York: Houghton, Mifflin, 1900);

Literary Friends and Acquaintance (New York & London: Harper, 1900);

A Pair of Patient Lovers (New York & London: Harper, 1901);

Heroines of Fiction, 2 volumes (New York & London: Harper, 1901);

The Kentons (New York & London: Harper, 1902);

The Flight of Pony Baker (New York & London: Harper, 1902);

Literature and Life (New York & London: Harper, 1902);

Questionable Shapes (New York & London: Harper, 1903);

Letters Home (New York & London: Harper, 1903);

The Son of Royal Langbrith (New York & London: Harper, 1904);

Miss Bellard's Inspiration (New York & London: Harper, 1905);

London Films (New York & London: Harper, 1905);

Certain Delightful English Towns (New York & London: Harper, 1906);

Through the Eye of the Needle (New York & London: Harper, 1907);

Between the Dark and the Daylight (New York: Harper, 1907; London: Harper, 1912);

Fennel and Rue (New York & London: Harper, 1908);

Roman Holidays and Others (New York & London: Harper, 1908);

The Mother and the Father, Dramatic Passages (New York & London: Harper, 1909);

Seven English Cities (New York & London: Harper, 1909);

My Mark Twain (New York & London: Harper, 1910);

Imaginary Interviews (New York & London: Harper, 1910);

Parting Friends, A Farce (New York & London: Harper, 1911);

New Leaf Mills (New York & London: Harper, 1913);

Familiar Spanish Travels (New York & London: Harper, 1913);

The Seen and Unseen at Stratford-On-Avon (New York & London: Harper, 1914);

The Daughter of the Storage and Other Things in Prose and Verse (New York & London: Harper, 1916);

The Leatherwood God (New York: Century, 1916; London: Jenkins, 1917);

Years of My Youth (New York & London: Harper, 1916);

The Vacation of the Kelwyns (New York & London: Harper, 1920);

Mrs. Farrell (New York & London: Harper, 1921);

Prefaces to Contemporaries (1882-1920), edited by George Arms, William M. Gibson, and Frederic C. Marston, Jr. (Gainesville, Fla.: Scholars' Facsimiles & Reprints, 1957);

Criticism and Fiction and Other Essays, edited by Clara Marburg Kirk and Rudolf Kirk (New York: New York University Press, 1959);

The Complete Plays of W. D. Howells, edited by Walter J. Meserve (New York: New York University Press, 1960).

COLLECTION: *A Selected Edition of W. D. Howells*, edited by E. H. Cady, Ronald Gottesman, Don L. Cook, and David Nordloh, 20 volumes (Bloomington: Indiana University Press, 1968-).

William Dean Howells, whose literary career began on the eve of the Civil War and ended after World War I, is one of the three most important American writers of the late nineteenth century. Samuel Clemens and Henry James, both of whom were his close friends, may be said to rank higher in the critical esteem of the 1980s, but Howells in his own day was generally regarded as the leading American man of letters. When the magazine *Literature* in 1899 asked its readers to name the ten writers most worthy to become members of an American Academy, Howells's name headed the list. He later was one of the original seven elected to the American Academy of Arts and Letters when it was founded in 1904, and he served as its president from 1908 until his death twelve years later. In 1912 President William Howard Taft, a fellow Ohioan, who attended Howells's seventy-fifth birthday dinner, remarked: "I have traveled from Washington to New York to do honor to the greatest living American writer and novelist." Howells himself, however, assessed his accomplishments more modestly and once wondered in a letter to Clemens if he would not be remembered chiefly because he had been Clemens's friend.

Though his reputation today is neither as high as it was in 1900 nor as low as it fell in the 1920s, it rests solidly on his undeniable merits as a prolific, versatile, and influential author during half a century of American literary life. He not only wrote forty-three novels and story collections, of which a handful have won a permanent place in American letters, but he also was an important editor, critic, and literary arbiter for two generations. Although he was a self-educated Midwesterner, he slipped effortlessly into the cultural life of literary Boston, where as editor of the *Atlantic Monthly*, he forged a link between the older writers of New England's flowering and his post-Civil War contemporaries. Later, as occupant of the "Editor's Study" and the "Editor's Easy Chair" columns in *Harper's Weekly*, he vigorously promulgated his theories of literary realism and helped shape the course of American literature. He also influenced the taste of a generation of readers by introducing them to little-known foreign authors, and he helped some of the younger generation of writers, such as Hamlin Garland and Stephen Crane, launch their own careers. He wrote a large number of plays in addition to his fiction, some ten travel books, several collections of poetry, several volumes of autobiographies, campaign biographies of two presidents, and about a dozen volumes of literary reminiscence, sketches, and collected essays.

Inevitably, such a vast torrent of writing contained much that was ephemeral, and inevitably its author invited attacks against his commanding position in American letters. Howells had to write steadily throughout his career to make a living in those decades after the Civil War when professional authorship was just becoming possible. Nevertheless, there is integrity, style, and craftsmanship in all his writing, though he rose only sometimes to the highest levels of creative imagination. The denigration of his work in the years after his death is more a commentary on the times and his achievement than an objective appraisal of his career. The battles that he had fought for realism as a young man had long since been won by the time he became an octogenarian and the bete noire of the young Turks.

Howells's chief importance today lies in his leading role as theoretician and practitioner in the movement toward literary realism. Early in his career he committed himself to the cause of realism, which he defined simply as "the truthful treatment of material," and throughout his career he practiced and preached this doctrine. His best works, novels such as *A Modern Instance* (1882), *The Rise of Silas Lapham* (1885), *Indian Summer* (1886), and *A Hazard of New Fortunes* (1889), exemplify his principles and achieve remarkable verisimilitude in their depiction of character and setting. From reading Howells, one gets a real sense of what people thought, felt, and did in the late nineteenth century, for his effects are achieved by a careful attention to ample, accurate detail and reasonable motivations. Let fiction "portray men and women as they are," argued Howells; "Let it leave off painting dolls and working them by springs and wires; . . . let it not put on fine literary airs; let it speak the dialect, the language, that most Americans know."

Howells's realism, however, does not embrace an amoral attitude toward its material, as does naturalism, its later progeny. If the object of a novel is "to charm through a faithful representation of human actions and human passions," wrote Howells, the effect can never be solely an aesthetic experience. "Morality penetrates all things, it is the soul of all things." Beauty clothing false morality will corrupt rather than edify: "We cannot escape from this; we are shut up to it by the very conditions of our being." Thus Howells felt a responsibility toward his readers that twentieth-century novelists seldom feel, but the didacticism in his fiction is always subtle, and one does not close a Howells novel feeling that he has listened to a sermon. Howells has a clear vision of the joys and sorrows, the triumphs and tragedies of life and does not gloss over human imperfections or avoid painful situations.

There is not, however, the tragic vision of a

Dostoevski in his work, for his theories required representation of typical American life. In commenting on *Crime and Punishment*, he wrote that American novelists "concern themselves with the more smiling aspects of life" because "whatever their deserts, very few American novelists have been led out to be shot, or finally exiled to the rigors of a winter at Duluth." In a land where "journeymen carpenters and plumbers strike for four dollars a day," Howells also wrote, "the sum of hunger and cold is comparatively small." But he began to have doubts, and when he edited this statement from an 1886 *Harper's Weekly* column to include it in *Criticism and Fiction* (1891), he added to the opinion that "the wrong from class to class has been almost inappreciable" in the United States the conclusion, "though all this is changing for the worse." His social conscience in the late 1880s was profoundly aroused by economic events and the increasingly sharp confrontations between labor and capital. The result of these events and concomitant reading of Tolstoy was doubt in the fulfillment of the American promise, a darker note in his fiction, and a belief that the salvation of America lay in a kind of Christian socialism.

Howells believed also that the course of literary history was moving toward realism and away from earlier artificial forms. At the beginning of the nineteenth century, Howells said, romanticism had to fight its way free from neoclassicism in order to "widen the bounds of sympathy, to level every barrier against aesthetic freedom." Romanticism exhausted itself in this struggle and it remained for realism to "assert that fidelity to experience and probability of motive are essential conditions of a great imaginative literature."

In addition he thought that for the realist nothing in life is insignificant, nothing unworthy of notice. But one has to point out that Howells was a product of the Victorian Age with its taboos and delicacies, and he neither could nor would treat sex with the candor allowed the twentieth-century novelist. In fact, he believed that since the novel had been developed in the eighteenth century, its morals had improved along with society's so that both were less indecent than they once were. This is not to say that Howells was unaware of man's sexual nature and avoided it. He did not, but one has to read between the lines. What he could not do himself, however, he defended in others if they were serious writers. Emile Zola's novels, for example, he would not let his daughters read, but he defended Zola's art because he saw the Frenchman as a serious moralist.

For Howells there were three ways to represent life in fiction: the novel, the romance, and the romanticistic novel. The novel was the supreme form of fiction and was represented in work like Jane Austen's *Pride and Prejudice* or Tolstoy's *Anna Karenina*. The romance, he thought, dealt with life allegorically, in terms of types and ideals, and Nathaniel Hawthorne's novels represented this kind of art. It should be judged as poems are judged and not by the rules that apply to novels. The romanticistic novel was a form he deplored because its motives were false. It reveled in the extravagant, the extreme, the bizarre and sought effect rather than truth. Charles Dickens and Victor Hugo were practitioners of this kind of novel.

In narrative structure Howells's novels usually take what he called the historical form, which he thought was the greatest way to create fiction. By this form he meant a novel written as if it were history. Here the novelist enters into the lives and minds of his characters. As omniscient narrator, he invents speeches for them, gives them their innermost thoughts and desires, and has their confidence in hours of passion or remorse or even of death. Howells also thought there were two other possible forms for the novel, the first-person narrative point of view, which he believed too narrow in its range and avoided, and the third-person limited, biographical perspective, in which the author's central figure reflects all the facts and feelings involved. This form too he felt was cramping and did not use, though he thought that James was achieving remarkable success with it.

Howells was born in Martin's Ferry, Ohio, and spent all of his boyhood in Ohio. His paternal ancestors were Welsh and his mother's people Pennsylvania German and Irish. His middle name was the maiden name of his mother, Mary Dean. His grandfather Howells had emigrated from Wales when his father was an infant and after moving about restlessly finally had settled in Hamilton, Ohio, gone into the drug and book business, and become an abolitionist. Howells's father was a printer and small-town newspaper editor in Hamilton where the family lived from William Dean's third to twelfth year. These were the happy days of his childhood, which he recounts engagingly in *A Boy's Town* (1890), but they did not last, for William Cooper Howells plunged into debt in an unsuccessful effort to become a daily newspaper publisher in Dayton. Formal schooling ended for Howells when this adventure began, for both William Dean and his older brother Joseph had to work cruel hours on the paper. "Until eleven o'clock I helped put the telegraphic dispatches . . . into type and between four and five o'clock in the morning I was up and carrying papers to our subscribers," Howells recalled in *Years of My Youth* (1916). There was a large family to support, seven children in all, four boys and three girls.

The printing shop became Howells's schoolroom, as it also was for Samuel Clemens in Missouri and had been earlier for Walt Whitman and Benjamin Franklin. As an adult, Howells could remember when he could not read, but he could not remember when he could not set type. By the time he was ten he was a competent typesetter and he did not write his first attempt at literature but first set it in type and printed it off himself. His father was a cultivated man, owned books, and delighted in reading aloud to the family. Howells recalled in *My Literary Passions* (1895) that his home held more books than any other house in town, and while many of the books were devoted to theology (William Cooper Howells was an ardent follower of Swedenborg), there were many volumes of poetry: Lord Byron, Robert Burns, Thomas Moore, Walter Scott, Alexander Pope. But he soon developed an interest in prose and discovered on his own the works of Oliver Goldsmith, Miguel de Cervantes, and Washington Irving. *Don Quixote* became the favorite book of his childhood.

The vicissitudes of the Howells family next took them to the countryside where William Cooper Howells tried to become a miller on the Little Miami River near Xenia. Life in the country was good for the children, but after a year of wasted effort Howells's father became a clerk for the Ohio legislature, and William Dean set type on the *Ohio State Journal*, the paper for which he later became reporter, news editor, and editorial writer. When he was fifteen the family moved again, this time for good, to Ashtabula County between Cleveland and Buffalo, and the elder Howells began publishing the *Sentinel*. William Dean Howells's literary career begins at this time with the appearance of his first known publication, a poem printed in the *Journal* on 23 March 1852. It begins: "Old winter, loose thy hold on us/ And let the Spring come forth," conventional newspaper verse, of course, reflecting the romantic poetry he had absorbed, but not bad for a fifteen-year-old. During the next four years he had more poems published and tried his hand at fiction, using mostly the family paper as his medium, but his real job was as printer.

His move to Columbus in 1857 marks his graduation from the compositor's table to journalism. He lived in the Ohio capital, then a city of

12,000, corresponded with the *Cincinnati Gazette*, wrote for the *Journal*, contributed occasionally to the *Sentinel*, the *Ohio Farmer*, and the *National Era*, and read omnivorously far into the night. He already had taught himself Spanish and now he added German so that he could translate Heinrich Heine, a poet "who dominated me longer than any one author that I have known." His interest in the nineteenth-century romantics, which also included a passion for Henry Wadsworth Longfellow, fueled his impulse to write verse. The result was his first book publication, *Poems of Two Friends* (1860), a collaboration with his friend J. J. Piatt, in which he included thirty-two poems reflecting the influences of his literary idols.

By this time Howells was aspiring to a literary career. As he remembered in *Literary Friends and Acquaintance* (1900), "I was a poet, with no wish to be anything else." He was contributing to the *New York Saturday Press*, a weekly organ of literary bohemia, and in the same year that his book of poems came out James Russell Lowell, editor of the *Atlantic Monthly*, had accepted four of his verses. This was an exciting event for a young man from the provinces where "the literary theories we accepted were New England theories, the criticism we valued was New England criticism." The *Atlantic Monthly* was the authentic voice of Boston, the literary center of New England. But Howells's verse was so derivative of his models that Lowell had kept his first contribution a long time before acknowledging it in order to make sure it was not a translation. Later he told Howells, "You must sweat the Heine out of you as men do mercury."

The chance to make a literary pilgrimage to Boston came later that year when Howells wrote a campaign biography of Lincoln and used the money he made from it to finance his journey. The visit was memorable in every way, for Lowell treated him as a young writer of promise whom he had discovered. He arranged a dinner for him at the Parker House, to which he invited James T. Fields and Oliver Wendell Holmes, and during the dinner the witty Dr. Holmes leaned over toward his host and said: "Well, James, this is something like the apostolic succession; this is the laying on of hands." It was a prophetic remark, but the succession did not take place for another six years. Meantime, Howells had to return to Ohio, but before he left Boston Lowell gave him a letter to Hawthorne, and Hawthorne passed him on to Ralph Waldo Emerson. He also looked up Henry David Thoreau while he was in Concord; then he headed for New York and home, but his stop-off in New York was anti-

climactic, for the bohemian editors of the *Saturday Press* repelled him, and he was not much impressed with Walt Whitman, whom he met in Pfaff's beer cellar.

When the Civil War began, Howells felt no urge to join the Ohio volunteers. Instead he used his campaign biography of Lincoln to secure an appointment as consul at Venice, a position he held from late 1861 until after the war ended in 1865. As Clemens went off to the big bonanza and Virginia City and James sat out the war in Newport, Howells embarked for Europe to begin the pivotal experience of his life. In a real sense Venice was his college education, for his duties as consul were minimal and wartime trade with Venice, never an important port in the nineteenth century anyway, was almost non-existent. Occasionally he had to look after traveling Americans, but most of his time he could devote to study and writing.

For the first couple of years he persisted in writing poems which he "sent to the magazines in every part of the English-speaking world, but they came unerringly back." Thus it was editorial rejection that turned him from a mediocre poet into a successful prose writer, that and the discovery of Venice as a source of material for prose sketches. As a journalist he already was a trained observer of the world about him, and the exotic setting of Venice supplied material of undeniable interest. Then he discovered the Italian dramatist Carlo Goldoni, who became another literary passion, one whose faithful record of Venetian life in his plays suggested that one's literary objective might well be "the truthful treatment of material." Howells wrote a series of sketches of life in Venice and sent them to the *Atlantic Monthly*, but Lowell was no longer editor, and James T. Fields, who had succeeded him, did not want the pieces. But the *Boston Advertiser*, a newspaper that Lowell and other Boston literati read, did buy them, and during 1864 seventeen appeared in print. The following year Howells revised the sketches for book publication, and *Venetian Life* (1866) became his first literary success, a book that was printed and reprinted throughout his life.

Between the writing of the sketches and the book publication, however, Howells came to what he later called the turning point of his life. After acquiring a fluency in Italian, he had plunged into extensive reading of nineteenth-century Italian writers, and in the spring of 1864 he began writing his first important piece of criticism, an essay on "Recent Italian Comedy." He sent it to Lowell, who was then editing the *North American Review* with Charles Eliot Norton, and awaited its fate. In August he received an electrifying letter from Lowell: "Your article is in print, and I was very glad to get it . . . Write us another on 'Modern Italian Literature,' or anything you like. I don't forget my good opinion of you . . . I have been charmed with your Venetian letters . . . They make the most careful and picturesque *study* I have ever seen on any part of Italy. They are the thing itself."

In the months after receiving Lowell's letter, Howells became increasingly restive in Venice and was eager to return to America to get on with his career. During his years in Italy he had acquired a wife and a child, put in four years of study and writing, and prepared himself for the life that was to follow. In 1862 he had gone to Paris to meet and on 24 December to marry Elinor Gertrude Mead of Vermont, who had captivated him during an Ohio visit a couple of years before. He escorted her back to his apartment in a palace on the Grand Canal and Winifred Howells was born a year later. By late 1864 he felt that he had gotten all he could from Venice, and when the war ended the following spring, he asked to be relieved of his consular duties.

The Howells menage arrived in New York late in the summer of 1865, and while Elinor went to visit her family in Vermont, William Dean looked for a job. First he did some free-lance writing for the *New York Times*; then E. L. Godkin offered him a position on the *Nation* at forty dollars a week. He jumped at the job but was barely settled in it before Fields asked him to become assistant editor of the *Atlantic Monthly*. Then he was off like a shot for Boston, the city of his heart's desire, and his subsequent career was inseparably linked with that city for almost a quarter of a century.

With Fields as his employer, Lowell as his sponsor, and Holmes as friend and confidant, Howells settled down in Cambridge as assistant editor of the most influential journal in the literary capital of America. Hawthorne and Thoreau were dead by this time, but he was passing judgment on contributions by Emerson, John Greenleaf Whittier, and a good many others who were established writers when he was a youth in Ohio. Norton took him house hunting as soon as he arrived and introduced him to Longfellow, who became a close friend and not-too-distant neighbor. Within a month Howells was invited to attend the weekly sessions of the Dante Club, which met at Longfellow's home and listened to the poet read the translation he was then making of *The Divine Comedy*. Howells had taken Lowell's advice and studied Dante while in Venice, and his knowledge of Italian literature and culture gave him an immediate en-

tree into the society of Cantabrigian Italophiles. Lowell wrote of his protege: "Venice has been the university in which he has fairly earned the degree of Master." The meetings of the Dante Club were among his richest experiences, and he recalled thirty years later that they were the one episode in his life he would most like to live over. The members of the club were "the men whom of all men living I most honored, and it seemed to be impossible that I at my age should be so perfectly fulfilling the dream of my life in their company."

Soon after Howells's settling down in Cambridge, *Venetian Life* appeared in book form and received enthusiastic reviews with Lowell leading the group. Readers of the book found that Howells had avoided the Venice of romance, the Venice of Lord Byron, Samuel Rogers, or James Fenimore Cooper, and he did not try to compete with John Ruskin's study of Venetian art and architecture. What he did was study Venetian life, not high society but everyday life, Venetian customs, Venetian character. He described his apartments on the Grand Canal, his life as a bachelor, then as a married man and father, his servants, walks through the city, trips to islands in the lagoon. He was trying in this work to find a literary form that would break away from the genteel restraints of sentimentality and ideality in the novel of the earlier nineteenth century. Henry Nash Smith sees both Howells in *Venetian Life* and Clemens in *The Innocents Abroad* working toward the same objective. And for Howells there are foreshadowings of the novelist to come, in the narrative voice, the character portrayals, the self-contained episodes.

The success of *Venetian Life* spurred Howells to continue using his Italian experiences in his next book, *Italian Journeys* (1867). In this work Consul Howells and his wife travel from Venice to Naples and back, going by train, boat, and carriage. The book is nonfiction, but there is continuous narrative and a plot fashioned from the travel framework. He had traveled with notebook in hand, observing and recording the life about him in the manner of the realistic novelist. The material subsequently worked up for the published book departs in many respects from the actual events: it is rearranged, shaped, embellished, dramatized. There are numerous episodes that read like chapters from Howells's later novels, scenes filled with the realistic dialogue that is one of his trademarks. Again reviewers were pleased with his work, and one wrote: "Mr. Howells is, in short, a descriptive writer in a sense and with a perfection that, in our view, can be claimed for no American writer except Hawthorne."

The writer of that review was young Henry James, whom Howells had met in Cambridge soon after joining the *Atlantic Monthly*. James, six years Howells's junior, was just beginning his literary career, having sold his first story to the *Atlantic Monthly* the year before, and the two men began a friendship that ended only with James's death in 1916. As assistant editor, Howells enthusiastically championed James's fiction in the magazine, and, as editor, later eagerly solicited his work. Both men were then working out their literary principles and held long, earnest discussions. Howells wrote his New York friend E. C. Stedman on 5 December 1866: "Talking of talks: young Henry James and I had a famous one last evening, two or three hours long, in which we settled the true principles of literary art. He is a very earnest fellow, and I think extremely gifted—gifted enough to do better than any one has yet done toward making us a real American novel."

One of Howells's principal duties as assistant editor of the *Atlantic Monthly* was the writing of book reviews, and one day in 1869 he received a copy of *The Innocents Abroad* for review. Recognizing its

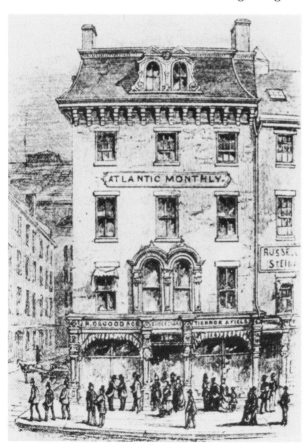

The Atlantic Monthly *office, 124 Tremont Street, Boston, where Howells served as editor-in-chief from 1871 to 1881*

quality, he wrote a favorable notice, which appeared in the magazine unsigned, as was the custom. Late in the year when Clemens turned up at the *Atlantic Monthly* office to thank Fields for the review, the editor introduced him to Howells. The two men, only two years apart in age and both from similar Midwestern backgrounds, immediately found each other congenial and struck up a friendship that lasted until Clemens's death in 1910. Both writers visited each other back and forth between Cambridge and Clemens's home in Hartford and occasionally collaborated on literary projects. Howells published some of Clemens's best work in the *Atlantic Monthly* during his editorship, and after Clemens's death wrote in *My Mark Twain* (1910) a memoir described by Edmund Wilson as the best "character" of Clemens that readers have.

The two Italian books moved Howells along the path toward his first novel, but he was not quite ready to write it. Meantime he worked prodigiously, becoming the de facto editor of the magazine and continuing to write many sketches, stories, articles, and reviews. His expertise in Italian literature brought him an honorary M. A. from Harvard in 1867 and an invitation from the new president, Charles W. Eliot, to be a special lecturer on contemporary Italian literature, an assignment that he carried out for two years and interspersed with another series of lectures at the Lowell Institute. Ever since the *North American Review* had published his article on "Recent Italian Comedy," he had been writing essays on Italian poetry. This interest, stimulated both by Lowell's encouragement and a keen sympathy for the Risorgimento, eventually culminated in *Modern Italian Poets* (1887), a critical survey with many translations of a century of Italian verse. Meantime he had managed to find a publisher for a long poem in unrhymed hexameters, *No Love Lost: A Romance of Travel* (1868), that he had written in Venice more than five years before.

In 1871 Howells became editor-in-chief of the *Atlantic Monthly* and produced another book. This was *Suburban Sketches*, not one of his major productions but his last work before attempting a novel. As the title implies, it is a collection of miscellaneous pieces, all of which had previously been published in the *Atlantic Monthly*. It does for Cambridge what Howells earlier had done for Venice. He describes Mrs. Johnson, the cook, as he had described Giovanna, his Venetian servant, and he relates conversations with Italian scissors grinders and chestnut roasters in Cambridge as he had reported his talks with gondoliers and porters. Howells later recalled that this book was one "where I was beginning to study our American life as I have ever since studied it." Lowell again led the chorus of praise from reviewers, comparing the character sketches to those in *The Canterbury Tales* and finding the style and powers of observation worthy of comparison with Hawthorne.

With such accolades ringing in his ears Howells took the next step and wrote his first novel, *Their Wedding Journey* (1872). As in *Italian Journeys*, the

THEIR WEDDING JOURNEY

BY

W. D. HOWELLS,

AUTHOR OF "VENETIAN LIFE," "ITALIAN JOURNEYS," ETC.

WITH ILLUSTRATIONS BY

AUGUSTUS HOPPIN.

BOSTON:
JAMES R. OSGOOD AND COMPANY.
LATE TICKNOR & FIELDS, AND FIELDS, OSGOOD, & CO.
1872.

Title page for Howells's first novel, which grew out of his travel sketches of the late 1860s

plot is draped on a framework of travel, but unlike the earlier travel book, Mr. and Mrs. Howells now become Basil and Isabel March, fictional characters that Howells was to use nine more times in later novels and stories. In December 1870 he had written his father: "At last, I have fairly launched upon the story of our last summer's travels, which I'm giving the form of fiction so far as the characters are concerned. If I succeed in this—and I believe I shall—I see clear before me a path in literature which no one else has trod, and which I believe I can make most distinctly and entirely my own. I am going to take my people to Niagara, and then down

the St. Lawrence, and so back to Boston." The book was serialized in the *Atlantic Monthly* during his first year as editor, and again the critical reception was favorable.

The novel is low-keyed throughout, lacking any sort of melodrama but filled with sharp observation of people and places and authentic dialogue. There is quiet humor, understatement, irony, and the supple style that his readers had come to expect. Henry Adams, who reviewed it for the *North American Review*, found in it "extreme and almost photographic truth to nature, and remarkable delicacy and lightness of touch." He thought the book would have a long life and that "our descendants will find nowhere so faithful and so pleasing a picture of our American existence, and no writer is likely to rival Mr. Howells in this idealization of the commonplace." Howells writes, as Basil and Isabel observe some silly byplay between a young man and woman on the night boat to Albany: "Ah! poor Real Life, which I love, can I make others share the delight I find in thy foolish and insipid face?" Apparently he could, though the novel is flawed if compared with his mature fiction of a decade later; yet it marches toward realism. Howells still had a considerable distance to go, however, in perfecting his narrative technique, in learning how to dramatize his material better, and in keeping out authorial intrusions.

The decade of the 1870s was a time of gathering powers. The *Atlantic Monthly* flourished under his editorship and at one time was simultaneously carrying Twain's "Old Times on the Mississippi" and James's *Roderick Hudson*. Howells also was encouraging and publishing the work of younger writers such as Sarah Orne Jewett, engaging Bret Harte to write for him, and readmitting to the magazine the poems of his older contemporary, Southerner Paul Hamilton Hayne. His abilities as a novelist grew steadily as he turned out six works of long fiction in this period, and he tried his hand at playwriting, both one-act farces and full-length comedies. As if all this activity were not enough, he still managed to write stories and sketches, introduce works by other authors, bring out a volume of poems, and write a campaign biography of Rutherford B. Hayes.

His second novel, *A Chance Acquaintance* (1873), was a superior performance to *Their Wedding Journey* and introduced into the comedy of manners of the earlier book what was to become a new characteristic dimension, the clash of differing social values. Again the novel's plot depended in part on a travel framework, for the characters are presented as traveling in Canada, in Quebec, and on the St. Lawrence and Saguenay rivers. Again Howells uses Basil and Isabel March, though they are not the leading figures this time. The real interest lies in the invention of Kitty Ellison, a girl from western New York State, and Miles Arbuton, a Boston snob. Kitty, Howells's best characterization so far, had played a walk-on part in the first novel as one of the passengers on the boat traveling down the St. Lawrence. Now she is the heroine, dramatically presented alone on deck as the novel opens. She is marveling at the lucky chance that has given her the opportunity to travel from Buffalo to Quebec and eventually back home by way of Boston with her Milwaukee cousin and his wife. Howells gives her the same awed respect for Boston that he himself had had as a young man visiting the city for the first time.

The social comedy in the novel develops in the relationship between Arbuton, who is attracted to Kitty but who cannot get over his conviction of social superiority. He falls for her, however, and proposes, but she puts him off, which offends his pride; he had expected her to swoon in his arms. He pursues her further, but when he meets some Boston friends and does not introduce her, she realizes that he is ashamed of her low origin (her father had been killed in a frontier brawl) and rejects him finally.

All this is handled with a light touch and nice irony, and it is interesting to note that Howells has avoided the sentimental ending that his magazine readers would have preferred. He also still is working out his ideas about realism and the use of commonplace material. He has Kitty tell Arbuton: "If I were to write a story, I should want to take the slightest sort of plot, and lay the scene in the dullest kind of place, and then bring out all their possibilities. I'll tell you a book after my own heart: 'Details,'—just the history of a week in the life of some young people who happen together in an old New England country-house; nothing extraordinary, little, every-day things told so exquisitely, and all fading naturally away without any particular result, only the full meaning of everything brought out." This is a fair description of what Howells was trying to do, though he allowed himself a more exotic setting in his use of French-speaking Quebec than his theory called for.

Howells had to write three novels before he produced one that did not depend on travel to give it movement. His next effort was *A Foregone Conclusion* (1874), a novel that takes place in Venice. The setting is exotic, and the heroine is an American girl sojourning in the Italian city, but the story is worked out within the confines of the *calle*, the palazzi, and the lagoons of Venice. As early as 1866 he had thought of writing a novel laid in Venice, but nothing had come of his idea. Now he had the experience and ability to do it, and the result was his most artistic and best-realized novel so far. At the end of its serialization in the *Atlantic Monthly*, his friend Stedman wrote: "I have read the closing chapters of *A Foregone Conclusion*, having followed it along the *Atlantic*, and like it the best of all your books. Indeed it has been of curious interest to me to see your *gradual* but steady progress in *construction*— invention of plot and management of separate characters. . . . Each of your books has had a little more *story* to it, and this is a story throughout and therefore the best of all. Of course you had nothing to gain in style or insight of character."

A Foregone Conclusion is the story of an Italian priest who falls in love with an American girl, mistakes her kindness and open American manner for a serious interest, decides to leave the Church and marry her. The girl, Florida Vervain, has encouraged the priest, Don Ippolito, to leave the Church and immigrate to America because she knows he is miscast as a priest and at heart is a frustrated inventor. But when he proposes to her, she is shocked at the idea of a priest's proposition and rejects him summarily. The priest conveniently dies of a fever, and later back in America Henry Ferris, the American consul who had introduced the two, gets the girl. In this novel Howells gave in to his readers' desires for a happy ending, though he felt apologetic about it, but he must have felt that to end with the death of the priest, which he knew was the logical conclusion, would have made the story more tragic than he intended it to be.

A Foregone Conclusion was the most successful of Howells's early novels. Fourteen printings appeared in the next thirteen years, and the book was republished as late as 1916. It was translated into German and put into the English Tauchnitz library for Continental travelers. It also was dramatized and produced both in London and New York, but it was not a hit on the stage. Don Ippolito, suggested by a priest Howells had known during his consulship in Venice, was the most ambitious characterization he had yet tried, and the critics were properly impressed. He came across to James as "a real creation"; Robert Dale Owen, who had been American minister to Italy, thought him "an admirable portrait"; John Hay called the priest "the best thing of the sort that has been done." There is a fair amount of anti-Catholicism in the novel, particularly in its criticism of celibacy for the priesthood, and the editor of the *Boston Pilot*, John Boyle O'Reilly, registered a protest against the reflection on the priesthood cast by the Don. Finally, the novel is Howells's first attempt at the international novel, a genre that both he and James found exceptionally attractive.

Howells's next novel is hardly known at all because it never appeared in book form until 1921, after his death. Published serially in the *Atlantic Monthly* as "Private Theatricals," Howells suppressed its book publication under circumstances that still are mysterious. His biographer, E. H. Cady, reports that Howells was threatened with a lawsuit by the people who ran the "Mountain Farm," where he had taken his family in the summer of 1874. He had vacationed in the White Mountains, as was becoming the custom for affluent Bostonians in the years following the Civil War, near Jaffrey, New Hampshire, and the setting of his novel was apparently too recognizable. If his denigrators of the 1920s had read the novel in 1921, when it finally appeared as *Mrs. Farrell*, they might have been surprised, for its title character is a femme fatale, something of a bitch, and a very well-drawn character.

The action is laid in a summer boardinghouse kept by a retired minister's family. One of the guests is Mrs. Farrell, who is fatally attractive to men and enjoys the fact. She causes the alienation of two young men, both of whom fall in love with her, allows one of them to woo her, but ends up casting him off and going on the stage. When she turns out to be no big hit in the theater, Howells has one of his minor characters comment that perhaps her real talent was for "private theatricals." He also uses the novel as a vehicle to attack the romantic ideals of love and courtship as they existed in sentimental romance. Here the militant realist in him was fully engaged.

After serializing "Private Theatricals," Howells turned to a literary genre that often has had an almost fatal allure for novelists—the drama. His interest in the theater began in his childhood during the terrible year and a half that his father was trying to publish a daily paper in Dayton. A traveling company of players paid for printing handbills with free tickets to their plays, and he remembered going every night to performances of *Macbeth*, *Othello*, *Richard III*, plus popular dramas now forgotten. Later in Venice Howells made his delighted discovery of Goldoni, whose lighthearted dramatizations of Venetian life left an indelible impression, and he attended the theater there regularly. Back in the United States his interest continued, and once he

was well established on the *Atlantic Monthly*, he turned his hand to writing plays. Drama never became a major preoccupation, but Howells is more important as a dramatist than most people know. His pioneering in realistic fiction carried over into his dramatic writing, and Arthur H. Quinn, historian of the American drama, writes: "His example and his critical judgments and inspiration, guided and encouraged [Edward] Harrigan, [James A.] Herne, [Augustus] Thomas, and [Clyde] Fitch, who have expressed their obligation to him directly and implicitly."

His first foray into the theater occurred in 1874 when he translated an Italian play, *Sansone*, by Ippolito d'Aste for Charles Pope. Not much came of this venture, but three years later Lawrence Barrett produced his full-length comedy, *A Counterfeit Presentment* (1877), with considerable success. This is a lighthearted comedy of manners laid in a summer hotel and involving the vicissitudes of young love. Though it is of minor importance among Howells's works, it is full of sharp, witty dialogue and again shows his acute understanding of human nature. When it opened in Boston Howells wrote his father: "The first night was a superb ovation, a gurgle of laughter from the beginning to end, and a constant clapping of hands. They called me up at the end of the third act, and *roared* at me. I never had my popularity at arm's length before, and it was very pleasant." But this never happened to him again, and his only other full-length comedy, *Out of the Question*, also published in 1877, with the same setting and similar action, never was performed professionally. After several later efforts to write for the theater he gave it up and wrote one-act plays, mostly farces and comedies, for his magazine public and amateur theatricals.

Beginning with *The Parlor Car* (1876), Howells turned out twenty-six of these one-act dramas during the next thirty-five years. When he shifted over to *Harper's* in the late 1880s the magazine asked for one of his farces each year for the Christmas issue. "They made me a very amiable public there," he wrote in 1912, "with the youth who played in drawing-rooms and church parlors." Booth Tarkington recalled that "a college boy of the late eighties and 'golden nineties' came home at Christmas to be either in the audience at a Howells farce or in the cast that gave it." On a few occasions these plays were performed professionally as curtain raisers, one of which, *The Garroters*, G. B. Shaw reported seeing in 1895: "The little piece showed, as might have been expected, that with three weeks' practice the American novelist could write the heads off the poor bunglers to whom our managers appeal."

Shaw was right, and the plays, which are packed with witty dialogue and amusing situations, are still a pleasure to read. When Howells wrote *The Sleeping Car* six years after *The Parlor Car* (1876), he invented a group of characters that he carried through a dozen plays. The idea may have been suggested by Goldoni's use of the old commedia dell'arte stock characters in many of his comedies, but wherever the idea came from, it provided Howells with characters who could be expected to amuse from play to play: the garrulous Agnes Roberts and her absentminded husband Edward, Willis Campbell from California and the amiable Amy Somers, a Boston widow who is wooed and won by Willis. Their antics range from slapstick farce to sophisticated comedy of manners.

After his playwriting interlude Howells returned to the international theme with *The Lady of the Aroostook* (1879), his most realistic novel yet. Like *A Chance Acquaintance* and *A Foregone Conclusion*, it presents an attractive, independent American girl in situations that test her character and contrast her values. As with Kitty Ellison in *A Chance Acquaintance*, Howells's new character, Lydia Blood, a schoolteacher from South Bradfield, Massachusetts, finds herself confronted with two sophisticated young Bostonians on board a ship sailing for Italy. Then in Italy she encounters, as did Florida Vervain in *A Foregone Conclusion*, the mores of European society. The idea for the story had come from Samuel Langley, the pioneer in aviation, who had visited Howells when he was consul in Venice. There had been an American girl traveling alone as the only woman aboard his ship on her way to visit an aunt in Italy. To the novelist of manners this situation had interesting possibilities, and Howells remembered it fourteen years later.

Nothing much happens in this novel either on board the ship or after Lydia is installed in her expatriated aunt's palazzo on the Grand Canal. The plot is also predictable, boy gets girl, but the novel is extraordinarily interesting and developed with great skill. Again there is superb dialogue and dramatic treatment of incident. Shipboard life is created with excellent use of closely observed detail, and the life of the expatriated American in Venice is vividly rendered. There are excellent minor characters, the captain, the cabin boy, the drunken passenger, the aunt and uncle. Howells was determined to make the novel as realistic as he could,

even giving his heroine a name as antiromantic as possible, Lydia Blood. Young James Staniford, the Bostonian who falls in love with her and proposes after they all get to Europe, is a far more attractive and subtle character than the Boston snob Arbuton in *A Chance Acquaintance*. Lydia is as naive as the Bostonians are sophisticated and has no idea that traveling without a chaperon in 1878 is something no innocent girl would do. Her expatriated aunt is shocked by her indiscretion, and the proper Bostonian Staniford has to wrestle with his sense of propriety before proposing.

The novel is a charming period piece that invites comparison with another more famous one, James's *Daisy Miller*, which appeared in the *Cornhill Magazine* in London four months before Howells began serializing his novel in the *Atlantic Monthly*. That James and Howells produced similar treatments of the unsophisticated American girl against a European background at the same time is not astonishing, however, given their frequent correspondence, similar literary theories, and common interests. *Daisy Miller* is the greater work of art, but *The Lady of the Aroostook* is very good, and one might argue that James gave his story a melodramatic ending by killing off Daisy, whereas Howells wrote a realistic conclusion by letting his main characters get married. James got a lot more critical attention than Howells because some thin-skinned Americans thought he had slandered the American girl, but Howells displeased critics and readers also. Those who liked ideality in their fiction found him too realistic, his characters too clinically studied, despite the happy ending.

The decade of the 1880s opened with the appearance in the *Atlantic Monthly* of *The Undiscovered Country*, Howells's first big novel and one of his best. Called an "American Pastoral" by Kermit Vanderbilt, the novel deals with matters of large scope upon which Howells had brooded a long time: the loss of faith amid nineteenth-century scientific skepticism, the moral and social disorder that he saw in the post-Civil War decade. His readers thought the book was mostly about spiritualism, which had enjoyed a considerable vogue in Boston in the mid-1870s, and the novel sold 8,000 copies in the first month. Then sales dropped off, the reviewers did not recognize the importance of the book, and it has remained for contemporary critics to point out the book's significance as a cultural document.

The story begins with Howells's most extensive use of Boston as a setting, then moves to a Shaker village in the country (where Howells had spent the summer in 1875). In the opening chapters Dr. Boynton, a spiritualist whose daughter Egeria serves as his medium, is conducting a seance, to which comes a Boston journalist named Ford, who wishes to expose the fraud that he thinks is being perpetrated. From this beginning develops a struggle for the possession of Egeria, who immediately senses in Ford's presence a force that opposes her father's hold on her. After the seance is disrupted by Ford, Boynton and his daughter decide to leave Boston and return to their home in Maine, but they take the wrong train and land in the country near the Shaker village. The Shakers take them in and after an illness Egeria finds that she no longer has the power to act as her father's medium. In the denouement Ford appears again, claims the girl, Dr. Boynton dies, and the two young lovers are married.

A bare summary of the plot does an injustice to the complexities and subtleties of this novel. The early reviewers who thought the love story was poorly integrated with the expose of spiritualism missed the overall design. The characters of Boynton, Egeria, and Ford all are lost souls wandering in exile from a rural America and the faith of their fathers. When they stumble into the religious community of the Shakers they undergo a spiritual rebirth. The doctor realizes that he was pursuing a pseudoscience in trying to maintain contact with the wife who died in childbirth; Egeria reawakens after her illness to a normal life and love, and Ford's rough skepticism is softened by his experiences. Thus a regional study of New England character and situation widens to a national analysis of America in an age of transition.

Another aspect of this novel that contemporary reviewers and readers missed is its bold psychological study of sexual passion. The relationship between Dr. Boynton and his daughter is a subtle pre-Freudian description of an Electra complex. Victorian taboos, of course, required sexual matters to be treated so obliquely that readers could ignore them, but Howells is not the timid depicter of sexual relations that he has been accused of being. One of the ironies of Howells criticism in the early twentieth century is that his critics read him so inattentively that they never suspected he was dealing in this novel with an incestuous relationship.

It is also interesting to note that *The Undiscovered Country* is a sort of updated version of *The Blithedale Romance*, Howells's favorite of Hawthorne's novels. Howells and Hawthorne had got on extremely well together when they met that afternoon in 1860, and both Lowell and James had seen affinities between the two. Vanderbilt characterizes this novel as follows: "Egeria is a spiritual Priscilla who blooms into a warm Zenobia and becomes a whole woman. Boynton is a grotesque Westervelt with some of the visionary zeal of Hollingsworth. Ford is a Coverdale with the added good fortune of overcoming skepticism and choosing his ideal lady in time."

The year 1881 was a time of decision, change, new directions, and serious illness for Howells. By the beginning of the year he was weary of the routine of editing a magazine, reading proof, writing book reviews, corresponding with contributors. Houghton, Osgood, and Company, publishers of the magazine and his books, had split up and were quarreling over his services and literary properties. Because he finally felt able to make a living without the drudgery of his editorial duties, he gave notice to Henry Houghton, now the sole owner of the *Atlantic Monthly*, that he would leave his editorship on 1 March. James Osgood, who was to continue in the publishing business alone, offered him a weekly salary and royalties to write one novel a year. He saw his way clear to a good deal of free time and the chance to travel again and accepted the proposal. But it was a distressing year in his personal life, for his daughter Winifred, whose health was always frail, was sick off and on, and at the end of the year Howells himself was down with a protracted illness from overwork.

That he had worked himself into a sickbed does not seem surprising when one notes that *A Fearful Responsibility* was serialized by *Scribner's* in June and July, *Dr. Breen's Practice* in the *Atlantic Monthly* from August through December, and *A Modern Instance* began in the *Century* in December. The first two works are modest productions, *A Fearful Responsibility* being a novella that drained the last of his Venetian experiences from his days as consul, and *Dr. Breen's Practice* being a novel about a woman doctor. The latter is an early study of women in the profession, but Grace Breen studies medicine only to retreat before male hostility and female disapproval and to leave medical practice for matrimony as soon as she can. The former novel was fashioned from a family situation that dated back to Venice in 1863 when Elinor Howells's sister Mary Mead visited Italy.

Professor Elmore and his wife are in Venice during the Civil War so that the professor may write a history of the city. When the professor's sister-in-law Lily comes to visit, the contrast between American and European mores again provides plot. The Elmores' fearful responsibility results from

A MODERN INSTANCE

A NOVEL

BY

WILLIAM D. HOWELLS

AUTHOR OF "THE LADY OF THE AROOSTOOK," "THE UNDISCOVERED
COUNTRY," "DOCTOR BREEN'S PRACTICE," ETC.

BOSTON
JAMES R. OSGOOD AND COMPANY
1882

*Title page for the first of Howells's realistic character studies.
Eleven years after publication Howells maintained "I have there
come closest to American life as I know it."*

Lily's indiscretion in striking up an acquaintance in a railway car with an Austrian officer and the professor's having to save her from the consequences. The Venetian background is authentic, but Howells had done it better in *A Foregone Conclusion* and *The Lady of the Aroostook*. One interesting bit in the novella has the professor expressing remorse over not taking part in the Civil War. Whether Howells felt this way himself, it would be worthwhile to know. The character in the story who most resembles the author is another fictional consul named Hoskins. Howells makes him a war veteran who was wounded early and given a medical discharge.

With the publication of *A Modern Instance* (1882) Howells carved himself a niche among the writers of enduring American classics. This novel, which remains in print and still is widely read, represents Howells at full artistic maturity, a fact that he recognized himself. He told an interviewer in 1893, when asked which of his novels he thought the best: "I have always taken the most satisfaction in 'A Modern Instance.' I have there come closest to

American life as I know it." He later elevated *A Hazard of New Fortunes* to top position, but there is no doubt that this novel is a mature and important work. As the first significant treatment of divorce in American literature, it deals with issues of large and lasting social importance.

Howells had thought about the subject for a long time. In 1875 he had seen a performance of Franz Grillparzer's *Medea*, which had suggested to him the possibility of his own adaptation of the Euripides tragedy to an American divorce case. Although he started work on it the next year, he did not get very far, and nothing remains of that early effort. After he left the editorship of the *Atlantic Monthly*, he settled down to write this story, and the work progressed quickly during the next six months. He had not quite finished by the time he fell sick late in the year, and the serialization began while he was struggling to complete the book. The sure command of the material shown in the first three-quarters of the novel falters toward the end and the artistry of the whole is marred.

The story traces the course of a deteriorating marriage in the years following the Civil War. Howells's earlier concern with the rise of religious skepticism and the loss of faith and the resultant effect on American society again motivated him to tell this story. Unlike *The Undiscovered Country* with its overt preoccupation with religion, *A Modern Instance* is a completely secular novel. It begins in the small town of Equity, Maine, where Bartley Hubbard, editor of the village newspaper, falls in love with Marcia Gaylord, daughter of a local lawyer. Bartley, though he has had a college education, has no social roots at all and an easy-going, hedonistic nature willing to make compromises. Marcia, raised in the circumscribed atmosphere of the small town, is the product of a free-thinking father and a self-indulgent and jealous nature. Bartley and Marcia elope, go to Boston where Bartley is hired by a newspaper. The marriage gradually goes to pieces, Bartley begins drinking, loses his job, deserts his wife and child, and the novel moves to an Indiana divorce court many months later. It ends as Marcia returns to a lonely life in Equity, and Bartley drifts off to Arizona where he is killed in a quarrel.

Besides being a splendid study of character, the novel is the picture of an age, what Clemens called "The Gilded Age" or V. L. Parrington "the Big Barbecue," the time of the Grant administration. The novel is told dramatically in one vivid scene after another, the method that both James and Howells had learned from reading Ivan Turgenev. The small Maine village, which in ordinary American mythology is the solid underpinning of national life, is here a town of chaotic liberality in religion. When Bartley and Marcia go to the city they are aliens, rootless, amid urban religious anarchy. Like Medea in Greek tragedy, Marcia, having left her father, lives in Boston in exile. Finally, the Indiana town where the divorce trial takes place is a copy of the Maine village only "more careless and unscrupulous" in appearance.

The novel made Howells a controversial figure, and the book received mixed reviews. Horace Scudder in the *Atlantic Monthly* hailed it as Howells's greatest achievement so far, "the weightiest novel of the day," but even he hoped that the author would go on to combine the serious matter of his novels with endings of "joyousness." Although the novel sold only 6,000 copies in the first six weeks, the sales satisfied the publisher, and Richard Watson Gilder, editor of the *Century*, was happy about the publicity the serial created. Inevitably, some reviewers thought Howells was writing a tract against divorce and charged him with undue polemicism, missing his real concern with larger issues. Scudder's review saw the point of the novel: "a demonstration of a state of society of which divorce laws are the index."

Fuel was added to the controversy the novel created when, a month after the book came out, Howells's article entitled "Henry James, Jr." appeared in the *Century*. In this essay he hailed James as the chief luminary of a new school of fiction, one in which "fiction had, in fact, become a finer art in our day than it was with Dickens and Thackeray," and he went on to add that "we could not suffer the confidential attitude of the latter now, nor the mannerism of the former, any more than we could endure the prolixity of Richardson or the coarseness of Fielding. These great men are of the past." These remarks raised a storm in England and no doubt tinctured some of the unfavorable reviews *A Modern Instance* received there. The essay was one of the opening salvos in the war for realism that Howells waged relentlessly later in the decade.

While the novel was still appearing serially, Howells fulfilled a long-standing desire to revisit Europe. He had written James in 1873 that the longing to return is "almost intolerable with me, and if I could see any way of keeping the bird in the hand while I clutched at those in the bush, I should go." He finally was able to do it, and before he left he arranged with Osgood, who was now both his publisher and his agent, to contract for the publication of a series of articles on Italian cities. He would make "each study as attractive as possible with anecdote and adventure. I should seek rather interest

than thoroughness, and I believe I should succeed and make some sketches which people would like. It is the ground I know, and I should work con amore." The proposal resulted eventually in *Tuscan Cities* (1886), a more modest project than the original plan to treat thirteen cities, but the book he did write is a superior travel book. It blends history and reporting with great skill and uses the craftsmanship of the novelist to make history come alive.

The Howells family sailed from Quebec in July and made their first stopover in London where James found them accommodations and was their host. The stay in London was pleasant, and Howells was wined and dined by artists and writers, but he left for the Continent before his essay on James appeared in the *Century*. He settled down in Switzerland for the fall in order to work on another novel, *A Woman's Reason* (1883), which is perhaps the worst novel he ever wrote. He had trouble writing in Europe and after leaving Switzerland took his family to Florence where they spent the winter and he finished the novel. The story sets out to study the life of a woman, who has no proper education with which to cope with life, trying to make her way after her father's death leaves her destitute. Howells keeps the heroine, Helen Harkness, separated from the man she eventually will marry by sending him off to China and then shipwrecking him for two years on a coral atoll in the South Seas. The novel is more romance than realism, and Howells's control of the material was at best faltering. He wrote Osgood while he was working on this book: "I find the strain of working out plots and characters amidst new and distracting scenes is awful."

Italy seemed older and dingier than when Howells was consul in Venice. His affection for the country remained unshaken, but he was unable to recapture the youthful charm. In April he took his family to Venice to show Winifred where she had been born, and to introduce his other children, Mildred and John, to Italy. He also wanted to look up old friends and former haunts and to roam the *calle* and canals of the city where he once had been "more intensely at home than in any other, even Boston itself." But the city was strangely shrunken, the churches and palaces shabbier than he remembered. Winifred, however, was enchanted by the city, but he took care not to let her get far from St. Mark's Square where there was a little "galvanic gaiety" and kept her away from the poverty and misery on the back *calle*.

After nearly a year in Europe Howells retraced his steps north toward England, stopping off again in London, this time to visit Lowell, American minister to England for whose appointment he had been responsible. Lowell took him to a reception at the home of the prime minister and then invited a roomful of titles to meet him. Howells could not do any writing in London because of the incessant round of socializing that made him "acutely miserable," and he was glad to board ship again to return to America. Once back home he settled down to write one of his best, but neglected, novels, *Indian Summer* (1886), the most important product of his return to Italy.

Indian Summer is an excellent example of the international novel, the genre that Howells and James both excelled in. Like James's *The American*, Howells's novel takes an American to Europe where he falls in love. In *Indian Summer*, however, the American Colville has traveled in Europe as a young man, become a newspaper editor, and he returns to Italy in order to write a book like *Tuscan Cities*. He is living in Florence when he meets the American Mrs. Bowen, who is his own age, and her young ward,

Imogene Graham. He at first falls in love with Imogene but in the end realizes that it is Mrs. Bowen he really wants. This plot provides Howells with the opportunity for a neat comedy of manners in his best manner. It also gave him a chance, as he wrote to Edmund Gosse, to study the "feelings of middle-life in contrast with those of earlier years." Howells had thought his return to Italy would renew his youth, but he found that impossible. Colville, who is just three years younger than Howells, reflects the author's realistic reassessment of middle age.

The novel has good unity of time, place, and character and creates a singleness of effect that often is lacking in Howells's novels. He liked the foreign setting for fiction because "you can segregate your characters so nicely, and study them at such long leisure." He worked over his manuscript carefully and for once had time to revise adequately. The novel did not begin appearing serially until eighteen months after he had completed the first draft, a unique experience for him, and when it did come out, the serialization of *The Rise of Silas Lapham*, written later, almost had been completed.

He was disappointed in its reception, however, because he thought it one of his most mature and artistic creations. He remembered in his old age that J. W. Harper had been somewhat dismayed to receive a manuscript which opened on the Ponte Vecchio in Florence when he had expected to get a Boston story. He wrote a friend: "To tell the truth, I like the story altogether, and I enjoyed doing it better than anything since *A Foregone Conclusion*. But our people don't want one on foreign ground, and I shall hardly venture abroad again in fiction." He did not quite stick to his resolve, but he never again placed a story completely in a foreign setting. This was, however, his last major use of Italy except for *Ragged Lady* (1899), a mediocre novel that again takes a New England girl to Venice where she meets her future husband.

While the reviewers found the book clever and neat but lacking in drama, Howells's friends read the novel with pleasure. Among the letters he received, none pleased him more than Clemens's: "You are really my only author; I am restricted to you; I wouldn't give a damn for the rest . . . It is a beautiful story, & makes a body laugh all the time, & cry inside, & feel so old & so forlorn; & gives him gracious glimpses of his lost youth that fill him with measureless regret." He ended his letter saying that he would rather "be damned to John Bunyan's heaven" than read James's *The Bostonians*, which appeared the same year. And despite J. W.

Howells's house at 302 Beacon Street, Boston, where he wrote The Rise of Silas Lapham

Harper's disappointment, the editor of *Harper's*, Henry Mills Alden, wrote that he was "much delighted with the novel. It seems to me to be in your best vein."

creative powers in the middle of his most fruitful decade.

In this novel Howells combines a study of business and a study of society in a skillful inter-

Howells in his Boston library at the time he was writing The Rise of Silas Lapham

The Boston story that Harper had hoped for to inaugurate Howells's new relationship with *Harper's Magazine* and his publishing firm was *The Rise of Silas Lapham*, but it was promised to the *Century*. Howells wrote it in the spring and summer of 1885, and it began appearing in the magazine in November. By the time it came out he had developed a large following, and a new Howells novel was eagerly awaited. Booth Tarkington remembered that he, at fifteen, was one of "a 'coast-to-coast' network of readers [who] hung upon every issue of the fortunate magazine that printed it." When one particular installment came, he waited at the door for the postman "so that I should be the first of the household to learn what happened to 'Silas Lapham' at the catastrophic dinner." Roswell Smith, publisher of the *Century*, told Howells that an estimated one million people were reading the story as it appeared in the magazine, and tourists in Boston began asking to see where the Laphams lived. The novel represents Howells at the peak of his

locking narrative. Writing a pioneering novel of business, he creates Silas Lapham, a self-made paint manufacturer who has returned from the Civil War, discovered a paint mine on the family farm in Vermont, gone into business, and prospered. Lapham is not a Carnegie or Rockefeller but reasonably rich and successful. The reader first sees him in a vivid dramatic scene in which he is being interviewed for the "Solid Men of Boston" series by journalist Bartley Hubbard. Lapham is brought down, in the course of the novel, however, through the accidental burning of his new house on Back Bay, into which he has poured a fortune, foolish stock speculations, and financial reverses in a time of economic dislocation. After his fall in fortunes, his "rise" takes place when he refuses to save his business through unethical means, and at the end he is back in Vermont starting over.

Coupled with the business story is a social plot in which the Laphams attempt to get into Boston society. The house is the symbol of their striving, and its burning ends their hopes. To bring the two plot threads together Howells invents the Corey family, Boston Brahmins who live on inherited wealth. Young Tom Corey, however, wants to do something with his life and gets a job in Silas's office. This brings Tom into contact with Silas's daughters, Irene and Penelope. Howells combines the business plot with a comedy of manners in the mix-up over which daughter Tom is in love with.

On the social side of the novel Howells wrote one of the great scenes in nineteenth-century American literature. This is the dinner party scene over which young Tarkington cried when Silas got drunk. The socialite Coreys, after Tom enters the paint business, feel they must invite the nouveau riche Laphams to dinner, but the Laphams neither know how to dress nor how to conduct themselves. Silas, who drinks water at home with his meals, allows his wine glass to be refilled far too often, and the result is disaster—a painful scene for Silas and the readers alike.

The novel has a great many attractive elements. The abundance of closely observed detail makes this novel an authentic picture of Boston in the later 1870s. The Laphams' house in unfashionable Nankeen Square, the Coreys' house, the summer cottage at the beach, particularly the new house that Silas builds, the details of Silas's business, the sights and sounds of Boston—all these are rendered superbly and give the novel verisimilitude. In fact the work has sociological interest quite apart from its artistic merits. The only weakness in the novel is its ending, in which Howells has to blend the social comedy of the love story, in which Tom and Penelope finally get together, with the business plot, which requires Silas's financial smash. The two elements do not mix very well, and the reader is left with the feeling that it all did not quite come off at the end.

The reviewers of *The Rise of Silas Lapham* were not very happy with the novel, and it has remained for later readers and critics to give it a high place in American letters. As Howells was the most prominent novelist of his day, the critics spent much of their energy finding flaws in the work. The ending came under attack, but the general tenor of the criticism was directed against Howells's uncompromising realism. As the reviewer for the *New York Herald* put it, Howells "always pleases, often charms us, but he never inspires." In short, Silas was neither a tragic figure whose downfall could bring catharsis, nor a noble character whose career fitted the stereotypes of the American success story. He was just an ordinary kind of person, and Howells, in

creating him, seemed too clinically detached from his material.

The years from 1886 to 1891 were a crucial half decade in Howells's career. The appearance of *Indian Summer* in *Harper's Weekly* marked the beginning of an association with the magazine and the publishing firm that lasted the rest of his life. Not only did Harper and Brothers begin to publish his books, but Howells created the "Editor's Study" column in the magazine, where he carried on a vigorous battle for literary realism. At the time his first column came out he wrote Edmund Gosse that "it's fun having one's say again, and banging the babes of Romance about." Also in this quinquennium Howells became deeply involved in social issues, found himself leaning more and more toward socialism, and grew sharply critical of the social and economic injustice suffered by working people. He was so outraged over the miscarriage of justice that followed the Haymarket riot in Chicago in 1886 that he wrote a public letter of protest. This brought him nationwide ridicule in newspapers and magazines.

Not only the deepening struggle between labor and capital changed his thinking, but also he

THE

RISE OF SILAS LAPHAM

BY

WILLIAM D. HOWELLS
AUTHOR OF "A MODERN INSTANCE," "A WOMAN'S REASON," ETC.

BOSTON
TICKNOR AND COMPANY
1885

Title page for Howells's most enduring novel, a pioneering examination of the American businessman

had recently discovered the writings of Tolstoy. He wrote his sister that Tolstoy's "heart-searching books" were "worth all the other novels ever written," and in *My Literary Passions* he said that Tolstoy had influenced him not only in aesthetics but in ethics also, "so that I can never again see life in the way I saw it before I knew him." It bothered him a great deal that his creature comforts conflicted with his belief in Tolstoy's Christian socialism. He wrote James that "after fifty years of optimistic content with 'civilization' and its ability to come out all right in the end, I now abhor it, and feel that it is coming out all wrong in the end, unless it bases itself anew on real equality. Meantime, I wear a fur-lined overcoat, and live in all the luxury my money can buy."

The final shaping events of this half decade were the death of his daughter, Winifred, and his move to New York. Both Howells and his wife watched helplessly as Winny's health deteriorated and no medical skill of the time was able to stop her decline. When she died in 1889, both parents were devastated, and Mrs. Howells lapsed into semiinvalidism for the rest of her life. Soon after that event Howells decided to edit a magazine again and accepted a coeditorship of the *Cosmopolitan* when his contract with Harper and Brothers expired in 1891. He was unable to endure the grind of editorial duties, however, and resigned after six months. In 1900 he went back to writing a column, "The Editor's Easy Chair," for *Harper's*, but in the meantime the firm had continued to publish his novels. The editorship of the *Cosmopolitan* had necessitated his move to New York where he lived, except for summers, for the rest of his life. New York was the place for a writer to be by 1891, for it had become the literary capital of the nation and the center of the publishing industry.

It is not surprising that three out of the next four novels that Howells wrote reflect his social concerns and his feeling that civilization was coming out all wrong. The first, *The Minister's Charge* (1886), which at one point he called "The Country Boy in Boston," develops for the first time his doctrine of complicity. Stated by the Reverend Mr. Sewell, it holds that "no one for good or evil, for sorrow or joy, for sickness or health, stood apart from his fellows, but each was bound to the highest and the lowest by ties that centered in the hand of God." The minister, who is a major character along with his charge Lemuel Barker, arrives at this realization through having been responsible for Barker's coming to the city. The story begins during a summer vacation when Sewell praises the poetry of Barker, a country boy, while really believing the lad

has no talent. Barker subsequently comes to the city to seek his fortune and becomes the minister's charge. Barker comes to terms with his predicament, takes whatever work he can do, ends up trying to drive a horsecar, is badly injured, and ultimately returns to Willowby Pastures.

Although Howells always denigrated polemical novels, he skates close to writing one here. He explores the life of working people in order to prick the consciences of the rich whom he felt should be more concerned with problems of unemployment, bad working conditions, and poverty. The novel is saved from didacticism, however, by good characterization and dramatization of social conditions rather than authorial moralizing, and the complicity doctrine comes at the end in one of Sewell's sermons. The reviewers sharpened their knives when the novel appeared and slashed at Howells for his treatment of "scenes of common and sordid life." The *Nation*'s reviewer asked: "Are the qualities in men that we know to be fine not real? Are trivial baseness, petty viciousness, the only truths?" In short the antirealists rose to the challenge presented both by the novel and by Howells's monthly columns in *Harper's*. Howells had turned upside down the American success story of the poor country boy seeking his fortune in the big city.

April Hopes (1887) was a change of pace, for it posits no social theories and grinds no axes. Set in Cambridge, Boston, Campobello, Washington, and Old Point Comfort, it is an excellent novel of manners in which boy gets girl. The characters are people from Howells's own social class. Of all Howells's work this is the most like the novels of Jane Austen, one of his oldest and greatest literary passions. It starts at Harvard Class Day where Dan Mavering meets Alice Pasmer, then moves to Campobello where Dan and Alice both vacation; Dan proposes and is rejected. When the couple accidentally meet again in Boston in the fall, they become engaged, but there are more vicissitudes before they finally get married.

Again Howells is the thoroughgoing realist. With consummate skill he mangles all the cliches of love and courtship in showing two unsuited temperaments sexually attracted going through an on-again, off-again romance. As they drive off together from the church after the marriage ceremony, Howells makes it perfectly clear that this couple will not have an easy time making the compromises necessary for a successful marriage. Howells later said that this novel was the first he wrote "with the distinct consciousness that he was writing as a realist." By this he meant that it was the first written after he had begun his monthly columns in *Harper's* "banging the babes of Romance about." Reviews of *April Hopes* were decidedly mixed, and the novel never has attained the status of a major work, but reading it today one is inclined to agree with Cady that it is a "neglected little masterpiece."

APRIL HOPES

BY

W. D. HOWELLS
AUTHOR OF
"INDIAN SUMMER" "THE RISE OF SILAS LAPHAM"
"MODERN ITALIAN POETS" ETC.

NEW YORK
HARPER & BROTHERS, FRANKLIN SQUARE
1888

Title page for Howells's comedy of manners, which he claimed was his first novel composed "with the distinct consciousness that he was writing as a realist."

In *Annie Kilburn* (1888) Howells returned to social themes, writing a story laid in a New England mill town and creating characters that include a female philanthropist, a minister who expounds Tolstoy's Christian socialism, a greedy hypocritical businessman, an alcoholic lawyer who defends the mill workers, and a sensible, nonpolitical doctor. Annie, who returns to her native Hatboro after living abroad for eleven years, is determined to help the people in her hometown. She sees herself as Lady Bountiful, but in the course of the novel she discovers that creating a social club for mill workers is not going to solve the problems of social injustice. While Annie learns a few things about the real world, she ends up marrying the doctor and substituting a happy marriage for philanthropy.

Although this novel is a tract for the times, it does not pose solutions for the problems it treats. Howells's Socialist minister Peck sees the ultimate salvation of society in Christian brotherhood, but he has no solution for getting to that utopia, and Howells finishes him off by having him step absentmindedly in front of a locomotive, symbol of the industrialization that no one knows how to control. What Howells has done superbly in this novel is to dramatize the social and economic problems of the late nineteenth century. In this way he hoped to move his readers to compassion and understanding. Edward Everett Hale wrote him a letter of thanks for being willing "to attack such problems" and to do so in a manner "so wise—so kind—so direct." He added: "It is a pulpit indeed—to write such a book for a million readers." Many of the reviewers again savaged his novel, but he did indeed have a pulpit in *Harper's* from which to reach a large audience.

A Hazard of New Fortunes (1889) is Howells's longest novel and his largest canvas. Previously he always had selected a small group of characters and shown them in their relationships to one another. This time he was inspired by having recently read *War and Peace* to write a "big" book with many characters and a wide-angled view of society. His setting was also a first, New York, where he had spent the winter of 1888-1889 before moving to the metropolis permanently and where most of the writing was done. The novel continues his concern with social issues and makes significant use of his growing interest in socialism. His lifelong habit of work enabled him to begin the novel during the agonies of Winifred's failing health and to finish it after her death. The despair he felt over this loss undoubtedly tinctures the novel and heightens its sobering impact. For many Howells critics this is his most important work.

Basil and Isabel March appear in this novel again as two of the fifteen major characters in the story. At the outset Basil, who is in the insurance business in Boston, is persuaded by Fulkerson, promoter of a newspaper syndicate, to come to New York to edit a new magazine that he proposes to launch. The angel of the venture is Dryfoos, an ex-farmer from Indiana who has struck it rich in gas wells and now is in New York with his family looking for investments. The starting of the magazine requires the hiring of a staff and the recruiting of contributors, and this device allows Howells to cleverly bring together his large cast and to involve them in each other's lives.

One of them is Lindau, German immigrant

who has lost his hand in the Civil War. He is an ardent Socialist whose linguistic competence makes him an ideal translator for foreign contributions. His socialism brings him into conflict with old Dryfoos, arch conservative who equates socialism with anarchy and violence. In a crucial episode in the center of the novel Lindau expresses his radical views at a dinner being held to celebrate the success of the magazine. Dryfoos orders March to fire Lindau, but March refuses on principle and Fulkerson, who is more interested in the magazine than in Lindau's right to his opinions, has to back his editor. The crisis ends when Lindau refuses to have anything more to do with Dryfoos. The old man's son, Conrad, who is a Christlike Tolstoyan socialist and a worker among the poor, is installed as business manager at his father's insistence, though he would like to become a minister. The novel reaches its climax when Conrad is killed in a futile effort to stop mob violence during a streetcar strike.

Other important characters are the Dryfoos women, the mother who is hopelessly out of place in New York and two daughters who want to get into society, and Alma Leighton and her mother, who come to the city so that Alma can study art. Alma supplies artwork for the magazine and is courted by Angus Beaton, the hedonistic art editor whom she rejects. There also is Colonel Woodburn and his daughter Madison, the former an anachronism whose solution for social ills is a return to a patriarchal agrarian society and the latter a witty girl who is wooed and won by Fulkerson. Finally, Margaret Vance, rich socialite who shares Conrad's social work and his Tolstoyan opinions, provides a glimpse into the lives and homes of New York's very rich. All the characters are well drawn and clearly differentiated.

Although Howells dramatizes the ideas and issues of 1890 in this well-structured novel, he does not try to solve the problems of society. Indeed he does not know the answers. Lindau often speaks for Howells in expressing his socialist philosophy, but he clearly carries his principles too far when they impel him to taunt the police as they club the strikers, an act that leads to Conrad's death. Conrad's Christlike martyrdom does not solve any problems either and is a needless sacrifice, though March, who speaks for Howells, says, "it was his business to suffer there for the sins of others." His death softens the father, however, but March does not believe that old Dryfoos really has changed. Yet March must believe something and concludes: "*I* don't know what it all means, Isabel, though I believe it means good." At the end of the novel the Dryfoos

family, who not only have lost their son but also have been frustrated in their efforts to get into society, go off to Europe leaving Fulkerson and March as proprietors of the magazine. Margaret Vance, who feels responsible for Conrad's death, enters a religious order. Meantime, the life of New York, depicted with all Howells's skill and with all its color and movement and variety, flows endlessly on.

Howells's career also flowed on for another thirty years during which his creative imagination diminished only gradually. In these final three decades he wrote an astonishing number of novels and story collections—twenty-six in all—and continued his steady production of critical essays, plays, travel books, introductions, and memoirs. At least eight of his novels written after he was fifty-three are important enough to deserve attention, and a few more are worth brief mention.

Two short novels written about the same time and now published in one volume of the Indiana Howells Edition, *The Shadow of a Dream* (1890) and *An Imperative Duty* (1891), are extraordinarily good novels that deserve to be better known. The first is Howells's most Hawthornesque fiction, and the second is a powerful pioneering study of black segregation and miscegenation. *The Shadow of a Dream* is also experimental in form for 1890, for it examines

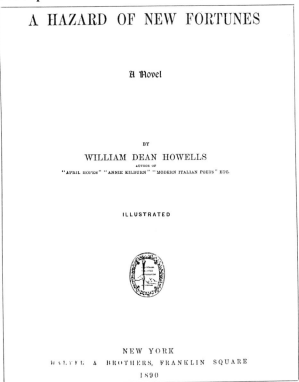

Title page for Howells's longest novel and his first about New York

its story from three different points of view. Howells wrote it immediately after he finished *A Hazard of New Fortunes* while his creative energies were strong and his speculations about the meaning of life and death were insistent. Was the realist's demand for empirical fact enough? Was there substance beyond reality in our unconscious lives? Winifred's death and suffering no doubt inspired this fine pre-Freudian study of dreams and their impact on his characters.

Basil March is a first-person narrator in this story, which has three parts, each devoted to one of the three main characters. March visits an old friend Douglas Faulkner, who is slowly dying of a hopelessly incurable disease, and finds him living in a menage a trois with his wife Hermia and a clergyman friend James Nevil. In part one, which is devoted to Faulkner, the dying man confesses to March that he is obsessed with a recurrent dream. March realizes that this obsession is one of the things killing him, and Faulkner dies soon after. Part two examines the wife's story, in the course of which the reader learns what the dream was when Hermia and Nevil become engaged and Hermia insists that her deceased husband's doctor tell her. The dream was that Faulkner saw his wife and Nevil in love and waiting for him to die and he further saw his funeral and the marriage taking place in the same church at the same time. Part three deals with Nevil and the working out of the impact of this revelation. Both lovers are destroyed by this knowledge, and the novel ends with Howells leaving the reader to decide whether the dream was a dying man's illusion or an intuitive glimpse into reality.

An Imperative Duty, a surprisingly early and bold treatment of race relations, is compact, tightly structured, and well executed. There are only three main characters: Dr. Olney, Mrs. Meredith, and her niece Rhoda, all of whom have just returned from living abroad. Dr. Olney is called from his hotel room to treat Mrs. Meredith, who has come to a crisis in her life. Following a proposal of marriage to Rhoda by a white minister, she feels it her imperative duty to reveal a secret, until now concealed, that her niece's grandmother was a slave. When Rhoda learns her history, she writes a letter dismissing her suitor and rushes off into the night. The aunt is so distraught that she takes an overdose of sleeping medicine. Dr. Olney takes charge of the girl, sees that she is cared for, and after his initial reaction of disgust over the girl's origin, which he recognizes as irrational prejudice, talks Rhoda out of her self-pity, proposes, and marries her. Early in the novel before the secret is revealed, Dr. Olney had reacted

to the blacks he saw in Boston on his return as "the only people left who have any heart for life here." "They all alike seemed shining with good-nature and good-will," and he felt that segregation was one of the "the most monstrous things in the world." At the end of the novel Howells adopts a realistic solution for an interracial marriage in 1892 by sending his couple back to Italy to live.

Howells in his apartment on Fifty-ninth Street in Manhattan at the time he was writing My Literary Passions

About the time Howells was writing this novel he received an offer from S. S. McClure to become editor of a new magazine, suggested perhaps by *Every Other Week*, the fictional magazine in *A Hazard of New Fortunes*. It was a case of life imitating art, for the ebullient McClure, who ran a newspaper syndicate, was a Fulkerson importuning Basil March's alter ego with the same sort of proposition. Howells was not tempted, even though he was to have a free hand in running the magazine and the contract was better than his arrangements with Harper and Brothers. In 1893 McClure started *McClure's Magazine* with himself as editor and achieved a phenomenal success, but it is unlikely that Howells had any regrets. McClure's only accomplishment in approaching Howells was to get him to write an extra novel that year. This was *The Quality of Mercy* (1892), one of Howells's best-plotted, liveliest long novels. McClure syndicated it in six newspapers with great success.

Subtitled in the newspaper version "a story of contemporary American life," it deals with a prominent businessman, Northwick, who has embezzled money from his company and been found out by his board of directors. His options are to commit suicide, go to jail, or flee the country. He takes the easy way out and goes to Canada (there are no extradition treaties yet), but after living in exile for a time, he decides to come back to face the music. He dies, however, on the train returning home. The novel takes place in Annie Kilburn's Hatboro and reuses characters from that story. Then it moves to Quebec, which Howells knew well, also to Boston, where Bromfield Corey, the Reverend Mr. Sewell, and other familiar Howells characters appear. The novel also deals at length with the lives of Northwick's children and the impact of the defalcation on them. The novel had contemporary interest, as defaulters were often in the news, but it has perennial interest to anyone following the Robert Vesco case in the 1970s and 1980s.

That Howells wrote too much is perfectly clear; yet even his lesser works contain good characters, well-developed situations, provocative themes. The two novels he turned out in 1893, *The World of Chance* and *The Coast of Bohemia*, and a later one, *The Story of a Play* (1898), are cases in point. While only moderately successful overall, they deal interestingly with art and the marketplace. The first takes a young man from the provinces, Percy B. Shelley Ray, to New York to find a publisher for his first novel. The second brings an Ohio girl, Cornelia Saunders, to New York to study art and make her way in the art world among men. The third novel does for a young playwright what Howells had done for his youthful novelist in *The World of Chance,* and in writing it Howells had his own experiences with actors and theater managers to draw upon.

These lesser performances punctuate an interlude between the economic novels of the late 1880s and Howells's utopian romances, *A Traveler from Altruria* (1894) and *Through the Eye of the Needle* (1907). Here Howells, following the great popularity of utopian fiction generated by Edward Bellamy's *Looking Backward* (1888), tried his hand at the genre. It gave him another chance to put into fiction his social and political ideas by creating Mr. Homos, the traveler from Altruria, which is somewhere in

William Dean Howells, circa 1905

the antipodes, who visits the United States. At a New Hampshire summer hotel, where he is the guest of an American novelist, he is shocked at the social superiority the other guests assume over the hotel employees in a country where he has been told "all kinds of work are honored." Then he cannot understand why the owner of a stand of timber on the lakeshore near the hotel has been allowed to clear-cut the trees and deface the landscape. He is further appalled to have a manufacturer explain to him the social Darwinism of his business principles. The traveler, in describing his own society, explains that in Altruria the people, by the simple device of the vote, had finally taken control of the country and resolved to form a society based on the idea of the good for all rather than the good of the individual.

Although this novel is a thinly disguised polemic, it is extremely interesting to read today to compare the conditions Howells describes in 1894 with the social and economic evolution this country has undergone since then. Reviewers found *A Traveler from Altruria* to their taste or distaste according to their preconceived philosophies. The *Critic* noted: "The good-will of a gentle man toward his kind, the interesting speculations of Plato, Bacon and Sir Thomas More, the poetic dreams of William Morris and the prosaic nonsense of Mr.

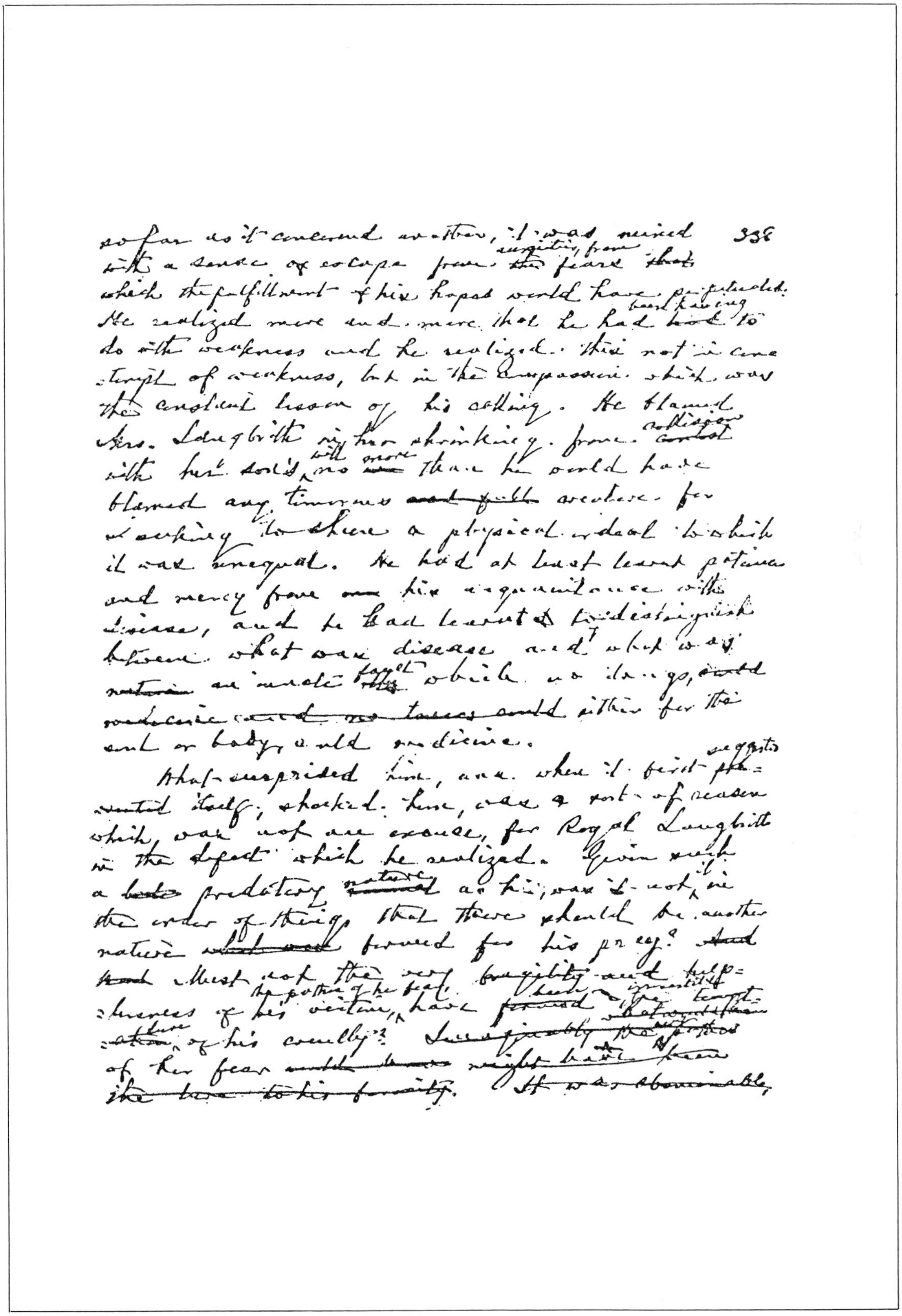
338

so far as it concerned another, it was seized with a sense of escape from the fears which the fulfillment of his hopes would have projected. He realized more and more that he had been having to do with weakness and he realized this not in contempt of weakness, but in the compassion which was the constant lesson of his calling. He blamed Mrs. Langbrith in her shrinking from collision with her son's will no more than he would have blamed any timorous creature for seeking to shun a physical ordeal to which it was unequal. He had at last learnt patience and mercy from his acquaintance with disease, and he had learnt to distinguish between what was disease and what was innate, for which no drugs, either for the soul or body, could medicine.

What surprised him, and when it first suggested itself, shocked him, was a sort of reason which was not an excuse, for Royal Langbrith in the defect which he realized. Given such a predatory nature as his, was it not in the order of things that there should be another nature formed for his prey? Must not the very helplessness of his victim, the pathos of her fear, have formed the temptation of his cruelty?

Page of the mauscript for chapter 23 of The Son of Royal Langbrith

Bellamy are all jumbled and shaken up together in Mr. Howells's book." On the other hand, the *Nation* wrote: "Mr. Howells speaks the thought of many men of his time with that clearness, force, and vivacity which have made his fame as a novelist." The sequel to this book, *Through the Eye of the Needle*, which was published serially in the *Cosmopolitan* after the original series, did not come out in book form until 1907 when Howells thought there was a revival of interest in utopian fiction. In it Mr. Homos falls in love with and marries an American; then he takes her back to Altruria, whence she writes letters home describing conditions in the utopian society where altruism is a way of life.

In the year that he was sixty Howells wrote another novel, *The Landlord at Lion's Head* (1897), that compares favorably with his best. It is a study of the selfish, amiable, amoral Jeff Durgin from the age of fourteen to his mid-twenties. He is seen through the eyes of a painter, Westover, who boards at the Durgin farm in the White Mountains one summer and becomes involved in the lives of the folks at Lion's Head. Jeff's doting mother converts the farmhouse into a summer hotel to put Jeff through Harvard, and Westover, from his Boston studio, observes the young man's unprincipled progress through life. Jeff gets engaged to Bessie Lynde, Boston socialite, while Cynthia Whitwell, his fiancee back home, waits for him. When both girls reject him, he goes off to Florence where he woos and marries a rich American. The old hotel at Lion's Head burns down under mysterious circumstances while Jeff is conveniently in Europe, and with the insurance and his wife's money he builds a more elegant establishment.

Although there are half a dozen good characters in this novel, the portrait of Jeff is outstanding. He is a complex figure whom any novelist would be glad to have created. He is a scoundrel in many ways but a likable one, a comical devil Cynthia's father calls him. Westover, who has observed him for a decade, does not fully understand him, but he actually is Howells's most naturalistic character. Howells would have denied that he was writing a naturalistic novel, yet Jeff Durgin is as amoral and egocentric as Theodore Dreiser's Frank Cowperwood. Westover recalls: "He once said to me, when I tried to waken his conscience, that he should get where he was trying to go if he was strong enough, and being good had nothing to do with it."

Of the seven novels that Howells had left in him after the turn of the twentieth century, two belong with his best work, and the third is a near miss. This last, which was produced first, is *The*

Kentons (1902), a story that begins better than it ends. Howells wrote a friend in 1904: "I know how [novels] are done better than ever, but I haven't the intellectual muscle I once had." The inspiration for *The Kentons* lay in Howells's Ohio background and his own family memories. He had had the idea to write an Ohio novel for half a dozen years; the death of his father in 1894 and visits to his brother and sister in Ohio strengthened his resolve. The result, however, is a novel of an Ohio family, which only begins in the village where Judge Kenton, retired from the bench, lives quietly with his wife and children. The family leaves Tuskingnum, Ohio, for New York to get Ellen away from an undesirable suitor and then continues on to Europe for the summer. On board ship Ellen meets a young clergyman who turns out to be the right man. Besides Ellen, the judge's younger daughter Lottie and his adolescent son Boyne are fully realized characters, and the use of Holland as his European setting is an interesting novelty.

Most critics have neglected this novel, and Howells was disappointed by its reception. He wrote Brander Matthews that the book had been killed by the "stupid and stupefying cry of 'commonplace people.' I shall not live long enough to live this down, but possibly my books may." In this hope he was correct, for the Howells revival of the past generation has found the mirror he held up to common human nature well worth preserving. Howells was incapable of compromising his principles of realism, and this novel, like most of his books of the previous decade, sold only about 10,000 copies. Discriminating readers appreciated the novel, however. James ended a letter praising the book: "It is in short miraculously felt and beautifully done."

The Son of Royal Langbrith (1904) is a major novel, the story of a son's delusion and its tragic consequence. James Langbrith cherishes the memory of his father, who died when he was an infant, as a great and good philanthropist, but the reality is that Royal Langbrith was a scoundrel and blackmailer who kept a mistress in Boston and tortured his wife physically and mentally. The son is a headstrong, selfish youth who has tyrannized his mother and insists that she never marry again. She is in love with her old friend Dr. Anther but afraid of her son. The question becomes: who shall enlighten the boy? Mrs. Langbrith finds she cannot, and the doctor also discovers that he cannot. A long-suffering uncle finally blurts out the truth, but it is too late. The doctor has died of typhoid fever contracted from a patient, and James, chastened and humbled, must live with the knowledge of his father's perfidy and his denial of happiness to his mother.

Howells's creative imagination burned brightly when he was writing this novel. The conception is strong and the execution sure. As psychological drama it compares well with *The Shadow of a Dream*. Howells had thought about the idea for a long time, for the notebook that was his "savings bank" for ideas has a paragraph written about 1894 containing the germ of the story. He spent nine months writing the novel, beginning it in his New York apartment and finishing it in his summer home at Kittery Point, Maine. The novel appeared serially in the *North American Review* the month after James's *The Ambassadors* ended and was widely and favorably reviewed. William M. Payne in the *Dial* thought *The Son of Royal Langbrith* one of the finest books that Howells had written.

Howells felt that he had one good novel left in him, and in 1916, a year short of his eightieth birthday, he published *The Leatherwood God*, which Cady describes as "his great unknown novel." It is unique in the canon of his works: his only historical fiction and his only real Ohio novel. Where *The Kentons* began as an Ohio story and ended up in the international category, *The Leatherwood God* plays out its story in Leatherwood Creek, Ohio, in pioneer times. It is a story, based on fact, of Joseph Dylks, who appears one August day in the frontier community and persuades a large number of people that he is God. It is the dramatic tale, full of life and action, of the rise and fall of this charismatic figure. Dylks is so successful at first that he begins to believe he may really be God; but the opposition gradually gathers strength, and when Dylks is unable to produce a promised miracle his downfall is assured.

Howells's success in telling this story lies in the invention of the skeptical Matthew Braile, who is the observer and commentator on the religious fanaticism that sweeps the community. This canny old man, who knows from the start that Dylks is an impostor, says in explaining the phenomenon: "He [God] doesn't want to keep interfering with man, but lets him play the fool or play the devil just as he's a mind to." He tells this to Nancy Billings, who had been married to Dylks and was deserted by him but who is unable to expose him because, thinking him dead, she has remarried. Howells was pleased with this novel and so were most reviewers. The *New York Times* noticed both Clemens's *The Mysterious Stranger* and *The Leatherwood God* in the same review and found both essentially contemporaneous works in their dealings with "humanity's religious strivings."

Howells felt the winds of change as he grew older and realized that he belonged to an earlier era. He wrote James in 1915 that "a change has passed upon things, we can't deny it; I could not 'serialize' a story of mine now in any American magazines. . . . I am comparatively a dead cult with my statues cut down and the grass growing over them in the pale moonlight." He was partly wrong, however, as the *Century* ran *The Leatherwood God* the next year, but partly right, as the attacks on him swelled to a considerable volume in the iconoclastic 1920s. They had already begun in 1917 with H. L. Mencken's blast in the *Smart Set*, which proclaimed as though Howells were already dead: "His psychology was superficial, amateurish, often nonsensical; his irony was scarcely more than a polite facetiousness; his characters simply refused to live."

Howells near the end of his life

But Mencken apparently did not bother to read Howells, for out of the five books he listed as forgotten novels, two are plays and a third poetry. In addition, one of the great ironies of American literary history is the attack that Sinclair Lewis made on Howells in accepting the Nobel Prize in 1930. He called him a writer who "had the code of a pious old maid whose greatest delight was to have tea at the vicarage." That moment was perhaps the highwater mark of Lewis's reputation, and the low point for

Howells. During the Depression 1930s Howells began to be rediscovered through his social and economic ideas, which seemed to anticipate the policies of the New Deal. Then after World War II he began to undergo a revival that has never ceased.

After writing *The Leatherwood God*, Howells never tried another novel, but he continued writing up to the time of his death. He turned out an "Editor's Easy Chair" column once a month for *Harper's Monthly Magazine* until the month before his death, wrote autobiographical and travel essays, introductions for works by others, and completed an important book, *Years of My Youth* (1916). The Academy of Arts and Letters awarded him its Gold Medal for fiction in 1915, an award now known as the Howells Medal. By 1920, however, he felt like the last leaf on the bough, for his wife was gone, and two of his best friends, James and Clemens, also had predeceased him. He caught a cold in Savannah where he wintered in 1919-1920 and could not shake it, and after returning to New York in April he died quietly in his sleep on 11 May 1920.

Letters:

Life in Letters of William Dean Howells, edited by Mildred Howells, 2 volumes (Garden City: Doran, 1928; London: Heinemann, 1929);

The Correspondence of Samuel L. Clemens and William D. Howells, 1872-1910, edited by Henry Nash Smith and William M. Gibson, 2 volumes (Cambridge: Harvard University Press, 1960);

Selected Letters, 1852-1872, edited by George Arms et al. (Boston: Twayne, 1979);

Selected Letters, 1873-1881, edited by Arms and Christof K. Lohmann (Boston: Twayne, 1979);

Selected Letters, 1882-1891, edited by Robert C. Leitz III (Boston: Twayne, 1980);

Selected Letters, 1892-1901, edited by Thomas Wortham (Boston: Twayne, 1981).

Interviews:

Ulrich Halfmann, ed., *Interviews with William Dean Howells* (Arlington, Tex.: *American Literary Realism*, 1974).

Bibliographies:

George Arms and William M. Gibson, *A Bibliography of William Dean Howells* (New York: New York Public Library, 1948);

James Woodress and Stanley P. Anderson, "A Bibliography of Writing about William Dean Howells," *American Literary Realism*, Special Number (1969): 1-139;

Vito J. Brenni, *William Dean Howells: A Bibliography* (Metuchen, N.J.: Scarecrow, 1973);

Clayton L. Eichelberger, *Published Comment on William Dean Howells through 1920: A Research Bibliography* (Boston: G. K. Hall, 1976).

Biographies:

E. H. Cady, *The Road to Realism: the Early Years, 1837-1885, of William Dean Howells* (Syracuse: Syracuse University Press, 1956);

Cady, *The Realist at War: the Mature Years, 1885-1920, of William Dean Howells* (Syracuse: Syracuse University Press, 1958);

Van Wyck Brooks, *Howells: His Life and World* (New York: Dutton, 1959);

Edward S. Wagenknecht, *William Dean Howells: The Friendly Eye* (New York: Oxford University Press, 1969);

Kenneth S. Lynn, *William Dean Howells: An American Life* (New York: Harcourt Brace Jovanovich, 1971).

References:

George N. Bennett, *The Realism of William Dean Howells: 1889-1920* (Nashville: Vanderbilt University Press, 1973);

Bennett, *William Dean Howells: The Development of a Novelist* (Norman: University of Oklahoma Press, 1959);

E. H. Cady and David L. Frazier, eds., *The War of the Critics over William Dean Howells* (Evanston, Ill.: Row, Peterson, 1962);

George C. Carrington, Jr., *The Immense Complex Drama: The World and Art of the Howells Novel* (Columbus: Ohio State University Press, 1966);

Carrington and Ildikó de Papp Carrington, *Plots and Characters in the Fiction of William Dean Howells* (Hamden, Conn.: Shoe String, 1976);

Everett Carter, *Howells and the Age of Realism* (Philadelphia: Lippincott, 1954);

Delmar G. Cooke, *William Dean Howells* (New York: Dutton, 1922);

James L. Dean, *Howells' Travels Toward Art* (Albuquerque: University of New Mexico Press, 1970);

Kenneth Eble, ed., *Howells: A Century of Criticism* (Dallas: Southern Methodist University Press, 1962);

Oscar Firkins, *William Dean Howells* (Cambridge: Harvard University Press, 1924);

Olov W. Fryckstedt, *In Quest of America: A Study of Howells's Early Development as a Novelist* (Cambridge: Harvard University Press, 1958);

William M. Gibson, *William D. Howells* (Minneapolis: University of Minnesota Press, 1967);

Robert L. Hough, *The Quiet Rebel: William Dean Howells as Social Commentator* (Lincoln: University of Nebraska Press, 1959);

Clara M. Kirk, *W. D. Howells: Traveler from Altruria, 1889-1894* (New Brunswick: Rutgers University Press, 1962);

Kirk, *W. D. Howells and Art in His Time* (New Brunswick: Rutgers University Press, 1965);

Kirk and Rudolf Kirk, *William Dean Howells* (New York: Twayne, 1962);

William McMurray, *The Literary Realism of William Dean Howells* (Carbondale: Southern Illinois University Press, 1968);

Kermit Vanderbilt, *The Achievement of Willian Dean Howells* (Princeton: Princeton University Press, 1968);

James Woodress, *Howells and Italy* (Durham: Duke University Press, 1952).

Papers:

The largest collection of Howells manuscripts is at Harvard, which has over 7,000 letters to and from Howells plus many manuscripts and journals. There are also significant collections at the Huntington Library, the Library of Congress, Yale and Columbia Universities, and the Rutherford B. Hayes Library in Freemont, Ohio.

Henry James

Robert L. Gale
University of Pittsburgh

BIRTH: New York, New York, 15 April 1843, to Henry James, Sr., and Mary Robertson Walsh James.

EDUCATION: Harvard Law School, 1862-1863.

AWARDS AND HONORS: Honorary degrees, Harvard University, 1911, Oxford University, 1912; Order of Merit, 1916.

DEATH: London, England, 28 February 1916.

SELECTED BOOKS: *A Passionate Pilgrim, and Other Tales* (Boston: Osgood, 1875);

Transatlantic Sketches (Boston: Osgood, 1875);

Roderick Hudson (Boston: Osgood, 1876; revised edition, 3 volumes, London: Macmillan, 1879);

The American (Boston: Osgood, 1877; London: Ward, Lock, 1877);

French Poets and Novelists (London: Macmillan, 1878);

Watch and Ward (Boston: Houghton, Osgood, 1878);

The Europeans (2 volumes, London: Macmillan, 1878; 1 volume, Boston: Houghton, Osgood, 1879);

Daisy Miller: A Study (New York: Harper, 1878);

An International Episode (New York: Harper, 1879);

Daisy Miller: A Study. An International Episode. Four Meetings, 2 volumes (London: Macmillan, 1879);

The Madonna of the Future and Other Tales, 2 volumes (London: Macmillan, 1879);

Confidence (2 volumes, London: Chatto & Windus, 1879; 1 volume, Boston: Houghton, Osgood, 1880);

Hawthorne (London: Macmillan, 1879; New York: Harper, 1880);

The Diary of a Man of Fifty and A Bundle of Letters (New York: Harper, 1880);

Washington Square (New York: Harper, 1881);

Washington Square, The Pension Beaurepas, A Bundle of Letters, 2 volumes (London: Macmillan, 1881);

The Portrait of a Lady (3 volumes, London: Macmillan, 1881; 1 volume, Boston & New York: Houghton, Mifflin, 1882);

The Siege of London, The Pension Beaurepas, and The Point of View (Boston: Osgood, 1883);

Daisy Miller: A Comedy in Three Acts (Boston: Osgood, 1883);

Portraits of Places (London: Macmillan, 1883; Boston: Osgood, 1884);

A Little Tour in France (Boston: Osgood, 1884; revised edition, Boston & New York: Houghton, Mifflin, 1900; London: Heinemann, 1900);

Tales of Three Cities (Boston: Osgood, 1884; London: Macmillan, 1884);

The Art of Fiction (Boston: Cupples, Upham, 1884);

The Author of Beltraffio, Pandora, Georgina's Reasons, The Path of Duty, Four Meetings (Boston: Osgood, 1885);

Stories Revived, 3 volumes (London: Macmillan, 1885);

The Bostonians: A Novel (3 volumes, London: Macmillan, 1886; 1 volume, New York: Macmillan, 1886);

The Princess Casamassima: A Novel (3 volumes, London: Macmillan, 1886; 1 volume, New York: Macmillan, 1886);

Partial Portraits (London & New York: Macmillan, 1888);

The Reverberator (2 volumes, London: Macmillan, 1888; 1 volume, New York: Macmillan, 1888);

The Aspern Papers, Louisa Pallant, The Modern Warning (2 volumes, London: Macmillan, 1888; 1 volume, New York: Macmillan, 1888);

A London Life, The Patagonia, The Liar, Mrs. Temperly (2 volumes, London: Macmillan, 1889; 1 volume, New York: Macmillan, 1889);

The Tragic Muse (2 volumes, Boston & New York: Houghton, Mifflin, 1890; 3 volumes, London: Macmillan, 1890);

The American: A Comedy in Four Acts (London: Heinemann, 1891);

The Lesson of the Master, The Marriages, The Pupil, Brooksmith, The Solution, Sir Edmund Orme (New York: Macmillan, 1892; London: Macmillan, 1892);

The Real Thing and Other Tales (New York: Macmillan, 1893; London: Macmillan, 1893);

Picture and Text (New York: Harper, 1893);

The Private Life, The Wheel of Time, Lord Beaupré, The Visits, Collaboration, Owen Wingrave (London: Osgood, McIlvaine, 1893);

Essays in London and Elsewhere (London: Osgood, McIlvaine, 1893; New York: Harper, 1893);

The Private Life, Lord Beaupré, The Visits (New York: Harper, 1893);

The Wheel of Time, Collaboration, Owen Wingrave (New York: Harper, 1893);

Theatricals, Two Comedies: Tenants, Disengaged (London: Osgood, McIlvaine, 1894; New York: Harper, 1894);

Theatricals, Second Series: The Album, The Reprobate (London: Osgood, McIlvaine, 1894; New York: Harper, 1895);

Terminations: The Death of the Lion, The Coxon Fund, The Middle Years, The Altar of the Dead (London: Heinemann, 1895; New York: Harper, 1895);

Embarrassments: The Figure in the Carpet, Glasses, The Next Time, The Way It Came (London: Heinemann, 1896; New York & London: Macmillan, 1896);

The Other House (2 volumes, London: Heinemann, 1896; 1 volume, New York & London: Macmillan, 1896);

The Spoils of Poynton (London: Heinemann, 1897; Boston & New York: Houghton, Mifflin, 1897);

What Maisie Knew (London: Heinemann, 1897; Chicago & New York: Stone, 1897);

In the Cage (London: Duckworth, 1898; Chicago & New York: Stone, 1898);

The Two Magics: The Turn of the Screw, Covering End (London: Heinemann, 1898; New York & London: Macmillan, 1898);

The Awkward Age (London: Heinemann, 1899; New York & London: Harper, 1899);

The Soft Side (London: Methuen, 1900; New York: Macmillan, 1900);

The Sacred Fount (New York: Scribners, 1901; London: Methuen, 1901);

The Wings of the Dove (2 volumes, New York: Scribners, 1902; 1 volume, Westminster: Constable, 1902);

The Better Sort (London: Methuen, 1903; New York: Scribners, 1903);

The Ambassadors (London: Methuen, 1903; New York & London: Harper, 1903);

William Wetmore Story and His Friends, 2 volumes (Edinburgh & London: Blackwood, 1903; Boston: Houghton, Mifflin, 1903);

The Golden Bowl (New York: Scribners, 1904; London: Methuen, 1905);

The Question of Our Speech, The Lesson of Balzac: Two Lectures (Boston & New York: Houghton, Mifflin, 1905);

English Hours (London: Heinemann, 1905; Boston & New York: Houghton, Mifflin, 1905);

The American Scene (London: Chapman & Hall, 1907; New York & London: Harper, 1907);

Views and Reviews (Boston: Ball, 1908);

Italian Hours (London: Heinemann, 1909; Boston & New York: Houghton, Mifflin, 1909);

The Finer Grain (New York: Scribners, 1910; London: Methuen, 1910);

The Outcry (London: Methuen, 1911; New York: Scribners, 1911);

A Small Boy and Others (New York: Scribners, 1913; London: Macmillan, 1913);

Notes of a Son and Brother (New York: Scribners, 1914; London: Macmillan, 1914);

Notes on Novelists with Some Other Notes (London: Dent, 1914; New York: Scribners, 1914);

The Ivory Tower, edited by Percy Lubbock (London: Collins, 1917; New York: Scribners, 1917);

The Sense of the Past, edited by Lubbock (London: Collins, 1917; New York: Scribners, 1917);

The Middle Years, edited by Lubbock (London: Collins, 1917; New York: Scribners, 1917);

Gabrielle de Bergerac, edited by Albert Mordell (New York: Boni & Liveright, 1918);

Within the Rim and Other Essays, 1914-15 (London: Collins, 1918);

Travelling Companions, edited by Mordell (New York: Boni & Liveright, 1919);

A Landscape Painter, edited by Mordell (New York: Scott & Seltzer, 1919);

Master Eustace (New York: Seltzer, 1920);

Notes and Reviews (Cambridge, Mass.: Dunster House, 1921);

The Art of the Novel: Critical Prefaces, edited by Richard P. Blackmur (New York: Scribners, 1934);

The Notebooks of Henry James, edited by F. O. Matthiessen and Kenneth B. Murdock (New York: Oxford University Press, 1947);

The Scenic Art: Notes on Acting & The Drama: 1872-1901, edited by Allan Wade (New Brunswick: Rutgers University Press, 1948; London: Hart-Davis, 1949);

The Complete Plays of Henry James, edited by Leon Edel (Philadelphia & New York: Lippincott, 1949; London: Hart-Davis, 1949);

Eight Uncollected Tales, edited by Edna Kenton (New Brunswick: Rutgers University Press, 1950);

The American Essays, edited by Edel (New York: Vintage, 1956);

The Painter's Eye: Notes and Essays on the Pictorial Arts, edited by John L. Sweeney (London: Hart-Davis, 1956; Cambridge: Harvard University Press, 1956);

Parisian Sketches: Letters to the New York Tribune, 1875-1876, edited by Edel and Ilse Dusoir Lind (New York: New York University Press, 1957);

Literary Reviews and Essays, edited by Mordell (New York: Twayne, 1957).

COLLECTIONS: *Novels and Tales of Henry James*, 14 volumes (London: Macmillan, 1883);

The Novels and Tales of Henry James, selected and revised by James, New York Edition, 26 volumes (New York: Scribners, 1907-1918);

The Novels and Stories of Henry James, edited by Lubbock, 35 volumes (London: Macmillan, 1921-1923);

The Complete Tales of Henry James, edited by Edel, 12 volumes (London: Hart-Davis, 1962-1964; Philadelphia & New York: Lippincott, 1962-1964);

The Bodley Head Henry James, edited by Edel (London: Bodley Head, 1967-);

The Tales of Henry James, edited by Maqbool Aziz (London: Oxford University Press, 1973-).

The first important fact in the life of Henry James is the wealth of his paternal grandfather, the Irish immigrant William James (1771-1832), who, when he died in Albany, New York, left a fortune of $3 million (based on salt, tobacco, real estate, and public utilities). A second significant circumstance in the life of the future novelist is his earliest recorded memory: he was less than two years old, was in Paris with his parents, and looked out their carriage window upon an impressive sight, the stately Place Vendôme with "its . . . tall and glorious column." A third fact always to be aware of in trying to

come to terms with James is suggested in a passage
from a letter which, as an old man, he wrote to his
gloomy old friend Henry Adams: "I am that queer
monster, the artist, an obstinate finality, an inexhaustible sensibility." These are the ingredients
for a unique Jamesian combination: family wealth,
travel abroad, and abiding artistic sensibility.

James's father, Henry James, Sr. (1811-1882),
revolted against the rigid Calvinism of the family
into which he had been born but was happy that the
family's money (though split among thirteen heirs)
enabled him to graduate from Union College
(1830) and then study for a couple of years at the
theological seminary in Princeton. He found orthodoxy just as unpalatable and American peda-
gogical methods thin: so he voyaged to England and
was soon influenced by Robert Sandeman, an anti-
Calvinist Scotsman whose letters the elder James
edited in 1838. A more positive source of religious
inspiration for him was Emanuel Swedenborg.
James was impressed by the Swedenborgian doctrine that God is a God of love not terror and by the
ideas that a spiritual cause lies behind every natural
object, that the Trinity is a division of essences only,
and that Christ's resurrection is emblematic of
man's glorious destiny. As for secular thought,
James followed the social philosophy of Charles
Fourier, who argued that individualism and competition are immoral, and that true happiness and
goodness come from an optimistic expression of
passion. Fourier sought to establish small social
units—humanistic agricultural communes which
would break down the unnatural restraints of so-
called civilized society. James associated informally
with many like-minded American intellectual leaders, among them Ralph Waldo Emerson, Ellery
Channing, Margaret Fuller, Henry David Thoreau,
Parke Goodwin, Charles Anderson Dana, Albert
Brisbane, and George Ripley. James lectured,
traveled, and wrote extensively on his views about
Christianity, morality, Swedenborg, social redemption, and God's pervasive power in human affairs.

Today the works of Henry James, Sr., are only
of antiquarian interest, but his influence upon his
family was enormous. He encouraged free and easy
chatter, dinner-table debating, freedom to attend
church—any church—or not, reading and travel
and museum attending—in short, an unmethodi-
cal, eclectic, intellectual foraging of the most
stimulating kind. His father's writings may have
influenced Henry James the novelist in some ways,
but the influence was probably indirect in the main.
After the old philosopher's death, his distinguished
son William James edited *The Literary Remains of the*

*Henry James at age nine, with his father. Photograph by
Matthew Brady*

Late Henry James (1884) and sent copies to Henry,
who replied with gratitude but added, "how beautiful and extraordinarily individual (some of them
magnificent) all the extracts from Father's writings
which you have selected so happily. It comes over
me as I read them . . . how intensely original and
personal his whole system was, and how indispens-
able it is that those who go in for religion should take
some heed of it. I can't enter into it (much)
myself—I can't be so theological nor grant such
extraordinary premises, nor throw myself into conceptions of heavens and hells, nor be sure that the
keynote of nature is humanity, etc. But I can enjoy
greatly the spirit, the feeling, and the manner of the
whole thing . . . and feel really that poor Father . . .
was . . . a great writer."

James's mother, Mary Robertson Walsh
(1810-1882), was from a prosperous upstate New
York family, Scottish-Irish in origin and Presbyterian (like her in-laws) in religious persuasion. She
accommodated her mind to her free-thinking husband's progressively more mystical thoughts with
no evident trauma, and long enjoyed her younger

sister Catharine (Aunt Kate) Walsh's loving presence in her household. Mary James was practical, unselfishly devoted to her husband and their five children, fair-minded, and sturdy. Upon her death, her devoted son Henry recorded this tribute to her in a private notebook: "She was our life, she was the house, she was the keystone of the arch. She held us all together, and without her we are scattered reeds. She was patience, she was wisdom, she was exquisite maternity. Her sweetness, her mildness, her great natural beneficence were unspeakable. . . . She is with us, she is of us—the eternal stillness is but a form of her love. . . . Thank God one knows this loss but once; and thank God that certain supreme impressions remain!"

Henry James was the second child. The oldest was William James (1842-1910), who turned out to be at least as brilliant as anyone else in the family. He studied painting under William Morris Hunt at Newport, Rhode Island, then science at Harvard University, then medicine at the Harvard Medical School (M.D., 1869). After a period of physical debilitation and intermittent nervousness, he became physiology instructor at Harvard, a professional experience which soon led him into psychology and then philosophy. Three of his most notable works are *The Principles of Psychology* (1890), which summarizes psychological knowledge to its date and incorporates his discoveries, insights, and hypotheses; *Varieties of Religious Experience* (1902), which insightfully relates religion, science, and common sense; and *Pragmatism* (1907), which persuasively suggests that ideas have meaning only when validated in the world of feeling and action.

After Henry James came Garth Wilkinson (Wilky) James (1845-1883), Robertson (Bob) James (1846-1910), and Alice James (1848-1892). None of these three achieved any sort of intellectual importance, although Alice James might have but for chronic ill health. Wilky and Bob volunteered for service during the Civil War. Wilky was wounded at Fort Wagner in 1863; Bob survived the siege of Charleston unscathed and emerged a captain. After the war, the two young brothers went to Florida and became unsuccessful cotton farmers for a time; then they headed west, to railroad jobs in Milwaukee. Wilky remained there, improvident and irresponsible, dying of a weakened heart and Bright's disease in his late thirties. Bob soon returned to the East, settled in Concord, Massachusetts, inveighed against railroad fortunes, considered becoming an actor, indulged himself in alcohol, and flitted from religion to religion without finding solace. Alice suffered under the lifelong

disadvantages of being the youngest child and the only daughter. She was neurasthenic, fainted often during her adolescence, and recorded in her remarkable diary that from the time she was twenty she felt dead. When she asked her indulgent father for permission to commit suicide and he freely gave it, she decided instead to confront the world's evils with him. Traveling a little, she lived with her parents until they died, then went to sanatoriums in southern England, with Henry James usually nearby, and devoted to her always. Cancer, compounding the misery of this intensely analytical and witty woman, finally killed her in 1892.

Henry James, Jr., was born on 15 April 1843 at 21 Washington Place (near Waverly Place), on the edge of Greenwich Village, in New York City. Very late in 1843 the parents took William and Henry to Europe. Once in London, James Senior made plans to meet his friend Emerson's distinguished friends Thomas Carlyle and John Sterling, and also the Swedenborgian J. J. Garth Wilkinson (for whom he was to name his third son). In the spring of 1844 the family was comfortably settled in Windsor, outside London, when the father underwent the horrifying experience of imagining that "some damned shape" with a "fetid personality" was "squatting invisible to me" in his room and "raying out . . . influences fatal to life." It was years before the shattered man felt normal, and water cures and doses of Swedenborg helped but little. Early in 1845 the Jameses visited Paris, then returned to New York City and Albany, which were to be their homes for the next decade. One of the most educational of Albany experiences was the presence of at least twenty first cousins, most of them presided over by their exceedingly sweet old paternal grandmother. Young Willy loved school in Albany from the first day, but the younger Harry cried and kicked. This contrast between the two illustrious brothers continued throughout their lives: William James always seemed the more assured and superior; Henry, less in the limelight, more in need of protection. It took Henry years before he struck out for independence.

Late in 1845 the growing James family moved to New York City, where the Fourierite father could be nearer to like-minded colleagues, lecture halls, and sympathetic publishers. The James residence at 58 West Fourteenth Street was to be at the center of many of the future novelist's fondest memories—of parental affection, sibling play, sprightly talk, reading, and forays into the incredibly bustling, noisy city. The boys' education teetered from attendance at a curious sequence of day schools and academies to being taught at home by polyglot governesses and tutors. The boys often dropped in on Grandmother Walsh, who had her home nearby, on Washington Square. In addition, they attended excellent dramatic and operatic performances on Broadway, as well as circuses and freak shows. Their father, meanwhile, was developing a formidable reputation as a lecturer and, to a lesser degree, as an author. Among the notables who visited in the Fourteenth Street mansion were Emerson, General Winfield Scott, and William Makepeace Thackeray. Young Henry profited from family sympathy and sincerity early in his life, and his natural expectation that he should move in important intellectual circles in due time must have been fostered quickly; but he fought juvenile shyness and later expressed slight regret at not only too much religious eclecticism but also at too little school discipline. Perhaps the result for a future novelist was generally beneficial, however, since, as James himself later described it, all this regimen constituted an "orgy of the senses and riot of the mind," both of which could only stimulate his imagination.

In the summer of 1855 the James family took a steamer from New York to Liverpool and went on to London, where young Henry had to recuperate from malarial ague before the group could get on to its destination this time—Geneva. All along the way, his vivid senses took in the varied scenes—the Channel crossing, a Parisian balcony, the train, the coach, the Alps, and mutedly glorious Switzerland. James remained too sick to attend the rigorous day school which his father had found for the other boys, and this fact only reinforced young James's sense of uniqueness and passivity. After only three months, the educational experiment palled; so the family returned to London, where the children had milder tutors and relished visits to museums, theaters, public gardens, churches, and old London monuments. James later recalled that everything in London at this time was redolent of Charles Dickens, George Cruikshank, William Hogarth, Thackeray, and old issues of *Punch*. Henry Senior, though enjoying his friendships with Carlyle, Thackeray, and Arthur Hugh Clough, among others, was beginning to think more highly of America again, just as Henry Junior, now a teenager, was inexorably if as yet all unconsciously inclining toward the residential preference of his adult life—the Old World.

June 1856 found the Jameses not yet back home but in Paris, which at that historical moment was perhaps artistically the most stimulating city in the world. Young James took full advantage of his opportunities. Tutors did what they could to regulate his study habits. But his real education during the next two years lay in his perfecting his uncanny fluency in the French language, summering and studying in Boulogne-sur-Mer (at the Collège Impérial), and isolating himself from his siblings to read and scribble. Henry Senior wrote home to his mother as follows: "Harry is not so fond of study, properly so-called, as of reading. He is a devourer of libraries, and an immense writer of novels and dreams. He has considerable talent as a writer." Unquestionably the most momentous psychic experience of his life occurred when young Henry first visited the Galerie d'Apollon of the Louvre, during his Parisian residence of 1856-1857. The 200-foot-long gallery is full of paintings on mythological themes, by such artists as Eugène Delacroix, Charles Lebrun, and Joseph-Benoît Guichard, as well as tapestries, mosaics, sculpture, and jewelry, all of which evoked for young James the name Napoleon. James's response was twofold. First the lad regarded the sight as a "bridge over to Style," at the end of which he "inhaled little by little, that is again and again, a general sense of *glory*." But a few years later, memory of that Napoleonic gallery triggered one "summer dawn" what he called "the most appalling yet most admirable nightmare of my life." He dreamed that he was in a room with the door closed, locked, and barred. A "creature or presence" on the other side was trying to force his way in. James had his shoulder against the door, resisting. Suddenly he became the aggressor, burst out of the room, and chased "the awful agent" down a "tremendous, glorious hall" (like the Galerie d'Apollon)—all to the accompaniment of lightning and thunder. Leon Edel rightly says of this pivotal, prophetic dream, "*Sublimity* was indeed the word for it: to resist nightmare, to turn the tables and counterattack, was consonant with the sense of triumph and glory and conquest and power. Attacked, Henry James had fought back. And he had won." It is hardly too much to suggest that the inspiration for the disturbing dream was also the inspiration of James's entire professional life.

In 1858 Henry Senior took the family back to America. His decision was partly owing to his temporary dissatisfaction with European educational methods but also largely due to an income loss after the 1857 panic. In the summer of 1858 the family crossed the Atlantic and settled in Newport, Rhode Island, then a somewhat shabby place, not yet the pretentious resort area it became after the Civil War. William and Henry James attended a school run by a Newport minister, the Reverend William C. Leverett, who relished Latin and fancied his own oratory. Some of Leverett's pupils became more distinguished than he. At the school Henry met the future painter, watercolorist, and stained-glass expert John La Farge, of French and Catholic background, who persuaded him to read Honoré de Balzac, Prosper Mérimée, Théophile Gautier, and the *Revue des Deux Mondes*. Henry also made another lifelong friend at this school. He was Thomas Sergeant Perry, later an editor, Harvard professor, and literary critic, and the recipient of some of James's most significant personal letters.

Henry James, Sr., uprooted his children once again in October 1859 and took the family to Europe for what was to be his own final foreign residence. His ostensible aim this time was to try yet another and different sort of school for his children, but the unacknowledged cause was more probably a continued intellectual restlessness and a vague fear about the approaching Civil War. This time they went to Germany and soon after to Geneva once more. The children were split up to a considerable extent. The family residence was a pleasant lakeside hotel, and Alice stayed with her parents. The two younger brothers went to a country boarding school nearby. William began to attend courses at the academy (later the University of Geneva), and Henry was required to take classes at the Institution Rochette, a preparatory school for engineers and architects. Henry James, Sr., seems to have hoped that he could wean William from his desire to paint and Henry from scribbling. It was not until spring that Henry was permitted to drop physics and mathematics, staying only with language classes until it was time for the family to go to Bonn for somewhat irregular study and then to wander in the Rhineland during the summer of 1860.

It was William's continued desire to paint that took the family back home for what was to be their longest American sojourn since 1845-1855. In September 1860, before the outbreak of the Civil War, they returned to Newport, so that William could formally study art at the Newport studio of William Hunt, who had followed his years at Harvard with study in Düsseldorf and Paris. While William worked hard at painting for a good six months, Henry tried sketching a while but soon turned back to more French literature, even translating Alfred de Musset's *Lorenzaccio* (1834) and Mérimée's *La Vénus d'Ille* (1841). Musset's work he adapted rather freely; he came to admire Merimee inordinately for the firmness of his narrative structures. James did not know it then, but even before the Civil War he was beginning to prepare himself for a life of creativity. Already he spoke French and German,

and he knew some Latin as well. He had had the mixed blessing of a dozen cosmopolitan homes and schools. His powers of observation were incredible. He had several brilliant young friends who would in differing ways make their mark in the arts. Also, family fortune and parental devotion would permit him to indulge himself for some years yet and to take his own slow time getting through a long post-romantic apprenticeship.

With the outbreak of war early in 1861, the James brothers had decisions to make. Now abandoning art, William decided on a scientific career and enrolled at Harvard. Wilky and Bob joined the Union army in due time. Henry wavered uncomfortably; then in October 1861 he suffered what he later called a "horrid even if an obscure hurt," which he added was "subsequently neglected." In trying to help extinguish a raging fire in a group of Newport stables near some houses, he manipulated a rusty water pump and, wedged between two fences, injured himself severely. Although some earlier scholars suggested that he castrated himself, Edel says that the hurt was in all likelihood a slipped disc or a strained back. Whatever it was, the injury pro-

Henry James, circa 1863

vided a valid reason for remaining on the sidelines during the war and was later a source of chronic pain for the man of letters who spent uncounted hours with his back bent over a desk. James, in his leisure after the fire, must have recalled that his father at the age of thirteen was so severely burned while trying to put out a stable fire that he lost a leg and spent two years convalescing in bed. The father had turned spectator and writer; now so might the son.

First Henry James, Jr., unaccountably entered Harvard Law School. He seems to have had no intention of becoming a lawyer. He later branded himself "a singularly alien member" of the place and attended for only a single academic year, 1862-1863. His enrollment there enabled him to attend James Russell Lowell's lectures in literature at Harvard College, to avail himself of Harvard's library, and—most important, perhaps—to make still more literary friends. Among them, in addition to Lowell, were Charles Eliot Norton, a distinguished professor of art history at Harvard and also a fine translator, biographer, editor, and letter writer; his knowledgeable, sensitive sister Grace Norton, to whom James later wrote some delightful letters; and Oliver Wendell Holmes, Jr., by then a dashing, wounded Civil War officer and later the eccentric, liberal associate justice of the U. S. Supreme Court.

From 1864 to 1869, James stayed mostly with his parents, first in Boston and, for the last three years, in Cambridge. Now determined to become a man of letters, he broke into print with an unsigned, melodramatic short story called "A Tragedy of Error" in the *Continental Monthly* for February 1864 and eight months later had an unsigned review of a forgotten book published in Norton's *North American Review*. James's first signed piece was "The Story of a Year," which appeared in James T. Field's *Atlantic Monthly* the following March and which is a disquieting piece about a wounded Civil War lieutenant and his confused fiancee. Fields and his vivacious wife, Annie Adams Fields, maintained a kind of Old World salon to which James soon quietly reported. But it was Field's young assistant editor, William Dean Howells, appointed shortly after he returned from spending the war years as consul in Venice, whom James ultimately came to treasure as his single most important American professional friend.

Howells became an editor and critic of incalculable influence, in addition to being a distinguished realistic novelist. He was an intimate friend of contemporary literary personalities as diverse as Henry Adams, John Hay, and Samuel Clemens, as well as Hamlin Garland, Stephen Crane, and Frank Norris later. He encouraged young James tremendously. James much later recalled somewhat inaccurately that it was Howells who first accepted his work: "You held out your open editorial hand to me at the time I began to write—and I allude especially to the summer of 1866—with a frankness and sweetness and hospitality that was really the making of me, the making of confidence that required help and sympathy and that I should otherwise . . . have strayed and stumbled about a long time without acquiring." In truth, by mid-1866 James had had twenty-two reviews, four short stories, and a couple of short critical notes published in five different journals, including the *Galaxy* and the *Nation*, the latter founded the year before by E. L. Godkin, a close personal friend of Henry James, Sr. The stream of Jamesian prose was gathering force, even though at this time James the critic, admiring the theory and practice of his French idols Auguste Sainte-Beuve, Balzac, and Gustave Flaubert, was ahead in theory of James the practicing story writer, whose early tales often display an apprenticeship fumbling with too much sentiment. All the same, within two years a reviewer in the *Nation* would define James as, within his own established limits, "the best writer of short stories in America."

By the time James went to Europe early in 1869, for his first adult trip abroad, he had written at least ten more short stories, in addition to twice that many reviews. The stories are still technically unsure and more moody than plotted. Two deal with the Civil War. They are "Poor Richard," in which the hero cannot compete with soldiers for the heroine, opts for alcohol, and then goes to war himself, and "A Most Extraordinary Case," which features a hero, already wounded in the war, who cannot compete with a civilian rival and opts for psychic, then real, death. Three other tales hint at the masterly James of the future. In "The Story of a Masterpiece" a painting seems almost alive, and the hero must stab it to assure his future tranquillity. With "De Grey: A Romance" James introduces his sacred-fount motif: in any intimate relationship, one, giving vitality to the other, is sucked dry in the vampiric process. In addition, "De Grey" concerns American travelers abroad. So does "A Light Man," the purpose of which, however, is to dramatize the corrosive effects of prospective money on friendship. James even wrote an unimportant little play called "Pyramus and Thisbe," involving talk in a boardinghouse, before leaving for Europe.

His fourteen months in England and on the

Continent, ending late in April 1870, established what was to become his lifelong pattern: travel, observation, and writing; much solitude, decorous friendships with men and women of the arts, homesickness, and mellow letters to loved ones. Bearded now and armed with a £1,000 letter of credit from his parents, James arrived in dingy Liverpool in February 1869 and went on to London, where friends introduced him to John Ruskin, William Morris and his wife, one of Dickens's daughters, Dante Gabriel Rossetti, Edward Burne-Jones, George Eliot, and Charles Darwin, among still other important Britishers. After brief treatment at a Malvern spa to try to set his chronically troubled digestive system in better order, James continued to France and Switzerland, both familiar countries from his childhood, and in September to Italy. Seeming incomparable from his first moments there, Italy soon became and always remained his favorite country. Germany was too harsh to suit him, although his parents wanted him to go straight there and although his brother William, home again after a year of study there, sternly recommended it. Swiss nature appeared raw and overly vigorous, and the country seemed barren of much art. By comparison, the Italian air and vineyards were soft; moreover, Italy had picturesque old ruins, incense-laden cathedrals, and art treasures in the galleries of Venice, Florence, and especially Rome. When James arrived in the Eternal City for the first time, on 30 October 1869, he became delirious with delight. "I went reeling and moaning thro' the streets, in a fever of enjoyment," he wrote home, adding at once, "In the course of four or five hours I traversed almost the whole of Rome and got a glimpse of everything . . . In fine I've seen Rome, and I shall go to bed a wiser man than I last rose. . . ." He felt wiser because, as he said about Rome, "I have caught the keynote of its operation on the senses." As a result, he was soon able to cast much fiction there—notably *Roderick Hudson* (1876), *Daisy Miller* (1878), and *The Portrait of a Lady* (1881)—and in addition to write many superb travel pieces about Italy.

Sick again, James made his way back north and west, to Genoa, Nice, Marseilles, Avignon, Paris, Boulogne, and still-wintry London. He was again at Malvern for the water cure when the saddest news of his life up to that time reached him. His beloved cousin Minny Temple, whom he had known since the old Albany days and adored for her spontaneity, wit, and radiance, had died of tuberculosis back home on 8 March 1870. She was only twenty-four. James was stunned, having thought that she was getting better even while he was slipping into poorer health himself. He vowed to immortalize the lithe, spirited girl in future fiction and later did so in his complex characterizations of Isabel Archer in *The Portrait of a Lady* and then Milly Theale in *The Wings of the Dove* (1902). Still later, he closed the second volume of his autobiography, *Notes of a Son and Brother* (1914), with the poignant cry that Minny's death was "the end of our youth." Perhaps his problem was psychosomatic, but in Malvern James became quite sick. So, after meeting his Aunt Kate in London, he returned gloomily to what he then called his "dear detestable . . . Cambridge" in May, in part to be examined by his brother William, now a medical doctor. James found New England culturally thin and uninspiring. His best new fiction to emerge at this time is "A Passionate Pilgrim," which concerns an American traveler much like James, exclaiming over Europe, specifically Oxford, which James always loved. His longest fictional effusion of this period is his first novel, *Watch and Ward* (not published in book form until 1878); later its author so little admired its thin plot, in which an older man rears an adopted child to be his bride, that he excluded it from the New York Edition of his selected fiction. "A Passionate Pilgrim," his sixteenth short story, is the earliest one to be included. Both of these works first saw print in Howells's *Atlantic Monthly* in 1871.

By 1872 James was again tired of America and was close to a decision to expatriate himself permanently. However, he was financially unable to do so. Nonetheless, he went to Europe again—this time, starting in May, as escort to his debilitated sister, Alice, and their Aunt Kate. Alice James soon grew not better but sicker; James took his charges from Paris over to the Liverpool dock, saw them off on a steamer headed west, and was free to take rooms back in Paris and write so steadily that he could reimburse his parents for their unceasingly generous allowance. *Nation* took five of his charming notes on England, Switzerland, and Italy, based on his travels in 1872. When fall came, James went to Rome again and made friends among the American expatriate community, of whom many were destined to become devoted to him for life. Among them were Fanny Kemble, a British actress, and her dazzling daughter Sarah Wister, the mother of Owen Wister, future author of *The Virginian* (1902). James also renewed his friendship with Francis Boott and his daughter, Lizzie. Their relationship may have partly inspired James's treatment of Gilbert Osmond and his pallid daughter, Pansy, in *The Portrait of a Lady*. Boott was a rather effete,

Europeanized American widower, and Lizzie later married the talented American expatriate painter-sculptor Frank Duveneck, whom James also knew.

In 1873-1874 James produced no less than fifty-eight pieces, mostly reviews and travel essays, but also some art gallery notes, items on Renaissance Italian art and Italian architecture, and seven short stories. The best fiction is "The Madonna of the Future" (published in *Atlantic Monthly*, 1873), a haunting fable of a procrastinating artist, his fading model, and his dusty, tattered canvas; "The Last of the Valerii" (*Atlantic Monthly*, 1874), a parable of the competing attractions of past and present; and "Madame de Mauves" (*Galaxy*, 1874), whose ambivalent heroine has recently been attracting and repelling readers of different critical persuasions. Now widening his outlets beyond the *Atlantic Monthly*, the *North American Review*, the *Nation*, and the *Galaxy* to include the *Independent* and *Scribner's Monthly*, James was quick to report home that his annual income approached $3,000—more than enough to support him in Europe indefinitely, independent at last of his indulgent parents.

When William, sick again with another of his periodic nervous disorders, descended in November 1873 upon his younger brother in Florence, Henry could now take the position of the more experienced: he wrote steadily through the morning hours, showed off his increasing knowledge of Italian to William (who was visiting Italy for the first time and did not know the language), and escorted him through museums and galleries. The two brothers were better for each other at a distance: when they were together, one seemed strong while the other waned; but when apart, they praised each other's professional efforts more fondly, although William tended to criticize his brother's increasingly complex fiction.

In the spring of 1874 James began work in Florence on *Roderick Hudson*, the first of his novels to be published as a book and the one he later enumerated as his first, and in September he returned to America to finish it. *Roderick Hudson* opens with a wealthy American named Rowland Mallet offering to become patron to a talented New England sculptor, Roderick Hudson. Once the two men are in Rome, Hudson learns quickly and even displays genius, but he is unstable and egocentric as well. He gambles in Germany, insults a rich would-be buyer, forgets Mary Garland—his fiancee back home—and falls in love with enigmatic Christina Light. Mallet urges her to stay away from Hudson, and her mercenary mother forces her to marry Prince Casamassima of Naples. Despondent in the

romantic Swiss Alps, even though his mother and Miss Garland have come to visit him, Hudson leaps or falls to his death. Roderick may be the titular hero, but Rowland is the central consciousness and, though perhaps too certain that everyone's will is free, an admirable force in the action. Christina Light is the first of many deadly females in James, who found her so intriguing that he made her the heroine of *The Princess Casamassima* a decade later. *Roderick Hudson* was respectfully reviewed in America, but James R. Osgood's first printing of 1,500 copies was enough to satisfy American sales. The book was far more popular in England. Roger Gard reports that it sold about 10,500 copies there and in America in James's lifetime.

After a few months in Cambridge, James went in January to live on East Twenty-fifth Street, near New York's old Madison Square, away from his parents and older brother. He worked hard at his varied writing, and in the winter of 1874-1875, as he ground out the concluding chapters of *Roderick Hudson* (which began to appear serially in the January 1875 issue of the *Atlantic Monthly*), he also contributed reviews to the *Nation* (at the rate of more than one a week through 1875), did other writing as well, and readied two books—*A Passionate Pilgrim, and Other Tales* and *Transatlantic Sketches* (twenty-five travel essays)—for publication by James R. Osgood and Company, Boston. James tried conscientiously to secure a niche for himself among the Manhattan literati but could not and found instead that he was both worried by the high cost of living in New York and homesick for Europe. So after staying under the parental roof in Cambridge a final time, from July until October, he made what his biographer F. W. Dupee calls "the great decision" and crossed the Atlantic yet again. James aspired to make Paris his residence for some years. By November 1875 he was there.

His long apprenticeship clearly behind him, James would strike for a position of equality among the literary titans of Europe and for financial independence. His French was as fluent as his English. Rather effortlessly he began to meet and associate with Ivan Turgenev (the influential emigre Russian novelist and ultimately his closest professional friend abroad), Flaubert (whom he defined as "kindly, and touchingly inarticulate"), Guy de Maupassant, Ernst Renan, the naturalists Edmond de Goncourt and Emile Zola, and Alphonse Daudet. James was sufficiently accomplished to appreciate their literary style but New Englander enough yet to decry their moral laxity. He soon began to feel like an unwanted outsider. Nor could he seem to please

Henry James in Rome, 1899

Andrew Lang, Richard Monckton Milnes (Lord Houghton), John Morley, Morris, Ruskin, Dr. Heinrich Schliemann, Herbert Spencer, Leslie Stephen, Alfred, Lord Tennyson, and Anthony Trollope. The son, however, already had a reputation which was beginning to eclipse that of the father. This young man of thirty-four years, serious, polyglot, of impeccable taste and formidable professional ambition, was known for his many short stories published in American journals, for his three books, which had been imported from Boston by Trübner and for his latest novel *The American*, installments of which had started to appear in the *Atlantic Monthly* the previous summer. It was published in Boston by Osgood in May 1877, and an unauthorized English edition appeared later that year.

The hero of *The American*, Christopher Newman, is a Civil War veteran and a rich ex-businessman, who brashly comes to Paris to buy the best wife on the market. Through an expatriated American matchmaker Newman meets a young widow, Claire de Cintré, whose proud French family, the Bellegardes, accept his suit but then squeeze the outsider back out, much as James was made to feel alienated a year earlier in Paris. Although Newman protests and lashes back, Claire's widowed mother and older brother remain inflexible. But Claire's younger brother is so ashamed of them that on his deathbed after a melodramatic duel he tells Newman that a family servant can tell him a secret he may use to extort permission to wed. James depicts the villainous French pair—mother and older son—as so defiant as almost to compel admiration. Claire enters a convent, and Newman, too noble to carry out his plan, burns the evidence. The main focus of the romantic novel is the contrast of American innocence and Old World experience, and it is hence the first substantial international novel.

In his preface to the revised version of *The American*, James said that the novel "unfurled . . . the emblazoned flag of romance," that it was a balloon with its cable wrongly detached from the real earth below, and that in real life the Bellegarde family "would positively have jumped . . . at my rich and easy American." Romantically inclined contemporary readers were sad when James's lovers manques were kept apart, but their creator privately opined that "they would have been an impossible couple." James was paid $1,350 for serial rights to *The American*, but it sold poorly thereafter in book form.

For the next four years James solidified his position as a sophisticated American writer in Lon-

the *New York Tribune*, whose assistant editor John Hay, soon to become another of James's closest friends, had obtained for him an assignment to write travel, society, political, and art notes from France. When the *Tribune* people urged James to make his efforts more chatty and gossipy, he replied, "they are the poorest I can do, especially for the money!," and quit. In December 1876 James moved from Paris to an apartment at 3 Boulton Street, near Piccadilly, in London, and eased into a productive pattern in that "great grey Babylon" for the next several years.

A list of the illustrious Britishers whom James met for the first time or with whom he renewed acquaintance is almost unbelievable. His father's books, even if not widely read, were a topic of conversation with many in London and helped to gain his son an entree into the highest circles. A list of James's old and new friends at this time would include Robert Browning, Sir Charles Dilke, George Eliot, G. H. Lewes, James Anthony Froude, William Ewart Gladstone, Alexander William Kinglake,

TWO SHILLINGS.

FAVORITE AUTHORS, BRITISH AND FOREIGN.

THE AMERICAN

BY

HENRY JAMES Jr

LONDON: WARD, LOCK, AND CO.

Front cover for the unauthorized first English edition of The American. *Though displeased by the publication, James admired the "wonderful picture on the cover."*

go boating to the Château de Chillon. They meet again in Rome; but Daisy's free and easy if harmless strolling with an opportunistic Italian named Giovanelli causes the girl to be cut socially by the American colony. After this, Daisy rashly visits Rome's miasmal Colosseum with thoughtless Giovanelli, becomes ill, and dies. Having discovered that Daisy was totally innocent after all, Winterbourne regrets his doubts about her virtue and admits, fatally late, that he has "lived too long in foreign parts." James's baffling little "study" of a modern American girl of the 1870s has taken on new meaning with the advent of women's liberation.

Washington Square (1881) brilliantly sets wealthy, widowered Dr. Austin Sloper of Washington Square, New York City, in opposition to his stolid daughter Catherine. When she meets Morris Townsend and is swept off her feet, her father judges (correctly) that Morris is a fortune hunter and volubly disapproves. Dr. Sloper's widowed busybody of a sister espouses the couple's cause even as the physician takes his daughter off to Europe. She remains passive but also determined; once home again, she declines Morris's selfish suggestion that she placate her father to avoid disinheritance. Catherine's misery, as caused by both father and "lover," is both poignant and lasting. *Washington Square* enjoyed what Gard calls a "good average sale (for James)," but the novelist excluded it from his New York Edition.

For occasional relaxation during this time, James traveled on a regular basis to France, Scotland, and Italy. Moreover, he maintained a dizzy social pace in London. He wrote to Grace Norton in June 1879 of "having dined out during the past winter 107 times!" No wonder he entitled one of his stories "The Siege of London" (1883).

Next came a monumental professional success followed by family sorrows. James found his income sufficient to permit him to plan and execute his longest novel, *The Portrait of a Lady* (1881), on which he pinned hopes for great renown. The novel concerns an American woman, from Albany, whose inherited wealth would make it possible for her sensibilities to be expanded by European travel and residence, but would also make her the prey of a serpentlike suitor in gardenlike Italy. Beginning the task of composing it in England in mid-1879, James worked on it in Florence in the spring of 1880 and in London from the summer of 1880 until February 1881, finishing it in Venice in the early summer of 1881. By this time it was appearing serially on both sides of the Atlantic: in England the first installment had been published in *Macmillan's Magazine* in Oc-

don. He wrote steadily and had his work published in rapid-fire order. *French Poets and Novelists* (1878) collected several of his sensitive periodical essays on such figures as Charles Baudelaire, Balzac, and *Théâtre Français* dramatists. *The Europeans* (1878) is a winsome study of the adventures of a Europeanized brother-and-sister combination visiting cousins back home in New England, judging their Puritanical strictures but also being quietly judged in return. New World innocence and moral rectitude come off rather well here.

Daisy Miller: A Study (1878), James's most popular success, was serialized in England and promptly pirated in two American periodicals before it was published as a book; the novelist thus lost much in royalties. In the story, expatriate American Frederick Forsyth Winterbourne meets attractive, enigmatically naive Daisy Miller, an American traveling with her vapid, gauche mother, while they are at Vevey. The two young people "improperly"

tober 1880, while the *Atlantic Monthly* began publishing it in November. These serializations, which ran into 1881, earned James about $5,000; book publication of the novel in England and the United States in late 1881 brought in still more money.

The Portrait of a Lady, James's first undisputed masterpiece, has a big cast of characters, several of whom might be construed as partly autobiographical. For example, James, like his heroine Isabel Archer, knew Albany as a child, traveled abroad on money which he had not earned, relished Europe enormously, and feared his own possible American provinciality. Like Isabel's cousin Ralph Touchett, James felt debarred from much normal activity through mysterious physical debility. And like Henrietta Stackpole, James sent journalistic travel letters from Europe, was loyal to America, but succumbed to the Old World at last. *The Portrait of a Lady*, however, is much more than veiled autobiography. Its simple, fairy-tale plot presents a callow, willful, charming American girl who is approached by three attractive suitors in Europe: Caspar Goodwood, a rich American manufacturer; Lord Warburton, aristocratic, ruddy, and political; and the successful Gilbert Osmond, fatally suave, superficially cultured, and as deeply corrupt as any villain in Hawthorne, Melville, or Faulkner. This rich and subtle novel is a study of deception and conceit, but also a portrayal of social and familial responsibility, and the possibility of triumph through renunciation of self, as Isabel chooses to remain with Osmond for the sake of his daughter, Pansy.

Once the first chapters of this great novel were being printed for book publication, James began to relax a good deal. He traveled in the British Isles and then in October returned, half fearfully, to America to see his aging parents in Cambridge. Independent now and enjoying the profits of *The Portrait of a Lady*, he took residence in a Boston hotel, where on 25 November 1881 he sat down and took stock of his life, recording his thoughts in a notebook: "I am glad I have come—it was a wise thing to do. I needed to see again *les miens*, to revive my relations with them . . . Such relations . . . are a part of one's life, and the best life . . . is the one that takes full account of such things. . . . Apart from this . . . it was not necessary I should come to this country. . . . I have made my choice, and God knows that I have now no time to waste. My choice is the old world—my choice, my need, my life. . . . the problem was settled long ago, and . . . I have now nothing to do but to act on the settlement." During his ample leisure, James went to New York, which seemed dull, and then paid his first visit to

Washington, D.C., calling on Henry Adams, whom he knew well by now, and on Adams's wife, Marian. On the evening of 29 January 1882 James was urgently called home from Washington; before he reached Cambridge, the greatest sorrow of his middle years had already happened: his beloved mother had died.

James recorded his impressions of winter in New England during his mother's funeral, later incorporating some of them in a weak short story called simply "A New England Winter" (1884). He stayed on at home, offering what comfort he could to his feeble old father, bereft but gently stoical. James piquantly wrote a family friend that "My father . . . has a way of his own of taking the sorrows of life—a way so perfect that one almost envies him his troubles." Then in May James went back "home" to Europe—first to Ireland, then to Bolton Street, London. His father sent a touching letter after him, "Good-bye then again, my precious Harry! . . . We [he and Alice James] shall each rejoice in you in our several way [*sic*] as you plough the ocean and attain to your old rooms, where it will be charming to think of you as once more settled and at work."

And work he did. He went carefully through familiar France and new spots there in the fall in preparation for *A Little Tour in France* (1884), one of his most remarkable books of travel. Ensconced back in London again for what he thought would be a winter of much writing, James was called to Massachusetts a final time. His father, no longer desirous of living, was slipping fast, and he died and was buried before the novelist docked in New York. Alice James seemed in somewhat better health at this time. Her friendship with Katherine Peabody Loring, later her traveling companion and private nurse, was a distinct help. The father had named Henry James rather than William James (then on research abroad) as executor of his will. Only the novelist's combination of tact and generosity prevented a family squabble, since William—now married and with a family—thought he should have more than an equitable fraction of their father's $95,000 estate.

After a stay in Cambridge, visiting his unsuccessful younger brothers in Milwaukee, and seeing old friends and familiar haunts in the Boston environs, James in August 1883 resolutely turned his face toward Europe once again. This time he was to remain abroad for the next two decades and more. He had found leisure to write a good deal while in America. Now his pace became fantastic. In 1881 he had no fiction published except *The Portrait of a Lady*. In 1882 he produced one story. In 1883 he had published two stories and an ill-starred dramatic version of *Daisy Miller* with a new and incongruous happy ending. But in 1884 he had six stories published, including the splendid "Lady Barbarina," "The Author of Beltraffio," and "Pandora." In addition, in November 1883 his friend Frederick Macmillan brought out the first collected edition of James's fiction in fourteen inexpensive little volumes. The first ten volumes republished *The Portrait of a Lady*, *Roderick Hudson*, *The American*, *Washington Square*, *The Europeans*, and, oddly, one of his weakest novels, *Confidence*. The last four volumes contained thirteen short stories, which illustrate international sexual relations, the contrast of American social gaucherie and European suavity, sad heroines, and what might be called societal incongruities in general. It must have gratified the forty-year-old expatriate American to see this selection of nearly 3,000 pages (well over 900,000 words) of his best fiction; excluded from it are some twenty-seven stories and his apprentice novel *Watch and Ward*.

James solidified his growing reputation with a significant manifesto of literary realism called "The Art of Fiction" in 1884. Started as a rebuttal to a recent lecture by critic and novelist Walter Besant, who had said that novels should have moral purpose and that novel writing can be taught like harmonics and perspective in other art forms, James's essay contends persuasively that fiction, like the best history and painting, should project a direct impression of real life, indeed, that the most artistic fiction competes with reality and—more—makes life worth living. James notes that saccharin fiction, with happy endings, is a base falsification of the real world, in which lives do not end thus. Rules for writing fiction injuriously restrict experiment. Far from limiting himself to his immediate range of experience, the writer should be allowed to project himself by his imagination, which "takes to itself the faintest hints of life, . . . converts the very pulses of the air into revelations." And far from being urged to decide whether to write novels of character or novels of incident, a new writer should be encouraged to make the most of reality seen all around him from his unique point of view. Finally, far from wanting novels to be didactic, James begs critics to let the writer freely choose his subject—his donnee—to find fault only with craftsmanship and execution, and to agree that "no good novel will ever proceed from a superficial mind." In addition, James argued for the theory, later very popular, that a piece of fiction is a living, organic entity with interdependent parts. James's own fiction generally

practices what is preached here.

The later years of the 1880s start James's middle period, during which the novelist continued to visit the Continent regularly, remained a loving brother, and worked hard. His mentor Turgenev had died in Paris in 1883; now James seemed to appoint himself mentor in his turn to talented novices. At about this time, in Paris and elsewhere, he made the acquaintance of the younger French writers Pierre Loti and Paul Bourget, the sickly Robert Louis Stevenson, and the expatriate American painter John Singer Sargent, among others. Late in 1884 Alice James voyaged to England, with Katherine Loring and that energetic woman's invalid sister. James, who had made over to Alice $1,200 per year from his patrimony, met the group in Liverpool and helped them settle in London and then Bournemouth. Alice's arrival reinforced Henry's belief that England was now his home; so the novelist leased larger quarters, at 34 De Vere Gardens, in Kensington, London, early in 1886. Meanwhile, 1885 and 1886 saw perhaps the most remarkable publishing event of his life. Appearing at about the same time were American serializations of two of his longest novels, *The Bostonians* and *The Princess Casamassima*. *The Bostonians* appeared in the *Century* (formerly *Scribner's Monthly*) February 1885-February 1886; *The Princess Casamassima*, in the *Atlantic Monthly* September 1885-October 1886.

These two novels represent substantive though not stylistic departures for James. *The Bostonians* concerns the post-Civil War feminist movement in New England, particularly Boston. It features an oratorically dazzling heroine named Verena Tarrant, who, somewhat stunted by wretched parental influences, becomes a passive object of contention between an old-fashioned, graciously sensual Confederate army veteran, Basil Ransom, now living in New York (and occasionally visiting Boston), and a possibly lesbian, well-to-do Bostonian political activist, Olive Chancellor. The novel also depicts many other female types, including a no-nonsense physician, a rich widow on the prowl, a vociferous organizer, and a dottering old reformer—Miss Birdseye—with memories as hoary as those of Elizabeth Peabody (Hawthorne's reform-minded sister-in-law), whom James too loudly denied using as his model. The male characters in *The Bostonians* are stereotypically chauvinistic, sinister, or foolish. It was as unpopular in book form as it had been when it was serialized. James earned less than £500 in all, from serial and book rights, but it has recently engaged the attention of many fine critics, especially feminist ones.

Moreover, most readers now praise it for its evocation of old Boston, for its murky depiction of the eternal battle of the sexes, and especially for its prescience with respect to aspects of women's liberation—for example, the misery of male parental dominance, the victimizing of women by women, marriage as cop-out, and the need for radicalism among reformers.

Political also is *The Princess Casamassima*, which is set in poverty-stricken sections of London, a la Dickens. It deals with international anarchism. Its hero is illegitimate Hyacinth Robinson, whose parents—a French adventuress and a British lord whom she stabbed to death—symbolize his psychic schism. An artistic little bookbinder in early manhood, Hyacinth pledges to assassinate a parasitic aristocrat, but then he is enabled by a small inheritance to have a taste of cultured Paris and Venice. Also wrenching him this way and that are the two loves of his brief life: the cultured but politically radical Princess Casamassima (who proved fatal to Roderick Hudson a decade earlier) and the grandly vulgar shopgirl Millicent Henning, James's most sensual female. Ultimately both women and other friends prove inconstant to Hyacinth; and so, unable to strike a blow against European aristocracy—rotten though it is—which produces sumptuous art, he puts a bullet through his own heart.

In book form *The Princess Casamassima* did not earn the advance of £ 550 which James received, and contemporary critics ridiculed it on the grounds that its author could not personally know about European anarchists. But in recent years the novel has perhaps been too extravagantly acclaimed for its exciting portrayals of would-be dynamiters and Dickensian have-nots.

Italy called James yet again. Feeling fatigued, without new ideas, and depressed by his books' lack of popularity, he went to Venice at the very end of 1886, stayed a couple of months, then moved on to Florence, where he shared a villa in the gentle hills outside town with Constance Fenimore Woolson, an unmarried expatriate American writer whom he had long known and who evidently cared for him more than he did for her. Here James wrote much of "The Aspern Papers," one of his most beautiful long short stories, inspired by the image of Claire Clairmont, the dead Lord Byron's aged former mistress, clinging to his letters. Wending his way north, James visited Venice again and returned to London after eight months, thoroughly refreshed. His next year's publishing record proves as much: in addition to "The Aspern Papers," the short novel *The Reverberator* (satirizing gossip columnists), six

short stories (including "The Liar" and "The Lesson of the Master"), and some critical and travel items.

The unpopularity of his last two lengthy novels had turned James against that form for the next couple of years. But in 1888 he started yet another piece of extended fiction, which he called *The Tragic Muse* and serialized in the *Atlantic Monthly* in seventeen installments, January 1889-May 1890. Its complex plot concerns a successful British politician who gives up his promising political career to study painting and a talented Jewish actress who, after studying in Paris, gives up marriage to a dashing British diplomat for success on the London stage. Art has its muse, says James, while politics and diplomacy do not, but serving the muse can be tragic for an artist's personal life.

James had long been a devotee of the theater—in America, London, and especially Paris—and he knew many actors and actresses. His next step was a new, daring, and partly damaging one. He vowed to write successful plays and spent five long years trying to do so. The lack of immediate popular or critical success of *The Tragic Muse* served only to push James harder toward playwriting. First, he accepted the invitation of an actor named Edward Compton to turn his melodramatic novel *The American* into a play. He did so in 1890, and it opened just outside Liverpool, with Compton in the leading role, with James's young American friend Elizabeth Robins (famous for her Ibsen roles in England) as Claire de Cintré, and with a happy ending. After Compton moved the troupe to London, the play was not well received, played only seventy nights, earned James only a moderate sum, but did not deter him from further efforts. By 1892 he had completed four new plays. He was led to believe that the famous American theatrical wizard Augustin Daly would convert one of them, called *Disengaged*, into a successful vehicle for his popular actress Ada Rehan. But so many troubles ensued that James, refusing to compromise with excessive production changes, demanded his script back and quit Daly. Never one to waste his materials, James had the four plays published in pairs as *Theatricals* (1894) and *Theatricals: Second Series* (1894). Meanwhile, in 1893 he completed yet another drama, this one entitled *Guy Domville*. The popular actor and producer George Alexander took it on. It opened on 5 January 1895; and, although James ultimately netted £ 750 on the play, it was a dismal failure. The play is set in the year 1780 and pits religious conviction against family responsibility, features melodramatic villainy, and rings with hollow lines (curiously James's fiction is filled with intensely dramatic

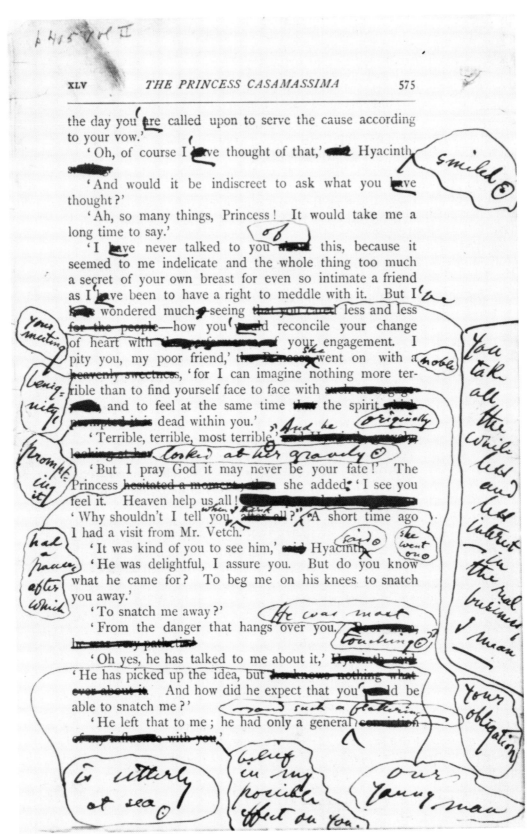

Pages from James's revision of The Princess Casamassima *for the New York Edition*

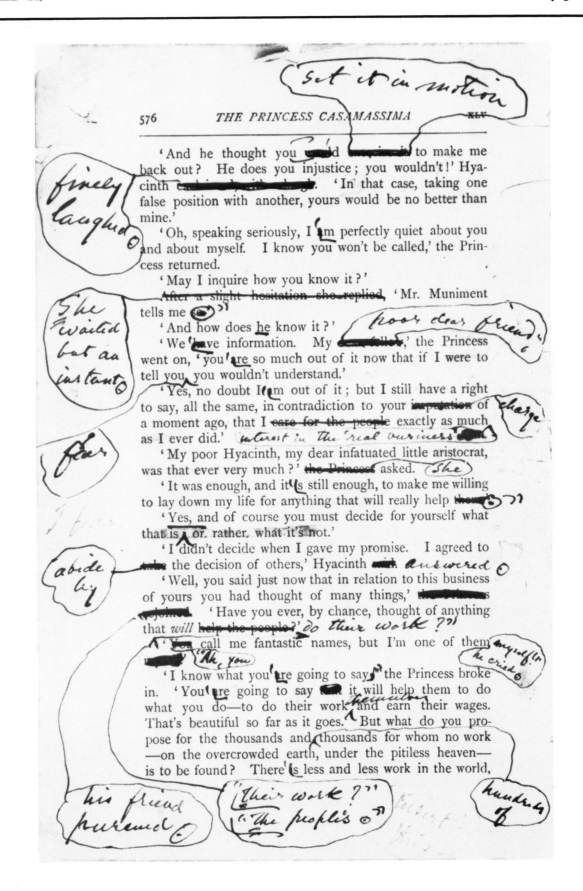

dialogue). James's friends in the first-night audience—including William Archer, Burne-Jones, Edmund Gosse, Sir Frederick Leighton, Sargent, and George Bernard Shaw—gave the opening a certain tone but could hardly save the play. When James appeared onstage at final-curtain time, he was booed. The play closed after one month.

It took James almost no time to recover his composure from this blow and to return to writing fiction, which, indeed, he never had abandoned during his dramatic years. Late in January 1895 he confided in his private notebook, "I take up my *own* old pen again—the pen of all my old unforgettable efforts and sacred struggles. To myself—today—I need say no more. Large and full and high the future still opens. It is now indeed that I may do the work of my life. And I will." At about the same time he found confidence enough to boast in a letter to William James that he was superior as a playwright to such popular contemporary dramatists as Oscar Wilde, noting of himself that "you can't make a sow's ear out of a silk purse." During his playwriting period James had published a number of splendid short stories: "The Pupil," about young male friendship and possible betrayal within a seedy expatriate family from America; "Sir Edmund Orme," a sophisticated ghost story; "Nona Vincent," about a playwright and an actress; "Owen Wingrave," about nonmilitary courage in a military family and the closest James ever came to writing naturalistic fiction; "The Middle Years," about second chances for aging novelists; "The Death of the Lion," about society's lionizing writers but ignoring their work; and "The Coxon Fund," about the risk of subsidizing an unstable genius—among other less distinguished pieces. Now James turned to writing more and possibly even greater fiction.

The half-decade now past had brought him personal sorrows enough to make even more profound his sharp probing of psychological reality. His old friend James Russell Lowell died in 1891. James's much-loved sister Alice died in London of breast cancer in 1892, with the novelist at her side. (She left a diary which was so personal and frank that James destroyed his copy of the privately printed edition.) Constance Fenimore Woolson, long sick in Venice, died there early in 1894 under curious circumstances, indicating the possibility of suicide; the news and then subsequent details alarmed James profoundly. (He avoided her funeral in Rome but obtained her family's permission to sort through the dead woman's private papers.) Late in 1894 Robert Louis Stevenson, whose vital

personality and adventuresome fiction James relished, died in faraway Samoa, in the South Seas. On top of these losses, the blow to his professional vanity occasioned by the collapse of his play *Guy Domville* was a heavy one.

A badly needed lift to his spirits came in the summer of 1896, when James vacationed in Rye, a little coastal town in Sussex, southeast of London, saw Lamb House there, and the following year took a long lease on the solid, cozy early eighteenth-century mansion. When he had the opportunity to purchase the delightful place two years later, he willingly paid the £2,000 asked. He quickly made it his home, entertained a succession of illustrious guests there, and fashioned some of his finest literary efforts in his garden-house studio adjacent. Numerous photographs show James in his well-manicured garden, alone and happy, or strolling with relatives and other visitors. Lamb House remained his residence for the remainder of his life. The aging James continued to visit old locales and many friends on the Continent, particularly in summer, and to participate in London social and theatrical seasons. He retained rooms in the London Reform Club for London visits and often went there to avoid Rye's damp and isolated winters or its muggy summers. But Lamb House was home now.

Much of the fiction which James wrote during this time is challenging, daring technically. He was now approaching the end of his so-called middle phase. The titles of two of his collections of short fiction, written before his move to Lamb House—*Terminations* (1895) and *Embarrassments* (1896)—may be an enigmatic comment on the wretched dramatic years of the author, who then plunged ahead with *The Spoils of Poynton* (1897), *What Maisie Knew* (1897), *The Turn of the Screw* (1898), and *The Awkward Age* (1899)—his first work written entirely at Lamb House. These fictional productions are remarkable, each in a different manner.

The Spoils of Poynton turns on an unfortunate British law: when a man dies, his widow must release his property to his oldest son. Not content to use this donnee merely to occasion a fictive family squabble, James dramatizes a brilliant development: have the widowed mother a fighter and her property include a dazzling collection of art objects, make the son bumbling and uncertain, and have a pair of contrasting young women both interested in him. The action continues mostly through the consciousness of Fleda Vetch, a somewhat impoverished young woman with taste enough to appreciate "the spoils." She is gently enamored of young Owen Gereth, but ruinously high principled and hence a match for neither her materialistic rival nor Owen's vindictive mother. The nature of Fleda's sexuality has puzzled readers and critics to this day. Does the young woman have good taste in men? Is she fatally negative, perverse? Does she allow too rigid scruples to make her seem inconsistent? Does she fear profound sexual arousal? Is "Victorianism" responsible for her final desolation?

What Maisie Knew centers in the emerging moral consciousness of an adolescent girl named Maisie Farange whose parents get divorced, marry others, and always treat the child selfishly. What Maisie gradually gains knowledge of is the baseness of some adults, the morality of one eccentric governess, and something which ought to be called love for her father's second wife's lover, who has become Maisie's mother's second husband. Poignant ambiguity results from innocent little Maisie's incomplete ability to verbalize her bewildering conceptions.

The Turn of the Screw, perhaps the world's finest ghost story, is the most satisfyingly ambivalent and provocative piece of fiction James ever wrote. In it, an unnamed governess, who narrates the main action with at least initial credibility, accepts the challenge of tutoring and overseeing the well-being of two young children, Miles and his little sister Flora. Their parents are dead, and their well-to-do uncle is altogether indifferent to them, except financially. He hires the governess (who seems immediately enamored of him and anxious to impress him) and dispatches her to stay with the children at his estate, Bly, in the remote English countryside. The governess is bright but possibly unstable. Suddenly one ghost, and then another, appears before her. One is that of the absent uncle's deceased valet; the other, that of the governess's (presumably) dead predecessor, who may have known the valet intimately. Curiously, only the governess sees the ghosts. Or is that the case? Are the ghosts real? Are they figments of the governess's imagination? Are they projections from her reading, or from her unrequited passion for the children's uncle? James himself is uninformative in critical comments on the puzzling work, which, in his preface to it in the New York Edition, he labels "a piece of ingenuity pure and simple, of cold artistic calculation, an *amusette* to catch those not easily caught. . . , the jaded, the disillusioned, the fastidious." The critical battle is still raging, and it is likely to do so indefinitely, since James seems consciously to have salted his text with veins leading in different directions.

In *The Awkward Age*, which also deals with children, two girls "come out" together in London society, which is a veritable horse fair parading marriageable young females before potential customers. James chose to write the story mostly in dialogue—complete with tersely narrated entrances and exits—and with a minimum of authorial explanation. The technique evidently puzzled early readers of *The Awkward Age*, which sold poorly in James's lifetime, but James's young protege Percy Lubbock later praised the novel for its "pure drama."

In 1900, at the start of the century whose literature he was to influence so spectacularly, Henry James shaved off his beard, thus greeting the new age more openly, and then proceeded to launch himself into what may well be the most impressive siege of writing, lasting through 1904, in the annals of American literary history. A collection of twelve short stories, *The Soft Side* (1900), was followed by *The Sacred Fount* (1901), *The Wings of the Dove* (1902), eleven more short stories in *The Better Sort* (1903), *The Ambassadors* (1903), a two-volume biography, *William Wetmore Story and His Friends* (1903), and *The Golden Bowl* (1904). This unprecedented burst of creativity, amounting to more than 3,000 pages, is all the more remarkable when one considers that James, from his earliest Lamb House days, had been in the habit of dictating most of his "writing" to a typist, not only because of a slight weakness in his right wrist but also because the volume of his personal correspondence had become almost unmanageable.

The Soft Side includes an innocuous ghost story about decorous smuggling, "The Third Person," set in and near Lamb House. *The Sacred Fount* fictionalizes the theory that in any interpersonal relationship one partner takes while the other is tapped dry of vitality. It is told in the first person by a possibly unreliable narrator who may not be sane and it has been seen as a parable of the artistic life. To some readers, it is prolix and otherwise unsatisfactory; others, however, feel that probing it successfully is tantamount to fathoming James himself. *The Better Sort* includes "The Beast in the Jungle," which, incredibly, James could not place in any journal before its book publication. This matchless story deals with John Marcher, who keeps himself aloof from life because he fancies that life plans to spring something uniquely special on him eventually. He insufficiently commits himself to May Bartram, who guesses the nature of "the beast" in Marcher's life but agrees to wait with him to see.

Henry and William James, circa 1901

Too late the foolish egoist learns that he is fated to be the one man on earth to whom nothing happens. The story has compelling imagery of masks, fire, and ice, and its syntax is as sluggish as its absurdist hero.

Entering what is now known as his major phase, James, with *The Wings of the Dove*, *The Ambassadors*, and *The Golden Bowl*, wrote a Dantesque commedia, a monumental triptych, three incomparable novels of expatriate Americans in England, Italy, and France. These tangled fables tell us much about renunciation and generosity, the value of studying new modes of moral behavior, and the price of love; the backgrounds of these actions inspire James to some of his best pictorial effects, especially when he limns glittering Paris and mouldering Venice.

Milly Theale, heroine of *The Wings of the Dove*, is like James's long-dead cousin Minny Temple, "heiress of all the ages," in the sense of being sensitive, cultured, bright, and well-to-do. But Milly is also dying. When British journalist Merton Densher is encouraged by his materialistic, egocentric fiancee Kate Croy to woo Milly for an eventual legacy, he agrees. Milly eventually finds out from the young man's rival, "turns her face to the wall," and dies—leaving Merton a vast sum. Meanwhile, her dovelike

generosity changes him, although Milly's bequest may have been a subtle form of revenge. The conscience-stricken Densher tells Kate he will marry her only if he refuses the bequest, but she refuses to marry him unless he takes it. The first part of the novel is cast in England, with beautiful late Victorian settings in and near London. Later, as Milly grows sicker, the scene shifts to sinister Venice.

The Ambassadors, which James called "quite the best, 'all round,' of all my productions," was inspired by his hearing that Howells, while in the painter James Whistler's Parisian garden, had cautioned a young acquaintance, "I'm old. It's too late. It has gone past me—I've lost it. You have time. You are young. Live!" From that "wind-blown seed," as he often called the inspiration of a plot, James nurtured his finest, most artistically integrated novel. Lambert Strether, a partly autobiographical New England editor, undertakes an ambassadorial mission to Paris for his domineering, widowed fiancee. He is to learn why her son Chad Newsome is dallying abroad and to bring him home to the family business. Strether finds the young man much improved in appearance, manners, and intellect, and soon wonders whether Chad loves married Marie de Vionnet (a bit too old for him) or her lithe daughter Jeanne (too young). Since every one is evasively genteel, it takes Strether so long to make a determination that a squad of new "ambassadors" is dispatched by the absent mother. By this time, Chad has grown willing to detach himself, but Strether has now espoused not only the Vionnets' cause but Gallic ethical relativism in general. Strether begins to change for the better, as Chad must have done for a while earlier. Strether's discovery that Chad and Marie are lovers is so beautifully orchestrated that it is a high point in American fiction, complete with French impressionistic backdrop. Character balances render the entire novel as modulated as a minuet: Strether learns graceful Old World steps, as Chad backs away into American awkwardness again; Chad advances toward little Jeanne, then minces away with her mother. James's high opinion of *The Ambassadors* is fully justified—by all evidence, that is, except initially poor book sales. A notable stylistic element in the novel is the manner in which the reader is permitted to learn, which is largely by seeing what and as Strether does, by tentatively concluding with him: as Strether sympathizes with others, so the reader empathizes.

Many critics regard *The Golden Bowl* as its author's finest novel. It offers the reader a plot of mathematical neatness wrapped in Jamesian syntax at its most difficult. A rich American widower and art collector named Adam Verver is traveling with his young adult daughter Maggie, who marries suave Prince Amerigo of Rome, formerly the lover of Charlotte Stant, whom Maggie once knew as well. Sensing her father's loneliness, Maggie throws Charlotte in his path, and Adam and Charlotte soon marry. But father and daughter remain too close. So Amerigo and Charlotte resume their sexual liaison. Earlier, Amerigo and Charlotte, while shopping for a wedding present for Maggie, rejected a beautiful golden bowl because it was flawed. Later Maggie happens upon it and learns indirectly through the shopkeeper of the intimacy of her husband and the young woman who is now her stepmother. Maggie now has an awesome moral problem. She wants her husband, but she also wishes to hurt neither her father nor her rival. James shows the intimacy of Adam and Maggie and depicts the adultery of the Prince and Charlotte with what must be called sympathy by resorting to the technical device of the confidante. He gives Maggie a sympathetic ear in the person of Fanny Assingham, an old family friend. Long-winded Fanny in turn makes a patient confidant of her husband Colonel Bob. But mainly James manages difficulties through indirections and even silences in dialogue,

ambiguities in narration, and operatic inner scenes first in the Prince's mind and later in Maggie's. That James could keep these gossamer-fine subtleties in mental suspension as, month after month, he dictated this 192,000-word novel in his Lamb House chambers, is amazing. *The Golden Bowl* enjoyed a modest success in England, outselling every other one of his London-published books except his controversial *Hawthorne* (1879).

Next James reluctantly agreed to put together *William Wetmore Story and His Friends* from masses of papers which his friend's family made available to him. Story (1819-1895), who had given up his position as a lawyer at Harvard and Boston for expatriation in Rome, where he was sculptor, painter, poet, musician, and travel writer, seemed to James a dilettante; but he nonetheless strung together his subject's papers with fascinating narrative commentary, valuable today only because in it James discusses his own memories of Rome in Story's day.

With his symphonically sustained fiction of the last five years now behind him, James turned his thoughts to rest, travel, lecturing, and note taking in the United States. He projected a travel book on his American sightseeing. Late in August 1904 he sailed from England and was soon enjoying a New England autumn with William James and his family. James stayed with them first in their summer home at Chocorua, New Hampshire, and then at Cambridge. During the Christmas season he went to New York, which seemed to him deplorably altered by tall buildings and noisy commerce. While there, he attended a Harper and Brothers banquet, where the guest list also included Samuel Clemens and Hamlin Garland. Next he went to Philadelphia, where he read his paper called "The Lesson of Balzac" to a culture club for $250. (He later commanded even higher fees—up to £1 per minute, as he once gloated.) He continued on to Washington, D.C. where, through the influence of his old friends John Hay (now secretary of state under President Theodore Roosevelt) and Henry Adams, he had dinner at the White House. (Roosevelt privately regarded James as "a miserable little snob," while the novelist privately called the wielder of the Big Stick "a dangerous . . . jingo.") After a visit to Virginia, blanketed by late snows which spoiled James's hope of seeing a Southern spring there, the traveler returned to the Philadelphia area to lecture at Bryn Mawr College and then went on to Richmond, Charleston, where he called upon Owen Wister, and Florida. James capitalized on his unexpected podium popularity by lecturing successfully in St. Louis, Chicago, Notre Dame, Indianapolis, and Los Angeles. He reveled in California, seeing it from the point of view of one familiar with Mediterranean coastal regions and noting resemblances. Soon he headed north to Oregon and Seattle, then traveled east as quickly as possible early in the spring, going through St. Paul and Chicago, loathing most of what he saw and heard—the clatter, aliens, unpleasant ghettos, and what he regarded as the mangling of the English language.

For the 1905 commencement at Bryn Mawr, James was the principal speaker, and he tactlessly chose "The Question of Our [American] Speech" as his subject. He attacked the natives for their slipshod speech patterns and was counterattacked in return for his syntactical complexities. Soon he ran up to Boston—though not again to see William James, who had mysteriously avoided him by going to Greece. The two had drifted apart since the death of their parents. Curiously, while William was in Greece he was elected to membership in the American Academy of Arts and Letters, but he was elected two months after his younger brother Henry had been. Learning this only upon his return home, William declined the honor, writing the Academy that the James family was sufficiently represented by "my younger and shallower and vainer brother."

Henry James went on to Maine, to enjoy a reunion with the vacationing Howells. Moving south again, James spent a while with Edith Wharton in her American home at Lenox, Massachusetts, and conferred with representatives at Charles Scribner's Sons for a sumptuous selected edition of his best fiction. July found him steaming east to Liverpool. His ten months back in America had been refreshing, impressive, enervating, and lucrative. He was now ready for his real home again, in Sussex. While still aboard the ship, he began the task of revising *Roderick Hudson* for the New York Edition. At the same time his memory was teeming with impressions which he was impatient to focus into a book on America.

Once back at Rye, James had to assert his authority in Lamb House, where problems arose with two of his servants. More happily, he soon reestablished his British friendships after his long absence. Next he began converting his American travel notes into *The American Scene*. He also started rereading the bulk of his enormous fictional productions, eventually selecting sixty-seven novels and tales as suitable, with revision, for inclusion in the New York Edition and rejecting the rest. At the same time, he planned to write a series of critical prefaces for the edition. Minor publishing ventures distracted him a trifle: early in October 1905 he put

together his lectures on Balzac and American speech patterns in a small book. Later in the same month he gathered fourteen old essays and two new ones on English scenes in *English Hours*.

The American Scene (1907) is James's most penetrating travel book, and one of the best of its

Editorial cartoon at the time of James's 1905 American tour

genre in world literature. James limited himself to his observations of the Eastern seaboard. (He hoped to write a follow-up volume on his Western travels but did not live to do so.) He reveals uncanny powers of visual perception in the present and with it tender sensory memories of his fading past. Since the purpose is personal evocation, the book usually lacks the social background normally found in an effort, as James puts it, to depict "a society reaching out into the apparent void for the amenities . . . after having earnestly gathered in so many of the . . . necessities." From New England to Florida James ranges, sees, and records his impressions. He is at his depressing best in describing New York City, which he found so grossly, energetically materialistic that it would take a potent Zola, not a squeamish James, to embody it in fiction. As they disturbed Howells earlier, the slums dismayed James and in his book he therefore contents himself with commenting on the threat to spoken English there and then the charm of adjacent stores. Better far is his treatment of Manhattan architecture, the eclectic clutter of which symbolizes the city as explosive chaos.

Pathetic nostalgia combines with an implicit admonition in James's eloquent description of his lost Newport: "it had simply lain there like a little bare, white, open hand, with slightly-parted fingers, for the observer with a presumed sense for hands to take or to leave. The observer with a real sense never failed to pay this image the tribute of quite tenderly grasping the hand, and even of raising it, delicately, to his lips. . . . The touchstone of taste was indeed to operate, for the critical, the tender spirit, from the moment the pink palm was turned up on the chance of what might be 'in' it. For nine persons out of ten, among its visitors, its purchasers of sites and builders. . ., there had never been anything in it at all—except of course an opportunity . . . The pink palm being empty, in other words, to their vision, they had begun . . . to put things into it, things of their own, and of all sorts, and of many ugly, and of more and more expensive, sorts; to fill it substantially, that is, with gold, the gold that they have ended by heaping up there to an amount so oddly out of proportion to the scale of nature and of space."

The sections on the South in *The American Scene*, though gracefully composed and predictably observant of architecture and setting, lack the sociological acumen demonstrated in those few chapters on regions James knew best and dreamed of most fondly: New England, New York, and the Hudson River region. The book is valuable today for its timeless warning to all Americans: treasure old local color, avoid ravaging the land, resist placing commerce above all else, respect your best art, look about, look out. The often gloomy message is lightened by glints of Jamesian humor and decidedly resembles the prophetic admonitions of Henry David Thoreau.

Preparing the splendid New York Edition cost James about four years. In his short story "The Real Thing" (1893) he had described tardy justice finally rendered to a neglected writer by means of a well-illustrated *édition de luxe*. Here was James's own chance. The aging novelist extensively revised earlier tales, making them more subtle in the eyes of critics who prefer his major-phase style, but veiling their romantic crispness according to those who like the early James best. He rejected works which neither could be cleaned by "the tentative wet sponge" and then "varnish[ed] . . . anew" (as he

puts it in his preface to *Roderick Hudson*, the edition's first volume) nor could be fitted into Balzacian thematic units. James collaborated with a pioneering young American photographer, Alvin Langdon Coburn, for frontispieces which might hint at fictive contents without being blatant and delimiting. Best of all, James wrote eighteen prefaces in which he discusses individual works as to their inspiration and compositional difficulties, includes relevant personal anecdotes, and mentions laudable successes and technical aspects where germane. His self-evaluation, sparkling with fine imagery, amounts to subjective literary criticism of the very highest order.

Twelve volumes of the New York Edition were devoted to six of James's best novels: *The Portrait of a Lady*, *The Princess Casamassima*, *The Tragic Muse*, *The Wings of the Dove*, *The Ambassadors*, and *The Golden Bowl*. *Roderick Hudson*, *The American*, and *The Awkward Age* took another volume each. Other novels and also long short stories and shorter tales accounted for the rest, bringing the total edition to twenty-four volumes. (After James's death, his unfinished novels *The Ivory Tower* and *The Sense of the Past* were added, in a volume each.) James labored hard to group the shorter works he had selected into fiction about English life, international manners, artists and writers, and things supernatural. Omitted therefore were *The Europeans*, *Washington Square*, and *The Bostonians* (all set in America), most of the American-based short stories, the weak novels *Watch and Ward*, *Confidence*, and *The Sacred Fount*, and dozens of early tales.

Volumes of the New York Edition appeared regularly from late 1907 until mid-1909. James had had such high hopes for good sales that low royalty reports—as little as £85 in all!—plunged him into gloom. He had worked frantically on revisions and prefaces alike, allowing himself only one good-sized vacation, in 1907, when he traveled by automobile with Edith Wharton and her husband through southern France, and then went on alone to Italy for a final time. During the same year he had made the mistake of dabbling in more playwriting, with no more success than in the early 1890s. He collected a volume of his critical essays, *Views and Reviews*, in 1908 (but some of these pieces were forty years old). *Italian Hours* (1909), James's last travel book, gathers more than a dozen previously published essays and adds five new ones. The volume is beautifully illustrated by Joseph Pennell and is one of the most delightful literary works on Italy by any American.

As for writing new fiction, in the next few

years James slowed down but was never idle. Despite his other work and then his depression over poor sales of his New York Edition, he wrote eight more tales. Three were in time for inclusion in that edition. One, "The Jolly Corner," is a captivating story of an expatriate's return to the Manhattan neighborhood of his childhood. The hero wonders with such intensity what he might have been like had he remained at home that he actually sees his alter ego. Among the last five tales that James wrote are "The Bench of Desolation," a surreal fable recently evoking splendid readings, and "A Round of Visits," a story about betrayal, crime, and suicide, set in New York City. James included these last five stories in *The Finer Grain* (1910)—an appropriate choice of title for the master of fictive subtlety.

James suffered through a long period of nervous sickness beginning in 1909. William James, though sick himself—with severe heart trouble—and his wife, Alice, came to Lamb House in the summer of 1910 to be of moral support. The three journeyed to Germany and Switzerland in search of health. But William became worse, so, sick though he was, Henry decided to return with him and his wife to New Hampshire, where William died in August. Henry was now the only survivor of the five children. He was desolate and wrote his old friend T. S. Perry, "I sit heavily stricken and in darkness—for from far back in dimmest childhood he had been my ideal Elder Brother, and I still, through all the years, saw in him, even as a small timorous boy yet, my protector, my backer, my authority and my pride. His extinction changes the face of life for me. . . ."

James remained in America for a year, during which time he accepted an honorary degree from Harvard University (Oxford University followed suit in 1912), consulted physicians in the hope of curing his partly psychosomatic disorders, and evidently tried, while staying in dead William's Cambridge house, to communicate with his brother's spirit. He also saw Edith Wharton and Howells again. August 1911 found James steaming back to England. His traveling days were over.

His widowed sister-in-law, Alice James, was so impressed by his ability to evoke the distinct family past through tender reminiscences that she persuaded James to write them down. Finding Lamb House something of a cage that aggravated his depression, he let his secretary engage him a room or two in her apartment building in Chelsea, London, near the Reform Club, where he slept; soon he was pouring forth an almost unstoppable stream of autobiography at her. It was great therapy. In *A*

Small Boy and Others James shares his earliest recollections, then slowly describes his teens to the point where he suffered from typhoid at Boulogne. By the time the book was published in 1913, James was well into *Notes of a Son and Brother,* which draws on masses of old family letters, portrays his father and favorite brother, and brings the author into his mid-twenties. It was published in 1914, during which year James also gathered *Notes on Novelists with Some Other Notes*, an important collection of eighteen critical and travel pieces, all of which had previously appeared in journals. His subjects include Balzac, George Sand, Stevenson, Zola, the new generation of novelists (most of whom James prize[d] not"), and London.

James had now reached seventy years of age. He was living in an apartment at 21 Carlyle Mansions, Chelsea, with three servants, staying at Lamb House only during the summer. His poor royalties were slipping even more; so Edith Wharton, with more good intentions than good sense, tried secretly to make up a birthday purse for him through friends. James got wind of the plan and furiously stopped it. However, he accepted, as a seventieth-birthday gift, an expensive silver bowl and dish plated with gold (a Golden Bowl) from 300 distinguished friends; he also sat for a portrait by John Singer Sargent, and donated it to the National Portrait Gallery, London.

The publication of *Notes of a Son and Brother* carried James by its momentum into further autobiographical dictation. The book was to be followed by a third volume and possibly two more. But *The Middle Years* (1917), starting with his first adult trip to Europe, remains a fragment of only 120 pages because in the summer of 1914 World War I crashed into James's tenuously cohering world and wrenched it irretrievably. Describing the war, James wrote a close friend about "the appalling blackness of it all, and the horror of having lived to see it!" He threw himself into what war work he could manage, given his age and his now weakened heart. He visited hospitals and comforted the wounded, made his quarters available to soldiers in transit, supported an American ambulance corps, and wrote to denounce German atrocities and to praise British and French courage. On 26 July 1915, James became a British citizen (sponsored by Prime Minister Herbert Asquith), not only to put a stop to the inconvenience of having to get permission from the police to go to Lamb House in coastal Rye as an alien but also to protest his native country's continued neutrality.

Not even the war could silence James the

writer. Curiously, he had begun his professional writing during the Civil War; he was destined to end it during another war. He had started a new long novel some years earlier, perhaps in 1908. Set in gracious Newport, it was to dramatize the reconciliation of rich, disputatious former business partners and also to concern a Europeanized American returning to an inheritance and quickly becoming entangled in financial betrayal and sexual intrigue. Early in 1914 James felt well enough to resume work on this novel to which he had given the title *The Ivory Tower*. If completed, it might have been an almost Theodore Dreiser-like study of wealth, culture, and temptation. But the war came; James, now back in Lamb House, found it impossible to address a contemporary problem, and so he abandoned the work when it was about thirty percent complete. But he still did not quit. Instead, he turned to another long-delayed project, a historical novel to be called *The Sense of the Past*, begun about fifteen years before in his excitement following the success of "The Turn of the Screw." This new long fiction would combine James's interest in extrasensory phenomena, international social relations, and the past. In it a young New York historian named Ralph Pendrel writes a book which so pleases an English relative that he wills the American an eighteenth-century mansion in London. Taking possession of it, Pendrel is deeply stirred by evidence of the past in its portraits, furniture, appointments, and very atmosphere—so much so that one day as he steps across the threshold he finds himself in the eighteenth century communing with his eighteenth-century alter ego, whose picture has been on the wall. Later he becomes that earlier Pendrel and converses with his fiancée, Molly Midmore, who is also exactly like her portrait. He meets his prospective sister-in-law Nan Midmore and quickly feels an affinity to her because of her—their—modernity. Rivalry starts between Pendrel and Nan's suitor, at which point the fragmentary novel breaks off.

Two unpleasant circumstances intervened to disturb James while he was writing the early parts of *The Sense of the Past*. In *Boon* (1915) H. G. Wells made a stinging attack on James's mannered style. He compared a Jamesian novel to "a church lit but without a congregation. . . , with every light and line focused on the high altar. And on the altar, very reverently placed, intensely there, is a dead kitten, an egg-shell, a bit of string. . . . [James] splits his infinitives and fills them up with adverbial stuffing. He presses the passing colloquialism into his service. His vast paragraphs sweat and struggle . . . And all

Henry James, circa 1905, when he was working on
The American Scene

for tales of nothingness. . . . It is leviathan retrieving pebbles. It is a magnificent but painful hippopotamus resolved at any cost . . . upon picking up a pea which had got into a corner of its den."

A second unpleasantness came in the form of violent denunciation in America of James for his supposed disloyalty in giving up his American citizenship to become a British citizen. He did not trouble to explain. He might have reminded his Yankee readers of his Christopher Newman, Daisy Miller, Isabel Archer, Milly Theale, Lambert Strether, and Adam and Maggie Verver—Americans all, and mostly innocent, decent, attractive, and eager to confront reality, and probably all moral victors in their clashes with smooth Europeans. But James let his fiction debate in his stead.

To Wells, however, James wrote a series of epistolary rejoinders, at first protesting, then explaining, and finally theorizing that "It is art that *makes* life, makes interest, makes importance, . . . and I know of no substitute whatever for the force and beauty of its process."

On 2 December 1915 James was in his apartment on 21 Carlyle Mansions when he sustained a stroke, which paralyzed his left side. His maid heard him say that the beast in the jungle had sprung. He later told a friend that as he fell he thought, "So it has come at last—the Distinguished Thing." The next day, he had another stroke. William James's widow, Alice James, received the news and crossed the wintry Atlantic at once to be with James until the end. Delirium upset his sense of place, and he grew frantic, but by mid-January he had improved. In moments of confusion, he dictated rambling thoughts of Robert Louis Stevenson and Henry Adams. James was mentally wandering and sometimes spoke of cities in Ireland and Italy. But more awesome and suggestive were letters which James in his delirium dictated from Napolean Bonaparte to relatives, concerning renovations of the Louvre and the Tuileries. The Louvre was again on James's mind, decades after his momentous dream of its Galerie d'Apollon.

Meanwhile, regal machinery of another sort was being set in motion. Prime Minister Asquith recommended to King George V that James be granted the Order of Merit. The award was announced on 1 January 1916, and James was lucid and delighted when his old friend the historian-diplomat James, Lord Bryce brought the insignia from the king. Through February James rambled much about William. During the afternoon of 28 February 1916, Henry James quietly died, technically of edema. After a funeral service in Chelsea Old Church and subsequent cremation, his ashes were transported to the United States and placed in the James family plot in Cambridge, Massachusetts.

After James's death, his works continued to decline in popularity for about a quarter of a century. But roughly with the outbreak of World War II, a new generation of readers began to see the value of his psychological profundity and of his perceptions about international manners. During the early 1940s, and especially in 1943, on the occasion of the centenary of his birth, the so-called James boom began. It has shown no letup in the succeeding decades. Some of the important commentators on James in his lifetime and shortly after his death are William Dean Howells, Joseph Conrad, Ford Madox (Hueffer) Ford, Ezra Pound, T. S.

Eliot, Joseph Warren Beach, and Percy Lubbock. Contributing to the James boom were R. P. Blackmur, Philip Rahv, Stephen Spender, Edna Kenton, Edmund Wilson, and F. O. Matthiessen. In the last quarter of a century more than 100 books and close to 2,000 chapters and journal essays have added to the ongoing boom. It would be impossible to name the best five or ten modern Jamesian critics without committing a tasteless sin of omission. Perhaps it should be added that in addition to H. G. Wells, two voices raised against the chorus of praise for James are those of Van Wyck Brooks and Maxwell Geismar. In truth, James left a legacy which is well worth the most serious, varied, and conscientious study.

James's literary production was staggering. His fiction alone amounts to twenty-two novels and 113 short stories. In addition, he wrote enough critical essays to fill about ten books, seven books of travel, three of autobiography, fifteen plays, and two critical biographies. Fifteen thousand of his personal letters are extant. On an average, one item by James was published every three weeks for more than half a century, in total volume possibly not much short of eight million words.

Of more lasting importance than prodigious quantity and selective popularity, however, are the high quality of James's work and its influence on other writers. James wrote on a limited range of themes but with subtlety and charm. He frequently depicts the clash of American inexperience and European sophistication. Often the American is an innocent person of wealth and intelligence, traveling in Europe and seeking to penetrate its cultural, social, and ethical mysteries. James sometimes complicates his conflicts by making his representatives of European culture Americans living abroad—hence at times trying to be more European than their native friends and neighbors. James's American naifs usually fail to achieve personal and social happiness and success, but they gain in moral esteem, in their eyes and those of their friendly readers. James always combines the international theme with other themes. He may stage with international overtones a drama which illustrates not only the virtue of a forgiving consideration for others but also the vices of meddling, coercion, or revenge. Or he may have the clash of personalities from different countries and social milieus effectuate in an exposure of such false values as social ambition, patriotism, exertion for fame, and pride—pride in one's pedigree, appearance, social renown, or connections. Sometimes these fictive dramas involve only Americans; sometimes, only Englishmen and

Englishwomen. James constantly placed his faith in art, rather than in formal religion, political power, wealth, or possessions; and he preferred professional independence rather than personal "love," involvement rather than smug aloofness, or fear of variety, or secondhand living. James was steadily unromantic and individualistic.

James's work is stylistically complicated, demanding much of the reader. He is verbally subtle and delicately comic. His use of the restricted point of view, especially in his later, more realistic work, makes his plots hard to follow but exciting because the reader shares the same delusions, limited perceptions, and dawning awarenesses as the character through whose consciousness the story is filtered. James's imagery adds a poetic dimension to his prose, and individual similes and metaphors cluster into patterns which elucidate human conduct. James's plots are precise and usually quite simple. His purpose is not to tell a story so much as it is to show the interaction between character and character and between character and setting, which is often presented pictorially and usually has symbolic import.

James's fiction is like life. It presents challenges, not answers. It deals in tension resulting from the collision of personalities having different backgrounds and degrees of decency. His endings are almost always unhappy and often unjust, and readers used to final wrap-ups often complain. But James once said that an entire story can never be told, that the novelist should therefore present only what harmonizes.

James's heroines are better than his heroes, more vibrant as artistic creations and finer models for the reader to emulate. James's settings and props are impressionistically painted in, and appreciating his artistry here sharpens the reader's vision for the appreciation of his own surrounding reality. James's concomitant love of fiction, poetry, drama, biography, painting, and sculpture inspires his devotees to try to see for themselves the unity of all art. Awareness of James's sturdy defense of his profession, his craft, is noble and worthy of emulation.

James was forward-looking and hence his work wears well. He tentatively explored eroticism (especially in the young), imaginative quests through time, nihilism, and absurdist disorientations. James disliked shapeless novels, bulky with social or personal protest and holding up a mirror to chaotic reality; he preferred those with balanced parts and a tidied appearance that please through subjective probing and unusual artistic tension and

balance. He has a character in *The Tragic Muse* say, "The book of life's padded, ah but padded—a deplorable want of editing." James sought to edit and thus order the reality he knew. Nearly every artistically shaped novel in English since James, and perhaps many not in English too, have probably been at least indirectly influenced by his example. What James ignores in his fiction would make a long list. Among many other things, a James character rarely works for a living or grabs a quick breakfast. His characters are usually rich enough, instead, to indulge their imaginations more sedately. Joseph Conrad once said that James is "the historian of fine consciences."

Henry James has frequently been compared to other writers. He belongs in a distinguished company which includes Nathaniel Hawthorne, Mark Twain, William Dean Howells, Edith Wharton, George Eliot, Joseph Conrad, Ivan Turgenev, Marcel Proust, Anton Chekhov. He lacks the sweep of Tolstoy, the humanitarianism of Dickens, the animal energy of Balzac. In the American Pantheon, he belongs with Hawthorne as a moral fabulist, Melville as a tragic-comic stylist, and Twain as a painter of innocents at home and abroad.

Letters:

The Letters of Henry James, edited by Percy Lubbock, 2 volumes (London: Macmillan, 1920; New York: Scribners, 1920);

Henry James: Letters to A. C. Benson and Auguste Monod, edited by E. F. Benson (London: Mathews & Marrot/New York: Scribners, 1930);

Theatre and Friendship: Some Henry James Letters with a Commentary by Elizabeth Robins (London: Cape, 1932; New York: Putnam's, 1932);

Henry James and Robert Louis Stevenson: A Record of Friendship and Criticism, edited by Janet Adam Smith (London: Hart-Davis, 1948);

Virginia Harlow, *Thomas Sergeant Perry: A Biography and Letters to Perry from William, Henry, and Garth Wilkinson James* (Durham, N.C.: Duke University Press, 1950);

Selected Letters of Henry James, edited by Leon Edel (New York: Farrar, Straus & Cudahy, 1955);

Henry James and H. G. Wells: A Record of Their Friendship, Their Debate on the Art of Fiction, and Their Quarrel, edited by Edel and Gordon N. Ray (London: Hart-Davis, 1958);

Edel and Lyall H. Powers, "Henry James and the *Bazar* Letters," *Bulletin of the New York Public Library*, 62 (February 1958): 75-103;

Henry James: Letters, edited by Edel (Cambridge: Harvard University Press, 1974-   ).

Bibliographies:

Richard N. Foley, *Criticism in American Periodicals of the Works of Henry James from 1866 to 1916* (Washington, D.C.: Catholic University Press, 1944);

Leon Edel and Dan H. Laurence, *A Bibliography of Henry James*, revised edition (London: Hart-Davis, 1961);

Maurice Beebe and William T. Stafford, "Criticism of Henry James: A Selected Checklist," revised list, *Modern Fiction Studies*, 12 (Spring 1966): 117-177;

Robert L. Gale, "Henry James," in *Eight American Authors: A Review of Research and Criticism*, revised edition, edited by James Woodress (New York: Norton, 1971), pp. 321-375;

Beatrice Ricks, *Henry James: A Bibliography of Secondary Works* (Metuchen, N.J.: Scarecrow, 1975);

Kristin Pruitt McColgan, *Henry James 1917-1959: A Reference Guide* (Boston: G. K. Hall, 1979);

Dorothy McInnis Scura, *Henry James 1960-1974: A Reference Guide* (Boston: G. K. Hall, 1979).

Biographies:

Theodora Bosanquet, *Henry James at Work* (London: Hogarth Press, 1924);

Pelham Edgar, *Henry James: Man and Author* (London: Richards, 1927);

Clinton Hartley Grattan, *The Three Jameses: A Family of Minds: Henry James, Sr., William James, Henry James* (New York: Longmans, Green, 1932);

Simon Nowell-Smith, *The Legend of the Master: Henry James* (New York: Scribners, 1948);

F. W. Dupee, *Henry James* (New York: Sloane, 1951; revised edition, Garden City: Doubleday, 1956);

Leon Edel, *Henry James: The Untried Years, 1843-1870* (Philadelphia & New York: Lippincott, 1953);

Robert Charles LeClair, *The Young Henry James, 1843-1870* (New York: Bookman, 1955);

Edel, *Henry James: The Conquest of London, 1870-1881* (Philadelphia & New York: Lippincott, 1962);

Edel, *Henry James: The Middle Years, 1882-1895* (Philadelphia & New York: Lippincott, 1962);

Edel, *Henry James: The Treacherous Years, 1895-1901* (Philadelphia & New York: Lippincott, 1969);

H. Montgomery Hyde, *Henry James at Home* (London: Methuen, 1969);

Edel, *Henry James: The Master, 1901-1916* (Philadel-

phia & New York: Lippincott, 1972);

Harry T. Moore, *Henry James* (New York: Viking, 1974).

References:

Charles R. Anderson, *Person, Place, and Thing in Henry James's Novels* (Durham: Duke University Press, 1977);

Quentin Anderson, *The American Henry James* (New Brunswick: Rutgers University Press, 1957);

Osborne Andreas, *Henry James and the Expanding Horizon: A Study of the Meaning of James's Fiction* (Seattle: University of Washington Press, 1948);

Martha Banta, *Henry James and the Occult: The Great Extension* (Bloomington: Indiana University Press, 1972);

Joseph Warren Beach, *The Method of Henry James* (New Haven: Yale University Press, 1918);

Millicent Bell, *Edith Wharton and Henry James: The Story of a Friendship* (New York: Braziller, 1965);

Nicola Bradbury, *Henry James: The Later Novels* (Oxford: Clarendon Press, 1979);

Peter Buitenhuis, *The Grasping Imagination: The American Writings of Henry James* (Toronto: University of Toronto Press, 1970);

Henry Seidel Canby, *Turn West, Turn East: Mark Twain and Henry James* (Boston: Houghton Mifflin, 1951);

Oscar Cargill, *The Novels of Henry James* (New York: Macmillan, 1961);

Stephen Donadio, *Nietzsche, Henry James, and the Artistic Will* (New York: Oxford University Press, 1978);

Robert L. Gale, *The Caught Image: Figurative Language in the Fiction of Henry James* (Chapel Hill: University of North Carolina Press, 1964);

Gale, *Plots and Characters in the Fiction of Henry James* (Hamden, Conn.: Archon, 1965);

Roger Gard, ed., *Henry James: The Critical Heritage* (London: Routledge & Kegan Paul, 1968);

Maxwell Geismar, *Henry James and the Jacobites* (Boston: Houghton Mifflin, 1963);

Richard A. Hocks, *Henry James and Pragmatistic Thought: A Study in the Relationship between the Philosophy of William James and the Literary Art of Henry James* (Chapel Hill: University of North Carolina Press, 1974);

Laurence B. Holland, *The Expense of Vision: Essays on the Craft of Henry James* (Princeton: Princeton University Press, 1964);

Alice James, *Alice James: Her Brothers–Her Journal*, edited by Anna Robeson Burr (New York:

Dodd, Mead, 1934);

James, *The Diary of Alice James*, edited by Leon Edel (New York: Dodd, Mead, 1964);

Granville H. Jones, *Henry James's Psychology of Experience* (The Hague: Mouton, 1975);

Cornelia Pulsifer Kelley, *The Early Development of Henry James* (Urbana: University of Illinois Press, 1930; revised, 1965);

James Kraft, *The Early Tales of Henry James* (Carbondale: Southern Illinois University Press, 1969);

Dorothea Krook, *The Ordeal of Consciousness in Henry James* (London & New York: Cambridge University Press, 1962);

Glenda Leeming, *Who's Who in Henry James* (New York: Taplinger, 1976);

Robert Emmet Long, *The Great Succession: Henry James and the Legacy of Hawthorne* (Pittsburgh: University of Pittsburgh Press, 1979);

F. O. Matthiessen, *Henry James: The Major Phase* (New York: Oxford University Press, 1944);

Matthiessen, *The James Family: Including Selections from the Writings of Henry James, Senior, William, Henry & Alice James* (New York: Knopf, 1947);

Bruce R. McElderry, Jr., *Henry James* (New York: Twayne, 1965);

James E. Miller, Jr., *Theory of Fiction: Henry James* (Lincoln: University of Nebraska Press, 1972);

George Monteiro, *Henry James and John Hay: The Record of a Friendship* (Providence: Brown University Press, 1965);

Elsa Nettels, *James & Conrad* (Athens: University of Georgia Press, 1977);

Sergio Perosa, *Henry James and the Experimental Novel* (Charlottesville: University Press of Virginia, 1978);

Ralph Barton Perry, *The Thought and Characters of William James*, 2 volumes (Boston: Little, Brown, 1935);

Dale Peterson, *The Clement Vision: Poetic Realism in Turgenev and James* (Port Washington, N.Y.: Kennikat Press, 1975);

Richard Poirier, *The Comic Sense of Henry James: A Study of the Early Novels* (New York: Oxford University Press, 1960);

Lyall H. Powers, *Henry James and the Naturalist Movement* (East Lansing: Michigan State University Press, 1971);

Strother B. Purdy, *The Hole in the Fabric: Science, Contemporary Literature, and Henry James* (Pittsburgh: University of Pittsburgh Press, 1977);

S. Gorley Putt, *A Reader's Guide to Henry James* (Ithaca: Cornell University Press, 1966; Lon-

don: Thames and Hudson, 1966);

John Carlos Rowe, *Henry Adams and Henry James: The Emergence of a Modern Consciousness* (Ithaca: Cornell University Press, 1976);

Charles Thomas Samuels, *The Ambiguity of Henry James* (Urbana: University of Illinois Press, 1971);

Daniel J. Schneider, *The Crystal Cage: Adventures of the Imagination in the Fiction of Henry James* (Lawrence: Regents Press of Kansas, 1978);

Sallie Sears, *The Negative Imagination: Forms and Perspective in the Novels of Henry James* (Ithaca: Cornell University Press, 1969);

Sister M. Corona Sharp, *The "Confidante" in Henry James: Evolution and Moral Value of a Fictive Character* (Notre Dame: University of Notre Dame Press, 1965);

Muriel G. Shine, *The Fictional Children of Henry James* (Chapel Hill: University of North Carolina Press, 1969);

Mary Doyle Springer, *A Rhetoric of Literary Character: Some Women of Henry James* (Chicago: University of Chicago Press, 1978);

William T. Stafford, *A Name, Title, and Place Index to the Critical Writings of Henry James* (Englewood, Colo.: Microcard Editions Books, 1975);

Elizabeth Stevenson, *The Crooked Corridor: A Study of Henry James* (New York: Macmillan, 1949);

H. Peter Stowell, *Literary Impressionism, James and Chekhov* (Athens: University of Georgia Press, 1979);

Krishna Baldev Vaid, *Technique in the Tales of Henry James* (Cambridge: Harvard University Press, 1964);

William Veeder, *Henry James—The Lessons of the Master: Popular Fiction and Personal Style in the Nineteenth Century* (Chicago: University of Chicago Press, 1975);

Edward Wagenknecht, *Eve and Henry James: Portraits of Women and Girls in His Fiction* (Norman: University of Oklahoma Press, 1978);

J. A. Ward, *The Imagination of Disaster: Evil in the Fiction of Henry James* (Lincoln: University of Nebraska Press, 1961);

Ward, *The Search for Form: Studies in the Structure of James's Fiction* (Chapel Hill: University of North Carolina Press, 1967);

Christof Wegelin, *The Image of Europe in Henry James* (Dallas: Southern Methodist University Press, 1958);

Philip M. Weinstein, *Henry James and the Requirements of the Imagination* (Cambridge: Harvard University Press, 1971);

Joseph Wiesenfarth, *Henry James and the Dramatic*

Analogy (New York: Fordham University Press, 1963);

Viola Hopkins Winner, *Henry James and the Visual Arts* (Charlottesville: University Press of Virginia, 1970);

Walter J. Wright, *The Madness of Art: A Study of Henry James* (Lincoln: University of Nebraska Press, 1962);

Ruth Bernard Yeazell, *Language and Knowledge in the Late Novels of Henry James* (Chicago: University of Chicago Press, 1976).

Papers:

Most of James's manuscripts and other papers are deposited in the Houghton Library at Harvard University. Other materials are in the Collection of American Literature, Yale University, and in the Library of Congress. The libraries of the following institutions also have notable collections: the University of Leeds, Colby College, the University of Rochester, the University of Chicago, the University of California at Los Angeles, the British Museum, the archives of Charles Scribner's Sons at Princeton University, the Huntington Library, the Morgan Library, the New York Public Library, the Buffalo Public Library, and the Century Association in New York City.

Sarah Orne Jewett

(3 September 1849 - 24 June 1909)

Gwen L. Nagel
Harvard University

BOOKS: *Deephaven* (Boston: Osgood, 1877; London: Osgood, McIlvaine, 1893);

Play Days. A Book of Stories For Children (Boston: Houghton, Osgood, 1878);

Old Friends and New (Boston: Houghton, Osgood, 1879);

Country By-Ways (Boston: Houghton, Mifflin, 1881; London: Trübner, 1882);

The Mate of the Daylight, and Friends Ashore (Boston: Houghton, Mifflin, 1884);

A Country Doctor (Boston & New York: Houghton, Mifflin, 1884; London: Constable, 1911);

A Marsh Island (Boston & New York: Houghton, Mifflin, 1885; London: Low, Marston, 1898?);

A White Heron and Other Stories (Boston & New York: Houghton, Mifflin, 1886);

The Story of the Normans, Told Chiefly in Relation to Their Conquest of England (New York & London: Putnam's, 1887; London: Unwin, 1891);

The King of Folly Island and Other People (Boston & New York: Houghton, Mifflin, 1888; London: Duckworth, 1903);

Betty Leicester, A Story for Girls (Boston & New York: Houghton, Mifflin, 1890);

Tales of New England (Boston: Houghton, Mifflin, 1890; London: Osgood, McIlvaine, 1893);

Strangers and Wayfarers (Boston & New York: Houghton, Mifflin, 1890; London: Osgood, McIlvaine, 1891);

Sarah Orne Jewett

A Native of Winby and Other Tales (Boston: Houghton, Mifflin, 1893; London: Constable, 1911);

Betty Leicester's English Xmas. A New Chapter of an Old Story (Baltimore: Privately printed, 1894); republished as *Betty Leicester's Christmas* (Boston & New York: Houghton, Mifflin, 1899);

The Life of Nancy (Boston & New York: Houghton, Mifflin, 1895; London: Longmans, 1895);

The Country of the Pointed Firs (Boston & New York: Houghton, Mifflin, 1896; London: Unwin, 1896);

The Queen's Twin and Other Stories (Boston & New York: Houghton, Mifflin, 1899; London: Smith, Elder, 1900);

The Tory Lover (Boston & New York: Houghton, Mifflin, 1901; London: Smith, Elder, 1901);

An Empty Purse. A Christmas Story (Boston: Privately printed, 1905);

Verses, edited by M.A. DeWolfe Howe (Boston: Privately printed, 1916);

The Uncollected Short Stories of Sarah Orne Jewett, edited by Richard Cary (Waterville, Maine: Colby College Press, 1971).

Sarah Orne Jewett is best known as the author of *The Country of the Pointed Firs* (1896), a loosely structured novel that is considered by many to be the finest example of regional literature published in the nineteenth century. Jewett's reputation rests securely on this work, but during the course of her writing career she also wrote four other novels, nine collections of stories and sketches about village life in New England, a history of the Normans, and three books for children. Like other writers of the local-color school, she faithfully recorded the life of rural folk whose culture and idioms were threatened by a more urban and homogenized culture. As a regionalist, Jewett will be remembered most for her depiction of New England settings, those dying coastal villages and up-country farms, the woods and shores of southeastern Maine; her nostalgia for the grand but departed past of her region; her low-key humor; her understated rendering of regional idiom; and her portraits of old women.

Theodora Sarah Orne Jewett was born 3 September 1849 in South Berwick, an upriver port in southern Maine. She was the second of three daughters of Caroline Frances Perry Jewett and Dr. Theodore Herman Jewett, a wealthy country doctor. The Embargo Act of 1807 had virtually destroyed the shipping industry in Maine, but in Jewett's childhood, memories of the great seafaring days of the past remained. Jewett heard the tales of adventures at sea that her paternal grandfather, who had been a captain, shared with his old cronies as they gathered at his general store in South Berwick. The economic decline of the region, the burgeoning industrialism, and the proliferation of manufacturing centers, which endangered the rural backwaters, were social forces that had no small effect on Jewett, a member of a gentry that looked back nostalgically at the past days of greatness.

Jewett was formally educated at Miss Raynes's School and Berwick Academy, but she was often sick and sometimes skipped classes, preferring to accompany her father as he visited his patients. The best of her education, Jewett was later to tell an interviewer, "was received in my father's buggy and the places to which it carried me." Dr. Jewett acquainted his daughter with the flora and fauna of the region, as well as with the life histories of the people he treated. Her father also encouraged her to read Laurence Sterne, John Milton, Alfred, Lord Tennyson, Matthew Arnold, Henry Fielding, Tobias Smollett, among other writers, while at her mother's suggestion Jewett read Jane Austen and Margaret Oliphant. In her early teens Jewett also read Harriet Beecher Stowe's *The Pearl of Orr's Island* (1862), a piece of local-color writing set along the coast of Maine that was a major influence on Jewett early in her career. In 1866 Jewett graduated from Berwick Academy and, though she considered a medical career, her health was not strong and she gave up the idea. She continued to live with her family in the large, well-appointed house in the center of South Berwick. She made numerous trips to Boston in her late adolescence visiting relatives and friends and enjoying theater, parties, and concerts. Because she was financially independent all her life, writing was not, as she once acknowledged, "a bread and butter affair."

Jewett had written poetry throughout her girlhood, and by 1867 she was submitting stories to magazines under three pseudonyms, Alice Eliot, A. D. Eliot, and Sarah C. Sweet. Her first published story, "Jenny Garrow's Lovers," appeared in the January 1868 issue of the *Flag of Our Union*. The piece is uncharacteristic of Jewett's later work for it is set in England and is basically a melodrama with several twists of plot. The following year Jewett submitted "Mr. Bruce," a courtship story set in Boston, to the *Atlantic Monthly*, and William Dean Howells, then assistant editor, accepted the story for publication. For the next four years Jewett's stories and poems (written primarily for young girls and stressing the importance of proper deportment and self-improvement) appeared in such periodicals as *Riverside*, *Our Young Folks*, and the *Independent*. During this early stage in her writing career, Jewett traveled often to New York and Boston, and made trips to Cincinnati, Philadelphia, and Wisconsin. Though virtually all of her best work is set in rural Maine, Jewett's forays into the wider world gave her the comparisons of city and country that inform so much of her work.

In 1873 "The Shore House," one of three sketches about a Maine coastal village that inspired Jewett's first full-length book, was published in the *Atlantic Monthly*. With encouragement from Howells, Jewett gathered together this and the other Deephaven sketches he had accepted at the *Atlantic Monthly*, made additions and modifications, and submitted them to James R. Osgood and Company of Boston. *Deephaven* was published in 1877. In the preface to the 1893 edition Jewett indicated she had hoped that her book would help improve the strained relations between summer visitors from the city and the natives of country towns. She had, she said, adopted Plato's dictum that "the best thing that can be done for the people of a state is to make them acquainted with one another." To this end, Jewett introduced into a sleepy fishing village along the Maine coast two young girls from Boston: Helen Denis, the narrator of *Deephaven*, and her friend Kate Lancaster. The two girls spend a summer in an old house in Deephaven and meet a variety of the local characters, garrulous old sea captains, reticent fishermen, resourceful housekeepers, elderly spinsters, impoverished farmers, and an eccentric herbalist, all of whom impart their philosophies, superstitions, country wisdom, and tales of the past. The perspective of the young girls and the village setting unify this plotless, episodic work. Jewett would later employ a narrator from the city and focus on the friendship between the narrator and another character in *The Country of the Pointed Firs*, but in her mature work, the narrator does not resort to didacticism or exhibit the girlish, occasionally saccharine, qualities that mar this first attempt. *Deephaven* received mixed reviews; some critics found it lacking in plot, but others were charmed by its compelling characters and the rich detail of rural life. The strength of the volume, as is true of much of Jewett's work, is the skillful rendering of an isolated and deteriorating New England community and its people, their traditions, quaint idioms, values, and the innate dignity of their simple lives.

Front cover for Jewett's first book, a collection of local-color stories about a Maine seaport town

Jewett's next volume, *Play Days*, a collection of fifteen previously published stories for children, appeared in 1878. The stories are filled with whimsical talking spools, kittens, dolls, and pepper-shaker owls and with little girls learning to be proper mothers or housekeepers. Jewett does not hesitate to stress moral lessons or to extol the virtues of obedience, patience, honesty, or charity. The stories give some evidence of Jewett's interest in gender roles, in urban and country contrasts, and in relationships between the young and old, all motifs that may also be found in Jewett's fiction for adults. Despite their didacticism, the stories exhibit the playful side of Jewett's nature. She often admitted she was reluctant to give up her childhood, and when she turned forty-eight she wrote to a friend, "This is my birthday and I am always nine years old." Annie Fields, her companion for nearly three decades, recalled that Jewett never put her doll away and all her life preferred, in intimate company, to be called by her childhood name, Pinny. Jewett's interest in a child's world manifested itself again in two books she wrote for younger girls, *Betty*

Leicester and *Betty Leicester's English Xmas*, published in 1890 and 1894, respectively.

Jewett suffered a great personal loss in the fall of 1878 when Dr. Jewett died. She had been deeply attached to her father; he was the model for Dr. Leslie in *A Country Doctor* (1884), which Jewett once admitted was her favorite book. Late in the 1870s Jewett met James T. Fields, the Boston publisher and owner of the *Atlantic Monthly*, and his wife, Annie. Jewett soon became part of the literary circle that gathered at the Fields's Beacon Hill residence.

Jewett's last volume of the 1870s, *Old Friends and New*, appeared in 1879. It is a collection of stories previously published in periodicals, along with "Lady Ferry," a Gothic tale that Howells had refused at the *Atlantic Monthly*. The volume is filled with portraits of old women; Lady Ferry is an eccentric, aged woman who seems to have been cursed to live forever. Many of the other old women in the collection are fiercely independent, suffer from isolation or poverty, but ameliorate their conditions by establishing beneficial relationships with other women. The development of bonds of affection and sympathy among women of sometimes different ages or social classes is a recurrent pattern in Jewett's fiction. Jewett's male characters, on the other hand, are often outside the community of sympathetic women and frequently either contribute to, or are the cause of, a woman's distress. A common problem Jewett's women face is the loss of their homes and possessions, which are cherished because of their link with the past or because they offer the women a sense of independence. Mrs. Wallis, in "A Bit of Shore Life," for example, moves painfully about her property watching the possessions of her lifetime being sold at auction. Before the objects are finally dispersed, however, the other old women of the neighborhood preserve the dying homestead by "committing every detail of its furnishings to their tenacious memories." Two of the weakest stories in *Old Friends and New* are set in the city; in general, it was when Jewett turned to life in rural New England that she was at her best. The volume was generally well received and praised for its charm and felicitous description, though the reviewer for the *Atlantic Monthly* felt the pieces lacked plot development and thereby remained sketches or episodes.

The essence of Jewett's next collection, *Country By-Ways*, is indeed the plotless sketch. The volume, published in 1881 and dedicated to her father, "who taught me many lessons and showed me many things as we went together along the country byways," includes three weak stories, four sketches,

and one example of what Richard Cary calls a hybrid, the sketch-story. The sketches are a potpourri of anecdote, natural description, local history, philosophical meditation, and personal reminiscence. The narrator of the sketches is a Jewett persona who meanders through the New England landscape in autumn ("An October Ride," "An Autumn Holiday") and in winter ("A Winter Drive"). In "River Driftwood," the persona floats Huck-Finn style down the Piscataqua River, recording her observations of shore life and the river's history, digressing on a variety of subjects on nature, and describing one of Jewett's many memorable eccentrics, Madam Hovey, an aging aristocrat who exhibits nobility and grace under the stresses of old age and poverty. Jewett strikes an elegiac tone in these sketches and in "From a Mournful Villager," in which she regrets the extinction of colonial gardens and the corresponding loss of past culture and traditions. The lament for a lost world is a theme that pervaded Jewett's works throughout her life. In "An October Ride," when Jewett's persona plays a role like that of the prince in "Sleeping Beauty," rides into "silent, forgotten places," takes spiritual possession of a lost kingdom—an abandoned New England farm—and animates it through remembrance and anecdote, she is preserving a dying region.

In 1881 James T. Fields died and Annie Fields turned to Jewett for companionship. Their relationship was intensely close and affectionate, of a type known as a Boston marriage, and lasted through Jewett's lifetime. Jewett spent a good part of every year living with Annie Fields at her homes in Boston and Manchester-by-the-Sea. The two women took their first of four trips to Europe together in 1882 where they visited, among others, Thackeray's daughter, Christina Rossetti, and Alfred, Lord Tennyson. Back home in Boston the women wrote, read, entertained a great deal, and engaged in or supported a variety of philanthropic enterprises. Their circle of friends included Oliver Wendell Holmes, Thomas Bailey Aldrich, and many of the older generation of writers like Harriet Beecher Stowe, John Greenleaf Whittier, and James Russell Lowell. Jewett shared friendships with many women artists and writers of the day, including Celia Thaxter, Louise Imogen Guiney, Sara Norton, and Sarah Wyman Whitman, and she also knew and corresponded with other local colorists from New England, among them Mary E. Wilkins Freeman, Rose Terry Cooke, and Alice Brown. When Jewett was at home in South Berwick she wrote and spent time riding, skating, rowing, fishing, and simply walking about the countryside.

She also maintained a voluminous correspondence with her numerous friends.

The Mate of the Daylight, and Friends Ashore which Jewett dedicated to Annie Fields, was published in 1884. The volume contains two more sketches, an undistinguished courtship story, two tales that focus on father-son relationships, one tale about a lonely spinster, and one piece, "Miss Debby's Neighbors," which is a story within a story and which derives much of its comic effect from the teller's digressive recollections. "Tom's Husband" is one of a handful of Jewett's works that deals with role reversals. In the story Mary Wilson finds domestic work limiting so she gives it up to manage the family mill, something she does with both pleasure and success. Meanwhile, Tom, her husband, stays home and keeps house. He enjoys it at first, but he soon tires of housework, feels dependent on his wife, and worries that he has grown apart from her. At the end of the story the couple take a trip to get away from their problems and leave the future unresolved.

Jewett explored the issue of women's work in *A Country Doctor*, without resorting to the escapism of "Tom's Husband." This second novel, published in 1884, is Jewett's most feminist. The partly autobiographical work traces the maturation of Nan Prince, an orphan who becomes the ward of Dr. Leslie, a compassionate country doctor. The first half of the novel focuses on Nan's childhood in Oldfields and, like Jewett, Nan skips school and accompanies the doctor on his rounds. Few constraints are placed on her freedom as she enjoys a Wordsworthian education roaming the fields and woods. When she decides to pursue a medical career Dr. Leslie is supportive, though he is conscious of the difficulties she would face as a woman in medicine. In the second half of the novel Nan confronts an elderly aunt, Anna Prince, who encourages her to give up medicine, marry George Gerry, and be satisfied with being a wife and mother. Nan briefly struggles with her conscience, but finally recognizes that she is devoted to medicine and decides that instead of marriage and a family she will "make many homes happy instead of one." Though Nan's choice of a career is a radical one for that time, Jewett's description of a female doctor as one who performs the duties of wife and mother to the larger world is particularly feminine and domestic.

The critical reception of the novel was mixed. Many reviewers praised it for its realistic depiction of rural character and scene, but one reviewer felt the controversial argument about a woman's role detracted from the portrait of New England life. Others thought the novel lacked plot and dramatic action and that Jewett's portrayal of young love was timid. As is characteristic of Jewett's work, the novel lacks strong movement. It is essentially a Bildungsroman: a story of maturation that portrays a provincial childhood, a conflict between generations, a confrontation with the larger society, a romantic conflict, and the search for a vocation.

The novel's craft and feminism received attention in France from Marie Thérèse Blanc, who, writing under the pen name of Th. Bentzon, reviewed it for the *Revue des Deux Mondes*. Jewett and Madam Blanc soon became friends and corresponded and visited each other over the years. Madam Blanc continued to review Jewett's works and even saw some of them, including *A Country Doctor* in 1885, into French translation.

A Marsh Island, Jewett's third novel, was serialized in the *Atlantic Monthly* in early 1885 before it appeared later that year in book form. Set in northeastern Massachusetts not far from Manchester-by-the-Sea, the novel traces a summer romance between its heroine, Doris Owen, and Dick Dale, a wealthy young artist from the city. Until Dick Dale spends the summer with the Owen family, painting scenes of their marsh-island farm and the surrounding countryside, Doris has been content with her life on the farm and with her lover, Dan Lester, a country blacksmith. Dick becomes interested in Doris and discovers that there are simple, rustic pleasures and great natural beauty to be found in this idyllic world, but he finally decides that the country does not offer him what the city provides. In contrast, when Doris visits an estate owned by some summer people from the city, she feels out of her natural element. Meanwhile, her reticent lover, Dan Lester, has been jealous of the interest Doris has shown the interloper from the city and has decided to go to sea, but Doris, having concluded that she prefers Dan and life on the farm, makes a treacherous predawn journey to town to declare love to Dan. They marry and remain on the marsh-island farm while Dick returns to the city, where he enjoys a successful showing of his paintings. This courtship novel reflects one of Jewett's long-standing interests, the confrontation of urban and rural values, with the possibility of reciprocal sharing between city dwellers and country folk. Again, Jewett refrains from depicting turbulent passions in this novel. *A Marsh Island* remains a serenely drawn portrait of simple, virtuous life in a pastoral setting, a life that is both threatened and enriched by a visitor from the city. Reviewers

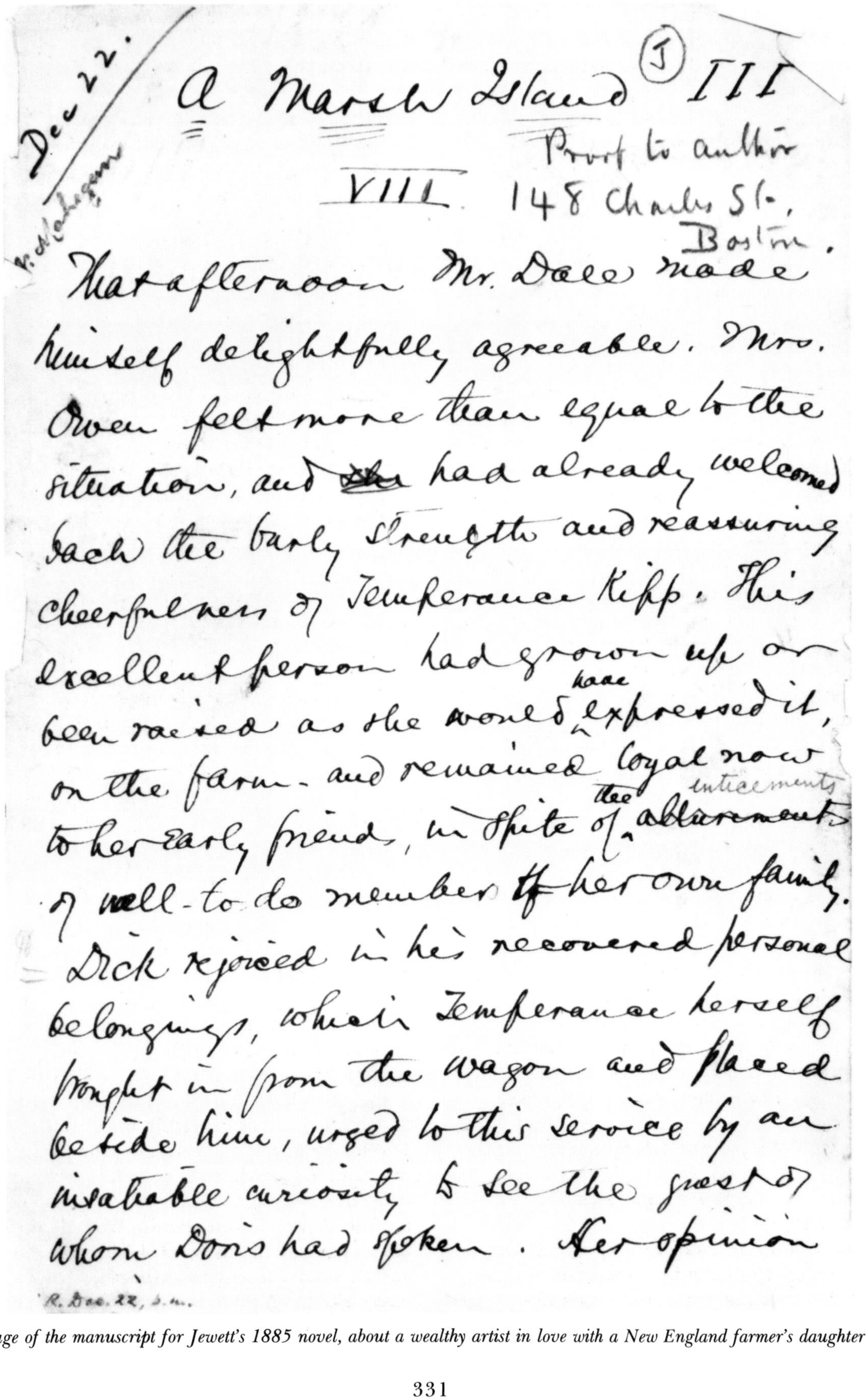

Dec 22

A Marsh Island ⓙ III

VIII.   Proof to author

148 Charles St.,

Boston.

That afternoon Mr. Dale made himself delightfully agreeable. Mrs. Owen felt more than equal to the situation, and she had already welcomed back the early strength and reassuring cheerfulness of Temperance Kipp. This excellent person had grown up or been raised as she would have expressed it, on the farm - and remained loyal now to her early friend, in spite of the enticements of well-to-do members of her own family. Dick rejoiced in his recovered personal belongings, which Temperance herself brought in from the wagon and placed beside him, urged to this service by an insatiable curiosity to see the guest of whom Doris had spoken. Her opinion

R. Dec. 22, s.m.

Page of the manuscript for Jewett's 1885 novel, about a wealthy artist in love with a New England farmer's daughter praised Jewett for her exquisite description of the novel's setting and her depiction of the quiet charm of rural life, but some also found the book lacking in dramatic action.

Jewett's next collection of stories, *A White Heron and Other Stories* (1886), contains some of her strongest fiction. There are no real departures in theme or technique here, but there is evidence of increasing control in such stories as "The Dulham Ladies," a much anthologized comic tale about two elderly sisters with social pretensions who try to regain their youth and their stature in the town of Dulham by donning hair pieces to cover their thinning gray hair. Jewett alternates comedy with pathos, for in "A Marsh Rosemary," Ann, a lonely spinster, marries a young and irresponsible man who eventually deserts her for a younger woman. Jewett portrays younger heroines as well in this collection. In "Farmer Finch," another role-reversal story, a resourceful young woman takes up farming instead of housekeeping when her father is no longer able to care for his family. Sylvia, in "A White Heron," is a little country girl who faces a test of her loyalty to the woodland creatures when an ornithologist from the city asks her help in locating a white heron for his collection of stuffed birds. She wavers for a time, but after a heroic climb up a landmark pine, Sylvia spots the heron and, rediscovering her kinship with the soaring bird, decides she cannot tell the hunter the location of its nest. Sylvia is a young version of a type found often in Jewett's work, a woman who feels a mystical kinship with the natural world and who preserves that which is threatened. This story has been anthologized often and is probably her best known.

Between *A White Heron* and her next collection of stories, Jewett turned to writing history. *The Story of the Normans*, a volume in the Story of the Nations series published by G. P. Putnam's, appeared in 1887. The book represents an unfortunate departure for Jewett, for it is a poor mixture of history, legend, and anecdote. It is informally narrated and espouses one of Jewett's pet theories, that the Norman race exhibited qualities superior to other races. With the publication of *The King of Folly Island and Other People* in 1888, Jewett returned to safer territory, to New England and to fiction. In this collection Jewett tries her hand at a story with French-Canadian characters, draws two portraits of pathetic women who are dominated by their tyrannical fathers, and, as if to balance these portraits of victimized women, she presents three of her most memorable strong women characters. Mrs. Goodsoe in "The Courting of Sister Wisby," a forerunner

of Almira Todd of *The Country of the Pointed Firs*, is an herbalist who shares an afternoon with the narrator of the tale, sharing as well her strong opinions about all things modern, denouncing doctors as "bookfools" and applauding an earlier generation of women whose superior wisdom derived from intuition and their close ties to the natural world. Mrs. Goodsoe also narrates a story within the story, a comic tale about the courtship of a strong-minded woman who gets her man. "A Village Shop" offers an elderly aristocratic woman who is forced by reduced circumstances to open a notions shop in one room of her ancestral home. When her ineffectual brother finally lands a job and insists she give up the shop, she proudly refuses him. Another of Jewett's strong female characters is Miss Tempy Dent of "Miss Tempy's Watchers." Typically, there is little plot; the story consists primarily of a simple conversation between two women of different social classes who keep watch in the house of their late friend, Miss Tempy, the night before her funeral. As they reminisce about the dead woman, her spirit is resurrected and affects them so that they emerge from their night together with greater understanding of each other. The story is one of Jewett's masterpieces, a superb study of character, atmosphere, and tone.

The 1890s were as prolific a period for Jewett as the preceding decade. From 1890 to 1900 she produced four more collections of short stories, a children's book, and her masterpiece, *The Country of the Pointed Firs*. She and Annie Fields vacationed in Florida, cruised the Caribbean, attended the Columbian Exposition in Chicago, and sailed twice to Europe where they visited, among others, Madam Blanc, Mrs. Humphrey Ward, Rudyard Kipling, and Henry James.

Jewett's first work of the 1890s was *Betty Leicester*, a story for young girls set in a small town in Maine. The resourceful young heroine, raised abroad by a peripatetic father, learns to value her old maiden aunts and the simple life in a New England village. A sequel, *Betty Leicester's English Xmas*, followed four years later and portrays Betty as she exhibits exemplary behavior on a Christmas holiday abroad. Jewett never quite gave up on moralizing in her fiction for the young, but in some ways Betty is a simple and youthful version of Jewett's older, more complicated women who fill her fiction for adults: ladies of either aristocratic origins or rustics of lesser pedigree who display resourcefulness and strength of character even under the most trying of circumstances.

Willa Cather recorded that Jewett "once

laughingly told me that her head was full of dear old houses and dear old women, and that when an old house and an old woman came together in her brain with a click, she knew that a story was under way." Three stories in Jewett's next collection, *Strangers and Wayfarers*, published in 1890, depict old women who have lost their homes. Because of their father's neglect, the two Bray sisters in "The Town Poor" are living as wards of the town in the back rooms in the home of an ungenerous and unsympathetic couple. When two women of the village visit the

Jewett at her writing desk

sisters, see their misery, and feel their sense of bondage to the people they live with, they resolve to rectify the situation. Old Mrs. Peet of "Going to Shrewsbury" is uprooted from her farm by a disreputable nephew. The narrator of the story rides the train with the old woman as she, laden with all her portable worldly goods, goes to live with relatives in the city. Though she could have remained in her home, it would have been at too great a cost to her self-respect. Mrs. Peet, who declares that she "ain't goin' to sag on to nobody" and is willing to work for her keep, is one of a number of fiercely independent women who people Jewett's fiction. Mercy Bascom in "Fair Day" is another, though her

age has finally forced her to rent out her house and move in with her son. The story describes Mercy's solitary return to her house on a day when her son's family is away at a fair. The trip is a foray into the past as the widow drinks in all the familiar details of her home. The day ends in a renewal as Mrs. Bascom vows to reconcile with an old enemy, her sister-in-law. As in earlier Jewett stories these women are inextricably bound to houses that are repositories for cherished ancestral items, or grant them a sense of identity and independence. Though she varied her treatment of the theme, Jewett portrays again and again an old house that is threatened in some way and an old woman who successfully or unsuccessfully attempts to preserve it.

Strangers and Wayfarers also includes a tale of the Irish in America, one of a handful of stories Jewett wrote on this theme. She also turns to the South for the setting of "The Mistress of Sydenham Plantation," a study of an old woman whose home and mind are destroyed by the Civil War. The remaining stories of the volume are set in New England and one, "In Dark New England Days," bears the influence of Nathaniel Hawthorne. There are more Jewett stories of courtship between elderly gentlemen and persistent matrons and one poignant tale, "By the Morning Boat," whose central figure is a young lad who takes leave of his family and neighbors as he sets out for the city for the first time.

In 1893 *A Native of Winby and Other Tales* was published; Jewett added two more stories about Irish immigrants and another story set in the American South to her canon. One story, "Decoration Day," which depicts a town's memorial parade for its war dead, is the best of Jewett's occasional stories; others by her that appeared in holiday issues of the magazines of the day are often marred by sentimentality. The title story, a tale of a man's return to the town of his birth (a motif Jewett frequently employed), contrasts the ostentatious public celebration Sen. Joseph K. Laneway receives at the railway station with the quiet but enriching evening he spends in reminiscence with his childhood sweetheart, Abby Hender, who greets the distinguished senator warmly with "Why, Joe Laneway, *you same boy!*" Memories of the past bind these old friends together after years of separation. *A Native of Winby* also contains another of Jewett's many portraits of strong women in "The Flight of Betsey Lane." Betsey Lane, a sprightly old woman confined to the Byfleet Poor-house, unexpectedly receives a gift of money and secretly goes off to the

Philadelphia Centennial. Her two friends at the poorhouse are concerned about her absence and start to believe she may have drowned herself in a pond, but Betsey returns bringing them gifts and stories about her experiences in Philadelphia. It is a poignant tale of affection among three old women and a portrait of a determined woman who asserts her independence for a time by escaping from the constricted world of the poorhouse.

The title story of *The Life of Nancy* (1895) recounts a country girl's first visit to Boston, her long years of invalidism, and the return visit a city man pays to her years later. "Fame's Little Day" depicts another urban-rural confrontation but, unlike "The Life of Nancy," which is a study in pathos, this is a humorous tale and represents Jewett's contribution to the literature of the country bumpkin duped by the city slicker. This is one of several comic stories in the collection. Others are "All My Sad Captains," in which three marriageable men, all former sea captains, are helpless pawns in a woman's campaign to get herself married, and "An Only Rose," in which the prosaic Mrs. Bickford has difficulty choosing which of the graves of her three dead husbands she will honor with her meager garden's only rose. "The Guests of Mrs. Timms" is another comic tale and one of many in the Jewett canon that deals with the social ritual of visiting. The story describes how two women pay an unannounced and unwanted social call on a woman who snubs them. It is a study in social pretensions and one of Jewett's finest ironic stories. In "The Hilton's Holiday" a visit of a different sort takes place as a farmer takes his two young daughters to town for a day's pleasure. Of the two girls, only Katy Hilton learns to appreciate the past, exemplified in part by Judge Masterson, an old man who reminisces with her father. At dusk the family returns to the farm with stories and gifts for Mrs. Hilton and the memories of their great day. While the theme of the affirmation of tradition and the past is commonplace in Jewett's works, this story is especially notable for its simplicity of action and control of tone.

Jewett had spent numerous vacations in New-

Jewett in the front doorway of her house at South Berwick

port and Manchester until in 1889 Alice Longfellow introduced her to the Boothbay Harbor region of Maine. In July 1895 Jewett and Annie Fields visited the Thomas Bailey Aldriches at their summer cottage in Tenants Harbor, Maine, and in September of that year they rented a small guest house, the Anchorage, in nearby Martinsville for a month of reading, rest, and long walks. The rocky coast, the view of offshore islands, the fir trees of the St. George Peninsula in Maine bear striking geographical resemblance to Dunnet Landing, the village in Jewett's masterpiece, *The Country of the Pointed Firs*. In January through September of 1896 the novel was serialized in the *Atlantic Monthly* and in November *The Country of the Pointed Firs* appeared in book form.

As in *Deephaven*, Jewett's first published work, the narrator of *The Country of the Pointed Firs* is a city visitor, a writer who spends a summer in a quaint but devitalized village along the coast of Maine. The book, almost devoid of plot, presents this nameless narrator's observations about the people and customs she finds in Dunnet Landing. Her hostess for the summer is a widow, Almira Todd, a strong woman who possesses great inner resources and a large store of country and herbal wisdom that she uses to earn a living and serve the natives of her village. One of the people the narrator meets is Captain Littlepage, a former sea captain who, preferring "the old days" when the shipping industry was in full flower, denounces the decadence of the present age. He also tells a rambling tale of a journey he once took to an Arctic village peopled with supernatural beings and representing, to the addled and obsessed old gentleman, "a waiting-place between this world an' the next."

Soon after this encounter with the old captain, the narrator and Mrs. Todd sail to Green Island, the home of Mrs. Todd's mother, the hospitable Mrs. Blackett, and her shy and gentle brother, William. Mrs. Blackett's sense of anticipation and hope, her enjoyment of the present, and her memories of past times keep her youthful despite her many years. Unlike Captain Littlepage's chimerical island in the Northern Seas, Mrs. Blackett's Green Island, with its circle of pointed firs, is a locus of continuity and permanence. While on an expedition to look for the herb pennyroyal on Green Island, Mrs. Todd shares with the narrator some details of her tragic and secret love of long ago, an episode that deepens the growing relationship between the two women. Back in Dunnet Landing, the narrator hears Mrs. Fosdick reminisce about the past and tell the story of Joanna Todd, a woman crossed in love who had

retreated to the inhospitable Shell Heap Island where she lived in seclusion. The narrator pays a visit to this island as well, and is moved to observe, "In the life of each of us, . . . there is a place remote and islanded, and given to endless regret or secret happiness. . . ." In contrast to Joanna's isolation and barrenness, as represented by her island, the Bowden family reunion, which is held up-country and in which the narrator marches with the family and partakes of the ritual feast, is a celebration of community and family continuity. Back in Dunnet Landing the narrator spends an afternoon with Elijah Tilley, an aged, lonely fisherman whose sole purpose in life is to preserve the memory of his dead wife. As the narrator leaves Dunnet Landing at the end of the summer, she catches one last glimpse of Mrs. Todd from the deck of the steamer and watches as the town and the stony, fir-crowned coast fade from sight.

The Country of the Pointed Firs is essentially a series of episodes recorded by a sympathetic nar-

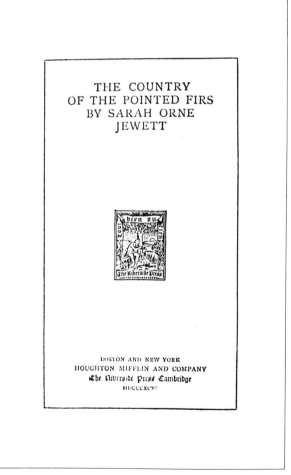

THE COUNTRY
OF THE POINTED FIRS
BY SARAH ORNE
JEWETT

BOSTON AND NEW YORK
HOUGHTON MIFFLIN AND COMPANY
The Riverside Press Cambridge
MDCCCXCVI

Title page for Jewett's 1896 book of connected sketches about life in a nineteenth-century settlement on the coast of Maine

rator who observes the simplicity and dignity of the sometimes noble, often eccentric people who live in and around a deteriorating coastal village. Unlike the girlish narrator of *Deephaven*, the narrator of Jewett's masterwork is mature and unobtrusive. Despite its episodic structure, the work derives unity from its setting, sustained tone, and a variety of thematic concerns that recur throughout the novel: the character and growth of the narrator; communal rites such as funerals, visiting, and reunions; the counterpointing of isolation and community, time and eternity, or past and present; the symbolic treatment of nature and its relationship with humanity; the presence and influence of the sea; the instinct to preserve and affirm values from the past; and the preserving function of memory, which is at the heart of the narrator's retrospective point of view and is a sustaining force in the lives of the characters who inhabit a dying world. Qualities and themes typical of Jewett's other works emerge here, and they are subtly evoked with great artistic skill.

Contemporary reviewers found much to praise in *The Country of the Pointed Firs*, and Jewett received accolades from personal and literary friends such as Rudyard Kipling and Henry James. In her preface to the 1925 edition Willa Cather ranked the novel, along with *The Scarlet Letter* and *Huckleberry Finn*, as an American work destined to endure, adding, "I can think of no others that confront time and change so serenely." Critics since have consistently judged *The Country of the Pointed Firs* to be Jewett's masterpiece and the finest achievement in local-color writing produced in the nineteenth century.

Between two more trips to Europe in 1898 and 1900, Jewett collected her last volume of short fiction. In *The Queen's Twin and Other Stories*, published in 1899, she includes two more Dunnet Landing sketches that have been incorporated as part of the novel in most editions of *The Country of the Pointed Firs* published since. "The Queen's Twin" relates a visit that the narrator and Mrs. Todd pay to Mrs. Abby Martin, an old widow who, because she shares a birthday with Queen Victoria, fancies herself a kind of spiritual twin. Her parlor, filled with pictures of the queen, is like a shrine. In "A Dunnet Shepherdess" the narrator and Mrs. Todd's brother, William, go trout fishing and then visit the aged Mrs. Hight and her daughter, Esther, a shepherdess and the love of William's life. Jewett worked on a story entitled "William's Wedding" in which the narrator returns to Dunnet Landing for the marriage of William and Esther. This story was incomplete at the time of Jewett's death but it appears in many editions of *The Country of the Pointed Firs* even though it disrupts the chronology of the collection. (Although "William's Wedding" takes place in May following the narrator's fall departure from Dunnet Landing, the story is often inserted before "The Backward View," the final episode of the original edition.) One other Dunnet Landing story, "The Foreigner," was published in the *Atlantic Monthly* in 1900. The story, which involves an element of the supernatural, is Mrs. Todd's reminiscence about the death of Eliza Tolland, a woman from whom she learned much of her herbal lore. "The Foreigner" was included in Richard Cary's *The Uncollected Short Stories of Sarah Orne Jewett* (1971) and in the 1962 edition of *The Country of the Pointed Firs*, edited by David Bonnell Green.

Of the other stories in *The Queen's Twin*, the two strongest are perhaps "Aunt Cynthy Dallett," in which Abby Pendexter gives up her own home to move in with her old Aunt Cynthy who, though self-reliant, can no longer live alone; and "Martha's Lady," which concerns the loyalty and affection a country maid, Martha, maintains for Helen, a girl from Boston who spends a summer in the country. Martha treasures the memory of this summer and only when they are reunited forty years later does Helen recognize the depth and constancy of Martha's love.

In 1901, at the end of nearly three decades of creativity, Jewett was delighted to be the first woman to be awarded an honorary doctorate by Bowdoin College, her father's alma mater. In this year as well, Jewett produced her last full-length work. Charles Dudley Warner had once suggested to Jewett that she write a historical novel about her hometown of Berwick. *The Tory Lover* (1901), a romance set during the American Revolution, was the result. Sections of the novel are set in Hamilton House, a Berwick mansion, and former citizens of the town appear as characters. The principal lovers are the beautiful and brave Mary Hamilton and Roger Wallingford, a handsome aristocrat who wavers between patriotism and Toryism. Roger finally asserts his loyalty to the colonies, however, when he sails with John Paul Jones on the *Ranger*. After Roger is betrayed by a villain, captured in England, and imprisoned, Mary and Roger's mother, one of Jewett's grande dames, sail to England and rescue him. The lovers are happily reunited and return to the colonies. The plot is contrived; most of the characters are unconvincing; and the scenes of dramatic action and violence lack realism. Finally, Jewett was never able to portray passionate love realistically. Her strengths were the muted tones of courtship among the elderly or deep feeling among women. The novel was a failed experiment, though it sold well. Various friends and critics voiced their disappointment, including Henry James who wrote, "Go back to the dear Country of the Pointed Firs, *come* back to the palpable present intimate that throbs responsive, and that wants, misses, needs you, God knows, and suffers woefully in your absence."

Jewett never did. On her fifty-third birthday she was thrown from a carriage and suffered serious head and spinal injuries. She never fully regained her strength and serious writing became impossible for her. A few of her poems were published (thirty of them were collected and published after her death) and in 1904 "A Spring Sunday," the last story published in her lifetime, appeared.

Jewett kept up her lifelong habit of letter writing in the years before her death, and she delighted in her new friendship with Willa Cather, whom she advised and encouraged in her work. But her writing career was at an end. She suffered a stroke in March 1909 and was moved to her home in South Berwick. Jewett had once said of this house, "I was born here and I hope to die here leaving the lilac bushes still green, and all the chairs in their places." On 24 June 1909 she died at home of a cerebral hemorrhage. She was buried with her parents and sisters in South Berwick and in 1931 her nephew bequeathed her house to the Society for the Preservation of New England Antiquities.

Jewett's reputation rests on *The Country of the Pointed Firs* and a body of short works that portray provincial life in nineteenth-century New England. Her fictive world is a limited one, but she perfected her craft, deepening her characterizations and gaining control of subtleties of tone and atmosphere. She has been declared one of the foremost writers of regional fiction, but she avoided the excesses of dialect and caricature that mar much of the work of the local-color school. She is a realist whose work bears the mark of a sympathetic and feeling observer. Like many of her fictive characters who confront change by guarding the artifacts, traditions, and values of the past, Jewett recorded for all time the essence of life in her country of the pointed firs. Her canon of finely wrought fiction will remain an enduring memorial to a way of life that has long since vanished.

Other:
Celia Thaxter, *Stories and Poems for Children*, edited

by Jewett (Boston & New York: Houghton, Mifflin, 1895);
The Poems of Celia Thaxter, edited by Jewett (Boston & New York: Houghton, Mifflin, 1896);
Letters of Sarah Wyman Whitman, edited by Jewett (Boston & New York: Houghton Mifflin, 1907).

Letters:
Letters of Sarah Orne Jewett, edited by Annie Fields (Boston & New York: Houghton Mifflin, 1911; London: Constable, 1912);
Sarah Orne Jewett Letters, edited by Richard Cary (Waterville, Maine: Colby College Press, 1956; enlarged and revised, 1967).

Bibliography:
Clara Carter Weber and Carl J. Weber, *A Bibliography of the Published Writings of Sarah Orne Jewett* (Waterville, Maine: Colby College Press, 1949).

References:
Richard Cary, ed., *Appreciation of Sarah Orne Jewett: 29 Interpretive Essays* (Waterville, Maine: Colby College Press, 1973);
Cary, *Sarah Orne Jewett* (New York: Twayne, 1962);
Josephine Donovan, *Sarah Orne Jewett* (New York: Ungar, 1980);
John Eldridge Frost, *Sarah Orne Jewett* (Kittery Point, Maine: Gundalow Club, 1960);
David Bonnell Green, ed., *The World of Dunnet Landing: A Sarah Orne Jewett Collection* (Gloucester, Mass.: Peter Smith, 1972);
F. O. Matthiessen, *Sarah Orne Jewett* (Boston: Houghton Mifflin, 1929);
Gwen L. Nagel and James Nagel, *Sarah Orne Jewett: A Reference Guide* (Boston: G. K. Hall, 1978);
Margaret Farrand Thorp, *Sarah Orne Jewett*, University of Minnesota Pamphlets on American Writers, No. 61 (Minneapolis: University of Minnesota Press, 1966);
Perry Westbrook, *Acres of Flint: Writers of Rural New England 1870-1900* (Washington, D.C.: Scarecrow Press, 1951), pp. 45-86.

Papers:
The largest depository of Jewett manuscripts, journals, and letters is the Houghton Library, Harvard University. Colby College in Waterville, Maine, also has a special collection of manuscripts, letters, and memorabilia.

Clarence King

(6 January 1842-24 December 1901)

Earl N. Harbert
Northeastern University

SELECTED BOOKS: *Mountaineering in the Sierra
Nevada* (Boston: Osgood, 1872; London: Low,
Marston, Low & Searle, 1872);
Systematic Geology, volume 1 of *Report of the Geological
Exploration of the Fortieth Parallel* (Washington,
D.C.: U. S. Government Printing Office,
1878);
Clarence King Memoirs (New York: Privately printed,
1904).

A spokesman for the best scientific realism in
the fiction and nonfiction of his day, Clarence King,
as both conversationalist and writer, was a persua-
sive influence on many important figures in late
nineteenth-century America, including John Hay
and Henry Adams. His personality and training
gave King an air of charm and erudition that
marked him as a symbolic representative of the new
and more consciously scientific age. Like Darwin, he
was regarded as a man of the new thought and new
culture. His presence, even more than his writing,
was welcomed everywhere, in the United States and
abroad. His friends did not suspect the marriage to
a black woman that King kept a secret from the
world and even from his closest friends. King
seemed to live as a public man only. In his published
writings, he succeeded in directing attention away
from himself, as if to underscore his most obvious
qualifications as a geologist, mining engineer, nature writer, mountaineer, art critic, and a trusted
adviser to men in high places.

Today, Clarence King is remembered chiefly
as Henry Adams's friend, whose life story becomes a
modern parable of failure in *The Education of Henry
Adams*. Even with the benefits of the finest scientific
education—a training for the world that Adams
claimed he lacked—King did not succeed in his
personal quest for order. Instead, his life, for
Adams, led finally to a demonstration of chaos. The
popularity of that book since 1918, when it was first
commercially published, some seventeen years after
King's death and a few months after Adams's, has
effectively served to hide King's own literary talent
and to obscure the historical facts of his international renown, as a geologist, mountaineer, finan-

cial speculator, gentleman-of-letters, and charming
social companion. At the time of King's death in
1901, he was far better known to the general public
than Adams, who had not yet written his most famous books, *Mont-Saint-Michel and Chartres* and *The
Education of Henry Adams*.

Clarence Rivers King was born in 1842, the
eighth-generation son in a prominent Rhode Island
family with a proud history in the China trade.
After the death of his father, James Rivers King,
when Clarence King was only six, the boy came
under strong maternal influence, which lasted at
least until he was forty-five. Even at that age, his
biographer concedes, "the anxious demands of a
doting mother" still continued to determine the
course of her son's life. Earlier, in 1868, Carolina
Florence Little King had succeeded in thwarting
her son's intentions to marry a Virginia City, Col-

orado, schoolteacher of whom she did not approve; and up to the moment of Clarence King's death, her influence remained strong. In fact, Mrs. King seems to have preferred from an early time in her son's life that he devote his attention to polite literature rather than to science. King's often-expressed but never-achieved ambition—to write a novel—was much indebted to her. Yet, while his interest in writing grew with his knowledge of the world, especially the exciting new world of post-Darwinian science, King never really accepted literature as a full-time vocation, any more than he limited himself to pure science in the form of research instead of more lucrative commercial application of his geologic knowledge in mining and engineering.

King showed early promise in science, as well as in languages and English composition. Perhaps the first important decision of his life was made in 1860, when he turned his back on the study of the liberal arts at Yale College and chose instead to attend the two-year course at Yale's six-year-old Sheffield Scientific School, which did not yet have the prestige of Yale College. On balance, however, except for the course at Sheffield and subsequent attendance at lectures by geologist Louis Agassiz at Harvard, King's formal education remained overwhelmingly classical and traditional, and throughout life his writing owed much to the old models. An impressive knowledge of scientific reality led to experiments in style. Yet the years in the new environment at Sheffield provided the young man with friendships that were more important than facts, with membership in the selective club of Sheffield graduates, who looked out for each other as they moved to put federal and state governments into the new business of large-scale science, such as extended geological surveys, during the boom years after the Civil War.

In 1863, Clarence King went west instead of to war; there he used his Sheffield connections to join the California Geological Survey, under the leadership of Josiah Dwight Whitney. What he saw and did from the time he left the East in 1863 until he completed the field work on the Geological Exploration of the Fortieth Parallel (often called the Fortieth Parallel Survey) in 1869 provided him with ample material for the writings that made his reputation as both a geologist and a man of letters. Appointed in 1867 by President Andrew Johnson as United States Geologist in charge of the Fortieth Parallel Survey, King was aware that he had secured a political and scientific plum at an unusually early age. While in the West, he met Bret Harte and began recording impressions of the geography,

animal life, and varieties of human habitation in essays for Harte's *Overland Monthly* and the *Atlantic Monthly*. King spent summers in the field and winters in an office, first in San Francisco and later in Washington, D.C. After enough data had been collected, he had to leave the exciting life of outdoor exploration to face the more routine office duties that would make his western work professionally respectable, as well as acceptable to his family and his eastern friends. During the 1870s King moved back and forth between West and East, first surveying and then organizing and editing all the publications deriving from the Fortieth Parallel Survey. He continued to see the world from the viewpoint of a practical geologist, but his writing and editing began to create the popular notion of Clarence King as a representative Western figure. He became both the author and the hero of a personal saga of frontier exploration. *Mountaineering in the Sierra Nevada* (1872) combines the realism of geological science with folklore and literary romance.

For that book King gathered together the es-

MOUNTAINEERING

IN THE

SIERRA NEVADA.

BY

CLARENCE KING.

"Altiora petimus."

BOSTON:
JAMES R. OSGOOD AND COMPANY,
Late Ticknor & Fields, and Fields, Osgood, & Co.
1872.

Title page for King's scientifically sound narrative accounts based on his experiences as a geologist in the West

says he had written in the West, and added some new material written after he returned to Washington and an office in 1869. *Mountaineering in the Sierra Nevada* sold well from its appearance, first in America and then in England. It has since become a classic of both mountaineering and western life, largely because the author's descriptions combine the keen perceptions of a geologist who can convey deep feelings about the grandeur of western topography, with skillful character description and storytelling. Each chapter is a separable jewel with a luster of its own, and readers have responded enthusiastically to King's informal invitation to admire each one, much in the same way they might admire a picture postcard. Visual appeal is a key ingredient in the book's popular success.

Although his other successful book of the decade was not the first volume of the *Report of the Geological Exploration of the Fortieth Parallel* to be published, King's *Systematic Geology* (1878) carried on its thick spine the designation of volume 1. In

Clarence King in Europe, circa 1882

Systematic Geology there is ample evidence of the author's imaginative leadership among his geological peers. What King wrote there, however, must now be considered as history rather than good science, since so much has changed in the theory and practice of geology during the past hundred years. At the time of its publication in 1878, however, the contents were new; so that serious reviewers and fellow scientists hailed King's masterly demonstration of a broad geological knowledge that rivaled any European's. King's chief biographer, Thurman Wilkins, finds that "Many agreed that *Systematic Geology* marked the highest point yet reached by government publishing in America," and the book remains both a monument to the value of the survey and a high watermark in the life and reputation of Clarence King. Unfortunately, he never again received the same acclaim that he enjoyed in 1879—as an author and a geologist.

What was publicly known of King during the years following the appearance of *Systematic Geology* may be described as a series of quick successes and even quicker financial failures. He made and lost fortunes in cattle ranching and mining, always spurning such quiet retreats as academic posts he was constantly offered by American universities. His friends, such as Henry and "Clover" Adams, welcomed his irregular appearances among them and did what they could to help him (as when Henry Adams recommended *Systematic Geology* as a textbook). Some wondered what King did when he was lost to view. Although he always claimed to be at work on some literary project—such as a novel to rival John Hay's *The Bread-winners* (1884) or Adams's *Democracy* (1880) in popularity and timely satire, or another masterwork of geology—no major publication from King's hand appeared during the 1880s to justify the promise of greatness shown in the works of the 1870s. Aside from an annual report of the survey, some compilations of mining statistics and mining laws, and a handful of reviews, King's literary work of the decade is a single magazine piece, "The Helmet of Mambrino," published originally in *Century* magazine for May 1886, and later in *Clarence King Memoirs* (1904). This tale, written in the manner of Washington Irving, derived from a European trip in 1882, during which King fell in love with the countryside and people of Spain. Instead of concentrating on the geological possibilities of the copper and iron mines at Río Tinto and Bilbao, the American visitor insisted on writing a continuation of *Don Quixote*, an additional chapter called "The Helmet of Mambrino." As readers of Cervantes' *Don Quixote* will recall, what

Don Quixote thought was Mambrino's helmet was in reality a barber's basin; and just such a basin, battered and scratched, King sent to his Spanish friend, Don Horatio Cutter, along with the manuscript of the tale. The story's ornate, old-fashioned style could hardly be more different from what one finds in *Systematic Geology*. Yet from the moment it appeared in *Century*, it was regarded as a charming if unrealistic demonstration of King's talent for nonscientific writing. Such promise was not to be sustained.

The story of King's private life after 1888 remained largely unknown, even to his mother and friends (and of course to the public). That story included a secret marriage to Ada Todd, a Negro nursemaid more than twenty-five years his junior, who maintained a residence with King in New York State, where their marriage was legally valid. Not only was their relationship kept secret from the world outside, but, as later became clear, Ada Todd King did not learn the real name or true identity of her husband (the father of her five children) until his death in 1901.

The burdens of supporting this New York household unquestionably played a part in creating the financial and personal crisis that sent the geologist to Bloomingdale Asylum in 1893, for recovery from a "mental disturbance" certified by his personal physicians. From this time until he died alone in Arizona, just after revealing his marriage and his wife's name to his doctor, King seems to have alternated between periods of hope and despair. The best of his life as a scientist and writer was long past, and he knew that he had failed to fulfill his potential. King was remembered chiefly as a brilliant conversationalist, never at a loss for words. His closest friend, John Hay, who may have been the only one to share part of King's secret, fondly recalled him, after his death, as "the best and brightest man of his generation." But Henry Adams, who began to write *The Education of Henry Adams* while his memory of King was still fresh, set down on paper the most memorable portrait of Clarence King, one that generously recounted his potential for success: "King had everything to interest and delight Adams. He knew more than Adams did of art and poetry; he knew America, especially west of the hundredth meridian, better than anyone; he knew the professor by heart, and he knew the Congressman better than he did the professor. He knew even women; even the American woman; even the New York woman, which is saying much. Incidentally he knew more practical geology than was good for him, and saw ahead at least one gener-

Clarence King (far right), with other members of the 1884 field party for the U.S. Geological Survey of California

ation further than the textbooks. That he saw right was a different matter. Since the beginning of time no man has lived who is known to have seen right; the charm of King was that he saw what others did and a great deal more. His wit and humor; his bubbling energy which swept everyone into the current of his interest; his personal charm of youth and manners; his faculty of giving and taking, profusely, lavishly, whether in thought or in money as though he were Nature herself, marked him almost alone among Americans. He had in him something of the Greek—a touch of Alcibiades or Alexander. One Clarence King only existed in the world."

Yet Henry Adams finally refused to make of his *Education* merely a polite compliment to a close friend now dead. From the real-life story of Clarence King, Adams fashioned instead an artistic indictment of American materialism in King's time. This unusual, didactic approach serves to temper King's personal failures with a powerful critical attack on the nation that had failed him: ". . . Much that had made life pleasant between 1870 and 1890 perished in the ruin, and among the earliest wreckage had been the fortunes of Clarence King. The lesson taught whatever the bystander chose to read in it; but to Adams it seemed singularly full of moral, if he could but understand it. In 1871 he had thought King's education ideal, and his personal fitness unrivalled. No other young American approached him for the combination of chances—physical energy, social standing, mental scope and training, wit, geniality, and science, that seemed superlatively American and irresistibly strong.... The result of twenty years' effort proved that the theory of scientific education failed where most theory fails—for want of money."

This shift away from individual responsibility leaves King's fate to larger, more deterministic forces. Yet this was the best that Adams could do for his close friend. For, while King's writing seems clear and scientifically advanced for his time, all too much about his life and thought remains mysterious. By turning King's experiences into one ironic "lesson" of the many in the *Education*, Adams managed to keep King's name alive. But like other parts of Adams's book, the passages about King raise more questions than they answer. Given what we do and do not know of the real Clarence King, this result seems most appropriate.

Periodical Publications:
"The Falls of the Shoshone," *Overland Monthly*, 5 (October 1870): 379-385;
"Active Glaciers Within the United States," *Atlantic Monthly*, 27 (March 1871): 371-377;

"Through the Forest," *Atlantic Monthly*, 27 (June 1871): 704-714;
"The Descent of Mount Tyndall," *Atlantic Monthly*, 28 (August 1871): 207-215;
"Wayside Pikes," *Atlantic Monthly*, 28 (November 1871): 564-576;
"Shasta," *Atlantic Monthly*, 28 (December 1871): 710-720;
"The Helmet of Mambrino," *Century Magazine*, 32 (May 1886): 154-159;
"The Education of the Future," *Forum*, 13 (March 1892): 20-33;
"The Age of the Earth," *American Journal of Science*, 45 (January 1893): 1-20;
"Shall Cuba be Free?" *Forum*, 20 (September 1895): 50-65;
"Fire and Sword in Cuba," *Forum*, 22 (September 1896): 31-52.

References:
Henry Adams, *The Education of Henry Adams* (Washington, D.C.: Privately printed, 1907; Boston: Houghton Mifflin, 1918);
Thurman Wilkins, *Clarence King: A Biography* (New York: Macmillan, 1958).

Papers:
A major collection of Clarence King's papers is on deposit at the Henry E. Huntington Library, San Marino, California.

Grace King
(29 November 1852-12 January 1932)

David Kirby
Florida State University

BOOKS: *Monsieur Motte* (New York: Armstrong, 1888; London: Routledge, 1888);
Tales of a Time and Place (New York: Harper, 1892);
Jean Baptiste le Moyne, Sieur de Bienville (New York: Dodd, Mead, 1892);
Balcony Stories (New York: Century, 1893; London: Warne, 1893);
A History of Louisiana, by King and John R. Ficklen (New Orleans: Graham, 1893; revised, 1905);
New Orleans: The Place and the People (New York & London: Macmillan, 1895);
De Soto and His Men in the Land of Florida (New York

& London: Macmillan, 1898);
The Pleasant Ways of St. Médard (New York: Holt, 1916; London: Constable, 1917);
Creole Families of New Orleans (New York: Macmillan, 1921);
La Dame de Sainte Hermine (New York: Macmillan, 1924);
Mount Vernon on the Potomac: History of the Mount Vernon Ladies' Association of the Union (New York: Macmillan, 1929);
Memories of a Southern Woman of Letters (New York: Macmillan, 1932).

Grace King

Grace King was a Southern writer whose career was set in the aftermath of the American Civil War. She has been described by Robert Bush as "an accomplished realist in the French tradition" as well as "the first important historian among Southern women." Her historical writings are still lively and readable accounts of early Louisiana life, and her fiction continues to be valuable because it provides a view of the Southern woman as she began to shed a passive role and to struggle for a more active one, and because it promotes an understanding of the sufferings of the South during Reconstruction, a subject largely ignored by better-known authors. Typically, the setting of her fiction is Reconstruction New Orleans, and the main character is a woman who not only has lost her worldly goods and position in life but also must do without the support of the men on whom she had relied before the war.

King experienced directly the hardships that are central to her fiction. As a child of nine, she watched from a window as the residents of New Orleans burned bales of cotton, broke open barrels of whiskey and poured their contents into the gutters, and otherwise prepared to surrender their city to Union troops in the late spring of 1862. Her father, William Woodson King, a prosperous New

Orleans lawyer, was able to escape to their outlying plantation, and later the family set out to join him. After a struggle to obtain the necessary passport from the commanding general, the same Benjamin F. ("Beast") Butler who achieved international infamy for the indignities he visited on the ladies of occupied New Orleans (whom he referred to collectively as "she-adders" and prostitutes), King's mother, Sarah Ann Miller King, started the family on its perilous journey. Their steamboat was fired on by Confederate guerrillas; they had to pass the night in a house that had been abandoned during an outbreak of scarlet fever; a ferry they had to take had been burned; and their skiff was grounded on a shallow. But the resourceful Sarah King kept everyone's spirits up and arranged for ways around every obstacle. Finally, they reached the plantation. In stark contrast with Sarah King's courage and activity was William King's sense of hopefulness. To Grace King he seemed passive and detached. King's fiction reflects consistently the hard truth she learned from this episode: in story after story, when the world goes awry, it is usually a woman who sets it right again. In an 1896 essay, King describes the French author Baronne de Bury as a "man of action"—a paradoxical epithet, yet one that makes sense in light of King's world view.

Following the war, the King family began life anew in New Orleans under much humbler conditions. The children studied at home and at the various French-language schools in the city; Grace attended the Institut St. Louis she later described in her story "Monsieur Motte." She was determined to make her way as a writer, and at this she eventually succeeded: she lived to see her fiction compared to that of Nathaniel Hawthorne, William Dean Howells, Theodore Dreiser, Willa Cather, and the French realists; her friends included Julia Ward Howe, Charles Dudley Warner, and Samuel Clemens. Late in life she enjoyed the praise of Sherwood Anderson and Edmund Wilson.

Her long and successful career had its beginning in a chance encounter. In 1885, Richard Watson Gilder, then editor of the *Century Illustrated Magazine*, asked King the reason for the rancor that so many New Orleanians seemed to feel for George Washington Cable and his writings. King told Gilder that Cable had proved a turncoat by treating his Creole characters unfairly in order to please his Northern readers. Gilder's reply was, "If Cable is so false to you, why do not some of you write better?" Stung by this response, King resolved to meet Gilder's challenge, and the result was her first published work, "Monsieur Motte," which appeared in the January 1886 number of the *New Princeton Review*.

"Monsieur Motte" is the story of a young girl named Marie Modeste who is about to graduate from an exclusive New Orleans boarding school. Her parents are dead (her father, like many of the fathers in King's fiction, has been killed in the Civil War), but an uncle whom she has never seen, Monsieur Motte, has assumed the cost of her upbringing. Presumably it is Monsieur Motte who will take Marie Modeste away following graduation, but he does not appear on the night of the ceremonies. As it turns out, Marie Modeste's education has been paid for by a black hairdresser named Marcélite, who was raised by Marie Modeste's family after her own mother was sold to a slaveowner who lived in another parish. Seeing that the orphaned child needed adult protection, yet realizing that she would never be able to raise Marie Modeste in her own home, Marcélite adopted the persona of an all-providing, though imaginary, uncle. King wrote

MONSIEUR MOTTE

By GRACE KING

NEW YORK
A. C. ARMSTRONG AND SON
714 BROADWAY
1888

Title page for King's first book, begun to counteract what she saw as the falseness in George Washington Cable's treatment of Creoles

three more sketches based on the same characters, and all four stories were published as a novel, *Monsieur Motte*, in 1888.

In this not-very-impressive first novel, Marie Modeste marries someone rather like herself, a young man who has lost his parents and has been raised by a faithful black female. In an astonishing conclusion, someone discovers that he has wrongly come to own a plantation that is Marie Modeste's, so he restores it to her. Overlooking this lapse in verisimilitude, a reviewer in the *Nation* found other things to praise in King's novel, especially her dialogue: "Her people speak an English which is French in idiom and incisive brevity, but which, instead of tormenting the reader, enables him to realize their passion, their piquancy, their folly and simplicity, as formal English never could." A second reviewer, writing in the *New Orleans Daily Picayune*, noted: "Miss King shows power, and after a time some really great work may be expected of her."

King's first collection of short fiction, *Tales of a Time and Place*, appeared in 1892. Of the five stories in this volume, "Bayou L'Ombre" is by far the greatest achievement and, indeed, is one of the best realized of all of King's short fictions. "Bayou L'Ombre" is the story of three young sisters who dream of winning the war for the Confederacy: "Black Margarets, Jeanne d'Arcs, Maids of Saragossa, Katherine Douglases, Charlotte Cordays, would haunt them like the goblins of a delirium; then their prayers would become imperious demands upon Heaven, their diaries would almost break into spontaneous combustion from the incendiary material enmagazined in their pages, and the South would have conquered the world then and there could their hands but have pointed the guns and their hearts recruited the armies." The girls have a chance to emulate their fictional heroines when a group of Union soldiers arrives at their plantation with some Confederate prisoners in tow. The girls courageously free the prisoners, but it turns out that, fearful of slave attack, the Southern guerrilla leader has compelled his Northern prisoners to switch uniforms with their captors in the hope that they will be allowed to rest at the plantation and depart in peace. No one has anticipated the daring and resourcefulness of the three sisters, who are shown to be as courageous as the men are bumbling. And the farcical "rescue" only underlines the sadly comic nature of that larger and more ludicrous male enterprise, war.

A reviewer in *Harper's Monthly* began by calling *Monsieur Motte* "as perfect a representation of creole conditions and social life as Hawthorne made of

New England" and then asserted that *Tales of a Time and Place* "increases this writer's reputation as an original force in American literature." Singling out "Bayou L'Ombre" for praise, the reviewer noted that it has qualities that "our critics have been accustomed to find only in the French masters of fiction."

King's second collection of short fiction, *Balcony Stories*, appeared in 1893. A prefatory sketch, "The Balcony," creates the ambience for the stories. The balcony is a place where women gather on summer nights to exchange stories: "experiences, reminiscences, episodes, picked up as only women know how to pick them up from other women's lives,—or other women's destinies, as they prefer to call them,—and told as only women know how to relate them." The thirteen stories that follow treat King's usual themes: male fallibility, female strength and calm in the face of despair, and mutual self-protection among women in a world of unreliable men.

Compared to the lengthy stories in *Tales of a Time and Place*, those in *Balcony Stories* are relatively brief, yet what they lack in complexity of plot and style they make up in artless simplicity. The most popular of her works, the collection was so well received that it was republished in 1914 and again in 1925; thirty-two years after the first appearance of *Balcony Stories*, the reviewer for the *Boston Transcript* found the stories "all well worth the re-reading." *Balcony Stories* remains King's most artistically accomplished work, both in the achievement of the individual stories as well as in the unity of the volume as a whole. These simple sketches have a high, even, nostalgic tone that transforms the past into a safe and moonlit dream.

The Pleasant Ways of St. Médard (1916) is King's first truly unified novel; certainly it is her most fully developed and successful full-length fiction. Perhaps its richness of texture and consistency of tone are owed to its autobiographical base. *The Pleasant Ways of St. Médard* is, in effect, a fictional retelling of the King family's return to New Orleans; Robert Bush writes that it might be called "a memoir thinly disguised as fiction." Like the best memoirs, this novel succeeds because it is so intensely personal that it transcends personality and becomes universal. As its author wrote in a letter to Edward Garnett, "Every woman who lived during Reconstruction says it is her own story." In *The Pleasant Ways of St. Médard*, the father, Mr. Talbot, is tortured by poverty and sickness. Only a coalition of dutiful relatives (notably the mother) and faithful friends saves him from ruin and death. Accepting

the novel for publication, Alfred Harcourt of Henry Holt and Company wrote to King, "I have spent some very pleasant evenings with your little group of loving and lovable people. At first, I didn't see the pattern, but I found its gradual unfolding very delightful; and thank heaven for the sense of humor that holds the balance all through."

William Lyon Phelps noted in the *Dial*: "Grace King really knows her New Orleans. . . . This new book gives her a definite place as a literary artist." A second reviewer wrote in the *New Republic*: "Something of the era hitherto unvoiced breathes in this exquisite memorial," and a third said in the *New York Times*: "Her work, which is not nearly so widely known as it should be, is among the best, in some of its features, that American writers have produced. . . . She is contemptuous of the artful aid of dramatic situations, the reader's suspense, and cumulative interest. But she can make a character alive in a single sentence." Edward Garnett went too far when he speculated that *The Pleasant Ways of St. Médard* would assume "a permanent place as an

THE PLEASANT WAYS OF
ST. MÉDARD

BY

GRACE KING

NEW YORK
HENRY HOLT AND COMPANY
1916

Title page for King's fictional retelling of her family's return to New Orleans after the Civil War

American literary classic," but the novel does describe accurately and often lyrically the broken world in which King and many like her lived.

King's final work of fiction, *La Dame de Sainte Hermine*, was published in 1924. This novel counterpoints the story of a young eighteenth-century French emigree, Marie Alorge, and the larger historical chronicle of Bienville's troubled governorship of Louisiana (already treated historically in King's 1892 biography of the French explorer). Jean Baptiste le Moyne, Sieur de Bienville, his partisans and enemies make the decisions that change the course of history; Marie Alorge and the other women of the colony perform the undramatic actions that keep the colony together. Unfortunately, the two parallel narratives never actually intertwine. Perhaps it was this lapse that caused the reviewer for the *New York Times* to complain that "a complete absence of narrative skill and a natural gift for storytelling make themselves keenly felt in 'La Dame de Sainte Hermine.'" Other critics found more to praise in the novel, but in retrospect, the fairest judgment, if a somewhat tepid one, seems to have been uttered by the reviewer who found *La Dame de Sainte Hermine* "agreeable if not strikingly dramatic."

In its faithfulness to ordinary life, King's fiction may be said to be realistic; in its attention to the limiting effects of poverty, disease, and human (notably male) frailty, it may even be called naturalistic. Yet there is undeniably much that is romantic in King's writing: her characters, particularly the female ones, emote, aspire, and strive as much as the heroines of romances. King herself addressed the paradox when she wrote: "I am a realist *à la mode de la Nouvelle-Orleans*. I have never written a line that was not realistic, but our life, our circumstances, the heroism of the men and women that surrounded my early horizon—all that was romantic." In her lifetime, King enjoyed a great deal of favor and attention. Following her death, she dropped from the view of all except a few scholars of Southern literature and Louisiana folkways; if she is mentioned at all in reference works, she is described as a representative, if minor, local colorist

and a social historian of the Reconstruction era. King's fiction is valuable because it describes a world that is little known. Her works have survived, even if they have been undervalued, and they speak tellingly of the postwar South and, particularly, of the Southern woman's struggle to adopt the demanding role that the war had thrust upon her.

Periodical Publications:
"Earthlings," *Lippincott's*, 42 (November 1888): 601-679;

"The Chevalier Alain de Triton," *Chautauquan*, 13 (July 1891): 409-464;

"A Quarrel with God," *Outlook*, 60 (6 March 1897): 687-694;

"Destiny," *Harper's Monthly*, 96 (March 1898): 541-548;

"Making Progress," *Harper's Monthly*, 102 (February 1901): 423-430.

Letters:
Robert Bush, "Charles Gayarré and Grace King: Letters of a Louisiana Friendship," *Southern Literary Journal*, 7 (Fall 1974): 100-131.

References:
Robert Bush, "Grace King (1852-1932)," *American Literary Realism*, 8 (Winter 1975): 43-49;

Bush, "Grace King and Mark Twain," *American Literature*, 44 (March 1972): 31-51;

Bush, "Grace King: The Emergence of a Southern Intellectual Woman," *Southern Review*, 13 (Spring 1977): 272-288;

Bush, Introduction to *Grace King of New Orleans* (Baton Rouge: Louisiana State University Press, 1973);

David Kirby, *Grace King* (Boston: Twayne, 1980);

Bess Vaughan, "A Bio-Bibliography of Grace Elizabeth King," *Louisiana Historical Quarterly*, 17 (October 1934): 752-770.

Papers:
The Grace King Papers are in the Louisiana State University Library Department of Archives, Baton Rouge, Louisiana.

Joseph Kirkland

(7 January 1830-28 April 1893)

David D. Anderson
Michigan State University

BOOKS: *Zury: The Meanest Man in Spring County* (Boston & New York: Houghton, Mifflin, 1887; revised, 1887);

The McVeys (An Episode) (Boston & New York: Houghton, Mifflin, 1888);

The Captain of Company K (Chicago: Dibble, 1891);

The Story of Chicago, volume 1 (Chicago: Dibble, 1891; revised, 1892); volume 2, by Kirkland and Caroline Kirkland (Chicago: Dibble, 1894).

Although Joseph Kirkland did not have his first novel published until he was fifty-seven and died seven years later after having produced two lesser novels, he, like his contemporary Edgar Watson Howe, was extremely influential in the development of the literature that came out of Chicago and the Midwest in the early years of this century and redirected the course of American literature. His *Zury: The Meanest Man in Spring County* (1887), together with Howe's one significant novel, *The Story of a Country Town* (1883), introduced the subject matter, the techniques, and the attitudes that were to find their culmination in Sherwood Anderson's *Winesburg, Ohio* (1919) and Sinclair Lewis's *Main Street* (1920) two generations later. While Anderson and Lewis were products of the Midwestern small town in the late decades of the nineteenth century after the Old Northwestern frontier had given way to order, stability, and a new respectability, Kirkland was a product of the frontier itself, of the westward movement and of the beginnings of Chicago as the trading, financial, and cultural center of the land west of the Appalachians.

Kirkland was born on 7 January 1830 in Geneva, New York, to William Kirkland, a schoolmaster educated at Hamilton College and the University of Gottingen, and Caroline Matilda Stansbury Kirkland, who was to win fame as the author of *A New Home–Who'll Follow?* (1839), *Forest Life* (1842), and *Western Clearings* (1845), sketches of life on the Michigan frontier where the family lived from 1835 until their return to New York City in 1843. Mrs. Kirkland's works have what has been called an "angry reality," a quality that was to influence her son's work a half-century later.

Kirkland was educated at home by both parents and after his father's death in 1846 by his mother. At seventeen he joined the crew on a transatlantic packet, traveled in England, Germany, and France as the opportunities arose, and returned a year later. During his year abroad, he kept a detailed journal written mostly in French. In 1852, after four years of working at various jobs in New York City, he became a clerk and reader for *Putnam's Monthly Magazine*, a New York publication that gave much attention to the West. Whether influenced by the journal's enthusiasm or dissatisfied with his progress, he moved to Chicago in 1855, becoming an auditor for the Illinois Central Railroad. He traveled extensively along the railroad's routes, in the process becoming acquainted with George B. McClellan, Judge David Davis, and Abraham Lincoln.

Joseph Kirkland

In 1858 he settled at Tilton, Illinois, where he became supervisor of a coal company. He also became active in Republican politics, serving as a member of the committee that notified Lincoln of his nomination in 1860. On 25 April 1861, he responded to Lincoln's initial call for volunteers, enlisting as a private in Company C of the Twelfth Illinois Volunteer Infantry. By August he had become a captain; during the course of the war he served on the staffs of Generals McClellan, Burnside, and Porter, who brevetted him major. When General Porter was cashiered on 21 January 1863 and his staff, including Kirkland, was reduced in rank, ostensibly for Porter's "willful disobedience" of orders, Kirkland resigned his commission on 22 February 1863, spent some months in New York and in Tilton, married Theodosia Burr Wilkenson on 29 December 1863, and returned to the coal business in Tilton.

Whether the result of his war experience, his mother's death in 1864, or the inspiration of his brother and sister, who moved to Tilton to live with him, he began to write. With his brother and sister he founded the *Prairie Chicken*, a literary paper whose profits would be given to the U. S. Sanitary Commission for soldiers' relief. The twelve issues of the paper, published from 1 October 1864 through 1 September 1865, contain numerous examples of his first known published writing.

His contributions include bits of doggerel, essays from a patriotic perspective on the war and its aftermath, eulogistic articles on corn and coal, two of Illinois's most abundant products, and a variety of miscellaneous sketches. He wrote earnestly and often graphically in a style much like his mother's unstudied prose, but not as good.

When the *Prairie Chicken* ceased publication Kirkland gave full attention to his coal company responsibilities, going into business for himself in 1865, first in Tilton, and then, after a family visit to Europe during the spring and summer of 1867, in Chicago, where he moved his wife and four children and opened a branch office. He did not write again until well after the Chicago fire of 1871 destroyed his home and business and left him virtually destitute. The panic of 1873 frustrated his attempts to reestablish himself in business. Later that year he went to work for the U. S. Internal Revenue Service and began to study law. He was admitted to the bar in 1880, at the age of fifty, and began to practice.

Kirkland's literary interests had been whetted by his return to Chicago, and in 1871 he was one of the founders of the Chicago Literary Club. In 1877 at the instigation of playwright James B. Runnion,

he and Runnion began writing a dramatic version of Alphonse Daudet's *Sidonie*. After several rewritings, the five-act play, which had been given the subtitle *The Married Flirt*, opened in Chicago on 10 December 1877, advertised for a two-week run. But it was harshly criticized in the *Chicago Tribune* for alleged moral lapses, and it folded before the announced run was complete.

Kirkland's first Chicago publication, a review of Benjamin Abbot's *Judge and Jury*, appeared in the *Dial* in August 1880. He reviewed regularly for the *Dial* and other journals for the next decade, and he tried other forms as well. His poem "The Lady or The Tiger? or Both?" was published in the *Century* magazine for June 1883. (The poem had been written as a reaction to Frank Stockton's short story, "The Lady or the Tiger," which had appeared in the *Century* in 1882 and had received a huge response.)

Around fall 1884 Kirkland began writing a novel that, he later recalled, had laid "long dormant" in his mind, a novel of rural life in the West, *Zury: The Meanest Man in Spring County*. After revisions recommended by the editors of Houghton, Mifflin were made, it was published in May 1887. Two weeks later the *Boston Transcript* published a review by Hamlin Garland, who called Kirkland's novel an example of "the inexhaustible wealth of native American material," material "as native to Illinois as Tolstoy's *Anna Karenina* and Torguenieft's *Fathers and Sons* are to Russia, its descriptions are so infused with life and so graphic . . . every character is new and native. . . ."

The novel also received praise from other writers, including William Dean Howells, who called it the work of "an artist with clear eyes and an honest hand . . . incapable of painting life other than he found it," but it was condemned by readers who found it immoral. Perhaps more important, however, Garland and Kirkland became friends, and Garland, obeying Kirkland's injunction that "You're the first actual farmer in literature—now tell the truth about it," began to work on *Main-Travelled Roads* (1891). In spite of its flaws—inconsistent point of view, sometimes insufficient motivation, lapses in technique—*Zury* had begun to reshape American fiction.

Garland's review of *Zury* led the way for the book's acceptance. Its readers appreciated not only its Western setting but its realism. Based on Kirkland's memories of his backwoods Michigan youth and his experiences in rural Illinois, *Zury* depicts the rise of Zury Prouder, the son of original settlers, who becomes the richest man in his county through hard work and sharp dealing, in the process be-

ZURY: THE MEANEST MAN
IN SPRING COUNTY

A NOVEL OF WESTERN LIFE

BY

JOSEPH KIRKLAND

BOSTON AND NEW YORK
HOUGHTON, MIFFLIN AND COMPANY
The Riverside Press, Cambridge
1887

*Title page for Kirkland's first novel, a realistic depiction of
pioneer life in the Midwest*

end of the novel. Kirkland's dialect is compounded of the rich, colorful language that came to the Old West by way of the rivers from Virginia and Kentucky, by land from New England, and was fused on the prairies of Illinois.

Kirkland is realistic, too, in his depiction of Zury himself. Kirkland's other characters—Zury's parents, earthy, hardworking pioneers who begin the transformation of prairie to farm; his first two wives, drab, ignorant, hardworking, their only assets land that Zury covets and their inevitable fate early graves; and the various neighbors—are equally realistic. Only Anne Sparrow, apparently altered from earlier versions, escapes the earthy image of the others.

Kirkland's style is terse and intense and he remains detached from the tragedies—the deaths of Zury's sister, his two wives, his children—that dominate the novel. He also recognizes, daringly, the reality of the sex impulse, although later, in "Realism Versus Other Isms" (*Dial*, 16 February 1893), he said about realism, "Let the truth be told, and not all the truth." In *Zury*, Kirkland transmitted the truth into fiction. Kirkland's first novel was also his best. Neither *The McVeys* (1888) nor *The Captain of Company K* (1891) approached either its impact or its influence.

The McVeys is a sequel to *Zury*, carrying its characters, including Zury, into the age of Illinois's emergence as a major political influence in the nation. Spring County has become relatively stable, and Zury becomes a legislator. When the circuit court comes to town, it is presided over by Judge David Davis, who hears arguments from a capable prairie lawyer named Lincoln. Like Kirkland's first novel, *The McVeys* contains scenes that truthfully depict life in Illinois at that time, but it is more episodic and repetitious and less realistic than *Zury*. Criticism of Zury's frankness about sex resulted in Kirkland's treating love sentimentally in this novel. Furthermore, because the use of the dialect that the readers of *Zury* found so interesting had diminished in Illinois by the period Kirkland was writing about, he used it less in this novel. *The McVeys* is a novel neither as realistic nor as exciting as *Zury*. Howells charitably commented in *Harper's* that Kirkland was too close to his characters to see them clearly; both the *Atlantic* and the *Overland Monthly*, however, found the novel plotless but realistic in incidents.

Kirkland was aware of the novel's shortcomings but concluded that he could do no better, and he regarded his third and last novel, *The Captain of Company K*, as "merely a potboiler." Nevertheless it

coming the meanest man as well. It is also the story of the stormy romance between Zury, who has already buried two wives, and schoolteacher Anne Sparrow, which ultimately results not only in their marriage, but in her transforming him into a kindly gentleman.

Kirkland's accomplishment in the novel is the fusion of two subject matters, that of the local colorists who emerged just after the Civil War, and the new realism then seeking its subject matter and techniques. (The melodramatic romance between Zury and Anne Sparrow is clearly in the local-color tradition in its departure from realistic characterization, while Zury's rise is realistic.) Kirkland's combination of melodrama and realism is sometimes unconsciously humorous.

Kirkland's dialogue attempts to recreate the dialect of (in Garland's term) the Illinois "sucker" through phonetic spelling, convoluted sentences, and a vocabulary so new to his readers that his editors insisted he include a detailed glossary at the

won first prize of $1,600 in a contest sponsored by the *Detroit Free Press*, in which it was serialized from 14 June through 10 July 1890, and its book publication in 1891 was greeted with good reviews, particularly in Chicago. Based on Kirkland's experiences in the Civil War, this episodic story of the adventures of the captain of a company of Illinois volunteer infantry is generally melodramatic; yet it nevertheless has realistic elements in its descriptions of camp life in combat, as it focuses on graphic individual reactions to regimentation and to fear and confusion in combat.

As in *The McVeys*, however, Kirkland overlays realism with the veil of romanticism, producing a novel that is too weak and confused to be true, and, aware of its shortcomings, he turned, in his remaining work, to factual and historical writing, only occasionally producing a short story or poem. His last major work was *The Story of Chicago*. The first volume was published in 1891, and the second, unfinished at his death, was completed by his daughter Caroline, and published in 1894. This history is of little more than antiquarian interest.

Kirkland's significance in American literary history lies not in what he accomplished. Far more productive and skilled writers are often ignored in literary history, whereas it is difficult to conceive of a study of the evolution of Midwestern and American realism that ignores the central role of *Zury*. For his contemporary Hamlin Garland as well as for those writers who came from Midwestern towns and farms later, he pioneered in the use of a new subject matter, a new language, and a new perception of reality.

Other:

The Chicago Massacre of 1812, includes contributions by Kirkland (Chicago: Dibble, 1893);

The History of Chicago, Illinois, 2 volumes, edited with contributions by Kirkland and John Moses (Chicago & New York: Munsell, 1895).

References:

Bernard Duffey, *The Chicago Renaissance in American Letters* (East Lansing: Michigan State University Press, 1954), pp. 93-98;

John T. Flanagan, "Joseph Kirkland, Pioneer Realist," *American Literature*, 11 (November 1939): 273-274;

Clyde E. Henson, *Joseph Kirkland* (New York: Twayne, 1962).

Jack London

Earle Labor
Centenary College of Louisiana

BIRTH: San Francisco, California, 12 January 1876, to William Henry Chaney (?) and Flora Wellman.

MARRIAGE: 7 April 1900 to Bessie Mae Maddern, divorced; children: Joan and Bess. 19 November 1905 to Clara Charmian Kittredge; child: Joy.

DEATH: Jack London Ranch, Glen Ellen, California, 22 November 1916.

SELECTED BOOKS: *The Son of the Wolf: Tales of the Far North* (Boston & New York: Houghton, Mifflin, 1900; London: Watt, 1900);

The God of His Fathers & Other Stories (New York: McClure, Phillips, 1901; London: Isbister, 1902);

Children of the Frost (New York: Macmillan, 1902; London: Macmillan, 1902);

The Cruise of the Dazzler (New York: Century, 1902; London: Hodder & Stoughton, 1906);

A Daughter of the Snows (Philadelphia: Lippincott, 1902; London: Isbister, 1904);

The Kempton-Wace Letters, anonymous, by London and Anna Strunsky (New York: Macmillan, 1903; London: Isbister, 1903);

The Call of the Wild (New York: Macmillan, 1903; London: Heinemann, 1903);

The People of the Abyss (New York: Macmillan, 1903; London: Isbister, 1903);

The Faith of Men and Other Stories (New York: Macmillan, 1904; London: Heinemann, 1904);

The Sea-Wolf (New York: Macmillan, 1904; London: Heinemann, 1904);

War of the Classes (New York: Macmillan, 1905; London: Heinemann, 1905);

The Game (New York: Macmillan, 1905; London: Heinemann, 1905);

Tales of the Fish Patrol (New York: Macmillan, 1905; London: Heinemann, 1906);

Moon-Face and Other Stories (New York: Macmillan, 1906; London: Heinemann, 1906);

White Fang (New York: Macmillan, 1906; London: Methuen, 1907);

Scorn of Women (New York: Macmillan, 1906; London: Macmillan, 1907);

Before Adam (New York: Macmillan, 1907; London: Werner Laurie, 1908);

Love of Life and Other Stories (New York: Macmillan, 1907; London: Everett, 1908);

The Road (New York: Macmillan, 1907; London: Mills & Boon, 1914);

The Iron Heel (New York: Macmillan, 1908; London: Everett, 1908);

Martin Eden (New York: Macmillan, 1909; London: Heinemann, 1910);

Lost Face (New York: Macmillan, 1910; London: Mills & Boon, 1915);

Revolution and Other Essays (New York: Macmillan, 1910; London: Mills & Boon, 1920);

Burning Daylight (New York: Macmillan, 1910; London: Heinemann, 1911);

Theft: A Play in Four Acts (New York: Macmillan, 1910);

When God Laughs and Other Stories (New York: Macmillan, 1911; London: Mills & Boon, 1912);

Adventure (London: Nelson, 1911; New York: Macmillan, 1911);

The Cruise of the Snark (New York: Macmillan, 1911; London: Mills & Boon, 1913);

South Sea Tales (New York: Macmillan, 1911; London: Mills & Boon, 1912);

The House of Pride and Other Tales of Hawaii (New York: Macmillan, 1912; London: Mills & Boon, 1914);

A Son of the Sun (Garden City: Doubleday, Page, 1912; London: Mills & Boon, 1913);

Smoke Bellew (New York: Century, 1912; London: Mills & Boon, 1913);

The Night-Born (New York: Century, 1913; London: Mills & Boon, 1916);

The Abysmal Brute (New York: Century, 1913; London: Newnes, 1914);

John Barleycorn (New York: Century, 1913; London: Mills & Boon, 1914);

The Valley of the Moon (New York: Macmillan, 1913; London: Mills & Boon, 1913);

The Strength of the Strong (New York: Macmillan, 1914; London: Mills & Boon, 1917);

The Mutiny of the Elsinore (New York: Macmillan, 1914; London: Mills & Boon, 1915);

The Scarlet Plague (New York: Macmillan, 1915; London: Mills & Boon, 1915);

The Jacket (London: Mills & Boon, 1915); republished as *The Star Rover* (New York: Macmillan, 1915);

The Acorn-Planter: A California Forest Play (New York: Macmillan, 1916; London: Mills & Boon, 1916);

The Little Lady of the Big House (New York: Macmillan, 1916; London: Mills & Boon, 1916);

The Turtles of Tasman (New York: Macmillan, 1916; London: Mills & Boon, 1917);

The Human Drift (New York: Macmillan, 1917; London: Mills & Boon, 1919);

Jerry of the Islands (New York: Macmillan, 1917; London: Mills & Boon, 1917);

Michael Brother of Jerry (New York: Macmillan, 1917; London: Mills & Boon, 1917);

The Red One (New York: Macmillan, 1918; London:

Mills & Boon, 1919);

Hearts of Three (London: Mills & Boon, 1918; New York: Macmillan, 1920);

On the Makaloa Mat (New York: Macmillan, 1919); republished as *Island Tales* (London: Mills & Boon, 1920);

Dutch Courage and Other Stories (New York: Macmillan, 1922; London: Mills & Boon, 1923);

The Assassination Bureau, Ltd. (New York: McGraw-Hill, 1963; London: Deutsch, 1964);

Jack London Reports: War Correspondence, Sports Articles, and Miscellaneous Writings, edited by King Hendricks and Irving Shepard (Garden City: Doubleday, 1970);

No Mentor But Myself: A Collection of Articles, Essays, Reviews and Letters, by Jack London, on Writing and Writers, edited by Dale L. Walker (Port Washington, N.Y.: Kennikat, 1979).

Jack London has been recognized as one of the most dynamic figures in American literature. Sailor, hobo, Klondike argonaut, social crusader, war correspondent, scientific farmer, self-made millionaire, global traveler, and adventurer, London captured the popular imagination worldwide as much through his personal exploits as through his literary efforts. But it is the quality of his writings, more than his personal legend, that has won him a permanent place in world literature and distinguished him as one of the most widely translated American authors. In 1914 Georg Brandes called him the best of the new twentieth-century American writers: "He is absolutely original," said the Danish critic, "and his style is singularly forcible and free from all affectation." Anatole France remarked that "London had that particular genius which perceives what is hidden from the common herd, and possessed a special knowledge enabling him to anticipate the future." More recently, Vil Bykov, comparing London favorably with Leo Tolstoy and Anton Chekhov, has observed that the "life-asserting force" in London's writings and particularly the portrayal of "the man of noble spirit" have "helped London to find his way to the heart of the Soviet reader." Among a number of contemporary European critics, London is considered "possibly the most powerful of all American writers."

London was, in fact, a writer of extraordinary vitality. He pioneered in the literature of social protest and apocalypse as well as in the fiction of escape and adventure. He excelled in the "plain style": the terse, imagistic prose so well suited to the depiction of physical violence and to the stringent demands of the modern short story. The publica-

London at age nineteen

tion of "An Odyssey of the North" in the January 1900 *Atlantic Monthly* and of his first book, *The Son of the Wolf*, a few months later was like a draft of bracing Arctic air: "Except for the similar sensation caused by the appearance of Mark Twain's mining-camp humor in the midst of Victorian America, nothing more disturbing to the forces of gentility had ever happened to our literature," says Kenneth Lynn, "and it decisively changed the course of American fiction." London was a major force in establishing for fiction a respectable middle ground between the saloon and the salon, and he blazed the way for such later writers as Ernest Hemingway, Norman Mailer, and James Dickey, as well as for George Orwell and Henry Miller. During the first fifteen years of the twentieth century, the golden era of the magazine, Jack London dominated the literary marketplace: scarcely a month passed without the appearance of his name in the newspapers and his stories in popular magazines like *Cosmopolitan* and the *Saturday Evening Post*. In less than two decades he produced some 400 nonfiction pieces,

200 short stories, and more than 50 books, fiction and nonfiction, that treat such varied subjects as architecture, astral projection, economics, gold hunting, penal reform, political corruption, prizefighting, seafaring, and socialism. His vitality seemed inexhaustible; yet he died before reaching his forty-first birthday, his body worn out by exertion and excess. In spirit, his brief career was a dramatic epitome of America's strenuous age; in mythic terms, his spectacular rise from rags to riches was paradigm of the American dream of success.

Jack London was born out of wedlock in San Francisco. His paternity has never been conclusively established. The biographical consensus is that his father was William Henry Chaney, a "Professor of Astrology" with whom his mother, Flora Wellman, was living in San Francisco as a fellow spiritualist and common-law wife in 1875. She named the child John Griffith Chaney—even though Chaney had deserted her in a rage of denial when he learned of her pregnancy. On 7 September 1876, she married John London, a Civil War veteran and widower who had been forced to place his two youngest daughters, Eliza and Ida, in an orphanage while he worked as a carpenter. Evidently it was a marriage of convenience rather than of love, providing a father for the infant boy and a home for the two girls.

Out of the circumstances of London's childhood were shaped the essential attitudes of his adulthood, and throughout his mature years he compensated, both creatively and self-destructively, for what he considered to have been a deprived youth. "My body and soul were starved when I was a child," he said; and he never fully outgrew his deep-seated resentment of his boyhood poverty and of his mother's detachment. Flora Wellman London was an unhappy, restless woman whose body had been dwarfed by a girlhood attack of typhoid fever and whose dreams of the genteel life had been aborted by the birth of an unwanted child. Too frail to nurse the infant herself, she had been forced to find a wet nurse, a black woman named Mrs. Virginia Prentiss, whose own baby had been lost in childbirth. What little maternal affection Jack received as a youngster, he got from his "Mammy Jennie" and from his older stepsister Eliza, not from his mother. One of the most significant factors in London's development was his conscious rejection of the occult, the supernatural, and the mystical— all of which he associated with his mother's cold spiritualism.

London's childhood was insecure financially as well as emotionally. The family moved often from one rented house to another in the Bay Area as John London tried desperately to make a living: contracting, selling sewing machines from door to door, storekeeping, and farming. On Jack's seventh birthday they moved from Alameda to a farm down the coast; as London recollected, "We had horses and a farm wagon, and onto that we piled all our household belongings, all hands climbing up on the top of the load, and with the cow tied behind, we moved 'bag and baggage' to the coast in San Mateo County, six miles beyond Colma." The next year, encouraged by his ambitious wife, John London bought an eighty-seven-acre ranch in Livermore; and they moved once again.

His loneliness led London at a very early age to seek companionship in books. "I always could read and write," he claimed, "and have no recollection antedating such a condition. Folks say I simply insisted upon being taught." Washington Irving's exotically romantic sketches in *The Alhambra* and Ouida's *Signa*, the story of a peasant girl's illegitimate son who rose to fame as a great Italian composer, were among his early favorites—as were Capt. James Cook's *Voyages* and Horatio Alger's success stories. In 1885, when the Londons moved back to the city, after an epidemic had destroyed their chicken flocks and forced John to give up his Livermore ranch, Jack found that he could check out books from the Oakland Public Library as fast as he could read them. "It was this world of books, now accessible, that practically gave me the basis of my education," he later wrote.

Other, coarser worlds also played notable roles in his education: the worlds of the gutter, the factory, the saloon, the sea. Although John London was a conscientious provider, his vitality had been sapped by war injuries and poor health, and his efforts to succeed in various business and farming enterprises were repeatedly thwarted by bad luck and by Flora London's instability. Consequently, even as a grade schooler, Johnny, as he was called, had been forced to help support the family, later attesting that "from my ninth year, with the exception of hours spent at school (and I earned them by hard labor), my life has been one of toil." At first the work was part-time: delivering newspapers, setting pins in a bowling alley, sweeping saloon floors, and doing whatever odd jobs would bring a few extra pennies into the family budget. When he finished grade school in 1889, he went to work full-time in a West Oakland cannery, spending as many as eighteen hours a day at ten cents an hour stuffing pickles into jars. It was a traumatic ordeal, impressing upon him a lifelong loathing of physical labor. Years later that trauma was translated into art in one of London's most powerful stories, "The Apostate." Describing the plight of his protagonist—a teenaged factory worker named Johnny—London wrote: "There was no joyousness in life for him. The procession of days he never saw. The nights he slept away in twitching unconsciousness. . . . He had no mental life whatever; yet deep down in the crypts of his mind, unknown to him, were being weighed and sifted every hour of his toil, every movement of his hands, every twitch of his muscles, and preparations were making for a future course of action that would amaze him and all his little world." That "course of action" was escape: just as London himself had done, the hero of "The Apostate" suddenly deserts the tattered army of "work beasts," abandoning the factory in favor of adventure.

The pattern of London's life, reflected in much of his fiction, might be viewed as a series of escapes—first from the drudgery of poverty, later from the monotomy of work: a constant alternation between commitment and escape, routine and recreation, work and adventure. At the age of fifteen, after borrowing $300 from Mammy Jennie to buy a sloop from one of the hoodlums who made their living by raiding commercial oyster beds, Jack (by now he had disavowed his childhood name of Johnny) achieved notoriety on the Oakland waterfront as "Prince of the Oyster Pirates." He followed this dangerous career for a year before, apprehensive that like a number of his comrades he would wind up dead or in prison, he switched sides to become a member of the California Fish Patrol. Many of his escapades during these two years were later fictionalized in *The Cruise of the Dazzler* (1902) and *Tales of the Fish Patrol* (1905).

London's maritime adventures continued into the next year when, a few days after his seventeenth birthday, he shipped out as an able-bodied seaman aboard the *Sophia Sutherland*, a sealing schooner bound for hunting grounds in the northwest Pacific. This seven-month voyage provided the raw materials not only for his novel *The Sea-Wolf* (1904) but also, more immediately, for his first successful literary effort: "Story of a Typhoon off the Coast of Japan," a prizewinning sketch published in the *San Francisco Morning Call* on 12 November 1893.

Subsequent experiences that winter working in a jute mill and at the power plant of the Oakland Electric Railway intensified his wanderlust: "The thought of work was repulsive," he recollected in his autobiographical *John Barleycorn* (1913). "It was a whole lot better to royster and frolic over the world

Front cover for London's first book, a collection of tales of the Northland

in the way I had previously done. So I headed out on the adventure-path again, starting to tramp East by beating my way on the railroads." At first he rode with the West Coast contingent of Coxey's Industrial Army, a group of unemployed men who went to Washington to petition Congress for relief following the Panic of 1893. After deserting this army at Hannibal, Missouri, on 25 May 1894, he hoboed northeast on his own. Arrested for vagrancy in Niagara, New York, in late June 1894, he served thirty days in the Erie County Penitentiary, then headed back home to Oakland, determined to raise himself out of what he perceived as "the submerged tenth" of American society.

London's tramping experiences, later recounted in *The Road* (1907), were profoundly influential in shaping his career. First, they helped develop his natural talents as a raconteur: "I have often thought that to this training of my tramp days is due much of my success as a story-writer," he said. "In order to get the food whereby I lived, I was compelled to tell tales that rang true. At the back door, out of inexorable necessity, is developed the convincingness and sincerity laid down by all authorities on the art of the short-story." Second, they transformed him from what he termed a "blond-beastly" bourgeois adventurer into a Socialist: "It is quite fair to say that I became a Socialist in a fashion somewhat similar to the way in which the Teutonic pagans became Christians," he recollected, "—it was hammered into me." Finally, they convinced him that to raise himself from "the shambles at the bottom of the Social Pit," he must resume his formal education. Consequently, he wrote, "I ran back to California and opened the books."

By 1895 London was reading Charles Darwin's *Origin of Species*, Herbert Spencer's *First Principles*, and Karl Marx's *Communist Manifesto*. At the first of the year he enrolled in Oakland High School and began contributing essays and sketches regularly to the student literary journal, the *High School Aegis*. The following spring he joined the Socialist Labor party, and his activism won him notoriety as Oakland's "Boy Socialist." In the late summer of 1896, after feverish cramming for the entrance exams, he was admitted to the University of California at Berkeley. Forced to withdraw after one semester for financial reasons, he launched his writing career in earnest: "Heavens, how I wrote!" he recalled in *John Barleycorn*. "I wrote everything—ponderous essays, scientific and sociological, short stories, humorous verse, verse of all sorts from triolets and sonnets to blank verse tragedy and elephantine epics in Spenserian stanzas. On occasion I composed steadily, day after day, for fifteen hours a day. At times I forgot to eat, or refused to tear myself away from my passionate outpouring in order to eat." But all his efforts earned him nothing but rejection slips, and he was forced to return again to manual labor, this time in the laundry at the Belmont Academy, a private boys' school. Escape came once again in July 1897, when he left for the Klondike gold rush with his brother-in-law, Captain J. H. Shepard, who had mortgaged his house for their stake.

His experience in the Klondike was the turning point in his career. "It was in the Klondike that I found myself," he confessed. "There you get your perspective. I got mine." Forced by an attack of scurvy to return home the next summer, he took back no gold, but a wealth of experiences—not only his own but also those of the argonauts and sourdoughs with whom he had spent the richest winter of his life, experiences which his artistic genius could then transmute into marketable fictions.

The fall of 1898 was for London a time of furiously intense work—an incredible outpouring of creative energy, subsequently documented in his autobiographical novel *Martin Eden* (1909) as well as in *John Barleycorn*. London had found his metier; and having discovered that, he was able now to find a market for his work. By January 1899 he had broken into print in the *Overland Monthly*; within a year his work was appearing in the most prestigious magazines in the country; and in the spring of 1900 his first book was published by a highly respected Boston publishing house. "Critics have complained about the swift education one of my characters, Martin Eden, achieved," London commented in *John Barleycorn*. "In three years, from a sailor with a common school education, I made a successful writer of him. The critics say this is impossible. Yet I was Martin Eden. At the end of three working years, two of which were spent in high school and the university and one spent at writing, and all three in studying immensely and intensely, I was publishing stories in magazines such as the *Atlantic Monthly*, was correcting proofs of my first book (issued by Houghton, Mifflin Co.), was selling sociological articles to *Cosmopolitan* and *McClure's*, had declined an associate editorship proffered me by telegraph

Front cover for London's early novel, drawing on his youthful experiences as the "Prince of the Oyster Pirates"

from New York City, and was getting ready to marry."

Bessie Mae Maddern was the woman London was "getting ready to marry" that spring. The daughter of an Oakland plumber, Bessie Maddern was an athletically attractive, quietly intelligent young woman who had graduated from business school and who made her living as a tutor. She had been engaged to London's friend Fred Jacobs, but he had recently died of food poisoning aboard a troopship en route to Manila during the Spanish-American War. London had known her for several years—in fact, she had tutored him in advanced mathematics during his intensive preparations for his university examinations in 1895—but there was evidently no stronger attachment than friendship between them when he decided that marriage and family life should be a part of his new-won success and impulsively proposed to her. They were married on 7 April 1900—the same day *The Son of the Wolf* was published by Houghton, Mifflin.

London's first book was an immediate success. A reading public tired of a cloying diet of sentimental romances welcomed the fresh, meatier fare that London had brought back from the Northland. "Where the 'artisan' Norris failed, London the 'artist' succeeds in giving us 'the real texture' of the Northland," wrote an anonymous reviewer in San Francisco's *Town Topics*. "The Klondike has waited three years for its storyteller and interpreter to set it in an imperishable literary mold," said the *New York Times Saturday Review of Books and Art*; "London catches the life and conflicts of the Far North with a sure touch, strong dramatic power, a keen eye for character drawing and a natural gift for storytelling." George Hamlin Fitch, reviewing *The Son of the Wolf* for the *San Francisco Chronicle*, awarded London "a foremost place among American short story writers," calling him "the Bret Harte of the Frozen North, with a touch of Kipling's savage realism. . . ." "His work is as discriminating as it is powerful," wrote Cornelia Atwood Pratt in the *Critic*; "it has grace as well as terseness, and it makes the reader hopeful that the days of the giants are not yet gone by."

The Son of the Wolf was the first volume of London's fabulous Northland Saga—the largest single facet of his complex literary achievement—comprising seventy-eight stories, most of which were collected in *The Son of the Wolf, The God of His Fathers and Other Stories* (1901), *Children of the Frost* (1902), *The Faith of Men and Other Stories* (1904), *Love of Life and Other Stories* (1907), *Lost Face* (1910), *Smoke Bellew* (1912), *The Night-Born* (1913), *The Turtles of Tasman* (1916), and *The Red One* (1918); four

novels—*A Daughter of the Snows* (1902), *The Call of the Wild* (1903), *White Fang* (1906), and *Burning Daylight* (1910); and one play—*Scorn of Women* (1906); along with a half-dozen nonfiction pieces (two of which, "The Shrinkage of the Planet" and "The Gold Hunters of the North," were collected in *Revolution and Other Essays*, 1910). The major themes of the saga are primitivism, atavism, Anglo-Saxonism, environmental determinism, stoicism, and humanism. What is perhaps most distinctive about the saga is the paradoxical intermingling of naturalism and supernaturalism. Born into an age when the larger religious structures of Western civilization were tottering, reared in a home without any formal religious orientation, and negatively conditioned by his mother's weird spiritualism, London gravitated logically toward the secular doctrines of Karl Marx, Ernst Haeckel, Charles Darwin, and Herbert Spencer, describing himself as a revolutionary Socialist and materialistic monist. But while he remained reasonably true to these convictions in theory, he betrayed himself time and again in fictional practice as an individualist and a philosophic dualist. And notwithstanding his asseverations to the contrary, the best of his creative writing is informed by an instinctive mysticism in what Carl Jung has called the "visionary mode." The following paragraph from "The White Silence," the first story in *The Son of the Wolf*, is exemplary:

> The afternoon wore on, and with the awe, born of the White Silence, the voiceless travelers bent to their work. Nature has many tricks wherewith she convinces man of his finity,—the ceaseless flow of the tides, the fury of the storm, the shock of the earthquake, the long roll of heaven's artillery,—but the most tremendous, the most stupefying of all, is the passive phase of the White Silence. All movement ceases, the sky clears, the heavens are as brass; the slightest whisper seems sacrilege, and man becomes timid, affrighted at the sound of his own voice. Sole speck of life journeying across the ghostly wastes of a dead world, he trembles at his audacity, realizes that his is a maggot's life, nothing more. Strange thoughts arise unsummoned, and the mystery of all things strives for utterance. And the fear of death, of God, of the universe, comes over him,—the hope of the Resurrection and the Life, the yearning for immortality, the vain striving of the imprisoned essence,—it is then, if ever, man walks alone with God.

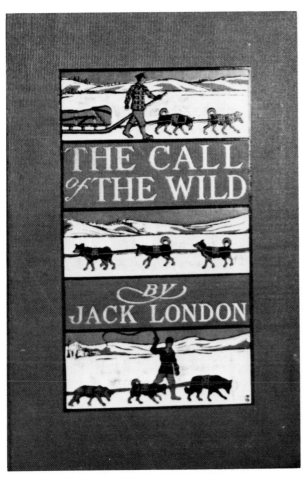

Front cover for London's best-known book, which has been translated into more than fifty languages

The modulating of naturalism into super-naturalism through the visionary mode is nowhere better illustrated than in *The Call of the Wild*, written at the bungalow London had rented in the Piedmont hills above Oakland during the winter of 1902-1903 when he had reached his full maturity as a prose craftsman. Read superficially, the story of Buck's transformation from ranch pet to Ghost Dog of the Wilderness is entertaining escape literature, often relegated to the children's sections in libraries. But to read the novel on this level is tantamount to reading *Moby-Dick* as a long-winded fisherman's yarn. Mere escape novels do not become classics—and *The Call of the Wild* has become one of the great books in world literature, published in hundreds of editions in more than fifty languages. In the strictest sense, London's book is not a novel at all but, as Maxwell Geismar has classified it, "a beautiful prose poem, or *nouvelle*, of gold and death on the instinctual level." Its plot is animated by one of the most universal of thematic patterns: the myth of the hero. The call to adventure, departure, initiation

through ordeal, the perilous journey to the "world navel" or mysterious life center, transformation, and final apotheosis—these are the phases of the myth—and all are evident in Buck's progress from the civilized world to the raw frontier of the Klondike gold rush, and then through the natural and beyond to the supernatural world. These rites of passage carry him not only through space but also through time and, ultimately, into the still center of a world that is timeless. London's style is modulated to conform to this transformation, becoming increasingly poetic as Buck progresses from the naturalistic world into that of myth. London's opening paragraphs are thoroughly prosaic: "Buck did not read the newspapers. . . . Buck lived at a big house in the sun-kissed Santa Clara Valley. Judge Miller's place, it was called." However, describing the death of one of the sled dogs when Buck arrives at the Dyea beach, London changes to the staccato cadence of violence: "It did not take long. Two minutes from the time Curly went down, the last of her assailants were clubbed off. . . . So that was the way. No fair play. Once down, that was the end of you." And, toward the end of the novel, the quest of John Thornton's gold-seekers into the mysterious "uncharted vastness" of the Northland wilderness is depicted in the softer rhythm of dreams: "In the fall of the year they penetrated a weird lake country, sad and silent, where wild-fowl had been, but where then there was no life nor sign of life—only the blowing of chill winds, the forming of ice in sheltered places, and the melancholy rippling of waves on lonely beaches."

This land is an appropriate setting for the "call to adventure," which, according to Joseph Campbell in *The Hero with a Thousand Faces*, "signifies that destiny has summoned the hero and transferred his spiritual center of gravity from within the pale of society to a zone unknown." This "fateful region of both treasure and danger," says Campbell, may be represented "as a distant land, a forest, [or as a] profound dream state"; but it is invariably an unearthly place of "superhuman deeds and impossible delight." This weird region in *The Call of the Wild* is a far cry from the pastoral ranch where the novel begins—and is remote as well from the raw frontier of the Klondike gold rush. Buck's party discovers at last a fantastically rich gold deposit at the heart of this "zone unknown," where "Like giants they toiled, days flashing on the heels of days like dreams as they heaped the treasure up."

His role fulfilled as guide, Buck's master John Thornton is killed by a raiding party of Yeehat Indians, thereby releasing the hero to complete his transformation into the awesome Ghost Dog of

Northland legend—an incarnation of the eternal mystery of creation and the life force: "When the long winter nights come on and the wolves follow their meat into the lower valleys," London concludes, "a great, gloriously coated wolf, like, and yet unlike, all other wolves . . . may be seen running at the head of the pack through the pale moonlight or glimmering borealis, leaping gigantic above his fellows, his great throat a-bellow as he sings a song of the younger world, which is the song of the pack." London's masterpiece—all rights to which he had sold to Macmillan for a mere $2,000—was an instant hit with the reviewers and the reading public alike. The *Athenaeum* was representative of the general response in calling it "London's best work so far. . . . an enthralling story, told ably, with restraint and artistry." In similar fashion the *Literary World* praised it as "a story of the robust variety which is never the work of any but a strong and original mind . . . first rank as to its conception and purport." J. Stewart Doubleday, in the *Reader*, wrote: "The Territory is brought home to us with convincing vividness; every sentence is pregnant with original life; probably no such sympathetic, yet wholly unsentimental, story of a dog has ever found print before; the achievement may, without exaggeration, be termed 'wonderful.' " "The telling thing in the book is its deep and underlying truth," observed Kate B. Stille in the *Book News Monthly*: "In this little drama we are brought face to face with that which we refuse to confess to ourselves, and are chilled by the realism of *The Call of the Wild*, and bidden by it to listen to the Voice of the Divine, which is also a part of our being."

While London had found the key to literary success in his Northland Saga, he was still searching for the key to domestic happiness during the years between the publication of *The Son of the Wolf* and *The Call of the Wild*. He had impulsively married Bessie Maddern because he believed he needed someone to tame his wildness, to give him a sense of roots and respectability, and to bear him "seven sturdy Saxon sons and seven beautiful daughters." Bessie Maddern, still trying to recover from the death of her fiance, wanted someone to make a home for. The marriage seemed to make a good deal of sense at the time—except for one fatal flaw: neither partner truly loved the other. Love apparently came to Bessie after the wedding—but not to Jack—and it became evident fairly early in the marriage that their personalities and interests were not, in fact, compatible. He was gregarious and fun-loving; she was prudish and humorless. He loved to fill their home with friends; she disliked company.

He had counted on a son as their firstborn: instead, she gave him a daughter, Joan, on 15 January 1901, and a second daughter, Bess (Becky), on 20 October 1902. Though he came to love both of the girls, his disappointment in not getting a boy was nonetheless acute.

A year or so after his marriage to Bessie Maddern, London fell in love with Anna Strunsky, a brilliant Stanford University student whom he had first met in San Francisco at a lecture by Socialist Austin Lewis in early December 1899. Two years younger than London, Strunsky had already won considerable notoriety as the "Girl Socialist" of San Francisco—just as London had earlier been called "Boy Socialist" of Oakland. London thought her a "beautiful genius" and quickly struck up a correspondence. "Take me this way: a stray guest, a bird of passage, splashing with salt-rimed wings through a brief moment of your life—a rude and blundering bird, used to large airs and great spaces, unaccustomed to the amenities of confined existence," he wrote to her on 21 December 1899. "And further, should you know me, understand this: I, too, was a dreamer, on a farm, nay, a California ranch. But early, at only nine, the hard hand of the world was laid upon me. It has never relaxed. It has left me sentiment, but destroyed sentimentalism. It has made me practical, so that I am known as harsh, stern, uncompromising. It has taught me that reason is mightier than imagination; that the scientific man is superior to the emotional man."

Some of the ideas in this early letter—most notably the dichotomy between the rational man and the emotional man—are central to much of London's work and constitute, particularly, the genesis of *The Kempton-Wace Letters*, an epistolary dialogue on love written in collaboration with Anna Strunsky in 1901-1902, and published anonymously by Macmillan in 1903. As Dane Kempton, Strunsky argues for the idealistic conception of love; behind the persona of Herbert Wace, a young economics professor at Berkeley, London contends that romantic love is nothing but "pre-nuptial madness," an emotional trap set by nature and idealized by man as simply "*a means for the perpetuation and development of the human type.*" A sensible union, he insists, "is based upon reason and service and healthy sacrifice." But these fine qualities, without love, were not enough to sustain a marriage, London subsequently realized. Because of his cold rationality, Herbert Wace's engagement to Hester Stebbins is broken; and by the time Jack and Anna had completed their collaboration on *The Kempton-Wace Letters*, London's marriage was clearly disintegrating. Writing to his friend Cloudesley Johns soon after his separation from Bessie in the late summer of 1903, London observed, "It's all right for a man sometimes to marry philosophically, but remember, it's damned hard on the woman."

Although Anna Strunsky was implicated when Bessie London filed suit for divorce in 1904, there is no real evidence that her affair with London was ever physically consummated; and she had apparently decided to end the romance when London left for England in the summer of 1902. They remained lifelong friends, but there was no passion in their letters after that summer, and Anna subsequently enjoyed a happy marriage to the wealthy socialist William S. Walling.

London went to England presumably en route to South Africa to report the aftermath of the Boer War for the American Press Association; that assignment was canceled, however, and he reported, instead, on the aftermath of the Industrial Revolution that he found in the London slums. Despite warnings from his friends that he would never be seen alive again, he spent ten shillings at a second-hand clothing shop in Petticoat Lane for a change of wardrobe; and, disguised as a stranded-and-broke American seaman, he disappeared into the black heart of the East End. On 16 August 1902, he wrote to Anna Strunsky, "Am settled down and hard at work. The whole thing, all the conditions of life, the immensity of it, everything is overwhelming. I never conceived such a mass of misery in the world before." The next week he wrote to her again, saying that his book was one-fifth done: "Am rushing, for I am made sick by this human hellhole called London Town. I find it almost impossible to believe that some of the horrible things I have seen are really so." When he emerged a month later, he had the vivid record—manuscript with photographs—ready for Macmillan.

The result was *The People of the Abyss* (1903), a pioneering work of creative nonfiction in the method now widely known among such contemporary writers as Tom Wolfe as the "New Journalism." This method involves the writer's total immersion in his subject, not merely as an objective reporter but, rather, as an active, sympathetic participant, so that his work achieves the immediacy of concrete human experience. "Of all my books on the long shelf," London said near the end of his career, "I love most 'The People of the Abyss.' No other book of mine took so much of my young heart and tears as that study of the economic degradation of the poor." What had affected him perhaps most deeply was the hopeless plight of the very old and

London dressed for research trip to the East End of London to gather materials for The People of the Abyss

the inevitable doom of the very young. For example, there were the two pathetic individuals called simply "the Carter" and "the Carpenter": decent, respectable tradesmen now too old to compete with vigorous younger men in a ruthless industrial system; their children dead and with no one left to care for them, they have been set loose without shelter or money, to scavenge for bits of garbage along filthy sidewalks and to drift aimlessly and painfully toward death. At the other end of this awful spectrum were the children, of whom 75 out of every 100 were doomed to perish before reaching the age of five. "If this is the best that civilization can do for the human, then give us howling and naked savagery," London concluded bitterly. "Far better to be a people of the wilderness and desert, of the cave and the squatting-place, than to be a people of the machine and the Abyss."

London returned home from Europe in November 1902, shortly after the birth of his second daughter, hoping to make his marriage work; but despite his efforts, it was increasingly obvious that he and Bessie could not live happily together. In May 1903 he took his family to Glen Ellen, California, a picturesque hamlet nestled in the heart of the Sonoma Valley (which London would call the Valley of the Moon in his novel of the same name) fifty-five miles north of Oakland. There he rented a summer cottage from Ninetta and Roscoe Eames, the managing editor of the *Overland Monthly*; and that summer he fell in love with Mrs. Eames's niece Clara Charmian Kittredge. Though she was four years older than he and though she was not beautiful, Charmian Kittredge was a comely, vivacious woman who not only knew how to make the most of her physical charms but also possessed an independent spirit that set her apart from the other young intellectuals, artists, and dilettantes who constituted The Crowd of London's acquaintances. The better he came to know her, the more it seemed to him that she was endowed with all the qualities he associated with the ideal comrade and "mate-woman" he had long dreamed about. In late July, without revealing that he was in love with another woman, he announced to his wife that he was leaving her. Shortly afterward he moved his belongings from their Piedmont bungalow into an Oakland apartment rented for him by his boyhood friend Frank Atherton. So discreet were he and Charmian in their affair that it was more than a year before Bessie London discovered the true identity of her husband's lover. In the meantime London was finishing his novel *The Sea-Wolf*, using Charmian as the model for Maud Brewster, and putting his own romantic sentiments into the mouth of the narrator-hero Humphrey Van Weyden. In combining the ingredients of the two major genres of the turn-of-the-century novel—the new naturalistic novel and the ever-popular sentimental novel—*The Sea-Wolf* proved to be one of London's most successful productions, rivaling *The Call of the Wild* in reprints and total sales (and even exceeding that classic with seven film versions). Soon after completing *The Call of the Wild* in late January 1903, London had written to George Brett, the president of Macmillan Company, about a new novel he had in mind: "My idea is to take a cultured, refined, super-civilized man and woman, (whom the subtleties of artificial, civilized life have blinded to the real facts of life), and throw them into a primitive sea-environment where all is stress & struggle and life expresses itself, simply, in terms of food & shelter; and make this man & woman rise to the situation and come out of it with flying colors." By this time fully aware of his market, he shrewdly added: "Of course, this underlying motif, will be *underlying*; it will be subordinated to the love motif. The superficial reader will get the love story & the adventure; while the deeper reader will get all this, plus the bigger thing lying underneath."

Essentially, *The Sea-Wolf* is an initiation novel, charting the progress of Humphrey Van Weyden from an effete upper-class sissy to full-blooded manhood. Cast to sea when the San Francisco-Sausalito ferryboat collides with a steamship in a heavy fog, Van Weyden is saved from drowning and pressed into sea duty aboard the sealing schooner *Ghost*. Though he is a highly educated literary critic, thirty-five years old, Humphrey is put to work as a lowly scullery boy and scornfully called Hump. During the course of his ordeal he learns for the first time in his life to stand on his own two feet amidst the rigorous brutalities of the seaman's world and eventually becomes first mate of the ship, earning the title of "Mr. Van Weyden."

The high priest of his initiation is Captain Wolf Larsen, one of the truly unforgettable characters in American fiction. "It is a rattling good story," wrote Ambrose Bierce in praise of the novel. "But the great thing—and it is among the greatest of things—is that tremendous creation, Wolf Larsen. . . . The hewing out and setting up of such a figure is enough for a man to do in a life-time." Van Weyden calls Larsen "a magnificent atavism, a man so purely primitive that he was of the type that came into the world before the development of the moral nature." This predatory character is not immoral, but simply amoral. He is a splendid physical specimen, capable of squeezing a raw potato into pulp with one quick grasp of his fist—or of killing a man with one blow of that same fist. Yet he is neither unusually large nor brutish—he is, in fact, quite handsome—and he is remarkably well read. His personal library includes Shakespeare, Tennyson, Browning, Darwin, and Herbert Spencer. He is a tragically flawed superman, doomed despite his intelligence and extraordinary physical strength. Larsen bridges the gap between the Byronic hero and the modern antihero: Like the earlier romantic rebel, he is sensitive, arrogant, uninhibited, actively contemptuous of conventional social mores and traditional beliefs, and—above all—alone. He rules alone; he suffers alone. But like the twentieth-century antihero, he lacks purpose and direction. Without a constructive goal or a meaningful quest into which to channel his great personal force, his energies are perverted into senseless brutality, brooding frustration, and finally self-destruction. "I believe that life is a mess," he confesses. "It is like a yeast, a ferment, a thing that moves and may move for a minute, an hour, a year, or a hundred years, but that in the end will cease to move. The big eat the little that they may continue to move, the strong eat the weak that they may retain their strength.

The lucky eat the most and move the longest, that is all." A hopeless materialist at home nowhere in the world, this rapacious loner, aptly named Wolf, epitomizes the plight of the naturalistic protagonist. Physically and morally, Larsen is a prototype of Eugene O'Neill's Yank Smith and of T. S. Eliot's ape-neck Sweeney; psychologically, he has more in common with Prufrock and Gerontion: he is cursed with a hyperrational sensibility. In his gradual deterioration—first headaches, then blindness and paralysis, and finally death from a brain tumor—he is symbolic of a modern type: the psychopathic overreacher who is alienated both from nature and from his fellow man by the disease of self. "The superman is anti-social in his tendencies," London observed, explaining Larsen's failure, "and in these days of our complex society and sociology he cannot be successful in his hostile aloofness."

The character best fitted for survival in *The Sea-Wolf* is not the *super* man but the *whole* man. It is a combination of adaptability, moral as well as physical courage, enhanced by a vital optimism and the capacity to love, that enables Humphrey Van Weyden to achieve wholeness in the course of his initiation. If Wolf Larsen is the high priest of his initiation, Maud Brewster—the great American poetess shipwrecked and rescued by the *Ghost* at midpoint in the novel—serves as priestess, or anima figure. It is through her influence and through their valiant escape from Larsen's hell ship that Van Weyden is able to put his newfound manhood to test. That manhood is confirmed when he manages not only to cope with the forces of nature, in the mode of Robinson Crusoe, on Endeavor Island, but also—and most significantly—to restep the masts of the derelict *Ghost* which is stranded there with its dying captain after the crew's desertion. Although the introduction of Maud Brewster midway through the plot has been disparaged by many critics as London's concession to sentimental popularity, such denigration overlooks what London called "the bigger thing lying underneath." A primary reason that his "man and woman rise to the occasion and come out with flying colors," while the great Wolf Larsen passes away in blind, impotent isolation, is that they have found the greater strength that comes from love, idealism, and cooperation. This was the underlying theme of much of London's work and was central to his socialistic beliefs. London "admired, even worshipped, strength," zoologist Conway Zirkle has remarked, "but he had learned that strength was increased by cooperation, by union. . . . Those who co-operated won because they were fit. The social virtues, altruism, co-

operation—even self-sacrifice—were justified biologically for they made gregarious living possible and the strength of the strong was the strength of the group."

In early January 1904, leaving the manuscript of *The Sea-Wolf* with Charmian Kittredge and his poet-friend George Sterling to edit and proofread, London sailed on the S. S. *Siberia* for Yokohama, to report the Russo-Japanese War for the Hearst Syndicate. He managed to get closer to the front than any other reporter but was continually frustrated by the Japanese officials, who had imposed strict censorship on reports of all military activities. "Personally, I entered upon this campaign with the most gorgeous conceptions of what a war correspondent's work in the world must be," London wrote. "I had read 'The Light that Failed.' I remembered Stephen Crane's descriptions of being under fire in Cuba. I had heard . . . of all sorts and conditions of correspondents in all sorts of battles and skirmishes, right in the thick of it, where life was keen and immortal moments were being lived. In brief, I came to war expecting to get thrills. My only thrills have been those of indignation and irritation." After six months of thwarted attempts to get into the action, London returned home with a high opinion of the Japanese soldier's toughness but only disgust for the Japanese military bureaucrat's obtuseness: "The Japanese does not in the least understand the correspondent or the mental processes of a correspondent, which are a white man's mental processes. . . . The Japanese cannot understand straight talk, white man's talk. This is one of the causes of so much endless delay."

The year following London's return from Japan was a crucially important one. In the spring of 1905, after his unsuccessful campaign for mayor of Oakland on the Socialist ticket, he took up permanent residence in the Sonoma Valley with Charmian Kittredge and in June purchased the 130-acre Hill Ranch, near Glen Ellen. Now happily engaged, they would be married as soon as his divorce became final. During those months he produced some of his best fiction, including "The Unexpected," "The Sun-Dog Trail," "All Gold Canyon," and what some critics consider the most artistically successful of his longer novels, *White Fang* (also, with a first printing of 48,195 copies in October 1906, one of his most commercially successful books).

The genesis of this novel may be found in a letter to George Brett, written 5 December 1904: London proposed a "complete antithesis" and "companion-book" to *The Call of the Wild*. "Instead of devolution or decivilization of a dog," he

To Build a Fire (alone......br

He travels the fastest who travels ~~alone~~ not
after the frost has ~~dropped~~ below
zero fifty degrees or more.   Yukon Code.

Day had just broken,
cold and gray — in-
finitely cold and gray — when
~~the man~~ turned
aside from the main
Yukon trail and climbed
the high earth-bank,
where a dim
and little-traveled trail
led eastward ~~through~~ the
fat spruce ~~timber~~
timber-land. ~~to the~~
~~eastward~~. It was a
steep bank, and he
paused for breath
at the ~~top~~, excusing
the act to himself by
looking at ~~his~~ his watch.
It was nine o'clock.
There was no sun nor
hint of sun, though there

2.

was not a cloud in the sky.
It was a clear day, and
yet there seemed an
intangible pall over the
face of things, a subtle
gloom that made the
day dark and that
was due to the absence
of sun. This fact did
not worry ~~the man~~.
He was ~~used~~ to the lack
of sun. It had been
days since he had
seen the sun, and
he knew that a few
more days ~~must~~
pass ere that cheerful orb,
~~~~ due
south, would just peep
above the sky-line and
dip immediately ~~from~~ ~~sight~~ view
The man
~~~~ flung a look
back along the way he

explained, "I'm going to give the evolution, the civilization of a dog—development of domesticity, faithfulness, love, morality, and all the amenities and virtues." Rather than being a true companion piece, however, this work would be, when finished, a completely different kind of book from *The Call of the Wild*. *White Fang* is a sociological fable intended to illustrate London's theories of environmental determinism and is therefore more thoroughly naturalistic than London's mythic classic. "I know men and women as they are—millions of them yet in the slime stage," he wrote to George Wharton James. "But I am an evolutionist, therefore a broad optimist, hence my love for the human (in the slime though he be) comes from my knowing him as he is and seeing the divine possibilities ahead of him. That's the whole motive of my 'White Fang.' Every atom of organic life is plastic. The finest specimens now in existence were once all pulpy infants capable of being moulded this way or that. Let the pressure be one way and we have atavism—the reversion to

Front cover for London's 1906 novel, conceived as a "complete antithesis" to The Call of the Wild

the wild; the other the domestication, civilization. I have always been impressed with the awful plasticity of life and I feel that I can never lay enough stress upon the marvelous power and influence of environment."

The power of environment is dramatically evident throughout *White Fang*. Born in the wild, the young cub sees his world through the eyes of the predator: "The aim of life was meat. Life itself was meat. Life lived on life. There were the eaters and the eaten. The law was: EAT OR BE EATEN." Later, after his mother has taken him with her from the wilderness back to her former Indian master, Gray Beaver, the young wolf dog is bullied mercilessly by Lip-lip, the leader of the camp dogs, and persecuted as an outsider by the other puppies, consequently becoming a fierce pariah. London makes it clear that environmental determinism is a crucial factor in the shaping of White Fang's character: that if Lip-lip had not tormented him, he would have "grown up more doglike and with more liking for dogs"; and that if his Indian master had been capable of affection, White Fang might have developed "all manner of kindly qualities." Unfortunately, such is not the case; instead, the dog has been perversely molded into a creature of hate, "morose and lonely, unloving and ferocious, the enemy of all his kind."

This hateful ferocity is intensified when Gray Beaver sells White Fang into the bondage of Beauty Smith, under whose sadistic tutelage he becomes the lethal Fighting Wolf. After a bloody and near-fatal career as a dog killer, the hero is redeemed by a new master, Weedon Scott, whose loving kindness converts him from vicious beast into loyal pet. The final stage of his initiation is accomplished when White Fang is taken to Scott's California ranch. Here he becomes properly domesticated; and—after saving the life of Judge Scott, Weedon's father, from the escaped convict Jim Hall (the man transformed into mad-dog killer by harsh social treatment)—he is renamed Blessed Wolf: "Not alone was he in the geographical Southland, for he was in the Southland of life. Human kindness was like a sun shining upon him, and he flourished like a flower planted in good soil."

In October 1905 London started east on tour for the Slayton Lecture Bureau, and on 19 November he and Charmian were married in Chicago. His tour climaxed with his famous lectures on revolution at Harvard and Yale that winter. "I went to the University. . . . but I did not find the University alive," he told his student audience. "If [collegians] cannot fight for us, we want them to fight against us—of course, sincerely fight against us, believing that the right conduct lies in combating socialism because socialism is a great growing force. But what we do not want is that which obtains today and has obtained in the past of the university, a mere deadness and unconcern and ignorance so far as socialism is concerned. Fight for us or fight against us! Raise your voices one way or the other; be alive!" That fall he was also elected first president of the Intercollegiate Socialist Society, with Upton Sinclair as vice president.

London's socialist enthusiasm reached its peak in 1905 and culminated creatively in his composition of *The Iron Heel* (1908) the following year. This apocalyptic novel purports to be a copy of the "Everhard Manuscript": a fragment written and hidden away by Avis Everhard, widow of the leader of the "Second [unsuccessful] Revolt," and edited seven centuries later by the historian Anthony Meredith in the year 419 B. O. M. (Brotherhood of Man). Mrs. Everhard's document covers the twenty-year period from 1912 to 1932 when the capitalist oligarchy, called "the Iron Heel" by her late husband, Ernest, rises to complete power, grinding all opposing political systems underfoot. In the early stages of the conflict, Ernest works against this oppression by use of democratic methods, winning election to Congress, where he is joined by a half-hundred Socialist representatives. This apparent victory is short-lived, however, for the oligarchy quickly consolidates its ranks and moves forcefully to suppress all political opposition. Union leaders are bought off; secret police and mercenaries are employed as terrorists; and political antagonists are arrested or murdered. Everhard's followers are forced to move underground and to fight violence with violence. The narrative reaches a bloody climax when an oppressed mob erupts from the great Chicago ghetto and is methodically slaughtered by the mercenaries of the Iron Heel. Although Ernest survives the holocaust and works to reorganize the forces of the revolution, the manuscript ends abruptly; and the reader is told in Professor Meredith's concluding footnote that Everhard has been mysteriously executed. Meredith says that the oligarchy held its power for another three centuries and throughout numerous revolts before Herbert Spencer's prophecy of socialist evolution was at last fulfilled.

No one seemed to care for *The Iron Heel*. Reviewers called it "pernicious" and "incendiary." The public bought only a few thousand copies. Even the socialist press gave it a mixed reception. "It was a labor of love, and a dead failure as a book," London

remarked about *The Iron Heel*. But if the novel was something less than a commercial and artistic success, it was nevertheless an important book, enthusiastically commended later by such noteworthy figures as Eugene V. Debs, Leon Trotsky, and Anatole France. Philip Foner asserts that it is "probably the most amazingly prophetic work of the twentieth century"; Robert E. Spiller calls it "a terrifying forecast of Fascism and its evils"; and Maxwell Geismar suggests that it is "a key work—perhaps a classic work—of American radicalism." Moreover, as a fictional articulation of London's private dreams of revolutionary glory, *The Iron Heel* is one of his most revealing works. The novel's "earnest" and "ever-hard" hero represents London's fantasy about himself, purged of his obsession to win to the good life of the American Dream. A "natural aristocrat" and a "blond beast" with blacksmith's biceps and prizefighter's neck, Ernest is the author's exact physical replica; with his Spencerian Weltanschauung and his Marxist rhetoric, he is also London's metaphysical replica; and the love affair between Avis and Ernest Everhard is virtually a carbon copy of that between Charmian and Jack London. "Few of Jack London's books, even those which were consciously autobiographical, are so intensely personal," remarked his daughter Joan London in her biography: "His best knowledge of the class struggle and the socialist movement, his best speeches and essays he gave to Everhard. . . ."

But "intensely personal" as it is, *The Iron Heel* is not so personal as *Martin Eden*, London's next novel, begun the following summer in Hawaii and completed in February 1908 in Tahiti, while he was sailing the South Seas on his much publicized cruise aboard the *Snark*. "Nowhere in London's fiction are the complexities and contradictions of his life and mind more intimately revealed than in *Martin Eden*," Jonathan Yardley has perceptively observed. Even London was not entirely sure how much of himself he was putting into this remarkable Bildungsroman, for in September 1907 he wrote to George Brett: "I am surging along with my new novel, for which I cannot find a name, and which is so totally different a novel from anything I have written, that I do not know quite how to make up my mind about it as I go along." Because of the author's deep personal involvement in the book, *Martin Eden* is an imperfect but powerful work.

The plot, unlike the novel's underlying theme, is fairly straightforward and uncomplicated. In much the same fashion that Jack London had fallen in love with Mabel Applegarth (the lovely sister of

London aboard his yacht, Roamer

Ted Applegarth, the closest friend of his college days), Martin Eden, a husky young sailor, falls in love with Ruth Morse, a fragilely beautiful Victorian lady. Though lacking in manners and formal education, Martin is a sensitive, intelligent young man who possesses extraordinary vitality. Inspired to make something of himself, he accepts Ruth as his cultural tutor and enters upon a rigorous program of self-education. He learns with astonishing rapidity and within a few months has become conversant not only with the best-known literary artists but also with such philosophers as Adam Smith, Karl Marx, and—above all—Herbert Spencer, who becomes his intellectual idol. Gifted with a natural talent for storytelling, Martin determines to make a career as a writer. Renting a typewriter, he sets himself to work in an eighteen-hour-a-day frenzy of creativity, churning out stories, poems, jokes, and articles by the dozens. For several months he gets nothing but rejection slips from the magazine editors and nothing but nagging from Ruth, his family, and his friends, all of whom insist that he get a steady job. His only encouragement comes from his poet-friend Russ Brissenden (modeled after George Sterling). Everything seems to go wrong for Martin. He is falsely publicized in the local newspapers as a

notorious revolutionary; under pressure from her mother, Ruth rejects him; a few weeks later he discovers that Brissenden, a world-weary consumptive, has taken his own life. Exhausted by his ordeal and profoundly depressed, Martin lapses into neurasthenic apathy. Ironically, at almost the same time, he starts to receive acceptances for the numerous manuscripts he has already sent out. His success snowballs; he becomes an instant celebrity; the publishers begin to clamor for his work; his friends invite him into their homes again, and even Ruth comes back, begging his forgiveness. But the recognition and the good fortune have come too late. Martin is thoroughly disenchanted. "It was work performed," he keeps repeating to himself. "And now you feed me, when then you let me starve, forbade me your house, and damned me because I wouldn't get a job. And the work was already done, all done. And now, when I speak, you . . . pay respectful attention to whatever I choose to say. . . . And why? Because I'm famous; because I've a lot of money. Not because I'm Martin Eden. . . ." All his dreams of love and success shattered, Martin books passage on a ship bound for the South Seas and, halfway across the Pacific, quietly squeezes through a porthole and drowns himself in the ocean.

"I am Martin Eden," London later professed. "I would not die but I went largely through Martin Eden's experience. Martin Eden died because he was an individualist, I live because I was a socialist and had social consciousness." But this novel was considerably more than an indictment of rampant individualism: a generation before Theodore Dreiser's *An American Tragedy* (1925) and F. Scott Fitzgerald's *The Great Gatsby* (1925), London had revealed the hollow core of the American Dream (his first preference for the title of his book had been *Success*). Ultimately, Martin is destroyed by the delusions that an ideal goal may be attained through material means and that success is synonymous with happiness—and by his failure to realize until too late that in America status derives more from image than from "work performed."

The deeper cultural implications of *Martin Eden* were generally overlooked by contemporary reviewers, who decried Martin's "turbulent egotism" and "defiance of the collective wisdom of mankind," denigrating his suicide as too pessimistic, "inartistic and unnecessary." William Morton Payne, in the *Dial*, remarked that Ruth Morse was "far more worth while than the man who has outgrown her in his own conceit" and concluded that it was "just as well" that Martin dropped out of the porthole at the end. Frederic Taber Cooper, in the *Bookman*, condemned London's "grotesque exaggeration of Martin's difficulties with his publishers," suggesting that the author was "out of his element" in trying to depict respectable social types. A few critics, however, perceived the merits of the novel. H. W. Boynton, in the *New York Times*, observed: "It is not a very sane or well-balanced book, but there is much wholesome truth in it." And Edwin Markham, in the *San Francisco Examiner*, praised it as London's "best novel—his story richest in the wisdom of the heart." More recently, Franklin Walker has concurred that despite its obvious flaws, *Martin Eden* remains an important novel: "Like all his books, it is uneven in structure, sometimes clumsy in expression, at times mawkish in tone. Yet it possesses great lasting power, having more vitality today than it did the day it issued from the press."

Martin Eden was written during the most highly publicized of all Jack London's adventures: the cruise of the *Snark*. The dream of circumnavigating the globe in their own boat had been inspired by Joshua Slocum's *Sailing Alone Around the World*, which Jack and Charmian had read at Wake Robin in summer 1905. London had calculated that the boat would cost him about $7,000, but in his careful planning he had anticipated neither the San Francisco earthquake of April 1906 nor the subtler disasters of twentieth-century production standards. Consequently, the *Snark* cost five times the original estimate, was a half-year late in leaving Oakland, and was so badly botched in the building that extensive repairs were needed when the boat reached Hawaii in May 1907. Moreover, the voyage, originally planned as a seven-year around-the-world cruise, lasted less than two years. By fall 1908, all seven members of the crew had been stricken with various tropical ailments—malaria, dysentery, Solomon Island sores—and, in addition to these, London himself suffered from a double fistula and a mysterious skin disease that caused his hands to swell and peel so badly that he could use them only with great pain. That December, on the advice of physicians in Sydney, Australia, he called off the voyage; and the following spring he and Charmian London departed for home, via Ecuador, Panama, New Orleans, and the Grand Canyon, arriving in Oakland on 21 July 1909.

While the *Snark* voyage had been disastrous from the standpoint of London's health and finances, it resulted in a book, *The Cruise of the Snark* (1911), and enriched the mythic element in his fiction. The impulse to escape from the dullness of work through travel and adventure, which informs

London circa 1912-1913

much of London's career, may be seen in his fiction as a revelation of the universal human yearning to recapture the condition of prelapsarian freedom and happiness. This archetypal motif, the quest for Paradise, recurs time and again throughout London's work. Its first significant manifestation is in the Northland Saga. There, civilized man might discover gold—and something even more precious than gold: "true comradeship," London called it. Confronted by the cold, implacable laws of the White Silence, those who were unfit—the morally weak, the selfish, the foolhardy—perished. Those who were fit candidates, however, might not merely survive but actually be improved by their adaptation to the Northland Code, which fostered such virtues as "unselfishness, forbearance, and tolerance." Still, the Northland wilderness was a far cry from Eden. Its spiritual wellsprings might be pure—but they were also frozen. Though an agent of moral reformation, the region offered neither warmth nor security—and the only serenity it provided was the stillness of death. In short, the Northland, London realized was a region to escape *from*—not *to*.

On the other hand, the South Seas—particularly Hawaii and Polynesia—held forth the promise of warmth, good health, and life abundant. When he first visited the Hawaiian Islands in 1904 en route to the Russo-Japanese War, London felt as if he had truly found Elysium, a paradise of flower-swept valleys peopled by bronzed youths and golden maidens. "When Hawaii was named the Paradise of the Pacific, it was inadequately named," he wrote afterward in an article for *Cosmopolitan* (October-December 1916). "Hawaii and the Hawaiians are a land and a people loving and lovable. By their language may ye know them, and in what other land save this one is the commonest form of greeting, not 'Good day,' nor 'How d'ye do,' but 'Love'? That greeting is *Aloha*—love, I love you, my love to you.... It is a positive affirmation of the warmth of one's own heart-giving." London's further experience taught him, however, that Hawaii was, in truth, Paradise Lost: a lovely land whose economy had been commercialized, whose politics had been usurped, and whose inhabitants had been contaminated by the "civilized" haoles. "They came like lambs, speaking softly," remarks Koolau in London's "Koolau, the Leper": "They were of two kinds. The one kind asked our permission, our gracious permission, to preach to us the word of God. The other kind asked our permission, our gracious permission, to trade with us. That was the beginning. Today all the islands are theirs, all the land, all the cattle—everything is theirs." Also

theirs, insidiously shared with the Hawaiians, is the "rotting sickness" of civilization, the leprosy which has metamorphosed a beautiful people into hideous monsters with stumps for arms and gaping holes for faces: "The sickness is not ours," says Koolau. "We have not sinned. The men who preached the word of God and the word of Rum brought the sickness with the coolie slaves who work the stolen land" (*The House of Pride*, 1912). The situation was the same

London circa 1914

wherever London traveled in Polynesia. Expecting to find the natives of Typee as splendidly vigorous as Melville had described them two generations earlier, he found, instead, nothing but a handful of "wretched creatures, afflicted with leprosy, elephantiasis, and tuberculosis." Bitterly disappointed, he wrote in *The Cruise of the Snark*, "Life has rotted away in this wonderful garden spot, where the climate is as delightful and healthful as any to be found in this world. Not alone were the Typeans physically magnificent; they were pure.... When one considers the situation, one is almost driven to the conclusion that the white race flourishes on impurity and corruption." Echoing a similar disenchantment, Prince Akuli, the Oxford-educated narrator of one of London's Hawaiian stories, mutters, "This is the twentieth-century, and we stink of gasoline" ("Shin Bones," *On the Makaloa Mat*, 1919).

But if Polynesia was Paradise Lost, Melanesia, particularly the Solomon Islands, which the *Snark* reached in the summer of 1908, was an Inferno. "If I were a king, the worst punishment I could inflict on my enemies would be to banish them to the Solomons," London reminisced in *The Cruise of the Snark*. "On second thought, king or no king, I don't think I'd have the heart to do it." He was drawing from firsthand experience when he wrote that in the Solomons "fever and dysentery are perpetually on the walk about, . . . loathsome skin diseases abound, . . . the air is saturated with a poison that bites into every pore, cut, or abrasion and plants malignant ulcers, [and] many strong men who escape dying there return as wrecks to their own countries." It was this region, rather than the Klondike, which inspired London's bitterest naturalistic writing. Here the wilderness-as-Eden symbolism is wholly inverted. Unlike the golden youths of Polynesia, the Melanesians are ugly myrmidons of the Prince of Blackness himself—"a wild lot, with a hearty appetite for human flesh and a fad for collecting human heads." The moral effect of this rotting green hell, unlike the northland, is to bring out the worst in those who survive. Among the natives the "highest instinct of sportsmanship is to catch a man with his back turned and to smite him a cunning blow with a tomahawk that severs the spinal column at the base of the brain. It is equally true that on some islands, such as Malaita, the profit and loss account of social intercourse is calculated in homicides." The white man is reduced to like savagery: "I've been in the tropics too long," confesses a character in the title story of *A Son of the Sun* (1912). "I'm a sick man, a damn sick man. And the whiskey, and the sun, and the fever made me sick in morals, too. Nothing's too mean and low for me now, and I can understand why the niggers eat each other, and take heads, and such things. I could do it myself." The only salutary effect Melanesia had on London was to convince him that the paradise he sought was not halfway around the globe but at home. "I also have a panacea," he wrote after suffering through a half-dozen hellish ailments inflicted by the tropics. "It is California. I defy any man to get a Solomon Island sore in California."

His ranch in the Sonoma Valley seemed, indeed, to be the panacea London needed after the *Snark* cruise; and for a while after returning home he thrived as he devoted the major time and energy to fulfilling his agrarian dream. "I believe the soil is our one indestructible asset," he said. "I am rebuilding worn-out hillside lands that were worked out and destroyed by our wasteful California farmers. . . . Everything I build is for the years to come." Between 1909 and 1916 he increased the size of Beauty Ranch to 1500 acres, one of the largest in the Sonoma Valley; and during those seven years he came to be regarded by the agricultural experts as "one of California's leading farmers" whose ranch was "one of the best in the country." By combining modern agronomy with the wisdom of Oriental agriculture (using such techniques as terracing, drainage, and tillage), he succeeded in growing bumper crops of prunes, grapes, and alfalfa on land that had been abandoned by previous owners. He built the first concrete-block silo in California and constructed a "pig palace" which was a model of sanitation and efficiency. His livestock regularly took high honors in the county and state fairs and brought top breeding prices. One of the finest tributes he ever received was that of Luther Burbank in *The Harvest of Years* (1927): "Jack London was a big healthy boy with a taste for serious things, but never cynical, never bitter, always good-humored and humorous, as I saw him, and with fingers and heart equally sensitive when he was in my gardens."

London's agrarian enthusiasm manifested itself in his literary as well as in his agricultural achievements; in fact, the two fields of interest were reciprocal, each enhancing the other. Four major works—three novels and one play—reflect his agrarian vision. The first of these, *Burning Daylight*—begun in Quito, Ecuador, on 5 June 1909, and finished on the ranch that fall—is the story of a Klondike bonanza king, Elam Harnish, who, having made his fortune in the Northland, seeks new worlds to conquer in the civilized southland, only to discover that the naturalistic laws of survival are no less operative in the jungle of big business than in the Arctic wilderness. Here, as in the Northland, life "was a wild animal fight" in which "the strong trampled the weak," and the strong "were not necessarily the best"—merely the luckiest. Existence was a gamble, and "God was a whimsical, abstract, mad thing called Luck." There was no justice, no fairness, in any of it. "The little men that came, the little pulpy babies, were not even asked if they wanted to try a flutter at the game. They had no choice. Luck jerked them into life, slammed them up against the jostling table, and told them: 'Now play, damn you, play!' "

Harnish, nicknamed "Burning Daylight" because of his tremendous vitality, after being mulcted of $11 million by Wall Street robber barons, decides to match their ruthlessness—and their luck—with his own. He recoups his fortune, consequently amassing even greater wealth as a San Francisco street-railway magnate; but in the process he loses his soul, becoming even more ruthless than those who swindled him. At the end, however, he is redeemed by the love of a woman, his secretary Dede Mason (modeled after Charmian London), who persuades him to renounce his financial empire and to move onto a small ranch in the hills near Glen Ellen, California. The reading public and the critics alike, for the most part, responded favorably to *Burning Daylight*. The novel, with a first printing of 27,108 copies, sold better than any book London had written since *White Fang*, and the reviewers praised both his portrayal of Dede Mason ("a real human being . . . the best woman London has created," wrote Una H. H. Cool in the *San Francisco Sunday Call*) and his morally affirmative ending. A typical review, in the *Nation*, attested that "this is by all odds the most interesting, as well as the most wholesome long story Mr. London has written."

By this time in his career London's socialist enthusiasm had clearly begun to wane, and he envisioned a less violent solution to modern man's woes than social revolution: "Oh, try to see!" he exclaimed: "In the solution of the great economic problems of the present age, I see a return to the soil. I go into farming because my philosophy and research have taught me to recognize the fact that a return to the soil is the basis of economics . . . I see my farm in terms of the world, and the world in terms of my farm." This vision is the central theme of *The Valley of the Moon* (1913), generally considered the best of London's agrarian novels. "I am planning a serial, the motif is back to the land," he wrote to *Cosmopolitan* editor Roland Phillips on 30 May 1911: "I take a man and a woman, young, who belong to the working class in a large city. Both are wage-workers, the man is unskilled—a driver of a brewery wagon, or something of that sort. The first third of the book will be devoted to their city environment, their meeting, their love-affair, and the trials and tribulations of such a marriage in the working class. Comes hard times. The woman gets the vision. She is the guiding force. They start wandering over the country of California. Of course, they have all sorts of adventures, and their wandering becomes a magnificent, heroic detailed pilgrimage. After many hints and snatches of vision, always looking for the spot, they do find the real, one and only spot, and settle down to successful

Front cover for the best of London's agrarian novels. "The motif is back to the land," he wrote his editor.

small-scale farming."

The central characters of the novel, Saxon and Billy Roberts, have a stillborn child in the ugly, strike-ridden city of Oakland; but, like Dede and Elam Harnish, they find Eden in the Sonoma hills. The novel concludes with a promise of new life in Saxon's announcement of her pregnancy as she and Billy, standing beside a quiet pool in the heart of their pastoral sanctuary, gaze blissfully upon a doe and a newborn fawn at the edge of the forest.

The reviewers were enthusiastic in their reception of *The Valley of the Moon*, seeing in this novel a departure from the brutality and pessimism of London's earlier, more naturalistic fictions. E. F. Edgett, in the *Boston Evening Transcript*, recommended it as a novel "for all thoughtful readers," especially praising the author for his realistic treatment of industrial turmoil and for his subordination of socialism to art. The *Athenaeum* observed that London had grasped "the essential traits of humanity" in this "essentially American" novel.

London's third agrarian novel, *The Little Lady of the Big House* (1916), was a less happy work. Unlike Elam Harnish and Billy Roberts, who have purified themselves of all exploitive motives before entering the pastoral wilderness, Dick Forrest, the hero of *The Little Lady of the Big House*, is possessed with a mania for efficiency and profit. The wealthy owner of a large California ranch, Forrest is a success as a commercial farmer and as a scientific breeder of prize stock—but he is a failure as a husband and his marriage is barren. He is London's version of the twentieth-century clockwork man whose every hour is governed by his watch. His wife, Paula (the title character), neglected and starved for genuine affection, falls in love with Dick's best friend, the artist-writer Evan Graham, and dissolves the love triangle by committing suicide at the end of the novel.

Contemporary reviewers condemned *The Little Lady of the Big House* as a bad book that immorally portrayed the "erotomania of three persons who fiddle harmonies on the strings of sensualism." Many of London's critics have subsequently agreed that this is his worst novel—cynical, confused, and gratuitously if unconsciously titillating. And several of his biographers have suggested that the book was a mirror of London's own psychological state following the multiple disasters of 1913: an attack of appendicitis and the discovery that his kidneys were badly diseased; the loss of his fruit crop by a false spring and late frost; the accidental killing of one of his prize mares by a hunter; the threatened loss of his motion picture copyrights by the lawsuit of the Balboa Amusement Company; and, on 22 August, the burning of his great new mansion, the Wolf House. Although there is some truth to these allegations, they nevertheless tend to obscure the important thematic implications underlying the tragedy of the Forrests' marriage: While "a return to the soil" is vital, mere scientific efficiency in treatment of the land is not the ultimate answer to the "problems of the present age"—efficiency must be tempered with love; head must be balanced by heart.

This humanistic theme is explicitly dramatized in *The Acorn-Planter* (1916), a play which London began writing on Christmas Day 1914, two weeks after completing the manuscript for *The Little Lady of the Big House*. This play, replete with references to nature but with virtually no naturalism, is a mythopoeic fantasy beginning in "the morning of the world" and concluding with "the celebration of the death of war and the triumph of the acorn-planters," incarnated in Red Cloud, the philosopher-agrarian. California is celebrated as the place of Edenic possibilities, "A sunny land, a rich and fruitful land . . . warm and golden," where "In place of war's alarums . . . The New Day dawns, / The day of brotherhood, / The day of man!"

Jack London was by this time a dying man, stricken with fatal kidney disease. During the next two years, though he tried to maintain a vigorous public image, his body betrayed him: the symptoms of uremia—edema, swollen ankles, bloated body, kidney stones, gouty rheumatism—were increasingly evident. Yet he refused to heed the warnings of his physician that he must restrict his diet and get more rest. He spent several months in Hawaii in 1915 and 1916, trying to recapture his lost health in that benevolent climate; but his body continued to deteriorate.

Coincidentally, while in Hawaii in the spring of 1916, he discovered the recently translated work of Carl Jung and was immediately captivated: "I tell you I am standing on the edge of a world so new, so terrible, so wonderful, that I am almost afraid to look over into it," he announced to Charmian London. Suddenly, the Polynesian myths he had listened to with good-natured disbelief over the past several years came to life within the Jungian context of racial memory and the archetypes of the collective unconscious. The literary results of this new discovery were a series of extraordinary stories written during the last six months of his life, published posthumously in *The Red One* (1918) and *On the Makaloa Mat* (1919), and signifying not only an advance in his own work but a new dimension in twentieth-century literature: London became the first American fictionist to make use of Jung's

Front cover for London's 1919 collection of South Seas tales

theories consciously as well as creatively. "The Water Baby," for example, in *On the Makaloa Mat*, involves a dialogue between the world-weary narrator, John Lakana (the Hawaiian name for London), and Kohokumu, an ancient Hawaiian diver who claims the sea as his true mother. "But listen, O Young Wise One, to my elderly wisdom," the old man admonishes his skeptical listener:

> "This I know: as I grow old I seek less for the truth from without me, and find more of the truth within me. Why have I thought this thought of my return to my mother and of my rebirth from my mother into the sun? You do not know. I do not know. I do not know, save that, without whisper of man's voice or printed word, without prompting from otherwhere, this thought has arisen from within me, from the deeps of me that are as deep as the sea. . . . Is this thought that I have thought a dream?"
>
> "Perhaps it is you that are a dream," I laughed. . . .
>
> "There is much more in dreams than we know," he assured me with great solemnity. "Dreams go deep, all the way down, maybe to before the beginning. . . ."

London himself, the self-avowed materialistic monist, was evidently undergoing a change during the last months of his life, coming to terms at last with those nonrational psychic elements he had so rigorously rejected in his earlier years. He finished "The Water Baby" on 2 October 1916; seven weeks later, his meteoric career was ended by a fatal attack of what the attending physicians called "gastro-intestinal type of uraemia." In his copy of Jung, Charmian reports, London had underscored the following biblical quotation: "Think not carnally or thou art carnal, but think symbolically and then thou art spirit."

The nation mourned London's death as that of one of its heroes, the newspapers allotting more space to London than to Francis Joseph I, the Emperor of Austria, who had passed away on the preceding evening of 21 November. Yet, despite this enormous popularity, his rating as an artist was negligible among the members of the literary establishment. William Dean Howells, who had encouraged such other young writers as Stephen Crane and Frank Norris, never so much as mentioned Jack London in his hundreds of literary reviews and essays. Joan Sherman has remarked that London's reputation "exemplifies the split between 'high' and 'low' culture," that he was the victim of "critical standards established by the New England Sages and their New York heirs in 'The Age of Innocence,' 'The Age of Decorum,' 'The Genteel Decades,' 'The Purple Cow Period'—as the years from 1870 through the early 1900's were variously called." Those same critical standards were implicit in Arthur Hobson Quinn's attempt to write London's literary epitaph in 1936: "It is almost certain that his vogue is passing, for there is something impermanent in the very nature of the literature of violence." The New Critics of the succeeding generation relegated classics like *The Call of the Wild*, *The Sea-Wolf*, and *White Fang* to junior-high-school classes, ignoring the rest of his work altogether.

But a change in London's reputation began in the 1960s with the publication of *Letters from Jack London* (1965), edited by King Hendricks and Irving Shepard; Hensley Woodbridge, John London, and George Tweney's comprehensive *Jack London: A Bibliography* (1966); and Franklin Walker's *Jack London and the Klondike* (1966). At the same time, the publication of the *Jack London Newsletter*, edited by Woodbridge, provided a forum for London scholars. The London "renascence" was readily apparent in the following decade with the publication of book-length critical studies by Earle Labor and James McClintock, along with another primary bibliography by Dale Walker and James Sisson and a secondary bibliography by Joan Sherman, as well as biographies by Russ Kingman and Andrew Sinclair. In 1976, the centennial of London's birth, three scholarly journals—*Modern Fiction Studies*, *Western American Literature*, and the *Pacific Historian*—published special Jack London numbers, indicating that he had at last won the academic respectability so long awaited in his own country.

Letters:

Letters from Jack London, edited by King Hendricks and Irving Shepard (New York: Odyssey, 1965).

Bibliographies:

Dale L. Walker and James E. Sisson III, *The Fiction of Jack London: A Chronological Bibliography* (El Paso: Texas Western University Press, 1972);

Hensley C. Woodbridge, John London, and George H. Tweney, *Jack London: A Bibliography* (Georgetown, Cal.: Talisman, 1966; enlarged edition, Millwood, N.Y.: Kraus, 1973);

Joan Sherman, *Jack London: A Reference Guide* (Boston: G. K. Hall, 1977).

Biographies:

Charmian K. London, *The Book of Jack London*, 2 volumes (New York: Century, 1921);

Irving Stone, *Sailor on Horseback: The Biography of Jack London* (Boston: Houghton Mifflin, 1938);

Joan London, *Jack London and His Times: An Unconventional Biography* (New York: Doubleday, Doran, 1939);

Andrew Sinclair, *Jack: A Biography of Jack London* (New York: Harper & Row, 1977);

Russ Kingman, *A Pictorial Life of Jack London* (New York: Crown, 1979).

References:

Richard W. Etulain, *Jack London on the Road: The Tramp Diary and Other Hobo Writings* (Logan: Utah State University, 1979);

Earle Labor, *Jack London* (New York: Twayne, 1974);

James I. McClintock, *White Logic: Jack London's Short Stories* (Grand Rapids, Mich.: Wolf House Books, 1975);

Ray Wilson Ownbey, ed., *Jack London: Essays in Criticism* (Santa Barbara, Cal.: Peregrine Smith, 1978);

Franklin Walker, *Jack London and the Klondike: The Genesis of an American Writer* (San Marino, Cal.: The Huntington Library, 1966).

Papers:

The Henry E. Huntington Library in San Marino, California, houses the largest collection of Londoniana, comprising some 60,000 items: the major portion of London's manuscripts and letters, as well as scrapbooks, most of London's personal library, and Charmian London's diaries. The Merrill Library at Utah State University in Logan, Utah, has the second largest collection of London materials, including many letters, some manuscripts and notes, along with a significant portion of Charmian London's correspondence. The New York Public Library houses London's correspondence with George P. Brett and the Macmillan Company, as well as some manuscripts. The Clifton Waller Barrett Library at the University of Virginia includes more than 100 London letters (most of them to his agent Paul Revere Reynolds). The Jack London State Historical Park in Glen Ellen, California, houses the Holman Collection of London materials, including important letters to his friend Frederick Irons Bamford. Other smaller but noteworthy collections of London materials are on file at the following libraries: The Bancroft Library at the University of California, Berkeley; Stanford University; the Cresmer Collection at the University of Southern California; the Irving Stone Collection at the University of California, Los Angeles; and the Oakland Public Library.

Mary N. Murfree
(Charles Egbert Craddock)
(24 January 1850 - 31 July 1922)

Ruth Salvaggio
Virginia Tech

BOOKS: *In the Tennessee Mountains* (Boston & New York: Houghton, Mifflin, 1884; London: Longmans, Green, 1884);

Where the Battle Was Fought (Boston: Osgood, 1884; London: Trübner, 1885);

Down the Ravine (Boston & New York: Houghton, Mifflin, 1885; London: Ward, Lock, 1886);

The Prophet of the Great Smoky Mountains (Boston & New York: Houghton, Mifflin, 1885; London: Chatto & Windus, 1885);

In the Clouds (Boston & New York: Houghton, Mifflin, 1886; London: Ward, Lock, 1886);

The Story of Keedon Bluffs (Boston & New York: Houghton, Mifflin, 1887; London: Ward, Lock, 1887);

The Despot of Broomsedge Cove (Boston & New York: Houghton, Mifflin, 1888; London: Ward, Lock, 1889);

In the "Stranger People's" Country (New York: Harper, 1891; London: Osgood, 1891);

His Vanished Star (Boston & New York: Houghton, Mifflin, 1894; London: Chatto & Windus, 1894);

The Phantoms of the Foot-Bridge, and Other Stories (New

York: Harper, 1895);

The Mystery of Witch-Face Mountain, and Other Stories (Boston & New York: Houghton, Mifflin, 1895);

The Young Mountaineers (Boston & New York: Houghton, Mifflin, 1897);

The Juggler (Boston & New York: Houghton, Mifflin, 1897; London: Gay & Bird, 1898);

The Story of Old Fort Loudon (New York & London: Macmillan, 1899);

The Bushwackers, and Other Stories (Chicago & New York: Stone, 1899);

The Champion (Boston & New York: Houghton, Mifflin, 1902);

A Spectre of Power (Boston & New York: Houghton, Mifflin, 1904);

The Frontiersmen (Boston & New York: Houghton, Mifflin, 1904);

The Storm Centre (New York & London: Macmillan, 1905);

The Amulet (New York & London: Macmillan, 1906);

The Windfall (New York: Duffield, 1907; London: Chatto & Windus, 1907);

The Fair Mississippian (Boston & New York: Houghton, Mifflin, 1908);

The Raid of the Guerilla, and Other Stories (Philadelphia & London: Lippincott, 1912);

The Ordeal; A Mountain Romance of Tennessee (Philadelphia & London: Lippincott, 1912);

The Story of Duciehurst: A Tale of the Mississippi (New York: Macmillan, 1914).

Mary Noailles Murfree's writing career spans almost fifty years. During that period she wrote eighteen novels and six volumes of short fiction on a variety of distinctly American subjects: polite Southern society, the Civil War, colonial history, and Mississippi culture. But it was her fiction set in the Tennessee mountains that established her reputation as one of America's leading local colorists. Known to her readers by the pseudonym Charles Egbert Craddock, she enjoyed tremendous popularity during her own day, though she is known today only because a few of her short stories appear in American literature anthologies. Murfree is clearly a minor literary figure, but her small contribution was nonetheless significant. She helped establish realistic Southern fiction as a respectable and popular form, and she made stories of the life and culture of the Tennessee mountaineers a distinctive part of the American local-color movement.

Murfree lived the life of a well-bred Southern woman. Her family's claim to their Tennessee

Charles Egbert Craddock

home, Grantland, can be traced back to the American Revolution, and the towns of Murfreesboro in Tennessee and North Carolina both owe their names to the Murfree family. Her father, William Law Murfree, a lawyer, and her mother, Fanny Priscilla Dickinson Murfree, were both confirmed devotees of the arts and exposed their children to the finest literature and music. Though Mary Murfree was left partially paralyzed by a fever when she was four, this handicap served only to strengthen her determination as a writer. The experiences of her first twenty-two years gave her most of the material for her stories, and the intellectual atmosphere of her home provided the ideal environment for a woman who was to devote the remainder of her life to the writing of fiction steeped in her native territory.

When Murfree was seven, her family moved from Grantland to Nashville, where they remained for sixteen years. There Murfree attended Nashville Female Academy and received an education in the classical curriculum as well as in polite manners. She always led her class. From the time Murfree was five until she was twenty, she and her family spent summers in Beersheba Springs, a resort in the

Cumberland range. It was here that Murfree witnessed firsthand the beauty of the mountains and the life-style of the mountaineers. After her family had lived in Nashville only four years, the Civil War broke out, and in 1862 Grantland was destroyed in the war. In 1867 Murfree went to Philadelphia to attend Chegary Institute, a finishing school for girls, where she excelled in music and wrote some poetry. Two years later she returned to Nashville and to the social life of polite Southern society. It was not until 1872, when the family left Nashville to return to their reconstructed Grantland, that Murfree began her career as a writer. She was twenty-two.

During the next nine years, Murfree wrote several short stories. In 1881 the family again relocated, this time in St. Louis. Three years after the move Murfree's first volume of stories, *In the Tennessee Mountains* (1884), was published. Before she and her family had returned to New Grantland in 1890, Murfree had had six novels published, among them *The Prophet of the Great Smoky Mountains* (1885), one of her best books. She continued to write stories and novels until 1914, finally producing a total of twenty-five volumes of fiction. As Murfree's writing career began to wind down, she became active in social and community affairs, particularly the Daughters of the American Revolution. She was elected their state regent in 1912, and for a while she traveled and lectured throughout Tennessee. In her last days, however, she was confined to a wheelchair and blind. The University of the South awarded Murfree an honorary degree in 1922, the year of her death.

Murfree's first published story, "Flirts and Their Ways," which appeared in *Lippincott's* in 1874, was a literary excursion into social-manners fiction, an excursion which ended well before it had the chance to develop. She wrote only one other story of this kind, "My Daughter's Admirers," which *Lippincott's* published in 1875. Both appeared under the pseudonym R. Emmet Dembry, a name she abandoned when she turned her attention from manners fiction to local color. Though Murfree's experiment with social satire proved brief, her lively descriptions of Southern society show a firm control of all the major features of manners comedy—humorous characters such as Mr. Sparkle and Reverend Yawn-your-head-off, marital intrigue involving eligible young ladies and gentlemen, and an overriding tone of frivolity. Just such descriptions of society reappear in the Mississippi novels that she wrote much later in her life.

Murfree actually wrote her first mountain stories sometime after 1872, a couple of years before the society stories were published. It was not until 1878, however, that she had her first literary breakthrough with local-color fiction, when William Dean Howells published "The Dancin' Party at Harrison's Cove" in the *Atlantic Monthly*. In 1884, this story, the first to appear under the pseudonym Charles Egbert Craddock, was collected with seven other stories that had first appeared in the *Atlantic*, and was published under the title *In the Tennessee Mountains*. By this time her literary reputation was already established with readers across the country. Critics considered *In the Tennessee Mountains* to be among the best local-color fiction of the day. The volume went through seventeen printings in just two years and seven additional printings during Murfree's lifetime.

Murfree's most significant and popular mountain stories appear in this first collection. "The 'Harnt' That Walks Chilhowee," generally considered the best story in the volume, and "The Dancin' Party at Harrison's Cove," the story which appeared

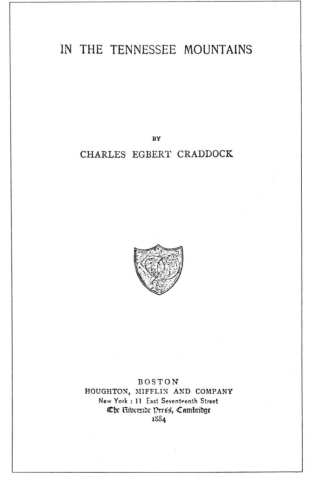

IN THE TENNESSEE MOUNTAINS

BY

CHARLES EGBERT CRADDOCK

BOSTON
HOUGHTON, MIFFLIN AND COMPANY
New York : 11 East Seventeenth Street
The Riverside Press, Cambridge
1884

Title page for Murfree's first book, a collection of dialect short stories

in the *Atlantic* and initiated her career as a local colorist, reveal several major characteristics and themes of the mountain tales: the brawling and feuding of the men, the domestic chores of the women, the courtship intrigues of the young. Though each story is constructed around a particular event, in these two stories a dancing party and the mysterious appearance of a mountain "harnt," they continually portray the same type of mountain life-style. Most characters tend to be stereotyped, and descriptions of the landscape tend to be colored by the same overriding pictorial perspective. The peculiar dialect of the characters, Murfree's distinctive contribution to the genre of local-color fiction, is a striking aspect of all the tales.

The stories typically begin with a sampling of this mountain dialect. In "A-Playin' of Old Sledge at the Settlemint," dialect sets the stage as one of the rough mountaineers speaks: "I hev hearn tell ez how them thar boys rides thar horses over hyar ter the Settlemint nigh on ter every night in the week ter play kyerds,—'Old Sledge' they calls it; an' thar goin's-on air jes' scandalous,—jes' a-drinkin' of apple-jack, an' a-bettin' of thar money." Murfree's own narrative language, careful and highly descriptive, offers a stark contrast to this crude mountain talk. Her most elaborate descriptions are of the mountain landscape, always overpowering and majestic: "No broad landscape was to be seen from this great projecting ledge of the mountain; the valley was merely a little basin, walled in on every side by the meeting ranges that rose so high as to intercept all distant prospect, and narrow the world to the contracted area bounded by the sharp lines of their wooded summits, cut hard and clear against the blue sky." Against the background of this landscape, characters engage in a variety of mountain intrigues. For example, in "The Dancin' Party at Harrison's Cove" there is the suspense surrounding the potential brawl between Rick Pearson and "the hot-headed Kossuth," and in "Electioneerin' on Big Injun Mounting" the intrigue revolves around the political fate of Rufe Chadd, who has recently lived among the "town folks" and has lost his status of "a mounting boy."

Character stereotypes are often indicated simply by personal names. Abel Stubbs is the typical stubborn mountaineer. Reuben Crabb, the one-armed "harnt" of Chilhowee, represents the devilish yet homespun figure who lives a secluded mountain life. Most of the male folk are described in strikingly similar terms: they are tall, gawky, weathered figures, confirmed in their prejudices, suspicious of change, and always ready for a brawl and a drink. The women tend to be consumed with domestic chores and familial matters, whether it be Mrs. Harrison worrying about the "wickedness of a dancing party" or Clarsie Giles consulting the ghost of Chilhowee about her marital fortunes.

Perhaps Murfree's outstanding feature as a local colorist was the way she combined character and setting in her stories. As Clarsie ponders her future in "The 'Harnt' That Walks Chilhowee," for instance, Murfree merges descriptions of the young girl's hair, the moon shining over the mountains, and the sounds of the mountain wind—"the voiceless sorrow of the sad earth." Rick Pearson, in "The Dancin' Party at Harrison's Cove," has a complexion "tanned by the sun, and roughened by exposure to the inclement mountain weather." Characters, like the mountain landscape, are a combination of earthy crudeness and rich mountain mystery. The image of the moon, which Murfree wove through nearly all of her tales, symbolizes the individuality of character and unchanging commitment to mountain custom. If the stories have any dominant theme, it revolves around the humanity of these mountain dwellers. When Rufe Chadd wins in the "Electioneerin'" contest, Murfree describes his victory as "That sympathetic heart of the multitude, so quick to respond to a noble impulse. . . ." This code of nobility provides the characters with their moral center and gives these simple tales about the Tennessee mountaineers an almost heroic dimension.

The favorable critical reception and popular success of Murfree's mountain stories paved the way for her first mountain novel, *The Prophet of the Great Smoky Mountains*, which received the praise of American and English critics alike. Particularly reviewers in the South considered her the best of Southern novelists, one reviewer comparing Murfree to Hawthorne, another comparing her to English novelist R. D. Blackmore. Before this book was published in 1885, two other novels by Murfree, *Where the Battle Was Fought* (1884), a Civil War story, and *Down the Ravine* (1885), a juvenile novel, were published. She would produce seven other mountain novels, including *In the Clouds* (1886), *The Despot of Broomsedge Cove* (1888), *In the "Stranger People's" Country* (1891), *His Vanished Star* (1894), *The Juggler* (1897), *The Windfall* (1907), and *The Ordeal; A Mountain Romance of Tennessee* (1912). Two of the local-color novels, *The Prophet of the Great Smoky Mountains* and *In the "Stranger People's" Country*, are Murfree's outstanding achievements.

Murfree begins *The Prophet of the Great Smoky Mountains*, as she had many of her stories, with a stately description of the mountains. Landscape permeates the book, intensifying the development of character and plot. Hiram Kelsey, the preacher-prophet, is a creature of the mountains. His spiritual doubts—the conflicting demands of flesh and spirit—are symbolized by the heights and depths of the Great Smoky Mountains which Murfree describes in the opening lines of the novel: they are a "barren ideal" contrasting "the vague isolations of a higher atmosphere" with "the material values of the warm world below." This double image of the mountains extends itself into several levels of the novel's social intrigue, especially Dorinda Cayce's dual commitment to Kelsey, the holy man of the mountains, and to Rick Tyler, a simple young mountaineer. Several other contrasting characters and situations enforce the dualistic thrusts of the story: there is the youthful, idealistic Dorinda and her commonsensical mountain mother; the burly, worldly Jake Tobin and the spiritualistic Kelsey; the unwritten code of mountain ethics and the written code of formal law. Several feuding factions complicate a plot which unfolds within the often opposing demands of religious faith and everyday realities.

The story has two basic plot lines: Kelsey's spiritual turmoil as he replaces his religious faith with a faith in man, and the intrigue surrounding Rick Tyler who is accused of murder and who unsuccessfully seeks Dorinda's hand. Murfree's various characters portray different types of the mountain people she came to know from her excursions through the Tennessee hills. Both Kelsey and Tyler are notable characterizations of the mountain man who must struggle to prove himself: Kelsey struggles with spiritual doubt, Tyler with real-world conflicts. And the stern mountain code, whether evidenced in Dorinda's idealism or the obstinacy of her father and brothers, colors nearly everything that happens in the novel. Only Kelsey transcends the mountain code when the Cayce men, who aim to kill the sheriff, mistakenly murder Kelsey. Kelsey voluntarily substitutes himself for the sheriff, predicting that the Cayces will repent, and thus ends his own spiritual struggle by sacrificing himself for his fellow man. Though the story of the prophet takes second place to the more realistic events associated with Tyler, Dorinda, and the Cayce family, Murfree achieved notable unity of the two plot strands and produced a tale filled with suspense and power.

The "Stranger People" of In the "Stranger People's" Country are only legend. Their tiny graves, thought by some of the novel's characters to be those of an extinct pygmy race or perhaps the tombs of Aztec or American Indian infants, are situated on the property of Fee Guthrie, one of Murfree's most complex characters. Like the prophet-preacher Kelsey, Fee Guthrie is a powerful mountain figure with a stern sense of honor to the mountain code. Also like Kelsey, he is plagued by religious doubts and is ultimately committed to human sympathy. Guthrie's loyalty to his fierce stepmother stems from a promise he made to his dying father, a promise which only the most fervent sense of honor compels him to keep. He is a man of his word, but also a man of tremendous physical appeal and power who ultimately meets a violent death. The portrayal of Guthrie is Murfree's major accomplishment in the novel, and the complexity of his character—his commitment to his stepmother, his love for Litt Pettingill, his personal doubts and struggles—makes him as compelling and curious as the tiny graves on his land.

Litt Pettingill, like Dorinda Cayce, has several suitors, and functions as the center point for most of the novel's social intrigue, while other characters are once again modeled on various mountain types. Fee's stepmother and Litt's mother are different variations of the stern, homespun mountain woman. Buck Cheever, almost a caricature of the scheming, bullish mountain man, recalls the stereotype of the Cayce men. The archeologist Shattuck, an outside urban figure, is Murfree's voice in the novel, as well as one of the objects of Litt's affections. He represents law and science, the obverse of mountain mystery and unwritten mountain code. The interaction of all these characters gives rise to one of Murfree's best-wrought plots. Everything from gunfights to parties supplies the story with its intrigue, and the rich descriptions of mountain landscape intensify the portrayal of character and demonstrate Murfree's firm belief in the interrelationship of nature and human nature.

Similar themes, characters, and plot lines appear in all the Tennessee mountain novels. Indeed, one of Murfree's artistic shortcomings was her tendency to vary only slightly the same types and incidents in story after story. She had clearly exhausted her talents in this area of fiction well before her public tired of her mountain novels. When the demand for local-color writing subsided around the mid-1890s, Murfree turned most of her attention to writing historical fiction, which was becoming increasingly popular. But she never entirely gave up local-color writing, eventually producing two more local-color novels and more than a dozen Tennessee mountain tales.

The Story of Old Fort Loudon (1899), *A Spectre of*

Power (1904), and *The Amulet* (1906) were Murfree's three historical novels depicting pioneer Tennessee. She also wrote seven short stories on this subject. Both the novels and stories were exercises in converting local-color writing into historical fiction by adding exhaustive historical detail including American Indian lore. *The Story of Old Fort Loudon* and *A Spectre of Power* suffer from a density of scholarly information which all but obliterates character and plot. Only *The Amulet* manages to merge historical fact and artistic richness. The fading of Murfree's imaginative powers, particularly in her descriptions of mountain landscape, is clearly evident in these novels and stories.

In 1905, a year before *The Amulet* appeared, Murfree returned to the subject of her first novel in *The Storm Centre*. *Where the Battle Was Fought* (1884), filled with autobiographical details and reflections of her own war experience, reveals much about

THE AMULET

A Novel

BY

CHARLES EGBERT CRADDOCK

AUTHOR OF
"THE STORM CENTRE," "THE STORY OF OLD FORT
LOUDON," "A SPECTRE OF POWER," "THE
FRONTIERSMEN," "THE PROPHET OF THE
GREAT SMOKY MOUNTAINS," ETC., ETC.

New York
THE MACMILLAN COMPANY
LONDON: MACMILLAN & CO., LTD.
1906

All rights reserved

Title page for Murfree's 1906 historical novel about pioneer Tennessee

Murfree's own artistic beginnings. When twenty years later she again wrote about the Civil War in *The Storm Centre* Murfree was both less personal and less forceful. The novel realistically portrays the horror of the war, but not as powerfully as does *Where the Battle Was Fought*. Though her local-color fiction is usually considered her finest writing, several critics have judged *Where the Battle Was Fought* to be among the best of her works.

At the end of her literary career, Murfree returned briefly to her familiar Tennessee setting in *The Ordeal; A Mountain Romance of Tennessee* (1912), and also wrote two novels set in Mississippi, *The Fair Mississippian* (1908) and *The Story of Duciehurst* (1914). In *The Ordeal*, her weakest novel, Murfree was unable to recapture the liveliness of her best subject. The two Mississippi novels, along with a couple of Mississippi short stories, depict a refined Southern society unlike that of the crude mountaineers, and recall some of the features of manners fiction that she had experimented with at the very beginning of her career. Murfree always showed promise in her manners fiction, but never developed her artistic talents in this area as she had in her best mountain novels. Descriptions of the river and its swampy banks are moving, but seem weak when compared to the intensity with which she portrayed the Tennessee mountains. Both Mississippi novels are notably lacking in character development and instead revolve around intricate plots. At this late stage in her long career, Murfree's artistic powers had weakened. Mississippi was not her homeland, and the Mississippi novels were no match for her Tennessee mountain fiction.

Mary Murfree will likely remain a minor American author, but will be remembered as a major part of the local-color movement which briefly dominated the American literary scene. The finest of her stories and novels, *In the Tennessee Mountains*, *The Prophet of the Great Smoky Mountains*, and *In the "Stranger People's" Country*, have established her reputation as a writer of significant accomplishment within the confines of a limited fictional world and a short-lived literary movement.

References:
Richard Cary, *Mary N. Murfree* (New York: Twayne, 1967);
Edd Winfield Parks, *Charles Egbert Craddock (Mary Noailles Murfree)* (Chapel Hill: University of North Carolina Press, 1941).

Frank Norris

Joseph R. McElrath, Jr.
Florida State University

BIRTH: Chicago, Illinois, 5 March 1870, to Benjamin Franklin and Gertrude Doggett Norris.

EDUCATION: University of California at Berkeley, 1890-1894; Harvard University, 1894-1895.

MARRIAGE: 12 February 1900 to Jeannette Black; child: Jeannette.

DEATH: San Francisco, California, 25 October 1902.

BOOKS: *Yvernelle: A Legend of Feudal France* (Philadelphia: Lippincott, 1892);
Moran of the Lady Letty: A Story of Adventure off the California Coast (New York: Doubleday & McClure, 1898); republished as *Shanghaied* (London: Richards, 1899);
McTeague: A Story of San Francisco (New York: Doubleday & McClure, 1899; London: Richards, 1899);
Blix (New York: Doubleday & McClure, 1899; London: Richards, 1900);
A Man's Woman (New York: Doubleday & McClure, 1900; London: Richards, 1900);
The Octopus: A Story of California (New York: Doubleday, Page, 1901; London: Richards, 1901);
The Pit: A Story of Chicago (New York: Doubleday, Page, 1903; London: Richards, 1903);
A Deal in Wheat and Other Stories of the New and Old West (New York: Doubleday, Page, 1903; London: Richards, 1903);
The Responsibilities of the Novelist and Other Literary Essays (New York: Doubleday, Page, 1903; London: Richards, 1903);
The Joyous Miracle (New York: Doubleday, Page, 1906; London: Harper, 1906);
The Third Circle (New York & London: John Lane, 1909);
Vandover and the Brute (Garden City: Doubleday, Page, 1914; London: Heinemann, 1914);
Collected Writings Hitherto unpublished in Book Form, volume 10 of *Complete Works of Frank Norris* (Garden City: Doubleday, Doran, 1928);
Frank Norris of "The Wave": Stories and Sketches from the San Francisco Weekly, 1893 to 1897, edited by Oscar Lewis (San Francisco: Westgate Press, 1931);
The Literary Criticism of Frank Norris, edited by Donald Pizer (Austin: University of Texas Press, 1964);
A Novelist in the Making: A Collection of Student Themes and the Novels Blix *and* Vandover and the Brute, edited by James D. Hart (Cambridge: Harvard University Press, 1970).

COLLECTION: *Complete Works of Frank Norris*, 10 volumes (Garden City: Doubleday, Doran, 1928).

Frank Norris is a central figure in American literary history mainly because of three novels, *McTeague* (1899), *The Octopus* (1901), and *The Pit* (1903). But he is also important because of what he indicates to the cultural historian: his works mirror changes occurring in his milieu during a remarkable period of intellectual and artistic transition at

Frank Norris

379

the end of the nineteenth century and the beginning of the twentieth. The need to redefine man's situation in the "new world" revealed by scientists, by antitraditional social theorists, and by modern schools of philosophical inquiry was a primary motivation for Norris as he shaped his more serious writings. Conventional Judeo-Christian "certainties" about man, God, nature, and society had waned. Norris realized just as dramatically as Henry Adams that the useful and comforting truths of traditional culture had become either defunct or dubious. In the cultural crisis resulting, Norris was one of many writers who sought to clarify the troubling questions of the age and to provide new explanations of life in their descriptions of characters and environments. What is unique about Norris, however, is that he ultimately transcended the iconoclastic attitudes popular among the turn-of-the-century avant-garde—as sardonically expressed by Stephen Crane and Ambrose Bierce when they ruminated over how little their unsophisticated contemporaries understood of life's complexities. After some similar flourishes of rebellion against his parent culture, he went on to anticipate, in his own fashion, T. S. Eliot's manner of dealing with the "modern predicament" by synthesizing what seemed to remain valid in the old thought and artistic methods and what seemed important in the new. The blending of the modern and the Victorian in his works once caused some confusion among literary historians: Norris's fiction was identified as a puzzling mixture of pessimism and optimism, realism and romanticism, progressive philosophy and regressive thought. The apparently paradoxical yoking of Darwin and St. Paul and the blending of Zola and Howells, however, was purposeful. Whether Norris always succeeded is debatable, but his intention was clearly that of a synthesizer attempting to wed the traditional and the modern in distinctive novelistic statements on the nature of life.

Born in Chicago on 5 March 1870, Benjamin Franklin Norris, Jr. was the son of a self-made businessman who prospered as the head of a jewelry business and who sought to improve his fortunes by moving the family to California in 1884. San Francisco provided new opportunities, and this entrepreneur flourished in his realm of interest. At home, Norris's mother, the one-time actress Gertrude Doggett Norris, pursued the genteel life, leading Frank and his younger brother Charles (1881-1945), who also became a novelist, down Victorian cultural byways. While Benjamin Franklin Norris, Sr., speculated in land acquisition and rental properties, Gertrude Norris shared the polite delights of Scott, Browning, and Tennyson with her children. Frank was given the appropriate upper-middle-class education: private schooling at the Belmont Academy south of San Francisco and then at the Boys' High School in the city; Episcopal Sunday School, some athletics (he broke his arm playing football) and training in art at the San Francisco Art Association. The well-to-do family made the socially requisite grand tour in 1887, and Frank remained in Paris at the Atelier Julien to study painting when the rest of the family returned to San Francisco.

As would later happen during his college years, Norris did not seriously apply himself. Subsequently an eclectic in his literary style, he early demonstrated his aversion to formality, consistency, and specialization by turning from sketch pad and canvas—too often—to delight in the potpourri of varied experience provided by Paris. Like the largely autobiographical hero of his novel *Blix* (1899)—who suffers from a lack of focus in his personal life and career—Norris was preoccupied with fencing, the opera, Jean Froissart's *Chronicles*, and the composition of tales about a character named Robert D'Artois, which he mailed in installments to brother Charles in San Francisco. None of these Paris tales, later described by Charles Norris, have survived but Frank Norris's strong fascination with things medieval and romantic is indicated in the 31 March 1889 issue of the *San Francisco Chronicle*. He had turned from the one ambitious painting project that he is known to have undertaken—an enormous, Froissart-inspired canvas devoted to the Battle of Crecy—to write an article on knightly appurtenances, "Clothes of Steel." It was his first publication, and Norris was clearly still under the spell of *Ivanhoe*. While progressive writers such as Balzac, Zola, Flaubert and the de Goncourt brothers may have come within the range of Norris's varied interests, the Paris experience mainly heightened his romantic view of life and art, which would soon come to dominate the character of his early poetry and fiction.

While Norris went on to do pen and ink illustrations for some of his later published writings, he failed as a painter, possibly because of a lack of talent but almost certainly because of a lack of self-discipline and personal commitment. (*Blix* suggests that such was Norris's personal predicament as late as 1897.) Details are sparse, but it would seem that the early choice of a career was largely one made by his parents and that Frank Norris had much in common with the undirected and weak-willed hero of another autobiographical work, *Vandover and the Brute* (1914), at this very self-indulgent stage of his life. Moreover, Norris's romantic imagination was hardly suited to the academic atmosphere of the late 1880s. His riotous delight in the dramatically forceful and the sensationally colorful, as evidenced in his writings, was hardly a trait of the sensibility encouraged by the French academy. The drama of Delacroix's canvases—which were *not* held up as models for imitation then—reflected Norris's tastes, while the academicians' preference was for a subdued, pre-impressionistic "realism" expressive of ideal concepts in tones of cool clarity. At the Atelier Julien there were the bohemianism of the students, the nude models of whom Gertrude Norris may not have been aware, and the fleshly fantasies of Bouguereau's canvases for stimulation. Norris described these conventional aspects of the offbeat world of art study in "Student Life in Paris" (1900); by 1900 the experience seemed to have mellowed in memory. In 1889, though, he yearned for something else, the "days of old / When swords were bright and steeds were prancing." Like Miniver Cheevy, Norris "missed the medieval grace / Of iron clothing." Finally he returned to San Francisco.

Although scholastically unprepared, Norris entered the University of California at Berkeley in 1890, initially playing the Parisian artiste and appearing the dandy. He maintained a position as one of the attractive young men in the better class of San Francisco society. He also associated with local artists—some decidedly in the decadent tradition. He was something of a fellow traveler with a group dubbed Les Jeunes which came to publish its own "Yellow Book," the *Lark*, in 1895-1897. Norris began to develop in new ways, though. It was not long before he became a boisterous fraternity man, a sworn foe of literary preciosity and effete cultural pretension in any form. He also turned his back on his one notable but commercially unsuccessful publication of the early 1890s: a Scott-like verse romance published in late 1892, *Yvernelle: A Legend of Feudal France*, which he gladly allowed to remain in oblivion when he began writing his quite different novels at the end of the decade. One may turn to any passage in *Yvernelle* and, with some surprise, note the difference between Norris's juvenilia and the typically less "literary" writing of his maturity. The substance of *McTeague* and *The Octopus* bears little resemblance to

> Time there was when squire, page and knight,
>> Portcullis, keep and barbican were real;

> When tournaments were things of daily sight,
>> And chivalry arrayed in flashing steel;
> And time there was when the brave errant-knight
>> Was not a fancy of a minstrel's tale,
> But fought in very earnest for the right,
>> Or wandered wide to find the Holy Grail.

The kind of artist and thinker who created that genteel piece of fine writing was the type that Norris would later lampoon with considerable spleen in five of his novels, especially in *The Octopus*.

The highly romantic short fiction that Norris produced during the early Berkeley years will disappoint readers looking for signs of originality or traces of genius: "Les Enerves de Jumieges" (1890), "The Son of a Sheik" (1891), "Le Jongleur de Taillebois" (1891), and "Lauth" (1893) are, at best estimation, pulp fiction in the sensational vein. Norris gave himself over to the marvelous somewhat lamely during the early years of his apprenticeship. "Le Jongleur," for instance, recalls Poe and Hawthorne in their most spectral, and slickly Gothic, moments. And poems such as "Crepusculum" (1892) did not indicate any great advance over the verse of *Yvernelle*. Of more significance and promise, however, were fictional sketches and dialogues which were drawn from Norris's personal experiences among the San Francisco debutantes and young gentlemen; the polite social comedies of Anthony Hope and Richard Harding Davis had a potent effect on Norris as he adopted their mannerisms to depict life among the swell set. The farcical play, *Two Pair* (1893), and short stories such as "Travis Hallett's Half-back" (1894) and "She and the Other Fellow" (1894) featured the urbane and witty characters of Hope's and Davis's society tales. Norris was clearly paying attention to the magazines and the stage to determine what worked and sold in the literary marketplace. By 1895, however, Norris was beginning to imitate other voices, such as those of Balzac and Zola, perhaps because he felt he had something more worthwhile to declare than did the popular drawing-room satirists. The turn toward the grimly realistic may also have been determined or accelerated in 1894 by the second great personal failure in Norris's life.

While Norris was trying his wings as a writer, he seemed to have little time for or interest in his studies. *Yvernelle* and the several short stories appearing in West Coast magazines counted for naught in academic life at Berkeley. Nor did his prominent role in fraternity high jinks, his participation in amateur theatricals, and his work for

Title page for Norris's first book, a melodrama in iambic tetrameter couplets

school newspapers and yearbooks. Berkeley had admitted him as a special student and expected him to make up for his shortcomings. But he did what he wanted rather than what was required. After some unsuccessful petitioning for even more special status on the ground that he had chosen to prepare himself for a career as a writer rather than a scholar, he had to leave Berkeley in 1894, carrying away a dislike for Macaulay, mathematics, and academic life in general. Only the evolutionary idealist, Professor Joseph LeConte, seems to have left a positive and deep impression upon his imagination.

LeConte was the exceptional professor for Norris: like Delacroix and two other influences, Robert Louis Stevenson and Victor Hugo, LeConte was an artist at vividly dramatizing concepts in a fully engaging manner. To the excitable imagination of his student he presented a grand spectacle in his interpretation of the evolutionary process and man's place in it. Like Stevenson, he acknowledged

the brutal side of man, the animalistic inheritance transmitted from generation to generation. Allusion to the "foul stream" of hereditary evil in *McTeague* would later recall this concept. LeConte also pictured the other side, demonstrating an inclination toward morality, spirituality, and the "upward movement" of man, a propensity for improvement of the individual and the race, which Emerson had described in his idealistic essays. To the melodramatically inclined Norris the tension between the two sides—the Dr. Jekyll *versus* Mr. Hyde dilemma—seemed confirmed by his own tendency toward self-indulgence and his simultaneous desire to live up to the "finer fabric" of his personality. In all of his novels, Norris mined the concept of man's dual nature as a source of story material, as is demonstrated in Donald Pizer's *The Novels of Frank Norris* (1966). LeConte's lectures, then, were the most important and positive intellectual experiences during Norris's largely negative Berkeley period.

He emerged from these troublesome years of 1890-1894—during which his parents' marriage failed—with one emotionally sustaining conviction: that he could make his mark as a writer. He then went to Harvard University for a final flirtation with the academy and, in 1894-1895, he wrote under the direction of Professor Lewis E. Gates and his assistants as a special student.

By this time he was already under the spell of Zola, whose work he viewed as a large step beyond the romanticism of Scott, Dumas and Hugo toward a progressive kind of romantic realism (or realistic romanticism). Norris was at this time taking the same step, away from *Yvernelle* and "Le Jongleur de Taillebois" toward *McTeague*. Gates, it seems, helped him to make the move forward by suggesting a more realistic aesthetic than the one he had been following. Gates's pronouncements in *Studies and Appreciations* (1900) are revelatory in this connection. When considering the failures of one of Gertrude Norris's saints, Alfred, Lord Tennyson, and charging him with an inability to relate literature to life, Gates articulated a literary criterion which remained at the front of Norris's mind and on the tip of his tongue throughout his career. Gates encouraged writers not to shrink from the "commonplace and from the crude" but to "interpret into fine significance life's puzzling complexities of motive, character, and passionate action." He proposed the achievement of a "renovating imaginative realism," and Norris's writing thenceforth was largely based on such an aesthetic foundation.

The immediate result was the forty-four

known themes Norris wrote as a course requirement, now collected in edited form in James D. Hart's *A Novelist in the Making* (1970). *McTeague*, *Blix*, and *Vandover and the Brute* were, in effect, begun by 1894-1895; for many of the sketches became sections of those novels. Indeed, chapter 2 of *Vandover and the Brute* is set in Cambridge, Massachusetts.

Another stage of apprenticeship completed, Norris returned to San Francisco, apparently expecting a rapid rise to national prominence. His envy-tinted comments about Stephen Crane in 1896 and 1897 suggest that he was very much aware of that young writer's leap to fame in 1895 with *The Red Badge of Courage*; and jaded allusions to another "boy wonder," Richard Harding Davis, indicate his full awareness of Davis's near overnight success when he was twenty-six years old. Norris—almost twenty-six—was ready for his turn, and he took the path that had led to Davis's *The West from a Car Window* (1892), *The Rulers of the Mediterranean* (1894), *Our English Cousins* (1894), and *About Paris* (1895)—impressionistic travel writing. Norris made arrangements with the *San Francisco Chronicle* and was off to exotic lands.

In November 1895 he traveled to South Africa and the Davis luck, initially, seemed to be his too. The Jameson Raid, an attempt to overthrow the Boer government of Transvaal, occurred while he was there. It was a story that filled newspaper columns throughout the Anglo-American world. Unfortunately, Norris failed to capitalize on the event. Only one of eight articles—"Street Scenes in Johannesburg During the Insurrection of January, 1896"—was placed in a national publication, *Harper's Weekly*; the rest, which appeared in the *San Francisco Chronicle* and the *Wave*, were undistinguished local-color pieces, such as "A Zulu War Dance" and "A Californian in the City of Cape Town." Norris could write *up* an event—sensationalize it in the manner of Davis and Zola to near-yellow journalism proportions—by this time. But he failed to draw much attention. He returned from his South African adventure to a dubious reward: two years as a copy writer for the *Wave*, a San Francisco weekly of small and local circulation.

Much of Norris's 1896-1898 writing for the *Wave* was worthy of a larger readership—a fact not yet obvious to many because the texts are still unavailable in collected form. He produced more than 150 prose pieces, many of which would have gained him a following had they been published in newspapers such as the *New York Evening Sun* or magazines such as *Harper's Weekly* or *Scribner's*, as

were Richard Harding Davis's during his early days. Quantitatively and qualitatively Norris's work was frequently superior to Davis's; and perhaps if he had enjoyed the kind of familial connections afforded to Davis his pieces would have been appearing in *Century* and *Harper's Monthly* rather than the *Wave*. Norris, however, was on his own. He conducted interviews, wrote sophisticated book reviews, theorized about literary movements and trends in pieces such as "Zola as a Romantic Writer" (1896), translated several tales from the French, and reported on many cultural, athletic, and civic events in the environs of San Francisco. His short fiction was largely in step with current fashions: a series entitled "The Opinions of Leander" (1897) wittily approximated Anthony Hope's *Dolly Dialogues* (1894); "The Heroism of Jonesee" (1896) and "Bandy Callaghan's Girl" (1896) were cut from the Davis cloth; and "The Third Circle" (1897) was a Stevensonian thriller. His originality manifested itself mainly in two ways. First, in journalistic pieces such as "On a Battleship" (1896) and "A Strange Relief Ship" (1897) he displayed considerable polish as an impressionist capable of vitalizing his subjects with a tone of awe and wonderment. His was the talent of making the ordinary seem extraordinary and thus interesting. Second, he displayed a de Maupassant-like sense of mordant humor, producing several noteworthy comic plunges into the bizarre. "A Salvation Boom in Matabeleland" (1896) is a near-bantering account of the crucifixion of a Salvation Army officer, on a telephone pole. "Judy's Service of Gold Plate" (1897) anticipates the sometimes grotesquely comical characterizations of Zerkow and Maria Macapa in *McTeague*. "Fantaisie Printaniere" (1897) is a Dickensian sketch dealing with the niceties of the fine art of wife beating—directly related to Trina and Maria's discussion of the same subject in *McTeague*. In 1897, as Norris was moving toward the completion of *McTeague*, he was developing a point of view and tone of his own, together with an interest in what may be termed the eccentric or, in 1897, the "improper" in literature. While the influences on his work would always remain clear, he dramatically declared his independence in the Christmas 1897 issue of the *Wave*: in "Perverted Tales" he parodied his masters with a skill equal to that of Bret Harte in his *Condensed Novels and Other Papers* (1867). His victims, predictably, were Rudyard Kipling, Stephen Crane, Bret Harte, Richard Harding Davis, Ambrose Bierce, and Anthony Hope. Then in January 1898 he once again attempted to break into the *real* world of publishing, centered in the East; and, finally, he succeeded, with *Moran of the Lady Letty: A Story of Adventure off the California Coast*.

He turned to *Moran of the Lady Letty*, though, after two more failures: a plan for a collection of short stories fell through; and *McTeague* was not accepted by a publisher. Late 1897 was marked by his depression. Norris felt that he had patiently served the appropriate apprenticeship, that he knew his craft from the critic's and the practitioner's points of view, and that he had something significant to say to the public—if he could only create a readership. Finally, he analyzed the market with his father's entrepreneurial eye, and he shrewdly chose a move that made a real career in writing possible. He stooped to conquer with a made-to-order thriller for the American audience then reveling in the melodramatic delights provided by Hope's *The Prisoner of Zenda* (1894) and Stevenson and Lloyd Osbourne's *The Wrecker* (1892). *Moran of the Lady Letty* began its serialization in the *Wave* in January 1898—with Norris sending the installments, as they appeared, to the S. S. McClure Syndicate in New York City. This sensational and luridly violent tale of Ross Wilbur's shanghai experience, blatantly echoing Davis's *Van Bibber and Others* (1892), Kipling's *Captains Courageous* (1897), and Stevenson's *Treasure Island* (1883), brought Norris to New York and a position with McClure. By the end of February he was living in a flat at 10 West Thirty-third Street, where he finished writing the final installments for the *Wave* at the end of March. McClure, in late spring, sent him to Cuba to cover the Spanish-American War. Like other journalists, he was stalled at Key West. He finally made it to Cuba, but while Crane and Davis enjoyed their finest, highly paid hours, Norris proved invisible. He returned to New York on 5 August with no publications to his credit except for two newspaper serializations of *Moran of the Lady Letty*. Malaria necessitated a lengthy recuperation in San Francisco. It was not until mid-October that he returned to New York, moving into a new apartment on Washington Square. Two articles about Cuba, "Comida" and "With Lawton at El Caney," were published in two first-rate magazines, *Atlantic Monthly* and *Century*, but too late to create a sensation—in March and June 1899. It was another lost opportunity and a setback. Still, *Moran of the Lady Letty* was trimmed and bowdlerized for book publication in September 1898; it proved a modest success with the reviewers and Norris was on his way. Doubleday and McClure next published *McTeague: A Story of San Francisco* in February 1899; and *Blix* was readied for serialization beginning in the March issue of a ladies magazine, *Puritan*, and

published by Doubleday and McClure in September 1899. The reviews—positive and negative—resulted in considerable visibility. None was a best-seller, but the adventure romance, the naturalistic novel, and the Howellsian love idyl—appearing almost simultaneously—made Norris look so versatile a writer that heads turned and eyebrows were raised.

Front cover for Norris's second novel, begun in 1895 when he was a student at Harvard

These books were the work of a young man. While *McTeague* is accounted a masterpiece, all three were the products of his apprentice years. He could have written *Moran of the Lady Letty* before the 1894-1895 sojourn at Harvard, so facile was the surface adherence to the adventure-romance formula as it had developed from Walter Scott to Robert Louis Stevenson. *Blix* is a pleasant boy-loves-girl romance cast in the genteel mold and it passed muster in the rigorously idealistic book-review section of the *Chautauquan*. Both did raise serious notions: *Moran of the Lady Letty* brutally rejects Judeo-Christian values and revels in post-Darwinian "survival of the fittest" thinking and "might makes right" sloganeering; *Blix* rejects hypocritical social conventions for the sake of more honest and thus more natural and ideal ways of living. But both fail to dramatize modern questions and predicaments in universally relevant and engaging fashion. Although William Dean Howells praised *Moran of the Lady Letty* in what were for him tones of marked enthusiasm, critics have typically viewed this novel and *Blix* as either youthful larks or potboilers. *McTeague* is different. It richly blends a de Maupassant-like fascination with the grim, a Dickensian sense of the ridiculous, a Zolaesque understanding of life's determinisms, and even a Bret Harte-inspired sense of "Western" color. It is a various tapestry in which the "novel of degeneration" narrative structure and theme stand in relief. As such, it is a masterfully worked counterpart to Zola's *L'Assommoir* (1877). In *McTeague* Norris makes what may be termed his first truly significant statement: he expresses an American truism emerging among the intellectual elite of the 1890s, that man is not the free creature whom Emerson described in "Self-Reliance." Rather, he is more like the pathetic creature described by Emerson in the essay "Fate"—a pawn of environmental determinisms, chance, and genetically inherited traits.

The composition of *McTeague* merits some special consideration in light of the long span of years some biographers have attributed to the process, extending back to late 1893 and the notorious murder of Sarah Collins by her husband in a San Francisco kindergarten, the setting for Trina McTeague's death. Donald Pizer's "The Genesis of *McTeague*" in *McTeague: A Norton Critical Edition* (1977) describes the long evolution of the work in as much detail as is now possible. Specific dates are difficult to determine with certainty; but, three states of mind and thus, in effect, three aspects of Norris's development from the mid-1890s through February 1899 seem preserved in *McTeague*. Norris begins it on Lewis E. Gates's serious and realistic note regarding the "commonplace and the crude." A day in the life of Polk Street, San Francisco, is rendered in a vital, detailed, colorful, and panoramic manner recalling (and surpassing) the first chapter of Zola's *L'Assommoir*. The crude dentist-hero McTeague is established in his milieu as a subject for study; he is the low-life character of limited intelligence suited to naturalistic treatment, and Norris is quick to provide an intellectual frame of reference within which the plot may develop with naturalistic significance. As chapter 2 progresses,

though, the comic sensibility that emerged in Norris's *Wave* writings of 1896-1897 comes to the fore. Through chapter 10 the stage is carefully set for the grim and inexorable developments typical of a degeneration tale; but much of the writing is comedy at the expense of McTeague, his friend Marcus Schouler, a maid named Maria, and the junkman Zerkow, who loom large as bumpkins and grotesques. There is a good deal of the vaudeville spirit in Norris's handling of his characters' antics. Like Zola in *Nana* (1880), Norris did not see comedy and pathos as inimicable. The drolleries cease and another sensibility comes to dominate, however, as Trina McTeague's latent, self-destructive traits are activated by worsening economic conditions and as McTeague's genetically inherited tendency toward alcoholism is triggered by his loss of occupation and disintegrating marriage. As McTeague begins his descent to what a LeContean would describe as his bestial state, Norris adopts a more sympathetic tone toward his character. Gradually, McTeague becomes a pathetic victim of heredity, environment, and chance. When McTeague beats Trina to death and steals her hoarded wealth, he seems as much a "victim" as the woman lying in a pool of blood.

By late 1897, just prior to the beginning of the *Moran* project, Norris had apparently taken the work this far, to chapter 20. In the fall he left San Francisco for Placer County in the Sierras where he finished the novel, transporting his hero in flight from legal authorities to that mountainous locale. The flight is sensationally and, in the conclusion, melodramatically handled as a piece of regional writing in the adventure romance tradition. His former friend, Marcus Schouler, pursues McTeague through Death Valley. Just before McTeague kills his nemesis, Marcus finds enough strength to handcuff their wrists. We last see McTeague chained to the dead man in Death Valley.

William Dean Howells and others noted this turn from the realistic and complained accordingly. Norris's eclectic mind of the Paris period was still in evidence; and when he was called upon to explain the long leap from the realistic to the romantic at the end of *McTeague*, he was unrepentant. He was convinced that the ending belonged. As he explained in conversation and indicated in "A Plea for Romantic Fiction" (1901) the conclusion was not the result of what would be termed today a "mood swing." While the various sensibilities informing *McTeague* described do make that term seem most relevant to the actual situation, Norris argued that the romantic seemed an essential in the most effective art. He

"no, it's not; no, it's not; no, it's not," cried Trina ve-
hemently. "It's all mine, mine. There's not a penny
of it belongs to anybody else. I don't like to have
to talk this way to you, but you just make me."
~~and besides when it~~ We're not going to touch a
penny of my five thousand nor a penny of that
little money I managed to save — that seventy-five."
~~in that two hundred, and fifty,~~ you mean."
~~in~~ That seventy-five. We're just going to live on the
interest of that and all what I earn from uncle
Oelberman — or just that thirty-one or two dollars."
"Huh! Think I'm going to ~~that~~ do, an' live in such
a room as this?"
Trina folded her arms and looked him squarely
in the face.
"Well, what are you going to do, then?"
"Huh?"
"I say, what are you going to do? You can get in
and find something to do and earn some more
money, and then we'll ~~talk~~ talk."
"Well, I ain't going to live here."
"Oh, very well, suit yourself. I'm going to. live here.")
"You'll live where I tell you," the dentist suddenly
cried, exasperated at the ~~reasoning~~ nemming tone she ~~tided~~.
"Then you'll pay the rent," exclaimed Trina, quite
as angry as he.
"Are you my boss, I'd like to know? who's the boss,
you or I?"   cried Trina, flushing to her pale lips.
"Who's got the money, I'd like to know? answer me
that, who's got the money?"   McTeague,
"You make me sick, you and your money. why,
you're a miser. I never saw anything like it. When
I was practising, I never thought of my fees as my
own; we lumped everything in together."
"Exactly; and I'm doing the working now; I'm
working for uncle Oelberman. and you're not

Page of the manuscript for McTeague. *A leaf of the 245-page manuscript was included in each copy of the 1928 Argonaut Manuscript Edition of Norris's works.*

never changed his mind on this point; and his later novels illustrate the conviction. What remained constant from 1896 and "Zola as a Romantic Writer" through 1902 and his death was Norris's allegiance to what he defined as the romantic.

Vandover and the Brute, although not published until 1914, was actually a fourth product of Norris's youthful phase. It was most certainly begun by 1895 when Norris was at Harvard and most probably finished before 1900. More relentlessly than *McTeague*, and without any leavening element of comedy, it pictures a young San Franciscan driven by forces—social, cultural, moral, commercial, and temperamental—toward a calamitous end. It was an end, some interpreters have suggested, toward which Norris feared he was moving before he attached himself to Jeannette Black in 1897 and enjoyed her stabilizing influence. The novel is largely autobiographical: the third-person narrator seems intimately familiar with the drawing rooms, barrooms, and places of assignation that the hero frequents. Vandover is a weak, maladapted individual bewildered by conflicts between instinctive appetites and social mores (particularly in regard to sexual matters). He cannot resolve conflicts between conclusions about life derived from practical experience and metaphysical "certainties" proffered by conventional society. The LeContean "brute" in him is constantly at odds with his "better self," and he is totally incapable of designing a rational balance between the two. While Norris indicates that the self-indulgently lazy and dismayingly unanalytical Van is largely responsible for his degeneration and that society cannot be totally blamed, the novel is a critical "Study of Life and Manners in an American City at the End of the Nineteenth Century" (the subtitle in the manuscript). Norris was critical of society's "laws"—again, sexual mores in particular—when they did not correspond to the actualities of human nature and human experience. That is, he was just as hostile toward morality unrelated to life as he was toward literature standing in the same relationship. Social criticism was minimal in *McTeague*; but in *Vandover and the Brute* Norris broadened his scope to picture San Francisco as representative of an entire society worthy of criticism. As Van degenerates and moves downward from the highest echelons of society to the lowest, the reader is presented with a total picture; and with this city as a metaphor for modern life, Norris offered a more widely relevant conclusion than *McTeague*'s. The theme is that late nineteenth-century American experience is fraught with social, moral and intellectual complexities not amenable to

any available solutions or even traditional explanations. Although Norris did not craft Van as the representative American, he did posit a disoriented and bewildered response to the world which recalls that of the correspondent in Crane's "The Open Boat," published in 1898 as the title story for a collection of Crane's short fiction. "The Open Boat" seems to have met with Norris's approval and may have both shaped the shipwreck episode of chapter 9 and informed its theme. This theme would be expanded and elaborated in the first work of Norris's mature phase, *The Octopus;* but before he wrote *The Octopus* between the spring of 1899 and the late winter of 1901, Norris involved himself in a project which the sympathetic critic would kindly term an experimental or transitional piece. Most critics simply label *A Man's Woman* (1900) Norris's worst.

By mid-1899 Norris turned from *Blix* to the composition of *A Man's Woman* (or, possibly its completion, since at least one scholar has concluded that it was begun in 1898). Once again, as with *Blix*, he was writing for the popular market: he exploited public interest in the quest to reach the North Pole; a fashionable new figure in the popular mind, The Nurse, was brought in as heroine; the horrors of physical suffering in the Arctic and a vivid description of a surgical technique provided sensation; and the muse of melodrama was called upon frequently. One reviewer noted that the novel contained enough crises to serve several novels. The novel also has a "serious" subject, however. Norris provides a psychological analysis of two American character types which is both profound and detailed. Less than enthusiastic about what he had done, Norris himself later termed it a "niggling analysis."

Ward Bennett is the opposite of the unfocused and unmotivated Vandover. A man of single ideas and absolute determination, he sets goals and brooks no opposition to reaching them. Although his field of action is Arctic exploration, he is essentially the self-reliant American cast in the heroic frontiersman mold. Lloyd Searight is the female counterpart, the "New Woman" of the 1890s, who pursues her vocation in the field of nursing with Brunhilda-like tenacity. Lloyd is Norris's opportunity to examine the social consequences of the newly "liberated" professional woman's emergence—a subject with which he had flirted in several *Wave* pieces and in *Blix*. But, while sympathetic to Lloyd, his response to her was distinctly traditional. Once Lloyd resolves her own psychological problems and feels fulfilled, she sees it as her duty to help her husband, Ward, realize his potential for greatness as an explorer. As the reviewer for the *Argonaut* observed, Lloyd ends up playing an updated version of the "angel in the house" role.

The most important focus of the novel, however, is on interpersonal relationships. In a post-Darwinian age, survival, success, and the positive evolution of the Anglo-American type (the spearhead of evolution in Norris's mind) depend upon the personality and accomplishments of "the fittest." In this class, unfortunately, one usually finds the most highly individuated and selfish types of humanity, such as the equally egotistical Ward and Lloyd. They are tough-minded achievers callous to the more tender-minded concerns that inform much of the nature of humane society, the family, and marriage—the essential institutions fostering sensitivity and countering the "laws of the jungle." The refrain of *Moran of the Lady Letty* was "To hell with the weak!" Ross Wilbur and Moran Sternersen derided Victorian sentiments regarding the value of Judeo-Christian civilization, and Norris appeared to condone the piratical behavior of the barbarically "fit." In *A Man's Woman*, though, the essentially Victorian thinker reemerged in Norris and he puzzled over the problem of humanizing his Darwinian exemplars. On the one hand, he saw the evolutionary vanguard, "the fittest," as absolutely necessary to the positive historical process in which he wanted to believe; on the other, he realized that the future of Anglo-American society was imperiled by the amorality and insensitivity manifested in the behavior of those in that category. True to the principles of Professor Joseph LeConte, Norris tried to demonstrate the need to synthesize vigor and fitness with ethicality and humaneness. He hoped to fashion his hero and heroine as instructive models of what may be involved in taking the difficult steps upward on the evolutionary ladder.

Unlike Ross and Moran, then, Ward and Lloyd are made to suffer the negative consequences of extreme self-interest and to temper their selfishness with concern for others' needs. Both overcome egotism and its debilitating effects; both move beyond the paralysis of self-pity in the face of failures; and both learn a new and constructive kind of sympathy. In their own ways, they become social creatures able to see beyond self. Needless to say, the novel ends happily.

Unfortunately, the unbridled melodrama, bombastic language, irritating anticlimaxes, and overwrought allegorical characterizations of *A Man's Woman* obscured the new and intellectually worthwhile theme. The author lamented in a letter to one reviewer that the novel was too "theatrical" and "slovenly put together." The central concept

was most progressive: rather than accept the antisocial implications of Darwinism, Norris had tried to reconcile man's "animal" heritage (energy and endurance being requisite for positive evolutionary action) with the best consequences of civilization. Norris seemed to hold as a point of faith that someone, at some time, should show how sensitivity to human needs had an essential place in the post-Darwinian Western world. To him the paramount question of the age was: how can Judeo-Christian values best exert their mollifying effects on a harsh world? In *The Octopus* he returned to this question—with much greater success. What he pictured was a Darwinian world, like that in Zola's *Germinal* (1885), crying out for humanizing influences.

As Zola had moved from an interest in objectively reporting the grimness of life in *L'Assommoir* to the more moralistic point of view and tone of *Germinal*, Norris was moving away from the largely amoral, naturalistic perspective of *McTeague* to a more traditional kind of fiction in which the author seeks to suggest a pragmatic solution to social and personal problems. The friendship he began in 1898 with the Reverend W. S. Rainsford, of St. George's Episcopal Church in New York City, is significant in this regard. Rainsford, as Pizer relates, held views similar to Joseph LeConte's; he was a social activist, and he may have encouraged Norris to strive for more constructive ends in his fiction. In one piece of literary criticism, "The Novel with a 'Purpose'" (1902), Norris advised against overt didacticism in novel writing, but in *The Octopus* he did not hesitate to raise the question of what one ought to do in regard to the social injustices and economic abuses typical of the late nineteenth century.

While *Blix* was in press and *A Man's Woman* was running as a newspaper serial, Norris visited California and began research on The Trilogy of the Wheat, the first volume of which was *The Octopus*. The trilogy was to be the most ambitious work of his career, and Norris became obsessed with its concept. After Norris's death, Frederic Taber Cooper recalled: "His friends are still fond of telling of the day he came to his office trembling with excitement, incapacitated for work, his brain concentrated on a single thought, his Trilogy of the Wheat. 'I have got a big idea, the biggest I ever had,' was the burden of all he had to say for many a day after." On 7 May 1899, he wrote to his old friend Ernest Peixotto, with whom he had studied in Paris, telling him how his research for *The Octopus* in California was proceeding: "The Wheat stuff is piling up BIG. Everybody is willing to help. . . . I

Front cover for Norris's 1899 novel, based on his courtship of Jeannette Black

may be here longer than I first expected. Mebbe til late in the fall, and I dunno why I should not write my immortal worruk at a wheat ranch any way. Tell [Gellett] Burgess I'm full of ginger and red pepper and am getting ready to stand up on my hind legs and yell big. . . ."

By the close of 1899 he was back in New York City with his notes in hand, ready to produce his prose epic. The focus of the California research was on socioeconomic conditions in the San Joaquin Valley and particularly the Southern Pacific Railroad's abuse of the wheat growers, which had triggered the infamous gun battle, the Mussell Slough Affair of May 1880. The railroad trust provided all the material that a muckraker might want: it had attracted farmers with the promise of cheap land ceded to it by the government. It was to sell the land at unimproved prices at some future date; but once the growers developed the properties agriculturally, the railroad priced the land at im-

proved rates. This change of policy, together with the railroad's high freight charges, meant economic ruination for the growers. Norris, however, did not resort to moral melodrama by pitting the noble husbandman of the soil against the malevolent trust. As a notebook-carrying Zolaist who had performed his field research—including an interview with C. P. Huntington, the head of the Southern Pacific—he sought instead to compose a trilogy representatively picturing the complexities of modern economic life, the unifying motif of which was the production, distribution, and consumption of an essential commodity. As a commentator he sought to shed some light on a lamentably junglelike society characterized mainly by rapacious interactions.

In late 1899 Norris began work as a reader for Doubleday, Page, a welcome position, making financially possible his marriage to Jeannette Black on 12 February 1900 in New York City. He seems to have spent little time at the office. In the spring he was hard at work on *The Octopus*. Reflecting on his data and writing at Greenwood Lake, New Jersey, in the summer of 1900, Norris maintained a nonsentimental point of view—in spite of the obvious temptations provided by the subject matter. Continuing the composition after he moved to Roselle, New Jersey, in October, Norris saw both the growers and the representatives of the trust as dominated by the same fixation: an insatiable mania for profit and self-aggrandizement. Wealth and power are the prime motivations in a dog-eat-dog order; it is a Darwinian world order that Norris sternly fashions. *The Octopus* graphically and unshirkingly lays out the apparently insuperable problem confronting the social ameliorist who might dare to offer a proposal for macrocosmic reform. As in *Vandover and the Brute*, Norris presents a harsh world defying any mollifications.

Norris, of course, attempts an enlightening response. Which is *his* response, however, has been a matter of heated debate for decades because some critics have perceived confusion in the novel regarding point of view. Adhering to the principles later enunciated in "The Novel with a 'Purpose'," Norris did not commit the literary sins of intruding upon the story and declaring his message to the world. Rather, he set up various characters, each with his own response to the central dilemma of the story—planning, most likely, to clarify his major theme in the never-written final volume of the trilogy. That is, *The Octopus* is not a fully independent work but a part of an intended but incomplete whole. When one reads the novel as an integral, separate work, with the expectations that naturally accompany such an approach, disappointment with Norris and disagreement with other interpreters may—and do—result.

Thus, a few critics have seen Shelgrim, the head of the railroad, as Norris's spokesman. This apologist for social Darwinism declares that events are beyond his control and that the economic order governs itself toward necessary and ultimately natural ends. "You are dealing with forces, young man, when you speak of Wheat and Railroads, not with men," he tells the character named Presley. "Complications may arise, conditions that bear hard on the individual—crush him maybe—*but the Wheat will be carried to feed the people* as inevitably as it will grow. If you want to fasten the blame . . . on any one person, you will make a mistake. Blame conditions, not men." Others have argued that the poet Presley and his mentor, Vanamee, a shepherd with mystical propensities, are more proximate to Norris's point of view. Both make what may be termed metaphysical responses to the disaster in the San Joaquin Valley and to life's problems in general: Vanamee asserts the illusory character of evils such as death, privation, and the abuse of the individual; Presley leaps to an Emersonian faith that the good produced by events compensates for evils and in the end, or "larger view," always dominates. Since these characters' thoughts and comments close the volume, critics judge that Norris was making a "transcendental" response to the human predicaments pathetically described in *The Octopus*.

There is yet another interpretive possibility remaining—that Norris experiments with a traditional assertion of Judeo-Christian values through the example of Annixter, one of the leaders of the growers in their fight against the railroad. Like Ward Bennett of *A Man's Woman*, Annixter is the epitome of selfishness in the first half of *The Octopus*. Like Ward, he is extraordinarily competent, fiercely competitive, and markedly insensitive toward others. He is famous for using and abusing everyone—until he experiences love for Hilma Tree. The consummation of his love requires a nearly total personality transformation, and that change occurs. He gradually becomes oriented toward others and develops an acute awareness of others' needs. Hilma and Presley are astounded at the emergence of the new man; and Annixter himself is surprised at the joy that comes with caring for his fellows. He is killed by railroad agents shortly after he begins to act as a new man, but during his brief experience of concern for Hilma and the other members of his immediate society, Annixter demonstrates what may have been the only pragmatic possibility for even minor social amelioration that Norris could imagine as of 1901. Annixter makes life better for those immediately around him; he is the only principal character in the whole of *The Octopus* to succeed in humanizing his environment.

Actually, the interpretive crux involves the choice of Vanamee, Presley, or Annixter as Norris's true hero. The choice of Vanamee or Presley involves positing an optimistic metaphysical response on Norris's part. The choice of Annixter implies that Norris was tentatively proposing a practical revival of Judeo-Christian values (relatively selfless living directed toward the end of love for one's neighbor). If one chooses Vanamee or Presley, though, he must deal with the fact that both are self-absorbed individuals; and Norris had identified that state as a negative condition in *A Man's Woman*. Moreover, in his next novel, *The Pit*, he would again make the same point.

With *The Octopus* in press by the early spring of 1901, Norris gave up his house at Roselle, New

The Epic of the Wheat

THE OCTOPUS

A STORY OF CALIFORNIA

BY

FRANK NORRIS

NEW YORK
DOUBLEDAY, PAGE & CO.
1901

Title page for the first novel in Norris's wheat trilogy, in which he planned to explore "(1) the production, (2) the distribution, (3) the consumption of American wheat"

Jersey, and traveled with Jeannette to Chicago, where he worked up the technical details and local color for the second stage of the trilogy. He was also writing short stories, contributing literary essays to the *Chicago American*, and dealing with the interruptions resulting from the critical and commercial success of *The Octopus*. By May he was in California, where he stayed for two months; then three months of privacy followed at Greenwood Lake, New Jersey. In September 1901 he was back in New York City, living in a West Side apartment, hard at work on *The Pit*. One year later it began its serialization in the *Saturday Evening Post*. The flow of wheat eastward is the background for the drama of *The Pit*; but, once more, it is human relationships on which the limelight is focused.

Curtis Jadwin is closely related to Ward Bennett and Annixter. Having made a fortune in real estate and occasional speculative sallies into the Board of Trade, Jadwin is a commanding figure, whom Norris adorns with much chivalric imagery, and whom he elevates to near-epic stature as the archetypal, achievement-oriented American. (Norris, too, was interested in writing the "Great American Novel," and the best-selling *The Pit* was his second attempt—as reviewers immediately recognized. Most praised it as an undeniably great novel.) Jadwin is not one who fails and, when he competes for Laura Dearborn's hand in marriage, he ignores rejection, routs his opponents, and wins the field. When he decides to seriously speculate in wheat futures, his relentless determination leads him to attempt a cornering of the entire wheat harvest. Obsessed with his goal, he wreaks havoc in a global population dependent upon reasonably priced wheat for its survival. In his personal life with Laura, calamitous consequences occur as well. With his marriage on the rocks because of his neglect, Jadwin suffers financial disaster and a nervous breakdown.

Laura is also an egotist with very grand expectations for herself. While Jadwin is the Darwinian exemplar, Laura is the epitome of another variety of a self-absorbed way of life—romantic narcissism, the other nineteenth-century manifestation of the "cult of the self." She requires a courtly lover who will dote upon her and see her as she views herself, as the grand heroine at center stage in the romantic drama that is life. Like the melodramatically self-conscious Lloyd Searight, she lives as though she is following the script provided by an operatic librettist. When Jadwin's obsession with the "battle" at the Board of Trade disqualifies him as the necessary idolizer, the spurned heroine turns to

another gallant and toward the traditional end of romantic love, adultery.

Laura comes very close to leaving Jadwin and, indeed, to going insane. Jadwin loses his immense future in his wheat speculations and discovers that he has ruined his life. With his two exaggerated symbols of nineteenth-century egotism on the brink of absolute tragedy, Norris stops the degeneration process and kindly allows them a second chance. Jadwin is not an intellectual, but he does realize that the path he has followed was the wrong one. His Titan-like energies were mischanneled. Laura, while not much clearer in her comprehension of what went wrong, is more conscious of the point that Norris wishes to convey to the reader. It is Ward's, Annixter's, and Lloyd's movements beyond self-absorption that come to mind when Norris relates Laura's final thoughts to the reader: "Self, self. Had she been selfish from the very first? . . . Whither had this cruel cult of self led her?" Familiar with Tennyson's *Idylls of the King*—to which there are overt allusions in *The Pit*—Norris allows his Guinevere time for reflection and reform. His Lancelot, Sheldon Corthell, is sent packing. And his Arthur escapes total defeat. It is to new possibilities in life that Jadwin, Laura, and Norris turn as *The Pit* closes.

Egotism, as encouraged by social Darwinism and fin de siecle romantic narcissism, was the villain of Norris's mature fiction. The world is harsh in all of Norris's novels, except in *Blix* wherein a clever heroine deftly checks the consequences of the hero's immaturity. This harshness Norris could accept as a hard fact. He could recognize the complexities and irremediable aspect of a world not especially amenable to positive change. What he could not accept or sanction was the way in which human beings regularly worsened conditions by engaging in destructive and self-destructive behavior. The laws of the universe could not be changed, and the socio-economic order could not be immediately redesigned, but individuals could alter and improve their lots, especially if they asked the question that occurred so late to Ward, Annixter, and Laura: what is *really* important? The answer demonstrated explicitly and implicitly in the last three novels was, relationships characterized by benign mutual concern. As an evolutionist the young Frank Norris echoed the "hard Darwinism" of Herbert Spencer; but as his thought matured, he gravitated toward the view of Peter Kropotkin in *Mutual Aid* (1902), which chastised Spencer for overlooking the "instinct of human solidarity and sociability" and its positive consequences. It was, possibly, an

Norris at the time he was working on his Trilogy of the Epic of the Wheat

old-fashioned answer that Norris came to when examining modern conditions. He echoed the positive theme in the final stanza of Matthew Arnold's "Dover Beach" (1867). But, to Norris's credit, he also anticipated the only hope for man seen by John Steinbeck and Albert Camus.

Norris died of appendicitis in San Francisco in October 1902, before the serialization of *The Pit* was concluded. He had not begun the final volume of the trilogy, "The Wolf." He might have planned to elaborate in "The Wolf" upon the negative effects of culturally sanctioned selfishness on the macro- and microcosmic levels; perhaps he would have clarified the situation in *The Octopus* and explained whether Presley's and Vanamee's transcendental visions of a good universe or Annixter's "helping hand" response to an imperfect world represented his final position.

When the reader turns from the novels of 1898 through 1902 to the post-*Wave*, nonnovelistic works for indications of what Norris may have planned to do in "The Wolf," he will meet with disappointment in this regard—and in other regards as well. While Norris dramatically improved as a novelist after he wrote *Moran of the Lady Letty*, and earned a permanent place in literary history as

a result, he did not fare so well in other types of writing. While *The Pit* was easily adapted by Channing Pollock for the stage in 1904, Norris never exploited his penchant for melodrama in this way. Writing poetry, like his banjo playing, he wisely allowed to remain something associated with his fraternity days. Indeed, his last poem was a bit of comic doggerel, "The Exile's Toast," addressed to his Phi Gamma Delta brothers when he could not attend the November 1900 reunion in San Francisco. He did continue to write short fiction, but it is obvious that his talent and energy were directed principally into novelistic writing. It is difficult to identify individual stories representing any advance over the quality of his 1896-1898 work. In fact, there is a falling off in quality and a frequent resort to easy formulas.

There were two posthumous collections of short fiction, *A Deal in Wheat and Other Stories* (1903), which includes stories published in periodicals between 1901 and 1903, and *The Third Circle* (1909), made up of magazine stories mainly from the mid-1890s. Neither of these books impressed contemporaneous reviewers. Viewing both collections one sees no growth of any sort in the early 1900s: all that is apparent is experiment with various formats, all of which have more in common with the features of pulp fiction than high art. The substance of *Yvernelle* became "The Riding of Felipe" (1901) with the hero saving the heroine at the last moment "from a fate worse than death." The lurid mystery of "The Third Circle" and "The House with the Blinds" (both 1897) anticipate "The Ship That Saw a Ghost" (1902) and "The Ghost in the Crosstrees" (1903)—two truly lifeless pieces in the Gothic vein. The earlier, pleasant humor of "This Animal of a Buldy Jones" (1897) proves superior to the heavy-handed comedy in "A Bargain with Peg-Leg" (1902), "The Passing of Cock-Eye Blacklock" (1902), and "Two Hearts That Beat as One" (1903). The 1900s stories, then, tell little about Norris's career except that he wrote twenty pieces, seemingly for pocket money. That the two collections were assembled and published was mainly the result of *The Pit*'s enormous success and the marketability of Norris's name.

"A Deal in Wheat" (1902) is, unfortunately, Norris's best known short story. Frequently anthologized because of its relationship to *The Pit*, it delineates the chicanery allegedly common in the daily activities of Chicago wheat speculators. Like Norris's later attempts at comedy in the short fiction, it is nothing more than a lengthy set-up for a snappy, surprise conclusion—one, in fact, borrowed from Richard Harding Davis's *The West from a Car Window*. Norris was not at his best when writing short stories; but he was better than "A Deal in Wheat" suggests, as a perusal of *The Third Circle* will indicate.

In his literary essays of the post-*Wave* period Norris may have spent the greater part of the energies he had left over from his novelistic enterprises. Today Norris is identified as "the most vocal expounder" of naturalistic critical theory at the end of the nineteenth century in America, according to Hugh Holman. But a study of his critical canon reveals something else. During the *Wave* period, he wrote only one essay truly "expounding" the virtues of "naturalism," and Norris did not even stress that term when he chose the title, "Zola as a Romantic Writer" (1896). If anything, Norris indicated that he did not find that term a useful one, especially since it was then synonymous with "dirty books" and "the French school" in the American reader's mind. The point of "Zola as a Romantic Writer" was that so-called naturalism "is a form of romanticism, not an inner circle of realism" as reviewers and essayists were then claiming. Norris wrote that in Zola's works everything "is extraordinary, imaginative, grotesque even, with a vague note of terror quivering throughout like the vibration of an ominous and low-pitched diapson. It is all romantic . . . closely resembling the work of the greatest of all modern romanticists, Hugo." To Norris in 1896, naturalism or Zolaism was romanticism set in the milieu of actual social conditions. And he allied himself with this school because it seemed the one most truthfully depicting the full "drama of the people" in real life.

In December 1901 he again held forth on the subject. By then he had in mind not only Zola's example but his own practice in five published novels—each a romance, or romance-novel (to use the term employed by Richard V. Chase in *The American Novel and Its Tradition*, 1957). The still young novelist was extremely close to his own works, and many of his literary essays are explanatory glosses on the volumes he had so recently completed. "A Plea for Romantic Fiction" further diminishes the emphasis on the term naturalism and more heavily emphasizes the Zolaesque-Norrisean concept of a romanticism transcending realism (as defined by Howells's practice) and popular romance writing (as exemplified by the cut-and-thrust and moonlight-and-golden-hair traditions). Norris's romanticism was a synthetic concept: by vitally blending a Hugoesque choice of remarkable incidents and characters with a Flaubertian concern for the specifics of actual human experience in the present, the truest kind of art became possible. For Norris, romanticism at its best was the ultimate form of realism in literature. The term denoted a full examination and presentation of the whole of experience from the trivial to the profound.

With such a redefinition of terms and concepts, Norris confidently entered the arena of American literary debate, somewhat unkindly hoisting Willian Dean Howells by his own petard. In the second chapter of *Criticism and Fiction* (1891), the dean of American letters warned of how realism might degenerate as a movement. "When realism becomes false to itself," Howells wrote, "when it heaps up facts merely, and maps life instead of picturing it, realism will perish." Norris saw Howells as guilty of such literal-mindedness and shallowness, and he damned the Howellsian tradition: "Realism stultifies itself. It notes only the surface of things." Romanticism, as practiced by Zola (and Norris), attended to surfaces in a documentary way, but it also penetrated to the depths of human nature and finally to Truth. As indicated in another essay, "The True Reward of the Novelist" (1901), Norris was as fixated on "the Truth" as Zola in his later years; and he celebrated Zola as *the* artist who knew how to use "romance" properly, as "an instrument with which [one] may go straight through the clothes and tissues and wrappings of flesh down deep into the real, living heart of things. . . . the unplumbed depths of the human heart, and the mystery of sex, and the problems of life, and the black, unsearched penetralia of the soul of man."

When Norris signed himself the "Boy Zola" in letters, he identified with a romantic. He does not even use the word *naturalistic* in "A Plea for Romantic Fiction." While historians will continue referring to Norris as a Naturalist (especially when viewing his thoughts in *McTeague* and *Vandover and the Brute*), it is necessary to acknowledge Norris's self-perception and his view—which was, ironically, anticipated by Howells in *Criticism and Fiction*—that the best literary art of the late nineteenth century is a manifestation of the noblest impulses of the romantic movement. That is, both Howells and Norris viewed remoteness from real life, which the romantics had found in neo-classicism, as negatively as Wordsworth did. Both championed greater fidelity to the natural and true—Howells declaring that at the beginning of the century "romance was making the same fight against effete classicism which realism is making to-day against effete romanticism." Norris too lamented degenerate romanticism, "the misuse of a really noble and honest formula of literature," and argued for the recognition of romance as "a teacher sent from God." In theory, Norris was, perhaps unwittingly, in harmony with Howells; but, in practice, of course, their differences were as obvious to Norris as they are to the modern reader.

Between 25 December 1897, when his last book review for the *Wave* was published and 25 May 1901, Norris wrote no literary essays except for "The Unknown Author and the Publisher," published in the *World's Work* in April 1901 and signed "A Publisher's Reader." One of the main reasons it is attributed to him is because of his work as a reader for Doubleday, Page and Company. The little time he actually spent at the office gave him enough experience to provide in "The Unknown Author" the first of several peeks-behind-the-curtains by one who was there in the New York publishing world.

One month later he had better credentials as a literary man and was sought after for essays on many topics. The homage generated by *The Octopus*, which was published in April, made all the difference. Norris was now a bona fide celebrity engaged by the *Chicago American* to write a series of articles entitled "Literature in the East" for its Saturday literary supplement. The feature ran from 25 May through 28 August 1901, missing only the 27 July issue. In the October issue of the *World's Work*, "The True Reward of the Novelist"—his most idealistic assessment of the artist's role in society—appeared. Then, on 6 November the *Boston Evening Transcript* welcomed him for twelve essays published through 5 February 1902. An as yet unidentified firm contracted with Norris for syndicated distribution of his work in January 1902, and he wrote at least eight essays for that company. A plateau was soon scaled: *The Critic* began a "Salt and Sincerity" series comprising seven essays published between April 1902 and February 1903. In November it printed his best known essay, "The Responsibilities of the Novelist."

Norris had become an authority. Yet, while he was clearly aspiring toward the status of William Dean Howells, he most often reached only the level of Hamlin Garland and frequently fell short of that. Many of the essays respectfully ushered into print were no better than what many Sunday supplement paragraphers were providing: inside scoops on what is really going on in the literary world, as in "New York as a Literary Centre" (1902) and "What Frank Norris Has to Say About the Unknown Writer's Chances" (1902); casual chat about "Why Women Should Write the Best Novels" (1901); and

gossip about luminaries such as Richard Harding Davis in "It Was a Close Call" (1902). Cultural analysis such as "The Frontier Gone At Last" (1902) exalts the Anglo-Saxon spirit in sincere tones but also in a manner designed to please the Rooseveltian mentality.

There were, of course, several truly interesting essays. As one who had tried to write the "Great American Novel" in *The Octopus* and had been praised for coming very close to it, his "The National Spirit: As It Relates to the 'Great American Novel'" (1902) made a good deal of sense in regard to how the regional orientation fostered by the local-color tradition might be transcended. "A Neglected Epic" (1902) notes the closing of the frontier chapter in American cultural history and laments the fact that no one had successfully responded to the epic subject matter of the frontier experience in the West—a notion touched upon through Presley in *The Octopus*. "The Novel with a 'Purpose'" (1902) addressed the difficulties of enlightening the public while avoiding the overt didacticism of genteel-ideal literature—another problem dealt with in *The Octopus*. It is especially

Norris's drawing of his dog Monk

Norris shortly before his death

clear in these essays that Norris was too close to his own work to develop the trait of catholicity in his expository prose. They are relevant to the cultural history of the United States, but they are more revelatory of the concerns that the author of *The Octopus* then had in mind.

Two essays stand apart. "Simplicity in Art" (1902) is a truly sophisticated statement of an aesthetic. Norris restates his detestation of the gingerbread style of late Victorian architecture and the overly ornate in all forms. He had originally expressed this point of view in the *Wave*, and he had laced *The Octopus* with similar commentary. In the essay he argued that elaborate phrasing, rhetoric, metaphor, and allegory—"rococo work"—too often disguise the "innate incompetence" of the writer. Quoting the narrative exposition in the King James translation of Luke 2: 6-7, he identified "the bare dignity of the unadorned" as the finest artistic trait. The essay is a curiosity among the others since its thesis seems to have nothing to do with Norris's own writing, which may fairly be termed "baroque"— with the Vanamee sections of *The Octopus* verging

toward the "rococo" itself. Norris buttresses his argument with these questions: "Does exclamation and heroics on the part of the bystanders ever make the curbstone drama more poignant? Who would care to see Niagara through colored fire and calcium light?" The irony is that, in January 1902, Norris was depicting the "Niagara" of wheat which would crush Curtis Jadwin in language which was colored, fiery, and sometimes too dazzlingly brilliant. Autobiographically viewed, then, the essay seems to speak of the writer's future: that Norris was planning, distantly, for a change of voice and method; that the author and redactors of Luke might someday join Norris's long list of literary influences.

The other essay of enduring value and interest is "The Mechanics of Fiction" (1901). It expresses a Poe-like concern for the particulars of effective craftsmanship in art. Recalling the mechanics of planning and execution described in "The Philosophy of Composition," Norris portrays the capable writer as one who behaves as a mosaicist— carefully choosing, shaping, and fitting into place the individual pieces of his picture. He intelligently proceeds with a plan, moved not by the frenzy of inspiration, but directed by practical intelligence and the knowledge that comes with experience. Norris's final revisions of *Blix* and *A Man's Woman* prior to book publication—the former especially indicating the degree to which Norris was a craftsman—make "The Mechanics of Fiction" seem more autobiographically significant than "Simplicity in Art." "The Mechanics of Fiction" also helps one to appreciate Norris's intentions in regard to the episodic structure of *McTeague* and the panellike or framelike arrangements of parts in *The Octopus*. Moreover, the essay is also relevant to modern critics because of the emphasis Norris placed upon fine craftsmanship. His points are ones that still have current value.

Donald Pizer's arrangement of the literary essays into thematically similar groups brings a good deal of coherence to the corpus. *The Literary Criticism of Frank Norris* (1964) identifies these main concerns: how the novelist might prepare for his profession; the need for literature to embody life rather than merely imitate prior "literary" portraits of the same; the methods of literary creation; and the role of the artist in society. The topics are worthy ones; but, again, Norris seemed a newcomer to the field, lacking in objectivity and breadth of vision. In 1903, when Doubleday sought to cash in on the success of *The Pit* and gathered twenty-eight pieces for *The Responsibilities of the Novelist and Other Literary Essays*, American and English reviewers panned it as derivative, contradictory, and sophomoric.

When appendicitis struck in October 1902, Norris was a successful novelist, and had been invited a few weeks before to give a reading at Berkeley, honored at the university he had attended but from which he never received a diploma. At thirty-two, he had risen to the prominent position of one addressing a national audience on literary matters through the *Critic*. Having moved to 1921 Broderick Street in San Francisco in July 1902, after he had finished writing *The Pit*, he was financially secure and was enjoying a stable marriage. He delighted in his daughter, born in February 1902; and it seems that he planned to proceed with his career at a less hectic clip. For instance, he canceled a planned trip around the world during which he was to gather data for "The Wolf." Friends related after his death that his new ambition was to settle down for good in the part of the country he loved and among the people whose friendship he cherished. According to Franklin Walker, Norris was thumping his chest as he announced to his friends, "*Main-*

tenant je suis bon bourgeois, moi–père de famille!" The enfant terrible who shocked the reviewers with a vengeance in *McTeague* was no more. Norris had become a vested member of the establishment.

Norris planned to build a country home in Gilroy, California. With "The Wolf" completed, he would write short stories set in that locale and begin a second trilogy dealing with the Battle of Gettysburg. As a literary critic he did not make any astounding contributions. As a short-story writer he rarely rose above the rank of adequate in his later years. But, as a novelist who finished seven novels before his death, he made a distinctive mark, and as a thinker increasingly interested in individual and social psychology he offered some truly unique insights, graphic delineations, and—true to his Victorian background—relevant "morals" grounded in the realities of human behavior.

Letters:

The Letters of Frank Norris, edited by Franklin Walker (San Francisco: Book Club of California, 1956).

Bibliographies:

Kenneth A. Lohf and Eugene P. Sheehy, *Frank Norris: A Bibliography* (Los Gatos, Cal.: Talisman Press, 1959);

William B. Dillingham, "Frank Norris," in *Fifteen American Authors Before 1900*, edited by Robert A. Rees and Earl N. Harbert (Madison: University of Wisconsin Press, 1971), pp. 307-332;

Joseph Katz, "The Shorter Publications of Frank Norris: A Checklist," *Proof*, 3 (1973): 155-220;

Jesse S. Crisler and Joseph R. McElrath, Jr., *Frank Norris: A Reference Guide* (Boston: G. K. Hall, 1974).

Biographies:

Franklin Walker, *Frank Norris: A Biography* (Garden City: Doubleday, Doran, 1932);

Joseph R. McElrath, Jr., "Frank Norris: A Biographical Essay," *American Literary Realism*, 11 (Autumn 1978): 219-234.

References:

Lars Ahnebrink, *The Influence of Emile Zola on Frank Norris* (Uppsala, Sweden: A. B. Lundequistska Bokhandeln, 1947);

Richard Allan Davison, ed., *The Merrill Studies in The Octopus* (Columbus: Merrill, 1969);

William B. Dillingham, *Frank Norris: Instinct and Art* (Lincoln: University of Nebraska Press, 1969);

Warren French, *Frank Norris* (New York: Twayne, 1962);

W. M. Frohock, *Frank Norris*, University of Minnesota Pamphlets on American Writers, No. 68 (Minneapolis: University of Minnesota Press, 1969);

Don Graham, ed., *Critical Essays on Frank Norris* (Boston: G. K. Hall, 1980);

Graham, *The Fiction of Frank Norris: The Aesthetic Context* (Columbia: University of Missouri Press, 1978);

Joseph Katz, "The Manuscript of Frank Norris' *McTeague*: A Preliminary Census of Pages," *Resources For American Literary Study*, 2 (Spring 1972): 91-97;

Ernest Marchand, *Frank Norris: A Study* (Stanford, Cal.: Stanford University Press, 1942);

Joseph R. McElrath, Jr., and Katherine Knight, eds., *Frank Norris: The Critical Reception* (New York: Burt Franklin, 1981);

Donald Pizer, *The Novels of Frank Norris* (Bloomington: Indiana University Press, 1966).

Papers:

The Frank Norris Collection at the Bancroft Library, University of California at Berkeley, contains the largest collection of letters and manuscripts, as well as Franklin Walker's notes for *Frank Norris: A Biography*. The Barrett Collection of the Alderman Library, University of Virginia, also contains manuscript material.

Thomas Nelson Page
(23 April 1853-1 November 1922)

David Kirby
Florida State University

SELECTED BOOKS: *In Ole Virginia* (New York: Scribners, 1887);

Befo' de War: Echoes in Negro Dialect, by Page and A. C. Gordon (New York: Scribners, 1888);

Two Little Confederates (New York: Scribners, 1888; London: Unwin, 1888);

On Newfound River (New York: Scribners, 1891; London: Osgood, 1891; enlarged edition, New York: Scribners, 1906);

Elsket and Other Stories (New York: Scribners, 1891; London: Osgood, 1892);

Among the Camps, or Young People's Stories of the War (New York: Scribners, 1891; London: Scott, 1892);

The Old South: Essays Social and Political (New York: Scribners, 1892);

Pastime Stories (New York: Harper, 1894);

The Burial of the Guns (New York: Scribners, 1894; London: Ward, Lock & Bowden, 1894);

The Old Gentleman of the Black Stock (New York: Scribners, 1897);

Two Prisoners (New York: Russell, 1897; revised, 1903);

Red Rock (New York: Scribners, 1898; London: Heinemann, 1899);

Santa Claus's Partner (New York: Scribners, 1899; London: Sands, 1900);

Gordon Keith (New York: Scribners, 1903; London: Heinemann, 1903);

Bred in the Bone (New York: Scribners, 1904);

The Negro: The Southerner's Problem (New York: Scribners, 1904);

The Coast of Bohemia (New York: Scribners, 1906);

Under the Coast (New York: Scribners, 1907);

The Old Dominion: Her Making and Her Manners (New York: Scribners, 1908);

Tommy Trot's Visit to Santa Claus (New York: Scribners, 1908);

Robert E. Lee, The Southerner (New York: Scribners, 1908; London: Laurie, 1909);

John Marvel, Assistant (New York: Scribners, 1909; London: Laurie, 1910);

Robert E. Lee, Man and Soldier (New York: Scribners, 1911);

The Land of the Spirit (New York: Scribners, 1913; London: Laurie, 1913);

Italy and the World War (New York: Scribners, 1920; London: Chapman & Hall, 1921);

Dante and His Influence: Studies (New York: Scribners, 1922; London: Chapman & Hall, 1923);

Washington and Its Romance (New York: Doubleday, Page, 1923; London: Heinemann, 1923);
The Red Riders (New York: Scribners, 1924).

COLLECTION: *The Novels, Stories, Sketches, and Poems of Thomas Nelson Page*, Plantation Edition, 18 volumes (New York: Scribners, 1906-1912).

One of the most popular authors of the Reconstruction South, Thomas Nelson Page not only articulated a consistent view of plantation life as he saw it but also served as a spokesman for his generation of Southerners. Page's contemporary, Southern novelist and historian Grace King, wrote that it was difficult to say in simple terms what Thomas Nelson Page meant to other Southerners at that time. "He was the first Southern writer to appear in print as a Southerner, and his stories, short and simple, written in Negro dialect, and I may say, Southern pronunciation, showed us with ineffable grace that although we were sore bereft, politically, we had a chance in literature at least."

The wide appeal of Page's vision, in the North

as well as in the South, seems directly related to its departure from historical reality. To readers everywhere, Page's daydreams were more desirable than the nightmares of war and Reconstruction. As a local colorist, Page sketched the minutiae of Southern life with unswerving fidelity, yet these details contribute to sentimental plots whose heroes are always noble beyond belief. At the center of Page's art is the code of Southern heroism, a system whereby men are loyal to their friends, fair to their enemies, and worshipful of women. It is a code which sees glory in the past, calls for the practice of military virtues in the present, and envisions a future that is ideal—a state of culture and leisure, albeit one that is, like Pericles' Athens, founded on a slave proletariat. This harsh necessity notwithstanding, Page offered his public so attractive a portrait of Southern life that even those who had been implacable foes of the South succumbed to it. Not untypical was Thomas Wentworth Higginson, the Northern writer and progressive social thinker who had commanded a regiment of black soldiers and who, when he read Page's story "Marse Chan" thirty years after the war ended, wept over the death of the slave owner hero.

Page's photographic exactitude as to the details of Southern life stems from the years he spent in and the affection he felt for a setting which he duplicated in story after story. In his introduction to the Plantation Edition of his works, Page recalls that his childhood home, Oakland Plantation in Hanover County, Virginia, was "within the sounds of the guns of battles in three great campaigns in which not less than three hundred thousand men fell, and during [my] boyhood and youth the recollection of the great Civil War was the most vital thing within [my] knowledge." Following a desultory education, Page attended Washington College (1869-1872) while Robert E. Lee was its president and took a law degree from the University of Virginia in 1874, thus preparing himself for the profession that was followed by many Southern authors of his day. From 1874 to 1893 he practiced law in Virginia and then retired to full-time authorship. In 1886 he married Anne Bruce, who died in 1888, and he was married again in 1893 to Florence Lathrop Field. As his popularity both as author and lecturer grew, Page became active in politics and in 1913 was appointed ambassador to Italy by Woodrow Wilson. In his later years he led a cosmopolitan life in London, Paris, Rome, and the Riviera, far removed from the bucolic world of his fiction. Page was elected to the American Academy of Arts and Letters in 1908.

Oakland, Page's birthplace in Hanover County, Virginia

Page's first book, a collection of stories entitled *In Ole Virginia* (1887), is acknowledged by many critics to be his best single work. It includes "Marse Chan," the story that brought Page national recognition when it appeared in *Century* in 1884. The donnee for the story is given in Page's introduction to the Plantation Edition. In 1880 he was shown a letter which had been taken from the pocket of a dead Confederate soldier. The author of the letter was the young man's fiancee, who "told him that she had discovered since he left home that she loved him, and that she did not know why she had been so cruel to him before he went away; that, in fact, she had loved him ever since they had gone to school together in the little school-house in the woods, when he had been so good to her; and that now if he would get a furlough and come home she would marry him. This was all, except, of course, a postscript. As if fearful that such a temptation might prove too much even for the man she loved, across the blue Confederate paper were scrawled these words: 'Don't come without a furlough; for if you don't come honorable, I won't marry you.' " This is essentially the story that is told to a first-person narrator, who is sojourning in the dream world of once-proud plantation owners. The narrator guides the reader into this fantasy of defeated aris-

tocrats: "Their once splendid mansions, now fast falling to decay, appeared to view from time to time, set back far from the road, in proud seclusion. . . . Distance was nothing to this people; time was of no consequence to them. They desired but a level path in life, and that they had, though the way was longer, and the outer world strode by them as they dreamed."

On one such plantation, Marse Chan's body servant tells the narrator the story of his young master's tragic love affair and death in the war, a Romeo-and-Juliet type of tale that Page used again and again, with increasing success. Marse Chan, a Whig, who wants Virginia to remain part of the Union, loves Anne Chamberlain, whose father is a Democrat and a secessionist. After Marse Chan bests him in a political debate, Colonel Chamberlain becomes insulting and finally issues a challenge. On the morning of the duel, the Colonel fires early but misses. The noble Chan discharges his pistol in the air and then refuses to duel again, a humanitarian act which, in its violation of the code of Southern heroism, angers Anne, who believes that Marse Chan insulted her father originally and is now compounding the insult by denying the Colonel satisfaction. Virginia secedes, and Marse Chan, who has opposed secession, puts aside his feelings and enlists as a private. One night a fellow soldier makes light of the Chamberlains, and Marse Chan gives him a thrashing. Word of the incident gets to Anne, who relents and confesses her love in a letter much like the one Page had been shown. But too late—Marse Chan is killed in battle, and the story ends tragically, like Shakespeare's play, with Anne's death and her burial beside Marse Chan.

The Romeo and Juliet model is used again in another story from *In Ole Virginia*, "Unc' Edinburg's Drowndin'." The narrator, much like the one in "Marse Chan," is a bemused sojourner and something of a connoisseur. He is in the story yet not of it; thus he, and the reader as well, is given a full sense of the war and its aftermath yet is never touched by it, never threatened. Again, as in the previous story, there is a second narrator, a faithful servant, Unc' Edinburg, who tells the traveler a tale of star-crossed lovers. As in "Marse Chan," there are strong personal and political differences between these latter-day Montagues and Capulets, and the story ends with a similarly tragic misunderstanding.

In his introduction to the Plantation Edition, Page noted: "The writer feels that he may without impropriety claim that with his devotion for the South, whose life he has tried faithfully to portray, and his pride in the Union, which he has rejoiced to see fully restored in his time, he has never wittingly written a line which he did not hope might tend to bring about a better understanding between the North and the South, and finally lead to a more perfect Union." Certainly no vehicle could have served Page better in this pursuit than the basic model offered by Shakespeare's play, though commercial motives (in addition to patriotic ones) may have figured in Page's reasoning as well. Grace King once discussed with Page the difficulty of getting her work published, and he suggested that she follow his formula: "Get a pretty girl and name her Jeanne, that name always takes! Make her fall in love with a Federal officer and your story will be printed at once! The publishers are right; the public wants love stories. Nothing easier than to write them." *In Ole Virginia* also contains "Meh Lady: A Story of the War," a tale that stands as a transition between Page's stories of tragic love between Southerners and such novels as *Red Rock* (1898), a story of intersectional marriage, the union that symbolizes "a more perfect Union." Wilton, the hero of "Meh Lady," is a Federal officer and only half Virginian. As in the other stories, complications and misunderstandings abound, but Wilton is a successful suitor, unlike the ill-fated Chan and George. Ultimately he is accepted by Meh Lady. They marry,

IN OLE VIRGINIA

OR

MARSE CHAN AND OTHER STORIES

BY

THOMAS NELSON PAGE

NEW YORK
CHARLES SCRIBNER'S SONS
1887

Title page for Page's first book, which, according to Albion Tourgée, helped make the Confederate soldier a "popular hero"

and two fine children ensue, members of a new and presumably more peaceful generation. Perhaps the major difference between this story and the two discussed previously is that here the impediments of family are removed. His is distant, hers is dead. These two lovers work out their destiny alone, without external pressures.

In Ole Virginia achieved for Page a success beyond his own imagining. Within a year of the publication of *In Ole Virginia* the Radical Republican author Albion W. Tourgée was able to say that because of Page's book, "not only is the epoch of the war the favorite field of American fiction today, but the Confederate soldier is the popular hero. Our literature has become not only Southern in type but distinctly Confederate in sympathy." Theodore Gross echoes the majority of modern critics when he notes that "the stories in *In Ole Virginia* represent the author's lasting contribution to American literature. . . . The major themes are formulated and fully realized in this first published work."

Of Page's full-length fictions, *Red Rock* (1898), though flawed, is one of the more successful, and certainly it is his most representative novel, his most sustained and panoramic attempt to vindicate the Reconstruction South. *Red Rock* begins in the "seething ferment . . . before the great explosion in the beginning of the Sixties—that strange decade that changed the civilization of the country." When it comes, the battle is not between the South and the North; as one of Page's characters says, "We are at war now—with the greatest power on earth: the power of universal progress. It is not the North that we shall have to fight, but the world." In chapter 4, "In Which A Long Jump is Taken," the narrator despairs of describing the war itself ("What pen could properly tell the story of those four years," he asks) and notes that "it is what took place after the war rather than what occurred during the struggle that this chronicle is concerned with." As in Page's other novels of the South, the characters consist primarily of sympathetic Southerners, notably Jacquelin Gray of Red Rock, his cousin Steve Allen, and the beautiful Blair Cary. There are also Yankee scoundrels, such as Jonadab Leech of the Freedman's Bureau, and noble Northerners, including Lawrence Middleton, the ranking officer in the district which includes Red Rock. After Middleton

is sent to the Northwest "to keep the Indians down," Leech conspires against the Southerners he hates, and much of *Red Rock* is taken up with his plot to imprison Steve Allen on charges involving Ku Klux Klan activities. Although Allen was a Klan leader only at its very beginning and became a foe of the organization when it turned violent and racist, Leech plans to call Ruth Welch, the daughter of a Union officer, as a witness against Allen. But the two have fallen in love and they marry. The marriage, of course, precludes Ruth's testimony, as a wife may not be forced to testify against her husband. But this marriage has another larger purpose than the rescue of the hero, for it is one of the many intersectional marriages in Page's novels, all designed to lead, according to Page's punning plan for harmony, "to a more perfect Union." The scene in which Steve announces to Jacqueline Gray his intention to marry Ruth Welch begins as Steve is reading Tennyson's *Idylls of the King* under a tree, and the great lovers of legend come to his mind for a moment before thoughts of Ruth dispel them. "A line from Dante flashed through his mind," and then the names of "Launcelot and Guinevere; Tristram and Isolt; Geraint and Enid" occur and are put aside. Steve Allen might have added "Romeo and Juliet" as well, since his and Ruth's story has much in common with that of Shake-

Page in 1917, during his tenure as ambassador to Italy. This photograph is inscribed to his brother, Rosewell Page.

speare's lovers, even if it ends more happily. The love story pleased the majority of contemporary reviewers, but critical opinion of the book as a whole darkens as one moves away from Page's native region and the period in which he wrote. In William Malone Baskervill's *Southern Writers* (1903), for instance, *Red Rock* is praised without qualification, whereas in *A History of American Literature Since 1870* (1922) Fred Lewis Pattee calls the novel weak and says that "the materials are better than the construction." In Edmund Wilson's *Patriotic Gore* (1962), *Red Rock* is described as "Page's most ambitious novel" though ultimately a "boring" one.

In *Harvests of Change: American Literature, 1865-1914*, Jay Martin notes that there are three tendencies on the part of local colorists: to romantically reconstruct the myth of the past, to realistically destroy it, and to embody both of the first two tendencies because of a "need to reconstruct a glorious past, along with a simultaneous recognition that such a paradise never existed." Page was a local colorist of the first type. Page's heroes are completely noble and pious without even minor vices, his villains totally Satanic without even occasional virtues. Romantic to a fault in his unbelievable characterizations, Page is realistic in his attention to such externals as dress, setting, and speech. Unfortunately, his attempts to reproduce with exactitude the details of Southern life result in dialogue that had a certain vogue in Page's day yet which is all but unreadable now. His story "Meh Lady" begins with a character saying "Won' dat Phil go 'stracted when he gits a pike on de een o' dis feller," a sentence that defies comprehension. With a language in which "urr" means "our," "nurr" means "neither," and " 'nurr" means "another," one proceeds as if cracking a code.

Because of this curious mixture of romance and realism, Page's writings are not to be taken as accurate accounts of life during and after the Civil War. On the other hand, they have great value insofar as they define the outlook of Page's own generation. Unable to alter the historical nightmare of the war, Page did what a more conscious artist would have feared to try: he rewrote the imaginary nightmare of *Romeo and Juliet* until it became a pleasant daydream, the misunderstandings smoothed away, the tragic deaths forgotten. The result is not great art, but Page's sustained and widely accepted attempt to substitute his own version of reality for the facts addresses a psychological dimension of history that more objective writings ignore.

References:
William Malone Baskervill, "Thomas Nelson Page," in *Southern Writers: Biographical and Critical Studies*, volume 2 (Nashville & Dallas: Publishing House of the M.E. Church, South, 1903), pp. 120-151;
Michael Flusche, "Thomas Nelson Page: The Quandary of a Literary Gentleman," *Virginia Magazine of History and Biography*, 84 (October 1976): 464-485;
Theodore Gross, *Thomas Nelson Page* (New York: Twayne, 1967);
Harriet Holman, "The Literary Career of Thomas Nelson Page, 1884-1910," Ph.D. dissertation, Duke University, 1947;
David Kirby, *Grace King* (Boston: Twayne, 1980);
Jay Martin, *Harvests of Change: American Literature, 1865-1914* (Englewood Cliffs, N.J.: Prentice-Hall, 1967);
Fred Lewis Pattee, *A History of American Literature Since 1870* (New York: Century, 1922);
Edmund Wilson, *Patriotic Gore: Studies in the Literature of the American Civil War* (New York: Oxford University Press, 1962).

Papers:
There is an extensive collection of Page manuscripts at Duke University and a collection of correspondence, photographs, and documents (pertaining mostly to Page's ambassadorship to Italy) at the College of William and Mary.

David Graham Phillips

(31 October 1867-24 January 1911)

Abe C. Ravitz
California State University, Dominguez Hills

BOOKS: *The Great God Success: A Novel*, as John Graham (New York: Stokes, 1901);

Her Serene Highness: A Novel (New York & London: Harper, 1902);

A Woman Ventures: A Novel (New York: Stokes, 1902);

Golden Fleece: The American Adventures of a Fortune Hunting Earl (New York: McClure, Phillips, 1903; London: Richards, 1903);

The Master Rogue: The Confessions of a Croesus (New York: McClure, Phillips, 1903; London: Richards, 1904);

The Cost (Indianapolis: Bobbs-Merrill, 1904; London: Laurie, 1905);

The Mother-Light (New York: Appleton, 1905);

The Plum Tree (Indianapolis: Bobbs-Merrill, 1905);

The Reign of Gilt (New York: James Pott, 1905; London: Watt, 1905);

The Social Secretary (Indianapolis: Bobbs-Merrill, 1905; London: Gay & Bird, 1907);

The Deluge (Indianapolis: Bobbs-Merrill, 1905);

The Fortune Hunter (Indianapolis: Bobbs-Merrill, 1906);

The Second Generation (New York: Appleton, 1907; London: Amalgamated Press, 1912);

Light-Fingered Gentry (New York: Appleton, 1907; London: Amalgamated Press, 1912);

Old Wives for New: A Novel (New York: Appleton, 1908; London: Newnes, 1917);

The Worth of a Woman: A Play in Four Acts, followed by a Point of Law: A Dramatic Incident (New York: Appleton, 1908);

The Fashionable Adventures of Joshua Craig: A Novel (New York: Appleton, 1909; London: Amalgamated Press, 1911);

The Hungry Heart: A Novel (New York & London: Appleton, 1909; London: Heinemann, 1909);

White Magic: A Novel (New York & London: Appleton, 1910);

The Husband's Story: A Novel (New York & London: Appleton, 1910; London: Newnes, 1917);

The Grain of Dust: A Novel (New York & London: Appleton, 1911; London: Newnes, 1918);

The Conflict: A Novel (New York & London: Appleton, 1911);

The Price She Paid: A Novel (New York & London: Appleton, 1912; London: Newnes, 1920);

George Helm (New York & London: Appleton, 1912);

Degarmo's Wife and Other Stories (New York & London: Appleton, 1913);

Susan Lenox: Her Fall and Rise, 2 volumes (New York & London: Appleton, 1917; London: Pilot, 1949);

The Treason of the Senate (New York: Monthly Review, 1953).

David Graham Phillips is often remembered by historians as the New York crusading journalist at whom Theodore Roosevelt directed his famous "Man with the Muck-Rake" speech of 14 April 1906, when the popular president, angered at Phillips's

David Graham Phillips

attack in *The Treason of the Senate* on Roosevelt's friend Senator Chauncey Depew, assailed "hysterical sensationalism" in the press and deplored what he regarded as indiscriminate, prodigal assaults on men in public life. During those turbulent days when epithets like "Undesirable Citizens, Mollycoddles, Rich Malefactors, Commercial Highwaymen, Dirty Infidels, Paid Prevaricators, and Holders-of-ill-gotten Gain" were an integral part of the nation's emotional landscape, David Graham Phillips wrote twenty-three novels which both illustrated the virtues of rugged individualism and dissected the American sociopolitical scene. He simultaneously clamored for reform of the nation's political system, spoke out strongly in behalf of "The New Woman," and achieved a popular blend of realism and romance in best-selling fictions. As an eloquent social Darwinist, David Graham Phillips, a "star" reporter as well as a widely read novelist, so precisely depicted the ethos of the so-called Strenuous Age that on his death he was eulogized as the "[Theodore] Roosevelt of our literature."

Phillips was born in Madison, Indiana, an Ohio River town, which had in 1867 several paved streets and a curious local diversion: watching the glamorous steamboats pass on their way to the metropolis of Cincinnati. His father, David Graham Phillips, Sr., was a banker who conducted early morning family prayers, and his mother, Margaret Lee Phillips, descended from a distinguished family that included Light-Horse Harry Lee, brought up her children ("Graham," three older sisters and a younger brother) in the old-fashioned way, which included regular home instruction in reading. By the time Graham Phillips was fifteen, the Bible, Dickens, Victor Hugo, Sir Walter Scott and even contemporary dime-novel scribes had become part of his rich, eclectic literary background. Within the family circle Graham developed an attachment to—perhaps even a dependence on—his sister Carolyn, eight years his senior. Their mutual love and devotion continued with a seemingly growing intensity until his death. Carolyn once noted that even as an eight year old her brother was "priest like in his attitude. His understanding was sublime."

In 1882, Phillips, having graduated from Madison High School, left home to attend Asbury College (now DePauw University) at Greencastle, Indiana, where the banker's son began an intensive study of oratory and debate, history and philosophy, politics and religion. Most significant for Phillips at DePauw, however, was his meeting with fellow undergraduate Albert J. Beveridge, a self-made man who later became an illustrious United States senator and powerful advocate of the rugged individualistic point of view. The college association developed into a lifelong friendship, with "Bev's" middle-border Darwinism, that fusion of frontier optimism with survival of the fittest, soon coming to influence Phillips's own opinions. When in 1885 Beveridge graduated, Phillips decided to move on as well, and without taking his degree he left to enroll as a junior at Princeton where, as a major in the arts, he found himself—along with the other eighty-five members of his class—immersed and struggling in the intellectual excitement generated by President James McCosh, a noted scholar of the day who had published widely on such diverse subjects as divine government and realistic philosophy. A dramatic, dogmatic instructor, McCosh took responsibly his charge to impart the whole truth: "I am pleased," he once wrote, "to discover that intelligent Christians are coming round gradually to the views which I have had the courage to publish." While the aggressive president was able to introduce Phillips to the Scottish school of Common-Sense Realism, he made few inroads on the Darwinist thought pattern that Beveridge had instilled in Phillips; in the yearbook Phillips listed "None" as his religious denomination. When he graduated in 1887 he had been thoroughly imprinted by an education of considerable philosophic depth. Nothing in his academic preparation, however, could have augured his immediate and incredible aptitude for newspaper work as a reporter in Cincinnati.

With pencil and pad in hand David Graham Phillips hit the streets of the Queen City. Fresh from Princeton he began learning the craft of writing and developing sympathy with people of all callings and from all walks of life. As early biographer Isaac Marcosson describes it: "He was absorbed in what he was doing. He went from fire to murder; from suicide to political sensation. He talked with policeman, fireman, criminal, cab-driver, actor, politician, capitalist. . . ." Phillips confided to Bailey Millard, editor of *Cosmopolitan*: "I have . . . avoided riding in a carriage or an auto, for I know that the man or woman who does it gets out of sympathy with the masses." Cincinnati soon was too small to contain his talent. In May 1890 Phillips, at a salary of fifteen dollars a week, was hired by Charles A. Dana to the staff of the *New York Sun*. The enthusiastic reporter wrote his father: "Here I am in this great city, and no man, woman, or child cares whether I am dead or alive; but I will make them care before I am done with them."

For the remainder of his life Phillips lived in

New York City and carved for himself a niche as journalist-novelist of considerable reputation. He was a frequent contributor to popular magazines and became "a legend" on Park Row, the street where New York's tabloids were published. He wrote rapidly and compulsively, scrutinizing with such care the fashions and foibles of the day that he came to be regarded by his own description, as America's recording secretary, keeping accurate minutes of the contemporary national experience. From 1894 on, Phillips, who remained a bachelor, lived under the same roof as his sister Carolyn Phillips Frevert, even after she separated from her husband Henry Frevert in 1900. A letter Phillips wrote in 1903 indicates his feeling for his loving sister: "I don't know what I should have done or whatever would become of me if it weren't for [Carolyn]." She had become the overseer and chief critic of his work. She maintained a comprehensive scrapbook of his writings; she encouraged his career steadily forward.

Shortly after he had joined the staff of Dana's *Sun*, Phillips began contributing human-interest pieces to magazines such as *Harper's Weekly*, *Cosmopolitan*, and *McClure's*, where he investigated the subject matter he later came to employ in his novels: the lower depths of big-city life, the psychological pressures inherent in modern marriage, and behind-the-scenes political chicanery from local ward to state house. Before long his work attracted the attention of Joseph Pulitzer, who hired Phillips to the staff of the *New York World*; there, by 1896 the initials D. G. P. had become familiar on the editorial page and were likewise seen frequently under many an office-rigged letter to the editor. Phillips additionally spent time as Pulitzer's London correspondent, as a gossip reporter, and as a self-styled political expert. The Pulitzer brand of journalism quickly claimed Phillips's energy and allegiance: the expose of criminal vice, the war on civic corruption, the crusade against disease and poverty absorbed his interest. Street learning was ultimately the education Phillips came to value most, and with sudden contempt for formal schooling, he observed that in his world of rough-and-tumble journalism there was not to be found "an ignorant professor . . . of some university where little of value is taught or learned." He left Pulitzer's organization determined to write fiction that would unify the senses of the reporter and the sensibility of the reformer.

First, Phillips told his own story. Under the pseudonym John Graham he wrote *The Great God Success* (1901), a loose tale of his entry into and early success in newspaper work, but unlike Phillips him-

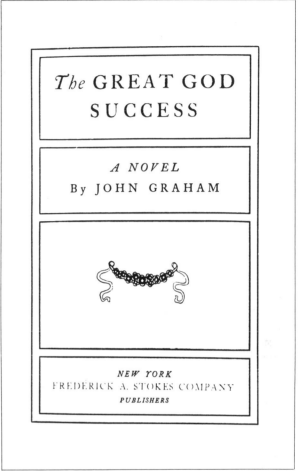

Title page for Phillips's pseudonymous first novel, based on his career as a journalist

self, the hero eventually turns into a rogue who sells out to the Coal Trust and is rewarded with an appointment as an ambassador to France. Most important for Phillips's career, the novel received Pulitzer's warm endorsement and caught the notice of George Horace Lorimer, publisher of the *Saturday Evening Post*, who immediately recruited the former reporter as regular contributor. Until the very end of his career Phillips and the *Post* were a consistent literary amalgamation.

The novels began to flow unceasingly. In 1902 Phillips produced *Her Serene Highness*, a perfumed tale of love and romance between a Chicago art collector and Princess Erica of Zweitenbourg. The tale, though primarily influenced by the romantic epidemic of the era (for novels to be set in the mythical kingdom of Graustark), introduced two motifs familiar in Phillips's fiction: the decadence behind great wealth and the independent woman in revolt. The same year saw the appearance of *A*

Woman Ventures, where Phillips brought a fully emancipated woman into the frenzied world of tabloid journalism, had her undergo a literal baptism of fire while at work covering bitter labor-capital warfare, and potently articulated a consistently developing Darwinist philosophy now being applied to economics as well as society: "Everywhere the law of the survival of the fittest—the best law, after all, in spite of its cruelty."

Next came *Golden Fleece: The American Adventures of a Fortune Hunting Earl* (1903), a piece of superficial satire which was first serialized in the *Post;* to Lorimer's delight Phillips held up to ridicule effete European titled men who prey upon wealthy American women. *The Master Rogue: The Confessions of a Croesus* (1903), on the other hand, indicts an American financial manipulator who without conscience annihilates opposition while he coerces and buys senators. An "inexperienced conscience" permits him easily to travel the pathway of plunder. The design of the David Graham Phillips universe was by now clear: a predatory world marked by vanity and corruption, it is propelled by a vicious plutocracy which quietly condones political marauding, and at the same time it spawns social parasitism. To survive with personal integrity intact by not behaving as man animalized and predatorily victimizing his peers in the struggle was perhaps the most admirable goal one might set. On occasion in the Phillips cosmos, a luminous character—usually drawn from the author's recollection of Albert J. Beveridge—would surpass such a goal by additionally seeking to protect the weak.

David Graham Phillips continued to focus his attention on the business world and its surrounding political arena. *The Cost* (1904), advertised as a "Romance of the Dollar Mark," featured a criminal Wall Street titan whose demeanor of "A wild beast" helps identify the hideous jungle in which he operates. Phillips depicts his death with heavy-handed symbolism: he is strangled by serpentine coils of stockmarket tickertape. In *The Plum Tree* (1905)—serialized in *Success Magazine*—Phillips continued to follow the careers of financial brigands, now up against an inspired political reformer, based on Beveridge, whose destiny is "to break up the mob that is being led on by demagogues disguised as . . . advance agents of prosperity." The metaphoric plum tree glistens with heavily laden boughs of corporate wealth, ready to be plucked by a ruthlessly ambitious speculator, who voices the credo of economic Darwinism: "I have had to use the code of the jungle." Phillips's incisive portrait of the collusion between big business and politics, however, drew a

sharp rebuke from President Roosevelt, who wrote to Lorimer that Phillips was "guilty" of "overstatement," that he "errs in making his big politicians think only of that which is directly to their own pecuniary interest"; and while "almost each individual fact brought forward by Phillips is true by itself . . . these facts are so grouped as to produce a totally false impression."

The ink was hardly dry on the first installment of Thomas Lawson's *Frenzied Finance: The Story of Amalgamated* (1904), a work exposing plunder by captains of industry, when Phillips brought out *The Deluge* (1905), inspired by Lawson's serialized text on disclosures of American capitalism and its "reckless viciousness." "The System" is successfully opposed by Phillips's hero, who precipitates a revolution of "the common man" turned against the monsters of high finance. At this time too Phillips, succumbing to another fin de siecle fashion, tried his hand at utopian fiction with *The Second Generation* (1907), a novel blistered by one critic as "So-

Phillips at work in his sister's Gramercy Park apartment. He characteristically wrote standing up.

cialistic" but lauded by others as Phillips's "strongest." Charting a socioeconomic experiment, not unlike the one Edward Bellamy set up in *Looking Backward* (1888), Phillips's tale portrays a "revolutionary scheme" to have labor participate in management decisions and to have capital and labor exist in a productive, noncompetitive harmony; he verbally punished "luxury-crazy, slave-driving" industrialists.

On the heels of this reformism came *Light-Fingered Gentry* (1907), Phillips's final examination of business. It is an incendiary expose of life-insurance fraud, a novel described by an anonymous reviewer in the *Outlook* as one in which "the yellow of the sensational journalist and the dismal black of the chronic pessimist are laid on with a prodigal brush." Under a sanctimonious stewardship, the Mutual Association Against Old Age and Death specializes in "robbing dead bodies [while] picking the pockets of calico mourning dresses." Opponents are branded as "anarchists" endeavoring to "tear down the social structure" of America. B. O. Flower in the *Arena* pointed up the timeliness of Phillips's book: "America's great Monte Carlo cannot continue as it has prospered during recent decades, and free institutions survive or the people escape the slavery of extortion, of remorseless greed."

The remainder of David Graham Phillips's literary production addressed itself to an examination of "The New Woman." Exploring this mystique he even wrote a play, *The Worth of a Woman*, which enjoyed a brief Broadway run early in 1908. In his preface to the drama Phillips stated the hypothesis he was to carry through the rest of his work on the subject: "Don't look on woman as mere female, but as human being. Remember that she has a mind and heart as well as a body." Phillips thus simultaneously studied two sides of the female sensibility: he looked at the American woman as parasite aspiring to a genteel, sterile leisure supported by her hard-working husband, and he looked at the woman who revolted against the stereotyped image of decorative lady and sought a place for herself as an independent entity free from the artificial trappings of the drawing room.

In *Old Wives for New* (1908) and *The Husband's Story* (1910) Phillips detailed manners and morals among plutocrats and their wives as they travel the road to American divorce courts. The former novel follows the decay of a woman of "luxury" whose complacency precipitates the deterioration of her body and mind. The latter tale traces the "gaudy gaddings" of another lady of leisure whose afflic-

tions include "social climbing," "toadyism," and "snobbishness." After her divorce she marries a worthless but titled foreigner. The American husbands of these women are genial, but shady, business men who feel that the only salvation for men and women in marriage is for both sexes to follow the advice of Roosevelt and pursue the strenuous life. Still, Phillips, while focusing on one so-called "battle of the sexes," never minimized those ever present Darwinist forces on hand to direct human behavior: "The truth is, we are like flocks of birds in a high wind. Some of us fly more steadily than others, some are quite beaten down. . . ."

A woman of refinement in Washington society is aligned against a senator (another derivative of Beveridge) fresh from the Great Plains in *The Fashionable Adventures of Joshua Craig* (1909) while *The Conflict* (1911) juxtaposes a plutocrat's daughter and a radical visionary socialist with whom she falls in love. Of a more serious nature are *The Grain of Dust* (1911) and *The Price She Paid* (1912) where Phillips dealt honestly with the woman who must earn her own way as well as deal with the obstacles facing women alone in early twentieth-century urban America. The alternatives for survival, Phillips vividly showed, were not numerous.

On the afternoon of 23 January 1911, Phillips left the Gramercy Park apartment for a stroll to the nearby Princeton Club to pick up his mail. He was accosted on the street by Fitzhugh Coyle Goldsborough, a professional violinist who had become obsessed with the notion that David Graham Phillips's novels, often reflecting real people and real events of the day, were little more than insidiously veiled attacks on the Goldsborough family of Washington, D.C. In his diary the distraught musician had characterized Phillips as "an enemy to society. He is my enemy." He had been silently shadowing Phillips for several days, and now he stepped before the unsuspecting novelist and fired several shots at short range into his body. Goldsborough immediately turned the revolver on himself and committed suicide. Phillips lingered one day; he died the following evening at Bellevue Hospital. One critic lamented that we had lost "the most distinguished American novelist" of our time.

Susan Lenox: Her Fall and Rise (1917), published in book form under the supervision of Phillips's sister Carolyn Frevert five years after the author's death, is a virtual compendium of his literary thought. The book achieved quick notoriety on its release when the *Boston Transcript* described it as "an extremely offensive addition to the literature of pornography" and the *New York Times* observed that "the story is . . . repulsive to the last degree [and is] a work of such thoroughly vicious romanticism masquerading as realism." John S. Sumner of the New York Society for the Suppression of Vice called 100 pages of the book "obscene" and demanded their

David Graham Phillips

SUSAN LENOX
HER FALL AND RISE

VOLUME I

WITH A PORTRAIT
OF THE AUTHOR

D. APPLETON AND COMPANY
NEW YORK   LONDON
1917

Title page for Phillips's most significant novel, which he worked on during the last seven years of his life

removal. The *Bookman*, however, favorably compared *Susan Lenox* to *The Scarlet Letter*. The novel is a straightforward deterministic tale of a woman who, abandoned by her family, must try to survive in the city. A traumatic marriage, her inability to make a living, and the hardness of fate in showing no respite for the victim, all lead Susan to affiliate herself with a series of exploitative men. She sinks into prostitution and drug addiction, and is brutalized, narcotized, and hopeless. Then, helped by fate and sheer accident, this unbelievable woman tenaciously turns her life completely around and finally reaches far beyond mere survival; she is free and she is a success. She becomes a Nietzschean *Ubermensch*, a

force herself. In a graphic picture of life in the depths, Phillips recalled all of his newspaper experiences following leads on New York's Lower East Side. Susan, blending common sense with her determinism, listened to a Salvation Army worker who warned, "The wages of sin is death"; the liberated Susan Lenox retorted, "The wages of weakness is death . . . but the wages of sin, well, it's sometimes a house on Fifth Avenue."

When David Graham Phillips wrote *The Reign of Gilt* (1905) and *The Treason of the Senate* (serialized in 1906) he delivered in the eye-catching vocabulary of tabloid journalism his fused aesthetic and ethical positions, wherein the ethic generated the aesthetic. He wrote of "Cast-Compellers," "Pauper-Making," "Snobism" [sic], "Democracy's Dynamo," and the "Common Man." He deplored the plutocratic "money-maniacs" in their marble palaces while he scathed "political and sociological quacks" who rely on "poets and poetical historians." Yet, Phillips himself was essentially a romancer, like Frank Norris, who similarly had realized that a "good read" lay in human warfare and whose view of American life fixed his philosophy on the struggle for survival. Phillips, too, tried, often unsuccessfully, to avoid the pessimism inherent in that point of view by tempering his fiction with elements of escapism. He was clearly one of the best novelists to come out of the muckrake movement, and, more important, his fiction gave American middle-class life and ideals serious treatment. Before Sinclair Lewis's *Babbitt* (1922), in Phillips's novels pedestrian materialism and a compromised idealism fuse in fictional harmony. Though often a captive of his own rugged individualism, David Graham Phillips was a faithful laureate of his times, the strenuous age.

Play:

The Worth of a Woman, New York, Madison Square Theatre, 12 February 1908.

Periodical Publications:

The Treason of the Senate, *Cosmopolitan*, 40 (March 1906): 487-502; 40 (April 1906): 628-638; 41 (May 1906): 3-12; 41 (June 1906): 123-132; 41 (July 1906): 267-276; 41 (August 1906): 368-377; 41 (September 1906): 525-535; 41 (October 1906): 627-636; 42 (November 1906): 77-84.

Biographies:

Isaac Marcosson, *David Graham Phillips: His Life and*

Times (New York: Dodd, Mead, 1932);

Eric F. Goldman, "David Graham Phillips: Victorian Critic of Victorianism," in *The Lives of Eighteen from Princeton*, edited by Willard Thorp (Princeton: Princeton University Press, 1946), pp. 318-332;

Louis Filler, *Voice of Democracy: A Critical Biography of David Graham Phillips, Journalist, Novelist, Progressive* (University Park: Pennsylvania State University Press, 1978).

References:

Elizabeth Janeway, Afterword to *Susan Lenox* (Carbondale & Edwardsville: Southern Illinois University Press, 1977);

Abe C. Ravitz, *David Graham Phillips* (New York: Twayne, 1966).

Papers:

Most of Phillips's papers are in the Princeton University Library.

William Sydney Porter
(O. Henry)
(11 September 1862-5 June 1910)

Eugene Current-Garcia
Auburn University

SELECTED BOOKS: *Cabbages and Kings* (New York: McClure, Phillips, 1904; London: Hodder & Stoughton, 1916);

The Four Million (New York: McClure, Phillips, 1906; London: Nash, 1916);

The Trimmed Lamp (New York: McClure, Phillips, 1907; London: Hodder & Stoughton, 1916);

Heart of the West (New York: McClure, 1907; London: Nash, 1916);

The Voice of the City (New York: McClure, 1908; London: Nash, 1916);

The Gentle Grafter (New York: McClure, 1908; London: Nash, 1916);

Roads of Destiny (New York: Doubleday, Page, 1909; London: Nash, 1916);

Options (New York & London: Harper, 1909; London: Nash, 1916);

Strictly Business (New York: Doubleday, Page, 1910; London: Nash, 1916);

Whirligigs (New York: Doubleday, Page, 1910; London: Hodder & Stoughton, 1916);

Sixes and Sevens (Garden City: Doubleday, Page, 1911; London: Hodder & Stoughton, 1916);

Rolling Stones (Garden City: Doubleday, Page, 1912; London: Nash, 1916);

Waifs and Strays (Garden City: Doubleday, Page, 1917; London: Hodder & Stoughton, 1920);

O. Henryana (Garden City: Doubleday, Page, 1920);

Postscripts, edited by Florence Stratton (New York &

London: Harper, 1923);

O. Henry Encore, edited by Mary S. Harrell (Dallas: Upshaw, 1936; New York: Doubleday, Doran, 1939; London: Hodder & Stoughton, 1939).

COLLECTIONS: *The Complete Writings of O. Henry*, 14 volumes (Garden City: Doubleday, Page, 1917);

The Biographical Edition, 18 volumes (Garden City: Doubleday, Doran, 1929);

The Complete Works of O. Henry, 2 volumes (Garden City: Doubleday, 1953).

When William Sydney Porter had his first book, *Cabbages and Kings* (1904), published he had only six more years to live. But, with his identity hidden beneath the legendary pen name O. Henry, the fame of his short stories was already firmly established in New York. By then he had written and had published in several magazines at least half of the nearly 300 stories that would fill eight more volumes before he died—and still another seven published within the two decades after his death. These sixteen collections of stories, however, were only a prelude to the avalanche of later editions, authorized and pirated, that would bring his works, in English and translated into dozens of foreign languages, to readers throughout the world as well as in the United States and other English-speaking countries. Since this process of dissemination is still going on, there is no way of estimating how many separate editions, let alone copies, of O. Henry's tales have been printed and distributed to date; but they have probably brought O. Henry's appealing image of America, however outdated, to tens of millions of foreigners. Yet, paradoxically, despite the worldwide popularity that O. Henry's writings still enjoy, the experiences and reputation of their author, William Sydney Porter, remain shrouded in pathos and mystery. Porter's life was fraught with pain, grief, and humiliation—ironic opposites to that joyous response to life's hardships which typifies so many of O. Henry's surprise endings. It can be argued, indeed, that O. Henry's enchanting fictive world offered a welcome refuge from Porter's unhappy life. Yet the psychic wounds of his childhood and his adult follies enriched his fiction.

Born in 1862, the second son of Dr. Algernon Sidney Porter and Mary Jane Virginia Swaim Porter, Will (as he was known to everyone) spent the first twenty years of his life in Greensboro, North Carolina. Shortly after the birth of a third son in 1865, his mother died, and with her death his father's world collapsed. Dr. Porter gave up his

home, moved to his widowed mother's house, and gradually abandoned his practice. The discipline of his two sons, Shirley and Will (the youngest, David, had died in infancy), was taken over by his mother and his maiden sister Evelina. "Miss Lina" was a forceful disciplinarian who served not only as Will's surrogate mother for the next seventeen years but also as the best teacher he ever had.

In the private primary school that Miss Lina kept as one means of providing the family income young Will learned respect for the written word. She inculcated in her young charges a love of learning by making them active participants in the learning process: among the devices she employed was that of beginning an original story herself and then calling upon each of her pupils in turn to contribute a part. And regularly throughout the school year she read to them, guiding and stimulating their minds through the example of good literature. Without question, her enthusiasm and discipline were the primary forces that aroused Porter's youthful passion for reading and his later desire to write.

Porter left his aunt's school at age seventeen to work in his Uncle William Clarkson Porter's drugstore, where he found an educational resource second only to that of Miss Lina's. During his three years as a pharmacist's apprentice, Porter mastered pharmaceutical techniques sufficiently to earn a state license as a practicing pharmacist in 1881. But most important for his future career as a writer, during these drugstore years he was meeting people and storing up countless impressions of their personal oddities, mannerisms, gestures, and modes of speech which were later to be reflected, along with his expert use of professional terminology, in many of his stories, notably such well-known tales as "Let Me Feel Your Pulse," "At Arms With Morpheus," "A Ramble in Aphasia," and "The Love-Philtre of Ikey Schoenstein."

In 1882 Porter left Greensboro and went to Texas, where he spent the next fifteen years, first on a cattle ranch near the Mexican border; then he served briefly as a bookkeeper and drug clerk in Austin. Following his marriage to nineteen-year-old Athol Estes Roach on 5 July 1887, he worked as a draftsman in the Texas Land Office for four years. Porter's years in the land office were probably his happiest, for his wife was a young woman of wit and high spirits, who is said to have stimulated and encouraged him in his ambition to become a writer and who shared his joys on receiving the first small checks his published skits occasionally brought in. But Athol Porter was not physically strong: her first child, a son born in 1888, lived but a few hours; and she herself survived the birth of her second child, Margaret, in 1889 by only seven years of steadily declining health. Soon after Porter's job at the land office folded in January 1891, he went to work as teller in the First National Bank.

While Porter worked as a bank teller he continued writing skits and short sketches; and in March 1894 he fulfilled a long-felt aim to publish them in his own humor paper by buying a cheap printing press and the rights to a local scandal sheet, the *Iconoclast*. Porter renamed the paper the *Rolling Stone*, changed it from a monthly to a weekly, and, while holding down a full-time job, managed to fill its eight pages each week with humorous squibs and satirical barbs on persons and events of local interest, most of them written, even set in type, by himself. Though never a commercial success, the *Rolling Stone* survived a full year, attaining a peak circulation of 1,500; but as Porter worked tirelessly to keep it rolling, the little paper gradually dragged him deeper into debt. Striving to shore up its sagging prospects, he borrowed heavily from his father-in-law and other friends; sometime during the year he also began taking funds he needed from the bank and altering his accounts with the hope that he could readjust them later upon replacing the money. When the shortages were discovered, Porter was obliged to give up his job in December 1894 and ordered to appear before a grand jury the following July on charges of embezzlement.

While awaiting trial Porter still tried futilely to keep the *Rolling Stone* alive, but the last issue of the humor sheet appeared on 30 March 1895 and was soon forgotten until O. Henry's fame a few decades later made it a collector's item. In this ephemeral little paper are to be found the origins of his later themes, plots, methods, and style. Porter continued developing these talents later in 1895 when, the grand jury having apparently closed the case in his favor, he took a job as a fill-in writer for the *Houston Post* and soon began running a daily feature column, "Some Postscripts," which resembled the kind of anecdotal humor he had written for the *Rolling Stone*. For the *Post* he also wrote longer sketches, many of them embryonic foreshadowings of his later, more famous stories. In the nearly sixty pieces identified as Porter's work, his facility for ringing changes on the familiar O. Henry themes of mistaken identity, false pretense, misplaced devotion, nobility in disguise, and the bitter irony of fate are plainly visible, along with such sentimental character types as the sensitive tramp, the ill-starred lovers, the starving artist, and the gentle grafter. Both

Porter in his teller's cage at the First National Bank of Austin, from which he embezzled funds to subsidize his humorous weekly, the Rolling Stone

the basic structure and tone of his stories, as well as the attitudes responsible for them were being shaped in the *Post* sketches.

In February 1896 the embezzlement case was reopened. He was arrested in Houston and obliged to face trial within six months. Despite the goodwill and support of friends in both Houston and Austin, he prepared no defense but instead fled the country, pausing first for a few weeks in New Orleans and then sailing to Honduras, where he remained for the rest of the year. His experiences in Honduras, like his others elsewhere, are veiled in legend and myth, the most romantic versions of which are presented in his own stories. Nearly thirty of these stories, written later, appeared in various popular magazines, and about twenty of them, reworked and tied together loosely, were published in 1904 as his first book, *Cabbages and Kings*. As a record of what actually happened to Porter they are wholly unreliable; but one of their special artistic merits, shared by most of his other stories as well, is their high concentration of realistic detail, captured chiefly in descriptive and dialogue passages. It is possible that Porter planned to remain in Honduras indefinitely and hoped to bring his wife and child to

Athol, Margaret, and William Porter, circa 1895

stories written and published in periodicals during this period (beginning with "Georgia's Ruling" in 1900), many others published later grew out of anecdotes and yarns Porter heard from his fellow prisoners. The Jeff Peters stories in *The Gentle Grafter* (1908), as well as many others involving the exploits of Texas outlaws and Mexican bandits in *Heart of the West* (1907), *Roads of Destiny* (1909), *Options* (1909), and still other volumes, came from the same sources. The most famous of them all was "A Retrieved Reformation," the tale of a light-fingered safecracker, Jimmy Valentine, first published in *Cosmopolitan* in April 1903. The story was dramatized with phenomenal success in 1910 at Wallack's Theatre in New York with Norman Hackett playing the lead. Hackett later took the play on the road; eventually "Alias Jimmy Valentine" appeared in many motion picture versions.

Porter entered the Ohio Penitentiary an amateur, but thanks to dedicated effort he emerged three years later as O. Henry, the professional literary artist. When he left the prison he had but nine more years to live, years that would be packed with personal triumphs, bringing him to the pinnacle of success as the self-anointed "Caliph of Bagdad-on-the-Subway." Yet, they were also to be years of suffering, loneliness, want, and guilt-ridden fear, as he tried vainly to elude the shadow of his past and to meet, through writing, his insatiable need for money to provide an expensive private education for Margaret Porter and to support a second, unsatisfactory marriage, hastily undertaken in 1907; as well as to satisfy his spendthrift indulgence in easy living, lavish gratuities, gambling, and alcohol.

After a brief hitch in Pittsburgh, during which he published nearly a dozen stories in such popular magazines as *Ainslee's*, *Munsey's*, and *Smart Set*, Porter went to New York in the spring of 1902. Quickly becoming an anonymous habitue of hole-in-corner hangouts and garish restaurants, he secluded himself in out-of-the-way hotels; prowled endlessly through New York streets to savor the varied color and texture of the city's life; but, fortified by his two-bottle average daily intake of alcohol, he also turned out the many stories (often six or more appeared simultaneously in different magazines) that soon made everyone wonder who O. Henry was. Porter's background had provided him a great variety of colorful types and adventures which, along with many new ones, he now swiftly transformed into the even more beguiling exploits of a multitude of fictive characters in O. Henry's glittering tales. The range of Porter's experience, from the provin-

live with him, at least until the statute of limitations might dispel his troubles at home. But he had to acknowledge the hopelessness of this plan when news that Athol Porter was dying obliged him to return in January 1897 and to face trial.

Ironically, it was also the year that first brought Porter a foretaste of the national fame to come when in December the McClure Company accepted his story "The Miracle of Lava Canyon"; but Athol would not live to know of this good fortune. She died on 25 July 1897. In February 1898 Porter was convicted of embezzling over $5,500 and of having attempted through flight to evade prosecution. He was given the lightest sentence possible under the prevailing terms of the law—a term of five years, which his good behavior as Prisoner Number 30664 in the Ohio Penitentiary at Columbus would reduce to three.

Humiliated by his imprisonment, Porter kept up an elaborate pretense in a long series of charming letters to young Margaret Porter (who was never told the real reason for his absence), and he also produced fourteen tales that bear the unmistakable stamp of the O. Henry style. While there are various versions of how and when Porter took his famous pen name, "O. Henry" was born during Porter's three-year stretch in prison. Besides the fourteen

cial limitations of boyhood in an embittered Reconstruction South to ultimate triumph in New York, seemed limitless as more and still more of O. Henry's stories appeared in print—113 of them in the weekly *New York Sunday World* alone between 1903 and 1905, and at least 25 longer ones published during the same period in monthly magazines such as *Everybody's*, *McClure's*, and *Munsey's*.

Appropriately enough, Porter's fame—as O. Henry—is most widely associated with his tales of New York's "four million," roughly the population of the metropolis in 1906, and shrewdly chosen as the title of his second collection of tales in response to Ward McAllister's claim in 1892 that "there are only about 400 people in New York society." For Porter's assertion that four million New Yorkers were well worth noticing in print touched a democratic chord that appealed to people everywhere. During his residence in New York he

CABBAGES
AND KINGS

BY

O. HENRY

NEW YORK
McCLURE, PHILLIPS & CO.
MCMIV

*Title page for Porter's first book, a collection of Latin American
adventure stories drawing on his experiences
as a fugitive in Honduras*

produced more than 140 stories (virtually half his total output), based on the appearance and behavior of the throngs he observed daily in shops and offices, restaurants and theaters, on street corners, park benches, and tenement fire escapes. He could select two or three individuals who had caught his fancy, invent imaginary situations and predicaments for them, and work out ingeniously unexpected solutions for their problems which rarely failed to satisfy his grateful readers. New York challenged the adventurous author to record its true voice and to penetrate its mystery; and also to show others that real worth and beauty were to be found even beneath Coney Island's spangled temples, since they too "offered saving and apposite balm and satisfaction to the restless human heart." O. Henry eagerly accepted the challenge and thus captured the essence of New York in story after story, quintessentially in such a pair of perennial favorites as "The Gift of the Magi" and "The Furnished Room," representing the polar opposites of joy and sadness with which his imagination clothed the domestic life of average New Yorkers.

When *The Four Million* appeared in 1906, Porter's fame was assured; besides strong public acceptance, this collection of twenty-five stories also received some favorable notice from serious critics in the *Atlantic Monthly* and the *Bookman*, who began comparing O. Henry to de Maupassant and other eminent writers. Porter could be sure that further volumes of his stories would be noticed, and these, indeed, appeared fairly regularly during his remaining years and after his death. In 1907 and 1908, *The Trimmed Lamp* and *The Voice Of The City* brought to seventy-five his total of New York stories in book form. Also published during these same years were *Heart of the West* and *The Gentle Grafter*, containing the tales based on Porter's experiences in Texas and in prison. In 1909 two volumes of stories with various settings, *Roads Of Destiny* and *Options*, appeared and another, *Strictly Business*—containing twenty-two more New York stories plus "A Municipal Report"—was published in 1910 shortly before Porter's death. More collections were published after his death.

Toward the end of 1907, however, though Porter's stories were in great demand, he was on the verge of a breakdown. Only 11 new stories were published in 1907 as against 19 in 1906 and 120 in the two years before that. Since his need for money was greater than ever following his marriage to Sara Lindsay Coleman, he drove himself remorselessly, producing 29 new stories in 1908 for an income of about $14,000; but the income was still insufficient for his lavish life-style. The strains and tensions in his marriage deepened as his health and energies declined. By the summer of 1909 all attempts to maintain a normal family life were abandoned, and, his health shattered, Porter could no longer summon up enough energy in a week to finish a short story which, a few years before, he could have written off in several hours. Virtually an invalid during the spring of 1910, he kept on trying to write until he collapsed on 3 June and was taken to the Polyclinic Hospital, where he succumbed two days later to cirrhosis of the liver. Owing thousands of dollars advanced to him by his father-in-law and his publishers, he died a pauper.

The "O. Henry Story," as it came in time to be recognized and admired, owed much of its popular appeal to Porter's sophisticated updating of two types of short fiction which had flourished in magazines and newspapers during the decades immediately preceding and following the Civil War:

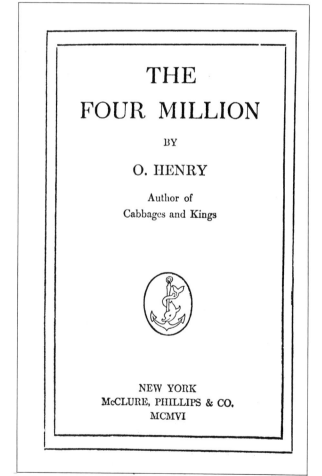

Title page for Porter's first collection of New York stories. The title reflects his notion that everyone in New York had a story worth telling.

namely, the boisterous tall tale of the Old Southwest frontier, and the more sentimental, romantic adventure story of the postwar local-color movement. During his long apprenticeship in Texas, Porter taught himself how to combine the most attractive features of both types by imitating and writing parodies or burlesques of other well-known writers' works and by turning his own personal encounters into farfetched legends. Experimenting with techniques and developing an individual style, he worked over in these sketches familiar old chestnuts like the disguise or imposter motif; and he presented such motifs in conjunction with the theme of disparity between rich and poor and the idea that destiny or fate imposes inescapable roles on the individual. This sense of determinism is treated, both seriously and comically, in many of his early pieces.

During Porter's three years in prison and the next two while getting his bearings in Pittsburgh and New York, he wrote about half of his eighty Western stories (excluding those published earlier in the *Houston Post* and *Rolling Stone*) that he produced throughout his career. Some two-thirds of the total number are stories with settings laid in Texas and Latin America, but virtually all of them reflect the conventional images associated with the "wild West." Despite realistic, specific details, the colorful characters presented in these stories are invariably romanticized: their actions are governed by a few basic passions—love, hate, fear, greed—as befitting a simplistic dichotomy of "good guys" and "bad guys." The prevailing situation in most of them is a variant of the boy-meets-girl problem, involving either rivalry between two men for the possession of a woman, or barriers between a man and a woman which, until removed by an unforeseen turn of events near the end, prevent a satisfactory resolution of the problem. Other situations concern the reformation or rehabilitation of criminals, or the opposing forces of crime and authority. O. Henry became increasingly skilled in setting up tightly knit plots with breathless tensions relieved in last-minute, quick reversals.

In his Western stories, O. Henry brilliantly shifted and rearranged pieces of his "cops-and-robbers" pattern, sometimes humorously, as in "A Call Loan" and "Friends in San Rosario," both of which dramatize the lax banking laws that victimized Porter himself by showing how they could be circumvented through the collusion of friendly bankers. And sometimes the pattern could be brutal, as in "The Caballero's Way," which combines the revenge and infidelity motifs in a gruesome plot involving the deadly Cisco Kid, O. Henry's most attractive villain, who "killed for the love of it— because he was quick-tempered—to avoid arrest— for his own amusement—any reason that came to his mind would suffice." The Cisco Kid must avenge the insult his honor has suffered from his mistress, Tonia Perez, who has conspired to turn him in to her new lover, Sandridge, the Texas Ranger who has been pursuing him; but his method of paying off her unfaithfulness is the "caballero's way" of tricking Sandridge into performing the dirty work instead. Coldly narrated, and almost totally free of sticky sentimentality, "The Caballero's Way" is a brilliant performance. Despite the liberal doses of "Western corn" in most of these tales, the plotting in them is often admirable, even more impressive because O. Henry repeatedly reworks hackneyed situations based on primitive forms of conflict and adventure.

The basic themes dramatized in all his later stories are fundamentally the same as those underlying the earlier ones. The four themes that recur most often have to do with pretense and reversal of fortune, discovery and initiation through adventure, the city as playground for the imagination, and the basic yearning of all humanity. The theme of pretense—the desire to pose as what one is not, if only for a few brief moments, and regardless of the price exacted—is the most persistent in nearly all O. Henry's stories from the earliest to the last few he left unfinished at his death. Yet in his later stories, O. Henry occasionally managed to tie it in brilliantly with the other three themes, as in his subtle response in "The Duel" to the implications of the city's glowing lights seen at midnight from a hotel window high above: "There arose the breath of gaiety unrestrained, of love, of hate, of all the passions that man can know. There below him lay all things, good or bad, that can be brought from the four corners of the earth to instruct, please, thrill, enrich, despoil, elevate, cast down, nurture, or kill. Thus the flavor of it came to him and went into his blood."

Within a decade after his death O. Henry's popularity had soared to unprecedented heights, and even scholarly critics such as Carl Van Doren, Archibald Henderson, and Hyder Rollins were praising him as one of the great masters of modern English literature. His writings became the norm against which other short stories were judged. Thanks to such mounting praise, his name was the inevitable choice when in 1919 Doubleday began publishing a selection of the year's best stories by American writers in American periodicals. To have a story published in *O. Henry Memorial Award Prize Stories* symbolized preeminence in the field, because his work stood—for the time being at least—as the highest standard of what the short story was meant to be.

By the mid-1920s, however, the O. Henry vogue began to wane as critics such as F. L. Pattee and N. Bryllion Fagin denounced the superficiality and falseness in his stories and his failure, as they saw it, to take himself and his art seriously. They felt, and subsequent generations of critics have agreed, that O. Henry's brilliant technical skills were misapplied. Over all his work, Fagin wrote, "there is the unmistakable charm of the master trickster, of a facile player with incidents and words," but while O. Henry has been ignored by academics, his stories are still read.

What contemporary critics tend to ignore is that O. Henry's techniques in isolated instances are less important than his technique as a whole; his individual imperfections and inadequacies are less significant than his pervasive literary personality. Moreover, his individual techniques, however limited and tricksterish, turn out to be quite impressive; carefully examined, they reveal a subtle artistry that Poe himself would have admired. The element of surprise or wonder that lies at the core of O. Henry's art, the motivating power instilled in virtually all his tricky endings even when shamelessly based on sheer coincidence, is more than just facile legerdemain. More often than not the surprise endings are logically contrived within the framework of the narrative. While the extraordinary compression of O. Henry's dialogue and descriptive details often trips the unwary reader into making wrong assumptions, his wit and verbal trickery, his fondness for puns, word coinages, sophistries, slang, and malapropisms of all sorts, appropriately sprinkled in the speech of all his romanticized types—even the dregs of humanity—make the characters seem authentic, funny, and important at the same time. Like Shakespeare and Sheridan, he enjoyed tampering with standard idioms; and his familiarity with their works, as well as with the ancient classics, is evidenced in the hundreds of sly allusions to them casually dropped into his stories.

O. Henry's typically romantic approach to life willfully chooses to ignore many sordid facts, yet there is something indestructibly appealing in the romanticist's creed which the world cherishes and clings to, and that is what explains O. Henry's hold on the world's reading public. The reader knows very well that things do not work out in real life as they do in O. Henry's stories, but often he would like to believe they might. Porter knew that too; he expressed it best, ironically, with a tribute to Milton's *Lycidas* in "Let Me Feel Your Pulse," the last story he completed just before he died. This story concludes allegorically that the only cure for human ills lies in the imagination: "What rest more remedial than to sit with Amaryllis in the shade, and. . . ?"—Amaryllis, symbol of love and poetic release since the days of Theocritus.

Letters:

Letters to Lithopolis, from O. Henry to Mabel Wagnalls (Garden City: Doubleday, Page, 1922).

Bibliography:

Paul S. Clarkson, *A Bibliography of William Sydney Porter* (Caldwell, Idaho: Caxton, 1938).

Biography:

Gerald Langford, *Alias O. Henry: A Biography of William Sydney Porter* (New York: Macmillan, 1957).

References:

Edward C. Echols, "O. Henry's 'Shaker of Attic Salt,' " *Classical Journal*, 43 (October 1947-May 1948): 488-489; "O. Henry and the Classics—II," *Classical Journal*, 44 (October 1948-May 1949): 209-210;

N. Bryllion Fagin, *Short Story Writing: An Art or a Trade?* (New York: Seltzer, 1923), pp. 36-42;

William B. Gates, "O. Henry and Shakespeare," *Shakespeare Association Bulletin*, 19 (January 1944): 20-25;

Gilbert Millstein, "O. Henry's New Yorkers and Today's," *New York Times Magazine*, 9 September 1962, pp. 36-38, 132-138;

F. L. Pattee, *The Development of the American Short Story* (New York: Harper, 1923), pp. 357-376;

William Saroyan, "O What a Man Was O. Henry," *Kenyon Review*, 24 (1967): 671-675.

Papers:

Greensboro Public Library, Greensboro, North Carolina contains the most complete collection of Porter's papers.

Frederic Remington
(4 October 1861-26 December 1909)

Ben Merchant Vorpahl
University of Georgia

*SELECTED BOOKS: *Pony Tracks* (New York: Harper, 1895);
Crooked Trails (New York & London: Harper, 1898);
Stories of Peace and War (New York & London: Harper, 1899);
Sun Down Leflare (New York & London: Harper, 1899);
Men With The Bark On (New York & London: Harper, 1900);
John Ermine of the Yellowstone (New York & London: Macmillan, 1902);
The Way of An Indian (New York: Fox, Duffield, 1906; London: Gay & Bird, 1906).

*This list excludes collections of Remington's art work.

Frederic Remington is remembered mostly as a painter, sculptor, and illustrator of western American subjects. His depictions of such figures as cowboys, frontiersmen, and Indians, many of which appeared in large national magazines such as *Harper's Monthly* and *Collier's* during his lifetime, continue to be popular. However, Remington was also a writer of essays, short fiction, and novels, which complement his paintings and sculptures, elucidating the darker side of Remington's complex thought. In these writings the settlement of the American West appears as a metaphor for diminishment and loss.

Remington was born at Canton, New York, a village not far from the St. Lawrence River, some six months after the beginning of the Civil War. His mother, Clara Sackrider Remington, was the daughter of a local hardware merchant. His father, Seth Pierre Remington, had founded the town's first newspaper in 1856, when he was about nineteen years old. Both sides of the family came from

sturdy Protestant stock. Shortly after Frederic's birth, Seth Pierre Remington left home to become an officer in the Union army. He served mostly in Virginia and Maryland, and did not return to Canton until his son was nearly six years old. During this time, Frederic Remington and his mother lived with her parents in Canton, where news of the war was anxiously received in newspapers and magazines. Seth Pierre Remington returned to Canton in 1867 and resumed his editorial duties, but without notable success, although Frederic admired him as a war hero.

Remington was thirteen when his family moved to nearby Ogdensburg, on the St. Lawrence River, where his father was appointed a customs officer at the port. There, Frederic Remington learned hunting, fishing, and woodcraft, and began to discover his artistic talent. Many of the pictures he made during his Ogdensburg years represented impressions he got from his reading, which in-

cluded the journals of Lewis and Clark, James Fenimore Cooper's Leatherstocking Tales, Washington Irving's accounts of the western prairies and mountains, and contemporary narratives of westering in magazines and popular books. He briefly attended the Vermont Episcopal Institute in Burlington, Vermont, in 1875. Eighteen seventy-six, the year he was sent to Highland Military Academy in Worcester, Massachusetts, to prepare for college, also marked Sitting Bull's massacre of General George Custer's troops at Little Big Horn Creek in Montana, an event that captured Remington's imagination at that time and held it. Although the mature artist and writer would address many subjects and events he had witnessed at first hand, he would never leave behind him the adventures he vicariously experienced as a youthful reader.

Remington entered the Yale School of the Fine Arts in 1878, acting against the advice of his parents, who wanted him to take a business course. He disliked his studies, and, after his father died early in 1880, he left the university. He spent the next five years in an unsuccessful search for a vocation. He went West in 1881 and visited the Custer battlefield site in Montana. When he came into his inheritance in 1883, he bought a small ranch near Peabody, Kansas, where he tried unsuccessfully to raise sheep. He sold this property in 1884 and promptly lost the money in unwise investments he made at Kansas City. That same year he married Eva Caten, a young woman from Gloversville, New York, whom he had courted since about 1880, when he met her at a county fair at Ogdensburg. With his marriage and the loss of his inheritance, he could no longer afford to be a vagabond, but his efforts to earn money by doing free-lance illustrations for eastern magazines did not seem promising in 1884. Early the following summer Eva left Kansas City, where the newlyweds had set up housekeeping, and returned to her parents in Gloversville, New York.

Remington spent the summer of 1885 sketching Indians and soldiers in southern Arizona, where the hostile Apache chief Geronimo had been conducting sporadic raids against white settlers for about five years. The pictures he made were energetic but crude, and when he went to New York City that fall, he had trouble selling them to magazine editors. He even became a student at the Art Students League; but his inability to sell his work ceased quickly, after U. S. and Mexican troops escalated their campaigns against Geronimo in the Southwest, and the so-called Apache War suddenly became newsworthy. Remington sold all of his Arizona sketches to *Outing* magazine and made

Remington in 1879 on the Yale fence. He was a lineman on the varsity football team.

other sketches for *Harper's Weekly*. By the time Geronimo surrendered in September 1886, Remington, whom Eva had rejoined in New York, was on his way to becoming well-known as a popular realistic illustrator of western subjects.

Remington soon became ambivalent about having his pictures published in popular magazines. He liked the money and the praise, but disliked the deadlines and the pressure to make his illustrations conform to prevailing genteel standards. Much of his writing was an attempt to formulate and explain his own standards, which were based jointly on his experience and his early reading of romantic writers such as Cooper and Irving. In 1888, he launched himself as a journalist with a series of four articles in the *Century*. The first of these articles, called "Horses of the Plains," deals with the various equine types that had developed in America from Spanish and Arabian strains, and demonstrates Remington's talent for careful observation. The last three articles—"A Scout With The Buffalo Soldiers," "On the Indian Reservations," and "Artist Wanderings Among the Cheyennes"—expressed his dismay at the degradation to which Indians were

being subjected on southwestern reservations. December 1890 found Remington in South Dakota reporting on the Sioux uprising that culminated in the Wounded Knee massacre, in which some 200 Sioux, many of them women and children, were killed by military units of the U. S. Seventh Cavalry. This event affected the artist so strongly that he soon afterward attempted to turn away from the American West as a subject, traveling to Africa and Europe in search of new interests. When he returned to the United States in 1892, and once more began to address frontier themes, his work was marked by a new impressionism. It was at about that time that his career as a writer began in earnest.

Remington's reputation as a writer rests on four volumes of collected short stories and two novels. A number of other short stories and nearly all of his essays and news dispatches remain uncollected. Most of the news dispatches concern battles between Indians and whites in the American Southwest, and, later, accounts of preparations for war with Spain. The essays, which cover a broad range of topics including horses, hunting, U. S. Indian policy, and the Cuban war, reveal Remington's shifting enthusiasms, his intelligence, and his abrasive wit. They also serve as background materials for his short stories and novels. As a writer, Remington more or less consistently tried to blur the distinctions between history and fiction.

"The Affair of the —th of July," the first of his published short stories, which appeared in *Harper's Weekly* on 2 February 1895, grows directly out of Remington's reports for *Harper's Weekly* on the 1894 Pullman strikes and riots in Chicago and is offered in the form of a letter from a military aide who watches while civil disorder erupts. A more successful application of the same epistolary technique is "Joshua Goodenough's Old Letter," published in the November 1897 *Harper's Monthly* and later collected in *Crooked Trails* (1898) and *Stories of Peace and War* (1899). Joshua writes to his son from Albany, New York, in 1798, recounting his participation in a series of conflicts over the previous forty years. He has fought with the British against the French at the Battle of Ticonderoga in 1758, against the Indians on the frontier, and against the British in the Revolution. As in "The Affair of the —th of July," the effect is somewhat grisly but strangely lacking in interest. Remington unknowingly stated the chief reason when, in a note to "Joshua Goodenough's Old Letter," he identified Goodenough as one of the "humble beings" who played a small part in creating the great republic. Using an epistolary technique to give his stories a flavor of history worked almost too well. The characters and incidents were so realistically mundane that they fell short of stimulating imagination.

However, Remington had already begun to explore other fictional techniques. By the time "Joshua Goodenough's Old Letter" was published, he had begun work on the two series of related stories that would later be collected as *Sun Down Leflare* (1899) and *Men With The Bark On* (1900). The tales that went into *Men With The Bark On* are based on actual events, such as the 1879 Dull Knife Indian fight in Nebraska and Wyoming, but they escape the tediousness of the epistolary stories by introducing characters such as Carter Johnson, the cavalry noncom who, in "A Sergeant of the Orphan Troop," leads the pursuit of Dull Knife and his band from Fort Robinson to the foothills of the Rockies. These characters are more aware than Goodenough of the consequences their actions bring about. Johnson, leading a charge on Dull Knife's band, knows not only that he is following orders, but that he is pitting himself against brave and determined men whom he admires. His heroism has a tragic dimension. The *Sun Down Leflare* narratives also express this tragic dimension, but in another way. They are all frame stories, in which an unnamed first-person narrator who resembles Remington provides the background for the tales told by Sun Down Leflare, a metis ("mixed blood") guide in Montana. The tragedy is that Sun Down has been reduced from a state of savage heroism to the semicivilized state in which he can only tell stories. Characters such as Goodenough and the narrator of "The Affair of the —th of July" are so humble that they seem mere counters in vast games of politics and social strife. Carter Johnson and Sun Down Leflare are certainly not pretentious, but they are ethical beings instead of humble ones. Because they are capable of making judgments about their own conduct and the conduct of others, they can see that something has gone wrong with historic processes—the same perception Remington became increasingly aware of in himself as he continued to examine the relationship between his romantic expectations of the West and his firsthand observations of it.

Remington completed only one of the Sun Down stories—a tale of the Crow Indians called "The Great Medicine Horse"—before the Spanish American War. When the war began in 1898, he went to Cuba as correspondent for *Harper's Weekly*, and there discovered that the conflict which he had eagerly anticipated was merely a larger and more horrible version of Wounded Knee. It was as an idealist, rather than as a pacifist, that he found himself disgusted. He missed, on actual battlefields, the personal sense of color and excitement he sought to express in his art. The remaining Sun Down stories, which he finished after his return from Cuba, reflect his disillusionment. In the first of them, "How Order No. 6 Went Through," Sun Down relates how he delivered a military order as a young man, at about the time of the massacre at Little Big Horn. It would be a relatively standard story of minor heroism, except for the frame which gives it perspective. The Sun Down who appears *in* the story is an Indian scout for General Miles. The Sun Down who *narrates* the story has become very much like the white Easterner to whom he tells it. He lives at a nearby white settlement, has domestic problems, and depends on the flour mill and commissary for his food. As one of Remington's illustrations shows, he even wears an ill-fitting suit of white-man's clothing.

"Sun Down Leflare's Money," the next story in the series, attempts to explain how the reckless young metis has evolved into the chunky, middle-aged yarn spinner. Sun Down, at some time after his service as a scout, made an alliance with an itinerant gambler, briefly acquired a considerable sum of money by cheating at cards and dice, and was run out of a Montana frontier settlement when the cheating was discovered. The story is a study of value systems. As an Indian, Sun Down measured wealth in terms of real objects actually possessed, and there were only three ways in which such wealth could be transferred: by gift, by barter, and by theft. All three ways were considered legitimate, because the real test of ownership was the owner's demonstrated ability to control what he owned physically. Under such a system, Sun Down contends, nobody had any money, but everybody was rich. White men brought confusing and catastrophic change by substituting artificial currencies for real wealth. Women may be (temporarily) bought with paper money or gold, but may not be traded for ponies. Card sharps practice guile and trickery, but without bravery, and receive nothing of real value in return. Significantly, Sun Down locates the source of the new evil in the railroad; after it came, he says, everything became "bad, all bad." The railroad not only brought whites into the land; it brought about his loss of innocence.

The last two Sun Down stories are thus more overtly bitter and pessimistic. In "Sun Down Leflare's Warm Spot," the aging guide gives an account of his various loves beginning with the best of them, a beautiful Gros Ventre woman for whom he

Frontispiece and title page for the book that established Remington's reputation as a writer. It was dedicated to "the fellows who rode the ponies that made the tracks."

had two decades earlier traded twenty-five ponies, and ending with the most recent, a white prostitute who has taken her money and departed by rail, leaving him with an infant son whom he is paying a white woman in the nearby settlement to care for. "Sun Down's Higher Self," the final story, focuses on the relationship between Sun Down and the narrator, whom Sun Down contemptuously calls a "white man." Whites, says Sun Down, foolishly believe that because they have built "de damn railroad" they can control the land. Indians, whose contact with the land is intimate and continuous, know "speerets" beyond white comprehension. However, Sun Down also confesses that he plans to take his son east and raise him as a white. The spirits may be remembered, but not revived. Although white men can see "no'ting," they have, in their bungling, unintended amorality, managed to destroy everything.

Sun Down Leflare brings into sharper definition Remington's many pictures of whites and Indians together. Although they may strike temporarily heroic poses, both races have an aura of pathos. The Indians' mystic spiritualism, founded on sensuous contact with nature, and the whites' technocratic hardness, founded on machine power, are both fleeting. The codes on which they base their heroic postures are beginning to wear out as their original meanings are forgotten or changed. Remington's concern with temporality as a subject reflects his concern that his work would not keep its interest over time. Despite some statements to the contrary (he boasted in 1895, shortly after completing the *Bronco Buster*, his first bronze, that he would be "d— near eternal") he was painfully convinced that his art would grow stale and be forgotten.

More than anything else, Remington was a

student of a failure of intention and a loss of meaning. His best short story, "When a Document is Official," published in the September 1899 issue of *Harper's Monthly*, demonstrates his keenly skeptical attitude about people's abilities to control their own destinies. William Burling, the central character, is a thirty-year-old cavalry sergeant stationed at a desert outpost in the Southwest during the 1870s. He has studied hard to be commissioned an officer, and, as the story opens, he has passed the examinations, but the document commissioning him a second lieutenant, already on its way from Washington, has not yet arrived. Meanwhile, Burling is sent to deliver another document to the commanding officer of an outlying desert camp. While he takes a drink of whisky at a makeshift saloon, this document is stolen from his saddlebag by a gang of "wolfish" buffalo hunters, who, though they cannot read, take it because they think it may be valuable. Burling overtakes the buffalo hunters, recaptures the document, and sets out toward his destination, but he is attacked and wounded by a band of hostile Sioux, who surround him in the dark. According to orders, he destroys the document by burning it, thus revealing his position to the Sioux, who fire toward the flame and kill him. Later, other Indians find the small pile of ash, with Burling's body beside it, the signs that Burling's horse had been picketed nearby, and, at the perimeter, the tracks and empty cartridge casings left by the encircling Sioux. At first, the story seems to be a study of acuity, because each of the characters is shown to be particularly skillful at some kind of interpretation. Burling is a model soldier who has studied military rules and who puts these rules into practice by following orders. The Sioux who kill him are, in their own way, equally proficient. They correctly interpret the flash of light made by the burning document as a sign of Burling's location. Likewise, the other Indians who come along later are able to reconstruct the whole story from the signs they find in the snow. Even the illiterate buffalo hunters are praised for their cunning in matters related to the hunt. However, all supposed sources of meaning, from the military rules Burling studied in order to be commissioned, to the empty cartridges left behind by his attackers, are quickly used up. If these signs are intentional, like Burling's commission or the document he attempts to deliver, they do not accomplish their intended objective. If they are unintentional, like the tracks in the snow or the flash of flame, they are dangerous—even fatal—revelations. More important, all signs, of whatever degree of intentionality, are shown to have only momentary significance.

The chief function of signs in the long term, then, is not elucidation but confusion. Remington seems to argue that to designate any document "official" is only to demonstrate ignorance.

"When a Document is Official" had personal implications for Remington which were real indeed. If even the relatively simple kind of communication Sergeant Burling tried to accomplish by delivering an official document was so difficult, then it seemed impossible to convey the nuances of meaning upon which art and literature depended. Yet Remington not only wrote into his stories his personal doubts about meaning and communication; he used his characters to work out provisional solutions. Carter Johnson, of "A Sergeant of the Orphan Troop," salvages something from the disgraceful episode of the Dull Knife fight by conducting himself in a soldierly fashion. Sun Down Leflare can remember the potent spirits, free ways, and wild loves of his youth, even though he cannot perpetuate them. His decision to renounce his Indianhood and rear his son in the East expresses a stark but courageous wisdom: red or white, men must change with the times or they will cease to be men. Even William Burling's death in the winter desert teaches a redemptive lesson. Courage, honor, steadfastness, and intelligence—the human virtues Burling espouses—save him from oblivion, even though they cannot preserve his life. These virtues are all the more valuable for being devised and practiced by human beings. This sense of value, finally, is what rescued Remington from the despair into which his thought about art and meaning threatened to plunge him. In his vision, manhood is difficult but not impossible, and for that reason it constitutes a standard of worth. The key to achieving it is the ability to accept transience without renouncing morality.

However, the idea of the formulated moral code does present something of a problem in Remington's two novels. John Ermine, the protagonist of the first of these novels, *John Ermine of the Yellowstone* (1902), is dead at the close, shot in the back by a jealous Indian as John attempts to kidnap the post commandant's daughter. John is only twenty-one years old, and the idea of transience disturbs him almost as much as does the idea of morality. Similarly, Remington's second novel, *The Way of An Indian* (serialized in *Cosmopolitan* in 1905-1906 and published in book form in 1906), closes as Fire Eater, the hero, carries the corpse of his infant son into the wintry foothills, accompanied by a ragged band of Cheyennes and pursued by General George Crook's cavalry. Like Ermine, he is no philosopher.

Indeed, he has lived mostly by lying, cheating, and killing. He attributes his current misfortune to the fact that he has lost a talisman he has carried with him since youth, a dried bat skin. Neither John Ermine nor Fire Eater fits the model established only a few years before in more heroic protagonists such as William Burling and Sun Down Leflare. The reason is that Remington, having begun his career as a realist, had become a naturalist. His two novels, favorably reviewed as examples of literary realism, were very much in the naturalistic mode.

The public was not prepared for Remington's shift from realism to naturalism. He had made his reputation as a popular illustrator and realistic painter. However, Remington's career as a realistic painter was largely over by the time he began to write fiction—brought to a close, perhaps, by his dismay at what he saw of reality at the Wounded Knee massacre. When his first attempt at fiction, "The Affair of the —th of July" came out in 1894, he had probably already begun planning the five vividly impressionistic oils he made to go with Owen Wister's essay, "The Evolution of the Cow Puncher," published the following year in *Harper's Monthly*. Because these pictures represented the same kinds of subjects Remington had addressed as a realist, critics and viewers tended to regard them as realistic, but comparing them with virtually any of the paintings Remington completed before 1890 shows that they are much different in form, color, composition, and conception.

As a writer, Remington probably modeled his earliest short stories after works by Mark Twain done in an epistolary or diary form. These short stories were the most clearly realistic of anything he ever wrote. When he abandoned the epistolary technique and began experimenting with other techniques—such as that of the frame stories he used in *Sun Down Leflare*—his fiction quickly acquired an impressionistic cast, much as his painting had already done. Not surprisingly, most readers and critics remained unaware that any change had taken place. The Sun Down stories and the other fiction Remington began writing in 1897 concerned types which were recognizable enough, even while they were exotic—cowboys, Indians, troopers, and frontiersmen. These were the same types that had been made popular by the fiction of Bret Harte and Owen Wister, the essays of Theodore Roosevelt, and Remington's early magazine illustrations. Yet while the popular conception of what these character types did was summed up in the title of Roosevelt's multivolume history, *The Winning of the West*, the same types performed very differently in

Remington's short stories. Here, the notion that the West might somehow be won is never even considered as a possibility. Instead, the West is always and irretrievably lost, enabling the characters to discover themselves. Carter Johnson discovers an "orphan"; William Burling finds an interpreter of meaningless signs; Sun Down Leflare finds a continuously fading range of ironic memories. In each case, the discovered self consists of a cluster of refracted impressions.

Perhaps it was inevitable that Remington should eventually turn to literary naturalism when he undertook to produce longer works. Asked in 1906 how he had decided to write novels, he offhandedly replied that he had done so mainly to explain to readers the intentions behind his paintings and sculptures. Significantly, his later paintings and sculptures had by then attracted the admiration of Ambrose Bierce, Stephen Crane, Frank Norris, and Theodore Dreiser, the chief writers of American literary naturalism. The distinguishing quality of the naturalism he practiced in his two novels is the same as the quality that Norris and Dreiser praised in his art. This quality may be described as a focus on the ironic tension between the protagonist

Remington, age forty-four, in his New Rochelle, New York, studio

Remington's house on his thirty-acre farm in Ridgefield, Connecticut, where he moved in 1909

and his environment—a tension that operates to transform the environment as perceived by the protagonist and also to transform the protagonist himself. Remington's literary naturalism may be described as an intensified impressionism, a more rigorous refraction of reality than he had attempted in even such stories as "When a Document is Official."

In the first of the two novels, blond, fair-skinned John Ermine has been raised from infancy in a band of Crow Indians who give him the name of White Weasel. As an adolescent he is given up to Crooked Bear, a deformed white recluse whom the Indians regard as an oracle. Crooked Bear renames the boy John Ermine, and reeducates him in white ways—including reading, writing, arithmetic, and moral philosophy—before sending him off to join General Crook in his pursuit of the Sioux during the winter of 1876, just after the massacre at Little Big Horn. Ermine proves a good soldier, although Crooked Bear has not prepared him for everything he will find in an army camp, such as liquor and cards. However, he earns the respect of his fellow soldiers, and soon attracts the attention of the commandant, who takes an almost paternal interest in him. When the unit returns to summer quarters on the Tongue River in 1877, he meets the commandant's pretty daughter, Catherine, and immediately falls in love with her.

Crooked Bear, supposedly because he is deformed, has never known women and has taught Ermine nothing about passionate love between the sexes. Flirtatious Catherine admires the young man's handsomeness and finds his discomfiture in her presence amusing. When he awkwardly blurts out a proposal, however, she is outraged, cruelly telling him that he would never be acceptable in her circle of society. After a stern lecture from the fatherly commandant, he skulks away, but eventually returns, overcome by lust, self-pity, and pride. This time he finds Catherine in the company of her fiance, a young staff officer who orders him away. Enraged, he fires on the young officer and wounds him before fleeing to Crooked Bear's lodge in the mountains. Despite Crooked Bear's advice, he decides to go back to the fort at night and steal Catherine, Indian fashion. He is discovered in this attempt by a jealous Crow and is killed.

In a way, Ermine's progress resembles that of the title character in Frank Norris's novel of four years earlier, *McTeague* (1898). Both men are born into impossible situations which force them to adopt a series of false roles, but a time comes for each when some inner self must assert itself against the sham and pretension society regards as order. Consequently, each hero is destroyed in a way that is luridly spectacular and ironic.

The Way of an Indian begins in about 1824, when a young Cheyenne named White Otter is being initiated into manhood. When he comes back from his fast in the mountains, he brings with him the body of a small bat he has caught, and which he adopts as his "medicine." Shortly afterward, he conducts a raid into Crow territory, where he steals two ponies and kills a young man innocently waiting for his mistress in a wooded creek bottom. For this, he is renamed the Bat. A series of similar exploits follow. In one of them, he leads the assault against white traders who defend themselves with dynamite. This earns him the name of Fire Eater. Secretly sure that his medicine has made him invulnerable, he becomes more and more reckless, at last leading a foolish charge from which he emerges the only survivor. Ashamed to go back to his own village, he joins the Shoshones. Years later, he rejoins the Cheyennes, having fabricated a story that presents him as a reincarnation of himself, a great hero.

By the summer of 1876, when Crook's troopers attack the village in the wake of Little Big Horn, but are repulsed, Fire Eater has married and fathered an infant son. He is still convinced of his own invulnerability. When the soldiers are driven off, he believes that he and his bat are responsible. However, the soldiers attack again during the winter. This time they surprise the Indians and destroy the village. Among the few survivors is Fire Eater who, when he discovers that the son he carries is dead, dramatically calls on the "Bad Gods" to come for him as well. Fire Eater has changed names, identities, and allegiances as easily as a con artist changes disguises, and with as little result. Indeed, he is a con artist so thoroughly taken in by his own con that he can never go beyond it.

John Ermine and *The Way of an Indian* may be faulted for being awkward, melodramatic, and needlessly gloomy, but Remington's two novels, along with his best short stories, demonstrate the artist's growing confidence in his own imagination.

Remington's final decade was his finest. After returning from Cuba in 1898, a victim of malaria, he worked with new vigor and confidence. He largely gave up doing illustrations for magazines and devoted himself to painting, sculpting, and writing. The thrust toward impressionism that had first begun to appear in his paintings after Wounded Knee became stronger and more assertive in all his work. His bronzes exhibited new harmony and power; his fiction boldly cast aside realistic conventions; he allowed the brush strokes to show in his oils and watercolors as never before. He was only forty-eight years old, and at the height of his powers, when he died of appendicitis at his newly completed home in Ridgefield, Connecticut, on the day after Christmas 1909. The year before, following a successful show, he had happily written to a friend, "I am no longer an illustrator."

Periodical Publications:
FICTION:
"The Affair of the —th of July," *Harper's Weekly*, 39 (2 February 1895): 105-107;

"Joshua Goodenough's Old Letter," *Harper's Monthly*, 93 (November 1897): 879-894;

"When a Document is Official," *Harper's Monthly*, 95 (September 1899): 608-622.

NONFICTION:
"Horses of the Plains," *Century*, 37 (January 1889): 332-343;

"Artist Wanderings Among the Cheyennes," *Century*, 37 (April 1889): 536-547;

"A Scout With The Buffalo Soldiers," *Century*, 37 (April 1889): 899-911;

"On the Indian Reservations," *Century*, 37 (July 1889): 393-406;

"Chasing a Major General," *Harper's Weekly*, 34 (6 December 1890): 946-947;

"The Art of War and Newspaper Men," *Harper's Weekly*, 34 (6 December 1890): 947;

"With the Fifth Corps," *Harper's Monthly*, 94 (November 1898): 960-978.

References:

Douglas Allen, *Frederic Remington and the Spanish-American War* (New York: Crown, 1971);

La Verne Anderson, *Frederic Remington: Artist on Horseback* (Champaign, Ill.: Garrard, 1971);

Peter Hassrick, *Frederic Remington* (New York: Abrams, 1973);

Atwood Manley, *Frederic Remington in the Land of His Youth* (Canton, N. Y.: Privately printed, 1961);

Harold McCracken, *Frederic Remington: Artist of the Old West* (Philadelphia: Lippincott, 1947);

McCracken, *The Frederic Remington Book: A Pictorial History of the West* (Garden City: Doubleday, 1966);

McCracken, *Frederic Remington's Own West* (New York: Dial, 1960);

Robin McKown, *Painter of the Wild West: Frederic Remington* (New York: Messner, 1959);

Ben Merchant Vorpahl, *Frederic Remington and the West: With the Eye of the Mind* (Austin: University of Texas Press, 1978);

Vorpahl, *My Dear Wister: The Frederic Remington-Owen Wister Letters* (Palo Alto: American West, 1972);

G. Edward White, *The Eastern Establishment and the Western Experience: The West of Frederic Remington, Theodore Roosevelt, and Owen Wister* (New Haven: Yale University Press, 1968).

Papers:
The Kansas State Historical Society in Topeka,

Kansas, has notebooks and letters from Remington to his wife; the Owen Wister Papers at the Library of Congress have Remington's letters to Owen Wister; St. Lawrence University Library in Canton, New York, has letters to friends; and the Remington Art Museum in Ogdensburg, New York, contains notebooks, diaries, and letters, as well as books from Remington's library, with the artist's notations.

Harriet Beecher Stowe
(14 June 1811- 1 July 1896)

Madeleine B. Stern

See also the Stowe entry in *DLB 1, The American Renaissance in New England.*

*SELECTED BOOKS: *Prize Tale: A New England Sketch* (Lowell, Mass.: Gilman, 1834);
The Mayflower; or, Sketches of Scenes and Characters among the Descendants of the Pilgrims (New York: Harper, 1843); enlarged as *The Mayflower and Miscellaneous Writings* (Boston: Phillips, Sampson, 1855);
Uncle Tom's Cabin; or, Life Among the Lowly, 2 volumes (Boston: Jewett/ Cleveland: Jewett, Proctor & Worthington, 1852);
Uncle Sam's Emancipation; Earthly Care, a Heavenly Discipline; and Other Sketches (Philadelphia: Hazard, 1853);
Sunny Memories of Foreign Lands, 2 volumes (Boston: Phillips, Sampson/ New York: Derby, 1854);
The Christian Slave. A Drama Founded on a Portion of Uncle Tom's Cabin (Boston: Phillips, Sampson, 1855);
First Geography for Children (Boston: Phillips, Sampson/ New York: Derby, 1855);
Dred; A Tale of the Great Dismal Swamp, 2 volumes (Boston: Phillips, Sampson, 1856); republished as *Nina Gordon: A Tale of the Great Dismal Swamp*, 2 volumes (Boston: Ticknor & Fields, 1866);
Our Charley, and What to Do With Him (Boston: Phillips, Sampson, 1858);
The Minister's Wooing (New York: Derby & Jackson, 1859);
The Pearl of Orr's Island: A Story of the Coast of Maine (Boston: Ticknor & Fields, 1862);
Agnes of Sorrento (Boston: Ticknor & Fields, 1862);

House and Home Papers, as Christopher Crowfield (Boston: Ticknor & Fields, 1865);
Little Foxes, as Crowfield (Boston: Ticknor & Fields, 1866; London: Low, 1866);
Religious Poems (Boston: Ticknor & Fields, 1867);

Queer Little People (Boston: Ticknor & Fields, 1867);

The Chimney-Corner, as Crowfield (Boston: Ticknor & Fields, 1868);

Men of Our Times; or, Leading Patriots of the Day (Hartford, Conn.: Hartford Publishing Company / New York: Denison, 1868); republished as *The Lives and Deeds of Our Self-Made Men* (Hartford, Conn.: Worthington, Dustin, 1872);

Oldtown Folks (Boston: Fields, Osgood, 1869);

The American Woman's Home, by Stowe and Catharine Beecher (New York & Boston: Ford, 1869); revised and enlarged as *The New Housekeeper's Manual* (New York: Ford, 1874);

Lady Byron Vindicated. A History of the Byron Controversy, from Its Beginning in 1816 to the Present Time (Boston: Fields, Osgood, 1870);

Little Pussy Willow (Boston: Fields, Osgood, 1870);

My Wife and I; or, Harry Henderson's History (New York: Ford, 1871);

Pink and White Tyranny. A Society Novel (Boston: Roberts, 1871);

Sam Lawson's Oldtown Fireside Stories (Boston: Osgood, 1872);

Palmetto-Leaves (Boston: Osgood, 1873);

Woman in Sacred History (New York: Ford, 1874); republished as *Bible Heroines* (New York: Fords, Howard & Hulbert, 1878);

We and Our Neighbors; or, The Records of an Unfashionable Street (New York: Ford, 1875);

Betty's Bright Idea. Also Deacon Pitkin's Farm, and The First Christmas of New England (New York: Ford, 1876);

Footsteps of the Master (New York: Ford, 1877);

Poganuc People: Their Loves and Lives (New York: Fords, Howard & Hulbert, 1878);

A Dog's Mission; or, The Story of the Old Avery House, And Other Stories (New York: Fords, Howard & Hulbert, 1880).

COLLECTION: *The Writings of Harriet Beecher Stowe*, 16 volumes (Boston & New York: Houghton, Mifflin, 1896).

*This list omits British editions.

Harriet Beecher Stowe's *Uncle Tom's Cabin* (1852) became not only a phenomenal best-seller but a moral instrument. Combining domesticity and sentiment with violence and realism, this novel was the target of vehement controversy upon publication and is still the subject of intense critical examination. Imbedded in fact, it was imbued by its author with moral fervor. Its influence on American attitudes toward slavery has become legendary.

Harriet Beecher Stowe was a product of New England, particularly of New England Calvinism. She was born in Litchfield, Connecticut, one of the eight children of Lyman and Roxanna Foote Beecher. When Harriet was four, her mother died, and two years later her father married Harriet Porter. The Beechers were a family driven to proselytize and convert, to teach and to preach. Lyman Beecher was a Congregational minister, and Harriet Beecher's brother, Henry Ward Beecher, later became well known as the pastor of Brooklyn's Plymouth Church. Harriet Beecher was reared in an atmosphere of "moral oxygen" charged with "intellectual electricity." Both these qualities would be injected into *Uncle Tom's Cabin*. In the parsonage where she grew up, the guiding principles of life were self-abnegation and spiritual regeneration. Harriet Beecher attended Miss Sarah Pierce's school in Litchfield for five years, and at the age of thirteen she went on to the Hartford Female Seminary, run by her sister Catharine. She subsequently taught there until 1832, when the family moved to Cincinnati upon Lyman Beecher's appointment as president of Lane Theological Seminary. She taught at the Western Female Institute, founded by Catharine Beecher, and in 1834 she won first prize

Harriet Beecher Stowe, Lyman Beecher, and Henry Ward Beecher

in a contest conducted by the *Western Monthly Magazine*. Her sketch appeared in the April 1834 issue of the magazine and was published separately as *Prize Tale: A New England Sketch* (1834).

In 1836 Harriet Beecher married a widower, Calvin Stowe, professor of biblical literature at Lane. During the first seven years of their marriage she bore him five children. To alleviate her domestic drudgery and overwork she occasionally wrote stories so that she could afford domestic help, and in 1843 a collection of her New England stories, *The Mayflower*, was published by Harper. While she was still living in southern Ohio Stowe witnessed the miseries of black freedmen who lived across the river from slavery. The subject of her famous novel began to take shape in her mind, and she was also aware that she must write to help her family financially. As she said in a letter to a friend, "When a new carpet or mattress was going to be needed or when . . . it began to be evident that my family accounts . . . 'wouldn't add up' then I used to say to my faithful friend and factotum, Anna, . . . 'now, if you will keep the babies and attend to the things in the house for one day, I'll write a piece and then we shall be out of the scrape.' " By 1850, when Calvin Stowe was appointed professor at Bowdoin College, Brunswick, Maine, the Stowes had two more children to support.

Stowe's New England and Beecher heritage had made her a crusader; her domestic needs provided financial motivation; her life in southern Ohio had given her knowledge, direct or second-hand, of the nature of slavery. Back in New England, spurred by the passage of the 1850 Fugitive Slave Law, she wrote *Uncle Tom's Cabin*. The story, for which she was paid $300, was written for the antislavery weekly, the *National Era*, which published it in forty installments (5 June 1851-1 April 1852). According to Charles Dudley Warner, "The installments were mostly written during the morning, on a little desk in a corner of the diningroom of the cottage in Brunswick, subject to all the interruptions of housekeeping, her children bursting into the room continually. . . . With a smile and a word and a motion of the hand she would wave them off, and keep on. . . . Usually at night the chapters were read to the family, who followed the story with intense feeling."

The story the family—and soon most of the world—followed with intense feeling began as polemical literature and became folklore. Designed to expose the evils of slavery—the evils to master as well as to slave—*Uncle Tom's Cabin* presented a series of characters who, as John William Ward has said,

have become "part of the collective experience of the American people."

According to Stowe, her object was to demonstrate black people's "wrongs and sorrows, under a system so necessarily cruel and unjust as to defeat and do away the good effects of all that can be attempted for them, by their best friends, under it." How well she succeeded in drawing attention to their plight is overwhelmingly demonstrated by the sales and publishing history of her work. Following its appearance in the *National Era*, *Uncle Tom's Cabin* (turned down by Phillips, Sampson who would not risk offending Southern readers) was published in two volumes by John P. Jewett of Boston in March 1852. During the first nine months, the first edition of 5,000 copies was quickly exhausted, and after a total of 100,000 sets of the two-volume edition had been sold, a cheap one-volume edition and an illustrated edition for the Christmas trade were published. Both the publisher's staff and his premises were enlarged to accommodate production of this single title, which was becoming a runaway bestseller. By March 1853, 300,000 copies had been sold. In January 1853, Charles Briggs commented in *Putnam's Magazine*, "Never since books were first printed has the success of *Uncle Tom* been equalled; the history of literature contains nothing parallel to it, nor approaching it: it is, in fact, the first real success in book-making. . . ." Maintaining sales of 1,000 copies a week, the book sold half a million copies by 1857. With pirated editions in England and translations into many languages, the historian Thomas Macaulay could accurately report to Stowe in fall 1856, "There is no place where Uncle Tom . . . is not to be found." Dramatic versions and "Tomitudes"—(Tom artifacts) all touted *Uncle Tom's Cabin*.

There were many ingredients in the success of *Uncle Tom's Cabin*. One of these was realism, derived from the author's firsthand observations and use of authentic source materials. While she was living in southern Ohio, "on the confines of a slave state," she had conversed with former slaves and, according to Annie A. Fields, Stowe had observed "the cruel sale and separation of a married woman from her husband" while she was aboard an Ohio River steamboat. Fields adds that Stowe's "husband and brother had once been obliged to flee with a fugitive slave woman by night . . . and she herself had been called to write the letters for a former slave woman, servant in her own family, to a slave husband in Kentucky." To this earlier personal experience, Stowe added what she had gleaned from her readings. For example, the source of the famous episode of Eliza

Part of the 1st Chapter of Uncle Toms Cabin
1st Drought

they are to be a fancy article entirely to sell for waiters to rich folks what can pay for a very handsome article — It sets off one of these stylish establishments you know — a handsome boy to open the door & wait & tend & all that — & they fetch a good round sum I can tell you

I would rather not sell him said Mr Selby thoughtfully — the fact is I'm a humane man & I hate to take the boy from his mother Sir —

— Oh you do — law sakes! — well it is unpleasant the fuss these women make about their children — I always hate these scraching screamin times they have & as I does business I commonly avoids em Sir — Cant you get the woman off for a day or two, for an errand or visit or some such & then the thing can be done quietly — your wife might buy her a new gownd & some ear rings or some such trap to make it up with her —

I'm afraid not —

Lor yes — bless you these cretures ant like folks you know — they gets over things — that is to say if you know how to manage them — Now they say my kind of trade is hardenin to the felins — but I never found it so — I never could do things up in the high

handed sort of way that some fellows manage
the business — I've seen em as would pull away
a womans baby out of her arms & set him up
to sell — & she scrunching like mad — so that it would
take two or three to hold her — bad policy that —
damages the article — makes em quite unfit for
service sometimes — I knew a real handsome girl
once as was entirely ruined by this kind of proceedin
— the fellow that was a tradin for her of course didn
want her baby & she was one of your real high sort
when her blood was up — & she squeezed her child
in her arms & talked reale awful — it kinder
makes my blood run cold to think ont — & when
they pulled away the baby & locked her up
— she just went ravin mad — & died in a week
— a clear waste sir of two thousand dollars —
just for want of a little management

And did you find that your way of managing
did the business any better said Mr Shelby —
— Certainly — to be sure — get em out of the
way — out of sight out of mind — & when the
things clean done & cant be helped & they
know it they naturally gets used to it — folks
can get used to any thing when they must

crossing the ice has been traced to an article in *A Friend of Youth*, a children's antislavery magazine edited by Mrs. Margaret Bailey, which in February 1851 carried an account of how a woman and her child escaped from Kentucky by crossing the ice of the Ohio River. Finally, Stowe pursued her research by seeking living sources. On 9 July 1851 she wrote to the freedman and abolitionist-orator Frederick Douglass about her project, explaining that because part of the book would be set on a cotton plantation, "I am very desirous, therefore, to gain information from one who has been an actual laborer on one, and it occurred to me that in the circle of your acquaintance there might be one who would be able to communicate to me some such information as I desire. I have before me an able paper written by a Southern planter, in which the details and *modus operandi* are given from his point of sight. I am anxious to have something more from another standpoint. I wish to be able to make a picture that shall be graphic and true to nature in its details." Thus, through personal experience and research, Stowe created a realistic account of her great subject.

To realism she added another major ingredient: the moral fervor that came from her Beecher inheritance and that could lead her to include in her novel pronouncements such as, "Not by combining together, to protect injustice and cruelty, and making a common capital of sin, is this Union to be saved—but by repentance, justice and mercy." Also demonstrated in *Uncle Tom's Cabin* is the skill of the increasingly professional writer who could wrest from the exigencies of writing for serial publication the triumph of suspense and who could reshape a sentimental story into what a British reviewer called an "Iliad of the blacks."

Many of Stowe's contemporaries appreciated her efforts. George Sand, perceiving that the book was "essentially domestic and of the family," went so far as to find its author endowed with the "genius . . . of the saint." A lengthy anonymous review in the *Times* (London) commented astutely that "the clever authoress . . . strikes at the convictions of her readers by assailing their hearts." At home, *Uncle Tom's Cabin* won the praise of Henry Wadsworth Longfellow and Ralph Waldo Emerson, who wrote in "Success" that the novel spoke "to the universal heart, and was read with equal interest to three audiences, namely, in the parlor, in the kitchen, and in the nursery of every house." Henry James later remembered that, as a young boy, he found the dramatic version of *Uncle Tom's Cabin* a thrilling "aesthetic adventure." As it aroused sup-

Harriet Beecher Stowe at the time of Uncle Tom's Cabin

port, the novel also stirred vituperative opposition primarily from the South. In the *Southern Literary Messenger* (October 1852) George F. Holmes wrote that Stowe "has shockingly traduced the slaveholding society of the United States." After exposing what he called "the inconsistencies and false assertions" of her "slanderous work," he concluded: "Indeed she is only entitled to criticism at all, as the mouthpiece of a large and dangerous faction which if we do not put down with the pen, we may be compelled one day . . . to repel with the bayonet."

In an attempt to silence her critics, Stowe made public her sources in *A Key to Uncle Tom's Cabin* (1853). This book contains documentary evidence for her statements: records of court cases, eye-witness reports, ephemeral handbills, all of which substantiated as realistic the graphic picture of slavery she had drawn.

Long after its author's death *Uncle Tom's Cabin* continued to be the object of critical examination. In 1896, the year of her death, Charles Dudley Warner provided the *Atlantic Monthly* with a detailed account of its history. Its artistry or the lack of it, the significance of its message, even its use of Negro dialect, have preoccupied critics, and the book has continued to be the subject of controversy. In a 1949 issue of the *Partisan Review*, James Baldwin assailed it as not only "a very bad novel" but a racist one. Three years later, Langston Hughes defended it as "a good story, exciting in incident, sharp in characterization, and threaded with humor," concluding that "the love and warmth and humanity that went into its writing keep it alive a century later from Bombay to Boston." There is no doubt that *Uncle Tom's Cabin* is a book unlikely to be forgotten.

Four years after the publication of *Uncle Tom's Cabin* Stowe resumed the antislavery theme in her novel *Dred* (1856). She was induced to return to the subject by three grave and almost simultaneous events in May 1856: the violent assault upon Charles Sumner in the Senate by Representative Preston Brooks of South Carolina; Henry Ward Beecher's staging of a mock slave auction in Plymouth Church to dramatize the antislavery protest; and the massacre in Pottawatomie, Kansas, of five proslavery men by John Brown and his followers. Set in North Carolina, Stowe's second antislavery novel describes Dred as a "tall black man, of magnificent stature and proportions," who is imbued with a passion for vengeance. Dred is balanced by the old slave woman Milly who, although she has lost fourteen children by death or sale, still believes in Christian love. The mulatto Harry Gordon faces the dilemma of choosing between these two forces of vengeance and patience. Although *Dred* has been called flawed and structurally disorganized, it paints such memorable scenes as the episode of "The Camp-Meeting," which Alice C. Crozier has called "a piece of historical realism . . . a valuable document." Instead of compiling a separate key to her sources as she had done for *Uncle Tom's Cabin*, Stowe included appendices of citations to substantiate her assertions. Not unexpectedly the novel drew strong adverse criticism from the South, the *Southern Literary Messenger* concluding a review with the remark: "Were she a woman, we should blush for the sex—luckily she is only a Beecher."

As a Beecher she assumed the task of recording her father's recollections, and in the course of her labors she became fascinated with his reminiscence of New England and the theological wrangling that characterized it. In 1857 she lost her firstborn son, a student at Dartmouth who had not yet been converted. When, still urged on by economic need, she began another novel, she naturally turned to the two interwoven themes of colonial New England and theological debate. Her series of New England novels begins with The

Minister's Wooing (1859). Set in Newport, Rhode Island, the novel reanimates Puritan life and explores the beginnings of the slave trade as it focuses on Dr. Samuel Hopkins, a forthright colonial minister subject to "those interior crises in which a man is convulsed with the struggle of two natures, the godlike and the demoniac." As Stowe wrote: "In no other country were the soul and the spiritual life ever such intense realities, and everything contemplated so much . . . 'in reference to eternity.' " In *The Minister's Wooing*, as in the novels that followed it, Stowe recreated realistically colonial New England and the theological warfare that was so much a part of it. Lawrence Buell has aptly referred to the novel's "creative uses of orthodoxy."

The Pearl of Orr's Island (1862) is the second in the series of Stowe's New England novels. Set on the coast of Maine, it portrays "the primitive and Biblical people of that lonely shore," among them the mystical heroine Mara, the pearl of the title. In 1869 Stowe expanded her chronicle of colonial New England with *Oldtown Folks*, one of whose most in-

OLDTOWN FOLKS

BY

HARRIET BEECHER STOWE,
AUTHOR OF "UNCLE TOM'S CABIN," ETC.

BOSTON:
FIELDS, OSGOOD, & CO.,
SUCCESSORS TO TICKNOR AND FIELDS.
1869.

Title page for Stowe's 1869 novel drawing on her childhood experiences in New England. It is one of the earliest examples of local-color writing in that region.

teresting characters is the patriot Ellery Davenport, a man "at war with himself, at war with the traditions of his ancestry." Theological issues still dominate the book, but Bret Harte, reviewing the novel rather disparagingly for the *Overland Monthly*, credited her with a "quaint Puritan humor." The final New England novel was published in 1878. In *Poganuc People* Stowe produced "a fictional memoir of her childhood years in Litchfield" and glorified the "millennium . . . ever the star of hope in the eyes of the New England clergy; . . . They were children of the morning."

By the time *Poganuc People* was published, Stowe had written several other books that engaged public attention. Perhaps the most sensational was her *Lady Byron Vindicated* (1870). Now famous and well-traveled, Stowe had seen a "beautiful and terrible ministry" at work in the life of her late friend Anne, Lady Byron. They had first met in 1853, and the friendship had deepened during Stowe's 1856 journey abroad. The two women shared not only religious interests, but, it appears, confidences: Lady Byron had revealed to Stowe Lord Byron's incestuous relationship with his half sister. After Byron's mistress, Countess Teresa Guiccioli, criticized Lady Byron in *My Recollections of Lord Byron* (1869), Stowe was prompted to retaliate with an article in the *Atlantic Monthly*. She later expanded this article into *Lady Byron Vindicated*, where she revealed the secret of Byron's incest, defended her late friend, and by defending one woman in particular, defended women in general. *Lady Byron Vindicated* aroused a storm of criticism. Justin McCarthy wrote in the *Independent*: "There is something positively painful about the sanctimonious imbecility of the manner in which Mrs. Stowe tries to regard her sickening task as a moral and religious duty." On the other hand, Elizabeth Cady Stanton reminded readers of the *Independent* that "the true relation of the sexes is the momentous question at this stage of our civilization, and Mrs. Stowe has galvanized the world to its consideration."

During the 1870s scandal came closer home. The scandal involving her beloved brother Henry Ward Beecher and two of his parishioners, the *Independent*'s editor Theodore Tilton and Tilton's wife, Elizabeth, culminated in Tilton's suing Beecher, charging him with adultery with Elizabeth Tilton. The jury was unable to reach a verdict, but Stowe believed in her brother's innocence. Her literary productions during this difficult period consisted primarily of post-Civil War society novels. In *My Wife and I* (1871), and *Pink and White Tyranny* (1871),

and *We and Our Neighbors* (1875), Stowe attempted to delineate realistically the life of the times: its business and its morals, its alcoholism and its prostitution, the domestic role of its women. She could not resist the temptation to caricature Victoria Woodhull, the woman editor who had first exposed the Beecher scandal, and in *My Wife and I* she satirized her as Miss Audacia Dangereyes. William Dean Howells, reviewing *My Wife and I* in the *Atlantic Monthly*, remarked that "the reality of Mrs. Stowe's best work is not here, as it is absent from the other books in which she deals with fashion and wealth in a moralistic spirit."

While her reputation will rest forever upon her masterpiece, *Uncle Tom's Cabin*, many of Stowe's other works are worthy of reading and analysis. She developed into a truly professional writer, producing at least a book a year between 1862 and 1884 and providing for her family and educating her children. Neither her New England novels nor her novels of society are comparable in moral power with her antislavery novels, although in all her novels she attempted to recreate realistically the themes, backgrounds, and characters that engrossed her. The crusade which she helped document and advance has become history, but her novels continue to interest scholars. Her artistry and literary craftsmanship, her aesthetics and her theology, her ideology and her realism are all being examined. Harriet Beecher Stowe has not lost her audience.

Other:

A Key to Uncle Tom's Cabin; Presenting the Original Facts and Documents upon which the Story is Founded, compiled by Stowe (Boston: Jewett/Cleveland: Jewett, Proctor & Worthington, 1853).

Letters:

Life of Harriet Beecher Stowe Compiled from Her Letters and Journals, edited by Charles Edward Stowe (Boston: Houghton, Mifflin, 1889);

Life and Letters of Harriet Beecher Stowe, edited by Annie A. Fields (Boston: Houghton, Mifflin, 1897).

Biographies;

Charles Edward Stowe and L. B. Stowe, *Harriet Beecher Stowe, The Story of Her Life* (Boston: Houghton Mifflin, 1911);

Forrest Wilson, *Crusader in Crinoline: The Life of Harriet Beecher Stowe* (Philadelphia: Lippincott, 1941).

References:

John R. Adams, "The Literary Achievement of Harriet Beecher Stowe," Ph.D. dissertation, University of Southern California, 1939;

Elizabeth Ammons, ed., *Critical Essays on Harriet Beecher Stowe* (Boston: G. K. Hall, 1980);

Alice A. Cooper, "Harriet Beecher Stowe: A Critical Study," Ph.D. dissertation, Harvard University, 1964;

Alice C. Crozier, *The Novels of Harriet Beecher Stowe* (New York: Oxford University Press, 1969);

Charles Foster, *The Rungless Ladder: Harriet Beecher Stowe and New England Puritanism* (Durham: Duke University Press, 1954);

Edward Charles Wagenknecht, *Harriet Beecher Stowe: The Known and the Unknown* (New York: Oxford University Press, 1965).

Papers:

Harriet Beecher Stowe's papers are in the Beecher-Stowe Collection at Schlesinger Library, Radcliffe College, Harvard University.

Edith Wharton
(24 January 1862-11 August 1937)

James W. Tuttleton
New York University

See also the Wharton entries in *DLB 4, American Writers in Paris, 1920-1939*, and *DLB 9, American Novelists, 1910-1945*.

SELECTED BOOKS: *Verses*, anonymous (Newport, R. I.: C. E. Hammett, Jr., 1878);

The Decoration of Houses, by Wharton and Ogden Codman, Jr. (New York: Scribners, 1897; London: Batsford, 1898);

The Greater Inclination (New York: Scribners, 1899; London: Lane/Bodley Head, 1899);

The Touchstone (New York: Scribners, 1900); republished as *A Gift from the Grave* (London: Murray, 1900);

Crucial Instances (New York: Scribners, 1901; London: Murray, 1901);

The Valley of Decision (2 volumes, New York: Scribners, 1902; 1 volume, London: Murray, 1902);

Sanctuary (New York: Scribners, 1903; London: Macmillan, 1903);

Italian Villas and Their Gardens (New York: Century, 1904; London: Lane/Bodley Head, 1904);

The Descent of Man and Other Stories (New York: Scribners, 1904; enlarged edition, London & New York: Macmillan, 1904);

Italian Backgrounds (New York: Scribners, 1905; London: Macmillan, 1905);

The House of Mirth (New York: Scribners, 1905; London & New York: Macmillan, 1905);

Madame de Treymes (New York: Scribners, 1907;

Wharton, age twenty-three, at the time of her marriage

London: Macmillan, 1907);

The Fruit of the Tree (New York: Scribners, 1907; London: Macmillan, 1907);

The Hermit and the Wild Woman and Other Stories (New York: Scribners, 1908; London: Macmillan, 1908);

A Motor-Flight Through France (New York: Scribners, 1908; London: Macmillan, 1908);

Artemis to Actaeon and Other Verse (New York: Scribners, 1909; London: Macmillan, 1909);

Tales of Men and Ghosts (New York: Scribners, 1910; London: Macmillan, 1910);

Ethan Frome (New York: Scribners, 1911; London: Macmillan, 1911);

The Reef (New York: Appleton, 1912; London: Macmillan, 1912);

The Custom of the Country (New York: Scribners, 1913; London: Macmillan, 1913);

Fighting France, from Dunkerque to Belfort (New York: Scribners, 1915; London: Macmillan, 1915);

Xingu and Other Stories (New York: Scribners, 1916; London: Macmillan, 1916);

Summer (New York: Appleton, 1917; London: Macmillan, 1917);

The Marne (New York: Appleton, 1918; London: Macmillan, 1918);

French Ways and Their Meaning (New York & London: Appleton, 1919; London: Macmillan, 1919);

The Age of Innocence (New York & London: Appleton, 1920);

In Morocco (New York: Scribners, 1920; London: Macmillan, 1920);

The Glimpses of the Moon (New York & London: Appleton, 1922; London: Macmillan, 1923);

A Son at the Front (New York: Scribners, 1923; London: Macmillan, 1923);

Old New York: False Dawn (The 'Forties), The Old Maid (The 'Fifties), The Spark (The 'Sixties), and New Year's Day (The 'Seventies) (New York & London: Appleton, 1924);

The Mother's Recompense (New York & London: Appleton, 1925);

The Writing of Fiction (New York & London: Scribners, 1925);

Here and Beyond (New York & London: Appleton, 1926);

Twelve Poems (London: Medici Society, 1926);

Twilight Sleep (New York & London: Appleton, 1927);

The Children (New York & London: Appleton, 1928); republished as *The Marriage Playground* (New York: Grosset & Dunlap, 1930);

Hudson River Bracketed (New York & London: Appleton, 1929);

Certain People (New York & London: Appleton, 1930);

The Gods Arrive (New York & London: Appleton, 1932);

Human Nature (New York & London: Appleton, 1933);

A Backward Glance (New York & London: Appleton-Century, 1934);

The World Over (New York & London: Appleton-Century, 1936);

Ghosts (New York & London: Appleton-Century, 1937);

The Buccaneers (New York & London: Appleton-Century, 1938).

While at the close of her career Edith Wharton was sometimes regarded as passe, a literary aristocrat whose fiction about people of high social standing had little to tell about the masses, particularly during the Jazz Age and the Depression, a countervailing view has begun to emerge in response to Edmund Wilson's call, after her death, for "justice" to Edith Wharton. In this counterview, Wharton is seen as a serious and deeply committed artist with a high respect for the professional demands of her craft, a woman praiseworthy for the generally high quality and range of her oeuvre, a novelist who wrote some of the most important fiction in the first quarter of the twentieth century, perhaps in American literary history. If this point of view has merit, her claim to attention arises from the clarity of her social vision, the particular angle of that vision (high society seen from the inside), and her subtle mastery of the techniques of fiction, which would be interesting to any reader concerned with the processes of writing. Recently the novelist Gore Vidal remarked in "Of Writers and Class: In Praise of Edith Wharton" that "At best, there are only three or four American novelists who can be thought of as 'major' and Edith Wharton is one." He regards Wharton and James as "the two great American masters of the novel." And he remarks that "now that the prejudice against the female writer is on the wane, they look to be exactly what they are: giants, equals, the tutelary and benign gods of our American literature." If that statement is not justice to Edith Wharton, it will be a long time in coming.

Born into the conservative, fashionable, and wealthy society of old New York in 1862, Edith Jones, the daughter of George Frederic and Lucretia Rhinelander Jones, was privately tutored, traveled extensively in Europe as a girl, and was married off on 29 April 1885 to Edward Wharton, a man considerably older than she and with few intellectual or artistic interests. During the early years of her marriage, she seems to have done little more than play the role of society matron and hostess in New York and Newport. Several years after her marriage, in 1894, she suffered a nervous breakdown, which resulted in convalesence in a sanatorium. There novel writing was prescribed therapy, and she thus commenced her professional writing career.

As a chronicler of the manners of New York society from the 1840s into the 1930s, an international novelist, and master of the short story, Wharton's principal focus, as indicated in her book *The Writing of Fiction* (1925), was the conflict between the desire of the individual and the authority of social convention. Blake Nevius has found the latent subject of her work to be two interlocking themes: "the spectacle of a large and generous nature . . . trapped by circumstances ironically of its own devising into consanguinity with a meaner nature"; and the related problem of trying to define "the nature and limits of individual responsibility, to determine what allowance of freedom or rebellion can be made for her trapped protagonist without at the same time threatening the structure of society." Since the publication of R. W. B. Lewis's

Edith Wharton: A Biography (1975), based on her private papers, it has become vividly clear the extent to which these intensely felt issues arose from her personal situation.

Her first publication was a book of poems, *Verses* (1878), privately published in Newport while she was yet a girl. Together with *Artemis to Actaeon and Other Verse* (1909), and *Twelve Poems* (1926), Wharton's verse suggests a very conventional poetic sense, sometimes passionately eruptive, but never in connection with the great poetic revolution of the twentieth-century avant-garde. *Verses* was followed by *The Decoration of Houses* (1897), a work on interior decor written with Ogden Codman, Jr. (apparently to bury the taste of her mother's generation). And her first book publications of fiction were *The Greater Inclination* (1899), *The Touchstone* (1900), and *Crucial Instances* (1901).

At the publication of *The Greater Inclination*, Henry James remarked that he was able to detect, in these eight short stories, the echoes of George Eliot sounding through the book. But many early reviewers, among them John D. Barry in the *Boston Literary World*, remarked that, unfortunately, she had been most influenced by James himself—a claim that Wharton came more and more to resent, although she and James were to develop a close friendship. Harry Thurston Peck was perhaps more discriminating in his observation that *The*

The Mount, the house Wharton built in 1901 on her 128-acre farm in Lenox, Massachusetts

Greater Inclination had caught the "English" manner of James's late style but had improved upon it. He concluded that "We have seen nothing this year that has impressed us so much as Mrs. Wharton's book." The stories in *The Greater Inclination* vary from a straight drawing-room scene written in dialogue, to a story—heavily freighted with psychological analysis—of a symbolic journey to death of a man and his wife. A number of the tales explore the power of social convention and the difficulty of transcending it; and a rather tough pragmatic attitude permeates Wharton's treatment of the theme. As one character remarks of conventions, "one may believe in them or not; but as long as they do rule the world it is only by taking advantage of their protection that one can find a *modus vivendi*."

In *The Touchstone*, Wharton tried her hand at the *nouvelle*, a form she was to bring to perfection in *Ethan Frome* (1911). *The Touchstone* involves a man who secretly sells intimate love letters once written to him by a now-deceased novelist, Margaret Aubyn. After their publication, he confesses to his wife the sale of the letters, identifying himself as the heartless recipient who allowed her anguished love to be published to the world; this confession achieves an alleviation of his guilt and the rehabilitation of his marriage. No longer, in the Jamesian phrase, a "publishing scoundrel," Glennard becomes the deeply sensitive and moral man Margaret Aubyn had seen *in potentia* and loved.

While some of her early critics were to condemn the "flatness" of her characters in the short story and *nouvelle*, Wharton always felt that it was the business of the novel gradually to develop character and that the business of the short story was to reveal a significant situation. If therefore her personae in the stories seem less than fully "rounded," her practice was premeditated. As she was to observe in *The Writing of Fiction*, "No subject in itself, however fruitful, appears to be able to keep a novel alive; only the characters in it can. Of the short story the same cannot be said. Some of the greatest short stories owe their vitality entirely to the dramatic rendering of a situation. Undoubtedly the characters engaged must be a little more than puppets; but apparently, also, they may be a little less than individual human beings." None of her early critics would have objected to her description of the short story as "a shaft driven straight into the heart of human experience," but her view of characterization in short fiction doubtless accounts for the recurrent conviction that, for all her brilliance, Wharton's tales lack the human warmth of great art. Still, in praise of Wharton's psychological realism in

The Touchstone, Aline Gorren remarked in the *Critic* that Wharton was to be praised for "the genius with which she will bring to the surface the underground movements of women's minds."

Crucial Instances was marked by a declining dependence on verbal irony and fin de siecle witticism and by a growth of her mastery of the short-story form. One of the predominant themes of this volume of tales is the futility of self-sacrifice (as in "The Angel at the Grave"); another was the aesthetic poverty of the American scene, particularly the New England small town, in contrast to Europe (as in "The Recovery"). These themes resonate throughout all Wharton's fiction, and the stories suggest, in their formal organization, what Wharton conceived short stories to be: "crucial instances" disengaged from "the welter of experience" that "illuminate our moral lives."

Wharton's annual excursions to Europe during her early married life account for the immediacy of the setting of her first novel, *The Valley of Decision* (1902), a long chronicle-novel set in settecento Italy on the eve of the Napoleonic invasion. Out of a passion for Italy were also to come *Italian Villas and Their Gardens* (1904), a serious examination of Italian villa and garden architecture, illustrated by Maxfield Parrish's drawings, and *Italian Backgrounds* (1905), a series of nine travel sketches recording the impersonal impressions of the Whartons, the Paul Bourgets, and others of their entourage. The title sketch of *Italian Backgrounds* recreates the color and variety of the settecento "world of appearances—of fine clothes, gay colours and graceful attitudes." *The Valley of Decision* was inspired by the same impulse to recreate that world in fiction, to vivify the colorful attitudes of the period. Like George Eliot's *Romola* (1863), however, the novel principally dramatizes the politics of a transitional age in which two political ideologies came into conflict with each other. An apt sense of the novel is suggested in Wharton's letter to William Crary Brownell, her Scribners editor. It was, she said, "an attempt to picture Italy at the time of the breaking-up of the small principalities at the end of the 18th century, when all the old forms and traditions of court life were still preserved, but the immense intellectual and moral movement of the new regime was at work beneath the surface of things.... I have tried to reflect the traditional influences and customs of the day, together with new ideas, in the mind of a cadet of one of the reigning houses, who is suddenly called to succeed to the dukedom of Pianura, and tries to apply the theories of the French encyclopedists to his small principality. Incidentally I have given sketches of Venetian life, and glimpses of Sir William Hamilton's circle at Naples, and the clerical milieu at Rome, where the suppression of the Society of Jesus, and the mysterious death of Ganganelli, had produced a violent reaction toward formalism and superstition. The close of the story pictures the falling to pieces of the whole business at the approach of Napoleon." Conservative in its social imagination, charged with contempt for radical Enlightenment political theorizing, *The Valley of Decision* thus took an indirect stand against the perfectibilitarian schemes for American social reform at the turn of the century, in the "progressive era." The general critical response was not favorable. Most reviewers felt it to be learned and labored and lacking in dramatic action, with characters put to the use of symbolizing various political positions. As an anonymous reviewer for the *Outlook* put it, "The story is not dramatic; it does not deal with the master passions in a masterly way; it is a carefully wrought study of a period and a temperament; an example of fine technique, a charmingly told story of deep and unusual interest."

Sanctuary (1903) deals once again with the theme of self-sacrifice. In this case, a woman marries a man guilty of fraud in order to prevent his unborn children from being "tainted" by their father's moral imperfection. In the end, Kate Orme saves their son Dick from replicating his father's financial dishonesty by having provided the sanctuary of love necessary to help him triumph over temptation where his father had not. In trying to render plausible Kate's motivation for marrying, Wharton writes of "mysterious primal influences," the "sacrificial instinct of her sex," and that "passion of spiritual motherhood that made her long to fling herself between the unborn child and its fate." But none of these phrases quite succeeds in making credible Kate's utterly fantastic motive in marrying Dick's father. As an anonymous reviewer in the *Independent* put it, *Sanctuary* is "the kind of book a woman writes when she conceives her characters all walking upon moral margins too narrow to be quite comfortable. And it does not demonstrate the growth of principles and manly stamina so much as it does a beautiful, tender sentimentality peculiar to women, whether they are writers, mothers or missionaries."

The Valley of Decision taught Wharton two principles about novel writing, she later observed. The first was that she ought to use the material she knew best; the second was that the value of any fictional subject would depend on how much significance

THE

HOUSE OF MIRTH

BY

EDITH WHARTON

London
MACMILLAN AND CO., Limited
NEW YORK: THE MACMILLAN COMPANY
1905

All rights reserved

Title page for Wharton's 1905 best-seller. Within the first three months of publication 140,000 copies were in print.

she could see in it. Was the New York beau monde too shallow to yield deep significance? Some critics, notably Van Wyck Brooks and V. L. Parrington, have thought so. But Wharton saw her task—in recreating this flat and futile commercial aristocracy in *The House of Mirth* (1905)—as that of extracting from New York society the human significance which would have universal meaning: as Wharton wrote in *A Backward Glance* (1934), "In what aspect could a society of irresponsible pleasure-seekers be said to have, on the 'old woe of the world', any deeper bearing than the people composing such a society could guess? The answer was that a frivolous society can acquire dramatic significance only through what its frivolity destroys. Its tragic implication lies in its power of debasing people and ideals. The answer, in short, was my heroine, Lily Bart."

The story of Lily Bart is the story of a beautiful but fastidious girl of inadequate means who tries to maintain her social position in the wealthy but dissolute New York beau monde while, at twenty-nine, trying to find a suitably rich husband. As she loses her tenuous position with the idle rich, Lily falls in the social order and eventually drops out of it, only to die of an overdose of chloral in a cheap boardinghouse.

The product of the social forces that have shaped her, Lily is too poor to run with a fast crowd but too much enamored of its luxuries to give up wealth and glamour and make an independent life with Lawrence Selden, the relatively poor young man who loves her. Lily's social values, so reminiscent of those of Dreiser's Sister Carrie, and Lily's tragic fall, so suggestive of Hurstwood's gradual deterioration and suicide in a New York flophouse, suggest that Wharton's world view might have been that of scientific naturalism. On this issue critics have frequently disagreed. Blake Nevius, for

Wharton in 1905, the year The House of Mirth *was published*

example, did call Wharton a writer of naturalistic tragedy, but Robert Morss Lovett found in her a "spirit of comedy." Marilyn Jones Lyde has tried to prove that Wharton's view of life was that of ethical tragedy. E. K. Brown, however, argued that Wharton saw life as more ironic than tragic.

What Louis O. Coxe says of *The Age of Innocence* (1920) has seemed true of her other works: that one of the graces and delights of Wharton's fiction lies exactly "in the multifariousness of its thematic material, in its refusal to tie itself down to 'meaning,' the while that it glitters with a density, a hardness of surface that only a truly novelistic eye could have seen and an informing mind recreate." This celebration of Wharton's philosophical ambiguity returns to Percy Lubbock's claim that Wharton was not committed to any one philosophical view, to Frances Russell's complaint that Wharton was "full of standards, viewpoints."

Wharton was not a thoroughgoing determinist. A close investigation of *Ethan Frome*, *The House of Mirth* and *The Age of Innocence*—those works that most frequently provoke the question of her world view—shows that free will is ordinarily present. Lily Bart, for example, realizes that Selden has preserved a detached view of the society she aspires to, that he has "points of contact outside the great gilt cage in which they were all huddled for the mob to gape at": "How alluring the world outside the cage appeared to Lily, as she heard its door clang on her. In reality, as she knew, the door never clanged: it stood always open; but most of the captives were like flies in a bottle, and having once flown in, could never regain their freedom. It was Selden's distinction that he had never forgotten the way out." Lily defines her goal in life as "success," getting as much as one can out of life. For Selden, however, it is personal freedom—what he calls the republic of the spirit: freedom "from money, from ease and anxiety, from all the material accidents. To keep a kind of republic of the spirit—that's what I call success."

But the problem of free will, the ability to choose between alternatives, is more complex than this analysis has suggested—principally because of the influence of Wharton's reading in the sciences. Her knowledge of the forces of heredity and environment, gained from writers like Charles Darwin, Thomas Huxley, Herbert Spencer, and John Locke, complicates her portraits. While according Lily Bart a measure of freedom and responsibility for her behavior, Wharton could also write of her in such a way as to suggest that Lily is the poignant victim of hereditary and environmental forces which she cannot understand and over which she

ETHAN FROME
BY
EDITH WHARTON

LONDON
MACMILLAN & CO
MCMXI

Title page for Wharton's 1911 novel, her first to reflect intensely personal emotions

moral decisions, in her awareness that in a very special sense character is destiny, Wharton must be called a "tender-minded determinist" who realized, like Lawrence Selden, that Lily "was so evidently the victim of the civilization which had produced her, that the links of her bracelet seemed like manacles chaining her to her fate." She learns too late the alternative order of values based on freedom that Selden describes. She cannot balance, as he apparently can, the epicurean's delight in pleasure with the stoic's indifference to it. The novel thus weighs both Lily and contemporary New York society in the balance and finds them wanting. To complete the biblical phrase to which the title alludes: "The heart of the wise is in the house of mourning; but the heart of fools is in the house of mirth" (Ecclesiastes 7:3). The point of the novel is suggested by Wharton's remark in her review of Howard Sturgis's novel *Belchamber* (1905): "A handful of vulgar people, bent only on spending and enjoying, may seem a negligible factor in the social development of the race; but they become an engine of destruction through the illusions they kill and the generous ardor they turn to despair." Surely Lily Bart was in her mind when Wharton wrote those lines.

Written rapidly under the pressure of a *Scribner's Magazine* deadline, *The House of Mirth* reflects weaknesses of style and plotting and a strain of sentimentality that often mar Wharton's best fiction. But the book was a best-seller in 1905 and 1906. While most reviewers deplored the vanity and vulgarity of high society, William Payne Morton was typical in praising the novel as "a work which has enlisted the matured powers of a writer whose performance is always distinguished, and whose coupling of psychological insight with the gift of expression is probably not surpassed by any other woman novelist of our time." The experience of writing the novel turned a drifting amateur into a professional writer, as Wharton herself confessed. It also revealed to her the possibilities inherent in the novel of manners set in New York. She celebrated her success by moving permanently to France in 1907, hoping to find in the exclusive Faubourg Saint-Germain quarter of Paris a literate and civilized high society lacking in New York.

Madame de Treymes (1907) dramatizes, after the manner of James's international tales (particularly *Madame de Mauves*, 1874), the conflict between the moral milieus of America and France. Set in Paris, which is celebrated for its physical beauty (Wharton always thought brownstone New York to be hideous), this *nouvelle* contrasts the individual goodness of the American with the moral and social com-

has little control: "Inherited tendencies had combined with early training to make her the highly specialized product she was: an organism as helpless out of its narrow range as the sea-anemone torn from the rock. She had been fashioned to adorn and delight; to what other end does nature round the rose-leaf and paint the humming-bird's breast? And was it her fault that the purely decorative mission is less easily and harmoniously fulfilled among social beings than in the world of nature? That it is apt to be hampered by material necessities or complicated by moral scruples?" But although the figurative language tends to suggest that Lily is a naturalistic victim, the irony in the rhetorical questions should not be lost on the reader.

In his Boston lectures on pragmatism in 1906, William James distinguished between a tender-minded and a tough-minded response to the question of free will and determinism. This distinction is relevant to Wharton's fiction. In her insistence that heredity and environment do strongly influence

plicities of a complex French social order. Henry James, who had just confessed in his preface to the New York edition of *The American* that he had not understood the French aristocracy in 1875, cautioned her about her subject matter: "All the same, with the rue de Varenne, &c, don't go in too much for the French or the 'Franco-American' subject—the real field of your extension is [England]—it has far more fusability with *our* native and primary material. . . ." But Wharton continued to feel more in command of the French scene than James had ever been. Even so, some reviewers wondered about *Madame de Treymes*'s sinister view of French familial solidarity, while Vernon Atwood claimed it to be "an absolutely flawless and satisfying piece of workmanship."

Wharton's third novel, *The Fruit of the Tree* (1907), sought to capitalize on the then-current vogue of muckraking and reform literature. This book abandoned the drawing-room milieu for the plight of the textile workers in a mill town in Massachusetts. Her aim, in telling the story of John Amherst, an assistant manager of a mill, was to expose and criticize the abuses of the industrial system, particularly the irresponsibility of managers who fail to look after the physical and spiritual welfare of their employees. That Wharton should have risked such a subject, about which she knew little, seems incredible. And, indeed, she got many of the details of factory life wrong. Then she shifted away from the reform topic midway through in order to explore the moral implications of euthanasia (Amherst's paralyzed wife is dispatched by an idealistic nurse who then marries him). The result is a structurally imperfect novel that concludes with the view that life is "not a matter of abstract principles, but a succession of pitiful compromises with fate, of concessions to old tradition, old beliefs, old charities and frailties." This observation, perhaps a latent theme of much of her fiction, suggests that the fruit of the tree is therefore a knowledge of the inextricable entanglements of good and evil.

A new invention, the motorcar, Wharton quickly discovered, had "restored the romance of travel." Her next book, *A Motor-Flight Through France* (1908), deals with a three-week tour taken by the Whartons and Henry James in the Whartons' new automobile. Perhaps the key to the work lies in what Wharton had to say about the effect of antiquities—like the Gothic cathedral at Reims—on the American traveler who has, in effect, no roots in the past: "Yes—reverence is the most precious emotion that such a building inspires: reverence for the accumulated experiences of the past, readiness

to puzzle out their meaning, unwillingness to disturb rashly results so powerfully willed, so laboriously arrived at—the desire, in short, to keep intact as many links as possible between yesterday and tomorrow, to lose, in the ardour of the new experiment, the least that may be of the long rich heritage of human experience." The operative terms for her point of view seem to be "enfranchisement of thought" combined with an "atavism of feeling." As an expression of medieval Catholicism, the cathedral represented both a bondage of superstition to be cast off in the modern age and yet a manifestation to be reverenced of the ancient attempt to struggle upward toward a clearer vision of the human condition. When the Germans shelled the cathedral at Reims in World War I, James wrote to her: "Rheims is the most unspeakable & immeasurable horror & infamy—& what is appalling & heart-breaking is that it's *'forever & ever!'* . . . There *it was*—and now all the tears of rage of all the bereft millions & all the crowding curses of all the wondering ages will never bring a stone of it back!"

Meanwhile, between 1904 and 1909, Wharton had been steadily producing short stories, amid frequent motor trips through France and Italy. *The Hermit and the Wild Woman and Other Stories* (1908) is a collection of seven tales ranging from a saint's legend (the title story) through Jamesian tales of art and life ("The Verdict" and "The Pot Boiler") to a tale of politics ("The Best Man"). Of these seven stories, perhaps "The Last Asset," about a divorced couple's momentary conspiracy to get their daughter married off, is the best, despite the interest of the title story which, in its study of the abnegations of a morbidly spiritual hermit, may be a portrait of Henry James as the high priest of art.

Wharton's next volume—*Tales of Men and Ghosts* (1910)—was a diversion from the two big novels then partially completed in manuscript—*The Reef* (1912) and *The Custom of the Country* (1913). Only two of the ten tales are about "ghosts"—"The Eyes" and "Afterward." But several other stories deal with fantasies, delusions, and hysteria in such a way as to suggest the impact of her breakdown in the 1880s and of her husband's neurasthenia, which was growing worse. At their best, Wharton's ghost stories always have a doubleness of significance, a miltiplicity of possible psychological interpretations that make the spectral tales plausible to the intellect.

In 1907 Wharton's knowledge of the French scene did not include a perfect command of a conversational idiom, even though she had spoken the language since childhood. At her request, Charles Du Bos found a tutor for her, but he turned out to be too amiable to correct her conversational errors. Instead, he asked her to prepare, for each of his visits, a written exercise, which he then corrected. In Wharton's exercise book is the germ of *Ethan Frome*: three chapters in French which introduce the three major characters and pose the complex relationship among them. The tragic ending of the story is nowhere in sight here: Wharton gave up her French lessons after a few weeks and the copybook, with its unfinished tale, was temporarily forgotten.

In the interim between the French version of the tale and the publication of *Ethan Frome* (1911) in English, there occurred perhaps the most passionate experience of Wharton's life—a brief but intense affair with Morton Fullerton, a ne'er-do-well American journalist then living in Paris. Her private diary suggests the intensity of her feelings: *"Wir waren zusammen. Die süssesten Stunden meines Lebens."* (*"We were together. The sweetest hours of my life."*) And again: "Sometimes I am calm," she wrote, "exalted almost, so enclosed and satisfied in the thought of you, that I could say to you truly, as I did yesterday, 'I never wonder what you are doing when you are not with me.' At such moments I feel that all the mysticism in me—and the transcendentalism that in other women turns to religion—were poured into my feeling for you. . . . I am a little humbled, a little ashamed, to find how poor a thing I am, how the personality I had moulded into such strong firm lines has crumbled to a pinch of ashes in this flame! For the first time in my life *I can't read! . . .* I hold the book in my hand, and see your name all over the page."

At the same time, Wharton was filled with guilt, for she believed in the marriage commitment and she knew that no relationship could be satisfactory that was not a total sharing of all the experiences of life. Besides that, Fullerton was an unstable scapegrace whose amorous escapades, with both sexes, scandalized their circle of friends. The affair was brief and intense; but this happiest moment of her life could not last. The 1909 poem "Terminus," published in Lewis's biography, suggests the inevitability of the end of the affair.

Ethan Frome, the *nouvelle* completed just after that intense liaison with Fullerton, deals less with character development than with the creation of an ironic situation—the entrapment of the three crippled victims of love and hate shut up together under one roof in a snowbound New England farmhouse: Ethan, his wife, Zeena, and his beloved Mattie Silver, now crippled, like Frome, in the wake of their suicidal toboggan ride into an elm tree. Stunning in the spare economy of its realistic detail, yet richly symbolic in its network of recurrent images, this work is frequently advanced as one of Wharton's most "naturalistic" studies of human defeat and despair. Lionel Trilling, for example, once observed that whenever a character suffers in a piece of fiction, he does so at the behest of the author, who must justify his cruelty "by the seriousness of his moral intention"; and he concluded that Wharton "could not lay claim to any such justification." For Trilling, the mind can do nothing with the "perpetuity of suffering" which memorializes "a moment of passion." It is true that the setting of Starkfield is grim, snowbound, and stony. But neither heredity nor environment serves to explain the fate of the characters, nor are determinist considerations invoked to account for them. If Ethan remains with these querulous and droning women, it is less because he is morally inert than because he is exceptionally responsible for them, if not constrained by his guilt. Looked at in the light of Wharton's anguish over the Fullerton affair, *Ethan Frome* is a stark projection, among other things, of Wharton's inability—much less her characters'—to escape the moral weight of self-punishment for illicit love. Contemporary reviewers seemed to grasp this point, in praising it as an analogue to Greek tragedy. As an anonymous reviewer for the *Nation* observed, "The wonder is that the spectacle of so much pain can be made to yield so much beauty."

Her next novel—*The Reef*—marked a significant departure from her characteristic mode as a novelist. It abandons the chronicle novel, like *The House of Mirth*, for a tightly constructed psychological drama focused on a central situation—again a love triangle—with a novelistic structure reminiscent of the manner of James's later works. Like *Ethan Frome*, *The Reef* deals with the power of sexual desire, the tortured frustrations of unrequited love, and the cerebrations of suspicion and jealousy that afflict Anna Leath, a "sheltered American girl" who has grown up, much like Wharton, in a repressive New York environment. Once again, the theme of the "monstrousness of useless sacrifice" is invoked, by George Darrow, but Anna Leath cannot think of herself as Darrow's wife without remembering that Sophy Viner has had an affair with him, without imagining what they must have done together. So trapped is she by her genteel aversion to physical sexuality that she cannot accept this virile man because it would compromise her ideal of perfect love and thus would be a desecration of its sanctity. *The Reef* glitters with felicities of psychological insight and precision. Henry James called it a "beautiful book," marked by "supreme validity and distinction" and quite "the finest thing you have done." For most reviewers, however, it was a failure.

In the long run, however, the Jamesian novel developing all sides of a central situation was not to be Wharton's metier. In her next novel, *The Custom of the Country*, she returned to the long, rambling chronicle of manners, narrating the rise of a vulgar and aggressive girl to social prominence in the East and in Europe. Undine Spragg, the heroine, is a dazzlingly beautiful girl from the Midwestern town of Apex City whose social ambition is so poisonous that it drives her to exploit everyone who crosses her path—her newly rich parents, whom she drags to New York and nearly bankrupts in her search for a rich husband; Ralph Marvell, the fashionable New Yorker whom she marries and drives to suicide; the Comte Raymond de Chelles, a French aristocrat of ancient family who seems more socially desirable as a husband than even Ralph; and finally Elmer Moffatt, an American billionaire railroad king with whom she eventually winds up. *The Custom of the*

Country recreates in a free-swinging satire the career of Undine Spragg, a type that Edmund Wilson once called the "international cocktail bitch," stripping off the skin of a decadent and lifeless New York social aristocracy, ridiculing the pretensions and provincialism of the American Midwest, and lambasting the American businessman as a crude materialist devoted only to mammon.

The year that *The Custom of the Country* was finished was in many ways a crucial one for Wharton. It marked, for one thing, the end of her marriage to Edward Wharton, whose mental derangement and embezzlement of funds in Wharton's trust made life with him unendurable. Her sense of liberation was reflected in what James called Wharton's "dazzling braveries of far excursionism" throughout the length and breadth of the Continent. Immediately after her April 1912 divorce she set out for Italy and then for Germany with her friends Walter Berry and Bernard Berenson, the art critic. In Germany she met Rainer Maria Rilke

Pages from the notebook Wharton kept while she was living in Paris at the beginning of World War I

and other German artists, visited the great museums, saw *Faust*, and discovered the magic of Richard Strauss's operas. "They were," she later wrote, "vernal hours," echoing Sigmund, *"es war der Lenz!"* She began a new novel, an ambitious *Künstlerroman* (a novel of education in which the hero becomes an artist) to be called "Literature." But when World War I broke out in 1914, she abandoned her compulsive travels, returned to Paris, and threw herself into journalism and war charities, organizing, among other things, a workroom for unemployed seamstresses in her arrondissement and finding food and lodging for refugees pouring out of Belgium.

Out of this work developed her next two books—*Fighting France: From Dunkerque to Belfort* (1915) and *The Book of the Homeless (Le Livre des Sans-Foyer)* (1915). The first recounts the experience of about six expeditions to the front line, where Wharton reported on trench warfare, the needs of the field hospitals, and the quiet heroism of the men and women who stood the rigors of frontline combat. Free of what she called "lyrical patriotism or post-card sentimentality," the book is nevertheless optimistic propaganda directed at the American public during the first fourteen months of the war. Her compilation, *The Book of the Homeless*, intended to assist the Children of Flanders Rescue Committee, contained poetry and music she solicited from such eminent artists as Rupert Brooke, Eleanora Duse, Sarah Bernhardt, Paul Claudel, Jean Cocteau, Thomas Hardy, William Dean Howells, George Santayana, William Butler Yeats, Igor Stravinsky, Joseph Conrad, Henry James, John Singer Sargent, and others. Like Wharton, Teddy Roosevelt—who wrote the introduction to the anthology—was concerned about America's continuing neutrality. "The part that America has played in this great tragedy is not an exalted part," he wrote, "and there is all the more reason why Americans should hold up the hands of those of their number who, like Mrs. Wharton, are endeavoring to some extent to remedy the national shortcomings." Meanwhile, in New York, Philadelphia, Boston, and Washington, "Edith Wharton" committees sprang up to collect funds for the perpetuation of her work.

Despite her inability to finish the manuscript of "Literature," Wharton did find time, amid her war work, to put together *Xingu and Other Stories* for publication in 1916. Most of the tales deal with typical Whartonian themes; some had been written well before the war commenced. "Xingu" is a broad satire on ladies' clubs which pretend to the mastery of "subjects" got up from week to week. "Kerfol" and "The Triumph of Night" are both ghost stories which hover between the occult and the psychologically aberrant. "The Choice" and "The Long Run" return to the theme of the moral ambiguities of love outside marriage in New York society. Surely Morton Fullerton must still have been in her mind when she protested to Charles Du Bos "the poverty, the miserable poverty, of any love that lies ouside of marriage, of any love that is not a living together, a sharing of all!" "Autre Temps . . ." and "Bunner Sisters" are the most brilliant tales in the collection; "Bunner Sisters" is comparable to *Ethan Frome* in the intensity of its vision of poverty and despair. Written at the fin de siecle, "Bunner Sisters" is a work of such powerful urban realism that Stephen Crane or Dreiser could not have done better.

In June of 1916, while the war raged on, she took a brief vacation at Fontainebleau, where she wrote *Summer* (1917). This New England tragedy, a companion piece to the wintry *Ethan Frome*, was a work as remote as possible from the combat scenes around her. *Summer* records the story of a poor young New England girl, Charity Royall, who is seduced by a handsome city architect who has come to her town to study its old houses. Predictably, their summer romance results in her pregnancy, abandonment, but rescue by Mr. Royall, the foster father who takes her in again and marries her. While its portrait of the inbred and degenerate mountain people of the Berkshires angered local residents and led the *Boston Evening Transcript* reviewer to call the book unconvincing, Wharton continued to insist throughout her life that she knew, from the inside, the impoverished rural lives of the Fromes and the Royalls. And she made a continuing claim for the realism of her New England tales, contrasting them to the idealizations of the New England local colorists. The *Bookman* reviewer concurred in praising the authenticity of Wharton's setting and characterization, which showed "all the virtue of her style and none of its weakness."

With the entry of the United States into the war in 1917, Wharton's hopes for the survival of France soared. Her new enthusiasm was reflected in *The Marne* (1918), a badly written, embarrassingly sentimental *nouvelle* about an underage American boy whose love for France is so impassioned that he joins the U.S. Army Ambulance Service as a driver, only to be killed at the Marne. Unfortunately, the book exudes an "Over There" enthusiasm suggesting that it is indeed sweet and dignified to die for one's adopted country.

A Son at the Front, not published until 1923 but

written at this time, is also a reflection of Wharton's war experience, specifically "that strange war-world of the rear, with its unnatural sharpness of outline and over-heightening of colour." In this novel, the artist-father John Campton reacts to the war personally and selfishly, as an inconvenience to his career, though he hopes that it may be the means by which his drafted son will gain a finer sense of values. When it becomes clear that the Allies will not win a quick victory, the defense of France becomes an obsession to him: "If France went, western civilization went with her; and then all they had believed in and been guided by would perish." The son is killed and the grieving father is much chastened by the experience. But the point is clear: the defense of France is the salvation of Western civilization. Wharton's continual call for American intervention in the war was like that of Henry James, who renounced his American citizenship in 1915 as a gesture of protest at America's seeming indifference to this assault on civilization.

The ways in which France stood for civilization is suggested in Wharton's *French Ways and Their Meaning* (1919), a work published toward the end of the war and intended for Americans, especially soldiers, in France. In this work, Wharton sought to explain her adopted country to those unfamiliar with its essential spirit, which she felt was typified by those "French" qualities of reverence, taste, continuity, and intellectual honesty. By "reverence" she meant the deeply rooted respect in France for old customs, traditions, rituals, and taboos—"les bienseances," the "always-have-beens," what she once called "the successive superpositions of experience that time brings." And by "continuity," she meant "the most homogeneous and uninterrupted culture" in the world. "France," she remarked, "has a lesson to teach and a warning to give [Americans]. It was our English forbears who taught us to flout tradition and break away from their own great inheritance; France may teach us that, side by side with the qualities of enterprise and innovation that English blood has put in us, we should cultivate the sense of continuity, that 'sense of the past' which enriches the present and binds us up with the world's great stabilising traditions of art and poetry and knowledge."

In *A Backward Glance* Wharton was to observe that "the really vital change" between 1870 and 1934 was that "in my youth, the Americans of the original States, who in moments of crisis still shaped the national point of view, were the heirs of an old tradition of European culture which the country has now totally rejected. This rejection . . . has opened a gulf between those days and these." In *The Age of Innocence*, a novel set in the old New York of her youth, Wharton sought to suggest some of those areas in which traditional society in old New York maintained the "old tradition of European culture" no longer characteristic of the postwar world. "To 'follow up' the traces of vanished old New York, Wharton felt, "one had to come to Europe"; there one found that the New York of the 1870s was very much like that of the English cathedral town or the French "ville de province" of the same era. In effect, she remarked on another occasion, "c'est seulement en ayant vu d'autres pays, étudié leurs moeurs, lu leurs livres, fréquenté leurs habitants, que l'on peut situer son propre pays dans l'histoire de la civilisation" ("it is only by having seen other countries, studied their customs, read their books, associated with the people, that one can place one's own country in the history of civilization").

Looking back, Wharton regarded old New York as having preserved an order of civilized values too precious to be forgotten in the age of jazz babies, flappers, and bathtub gin. Writing *The Age of Innocence* was therefore an act of piety for her, an attempt to atone for her youthful satire on the graceful, ordered civility of her parents' world. On one level the novel is a faithful record of the manners and mores of that New York City haut monde between 1870 and 1900: the opera evenings at the old Academy of Music, playgoing at Lester Wallack's theater, the formal dinners, the round of visits and leaving visiting cards, the betrothal visits, Grace Church weddings, the summers in Newport and winters in Washington Square, and the effect on her New Yorkers of "Arabian Night marvels" like the invention of electricity and the telephone.

The Age of Innocence interests today's readers, though, less for these archaeological exhumations than for the spiritual portrait of the age. What Wharton meant by innocence was partly sexual propriety and financial rectitude, but partly an aversion to the darker experiences of life, a fear of innovation, and a submissiveness to the power of social convention that characterized her parents' class. Wharton tests the value of this innocence in the character of Newland Archer, a young dilettante who grows bored with the stuffy, ordered world, falls in love with a Europeanized American, the Countess Ellen Olenska, contemplates running away to Europe with her but is maneuvered back into conformity within the dictates of his society when his rebellion threatens to destroy his marriage. Yet far from being the story of "a pathetic instance of vain frustration, of wasted forces," *The*

Age of Innocence demonstrates that beneath the surface dullness were things so fine and sensitive and delicate that Ellen Olenska's spontaneity and social iconoclasm seem almost crass by comparison. In fact, the epilogue of the novel, set in 1900, affirms the balanced virtues of both the older ways of Archer's generation and the newer openness of the turn-of-the-century period, in the widower Archer's declining to renew his interest in Ellen (out of respect to the memory of his marriage) and in the marriage of Archer's son, Dallas, to a girl of marginal social position.

While *The Age of Innocence* did not match the 100,000 plus sales record of *The House of Mirth*, it did achieve best-seller status. Some reviewers complained that Wharton's art was wasted on a negligible high society and trivial people. V. L. Parrington claimed that there was "more hope for our literature in the honest crudities of the younger naturalists," and Katherine Mansfield begged for "a little wildness, a dark place or two in the soul." But

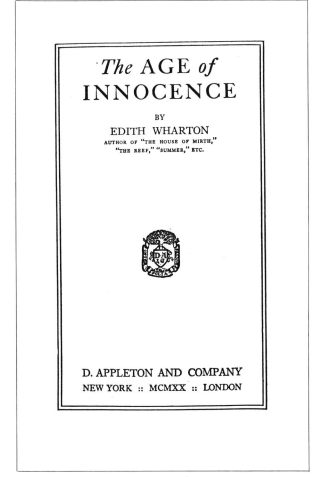

Title page for Wharton's Pulitzer Prize-winning novel about high society in the late nineteenth century. It earned her some $70,000 between 1920 and 1922.

readers generally agreed with the *Times Literary Supplement* reviewer, who described the novel as "a thorough mastery of the whole situation," and with William Lyon Phelps, who called her a writer who "brings glory on the name of America, and this is her best book." Indeed, it won for her the Pulitzer Prize in 1920.

The publication of *The Age of Innocence*—which Yvor Winters once called "the finest single flower of the Jamesian art; one which James fertilized but would have been unable to bring to maturity"—closed out the major phase of Wharton's career as a writer. Her best books were behind her, her war work was over, and many of her friends—Henry James, Howard Sturgis, Teddy Roosevelt, as well as young soldier-friends such as Ronald Simmons and her cousin Newbold Rhinelander—were gone. It no longer seemed possible to stay at 53, rue de Varenne. Even Paris seemed too much. So Wharton gave up her Faubourg apartment and bought a large estate outside Paris at Saint Brice-sous-Forêt. Henceforth, in the summer, Pavillon Colombe was to be her home; and in the winter she journeyed to her other estate, Sainte-Claire Le Chateau, at Hyéres, on the Riviera. Writing in the postwar world seemed highly problematical to her. Yet stories kept clamoring to be told, and young writers such as F. Scott Fitzgerald and Sinclair Lewis wrote admiringly to her. Perhaps something could yet be done to record the moral history of the postwar world, she decided.

Looking about her at this world, Wharton was disgusted at the spectacle of the wealthy, denationalized, deracinated cosmopolites rushing about Europe from London to Paris, to St. Moritz and the Riviera. *The Glimpses of the Moon* (1922) deals with the four cornerstones of their existence—money, luxury, fashion, and pleasure. Her young couple, Susy Branch and Nick Lansing, resemble Lily Bart and Lawrence Selden of *The House of Mirth* in that they are in love and want to marry, but, also like Lily and Lawrence, they do not have enough money to maintain themselves in the rich crowd. Despite their desire to remain part of this group, they decide to marry, while each scouts for a wealthier spouse: "Why shouldn't they marry; belong to each other openly and honourably, if for ever so short a time, and with the definite understanding that whenever either of them got the chance to do better he or she should be immediately released? The law of their country facilitated such exchanges, and society was beginning to view them as indulgently as the law." In the end, their experiment a failure, Nick and Susy return to each other, poor but happy. Written for the *Pictorial Review*, a slick periodical aimed at American housewives, *The Glimpses of the Moon* marked a steep decline in Mrs. Wharton's powers. While some reviewers gave the obligatory nod to Wharton's stylistic powers, Ruth Hale memorably defined the critical view that would seal the book's fate: "Edith Wharton has no business to be writing such trash."

Nor was *A Son at the Front*, largely composed during the war, any improvement. At sixty, living in her villa outside Paris, gardening and reading, Wharton wanted most to escape from the present. In 1923 she returned to the United States to receive an honorary doctorate from Yale University, but in many ways the trip was a failure. Most of her old friends were long dead or unrecognizable, and New York itself was measurably different from the prewar city she had left almost two decades before. Her parents' world, old New York, was gone without a trace.

In an effort to recreate that vanished world of her parents, Wharton produced in 1924 four *nouvelles* dealing with four decades of that vanished society's social history: *Old New York*, the collective title, is composed of *False Dawn (The 'Forties)*, *The Old Maid (The 'Fifties)*, *The Spark (The 'Sixties)*, and *New Year's Day (The 'Seventies)*. As glimpses of the social history of the time and place, *Old New York* is not compelling; but as a group of sharply realized moral dramas, the four parts do succeed as "crucial instances" of the complex struggle of four individuals in relation to the oppressive social order of a conventional society in the process of change.

The Mother's Recompense (1925) expands the theme of "Autre Temps . . ." in order to suggest certain transformations of moral and social values over two decades in contemporary New York. Kate Clephane, having abandoned her husband and child for a lover in Europe, returns to New York City eighteen years later to attend her daughter's wedding, only to discover that Anne's fiance is a young man with whom Kate has had an affair in Europe. Unable openly to oppose the marriage without revealing her own dissipation (except to a New York gentleman who is still willing to marry her), Kate acquiesces in the marriage to protect her daughter and returns to Europe alone. Hers is a drama of renunciation, her only recompense being that "whenever she began to drift toward new uncertainties and fresh concessions," she could remind herself that "once at least she had stood fast, shutting away in a little space of peace and light the best thing that had ever happened to her."

By 1925 Edith Wharton had become the

grande dame of American letters, had received an honorary doctorate from Yale, and was consistently identified as one of "the twelve greatest women in America." Few reviewers gave her really bad reviews, although there were veiled complaints at her "aristocratic status," her treatment of the beau monde rather than the toiling masses, her old-fashioned sensibility, the increasing slickness of her stories. Perhaps the *Independent* reviewer caught the general mood in his remarks about *The Mother's Recompense*: "Competent, skillful work, adequately chiseled and polished like a painting by a competent, but rather tired, artist."

Wharton had always felt that few English and American novelists had been really interested in the deeper processes of art. Perhaps with the exception of Henry James in mind, she had *The Writing of Fiction* published in 1925. A compilation of essays that had appeared in *Scribner's Magazine*, the work deals prescriptively with the craft of fiction, as she had meditated and practiced it. Emphasizing in Jamesian terms such issues as selection, psychology,

THE MOTHER'S RECOMPENSE

BY

EDITH WHARTON

AUTHOR OF
"OLD NEW YORK," "THE AGE OF INNOCENCE,"
"THE GLIMPSES OF THE MOON," ETC.

Desolation is a delicate thing.
SHELLEY.

D. APPLETON AND COMPANY
NEW YORK :: LONDON :: MCMXXV

Title page for the first of Wharton's novels in the middle and late 1920s about the relations between parents and children

and the moral sense, Wharton devoted chapters to "Telling a Short Story," "Constructing a Novel," and "Character and Situation." A concluding essay dealt with Marcel Proust. As a vade mecum for the aspiring writer, the volume has its uses, although the prescriptiveness suggests how conventional were her attitudes in the age of surrealism, dadaism, and stream-of-consciousness fiction. For she is a realist preeminently in the tradition of the early James, Howells, Honoré de Balzac, and Emile Zola.

Perhaps some episodes from her novels *Hudson River Bracketed* (1929) and *The Gods Arrive* (1932) will lay bare the theory implicit in her realistic art. In the former novel George Frenside, a literary critic and adviser, tells the aspiring novelist Vance Weston that he ought to get out and mix more often in society: "Manners are your true material, after all." This advice embodies Wharton's belief, as she put in *The Gods Arrive*, that "the surface of life was rich enough to feed the creator's imagination." This corresponds with the view she expressed in *The Writing of Fiction*—for the novelist "the proper study of mankind is man's conscious and purposive behaviour rather than its dim unfathomable sources." The point of interest in human behavior, for her, was "the conflicts . . . produced between the social order and individual appetites." The dramatization of such conflicts frequently produces the novel of manners, of which she was an expert practitioner. Her aim was like that of Vance Weston—not "to denounce or to show up, as most of the 'society' novelists did, but to take apart the works of the machine, and find out what all those people behind the splendid house fronts signified in the general scheme of things." Such an intention, well executed, delivers the novel of manners from the charge of superficiality in its treatment of society. In fact, Wharton's realism makes great demands on the insight of the writer, for the surface must be probed and dissected by one on whom nothing is lost. Like James, she remarked that "As to experience, intellectual and moral, the creative imagination can make a little go a long way, provided it remains long enough in the mind and is sufficiently brooded on." But her conception of experience was not impressionistic and inward, as was James's. For Wharton, the novelist's subject was the individual in full engagement with the social world, its manners and mores, its rites and traditions, its liberties and constraints. And she did not hesitate to criticize Howells for not probing deeply enough or the later James for severing his characters from "that thick nourishing human air in which we all live and move," for stripping them of "all the *human fringes*

we necessarily trail after us through life."

Between 1925 and her death in 1937, Wharton produced five more volumes of short stories, the final flowering of her art with the short tale: *Here and Beyond* (1926), *Certain People* (1930), *Human Nature* (1933), *The World Over* (1936), and *Ghosts* (1937). During this period she also wrote a volume of poems, her memoir, and five novels, one published posthumously.

Here and Beyond is composed of a half-dozen tales which deal about equally with this world and the next. Those which explore the supernatural— "Miss Mary Pask," "The Young Gentleman," and "Bewitched"—create, as always, an overpowering mood of occult strangeness, even while Wharton's steady rationalism usually provides us with a means of understanding the inexplicable. *Certain People* also offers six tales, of which the best is doubtless "After Holbein," a parable, in its way, of the fatal consequences of the life of social self-indulgence in New York City during the Gilded Age. *Human Nature*, dedicated to Bernard Berenson, whom she visited almost every year at his Villa I Tatti in Florence, contains only five tales, all but one of them ("A Glimpse") concerned with illness, disease, and death. Over seventy when the book was published, Wharton had been steadily deteriorating in health, and almost all of her contemporaries had died. Yet her theme was the inevitable fact that human nature had not changed as fast as Jazz Age social usages. Of the generally trivial group of tales in *The World Over*, one, "Roman Fever," is as good as anything she ever wrote. Again, the focus is on age, the function of memory, and death. The tale makes expert use of suspense; the controlled revelation of events which happened in the distant past has no equal in Wharton's oeuvre. It is at the same time a complex study of the sameness of, and the vital differences between, the generations, and a revelation of latent hatred which rises to a sudden and unexpected climax. In this tale, two widows in Rome, trying to keep up with their two fast-living, husband-hunting daughters, sit at a restaurant table overlooking the Palatine, the Forum, and the Colosseum. Constituted only of their conversation about the girls and their own girlhoods, and worked out against that vast Roman memento mori, the tale suggests that the real Roman fever is not the malaria that afflicted their grandmothers' generation, but that power of passionate love sufficient, once experienced, to nourish Mrs. Ansley through years of quiet obedience to the social forms of her New York City world. Leon Edel once observed that many of Wharton's stories suffered from "too close an adherence to the formula popular at the end of the nineteenth century, that of the sudden twist, the *coup de theatre*." Yet "Roman Fever" could not have succeeded as effectively with any other ending than the ironic bombshell that Mrs. Ansley quietly drops at the end, that Alida Slade's husband had also fathered Grace Ansley's daughter.

In *Ghosts*, Wharton collected eleven tales already published in magazines and book form, dedicating the book to Walter de la Mare. This collection contains a preface on the nature of supernatural fiction which, together with her comments in *The Writing of Fiction*, constitutes the rationale of her spectral tales. In the preface to *Ghosts* she remarks that while the rational mind may not believe in ghosts, "it is in the warm darkness of the pre-natal fluid far below our conscious reason that the faculty dwells with which we apprehend the ghosts we may not be endowed with the gift of seeing." Only two requirements were necessary, she felt, for the supernatural tale: silence and continuity. But with jazz, the wireless, "the conflicting attractions of the gangster, the introvert and the habitual drunkard," the ghost and the ghostly story, she predicted, may succumb "to the impossibility of finding standing-room in a roaring and discontinuous universe."

"It is useless, at least for the story-teller," Wharton had observed in 1927, "to deplore what the new order of things has wiped out, vain to shudder at what it is creating; there it is, whether for better or worse, and the American novelist can best use his opportunity by plunging both hands into the motley welter." None of the five novels published in the last decade of her life—*Twilight Sleep* (1927), *The Children* (1928), *Hudson River Bracketed*, *The Gods Arrive*, and *The Buccaneers* (1938, posthumously submitted to Appleton-Century by her literary executor, Gaillard Lapsley)—matches the greatness of *The House of Mirth*, *Ethan Frome*, or *The Age of Innocence*; but high claims have been made for *Hudson River Bracketed* and *The Buccaneers*.

The first of these five—*Twilight Sleep*—bids fair to be one of Wharton's weakest novels. A satire on modern manners and morals, this novel ridicules the hurried, frenetic quality of modern social life, the ceaseless pursuit of pleasure and the fear of pain (focusing on the new anesthetic used in childbirth that is indicated by the title), the secular substitutions for religious value in society, and the shallowness of love in the age of Freud, jazz, and "quickie" divorces.

If *Twilight Sleep* reveals how the irresponsible adults victimize the young, *The Children* makes the point even more explicitly. As she grew older, the

Wharton at age sixty-three

villains of Wharton's fiction became the middle generation of valueless hedonists—not irreverent youth, to whom society must now look for salvation. The final novels dramatize the fate in the modern world of young people who have rejected adults' inanities and who have discovered a value embedded in the cultural past unknown to their elders. Judith Wheater, a fifteen year old who tries desperately to keep her brothers and sisters together, despite the marryings and divorces and abandonments of parents and stepparents, is typical of all of the protagonists of the last five novels. They somehow develop the "memorial manner," which acknowledges and reverences the usable past, and a vivid moral sense (derived therefrom), by which their elders' conduct is weighed in the balance and found wanting. While many reviewers found the novel barely credible, Gorham Munson was perhaps typical in remarking that, although *The Children* "is not by the inspired Edith Wharton who wrote that finest of New England tragedies, *Ethan Frome*, it is a characteristically competent Wharton product, and the sun of Henry James, once refracted, still brings out the polish of pages that regret the decline in manners and record the new vulgarities."

The year *Hudson River Bracketed* appeared, thirty-one critics were asked to rank seventy-two contemporary American writers on the basis of literary merit. That Wharton still held her own was indicated by sixteen of them placing her in group 1 and ten in group 2, generally judging her work as "superior." *Hudson River Bracketed* confirmed her general reputation by expertly tracing the apprenticeship of a young American novelist of manners, Vance Weston, while offering some lively comment on American life, the international literary scene, stream-of-consciousness fiction, dadaism and surrealism, and the artist's imagination. In brief, the novel deals with the necessity of Weston's discovering in Willows—an old house designed in the Hudson River Bracketed style—a symbol of continuity, history, and tradition—just what is needed to nourish the artist's imagination, according to Wharton.

In *The Gods Arrive*, written as a sequel, Wharton has Weston go to Europe in further pursuit of American cultural roots and, at the same time, he descends deeper into himself to discover the source of his creative energies. The novel weaves together two interrelated themes: the age-old perplexing problem of love between men and women, both within and without the married estate; and the discovery of Europe and its old established traditions by a young writer inflamed with the recently discovered concept of continuity. Both books were received as competent and workmanlike, if old-fashioned in their literary attitudes, Isabel Paterson remarking how Wharton "satirizes the modernists in her own leisurely way, conceding not the fraction of an inch in either theory or practice to their literary claims."

One of the most interesting aspects of *Hudson River Bracketed* and *The Gods Arrive*, as well as of *The Buccaneers*, her last, uncompleted novel, is that they express an increasingly complex attitude toward the American Middle West, which she had consistently satirized in her earlier work. *The Buccaneers*, set in New York in the 1870s, deals with the efforts of the St. George family, indefatigable plutocrats from the Midwest, to launch their daughters into New York society. In Vance Weston and the St. George girls, who eventually discover the importance of the cultural roots and the traditions of an established society, Wharton celebrates the energy, passion, and power of the new Americans, especially as they try to assimilate cultural tradition. It is clear that, in Wharton's affection for the invading American beauties, who marry into the English aristocracy, in her satire upon the snobbishness of old New York,

and upon the inanities of life among the British aristocracy, Wharton was sharply revising her views about the Midwestern nouveaux riches to show how they might, after all, have a tonic effect on society and reinvigorate the meaning of the past and the value of tradition.

Vance Weston's successive experiments with several kinds of novels in *Hudson River Bracketed* and *The Gods Arrive* have the effect of highlighting what, to Wharton, were the limitations of novelistic genres. Even the naturalistic novel, for Wharton, had failed. The great French writers, she remarked, "invented the once-famous *tranche de vie*, the exact photographic reproduction of a situation or an episode, with all its sounds, smells, aspects realistically rendered, but with its deeper relevance and its suggestions of a larger whole either unconsciously missed or purposely left out." If they succeeded, she held, they did so only in spite of their theories. As early as 1914, she had left the hope that "some new theory of form, as adequate to its purpose as those preceding it, will be evolved from the present welter of experiment." But by the 1930s she did not find modernist theories of fiction to have produced a great narrative art. And in *The Gods Arrive*, she expressed her dismay at the literati in Paris who denounce tradition and argue that "fiction, as the art of narrative and the portrayal of social groups, had reached its climax, and could produce no more . . . —that unless the arts were renewed they were doomed, and that in fiction the only hope of renewal was in the exploration of the subliminal." For her, the realistic novel of manners, centering on the characters' conscious and purposive motives in the conflict between the social order and the individual's appetites, the novel of manners offering the social surface but probing for its deeper significance, would more than challenge the capacities of any artist.

In the process of dramatizing the vulgarity of the modern world and in defending the novel of manners against the emerging modernists, whom she largely misunderstood, Wharton lost, rather conspicuously, the sharp irony of her youthful style; and in its place readers increasingly encountered both the bitter distortions of satire and a mellow nostalgia for a vanished world that few could remember across the wreckage of the Great Depression and the war years. She was never at home in the postwar world. But although her novels became increasingly deprived of that rich and direct social experience that is the substance of the American novel of manners, she nevertheless tried to deal responsibly and realistically with her times up until her death in 1937. From this high seriousness and from her deep interest in the craft of fiction came a handful of superior novels—*The House of Mirth*, *Ethan Frome*, *The Custom of the Country*, and *The Age of Innocence*—and a score of excellent short stories—among them "Autre Temps . . . ," "Roman Fever," and "The Other Two." They will always be read with close attention and remembered with pleasure.

Other:

Hermann Sudermann, *The Joy of Living*, translated by Wharton (New York: Scribners, 1902);

The Book of the Homeless, compiled by Wharton (Paris, 1915; New York: Scribners, 1916);

Eternal Passion in English Poetry, edited by Wharton, Robert Norton, and Gaillard Lapsley, with a preface by Wharton (New York: Appleton-Century, 1939).

Periodical Publications:

"The Vice of Reading," *North American Review*, 177 (October 1903): 513-521;

"The Criticism of Fiction," *Times Literary Supplement*, 14 May 1914, p. 230;

"The Great American Novel," *Yale Review*, new series 16 (July 1927): 646-656;

"When New York Was Innocent," *Literary Digest*, 99 (15 December 1928): 27;

"Visibility in Fiction," *Yale Review*, new series 18 (March 1929): 480-488;

"Confessions of a Novelist," *Atlantic Monthly*, 151 (April 1933): 385;

"Permanent Values in Fiction," *Saturday Review of Literature*, 10 (7 April 1934): 603-604;

"Souvenirs du Bourget d'Outremer," *Review Hebdomadaire*, 45 (21 June 1936): 266-286.

Bibliographies:

Vito J. Brenni, *Edith Wharton: A Bibliography* (Morgantown: West Virginia University Library, 1966);

James W. Tuttleton, "Edith Wharton: An Essay in Bibliography," *Resources for American Literary Study*, 3 (Fall 1973): 163-202.

Biography:

R. W. B. Lewis, *Edith Wharton: A Biography* (New York, Evanston, San Francisco & London: Harper & Row, 1975).

References:

Louis Auchincloss, *Edith Wharton* (Minneapolis: University of Minnesota Press, 1961);

Auchincloss, *Edith Wharton: A Woman in Her Time* (New York: Viking, 1971);

Millicent Bell, *Edith Wharton and Henry James: The Story of Their Friendship* (New York: Braziller, 1965);

Irving Howe, ed., *Edith Wharton: A Collection of Critical Essays* (Englewood Cliffs, N. J.: Prentice-Hall, 1962);

Margaret McDowell, *Edith Wharton* (Boston: Twayne, 1976);

Blake Nevius, *Edith Wharton: A Study of Her Fiction* (Berkeley: University of California Press, 1953);

James W. Tuttleton, *The Novel of Manners in America* (Chapel Hill: University of North Carolina Press, 1972), pp. 122-140;

Cynthia Griffin Wolff, *A Feast of Words: The Triumph of Edith Wharton* (New York: Oxford University Press, 1977).

Brand Whitlock
(4 March 1869-24 May 1934)

David D. Anderson
Michigan State University

SELECTED BOOKS: *The 13th District* (Indianapolis: Bobbs-Merrill, 1902);

Her Infinite Variety (Indianapolis: Bobbs-Merrill, 1904);

The Happy Average (Indianapolis: Bobbs-Merrill, 1904);

The Turn of the Balance (Indianapolis: Bobbs-Merrill, 1907);

Abraham Lincoln (Boston: Small, Maynard, 1909; revised edition, London & New York: Nelson, 1919);

The Gold Brick (Indianapolis: Bobbs-Merrill, 1910);

The Fall Guy (Indianapolis: Bobbs-Merrill, 1912);

Forty Years of It (New York & London: Appleton, 1914);

Belgium: A Personal Narrative, 2 volumes (New York: Appleton, 1919); republished as *Belgium under the German Occupation: A Personal Narrative*, 2 volumes (London: Heinemann, 1919);

J. Hardin & Son (New York & London: Appleton, 1923);

Uprooted (New York & London: Appleton, 1926);

Transplanted (New York & London: Appleton, 1927);

Big Matt (New York & London: Appleton, 1928);

La Fayette, 2 volumes (New York & London: Appleton, 1929);

The Little Green Shutter (New York & London: Appleton, 1931);

Narcissus: A Belgian Legend of Van Dyck (New York & London: Appleton, 1931);

The Stranger on the Island (New York & London: Appleton, 1933);

Little Lion: Mieke (New York & London: Appleton-Century, 1937);

The Buckeyes, edited by Paul Miller (Athens: Ohio University Press, 1978).

Brand Whitlock successfully combined the careers of political activist and professional man of letters. A progressive politician, four-term reform mayor of Toledo, Ohio, and American minister (later ambassador) to Belgium during World War I, honored internationally for his services to that nation throughout its occupation by German troops, he preferred to think of himself as a man of letters

Brand Whitlock

and was determined to be, together with his friends Henry James and William Dean Howells, a great American novelist.

Born in Urbana, Ohio, of Scotch-English ancestry, to the Reverend Elias D. and Mollie Lavinia Brand Whitlock, Whitlock was raised in a series of Methodist parsonages in Ohio and was strongly influenced by his father's strong sense of personal responsibility as well as by his love of language and the great English novelists of the nineteenth century. Educated at home and later at a public high school in Toledo, he spent his summers with his maternal grandfather, Joseph Brand, an early abolitionist, a founder of the Republican party in

451

Ohio, and a lifelong reformer. Both Whitlock and his grandfather broke with the Republicans in 1888 over the protective tariff issue and became the only Democrats and supporters of Grover Cleveland in a family of staunch Ohio Republicans.

Although his family wanted him to prepare for the ministry at Ohio Wesleyan, from which his father had graduated and of which his uncle William Whitlock was president, Whitlock broke again with family tradition and in 1887 became a reporter on the *Toledo Blade*. At this time Toledo was becoming industrialized and was suffering the concomitant evils of its sudden transition from an agricultural trading center to a manufacturing center. Just after his twenty-first birthday, in 1890 he moved to Chicago and became a reporter on the *Chicago Herald*, Chicago's leading Democratic newspaper.

In Chicago Whitlock developed literary ambitions and a strong interest in reform politics. As a reporter he came to know such writers as George Ade, Peter Finley Dunne, Ben King, and George Barr McCutcheon. He became a member of the bohemian Whitechapel Club and began tentatively to write fiction. Sent to Springfield as political reporter for the *Herald* in 1892, he met reform politician John Peter Altgeld and saw at first hand the alliance between machine politics and corrupt industrialism. During that same year he courted and married Susan Brainerd of Springfield, who died four months after their marriage. Almost immediately after her death, he became active in Altgeld's first, successful campaign for the governorship of Illinois.

Upon his election, Altgeld offered Whitlock an appointment as his private secretary, which Whitlock refused, accepting instead the chief clerkship in the office of the secretary of state, a position that would give him time to read, to write, and to study law. During his four years in Springfield, from 1893 to 1897, he became close friends with Clarence Darrow and Altgeld, who later provided the inspiration for some of his fiction as well as for his political career. While both men encouraged Whitlock's ambitions, he accumulated rejection slips for his short stories, based upon his newspaper and political experience. Whitlock was admitted to the Illinois bar in 1894, and the next year he married Susan Brainerd's sister Ella, who was to survive him. Their marriage was childless.

Upon Altgeld's defeat in his bid for reelection to the governorship in 1897 Whitlock returned to Toledo to practice law and to write. In July 1898 his first published short story, "The Pardon of Thomas Whalen," appeared in *Ainslee's Magazine*. The story is based upon the events surrounding Altgeld's 1893 pardon of three of the men charged with conspiracy in the Haymarket labor riots of 1885. Altgeld believed that the men had been wrongfully convicted, but his action met with widespread criticism. The governor in Whitlock's story is the first of the idealized portraits of Altgeld that appear in Whitlock's fiction, and the story explores a theme that was also to recur in his later work: the necessary but difficult reconciliation of justice and legality.

Whitlock's *The Thirteenth District* was published in March 1902. Written in his office while he waited for his few clients, it is a fine study of human and political degeneration and one of the few successful novels dealing with grass roots American politics. Whitlock drew upon the traditions of late nineteenth-century partisan politics in a Midwest two generations removed from its frontier origins and upon his observations of the impact of corrupt business practices on politics in Springfield to plead for the substituting of direct primaries for party conventions in choosing candidates. The novel provides realistic vignettes of events and fictional portraits of some of the people he had known in Springfield. Among those he portrays are Altgeld, Darrow, and William Jennings Bryan.

Whitlock's skill as a novelist prevents the work from becoming a tract. In style and technique *The Thirteenth District* is realistic in the tradition of Howells. The characters are fully developed; and there are only occasional authorial intrusions to express Whitlock's beliefs about democracy. The novel, which remains one of Whitlock's best, marked the path that his work was to take in the future.

Whitlock's first published book was followed by two more political novels, both of them written before *The Thirteenth District* and revised as a result of the techniques he had learned in writing this novel. Neither *Her Infinite Variety* nor *The Happy Average*, both published in 1904, approaches the stature of *The Thirteenth District*, but each amplifies a theme touched upon in that novel.

Her Infinite Variety, an ironic social comedy dealing with the introduction of a woman's suffrage amendment in the Illinois legislature and the alliances of old-time political bosses and militant female antifeminists that lead to its defeat, satirizes traditional double standards. The novel also portrays the ideal young politician of the future and the new self-liberated woman and suggests that when these two types combine forces, they will inevitably secure the amendment's passage in the future.

The novel successfully combines the humorous irony of reversed positions, such as portraying the militant female antifeminist as a masterly, practical politician, with a serious consideration of a failure of democracy. The alliance that defeats the bill is shown to be vicious, and the double standard exposed as undemocratic, but Whitlock successfully uses humor rather than invective to accomplish his ends.

The Happy Average is set in the western Ohio town of Macochee, based upon Urbana, Ohio, a setting to which he would return in *J. Hardin & Son* (1923). Social rather than political in its emphasis, the plot of *The Happy Average* focuses on an idealized love affair and on the transition of Ohio from an agricultural to an industrial society. The impact of the new materialism contrasts strongly with the old Jeffersonian ideal of an open society, and the old narrow religious puritanism combines with a new social puritanism as what was once a democratic society becomes stratified by money and prejudice. Whitlock vividly illustrates the failure of the democratic dream: the town refuses to recognize the Irish residents of "Lighttown" or the blacks of "Gooseville" except when they can be exploited; a bishopric is gained by political acumen rather than religious faith; success is measured by money rather than by ability or personal worth.

Neither *Her Infinite Variety* nor *The Happy Average* is as complex or as successful as *The Thirteenth District*, but neither is a failure, and the three novels set forth the political and the literary philosophies that Whitlock was to follow in the future. In literature he was a realist, in politics a Jeffersonian idealist. Realism, he believed, was the only means whereby literature could approximate the truth of human experience; his Jeffersonian politics affirmed his conviction that the American ideal might become the American reality. All his life he rejected determinism and naturalism as denials of the reality he saw and the idealism he practiced.

In the summer of 1904 Whitlock reentered active politics as successor to "Golden Rule" Jones, reform mayor of Toledo and a close friend, who had recently died. He was reelected four times. During his eight years as mayor, he fought the monopoly of the Toledo Railways and Light Company, refused to enforce blue laws, and attempted to humanize the police force. Criticized strongly by the *Toledo Blade* and local clergymen because he insisted that prostitutes were not criminals but victims, he nevertheless became a popular speaker and writer for reform causes, writing such essays as "Thou Shalt Not Kill," an eloquent denunciation of capital punishment, and "On The Enforcement of

Law in Cities," an argument for compassion and mercy rather than force as effective means of bringing order to cities.

In 1907, while he continued to be embroiled in reform activities, Whitlock's most ambitious novel, *The Turn of the Balance*, was published. An indictment of the inequities and injustice in the American industrial city, the novel is based upon his observations of the criminal courts, the slums, the jails, and the new industrial aristocracy of Toledo. Although it contains strong social criticism, the novel reaffirms Whitlock's faith in human rather than legal justice, but his concluding optimism is not supported by the facts presented in the novel.

The Turn of the Balance is a study in contrasts: between the rich and the poor, the just and the unjust, the compassionate and the merciless; and it presents some of Whitlock's most profound observations on the nature of modern urban industrial society. The contrasts are portrayed through the interwoven stories of two families, the wealthy socialite Wards—father, mother, naive daughter,

THE TURN OF THE
BALANCE

By

BRAND WHITLOCK

Author of The Happy Average
Her Infinite Variety
The 13th District

With Illustrations by

JAY HAMBIDGE

INDIANAPOLIS
THE BOBBS-MERRILL COMPANY
PUBLISHERS

Title page for Whitlock's most ambitious novel, based on his observations in Toledo

and wastrel son—and the working class Koerners—father, mother, housemaid daughter, and unemployed son, a recently discharged veteran of the pacification campaign in the Philippines. The Wards, mindless exploiters, maintain and enhance their position, while their son's criminal embezzlement is covered up. The Koerners go down to destruction as the father loses a leg at work, receives no compensation, and the son, having learned violence in the army and having been victimized by society for minor crimes, is ultimately executed for a murder to which he is driven by police persecution.

Related in theme to Frank Norris's *The Octopus* (1901) and Upton Sinclair's *The Jungle* (1906), *The Turn of the Balance* is superior to both in structure and in the subtlety with which the contrasts are handled. Both powerful and eloquent in its condemnation of the abuses of an inhuman social and legal structure, it avoids both the didacticism and sensationalism of *The Jungle* and the deterministic optimism of *The Octopus* as it concludes, in progressive fashion, with the conviction that the system can be changed for the better if those in power are willing to make the attempt to do so.

This novel, Whitlock's last major work of fiction until after World War I, reflects his concerns as a reformer and political activist. In the remaining five years of his tenure in the mayor's office he wrote articles on the theory and practice of government, short stories, and a brief biography of Abraham Lincoln for Lincoln's centennial year. An interesting interpretation of Lincoln as a progressive reformer, *Abraham Lincoln* (1909) is perhaps the most significant of all the works that appeared on Lincoln during that year.

Whitlock also gathered his published short stories, many of them revised, and several new stories into two volumes, *The Gold Brick* (1910) and *The Fall Guy* (1912). *The Gold Brick* contains twelve stories unified by their political subject matter and set in Chicago, Springfield, or rural Ohio. Each story focuses on a political crisis and contrasts political corruption, which grows out of human weakness, with honesty, which is founded on strength. The stories in *The Fall Guy* are more varied, including stories of criminality, of Civil War reminiscences, of life in Macochee, and of human weakness exploited by materialism. Both collections contain a few first-rate stories, but many of them, in response to the commercial demands of the popular magazines in which they were published, are marred by sentimentality, trick endings, and by the oversimplification of complex themes.

Whitlock's autobiography, *Forty Years of It*

(1914) was intended as his farewell to political activism, and on 1 January 1914, he became American minister to Belgium, appointed by Woodrow Wilson and Secretary of State William Jennings Bryan. As senior American diplomat in Brussels, a political backwater before World War I, he expected much time to write, and immediately after his arrival he began a new novel. By the end of July he had completed twenty-five chapters, and the end of the first draft was in sight. But on 1 August Europe went to war, and Whitlock put the manuscript in a dispatch box, where it was to remain unfinished for more than a decade.

Whitlock's activities in World War I were attempts to counteract the inhumanity of modern total war, including his futile attempts to rescue Edith Cavell, a Red Cross nurse charged with aiding escaping Allied prisoners, from a German firing squad. *Belgium: A Personal Narrative* (1919) is based on his papers and journal from this period. Dominating the book are the Marquis de Villobar, Spanish minister to Belgium, and Cardinal Mercier, both of whom joined with Whitlock to mitigate the effects of the German occupation. *Belgium* records Whitlock's perception of the war as the continuation of the age-old struggle between the forces of mechanistic efficiency and exploitation, personified in his encounters with German officers, and humanism, with concern for the life of the individual, demonstrated by his two friends. *Belgium* ends on a note of hope and faith in people, rather than in governments, as the instruments of justice. Although his post had been raised to an ambassadorship upon the election of Warren G. Harding, a man he despised as a vulgar, weak politician, Whitlock, the recipient of many honors from Belgium and other countries, decided to resign his post and remain in Europe to write novels.

Of the eight works that Whitlock produced between 1923 and his death in 1934, only two, *J. Hardin & Son* and the two-volume biography *La Fayette* (1929), are significant accomplishments. His best novel, *J. Hardin & Son*, is set in Macochee. A study in contrasts between the two characters of the title, its contrasts are not merely between generations but between two Americas, that of the age of faith and causes, an age that saw a wilderness made orderly and slavery destroyed, and the new age, dominated by an ambiguous fusion of virtue and vice, by mindless exploitation, and by freedom become license.

J. Hardin & Son was well received and sold well. H. M. Fuller in *Literary Review* (20 October 1923) wrote that it is "An Ohio *Main Street*, but how

Albert, King of the Belgians, and Brand Whitlock

much more is Mr. Whitlock than Mr. Lewis." W. E. Woodward in the *Nation* (5 December 1923) called it "A real book—genuine, vitally sincere." But the novels that followed, *Uprooted* (1926), *Transplanted* (1927), both about Americans living in Europe, are technically excellent but derivative and ambiguous in subject matter. *Big Matt* (1928) and *The Little Green Shutter* (1931) are brief returns to the Ohio political and social scene. *Narcissus: A Belgian Legend of Van Dyck* (1931) is a historical novel based on Van Dyck's painting *Saint Martin*, and *The Stranger on the Island* (1933) is based on the brief domination of Beaver Island in Lake Michigan by "King" James Strang.

In *La Fayette* (1929) Whitlock destroys the myth of the romantic young French nobleman who rode with Washington and became enshrined in American history and in its place provides a portrait of a man whose life is compounded of victory and defeat and ultimate tragedy. Lafayette maintained his idealism in the face of exile, and, Whitlock says, he suffered the inevitable loneliness of a liberal reformer who is out of place in an age that rejects his ideals. *La Fayette* is not only a substantial, well-researched work, but it is a novelist's biography, written with the drama of fiction, portraying a great man and a great age, perhaps, Whitlock reflects, the last great age of man. With *Belgium* it remains his most substantial nonfictional work.

At his death in 1934 Whitlock left unfinished biographies of Jefferson and of Jackson and the manuscript of a novel, which has recently been published as *The Buckeyes* (1978), a story of Macochee in transition from frontier settlement to country town. In the years since his death, Whitlock has been remembered as a reform politician and diplomat rather than as a writer. In his careful realistic style he explored themes that were universal but not unique, themes that were often explored more sensationally if sometimes less artistically by his contemporaries. His contributions to literature, his continued concern with humanistic causes, and his faith in the ultimate triumph of principle over expediency are worthy of more attention than they have received.

Letters:

The Letters and Journals of Brand Whitlock, edited by Allan Nevins (New York & London: Appleton-Century, 1936).

References:

David D. Anderson, *Brand Whitlock* (New York: Twayne, 1968);

Robert M. Crunden, *A Hero in Spite of Himself* (New York: Knopf, 1969);

Jack Tager, *The Intellectual as Urban Reformer* (Cleveland: Case Western Reserve, 1968).

Constance Fenimore Woolson

(5 March 1840-24 January 1894)

Lynda S. Boren
Tulane University

BOOKS: *The Old Stone House*, as Anne March (Boston: Lothrop, 1872);

Castle Nowhere: Lake-Country Sketches (Boston: Osgood, 1875);

Two Women, 1862: a Poem (New York: Appleton, 1877);

Rodman the Keeper: Southern Sketches (New York: Appleton, 1880);

Anne (New York: Harper, 1882; London: Sampson Low, 1883);

For the Major (New York: Harper, 1883; London: Sampson Low, 1883);

East Angels (New York & London: Harper, 1886; London: Sampson Low, 1886);

Jupiter Lights (New York: Harper, 1889; London: Sampson Low, 1889);

Horace Chase (New York: Harper, 1894; London: Osgood, 1894);

The Front Yard and Other Italian Stories (New York: Harper, 1895);

Dorothy and Other Italian Stories (New York: Harper, 1896);

Mentone, Cairo, and Corfu (New York: Harper, 1896);

Constance Fenimore Woolson, volume 2 of *Five Generations*, edited by Clare Benedict (London: Ellis, 1930).

C. F. Woolson

Great-niece of James Fenimore Cooper, literary friend of Henry James and Clarence Stedman, Constance Woolson is best remembered for her perceptive rendering of character and her vivid descriptions of the American landscape. Her sketches of wilderness life in the remote areas of Northern Michigan and her faithful attention to character portrayal, dialect, and regional expression place her among the realists and local colorists of her day. Her artistry is often favorably compared with that of Mark Twain, William Dean Howells, and Henry James, and she also ranks high among such regional writers as Sarah Orne Jewett, George Washington Cable, and Bret Harte. Through her verse and short stories, most of which were published over a twenty-year span in *Harper's*, the *Atlantic*, *Appleton's*, *Galaxy*, *Scribner's*, and *Century* magazines, Woolson often impressed the readers and critics of her day with a force that is now rarely appreciated. But in any assessment of literary realism she must be given credit not only for her pioneer efforts in the local-color movement (stories of Ohio, the Great Lakes region, and the South) but also for her accurate depiction of small-town life, her creation of living characters, and her exploration of the international theme.

The deep love of nature revealed in all of her works was reinforced in Woolson by her New England heritage and her early attachment to the Great Lakes region. Born in Claremont, New Hampshire, she was the sixth child of Charles Jarvis and Hannah Cooper Pomeroy Woolson. Her mother was the daughter of Ann Cooper Pomeroy, an elder sister of James Fenimore Cooper. After a scarlet-fever epidemic, which claimed three of Constance's older sisters, the family relocated to Cleveland, Ohio, in the Western Reserve. There, as a manufacturer of stoves, Charles Woolson maintained the family, and Constance later attended Miss Hayden's School for girls and the Cleveland Female Seminary. With her first summer visit in 1855 to Mackinac Island in the Straits of Mackinac between Lake Huron and Lake Michigan, Constance fell in love with its scenic grandeur, making it the subject of her earliest sketches and later her first novel, *Anne* (1882). At eighteen she graduated at the head of her class from Madame Chegaray's New York School and was treated with her family to a sentimental tour of those Boston resorts her father had frequented in his youth. While Constance acted the part of a "great belle," as her younger sister Clara tells us, "the literary talent in her led her to do things that those *not* thus gifted, did not do." She exasperated her mother by running up and down the stairs in her lovely gowns while balancing an open inkwell on top of her portfolio. The inevitable occurred one day, resulting in a disastrous ink-stained conclusion at the bottom of the stairs.

Determined to fulfill her literary ambitions, Woolson turned her experiences into the usable material of art. The Civil War was a momentous event in her young life, and her activities during this period found their way into her early work, in verses and, most specifically, in her novel *Anne*. Engaging herself in the war effort by taking charge of a temporary post office in one of the sanitary fairs established for convalescing soldiers, Woolson fell in (and out) of love with a young officer, reveling in the romance and excitement. After the end of the war, Woolson remained unmarried, and the death in 1869 of her father, to whom she was extremely close, dealt her a severe psychological blow which may have been responsible in part for the periods of deep depression that overcame her from time to time throughout the remainder of her life. Now in her mid-twenties, Woolson turned to writing as a serious occupation, moving to New York after her father's death. The declining health of her mother, however, forced Woolson to become her mother's live-in companion, and from 1873 to 1879 she accompanied her mother to Florida for the winters, returning to New York only for the warmer months. On her initial trip to St. Augustine she met Clarence Stedman, who subsequently became her literary adviser, and her frequent visits to the Carolinas provided material for her finest sketches of Southern life and character.

After her mother's death in 1879, Woolson, now in her late thirties, with a small inheritance, was free to pursue her own interests and elected to travel in Europe. Her sojourn in the Old World lasted for fourteen years, most of which was spent in Italy. Henry James became her intimate friend in Florence in the spring of 1880 and, later, her adviser. As her deafness (inherited from her father) became increasingly more acute, she turned to the visual arts as a source of delight, and James escorted her through the galleries of Italy in 1880, charming her with his sensibility and perhaps unwittingly breaking her heart. As Leon Edel indicates in his biography of James, Woolson and James often shared literary plots and ideas. While according to John Kern "there is no direct evidence of indebtedness on either side," Edel points out that James did use plot structures or situations previously conceived by Woolson, the most specific instance being the plot of "The Figure in the Carpet." Woolson obviously adopted James's philosophy of character and circumstance and had certainly read most of his works by the time of their first meeting in 1880.

When Woolson began to contribute her writings, primarily sketches and verse, to American periodicals in 1870, she relied heavily upon description of natural setting; plot and character were secondary to her desire to capture the scenic moods of the Lake Country in Michigan, the Ohio Valley, and New York. Her sketches of the South and later of Europe also suggest a symbolic link between scene and character. The best of this fiction derived from her observations is collected in four volumes of short stories which demonstrate her development in the handling of setting: *Castle Nowhere: Lake-Country Sketches* (1875); *Rodman the Keeper: Southern Sketches* (1880); *The Front Yard and Other Italian Stories* (1895); and *Dorothy and Other Italian Stories* (1896). (Her first published volume was *The Old Stone House*, a book for children that appeared in 1872 under the pseudonym of Anne March and is largely autobiographical, incorporating much of Woolson's own family experiences.)

The Lake Country volume comprises nine tales, all but "Castle Nowhere" previously published in national magazines. As its title indicates, "Castle Nowhere" is an allegorical romance. It has a somewhat Gothic hero named Fog, an escaped murderer who defies all religious and moral conventions to maintain Silver, an orphaned child, in expiation for his sin. He cares for Silver in a log fortress, Castle

her own people. In the final story, "The Lady of Little Fishing," a beautiful missionary finds her almost supernatural effect upon the men of a crude trapping camp reversed when she brings about her own destruction by falling in love with Reuben Mitchell, the one man among them who cannot love her. In the end, Reuben returns thirty years later to view her grave, having been scorned in return by the one woman who could not love him. There is in these tales an intermingling of nature and allegory much akin to Nathaniel Hawthorne's, and the heavy romantic trappings are sometimes too starkly undercut by Woolson's attempts at realism.

The ten stories in *Rodman the Keeper* center on characters and settings in the Carolinas and Florida. In these stories of the early Reconstruction South, Woolson again connects scenery and psychology, creating in some cases her finest stories in this vein. In the title story Rodman is the keeper of a federal cemetery in the South, the caretaker of a tragic bounty. As the old Southern plantation near the

CASTLE NOWHERE:

LAKE-COUNTRY SKETCHES.

BY

CONSTANCE FENIMORE WOOLSON.

BOSTON:
JAMES R. OSGOOD AND COMPANY,
Late Ticknor & Fields, and Fields, Osgood, & Co.
1875.

Title page for Woolson's second book, a collection of nine local-color stories about French settlers in the Great Lakes region

Nowhere, deep in the Michigan swamps, providing for her by luring lake steamers to their destruction. A stranger from the outside world, Jarvis Waring, enters this domain, falls in love with Silver, and returns her to civilization to marry her. Fog dies before they depart, and his castle gradually succumbs to the elements: "The walls fell in, and the water entered. The fogs still steal across the lake, and wave their gray draperies up into the northern curve; but the sedge-gate is gone, and the castle is indeed Nowhere." The remaining sketches are less fantastic and less reminiscent of James Fenimore Cooper's themes, but they are still highly descriptive, evolving character from the atmosphere of setting. In these stories the differences between civilization and raw frontier life are marked, and Woolson often indicates her sympathy for the outcast in such tales, whether it be the Anglican priest in "Peter the Parson" or the French half-breed "Jeannette," who rejects a cultured suitor for one of

RODMAN

THE KEEPER:

SOUTHERN SKETCHES.

BY

CONSTANCE FENIMORE WOOLSON,
AUTHOR OF "CASTLE NOWHERE," "TWO WOMEN," ETC.

NEW YORK:
D. APPLETON AND COMPANY,
1, 3, & 5 BOND STREET.
1880.

Title page for Woolson's collection of ten stories set during Reconstruction in the Carolinas and Florida

like sending a letter immediately across the ocean to say "Thank You."

Yours very truly,

C. F. Woolson.

[H. H. Boyesen]

Care Sebastien Cirelli &c.
Lucerne. Switzerland.

Dear Sir,   August 7th

I have just received the notice of my "Southern Sketches" (in the Midsummer number of "Scribner's), and it has given me so much pleasure that I feel like writing a little private letter to say so.

I was especially pleased that "Miss Elizabetha" and "Felipa" were commended, because they are favorites of mine. The little word of censure about "Felipa" was quite deserved; I yielded, there, to temptation. You are right, too, as to the over-touch in "Rodman". As to the way my southern girls talk, I do not think it is over-drawn. They do — or did — talk in that way, when excited. Not all southern girls, of course; but the daughters, for

instance, of those old Virginia and Carolina families who ruled their own neighborhoods and their own state in the old days. Just before the breaking out of the rebellion, I was sent from Cleveland to an old-fashioned French school in New York;- that of Madame Chegaray. At that period, almost all her boarding-pupils were southern girls, and they were so entirely new to me. — I was so fascinated by their ways and grandiloquent style of talking that I spent most of my time listening to, and looking at, them. Later, when I went south myself, I met some of these girls again, and I noticed in what they said (as well as in the stories other southern ladies told me), that the same old grand-iloquence had survived through all their sorrows and sufferings. I do not deny that there was absurdity in

much of this old-time rhetoric. I have given it as it was, intentionally. But, they lived up to it in one way. The very girls who, at school, had grandly called themselves "The Daughters of Carolina," (to the astonishment of the new western pupil, who had never thought of styling herself "the Daughter of Ohio") proved themselves her daughters indeed, when the time came, suffering with her — although mistakenly — every privation.

That you call the book "convincing," gives me much gratification, because I tried hard to be accurate. It is much easier, I think, to imagine than to simply describe; and I called myself back many times, when at work on those sketches, from tempting exaggerations and fancies, to plain fact.

I do not know to whom I am writing; but the cordial and appreciative tone of the notice has made me feel

Letter from Woolson to H. H. Boyesen thanking him for his review of Rodman the Keeper: Southern Sketches

cemetery is about to be torn down, Rodman asks for the greenery

> that once screened the old Piazza.
> "Wuth about twenty-five cents, I guess," said the Maine man, handing them over.

And thus the story ends. While she uses the sort of Gothic elements apparent in many of Edgar Allan Poe's tales, Woolson avoids the sensational by just such touches of realism. In "The South Devil," however, Woolson uses pure description to transform the swamp into an uncanny force. Unlike Poe, she does not link her description to symbolic or moral suggestion. The swamp she portrays is a nonhuman, living spirit. "The atmosphere was hot, and heavy with perfumes. It was the heart of the swamp, a riot of intoxicating, steaming, swarming, fragrant, beautiful, tropical life, without man to make or mar it. All the world was once so, before man was made." In many of these tales, Woolson is fascinated with the view of the South held by aliens from the North and, therefore, builds up to her later stories of transplanted Americans, aliens in the Old World.

The Front Yard and Other Italian Stories, published after Woolson's death, contains six stories that previously appeared in national magazines from 1882 to 1892. While most of these tales do not have the power of her American stories, especially that of the Southern ones, they are stronger in their representation and analysis of character. The title piece is a study of Prudence, a New England woman who, taken in by the illusions of romantic Italy, marries a man who only wants her money. He brings her home to his poverty-ridden family, where she finds out that he has eight children by a previous marriage and a cowshed in the front yard. She dreams of one day replacing the shed with a flower garden and saves her money to do so, only to have it stolen by her stepson, Giovanni. Years later, she is discovered by an American tourist, who cares for her and who, removing the cowshed, gives her a proper front yard with flowers and a fence. The irony is that Prudence dies thinking only of the scoundrel stepson who ran away with her meager savings. Woolson's technique can be compared with James's. The emphasis is on the character's growing awareness as he enters the Old World, and less attention is given to plot than to psychological analysis and portraiture. In "The Street of the Hyacinth," Woolson manages to interweave scene and character in a Jamesian way, and this tale, with its inexperienced American heroine and maturing hero, is one of the finest in the collection.

The five stories in *Dorothy and Other Italian Stories*, all but one set in Italy, continue to display Woolson's preoccupation with Americans abroad. Interwoven with the lovers' tensions in these stories on the theme of love are discussions of art which often reveal much about the characters' perceptions. Some speculation has arisen concerning the autobiographical nature of these stories since they seem to echo Woolson's enchantment with Henry James when he escorted her about Florence in the 1880s. "A Transplanted Boy" (1894) is also similar to James's "The Pupil" (1891) in that it centers on a young American boy abandoned by a mother he adores. He almost succumbs of malarial fever on the death of his pet terrier (his last emotional resource) but is rescued by a compassionate expatriate, who informs his mother of the boy's condition.

Woolson's short stories and sketches offer a wide spectrum of scene and character. While many of the plots and situations appear to be strangely romantic and therefore dated, contrived, or unforgivably subordinated to description and character, the stories remain of interest to students of American realism.

Woolson produced five novels in her lifetime: *Anne*; *For the Major* (1883); *East Angels* (1886); *Jupiter Lights* (1889); and *Horace Chase* (1894). All of the novels, like her short stories, include much description of the geographical locales in which they are set and demonstrate, on a larger scale, Woolson's preoccupation with character analysis. The themes of her shorter works are also apparent in the longer fiction. Thwarted love, the danger of illusions, renunciation, self-sacrifice, alienation, and loneliness are all examined within social contexts and settings drawn from Woolson's own experiences.

An omnivorous reader all her life, Woolson admitted her indebtedness to Charles Dickens, George Sand, Ivan Turgenev, and George Eliot, but in the final analysis her fiction draws most heavily upon her own perceptions of life. Although her novels are notable for their descriptive passages, she devotes so much time to the building up of scene in her works that artistic unity is often sacrificed. The fact that she wrote her novels for serialization also contributed to the episodic structure of much of her work. Excerpts from her notebooks reveal her strong interest in character analysis, which eventually became her forte. With a satirical eye, Woolson often glanced behind the facade of human behavior to unearth the not-so-beautiful truth, as is revealed in this notebook entry: "Imagine a man endowed with an absolutely unswerving will; extremely intelligent, he *comprehends* passion, affection, unselfishness and self-sacrifice, etc., perfectly, though he is himself cold and a pure egotist. He has a charming face, a charming voice, and he can, when he pleases, counterfeit all these feelings so exactly that he gets all the benefits that are to be obtained by them." Woolson, like Jane Austen before her, perceived human psychology in its minute details, and her best work demonstrates this quality.

In *Anne* the action moves from Mackinac to New York to Cleveland and back to Mackinac, with each geographical move roughly corresponding to a shift in plot or character development. Anne Douglas, like most of Woolson's central figures, is an almost unbelievably angelic young woman with great powers of endurance. Her mother dies at an early age, and her father, William Douglas, remarries. His second wife, Angelique Lafontaine, is a woman with French and Indian blood, who bears him more children, the most compelling of whom is Tita, a dark, spritelike creature who refuses to relinquish the French patois spoken on Mackinac Island. She is envious of Anne who is the favored child of the family and well-liked socially. After the death of Tita's mother, William Douglas's old friend Miss Lois Hinsdale agrees to act as protector to the children. Secretly in love with Douglas and dominated by a severe New England puritanism, she despises Tita's mixed blood. "Tita is hideous," Miss Lois tells Anne. "She is dwarfish, black, and sly." Even Douglas seems half ashamed of his passion for Angelique and the marriage that produced Tita. A self-confessed dreamer, he shifts his burdens to Anne:

> "Stand by little Tita, child, no matter what she does. Do not expect too much of her, but remember always her—her Indian blood," said the troubled father, in a low voice.
>
> A flush crossed Anne's face. The cross of mixed blood in the younger children was never alluded to in the family circle or among their outside friends.

Fascinated with the outcast and the unusual situation, Woolson contrived in most of her novels to bring into the family those classical conflicts of secrets, dead wives, returning sons, or past marriages which resurface to haunt the living. The mother is often conveniently absent, with the eldest daughter having assumed her role. The ties between father and daughter are thus more significant, and Woolson is free to develop an often

idealistic heroine like Anne, who, conditioned to self-sacrifice and the protective mothering role, finds herself deceived and abandoned by men.

After her father's death, Anne agrees to become engaged to Rast Pronando, the village hero, before leaving for New York to attend Madame Moreau's School for women in Manhattan, there to be supported by her wealthy maternal great-aunt, Miss Katherine Vanhorn. She eventually breaks her vow to Pronando when she realizes that she does not love him, and the remainder of the story concerns itself with Anne's unfortunate love for Heathcote, an officer in the Union army who eventually marries her best friend. When his wife is mysteriously murdered, Heathcote is the prime suspect, but Anne, Miss Hinsdale, and Pere Michaux, a Catholic priest of Mackinac, discover the real killer. Heathcote returns to the Union army and Anne to Mackinac. At the conclusion of the war, two years later, Anne and Heathcote are married on the island. *Anne* was Woolson's most popular novel, selling more than 57,000 copies. The strength of this work lies in its accurate depiction of customs, speech patterns, and regional geography. Her rendering of dialect is excellent, and in spite of the novel's episodic structure, the strength of Anne's character holds it in focus.

Woolson's next work, *For the Major*, is considered the best of her longer fiction. Much shorter than *Anne*, it was not nearly as popular (it sold only around 5,000 copies), despite the critics' praise. Set in the village of Far Edgerley in the mountains of North Carolina, the novel centers on the town's first family, the Carroll's. Major Carroll, who is suffering from progressive senility, marries a woman whose husband (unbeknown to the major) abandoned her years ago, taking with him her only son. She agrees to marry the widowered major (keeping her desertion secret), vowing to be a perfect wife for him. The major expects her to appear eternally youthful and gay, and she manages to create this illusion for the major and for her visitors from Far Edgerley. Tension arises, however, when Madam Carroll's long lost son (now a young man) enters the community. She keeps her identity secret from her son, but shares this knowledge with her stepdaughter, who aids her in her desperate situation. If the truth were revealed it would destroy not only the major's image in the eyes of Far Edgerley but would render the frail boy she has borne to the major illegitimate. The secret of Madam Carroll's past and her age is kept, happily, and her elder son conveniently dies of a fever. After the major sinks into total senility, Madam Carroll is at last free to experience the comfort of being old. Needless to say, the tale is not without humor, as Woolson disregards the conventional mode of feminine self-sacrifice and places it in a fresh light. The depiction of minor characters and the careful painting of setting have led critics to praise Woolson's technique highly. According to James in his *Partial Portraits* (1888), Woolson achieves a type of legerdemain in making this fanciful tale credible: "We swallow Far Edgerley whole, or say at most, with a sigh, that if it couldn't have been like that, it certainly ought to have been." The novel was enthusiastically received by reviewers of its day.

East Angels, while not as finely wrought as *For the Major*, was more popular with Woolson's readers, selling over 10,000 copies. The setting is a small Florida village, and the central characters are Northerners with wealth and large hearts who come seeking the ease of the South and who end up rescuing the mistress of East Angels, a nearby plantation, and her beautiful daughter, Garda, from the genteel poverty brought about by their declining fortune.

Evert Winthrop purchases the plantation and also assumes responsibility for Garda, whose beauty reflects a tinge of Spanish blood. The remainder of the plot concerns Winthrop's love, not for the selfish Garda, who refuses his hand in marriage, but for Margaret Harold, a woman who is eternally bound to Lanse, a wastrel husband she will not leave. Both fall victim to their senses of duty, and the epilogue to the novel ends on a note of pathos as Margaret sits with her unworthy Lanse:

> Lanse was still crippled; but his face remained handsome. Save for his crippled condition, he appeared well and strong.
> After a while he turned from the moonlight and sat idly watching his wife's hand move over her work. "Do you know that you've grown old, Madge, before your time?"
> "Yes, I know it."
> "Well—you're a good woman," said Lanse.

The theme of renunciation is reminiscent of James's treatment of it; in fact, James felt that Margaret Harold was Woolson's finest character.

Jupiter Lights is more episodic than *East Angels* and suffers from this disunity, due in part to the frequent changes in setting, from the Georgia coast, to the Lake Country of Michigan, and finally to Italy. The central character, Eve Bruce, attempts to rescue her nephew and sister-in-law from the clutches of a wealthy dipsomaniac, Ferdie Morrison, who, one night in an alcoholic mania, attempts to murder them. Eve shoots him and, thinking she has killed him, flees with her sister-in-law, Cecily, and her nephew to the home of Paul Tennant in Lake Superior. Paul is Ferdie's half brother and his psychological opposite. When he proposes to Eve, she refuses because she still thinks she has killed his half brother. She retreats to Italy, away from Paul, who feels that her "sin" is not unpardonable. He pursues her to Italy, forcing his way into a fourteenth-century convent, where Eve is about to take her vows as a nun. Having discovered that his half brother has died of alcoholism, not by Eve's hand, Paul convinces Eve to marry him. Despite this contrived ending, Woolson's skill with the revelation of human psychology is evident in the work. Her analysis of Ferdie's alcoholism is accurate and horrifying and, once again, her depiction of setting is matchless. Both contemporary reviewers and more recent critics have been disturbed by the melodramatic, pathological tone of the work, however, and its awkward use of point of view.

In January 1894 Woolson, suffering from a high fever caused by influenza, either leapt or fell to her death from her bedroom window in Venice. A few years after her death, in words reminiscent of "The Beast in the Jungle," James called Woolson's grave "the most beautiful thing in Italy. . . . It is

Woolson's grave in Rome

tremendously, inexhaustibly touching—its effect never fails to overwhelm."

Horace Chase appeared in book form shortly after Woolson's death. In it she had attempted even more ambitiously to render the various aspects of human psychology, and most critics agree that she was not entirely successful. Once again, Woolson has transplanted a Northern family into a Southern setting, in this case, Asheville, North Carolina. Ruth Franklin, the youngest daughter, marries Horace Chase, who is close to forty at the time and a self-made millionaire. The marriage offers a solution to the genteel poverty of the Franklins, even though Chase is somewhat vulgar for their tastes. Inevitably, while vacationing in St. Augustine, Ruth falls in love with a younger man, Walter Willoughby. Chase innocently takes Walter on as a business partner, sending him to California. While he is absent for two years, Ruth controls her ardor, but when he returns and Chase is away on business, she goes to his rented lodge in the mountains, where she discovers to her dismay that he is betrothed to another woman. Caught in a mountain storm, she leaves without being seen. A friend finds her and takes her into a nearby home where Chase finds them, hears Ruth's confession, forgives her, and agrees to treat her less as a child and more as a wife and woman. Woolson obviously intended to create a benevolent self-sacrificing male character, but the focus of interest and point of view is that of Ruth. Chase, as a result, does not come to life as the main character should. Had Woolson been given the opportunity for revision, she might have developed Chase along the lines she intended for him.

While Constance Fenimore Woolson's work is rarely read or studied today, she has been given considerable attention by Alexander Cowie, F. L. Pattee, Jay Hubbell, A. H. Quinn, and Edward Wagenknecht in their studies of the development of American fiction. John Dwight Kern has pointed out her contributions to the local-color movement in his *Constance Fenimore Woolson: Literary Pioneer* (1934), and other critics of American literature are intrigued with her exploration of the international theme. Henry James praised her highly for her fine development of character, particularly her female ones; and her travel sketches, letters, and notebook entries offer interesting material for comparison with the memoirs of other American women abroad such as Alice James, Henry James's younger sister, and Edith Wharton. The publication of four of her hitherto unpublished letters to Henry James by Leon Edel in his third volume of James's letters should create new interest in the James-Woolson relationship, and perhaps the revival of her works, in such publications as the Garrett Press American Short Story Series, will eventually insure her an appreciative contemporary audience.

References:

Clare Benedict, ed., *Five Generations*, 3 volumes (London: Ellis, 1929-1930);

Alexander Cowie, *The Rise of the American Novel* (New York: American Book Company, 1948), pp. 568-578;

Leon Edel, *Henry James: The Middle Years, 1882-1895* (New York & Philadelphia: Lippincott, 1962);

John Dwight Kern, *Constance Fenimore Woolson: Literary Pioneer* (Philadelphia: University of Pennsylvania Press, 1934);

Rayburn S. Moore, *Constance Fenimore Woolson* (New York: Twayne, 1963);

Fred Lewis Pattee, *The Development of the American Short Story: An Historical Survey* (New York: Harper, 1923), pp. 250-255, 332;

Edward Wagenknecht, *Cavalcade of the American Novel* (New York: Holt, 1952).

Contributors

David D. Anderson ....*Michigan State University*
Lynda S. Boren ....*Tulane University*
Stephen C. Brennan...*Drexel University*
Martin Bucco...*Colorado State University*
James B. Colvert ....*University of Georgia*
Eugene Current-Garcia...*Auburn University*
Sara deSaussure Davis..*University of Alabama*
Robert S. Fredrickson..*Gettysburg College*
Robert L. Gale ....*University of Pittsburgh*
M. E. Grenander ....*State University of New York at Albany*
Earl N. Harbert...*Northeastern University*
Hamlin Hill..*University of New Mexico*
David Kirby..*Florida State University*
Michael Kreyling ....*Tulane University*
Earle Labor ....*Centenary College of Louisiana*
Joseph R. McElrath, Jr..*Florida State University*
George Monteiro..*Brown University*
Gwen L. Nagel ....*Harvard University*
John Pilkington, Jr...*University of Mississippi*
Donald Pizer...*Tulane University*
William Peirce Randel ....*Alfred, Maine*
Abe C. Ravitz..*California State University, Dominguez Hill*
Ruth Salvaggio...*Virginia Tech*
Charles W. Scruggs..*University of Arizona*
Madeleine B. Stern..*New York, New York*
James B. Stronks...*University of Illinois at Chicago Circle*
Tom H. Towers ....*University of Rhode Island*
James W. Tuttleton..*New York University*
Ben Merchant Vorpahl...*University of Georgia*
Linda W. Wagner...*Michigan State University*
Perry D. Westbrook..*State University of New York at Albany*
James Woodress...*University of California, Davis*
Robert H. Woodward ....*San José State University*

Cumulative Index

Dictionary of Literary Biography, Volumes 1-12
Dictionary of Literary Biography Yearbook, 1980, 1981
Dictionary of Literary Biography Documentary Series, Volumes 1-2

Cumulative Index

DLB before number: *Dictionary of Literary Biography*, Volumes 1-11
Y before number: *Dictionary of Literary Biography Yearbook*, 1980, 1981
DS before number: *Dictionary of Literary Biography Documentary Series*, Volumes 1-2

D

H

I

J

K